THE
CAMBRIDGE EDITION OF
THE LETTERS AND WORKS OF
D. H. LAWRENCE

THE LETTERS OF D. H. LAWRENCE

*Vol. I: September 1901 – May 1913
James T. Boulton

*Vol. II: June 1913 – October 1916
George J. Zytaruk and James T. Boulton

*Vol. III: October 1916 – June 1921
James T. Boulton and Andrew Robertson

*Vol. IV: June 1921 – March 1924
Warren Roberts, James T. Boulton and Elizabeth Mansfield

Vol. V: March 1924 – March 1927
James T. Boulton and Lindeth Vasey

Vol. VI: 1927 – 1928
James T. Boulton and Margaret H. Boulton, with Gerald M. Lacy

Vol. VII: 1928 – 1930
Keith Sagar and James T. Boulton

* Already published

THE LETTERS OF D. H. LAWRENCE

THE LETTERS OF D. H. LAWRENCE

VOLUME V
March 1924 – March 1927

EDITED BY
JAMES T. BOULTON
AND
LINDETH VASEY

The right of the
University of Cambridge
to print and sell
all manner of books
was granted by
Henry VIII in 1534.
The University has printed
and published continuously
since 1584.

CAMBRIDGE UNIVERSITY PRESS

CAMBRIDGE
NEW YORK PORT CHESTER
MELBOURNE SYDNEY

Published by the Press Syndicate of the University of Cambridge
The Pitt Building, Trumpington Street, Cambridge CB2 1RP
32 East 57th Street, New York, NY 10022, USA
10 Stamford Road, Oakleigh, Melbourne 3166, Australia

First published 1989

Printed in Great Britain at
the University Press, Cambridge

Library of Congress cataloguing in publication data

Lawrence, D. H. (David Herbert), 1885–1930.
The letters of D. H. Lawrence
(The Cambridge edition of the letters and works
of D. H. Lawrence)
Includes indexes.
Contents: v. 1. September 1901–May 1913. – v. 2.
June 1913–October 1916 / edited by George J. Zytaruk and
James T. Boulton. – [etc.] – v. 5. March 1924–March 1927 /
edited by James T. Boulton and Lindeth Vasey
1. Lawrence, D. H. (David Herbert), 1885–1930 –
Correspondence. 2. Authors, English – 20th century –
Correspondence. I. Boulton, James T. II. Zytaruk,
George J. III. Robertson, Andrew, 1945–
IV. Title. V. Series: Lawrence, D. H. (David Herbert),
1885–1930. Works. 1979.
PR6023.A93Z53 1979 823'.9'12 [B] 78-7531

British Library cataloguing in publication data

Lawrence, D. H. (David Herbert), *1885–1930*
The letters of D. H. Lawrence. – (The
Cambridge edition of the letters and works
of D. H. Lawrence).
Vol. 5: March 1924–March 1927
1. Fiction in English. Lawrence, D. H. –
Correspondence, diaries, etc.
I. Title II. Boulton, James T. (James
Thompson), *1924–* III. Vasey, Lindeth
IV. Series
823'.912

ISBN 0 521 22147 1 (v.1)
0 521 23114 0 (v.5)

SE

CONTENTS

ILLUSTRATIONS

Between pages 252 and 253

ACKNOWLEDGEMENTS

The generosity of holders of Lawrence manuscripts toward the Cambridge edition of his letters has continued; it is reflected in the list of cue-titles of manuscript locations; and the Editorial Board remain deeply grateful.

The volume editors have welcomed the advice and help given by their colleagues on the Board. They also wish to record their gratitude to Michael Black and the staff at Cambridge University Press for their unceasing and willing co-operation.

Many people have readily made their knowledge and assistance available to the editors. Among them the following are particularly deserving of thanks: Gui de Angulo; Dorothy Armstrong; Armin Arnold; Anna Lou Ashby; Jan Barnhart; Barbara Barr; Eugenie Beatty; Charles Bell; Jim Bitner; Derek Britton; Jean Curtis Brown; Tori C. Buchanan; Gretchen Byrne; Shirley Byrne; Charlotte Carl-Mitchell; John Carswell; Sharron G. Cassavant; Barbara Chavez; L. D. Clark; W. H. Clarke; Stephanie Cleveland; Brooke Cottam; Louis Cottam; Kenneth Craven; Philip Crumpton; Keith Cushman; Harry C. Davis; T. R. Davis; Vicki Denby; Marian Eames; Paul Eggert; David Ellis; Simonetta de Filippis; Eileen G. Foote; Leona Foster; Martha Freeman; E. Fröhlich; David Goodway; Richard E. Greenleaf; Jacqueline Guirand; Eddie Gussie; Michael Halls; Bonnie Hardwick; George W. Hardy; Walton Hawk; Michael Herbert; Kurt W. Hettler; Gregory J. Higby; Ron Hitchens; David J. Holmes; Kenneth Hopkins; Patricia M. Howell; Bruce Hunter; Frederick Jeffrey; Jerry Jensen; Lisa Jones; Anne Jordan; the late Noel M. Kader; Patricia Keeley; William A. Koshland; Carol Kroll; Rosalie A. Lang; Carolyn Law; George Lazarus; Miriam Librach; Library Staffs of the University of Birmingham and Harry Ransom Humanities Research Center, University of Texas at Austin; Local History and Archives Department, District Library, City of Westminster; Derek Lomax; Nancy Lutton; Barbara McCandless; E. D. McDonald; John P. McDonald; Philip M. J. McNair; Doris B. Mason; Anthony Matthews and Staff of the Department of Prints and Drawings, British Museum; Dieter Mehl; Harold L. Miller; Colin Milton; Loren Mozely; Margaret Needham; Margaret Oppenheimer; Marijane Osborn; Ann Parr; Harwood B. Picard; Gerald Pollinger; Ann Preston; Bridget Pugh; Bette Rae; Edward S. Riley; the late Alice Rossin; Anthony Rota; the late David Rundle; Halina Rusak; Sheila Ryan; John St John; B. E. de M. Seaman; Adrian Secker; Gerard Sharp; Lloyd Shively; Margaret Shively; Patty Shively; Gerry Slowey; Robert E. F. Smith; Richard L. Snyder; Alberto Sorani; Southwark Local Studies Library; Bruce Steele;

Ronald Toya; Wellcome Institute for the History of Medicine; Maria X. Wells; Iain White; W. van der Will; Elisabeth Ross Wills; Corinna Wiltshire; Phoebe Winch; Laurie Witkin; Dennis Wood; John Worthen.

Special thanks have been earned by Cornelia Rumpf-Worthen and John Worthen for translating the letters Lawrence wrote in German; Ross Parmenter for offering his detailed knowledge of Lawrence's stay in Mexico and his proof-reading; David Farmer for his early work on this volume; Anne Buckley for her continuous secretarial support; Ron Vasey for his computer expertise; Elma Forbes for producing the final index; and Margaret Boulton who meticulously checked the text of the entire volume and read proof.

For permission to use copyright material in the annotation, gratitude is expressed to Sylvia Secker (for letters written by Martin Secker) and the University of Illinois (for use of the Secker Letter-Book) and to Doris B. Mason for Harold Mason's and David Jester's correspondence.

Illustrations have been made available through the kindness of: Barbara Barr; Battye Library Pictorial Collection, Perth, Western Australia; Barbara Chavez; Louis Cottam; Eileen G. Foote; E. Fröhlich and the Carl Seelig-Stiftung, Zürich; Harry Ransom Humanities Research Center, University of Texas at Austin; David J. Holmes; E. D. McDonald; The New York Times (Ida Rauh); Ross Parmenter; Sara C. Quintanilla; Sarah Roberts; Keith Sagar; B. E. de M. Seaman; Adrian Secker; Margaret F. Secor; Barrie Unrath; Elisabeth Ross Wills.

NOTE ON THE TEXT

A full statement of the 'Rules of Transcription' and an explanation of the 'Editorial Apparatus' are provided in Volume I, pp. xviii–xx. The reader may, however, like to be reminded that the following symbols are used:

[ ]	indicates a defect in the MS making it impossible even to conjecture what Lawrence had written. Where a reconstruction can be hazarded or a fault corrected, the conjecture or correction is shown within the square brackets.
[. . .]	indicates a deletion which cannot be deciphered or a postmark which is wholly or partly illegible.
MSC	= autograph manuscript copy
TMS	= typed manuscript
TMSC	= typed manuscript copy
TSCC	= typescript carbon copy

Maps are provided to show the location of places which Lawrence visited for the first time during the period covered by this volume. No attempt has been made fully to repeat information given on the maps in earlier volumes.

CUE-TITLES

Cue-titles are employed both for manuscript locations and for printed works. The following appear in this volume.

A. Manuscript locations

Baker	the late Mr John E. Baker, Jr
BL	British Library
Bonsignore	Signora Silvia Carenzio Bonsignore
Booth	Mrs Gwyneth G. Booth
Brill	Dr Edmund R. Brill
Carswell	Mr John Carswell
Chavez	Mrs Barbara Chavez
Clark	Professor L. D. Clark
Clarke	Mr W. H. Clarke
ColU	Columbia University
Crichton	Mr Robert Crichton
Cushman	Professor Keith Cushman
DC	Dartmouth College

Dobrée	Miss Georgina Dobrée
Forster	Mr W. Forster
Foster	Mrs Leona Foster
Grover	Mr John Grover
GSArchiv	Goethe- und Schiller-Archiv, Weimar
Harvey	Mr John Harvey
Hirst	Mr W. Hirst
HU	Harvard University
IEduc	Iowa State Education Association
Jeffrey	Mr Frederick Jeffrey
KCC	King's College, Cambridge
Kimball	Mr Clark Kimball
King	Miss Joan King
Lazarus	Mr George Lazarus
LC	Library of Congress
McGuire	Mr Allan D. McGuire
Mason	Mrs Doris Mason
Moore	Mrs Beatrice Moore
NCL	Nottinghamshire County Libraries
Needham	Mrs Margaret Needham
Neville	Mr Maurice Neville
NWU	Northwestern University
NYPL	New York Public Library
OUP	Oxford University Press
Picard	Mrs Harwood B. Picard
PM	Pierpont Morgan Library
Sagar	Dr Keith Sagar
Schlaefle	Mrs Susan Schlaefle-Nicholas
Schorer	the late Professor Mark Schorer
Secor	Mrs Margaret Secor
SIU	Southern Illinois University
Smith	Charles H. Smith Collection, University of Indiana
StaU	Stanford University
Subun-So Book Store	Subun-So Book Store, Tokyo
SyrU	Syracuse University
UCB	University of California at Berkeley
UCin	University of Cincinnati
UCLA	University of California at Los Angeles
UIll	University of Illinois
UInd	University of Indiana

ULon	University of London
UN	University of Nottingham
UNYB	State University of New York at Buffalo
UT	University of Texas at Austin
UTul	University of Tulsa
WAPL	Western Australia Public Library
WHist	State Historical Society of Wisconsin
YU	Yale University

B. Printed works

(The place of publication, here and throughout, is London unless otherwise stated.)

Brett	Dorothy Brett. *Lawrence and Brett: A Friendship.* Philadelphia: J. B. Lippincott, 1933
Brett, *South Dakota Review*	Dorothy Brett, 'Autobiography: My Long and Beautiful Journey', *South Dakota Review*, v (Summer 1967), 11–71
Brewster	Earl Brewster and Achsah Brewster. *D. H. Lawrence: Reminiscences and Correspondence.* Secker, 1934
Bynner	Witter Bynner. *Journey with Genius: Recollections and Reflections Concerning the D. H. Lawrences.* New York: Day, 1951
Carswell	Catherine Carswell. *The Savage Pilgrimage: A Narrative of D. H. Lawrence.* Chatto and Windus, 1932
Centaur	*The Centaur Letters.* Austin: Humanities Research Center, 1970
DHL Review	*The D. H. Lawrence Review.* Fayetteville: University of Arkansas, 1968–
Frieda Lawrence	Frieda Lawrence. "*Not I, But the Wind . . .*". Santa Fe: Rydal Press, 1934
Gransden	K. W. Gransden, 'Rananim: D. H. Lawrence's Letters to S. S. Koteliansky', *Twentieth Century*, clix (January–June 1956), 22–32
Huxley	Aldous Huxley, ed. *The Letters of D. H. Lawrence.* Heinemann, 1932
Irvine, Brett	Peter L. Irvine and Anne Kiley, eds. 'D. H. Lawrence and Frieda Lawrence: Letters to Dorothy Brett', *D. H. Lawrence Review*, ix (Fayetteville, Spring 1976), 1–116

Lacy, *Seltzer*	Gerald M. Lacy, ed. *D. H. Lawrence: Letters to Thomas and Adele Seltzer*. Santa Barbara: Black Sparrow Press, 1976
Lawrence–Gelder	Ada Lawrence and G. Stuart Gelder. *Young Lorenzo: Early Life of D. H. Lawrence*. Florence: G. Orioli [1931]
Letters, i.	James T. Boulton, ed. *The Letters of D. H. Lawrence*, Volume I, September 1901–May 1913. Cambridge: Cambridge University Press, 1979
Letters, ii.	George J. Zytaruk and James T. Boulton, eds. *The Letters of D. H. Lawrence*, Volume II, June 1913–October 1916. Cambridge: Cambridge University Press, 1981
Letters, iii.	James T. Boulton and Andrew Robertson, eds. *The Letters of D. H. Lawrence*, Volume III, October 1916–June 1921. Cambridge: Cambridge University Press, 1984
Letters, iv.	Warren Roberts, James T. Boulton and Elizabeth Mansfield, eds. *The Letters of D. H. Lawrence*, Volume IV, June 1921–March 1924. Cambridge: Cambridge University Press, 1987
Luhan	Mabel Dodge Luhan. *Lorenzo in Taos*. New York: Knopf, 1932
Moore, *Intelligent Heart*	Harry T. Moore. *The Intelligent Heart: The Story of D. H. Lawrence*. New York: Farrar, Straus, and Young, 1954
Moore, *Poste Restante*	Harry T. Moore. *Poste Restante: A Lawrence Travel Calendar*. Berkeley and Los Angeles: University of California Press, 1956
Moore	Harry T. Moore, ed. *The Collected Letters of D. H. Lawrence*. 2 volumes. Heinemann, 1962
Murry, *New Adelphi*	John Middleton Murry, 'Reminiscences of D. H. Lawrence I–VII', *New Adelphi*, iii (June–August 1930–March 1931)
Nehls	Edward Nehls, ed. *D. H. Lawrence: A Composite Biography*. 3 volumes. Madison: University of Wisconsin Press, 1957–9
Parmenter	Ross Parmenter. *Lawrence in Oaxaca*. Salt Lake City: Gibbs M. Smith, 1984
Roberts	Warren Roberts. *A Bibliography of D. H. Lawrence*,

	2nd edition. Cambridge: Cambridge University Press, 1982
Sagar, Wilkinsons	Keith Sagar, 'The Lawrences and the Wilkinsons', *Review of English Literature*, iii (October 1962), 62–75
Secker	Martin Secker, ed. *Letters from D. H. Lawrence to Martin Secker 1911–1930*. [Bridgefoot, Iver] 1970
Skinner	M. L. Skinner. *The Fifth Sparrow*. Sydney, Australia: Sydney University Press, 1972
Tedlock, *Lawrence MSS*	E. W. Tedlock. *The Frieda Lawrence Collection of D. H. Lawrence Manuscripts: A Descriptive Bibliography*. Albuquerque: University of New Mexico, 1948
TLS	*The Times Literary Supplement*
Zytaruk	George J. Zytaruk, ed. *The Quest for Rananim: D. H. Lawrence's Letters to S. S. Koteliansky 1914 to 1930*. Montreal: McGill–Queen's University Press, 1970

MONETARY TERMS

tanner = sixpence (6d) = 2½p.
bob = one shilling (1/-) = 5p.
half-a-crown = 2/6 = 12½p.
quid = £1.
guinea = £1/1/- = £1.05.

LAWRENCE: A CHRONOLOGY, 1924–1927

11 March 1924	Lawrences arrive in New York City with Brett
post 11 March 1924	Writes and rewrites 'Jimmy and the Desperate Woman', 'The Last Laugh' and 'The Border-Line'
15 or 16 March 1924	Attends concert and visits Willa Cather, and to tea with her the next day
18 March 1924	Leaves for Taos; sees Harriet Monroe in Chicago
21 March 1924	Arrives in Santa Fe
22 March–5 May 1924	Taos at Mabel Luhan's
c. 26 March 1924	Finishes 'The Last Laugh'
c. 28 March 1924	Mabel Luhan returns to Taos with Ida Rauh
c. 30 March 1924	Lawrences move into two-storey house and Brett into studio
April 1924	Probably writes 'The Overtone'; 'A Review of *The Book of Revelation* by Dr. John Oman' in *Adelphi*
3 April 1924	Antonio Luhan and Jaime de Angulo arrive in Taos; Willard Johnson has typed 'The Last Laugh' and returns to Santa Fe
4 April 1924	Sends copies of 'Jimmy and the Desperate Woman', 'The Last Laugh' and 'The Border-Line' to Curtis Brown and A. W. Barmby; Mabel Luhan has given Frieda 'The Flying Heart' ranch
6 April 1924	Visits ranch
9 April 1924	To Taos pueblo for dance
10 April 1924	Sends jacket-design for *The Boy in the Bush* to Martin Secker; Brett's sent to Thomas Seltzer
ante 14 April 1924	Nina Witt and Ida Rauh arrive
ante 20 April 1924	Writes 'Indians and Entertainment'
20 April 1924	Easter; writes 'O! Americans!'; sends typescripts of 'Indians and Entertainment' to Curtis Brown and Barmby
22–3 April 1924	To Santo Domingo pueblo for dances; writes

	'The Dance of the Sprouting Corn'; de Angulo goes with them as first stage back to California
May 1924	'Liberty' in *Adelphi* (from *Little Novels of Sicily*); 'Dear Old Horse: A London Letter' and 'The Bad Girl in the Pansy Bed' (drawing) in *Laughing Horse*
2 May 1924	Sends his revised version of Brett's jacket-design for *The Boy in the Bush* and Martin Secker's duplicate proofs of *The Boy* to Thomas Seltzer
5 May–11 October 1924	At Lobo (later called Kiowa) Ranch
12 May 1924	Geronimo comes to Lobo in carriage; tries to finish first half of 'Pan in America' (completed after 14 May)
17–18 May 1924	To Taos via Arroyo Seco (setting for 'The Woman Who Rode Away')
19 May 1924	Shopping and return to Lobo with Luhans
20 May 1924	'Finish [rebuilding Lobo] this week-end, I hope'
24 May 1924	Lawrences move into their cabin; Mabel Luhan brings Clarence Thompson to Lobo
25 May 1924	Outing to Red River (with Mabel Luhan and Thompson)
27 May 1924	Luhans and Thompson return to Taos
28 May 1924	Washed and painted Luhans' cabin
31 May–1 June 1924	To Taos
June 1924	Writes revised version of 'Pan in America'; 'On Being a Man' in *Vanity Fair* (in *Adelphi*, September 1924)
3 June 1924	Reports 'The Border-Line' sold to *Smart Set*
4 June 1924	Adobes made for oven
6 June 1924	Mabel Luhan and Thompson bring supplies
6? June 1924	José takes Contentos and Cequa back to Taos
7 June 1924	'Finished all our hard work . . . after 5 weeks slaving'; returns contract for Magnus's *Memoirs of the Foreign Legion* to Curtis Brown
8 June 1924	Hawks visit Lobo
12 June 1924	'I began to write a story' (either *St. Mawr* or

	'The Woman Who Rode Away')
15 June 1924	To Del Monte Ranch to go fishing with Hawks and Gilletes at Cabresto Lake
16 June 1924	Geronimo builds oven (in use ante 28 June); Mabel Luhan and Thompson come to Lobo; Louis Cottam also comes
c. 17 June 1924	Brett typing 'The Woman Who Rode Away' on Mabel Luhan's typewriter
18 June 1924	Has heard 'The Border-Line' sold to *Hutchinson's Magazine*; 'The Woman Who Rode Away' 'finished' and *St. Mawr* 'being done again'
18–23 June 1924	To Taos; meets Alice Sprague; may have thought of *Altitude*
18 June 1924	Meets George Creel
19 June 1924	Reports *Theatre Arts* have 'The Dance of the Sprouting Corn' and two drawings
22 June 1924	To Shadybrook Inn for lunch
23 June 1924	Mabel Luhan reads 'The Woman Who Rode Away'
c. 28 June 1924	Lawrences sleep in Indian camp
c. 28 June–3 July 1924	Builds kitchen porch
28 June 1924	'I've written two stories'
July 1924	'The Dance of the Sprouting Corn' and *The Corn Dance* (drawing) in *Theatre Arts Monthly* (essay in *Adelphi*, August 1924)
5 July 1924	Luhans retrieve MS of *Sons and Lovers* from post office
7 July 1924	Sends typescripts of 'The Woman Who Rode Away' to Curtis Brown and Barmby; returns corrected proofs of Magnus introduction to Secker; Ferdinand takes Poppy
post 7 July 1924	Brett begins to type *St. Mawr*
c. 8 July 1924	Ufers visit Lobo
23 July 1924	'I go on slowly with my second long-short story' (*St. Mawr*)
30 July–7? August 1924	Johnson visits Lobo; Mabel Luhan drives him up but does not stay

30 July 1924	'Just winding up "St. Mawr"'
August 1924	'Rex' in *Stories from the Dial* (USA)
3? August 1924	Spits blood (in bed till at least 5 August); Dr T. P. Martin comes next day
ante 5 August 1924	Gaspards visit
ante 7 August 1924	Joseph Foster, Margaret Hale and Swinburne Hale visit Lobo
8 August 1924	'Nearly got to the end of my second "novelette –"'
by 9 August 1924	Renames ranch 'Kiowa'
13 August 1924	To Taos and Santa Fe
14–23 August 1924	To Hotevilla for snake dance on 17–18 August via Laguna (14 August), Gallup (15), St Michaels (16), Laguna (18), Chin Lee (19), Cañon de Chelly (20), Gallup (21), Santa Fe (22 August, Hotel de Vargas)
22 August 1924	Writes 'Just Back from the Snake Dance – Tired Out'
23 August 1924	To Taos and Kiowa (25 August)
26 August 1924	Writes 'The Hopi Snake Dance'
late August 1924	Trip to Columbine Lake with Brett and Hawks (setting for 'The Princess')
28 August 1924	*The Boy in the Bush* published in England by Secker (30 September in USA by Seltzer)
30 August 1924	Sends 'Hopi Snake Dance' to Nancy Pearn; rides to San Cristobal
September 1924	'The Border-Line' in *Smart Set* and *Hutchinson's*; 'Just Back from the Snake Dance – Tired Out' in *Laughing Horse*
1 September 1924	Writes 'Introduction to Bibliography' ('The Bad Side of Books') and sends to Edward McDonald on 10 September
10 September 1924	Death of his father, John Arthur Lawrence
by 12 September 1924	Writes 'Climbing Down Pisgah'
13 September 1924	'*St. Mawr* is finished and Brett is typing it out'
21 September 1924	Johnson to Kiowa
by 28 September 1924	Completes 'Epilogue' to *Movements in European History*

30 September 1924	Sends typescript of *St. Mawr* to Curtis Brown and Barmby; writing 'The Princess'; sends MSS to Barmby for safekeeping
29/30 September–1/2 October 1924	In Taos, for San Geronimo festival; stays in two-storey house
October 1924	'Jimmy and the Desperate Woman' in *Criterion*
1 October 1924	*Memoirs of the Foreign Legion* with Lawrence's 'Introduction' published in England by Secker (January 1925 in USA by Alfred Knopf)
8 October 1924	'The Princess' 'being typed now'; posted to Nancy Pearn c. 11 October
11 October 1924	To Taos
16 October 1924	To Santa Fe
19 October 1924	To El Paso
20–3 October 1924	To Mexico City
23 October–8 November 1924	Hotel Monte Carlo, Av. Uruguay, Mexico D.F.
25 October 1924	Lunch with Zelia Nuttall
26 October 1924	Lunch with Zelia Nuttall at Coyoacán, and dines with British Consul-General, Norman King at Tlalpam; 'Indians and Entertainment' in *New York Times Magazine* (in *Adelphi*, November 1924)
between 25 and 28 October 1924	Visits National Museum and Virgin of Guadalupe church with Brett
31 October 1924	Dines with P.E.N. at Oriental Café
post 31 October 1924	With Luis and Ruth Quintanilla to Sanborn's
2 November 1924	With Quintanilla to meet Edward Weston
4 November 1924	Weston photographs Lawrence
5 November 1924	Lunch with Somerset Maugham
8 November 1924	At Hotel Mexico, Tehuacán
9–18 November 1924	At Hotel Francia, Oaxaca; meets Rosalind Hughes
ante 14 November 1924	Calls on Governor Ibarra in palace
18 November 1924–14 February 1925	At Avenida Pino Suarez. #43. *Oaxaca* (Oax.), Mexico
19 November 1924	Begins second version of 'Quetzalcoatl' (*The Plumed Serpent*)

29 November 1924	'I am working again' (and Brett typing)
30? November 1924	To Mitla with Donald Miller via Santa María del Tule
December 1924	'The Hopi Snake Dance' in *Theatre Arts Monthly* (and in *Adelphi* January–February 1925)
7 December 1924	'I am working at my novel'; to opera house to see *The Thief of Baghdad* at Teatro Luis Mier y Teran
19?–25? December 1924	Writes four 'Mornings in Mexico' essays
21 December 1924	Walks to San Andrés Huayapan
24 December 1924	Writes 'Preface to *Black Swans*'
post 24 December 1924	Writes 'Resurrection' after reading Tolstoy's *Resurrection*
26 December 1924	Rosalind Hughes leaves Oaxaca
31 December 1924	Reaches p. 382 of 'Quetzalcoatl' (beginning of second notebook)
10 January 1925	Sends four 'Mornings in Mexico' essays to Barmby
by 10 January 1925	Rewrites Quintanilla's 'Mexico, Why Not?'
14 January 1925	Receives *Memoirs of the Foreign Legion*
19 January 1925	Brett to Mexico City (leaves for Del Monte on 8 February)
23 January 1925	Frieda: 'Lawrence is seedy . . . has a dread of Mexico'
c. 30 January 1925	'We had a little earthquake'; both ill
c. 1 February 1925	Finishes 'Quetzalcoatl'
c. 1–14 February 1925	Has influenza, recurrence of malaria and typhoid fever
14–24 February 1925	To Hotel Francia, Oaxaca
25–6 February 1925	To Mexico City via Tehuacán
26 February–25 March 1925	At Imperial Hotel, Mexico D.F.
27 February 1925	To British Consulate
March–May 1925	'The Princess' (I–III) in *Calendar of Modern Letters*
2 March 1925	'The Last Laugh' in *The New Decameron IV*
3 March 1925	Visits Norman King's office; has 'a very attractive scheme' for a play ('Noah's Flood')

6–11 March 1925	In bed; tested by doctors who decide against sea trip
9 March 1925	*Little Novels of Sicily* published in USA by Seltzer
11–19 March 1925	Dictates the first 9 pp. of 'The Flying-Fish' to Frieda
18 March 1925	Lunch at Conways'
21 March 1925	Lunch at Zelia Nuttall's
23 March 1925	Returns proofs of *St. Mawr* to Secker
25–9 March 1925	To Santa Fe (Hotel de Vargas)
31 March–1 April 1925	To Del Monte Ranch
1–5 April 1925	At Del Monte Ranch
6 April–9 September 1925	At Kiowa Ranch
10 April 1925	Tony Luhan and Nina Witt visit
14 April 1925	Has written six scenes of *David* and gives to Brett to type
16 April 1925	Frieda to Taos with Betty Cottam
17 April 1925	Agrees to 'a little book of uncollected essays' to be published by Centaur Press (*Reflections on the Death of a Porcupine*)
18 April 1925	Sends 'Accumulated Mail' to Barmby for Knopf
1 May 1925	*David* '⅔ done' (finished 7 May)
14 May 1925	*St. Mawr Together with The Princess* published by Secker in England
c. 16–20 May 1925	Ida Rauh to Kiowa to read *David*; Lawrence writes music for *David*
19 May–18 July 1925	Friedel Jaffe visits Kiowa
by 21 May 1925	Probably has received typescript of 'Quetzalcoatl'
23 May 1925	Agrees to title *The Plumed Serpent*
c. 30 May–ante 18 June 1925	Builds corral
June 1925	Writes 'Art and Morality', 'Morality and the Novel' and 'The Novel'
1 June 1925	Susan, the cow, arrives at Kiowa
3 June 1925	Receives copies of Knopf's *St. Mawr*
5 June 1925	*St. Mawr* published in USA by Knopf

June–early July 1925	Revises 'Quetzalcoatl' in typescript
14 June 1925	Sherman's review, 'Lawrence Cultivates His Beard', in *New York Herald Tribune Books*
18 June 1925	Brett finishes typing *David* (copies to Barmby and Ida Rauh); Trinidad leaves
19 June 1925	Friedel Jaffe and Frederico Alires to Taos
23 June 1925	*A Bibliography of the Writings of D. H. Lawrence* including 'The Bad Side of Books' published in USA by the Centaur Book Shop, Philadelphia
27 June 1925	Receives copies of *Bibliography*
29 June 1925	Sends 'The Novel' (revised) to Centaur Press
July–August 1925	'The Woman Who Rode Away' (I–II) in *Dial* (in *Criterion*, July 1925, January 1926)
12 July 1925	Margaret Hale and Dr Gertrude Light visit Kiowa
by 13 July 1925	Frieda has started translation of *David*
post 15 July–12 August 1925	Writes 'Reflections on the Death of a Porcupine', 'Him with His Tail in His Mouth', 'Blessed Are the Powerful', 'Aristocracy' and 'Note to "The Crown"'; Brett types 'Power' ('Blessed Are the Powerful'): 'I have been typing one on "Love" and another called "Power"'
24 July 1925	Brett in Taos and sees Tony Luhan
ante 29 July 1925	Willa Cather visits Kiowa
12–ante 22 August 1925	Revises 'The Crown' and 'Love' ('. . . . . . Love was Once a Little Boy')
ante 19 August 1925	Kyle and Mary Crichton visit Kiowa
30 August 1925	Secker receives *The Plumed Serpent* TS
9 September 1925	At Del Monte Ranch
10–13 September 1925	To New York City via Denver (11 September)
13–21 September 1925	At 71 Washington Place, New York (Nina Witt's apartment)
14 September 1925	At Greenwich Theatre to see *Outside Looking In*
18 September 1925	Meets McDonalds and Masons
21 September 1925	Sends corrected proofs of 'Accumulated Mail' to Blanche Knopf (published on 24 December in *The Borzoi* by Knopf)

21–30 September 1925	To Southampton on *S. S. Resolute*
30 September –8 October 1925	At Garland's Hotel, Suffolk Street, Pall Mall, London
4–5 October 1925	Visits Carswells near High Wycombe
7 October 1925	Visits Seckers at Bridgefoot, Iver
8–14 October 1925	With Emily King at Sneinton, Nottingham
13 October 1925	Completes review of Corvo's *Hadrian the Seventh*
14–22 October 1925	With Ada Clarke at Ripley, Derbyshire
by 20 October 1925	Proofs of *The Plumed Serpent* returned to Secker; review of Pickthall's *Saïd the Fisherman* completed
22–9 October 1925	In Gordon MacFarlane's flat, 73 Gower Street, London
23 October 1925	Meets William Gerhardie, Margaret Kennedy and Rose Macaulay
25 October 1925	Lunch with Lady Cynthia and Herbert Asquith
29 October 1925	Leaves London for Baden-Baden via Strasbourg
30 October–12 November 1925	At Baden-Baden with Frieda's mother
November 1925	'Art and Morality' in *Calendar of Modern Letters*
ante 12 November 1925	Receives proofs of *David*
12–15 November 1925	Stays with Carl and Maria Seelig in Kastanienbaum, near Lucerne
15–23 November 1925	At Hotel Miramare and then Albergo Ligure, Spotorno, Italy
17 November 1925	Returns 'mauled' copy of *Movements in European History* to Oxford University Press
21 November 1925	Sends review of Krout's *The Origins of Prohibition* to Curtis Brown
23 November 1925–20 April 1926	At Villa Bernarda, Spotorno
ante 25 November 1925	Writes 'Europe Versus America'
25 November 1925	Writes 'A Little Moonshine with Lemon'
December 1925	Review of Corvo's *Hadrian the Seventh*, and 'Corasmin and the Parrots' in *Adelphi*;

	'Morality and the Novel' in *Calendar of Modern Letters*
4 December 1925	To Alassio to see Barbara Weekley; she returns the visit over the weekend c. 13 December
7 December 1925	*Reflections on the Death of a Porcupine and Other Essays* published in USA by the Centaur Press, Philadelphia
ante 12 December 1925	Rewrites part of Mollie Skinner's story, 'The Hand'
12 December 1925	Receives typescript of 'Smile' from Brett; sends her the MS of 'Sun' for typing
by 12 December 1925–18 January 1926	Secker at Villa Maria, Spotorno
19 December 1925	Sends 'Smile' to Curtis Brown
24 December 1925	First part of 'Sun' typescript arrives from Brett
25 December 1925	Visited by Barbara Weekley 'for a few days'
27 December 1925	Review of Pickthall's *Saïd the Fisherman* in *New York Herald Tribune Books*
29 December 1925	'Glad Ghosts' finished and sent to Brett for typing
January 1926	'Pan in America' in *Southwest Review*; 'The Last Laugh' in *Ainslee's*
6 January 1926	Receives remainder of 'Sun' typescript and sends whole to Curtis Brown
19 January 1926	First part of 'Glad Ghosts' typescript arrives from Brett; more before 25 January; the whole to Curtis Brown on 29 January
20–6 January 1926	Visit from Barbara Weekley
21 January 1926	Finishes *The Virgin and the Gipsy*, and sends MS to Secker; typescript received from Secker on 30 January; *The Plumed Serpent* published in England by Secker (in USA by Knopf on 5 February 1926)
31 January 1926	Review of Krout's *The Origins of Prohibition* in *New York Herald Tribune Books*
February 1926	'Creative Evolution' in *Adelphi*
2 February 1926	'I've left off writing now'
10–22 February 1926	Visit from Ada Clarke and Lizzie Booth

12 February 1926	Frieda's daughters Elsa and Barbara arrive at Albergo Ligure, Spotorno; by 16th she has joined them
20 February 1926	'The Late Mr. Maurice Magnus' in *New Statesman*
22 February 1926	Lawrence, Ada Clarke and Lizzie Booth go to Hotel Beau Séjour, Monte Carlo, then drive to Nice on 25th before the women return to England; Elsa and Barbara Weekley move into Villa Bernarda with Frieda
25 February 1926	'The Rocking-Horse Winner' sent to Curtis Brown
25–6 February 1926	At Hotel Brice, Nice
26–7 February 1926	To Capri via Ventimiglia and Rome
27 February–c. 10 March 1926	Stays with Earl and Achsah Brewster at Villa Quattro Venti on Capri
March 1926	*David* published in England by Secker (in USA by Knopf on 23 April 1926)
c. 10–22 March 1926	At Hotel Palumbo, Ravello, initially with Brett
22 March–3 April 1926	In Rome with Millicent Beveridge and Mabel Harrison (22–5 March); then to Assisi, Perugia and Hotel Washington, Florence (25–30 March); and finally with them to Ravenna
April 1926	'The Gentle Art of Marketing in Mexico' in *Travel*; 'A Little Moonshine with Lemon', 'Mediterranean in January', 'Europe Versus America', 'Beyond the Rockies', 'Paris Letter' and 'Pueblo Indian Dancers' (drawing) in *Laughing Horse* (*D. H. Lawrence number*)
3 April 1926	Returns to Villa Bernarda, Spotorno
14 April 1926	Review of William Carlos Williams's *In the American Grain* in *Nation* (New York)
20 April–6 May 1926	To Pisa with Frieda and her daughters and then at Pensione Lucchesi, Florence (Elsa and Barbara Weekley leave on 28 April for London)
6 May 1926	Moves into Villa Mirenda, San Paolo Mosciano, Scandicci, the Lawrences' home until June 1928

ante 13 May 1926	Writes Introduction to William Siebenhaar's translation of *Max Havelaar*
13 May 1926	'Two Blue Birds' sent to Curtis Brown
16 May 1926	Reginald Turner and Giuseppe Orioli visit Villa Mirenda
ante 26 May–ante 14 June 1926	Types Frieda's German translation of *David*
2 June 1926	Visits Sir George and Lady Ida Sitwell at Castello di Montegufoni, Montagnana, near Florence
19 June 1926	'Smile' in *Nation and Athenæum* (and in *New Masses*, New York, June 1926)
25 June 1926	Writes 'Fireworks'
ante 27 June 1926	Writes 'The Nightingale'
27 June 1926	Writing 'The Man Who Loved Islands'
July 1926	'Glad Ghosts I' in *Dial* (Part II in August); 'The Rocking-Horse Winner' in *Harper's Bazaar*
1 July 1926	Lunches with Giorgio Chiavacci, the European fencing champion
ante 7 July 1926	Visited by Lord Berners
12 July 1926	To Baden-Baden
13–29 July 1926	Visits Frieda's mother in Baden-Baden
post 16 July 1926	Proofs of Irish edition of *Movements in European History* checked by Vere Collins
c. 29 July 1926	Probably wrote 'Mercury'
29 July 1926	To London via Strasbourg, Brussels and Ostend
30 July–28 August 1926	At 25 Rossetti Garden Mansions, Chelsea
5 August 1926	Visited by Nancy Pearn
7?–8 August 1926	Stays with Richard Aldington and Arabella Yorke at Malthouse Cottage, Padworth, near Reading
9–21 August 1926	Stays with Millicent Beveridge in Inverness (Frieda remains in London)
16–18 August 1926	Visit to Fort William, Mallaig and Isle of Skye
20 August 1926	Sends review of H. G. Wells's *The World of William Clissold* to Curtis Brown

21 August 1926	Leaves Inverness for Mablethorpe, Lincolnshire where Frieda joins him on 27th
28 August–13 September 1926	At Sutton-on-Sea, Lincolnshire
September 1926	Irish edition of *Movements in European History* published in Dublin; *Sun* published by 'E. Archer' (Charles Lahr) following its appearance in *New Coterie*, Autumn 1926
13 September 1926	To Emily King's in Nottingham (Frieda to London)
14–16 September 1926	Stays with Ada Clarke in Ripley (makes final visit to Eastwood)
16–28 September 1926	At 30 Willoughby Road, Hampstead
22 September 1926	Returns Benn's proofs of *Glad Ghosts* to Curtis Brown; sees Louis and Jeanette Untermeyer
23 September 1926	Visits Catherine Carswell in Parkhill Road, London
28 September 1926	'The Rocking-Horse Winner' in *The Ghost-Book*, ed. Lady Cynthia Asquith; leaves London for Paris via Folkestone and Boulogne
October 1926	*Twilight in Italy* issued in Cape's 'Travellers' Library'; review of Wells's *The World of William Clissold* in *Calendar*
1 October 1926	Leaves Paris for Lausanne
3–4 October 1926	Travels from Lausanne to Villa Mirenda, Florence via Milan
6?–11 October 1926	Visit from Richard Aldington and Arabella Yorke
16 October 1926	Sends music for *David* to producer
c. 18 October 1926	'More Modern Love' (later entitled 'In Love') to Curtis Brown
22–8 October 1926	Visits from Aldous and Maria Huxley
26 October 1926	Reaches p. 41 of *Lady Chatterley's Lover* (finishes first version c. 25 November)
November 1926	*Glad Ghosts* in Benn's 'Yellow Books'; 'Sunday Stroll in Sleepy Mexico' in *Travel*
6 November 1926	'The Woman Who Rode Away' in *The Best British Stories of 1926*
ante 11 November 1926	Painted *A Holy Family*

ante 23 November 1926	Completes painting *Men Bathing*
23 November 1926	Agrees title *Mornings in Mexico* with Secker
27 November 1926	Begins painting *Boccaccio Story* (finished by 19 December)
1 December 1926	Sends sketch, possibly 'Man is a Hunter', to Curtis Brown
c. 1 December 1926	Starts *Lady Chatterley's Lover*, second version (has finished by 27 February 1927)
12, 13, 19 December 1926	*The Widowing of Mrs. Holroyd* produced by Esmé Percy at the Kingsway Theatre, London
19 December 1926	Goes to Stenterello Theatre, Florence
c. 19–c. 28 December 1926	Painting *Fight with an Amazon*
24 December 1926	Gives party for twenty-seven local peasants
31 December 1926	Two poems, 'The Old Orchard' and 'Rainbow', to Curtis Brown
January 1927	Review of Cunninghame Graham's *Pedro de Valdivia* in *Calendar*
1 January 1927	Review of Tomlinson's *Gifts of Fortune* in *T. P.'s and Cassell's Weekly*
c. 8–25 January 1927	Painting *Red Willow Trees*
9 January 1927	Sends 'On being a Success' to Curtis Brown
10 January 1927	Visits Villa Curonia at Arcetri, near Florence, with Orioli
c. 12 January 1927	Finishes painting *Negro Wedding*
16–18? January 1927	Visit from Earl Brewster; with Brewster meets Alberto Magnelli on 18th
20 January 1927	Revised Irish edn of *Movements in European History* (OUP) for sale to 'Catholic Communities outside Ireland'
February 1927	'Mornings in Mexico, The Mozo' in *Adelphi*; 'Mercury' in *Atlantic Monthly*; Secker reprints *David*
6 February 1927	Painting *Flight Back into Paradise*
8 February 1927	Selects title *Lady Chatterley's Lover*
25 February 1927	Sends to Curtis Brown review of van Vechten's *Nigger Heaven*, White's *Flight*, Dos Passos's *Manhattan Transfer* and Hemingway's *In Our Time*

28 February 1927	Sends a Scrutiny on John Galsworthy to Curtis Brown
ante 8 March 1927	Begins painting *Resurrection*
11 March 1927	Sends 'The Lovely Lady' to Curtis Brown
17 March 1927	Frieda goes to Baden-Baden
19 March 1927	Lawrence to Rome en route to stay with the Brewsters at the Palazzo Cimbrone, Ravello

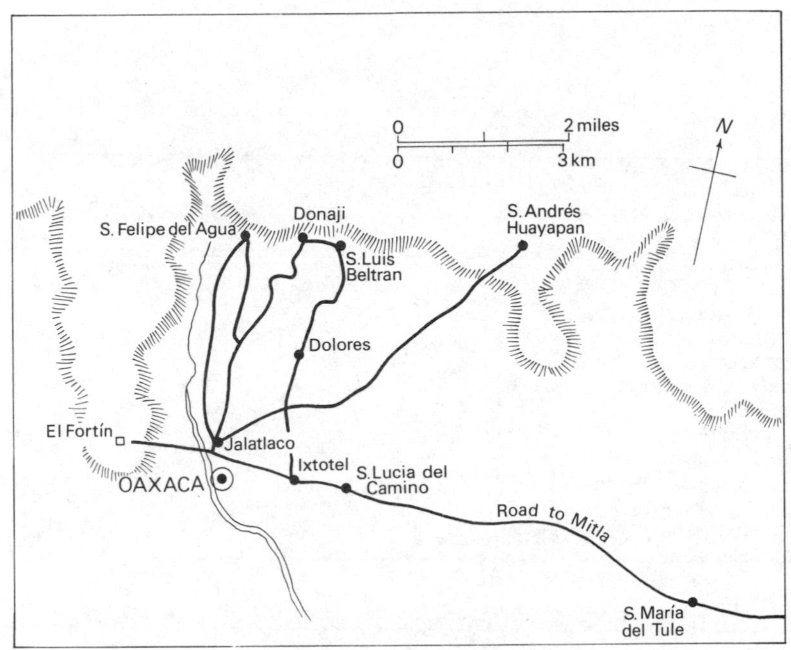

Oaxaca region (adapted from Parmenter)

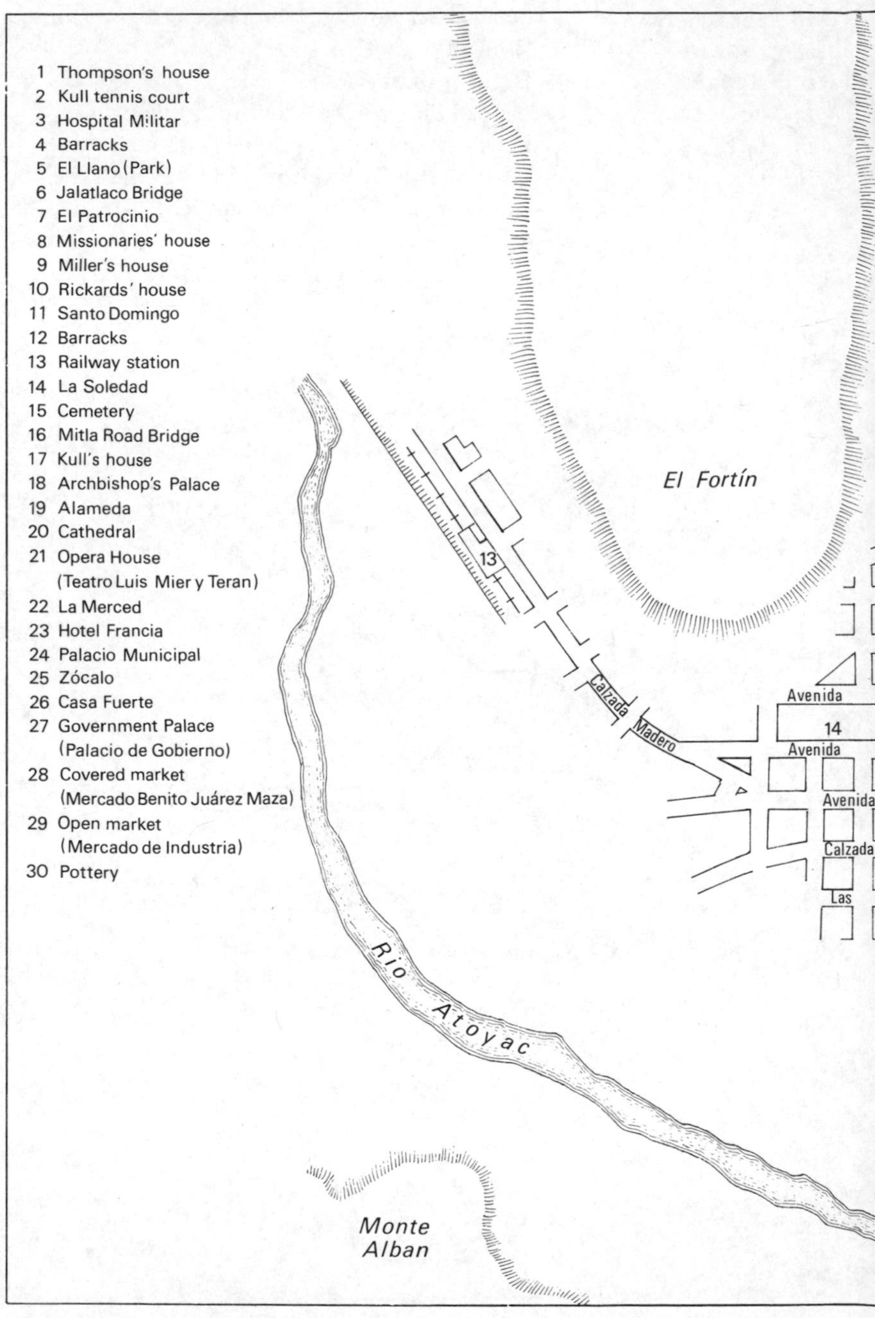
1 Thompson's house
2 Kull tennis court
3 Hospital Militar
4 Barracks
5 El Llano (Park)
6 Jalatlaco Bridge
7 El Patrocinio
8 Missionaries' house
9 Miller's house
10 Rickards' house
11 Santo Domingo
12 Barracks
13 Railway station
14 La Soledad
15 Cemetery
16 Mitla Road Bridge
17 Kull's house
18 Archbishop's Palace
19 Alameda
20 Cathedral
21 Opera House
(Teatro Luis Mier y Teran)
22 La Merced
23 Hotel Francia
24 Palacio Municipal
25 Zócalo
26 Casa Fuerte
27 Government Palace
(Palacio de Gobierno)
28 Covered market
(Mercado Benito Juárez Maza)
29 Open market
(Mercado de Industria)
30 Pottery
El Fortín
13
Calzada Madero
Avenida
14
Avenida
Avenida
Calzada
Las
Rio Atoyac
Monte Alban

City of Oaxaca

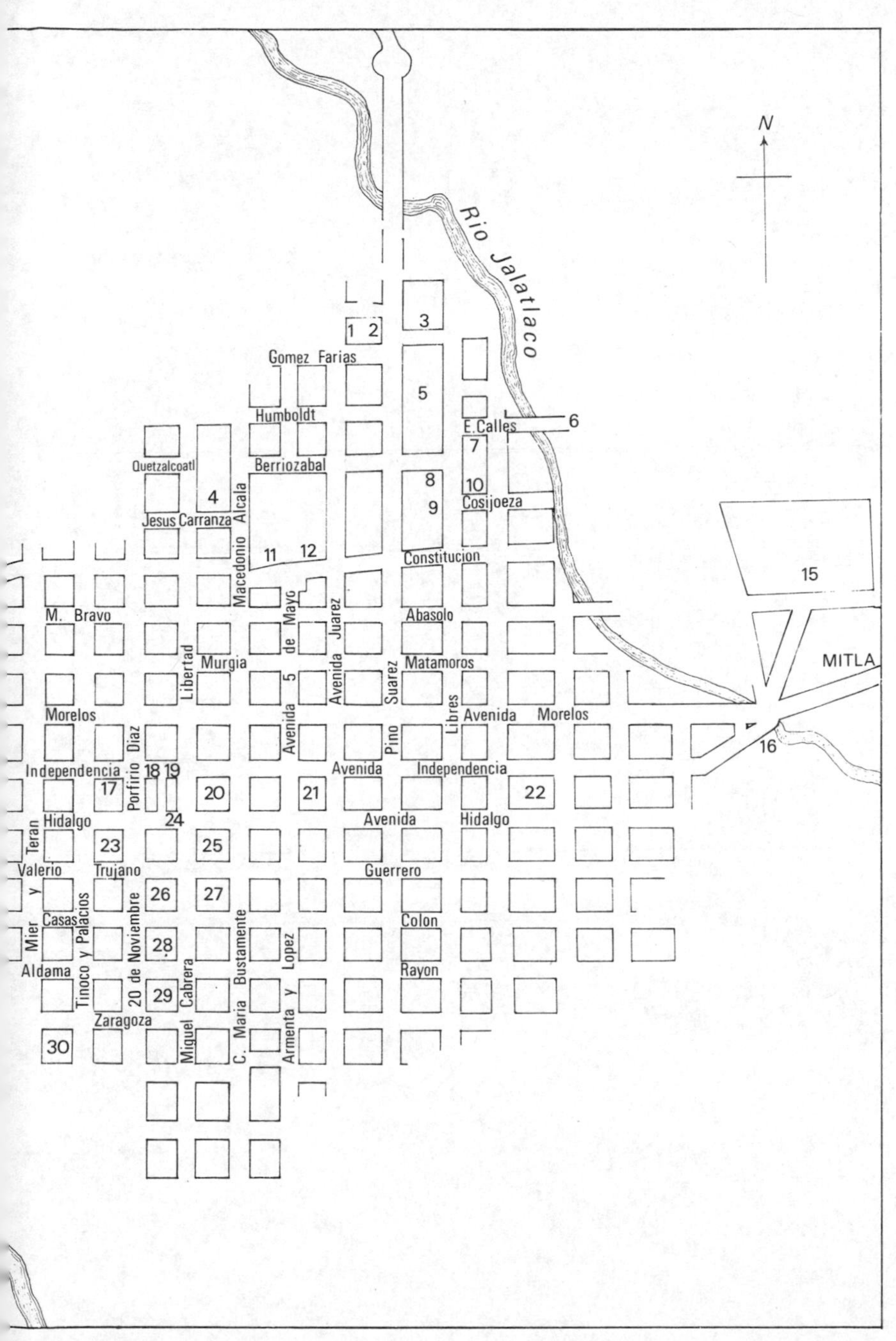

N
Rio Jalatlaco
Gomez Farias
Humboldt
E.Calles
Quetzalcoatl
Berriozabal
Jesus Carranza
Macedonio Alcala
Cosijoeza
Constitucion
M. Bravo
Abasolo
Murgia
Matamoros
Libertad
5 de Mayo
Avenida Juarez
Suarez
Pino
Libres
Avenida Morelos
Morelos
MITLA
Independencia
Porfirio Diaz
Avenida Independencia
Hidalgo
Avenida Hidalgo
Teran
Valerio
Trujano
Guerrero
Mier y Casas
Tinoco y Palacios
20 de Noviembre
Colon
Aldama
Rayon
Miguel Cabrera
C. Maria Bustamente
Armenta y Lopez
Zaragoza
1
2
3
4
5
6
7
8
9
10
11
12
15
16
17
18
19
20
21
22
23
24
25
26
27
28
29
30

INTRODUCTION

The volume opens with Lawrence's return to USA but the excited anticipation with which he had approached the New World eighteen months earlier had been dissipated. In March 1924 he returned principally for business reasons: to satisfy himself concerning the rumours he had heard about the precarious state of his publisher Thomas Seltzer's affairs; and to enable him to pay his American taxes. New York he now regarded as 'stiff, machine-made, and against nature' – but it was more stimulating than what he had left behind: 'a machine is perhaps less distressing than a dying animal: London'.[1] Europe had depressed him as is evident from three stories he had started just before leaving. 'Jimmy and the Desperate Woman', 'The Last Laugh' and 'The Border-Line' 'are the result of Europe, and perhaps a bit dismal'; they share a tone that is 'wintry' and bitter; and they reveal a fascination with calculated cruelty in human relationships.[2] Yet, before three months were out, Lawrence asked his English publisher Martin Secker to order two periodicals so that he could keep in touch with the popular literary scene in London; in Mexico, in November, he confessed to being 'a bit sick of the American continent' and sometimes 'a longing for Europe' came over him; and by June 1925 he was quite clear that, though America was rewarding for a short time, eventually it 'makes one feel leathery in one's soul'. 'It's time I was softened down a bit, with a little oil of Europe.'[3]

By 'Europe' we must understand the continent, principally Italy and, later, France, but excluding Britain. Lawrence's affection for the English countryside, especially that of the Midlands, remained strong (his detailed description of 'the country of my heart' in a letter to Rolf Gardiner, confirms that);[4] he felt nostalgia for the Lincolnshire coast where he had spent holidays as a boy with his mother; his attachment to his sisters continued firm; but he was determined never to live in England again. At the close of this volume he is found disenchanted with USA, too: 'America puts me off', he wrote in March 1927.[5] The American continent had become associated with illness and, particularly in the case of Mexico in February 1925, nearly dying; he would never visit it again. 'Whatever else I am, I'm European', he declared, 'my desire to go far has left me.'[6] This resolution persisted for the three years of life still left to him.

Lawrence's anxiety in 1924 concerning Thomas Seltzer was well founded. Early the previous year he had disregarded the warning from his then agent in

[1] Letters 3092, 3093. [2] Letters 3098, 3099. [3] Letters 3144, 3300, 3441.
[4] Letter 3904. [5] Letter 3970. [6] Ibid.

USA, Robert Mountsier, that Seltzer's publishing business was in jeopardy. Lawrence was grateful to Seltzer for having published *Women in Love* in 1920 – 'it has made us friends for life'[7] – and then defending it against the threat of suppression in the summer of 1922. Nor should it be forgotten that Seltzer published more first editions by Lawrence than any other American publisher has ever done. But eventually Lawrence had to admit that Mountsier had been right. He conceded in September 1924: 'We are having the struggle with Seltzer that you warned me about. You were right and I was wrong about him.'[8]

Mountsier himself had been dismissed as Lawrence's agent in February 1923; Lawrence then tried to act on his own behalf in USA. However he was glad to accept the advice of Albert Curtis Brown, his English agent, that Curtis Brown's New York office should negotiate with Seltzer and take over the responsibilities of agent in America. Soon after arriving in USA in March 1924 Lawrence established very friendly relations with the Yorkshireman, Arthur Barmby, who ran the New York office, and he was impressed when 'The Border-Line' was sold to *Smart Set* for $175 in June. In 1925 Barmby persuaded Lawrence to allow Alfred A. Knopf to publish *St. Mawr*: this effectively terminated the link with Seltzer.

It was obviously advantageous for Lawrence to use the same reliable agency in London and in New York. As had been the case for several years, he was frequently sought after by magazine editors, book publishers, critics and journalists. To have Barmby handling his American literary affairs and that 'golden' 'magazine girl, Nancy Pearn' handling the non-American, from Curtis Brown's office in London, meant that Lawrence profited from a consistent publishing policy as well as from business efficiency. 'I find them really very good', he assured Catherine Carswell.[9]

Nancy Pearn, for example, encouraged Lawrence (despite Secker's opposition)[10] to accept Ernest Benn's invitation to contribute to the firm's sixpenny series of paperback books of prose and verse. *Glad Ghosts* was included in the series devoted to short stories and later Lawrence readily agreed to publish a selection of poems in Benn's 'Augustan' series. When that appeared, in 1928, Humbert Wolfe wrote in his editorial preface: 'Readers require no introduction to Mr Lawrence, who has established himself as an integral part of modern literature.' This view – reinforced by the commercial interests of publishers and agents – had become generally accepted and Lawrence, acknowledged as a leading man of letters, was the focus of much public and critical attention. Herbert J. Seligmann published the first

[7] *Letters*, iii. 635. [8] Letter 3239. [9] Letter 3719. [10] Letter 3827.

American book on him in February 1924; a Swedish professor of English requested his co-operation towards the writing of a students' handbook of modern English literature in which Lawrence was intended to appear; the Italian critic Carlo Linati asked for his help with the preparation of a critical article on Lawrence's works, as did the Florentine littérateur Aldo Sorani whose 'critique' was published several years later.[11] Lawrence became the subject of a scholarly bibliography to which he contributed a prefatory essay.[12] He was fêted by P.E.N. in Mexico City and Frieda was 'thrilled' to see a caricature of her husband in a market bookshop in Oaxaca.[13] He was mentioned prominently in a pseudo-Joycean novel by an American author; he was invited by the young John Hayward to address the Cambridge 'Heretics'; and his photograph served as an illustration to articles on Capri in the *Tatler* and *Eve*, both in March 1926.[14] His friend 'Spud' Johnson devoted an entire issue of *Laughing Horse* to items by and about Lawrence; among several amusing advertisements Lawrence is listed (together with Kit Carson) among the 'Celebrities [who] have had their Ice-Cream Sodas and Coca-Cola' at La Botica de Capital in Santa Fe. Or, again, along with Belloc, Chesterton, Maugham, Shaw and others, Lawrence contributed at Compton Mackenzie's invitation to a 'Symposium' of 'distinguished men and women' who were willing to name their musical favourites for publication in the *Gramophone*.[15] Lawrence had come a long way since his schoolmaster days in Croydon: the nostalgic letter of 10 February 1927, the last (known) to his friend and teaching colleague at Davidson Road School, Arthur McLeod, brings this into sharp focus.[16]

It had been Lawrence's reputation as a writer which prompted Mabel Dodge (Luhan) to invite him to Taos in September 1922; now, in March 1924, he returned there. From New York Lawrence and Frieda were accompanied by the Honourable Dorothy Brett, daughter of Lord Esher; she was the first recruit to the ideal community 'Rananim',[17] which Lawrence hoped to establish in New Mexico. As could have been predicted, she and Mabel vied strenuously for the position of his chief disciple; Frieda herself was resolved that neither of them should occupy the position they both coveted. Brett's claim to it was strong since she alone among Lawrence's English friends had responded positively to his call for volunteers to found Rananim. She

[11] Letters 3113 and n. 1; 3186 and n. 3; 3731 and n. 2.

[12] Edward McDonald, *A Bibliography of the Writings of D. H. Lawrence* (Philadelphia, 1925). It was prefaced by DHL's essay, 'The Bad Side of Books'.

[13] Letter 3281 and n. 4; Frieda Lawrence 164.

[14] Letters 3569 and p. 359 n. 2; 3604 and nn. 1, 2; 3667 and n. 1.

[15] Letter 3879 and nn. 1, 2.

[16] Letter 3958.

[17] See *Letters*, ii. 252 and n. 3, 259.

abandoned nearly all and followed him. Lawrence's explanation to Mabel Luhan was that 'he had brought Brett along to be a kind of buffer between him and Frieda. "It's a little *too* hard, alone with her".' Mabel regarded Brett, with Toby her ear-trumpet, as 'a spy upon any influence near Lorenzo . . . She was more present and pervasive than the air around him . . . She paid all her attention to him, just as I did'.[18] For her part Frieda recalled:

> Lawrence said to me: 'You know, it will be good for us to have the Brett with us, she will stand between us and people and the world.' I did not really want her with us, and had a suspicion that she might not want to stand between us and the world, but between him and me.[19]

Brett's adoration of Lawrence and relative indifference to everyone else – both plain subsequently in her memoir, *Lawrence and Brett* – infuriated the other two women.

Brett was useful to the Lawrences; Frieda readily acknowledged that 'she did her share of the work'.[20] She helped to clean out and make habitable three filthy and primitive buildings on the ranch (which Mabel Luhan had given Frieda who later gave her in return the manuscript of *Sons and Lovers*); she assisted with cleaning the spring and making furnishings. Moreover Brett could type and thus be of direct value to Lawrence. She typed 'St. Mawr', the early chapters of the second version of *The Plumed Serpent*, short essays, 'The Woman Who Rode Away' and 'The Princess'. She designed several dust-jackets for Lawrence's books[21] and shared his keen interest in painting. These were, of course, activities which gave her precedence, thereby increasing Frieda's resentment. Frieda regretted the loss of privacy and was irritated by Brett's hero-worship of Lawrence balanced, as Frieda sensed it was, 'by a preconceived critical attitude towards me. He was always perfect and I always wrong, in her eyes.'[22]

Lawrence's arrival in Taos was soon followed by tension and then the break with Mabel Luhan. The atmosphere which precipitated it can be illustrated from her account and Brett's of the same disastrous visit from the ranch to Taos on 18–23 June 1924; the two versions of the occasion when Lawrence consented to dance also demonstrate the hazards of relying on tendentious reporting. According to Mabel, her protégé Clarence Thompson was dancing with Frieda; she herself was Lawrence's partner; and Brett, drunk, was dancing alone. Brett in her memoir, admits she was drunk but claims that she was Lawrence's partner: 'I feel you *warm*; I can feel the stream of quick life in

[18] Luhan 166–7. [19] Frieda Lawrence 168. [20] Ibid.
[21] Two were used: for the Seltzer edn of *The Boy in the Bush* (1924) and the Knopf edn of *The Plumed Serpent* (1926). [22] Frieda Lawrence 167–8.

you; it is like dancing with a faun'.[23] Both memorialists agree that Lawrence and his partner deliberately and roughly collided with the other dancers. Whatever the truth about this bizarre occasion, the next day Thompson denounced Lawrence as a 'devil' and warned Mabel Luhan: 'He *wants* you *dead*... to *know* that you are in the ground.'[24] Less than a fortnight later, Tony Luhan, her Indian husband, reclaimed the horses he had lent to the visitors; this in turn aroused Lawrence's anger as is shown in three letters all written on one day.[25] The friendships were patched up sufficiently for the Lawrences and Luhans to go together in August to the Hopi snake dance in Arizona, but no friendship can survive such strains unimpaired. 'We'll remain friendly at a distance', Lawrence told Mabel Luhan, and he kept his word.[26] In Italy in 1926–7, for example, he advised her about the writing of her memoirs; he also devoted much time and energy to sorting her books in the Villa Curonia (owned by Mabel's second husband, Edwin Dodge) and offering advice on what to do with them.

Frieda's irritation over Brett's stifling intimacy with Lawrence erupted into open hostility when the trio moved to Oaxaca, Mexico, for the winter 1924–5. Her feelings were made plain, as Brett herself recalled: 'Frieda is in a rage... She is attacking me... says I spoil all her fun, that I laugh at her and so on.'[27] Lawrence followed this, on 9 January 1925, with a letter which was unambiguous:

> You, Frieda and I don't make a happy combination now. The best is that we should prepare to separate: that you should go your own way. I am not angry: except that I hate 'situations', and feel humiliated by them. We can all remain decent and friendly, and go the simplest, quietest way about the parting, without stirring up a lot of emotions that only do harm. Stirred-up emotions lead to hate.[28]

He made clear his wish that Brett should leave Oaxaca and return on her own to the ranch in New Mexico. When the Lawrences themselves arrived back at the ranch in April 1925, Frieda insisted that Brett should distance herself from them but, despite even that, the disciple clung closely to the master and he felt obliged to write:

> You are, you know, a born separator. Even without knowing that you do it, you set people against one another. It is instinctive with you. If you are friendly with one, you make that one unfriendly to the others: no matter who it is. It's just a natural process with you. – But it usually turns everybody into an enemy, at last. – It's no use your talking about friendship . . . Among three people, always two against one.
>
> It's no good our trying to get on together – it won't happen. Myself, I have lost all desire for intense or intimate friendship. Acquaintance is enough.[29]

[23] Luhan 224–7; Brett 109.
[24] Luhan 238, 240. See also p. 60 n. 3.
[25] Letters 3156–8.
[26] Letter 3163.
[27] Brett 200.
[28] Letter 3330.
[29] Letter 3391.

This did indeed force a break. Yet Lawrence's anxiety about Brett on her solitary way via New York to Europe in October 1925 is evident from his letters to her. Frieda was reported to be implacably resolved never to speak to Brett again.[30] However, when the Lawrences were in Spotorno, Brett, in Capri, was typing 'Glad Ghosts'; when Lawrence angrily left Frieda in Spotorno in February 1926, it was to Capri that he eventually went, warning Brett by telegram that he was coming. Many years later she claimed that during his stay on Capri Lawrence attempted unsuccessfully to make love to her.[31] In April, when Brett's plan to return to New Mexico was known, Frieda made peace – though not without a touch of malice: 'dont think that we hate each other, only I am so impatient of any will that's put over me – You have given us much support also – But do get somebody to live with you at the ranch – You'll go queer alone'.[32] Brett and Lawrence were never to meet again. Lawrence's second attempt to establish Rananim had ended and his one convert went back to USA alone to live out her long life in Taos.

In March 1924 there had been a third reason for Lawrence's return to America: to rewrite his novel, 'Quetzalcoatl' (published as *The Plumed Serpent*). However, as early as 4 April he knew that he would not get to Mexico until late autumn 'which means I shall not finish "Quetzacoatl". . . this year'.[33] In the meantime he corrected proofs of *The Boy in the Bush* (rewritten from Mollie Skinner's novel), arranged for the publication of Maurice Magnus's *Memoirs of the Foreign Legion* (with Lawrence's own introduction) and wrote the three novelettes which have New Mexico settings: 'St. Mawr', 'The Woman Who Rode Away' and 'The Princess'. (Mabel Luhan claimed to recognise herself as the heroine who rode away; Brett was certainly the model for 'The Princess'.)[34] Lawrence had revised the novelettes and written two versions of the essay on the Hopi snake dance, together with several other short pieces, by the time he set out for Mexico in October 1924.

The day after the Lawrences moved into rented accommodation in Oaxaca, on 18 November, he began work on 'Quetzalcoatl'.[35] Into the first draft, which he had put aside in the summer of 1923, he incorporated details of his trip to western Mexico in September–November 1923 and of his present stay in Oaxaca. He wrote a number of other things, including four essays later included in *Mornings in Mexico* – but his main preoccupation until late January 1925 was the completion of the novel. It is the most compelling of what are referred to as Lawrence's 'leadership' novels; characteristically he

[30] Letter 3615.
[31] Brett II–III: in the Sunstone Press, Santa Fe reprint, 1974.
[32] P. 425 n. 1.
[33] Letter 3099.
[34] Luhan 237–8; see p. 136 n. 1.
[35] See p. 179 n. 2.

considered it his 'most important novel, so far'.[36] He had studied Aztec and earlier religions intensively and the work was specifically intended to provide a blueprint of a quasi-religious and political system to govern the country, a vision of how the world itself should develop. Its completion coincided with Lawrence's becoming very seriously ill. No wonder, then, that he told Amy Lowell in April: 'I daren't even look at the outside of the MS. It cost one so much.'[37]

In the period covered by this volume Lawrence's health became a matter of prime concern to him and others close to him. He refused to admit the seriousness of his illnesses but it was evident to Frieda and Brett. Brett remembered that, in August 1924 –

> You suddenly spit. You constantly spit, so there is nothing new in that: but this time a splash of bright red blood comes with it, which is new. You cast a look of consternation at Frieda: she looks flabbergasted – while I pretend not to see at all. You already have a bit of a cold, and during the morning this gets worse. After lunch, looking white and ill, you go to bed . . .
>
> The following day you are still in bed, and in the afternoon you spit blood again.[38]

He was irritated when Frieda called in a local doctor to examine him. Despite the signs, Frieda insisted – and Lawrence told his correspondents – that he was suffering only from a bronchial infection and sore throat.[39] But, after more colds and the traumatic break with Brett, Lawrence became so ill about 2 February 1925 that his life was feared for. The causes were probably various: possibly a recurrence of the malaria he contracted in Ceylon in 1922, combined with typhoid fever which was endemic in Oaxaca, and now tuberculosis, with the additional worry over Brett and exhaustion from completing *The Plumed Serpent*. Frieda also recalled an earthquake: it was not severe enough to merit a mention in the local newspaper but it was an added strain to her and Lawrence.[40] According to Frieda he thought he would die: 'that night he said to me: "But if I die, nothing has mattered but you, nothing at all."'[41]

After much nursing by new but devoted friends in Oaxaca, Lawrence was moved by train to Mexico City. There Frieda had influenza, he suffered another relapse or even two, and when she called in Dr Sidney Ulfelder, perhaps at the instigation of the poet Luis Quintanilla, tuberculosis was confirmed. Frieda claimed that the doctor told her his diagnosis in front of Lawrence – 'and Lawrence looked at me with such unforgettable eyes' –

[36] Letter 3439. [37] Letter 3385. [38] Brett 139.
[39] Ibid. 141; Letters 3184, 3185, 3193, 3234, 3256.
[40] Parmenter 318; Letter 3352 and pp. 210–11 nn. 3, 1; p. 209 n. 1.
[41] Frieda Lawrence 165.

whereas Quintanilla's account insists that Lawrence was not told. Frieda further remembered the doctor's prediction that Lawrence had only a year or two to live. 'After the great strain of his illness', Frieda wrote, 'something broke in me. "He will never be quite well again, he is ill, he is doomed. All my love, all my strength will never make him whole again."'[42] Lawrence had hoped to return to England but, as he told his sister Emily on 11 March: 'Another blow. After various examinations and blood tests, the doctor won't let me take a sea voyage nor go to England. He says I must stay in Mexico in the sun, or return to the ranch. So we shall go back to the ranch as soon as I can travel: am still in bed here.'[43]

Despite his precarious hold on life Lawrence's writing suffered only a brief hiatus in February – and even then he dictated the opening of 'The Flying-Fish' to Frieda. (Later he admitted that he could not bear to finish it because it had been written so close to death.)[44] In March he corrected proofs of Secker's *St. Mawr*; he then began two plays based on biblical stories, apparently at the suggestion of the actress Ida Rauh, a friend of Mabel Luhan. He started with *Noah's Flood* but quickly abandoned it in favour of *David*; he had Ida Rauh in mind for the part of David's wife, Michal, but when she read the play in June 1925 she thought herself quite unsuited for it.[45] Lawrence tried to interest members of the Theatre Guild in a production of *David* when he and Frieda were in New York en route for England in September 1925, but without success. The play was published in England and America in the early months of 1926, and had a London production in May 1927 (with Angela Baddeley as Michal).

At Kiowa Ranch, where they returned in early April 1925, Lawrence made a slow recovery and Frieda endeavoured to shield him from Brett and others as much as possible. 'I potter about and lie on a camp bed on the porch', he told Emily King on 21 April; 'I don't work yet'.[46] An Indian couple, Trinidad and Rufina Archuleta, were responsible for domestic chores, but by the end of May Lawrence was well enough to assist with projects on the ranch such as laying pipes for a waterway or building a corral, and daily jobs like milking Susan the cow. Nevertheless he was disinclined to see people and did not leave Kiowa even to go to Taos by car. Friedel Jaffe, Frieda's nephew, who was an exchange student from Germany and visited the ranch May–July, still recalls Lawrence's reluctance to have visitors that summer.

Kiowa was a source of great pleasure for Lawrence: he often told correspondents about the practical responsibilities it entailed and the animals he had acquired; and the restfulness of his surroundings, first noted when he re-

[42] Ibid. 166–7; Nehls, ii. 396. [43] Letter 3368. [44] Brewster 288.
[45] Brett 60, 220; Letters 3300, 3362. [46] Letter 3401.

turned to the ranch in 1924, was a perpetual delight. 'We are awfully glad to be back at the foot of the Rockies, on the desert', he assured William Siebenhaar in Australia, 'to smell the sage-brush, and hear the Indians' drums, and ride a pony once more.'[47] The Lawrences were experiencing for the first time some of the pleasures of working and living in a place which they (strictly speaking, Frieda) owned.

However, by mid-1925 Lawrence had, as so often in the past, become restive. His disappointment over Seltzer, the strained personal relationships with Mabel Luhan and Brett, his near-fatal illness, coupled with a growing distaste for 'this rather malevolent continent' and the conviction that 'One needs a *rest* after America': all such factors cumulatively generated 'a bit of a heimweh for Europe'.[48] Moreover he was perhaps aware that since his arrival in New York eighteen months earlier, though he had written some important pieces, none of them is in the first rank of his achievements. It was not surprising, therefore, that he was 'glad to be going out of America for a time: I feel like Europe.'[49] He wrote thus at the end of September 1925, on *S. S. Resolute*, just two days from Southampton.

London had depressed him before he left it in March 1924; his reaction to it on his return was even more scathing: 'it's much worse than when I was here last time, almost gruesome'. He caught up with some old friends, visited the Carswells 'buried alive in a hole of a horrid little cottage in damp and dismal Bucks', entertained Compton and Faith Mackenzie, discovered that Mark Gertler was in the Mundesley sanatorium, failed to find Koteliansky and concluded: 'There's no *life* in anybody.'[50] His principal visits were made outside the capital – to his sisters, Emily King in Nottingham and Ada Clarke in Ripley, spending a week with each. This marked concern for them was normal: he invariably interested himself in their financial state and business affairs, their general welfare or their children's health and education, and regularly remembered their birthdays; and since his father's death a year before, they were the closest members of his immediate family. Many old friends were also still in the Eastwood area; one for whom he felt a special anxiety was Gertrude Cooper whose tubercular condition gave them a shared misfortune and drew from Lawrence some particularly sympathetic letters. He was extremely affectionate, too, towards Frieda's mother and after a second week in London, following the fortnight in the Midlands, the Lawrences headed for Baden-Baden to see her. He could be humorous about the 'departed grandeur' surrounding the Baroness Anna von Richthofen and the whist he played with her ancient friends,[51] but his tender concern for her was

[47] Letter 3112. [48] Letters 3296, 3318, 3438.
[49] Letter 3489. [50] Letter 3501. [51] Letter 3529.

manifest. It provided the impetus for some of Lawrence's most engaging letters.

Family relationships were, then, important to both Lawrence and Frieda; they could, however, be the cause of considerable tension between them. A vivid illustration of this occurred with the simultaneous arrival of Ada Clarke and a friend on the one hand, and Frieda's daughters on the other, in February 1926, half-way through the Lawrences' stay in the Villa Bernarda rented from Angelo Ravagli in Spotorno. Lawrence had issued a threat, if the young Weekleys came: 'When they appear, I shall disappear.' 'I can't stand Frieda's children', he told Brett. 'They have a sort of suburban bounce and *suffisance* which puts me off.'[52] The knowledge that their father, Ernest Weekley, preferred them not to stay with the Lawrences was additionally galling. For her part Frieda believed that Lawrence had invited his sister in order to provide a counterbalance to her daughters: 'Ada felt he belonged to her and the past', Frieda wrote; 'I had, of equal necessity, to fight that past'.[53] The result was an explosion of anger and hostility between Lawrence and Frieda. She joined Barbara and Elsa Weekley in their hotel; he, 'absolutely swamped out', left for Monte Carlo and Nice with Ada and her friend; then for the whole of March he made a 'little "giro" round Capri and Ravello and Rome and Umbria and Ravenna' with a variety of friends, mainly female.[54] Reconciliation was gradually achieved, Frieda taking the intelligent view that 'we must live more with other people . . . and not cut ourselves off'.[55] When he returned to Spotorno on 3 April Lawrence found 'all very quiet and welcoming'; 'for the moment I am the Easter Lamb', he told Frieda's mother.[56] With Ada gone he discovered that he enjoyed the company of the Weekley daughters; he and Frieda had a brief holiday with them in Pisa and Florence. The explosion was over.

At Spotorno from November 1925 till he temporarily 'left off writing' in early February 1926,[57] Lawrence was as productive as usual. Several reviews and essays were written for America and England; 'Sun' and 'Glad Ghosts' were written and then typed by Brett; 'The Virgin and the Gypsy' was completed and sent to Secker in London for typing; and *Reflections on the Death of a Porcupine and Other Essays* (largely written at Kiowa in mid-1925) was published in Philadelphia. The publication of 'Sun', first in *New Coterie*, Autumn 1926, and then separately by 'E. Archer' in September, marked the

[52] Letter 3535. [53] Letter 3563; Frieda Lawrence 194.
[54] Letters 3622, 3667. [55] Letter 3646.
[56] Letters 3659, 3661. (Ada Clarke was told, on 20 April 1927: 'I have made a permanent agreement with Frieda that . . . This mix-up of relations is no good – we'll keep them apart. And that's final.') [57] Letter 3614.

beginning of Lawrence's association with Charles Lahr; he was the publisher responsible for both and, in 1929, for the unexpurgated edition of *Pansies*. Lahr, an anarchist, was one of the most vivid and eccentric publisher–booksellers of this century, with whom Lawrence had an extensive correspondence until a fortnight before his death. Lawrence was immediately attracted by the tone of *New Coterie*, a journal which, even in its brief life, included among its contributors Augustus John, Stanley Spencer and William Rothenstein.

'We are getting to the age when we shall really have to think of establishing ourselves some little spot on the face of the earth.'[58] This uncharacteristic remark was written in July 1926 at the Villa Mirenda in the tiny, remote hamlet of San Paolo Mosciano outside Scandicci, itself on the edge of Florence. Mirenda did not become a permanent residence for the Lawrences, but its upper floor provided them with a home until June 1928 and that, in Lawrentian terms, was as near permanence as any spot on earth. Lawrence took great pleasure in the Mirenda, living in it and describing it and his neighbours to his correspondents – as on one occasion to his niece Margaret King:

> there are two gardens, and lovely slopes of vines and olives, and three families of peasants to work the place – It is quite lovely in its way. – We have one family of English neighbours, who would sent you into fits if you saw them: he's got the wildest red beard, sticking out all round – and wife and daughter and son, all with sandals and knapsacks. But they're jolly and very clever . . .[59]

Near Christmas 1926 Frieda told Mabel Luhan: 'We are very cosy and quite "elegant" for us, rushmatting all over the floor in a big, good room with bright, light things in it, and a piano and cyclamens, Lawrence painting on an easel – a Boccaccio picture *not at all* proper.'[60] They had a good-humoured, tolerant relationship with the eccentric Wilkinsons and Lawrence wrote them many high-spirited letters; the Lawrences enjoyed entertaining their peasant neighbours on Christmas Eve, 'with the children washed beyond recognition';[61] and, despite some disclaimers, Lawrence's social life was as energetic and varied as he wished it to be. He used the well-known Vieusseux circulating library in Florence, frequently lunched with the bookseller–publisher 'Pino' Orioli and the English expatriate novelist 'Reggie' Turner, and dined regularly with Norman Douglas 'and the boys', probably at the Gambrinus bar.[62]

[58] Letter 3743.
[59] Letter 3705. The English family consisted of Arthur Gair Wilkinson, his wife Lilian and their two children.
[60] Letter 3909. [61] Letter 3932.
[62] Letters 3700, 3919, 3924, 3855 and see p. 445 n. 1.

He and Frieda lunched with Sir George and Lady Ida 'parents of the writing Sitwell trio' at their Castello di Montegufoni about fourteen miles away; they gave tea at the Mirenda to the wealthy writer, composer and painter Lord Berners.[63] They went to the popular theatre in Florence with friends; they took tea with the writer Helen Zimmern in the Via dei Bardi; and on one occasion Lawrence lunched with Giorgio Chiavacci whom he described (slightly inaccurately) as 'the world's champion fencer'.[64] In the light of this evidence, Frieda's comment to Mabel Luhan – 'I think in Florence we're a myth. We hardly see anybody' – was somewhat exaggerated.[65]

In February 1927 Lawrence quite excitedly informed some of his correspondents that 'the two Misses Beveridge and Mabel Harrison' were about to move into 'a little villa across the dip' from San Paolo Mosciano. He had known them for several years so there was a general pleasure to be expected from their company but, more significant, Millicent Beveridge and Mabel Harrison were painters (the former painted Lawrence's portrait in Sicily in 1921). 'There'll be great competitions painting!' he told his sister Emily.[66] This was of particular importance to Lawrence. Since November 1926 he had become more than ever absorbed by his love of painting, 'a much more amusing art than writing'.[67] He loved 'discovering one can paint one's own ideas and one's own feelings'; he found Tuscany '*beautiful* painting country'; and he had the good fortune to be given by Maria Huxley several canvases 'that her brother had daubed on' but that could be re-used.[68] He found himself 'bursting into paint'.[69] The result was that, in three months, Lawrence completed *A Holy Family, Men Bathing, Boccaccio Story, Fight with an Amazon, Red Willow Trees, Negro Wedding* and *Flight Back into Paradise*.

Lawrence had stayed with Millicent Beveridge in Inverness during a visit to Britain in the previous August and September (which in turn followed the visit he and Frieda paid to Baden-Baden for his mother-in-law's seventy-fifth birthday). The northern dampness made him shrink 'a trifle inside [his] skin', he told Brett;[70] nevertheless on 'one perfect day' the Scottish landscape was quite enthralling:

There is still something of an Odyssey up there, in among the islands and the silent lochs: like the twilight morning of the world, the herons fishing undisturbed by the water, and the sea running far in, for miles, between the wet, trickling hills, where the cottages are low and almost invisible, built into the earth. It is still out of the world, and like the very beginning of Europe. . .[71]

[63] Letters 3732, 3749.
[64] Letters 3921, 3924, 3741.
[65] Letter 3909.
[66] Letter 3963.
[67] Letter 3938.
[68] Letters 3897, 3934.
[69] 'Making Pictures', *Phoenix II* 602.
[70] Letter 3785.
[71] Letter 3791.

The opportunity to 'get outside the made world, if only for a day' refreshed him, but that world insistently impinged upon him. Leaving Scotland he, with Frieda, took a fortnight's holiday on the Lincolnshire coast and then, alone, in mid-September he briefly called on his sisters in Nottingham and Ripley. This was the occasion when he made what proved to be his final visit to Eastwood. There in the Nottinghamshire–Derbyshire coalfield, Lawrence was confronted by the disastrous political and social, as well as economic, consequences of the prevailing miners' strike; he was profoundly disturbed by what he saw and intuitively grasped. 'I'm afraid it's a wound in the famous English unity, our dear Body Politic, this strike . . . I wish they'd come to a settlement. I am afraid of the class hatred which is the quiet volcano over which the English life is built.'[72] For the first time in his experience the miners seemed 'class-conscious, and full of resentment'; 'this will be the beginnings of a slow revolution . . . but a serious one', he told Arthur Wilkinson; and in October, back in Italy, from the perspective of the Villa Mirenda the strike appeared 'one of the greatest disasters that has ever happened to England'.[73]

On 26 October 1926, two days before that last letter was written, a dog belonging to one of the peasant families near the Mirenda had smudged page 41 of the manuscript on which Lawrence was working. He was writing 'a story – shortish – don't feel like a long effort'.[74] By mid-November he was describing it to Martin Secker as 'a novel in the Derbyshire coal-mining districts – already rather improper'; on 8 February 1927 Secker was told: 'It won't take me very long, I think, to finish the novel . . . I want to call it *Lady Chatterley's Lover*.'[75] Into that novel, the second version of which was completed by 27 February, went much of the apprehension Lawrence had felt on his recent visit to the Midlands. It is more than mere coincidence that Connie Chatterley raises the question of whether there will be 'a coal strike', or that Parkin's response to the oppressive industrial system is to become a Communist, or that Duncan Forbes – exactly like Lawrence himself in September 1926 – gets 'an awful feeling of hopelessness, of death, in [Connie's] part of the country.'[76] In September, too, on a walk with his old Eastwood friend Willie Hopkin, Lawrence had recognised the spot where 'a forest ranger's cottage' had stood; he also visited Robin Hood's Well.[77] The novel in which he made use of those and other experiences in 'the country of [his] heart', and turned to creative effect his perception of 'resentment' and

72 Letter 3796. 73 Letters 3824, 3826, 3874.

74 Tedlock, *Lawrence MSS* 20; Letter 3872. 75 Letters 3890, 3956.

76 *The First Lady Chatterley* (New York, 1944), pp. 119, 299, 306 (Parkin in the first two versions of the novel becomes Mellors in the third.)

77 W. E. Hopkin, 'D. H. Lawrence's Last Visit Home', *Nottingham Journal*, 11 September 1942.

class-consciousness among the mining population, would occupy his attention beyond the period covered by the present volume. The need for a 'flow of life from one to another' which Duncan Forbes recognises was later to be central in Lawrence's own 'message' to the miners in December 1928: 'We want a revolution not in the name of money or work or any of that, but of life.'[78]

[78] *The First Lady Chatterley*, p. 306; Letter to Charles Wilson, 28 December 1928.

THE LETTERS

3091. To Harriet Monroe, 12 March 1924

Text: TMSC NWU; Huxley 598.

c/o Thomas Seltzer, 219 West 100th St., New York City
12 March 1924

Dear Harriet Monroe:[1]

We got here yesterday.[2] I think we shall be going through to Taos on Tuesday or Wednesday – myself and my wife and a friend the Hon. Dorothy Brett.[3] I should like to see you, if you would tell me where – perhaps at *Poetry*'s office for a cup of tea.

Yours sincerely D. H. Lawrence

3092. To S. S. Koteliansky, [13 March 1924]

Text: MS BL; Postmark, New Yor[k] MAR 13 [. . .]; cited in Gransden 29.

[219 West 100th Street, New York][4]
14 March 1924

My dear Kot.[5]

We landed here in a gale, and snow, cold and horrible. But today there is brilliant sunshine. New York looks as ever: stiff, machine-made, and against nature. Still it is more stimulating than Europe. It is so mechanical, there is not the sense of death. And another destiny. Brett so far is very nice: self contained and detached, which is the best. – Seltzer and Mrs Seltzer are not so

[1] Harriet Monroe (1860–1936), American poet and editor; she founded *Poetry: A Magazine of Verse* (Chicago) in 1912. See *Letters*, ii. 167. DHL's poetry appeared in *Poetry*, 1914–23.

[2] DHL, Frieda and Brett sailed from Southampton on the *R. M. S. Aquitania* on 5 March 1924. They landed in New York on 11 March, staying with the Seltzers (see p. 16 n. 1), on their way to Taos, New Mexico.

[3] Hon. Dorothy Eugenie Brett (1883–1977), painter; daughter of Viscount Esher; studied at the Slade School of Art and first met DHL in 1915. See *Letters*, ii. 427. Author of *Lawrence and Brett: A Friendship* (Philadelphia, 1933).

[4] This letter and the following one are written on headed paper.

[5] Samuel Solomonovich Koteliansky ('Kot') (1880–1955), was Russian-born but naturalised British. He produced over thirty translations of Russian works, some of them with DHL acting as 'editor'. Kot was a close friend and correspondent of DHL's, 1914–30. See *Letters*, ii. 205 n. 4.

nice.[1] She is the bad influence. He says he lost $7.000 last year.[2] And simply no money in the bank, for me. I don't like the look of their business at all. – But Curtis Brown's man here seems very decent and reliable: a north of England man.[3] He'll attend to the thing for me.

We shall leave next week for Taos, as soon as this is a bit straightened out. – My dear Kot, it's no good thinking of business unless you will go at it like a lion, a serpent, and a condor. You're well out of publishing.[4] The world is a very vast machine, that grinds the bones of the good man gladly, if he's fool enough to let it.

DHL

3093. To John Middleton Murry, 14 March 1924

Text: MS NYPL; Moore 784–5.

[219 West 100th Street, New York]
14 March 1924

Dear Jack[5]

Seltzer says he sent to you Magnus' *own* MS of *Foreign Legion*, 'Dregs.'[6] Will you please turn it over to Martin Secker – he may publish it.[7]

[1] Thomas Seltzer (1875–1943), journalist, translator and publisher; DHL's chief American publisher, 1920–5. m. 1906, Adele Szold (1876–1940). See *Letters*, iii. 390 n. 2 and Lacy, *Seltzer* 171ff.

[2] From 7 February, DHL wrote about his concern that he had not heard from Seltzer since the first of the year (*Letters*, iv. 572, 588): he must return to New York to pay his USA income tax by 15 March, Seltzer had not paid his royalties, DHL had little money and Seltzer might have 'gone all wrong' (*Letters*, iv. 579).

[3] Arthur William Barmby (1880–), b. in Sculcoates, Yorkshire, was on the staff of Curtis Brown's New York office. DHL had not had an American agent since he broke with Robert Mountsier in February 1923 (see *Letters*, iv. 376, 377–9), but now after his difficulties with Seltzer (against whom Mountsier had warned DHL), he was ready to let the New York branch of Curtis Brown take over (see p. 19 n. 3).

[4] Kot had experience as business manager for John Middleton Murry when he started publishing the *Adelphi* in June 1923 (see *Letters*, iv. 565 and n. 1).

[5] John Middleton Murry (1889–1957), journalist and critic; founder and editor of *Adelphi*. See *Letters*, ii. 31 n. 6.

[6] Maurice Magnus (1876–1920), American, joined the French Foreign Legion during World War I and deserted after it. DHL met him through Norman Douglas in Florence, November 1919; Magnus committed suicide in Malta, November 1920. See also Letter 3108. DHL wrote an introduction to Magnus's 'Dregs', which he persuaded Secker to publish as *Memoirs of the Foreign Legion*.

[7] Murry sent the MS to Martin Secker on 24 March 1924; Secker wrote to DHL the next day (Secker Letter-Book, UIll):

Dear Lawrence

Many thanks for yours of the 14th. I hope you have now settled down comfortably to finish your book. Murry sent me round yesterday the Magnus typescript, and I shall be very pleased to publish it, with your introduction, during the coming autumn. I think it would be fair if I

I don't care much for the Seltzer outlook. His business is on the wane – Mrs Seltzer's poison-streak. Curtis Brown's man here seems a very decent sort, no fool: his name is Barmby A.W., if ever you want him:

c/o Curtis Brown Ltd, 116 W. 39th St

I think we shall go on Monday, to Chicago, and Taos. Bretts' money from Windsor is not here: but she will have enough. She and Frieda are in the Seltzers' flat, I am in an hotel. The snow has gone again, it is bright, strong sunshine, but frozen still. I haven't much respect for New York: but a machine is perhaps less distressing than a dying animal: London. Brett is quite calm, not much impressed, but feels an adventuress. New York jeers[1] at us all, and we look down our noses.

DHL

I cashed your cheque at 4.29.[2]

3094. To Catherine Carswell, [16 March 1924]

Text: MS YU; Postmark, [. . .] N.Y. MAR 16 [. . .]924; cited in Carswell 216–17.

New York
Sunday 16 March

Dear Catherine[3]

We landed in a sort of blizzard on Tuesday, about 2.0 o clock: New York looking hideous. But since then, the strong American Sunshine. We had a very

paid a royalty of 10% on the first 2000 copies and 15% after that, and I assume that you will let me have the American market so that I may sell an edition in sheets there. Shall I make the contract with you, or through Curtis Brown? There will have to be a few excisions made in the text, and I would not propose to call the book "Dregs", but "Memoirs of the Foreign Legion". I think that you should share to the extent of 50% in the proceeds, for it is your introduction which gives value to the document and makes the author of it live.

Everything continues to go on very well indeed at home, I am most thankful to say. All send their kindest regards to you both.

Yours sincerely Martin Secker

D. H. Lawrence Esq

(Most of Secker's letters were published, but even then not always completely, in Martin Secker, *Letters From a Publisher: Martin Secker to D H Lawrence & Others 1911–1929*, 1970.)

Martin Secker (1882–1978), London publisher. *New Poems* (1918) was the first of DHL's books to appear under his imprint; Secker continued as his publisher throughout DHL's lifetime and beyond. See *Letters*, i. 275 and nn. 1 and 2.

1 jeers] laughs

2 Possibly payment for 'On Being Religious' or 'On Human Destiny' in *Adelphi* of February and March 1924 respectively (i, 791–9, 882–91), but DHL had an article in every issue September 1923–May 1924.

3 Catherine Roxburgh Carswell (1879–1946), novelist, biographer and journalist, and her husband, Donald Carswell (1882–1940) – barrister and journalist – had been friends of the Lawrences since 1914. (See *Letters*, ii. 187 n. 5.)

good voyage – but I don't care for the atmosphere on those huge boats. And it's vile being shut in with all the people. Most people are unpleasant nowadays, particularly those going to America to make a fortune. However, it didn't last long. And the disembarking quite simple – no Ellis Island: customs people very nice.[1]

One of Seltzer's clerks took the Max Beerbohm book round to Ethel Bell:[2] but returned with book and news that there was no such person at that address. Seems queer – because it was the same wrapper you put round – and your address-writing. The book lies in Seltzer's office, awaiting instructions from you. Will you write him: Thomas Seltzer. 5. West 50th St. and tell him what you want.

New York, of course, is no better than London, save that the climate, even the cold wind, gives one one's energy back again. It's just that. Humanly, rather awful.

Brett looks at it all very calmly, just a trifle uneasy – says the town is all 'against nature' – but by no means bowled over, and a bit disappointed in this city: not so impressed as she thought she'd be.

I've been busy seeing Curtis Brown's man and the lawyer.[3] At the moment I have no money at all in the bank. Seltzer had a bad year, lost $7,000.00, paid me nothing in. But he's going to scrape a few hundreds together,[4] and we're going west on Tuesday morning. Write to me *Taos*: New Mexico. U.S.A. – Meanwhile the agent and lawyer will collect the money bit by bit: friendly relations preserved.

We'll see what it's like in Taos and let you know. Apparently plenty of

[1] The officials came on the ship, rather than the passengers having to wait in queues at the examination centre for immigrants on Ellis Island. But Brett did have trouble with immigration officials because of her deafness and travelling alone and her surname not matching her father's title, and with customs officials who wanted to make her pay duty on her painting supplies. See *Letters*, iv. 600–1 and Brett 37 and n. (in the 1974 re-issue of Brett by Sunstone Press, Santa Fe, New Mexico).

[2] Possibly *Things New and Old* (1923) or *Yet Again* (1909; republished in 1923). Ethel Bell is unidentified; there may have been some confusion with Catherine Carswell's distant cousin, Enid Bell.

[3] Possibly Benjamin H. Stern of the legal firm Stern and Ruben who had earlier assisted DHL in retrieving copyrights from another delinquent American publisher, Benjamin Huebsch (*Letters*, iv. 182 and n. 2).

[4] In the middle of DHL's diary (MS UCB) are two pages of 'Accounts with Seltzer & *National Chase Bank*, Met. Branch' which DHL recorded on 13–14 March 1924. Deposits, probably from Seltzer, were noted: $1000 on 15 August 1923, $500 on 26 September, $100 on 6, 11, 13, 18 and 23 October; no further deposits from Seltzer were made until 4 April 1924 ($200) which was paid via Barmby.

After DHL cashed a cheque for $100 on 12 March, he had a balance of $17.50 in his account. He drew a $500 cheque 'from Seltzer's office' on 17 March.

houses going begging. Tell me about your farm.[1] It was such a lovely day when we left England.

I'm not seeing people here: feel a nausea for people. Greet Don and the boy.[2]

DHL

3095. To Curtis Brown, 18 March 1924

Text: MS UT; Unpublished.

New York.
18 March 1924

Dear Curtis Brown[3]

We leave New York today, for Taos: address simply *Taos*. New Mexico.

I have seen Barmby several times, and we get on together. Apparently it *was* time I came. But I think Barmby will gradually get my things shipshape.

Fix a date with Secker for *Boy in the Bush*.[4] Seltzer hasn't sent it to print yet. I don't really mind if they hold it over till autumn, but it is as Secker wishes, in the first place.

I want to get quiet, and do some stories.[5]

Yrs D. H. Lawrence

3096. To Curtis Brown, 24 March 1924

Text: MS UT; Unpublished.

Taos. New Mexico
24 March 1924

Dear Curtis Brown

I asked Barmby to cable *Accept Secker*. If the advance is small, if Miss Skinner writes you that she would like it, let her have it all. Otherwise we halve it.[6]

1 '[DHL] was anxious to hear all about our venture in the country. He knew we had thoughts of a small farm . . . Our farm idea dissolved into a very small cottage in Bucks . . .': Hawthorne Cottage, Great Kingshill, near High Wycombe (Carswell 217).

2 John Patrick Carswell (b. 1918).

3 Albert Curtis Brown (1866–1945), managing director of Curtis Brown Ltd, became DHL's English literary agent in April 1921. m. 1890, Caroline Louise Lord. See *Letters*, iii. 566 n.

4 Mollie Skinner's novel originally entitled 'The House of Ellis' was published as a collaboration after DHL rewrote the MS as *The Boy in the Bush*. See n. 6 below. Secker published it on 28 August 1924; Seltzer in September.

5 Possibly 'Jimmy and the Desperate Woman', 'The Last Laugh' or 'The Border-Line', all begun in January–February 1924 (see *Letters*, iv. 564 and n. 2, 568). See also Letters 3098 and 3100.

6 Curtis Brown must have forwarded details of Secker's letter of 6 March (Secker Letter-Book, UIll):

Secker can do as he likes about Australia, both with the *Boy* and with *Kangaroo*.[1]

I am just finishing a short story, for Blackwell if he likes it.[2] Let you have it in a day or two. Ask him – Basil Blackwell – his intentions regarding Verga's *Novelle Rusticane*, will you:[3] and then let Seltzer know at once. Blackwell talked of sending the MS to print. – Suggest the title *Sicilian Novelettes*.

Sun shines here in a blaze, thank the Lord, and I'm already riding my own little mare,[4] and beginning to feel a bit like myself again. Oh those cities!

Do hope your family troubles are smoothing out.[5]

Yrs D. H. Lawrence

3097. To Mollie Skinner, 4 April 1924

Text: MS WAPL; Postmark, Taos APR [. . .] 1924; Moore 785–6.

Taos. New Mexico. U.S.A.
4 April[6] 1924

Dear Miss Skinner[7]

Your letter about the *Boy* MS. has come here. I have written to Secker and Seltzer to make the alterations you wish, if it is not too late. Also I tell them

I am now able to write more fully about "The Boy in the Bush". I do not think it is entirely equitable for the terms to be identical with "Kangaroo", for this book cannot pretend to be an authentic Lawrence work, and it will bear the collaborator's name on its title-page. I think, moreover, that it is extremely doubtful whether the circulating libraries will admit it to their shelves. However, I do not wish to discuss the terms in detail, and I am ready to agree to the scale of royalties you suggest, but only paying on publication the amount of the accrued royalties to that date.

I should be glad to have the Australian rights, and will do my best to sell a special edition of 1000. I think it very likely I can do this, if I guarantee the Austral[as]ian market. I would pay either 4[?]d per copy or 15% of the proceeds, whichever you prefer.

If you will agree to this, and will kindly alter the contract in accordance I shall be very pleased to put the work in hand at once.

Yours sincerely

[1] DHL at Mountsier's suggestion had wanted to have a separate Australian edition of *Kangaroo* (1923) published, but acceded and allowed Secker to sell sheets (see *Letters*, iv. 319 n. 3).

[2] 'The Last Laugh', first published in *The New Decameron IV* by Basil Blackwell on 2 March 1925 (Roberts B15); it was collected in *The Woman Who Rode Away* (1928). See also Letter 3100.

[3] DHL translated *Novelle Rusticane* (1883) by Giovanni Verga (1840–1922) in April–May 1922 which Blackwell published as *Little Novels of Sicily* in April 1925; Seltzer published on 9 March 1925.

There is a note in an unidentified hand on DHL's letter, in pencil: 'I wrote to A.W. B[armby] a little while ago, asking him to get Seltzer to quote Blackwell for sheets – at Blackwell's request. We ought to be hearing soon.'

[4] Poppy, lent by Tony Luhan (see Letters 3156ff.).

[5] Curtis Brown's son had 'lung trouble' and considered going to New Mexico (see *Letters*, iv. 546). [6] April] March.

[7] Mary Louisa ('Mollie') Skinner (1876–1955), Australian nurse. The Lawrences stayed in her guesthouse 'Leithdale' in Darlington, Western Australia, 6–18 May 1922. In addition to rewriting her novel and getting it published as *The Boy in the Bush*, DHL wrote a preface for

they may leave out both chapters at the end, if they wish. But here, if the book is set up, the publishers will not agree unless they wish to of their own account.[1] We shall see. I asked them both to write you what they are doing. The book should be out end of May. It is between-seasons, but I think perhaps it is just as well. Book trade alas is very bad.[2] I have arranged with Curtis Brown's representative in New York to conduct all my business this side. He is

A. W. Barmby. Curtis Brown Ltd. 116 West Thirty-ninth St, New York. Write to him for anything you want to know. And I will see he sends you your half of the royalties, and the statements, as they come due.

I think myself *The Boy* is a fine book. It runs on to its inevitable conclusions. But I know the world doesn't like the inevitable. – Anyhow I am glad you like it on the whole. I wanted you to say just what you felt – and I do understand your feeling about the things you would like modified. It is a pity we were so far apart, that we could not have worked a bit together. – Now, the next phase is in the hands of the public.

I had a letter also today from Mrs Throssell.[3] I hope you will get to know her.

Black Swans (not published with it; see *Letters*, iv. 496 and n.) and revised extensively her unpublished novel 'Eve in the Land of Nod'.

[1] Secker wrote to DHL on 3 April about Mollie Skinner's alterations (Secker Letter-Book, UIll):

Dear Lawrence

I have posted to you today two sets of proofs of "The Boy in the Bush" which I hope will reach you safely. We received from Curtis Brown (but after the book had gone to the printer) a second typescript which contained some small alterations and suggestions, presumably from Mrs Skinner. These have been transferred to the marked set, and you will also find among its pages some of the suggestions, which you may like to adopt. When you have corrected this will you transfer the alterations to the second set, which will do for Seltzer to set up from. As to the date of publication, I think that unless you would like it to appear sooner, we might fix September 1. This will give Seltzer plenty of time to prepare his own edition and make simultaneous publication.

I hope all is well with you both and with the new book. All continues to progress satisfactorily at home.

Yours sincerely

and about the final two chapters he also wrote on 25 April:

As to "The Boy", no doubt by this time you will have received proofs, in one copy of which you will find Miss Skinner's suggestions. They seem to me quite unimportant, but I do very strongly feel that the last two chapters should not be scrapped. As soon as I get back your proofs I will write fully to Miss Skinner, giving her all information, probable date of publication, etc.

See also Letter 3099. DHL had thought Mollie Skinner might disapprove of his changes: see *Letters*, iv. 524 and n. 2.

[2] There was a general concern among American publishers and booksellers about 'overproduction' of new books, especially novels.

[3] Katharine Susannah Prichard (1884–1969), Australian author. m. Hugo Vivian Hope Throssell (1884–1933), V.C., son of George Throssell, briefly Premier of Western Australia. Katharine Throssell sent copies of some of her books to DHL while he was in Australia, and they corresponded. See *Letters*, iv. 251 n. 2.

We are here again at the foot of the Rockies on the desert, among the Indians – 7,000 feet up.[1] I am glad to be away again. The winter in Europe wearied me inexpressibly. There seems a dead hand over the old world.

Tell me what you are doing about a new book.[2]

Many greetings from my wife and me.

D. H. Lawrence[3]

3098. To Thomas Seltzer, 4 April 1924

Text: MS UT; Postmark, [. . .] APR 7 1924; Lacy, *Seltzer* 130–1.

Taos. New Mexico.
4 April 1924

Dear Thomas

I enclose a letter from Molly Skinner.[4] If you have time, I wish you would make the alterations she wishes: at least the smaller ones. If you want to omit the last two chapters, I don't care. What do I care any more about the pruderies or not the pruderies? I wish you'd send her just a line, to say what alterations you *are* making, at her request, so she knows she is not ignored. She is nice, anyhow. Send her a little letter of information, please.

Taos is very nice: alternates between hot sun and birds singing, and deep snow and silence. Mabel is very mild: no longer mythological. F[rieda] and I are in the two-storey house, Brett in the studio, and we eat in the big house. All goes smoothly: Mabel is wiser,[5] has had a very bad time last year. And she was never small. Seems to me quite all right now. Touch wood! – As for Lee Witt, he is addled. Nina is divorcing him – rightly.[6] – Tony arrived with the car, and

[1] The Lawrences stayed with Mabel Luhan 11 September–1 December 1922 in Taos and then on Del Monte Ranch, n. of Taos until 18 March 1923. Rachel Hawk (see p. 440 n. 1) and Brett (in *South Dakota Review*) give the name as 'Delmonte'.

[2] Mollie Skinner took her first novel 'Lettie' (published as *Black Swans*) with her to London: see Letter 3161.

[3] Note on envelope: 'ans 1st July'.

[4] The letter is unlocated.

[5] When Mabel and Tony Luhan returned from California a few days after the Lawrence party arrived, the latter moved from the main house to other houses on Mabel Luhan's compound.

Mabel Dodge Luhan, née Ganson (1879–1962), American patroness of the arts; at her encouragement DHL had originally come to Taos. Published *Lorenzo in Taos* (New York, 1932). See *Letters*, iv. 110 n. 4.

[6] Lee Witt (1871–1929), formerly a sheriff, and Cornelia ('Nina') Rumsey Wilcox (1880–1968) were married in 1921 and divorced in 1923. See *Letters*, iv. 332 and n. 4.

Jaime de Angulo, last night: same as ever.[1] He's a good soul – but, Brett says, a bit like an old nurse. Verdad![2]

Will you please send to

Willa Cather.[3] 5. Bank St. Washington Square, New York

a copy of *Kangaroo* and a copy of *The Captains Doll*.[4] – And please send to Walter Ufer.[5] Taos. New Mexico a copy of *The Lost Girl*.

I am busy doing a few short stories – I wish they'd stay shorter. But they are the result of Europe, and perhaps a bit dismal.

I do hope business will go better.

DHL

Mabel has given Frieda the ranch above Lobo – legally made over.[6]

Miss M. L. Skinner, 'Leithdale'. Darlington nr Perth. West Australia.

3099. To Martin Secker, 4 April 1924

Text: MS UInd and IEduc; Postmark, [. . .] APR 7 1924; Secker 56–7.

Taos. New Mexico
4 April 1924

Dear Secker

We were glad to know that *Adrian* is safely entered into the family. I drank a

[1] Antonio ('Tony') Luhan (d. 1963), a Taos Pueblo Indian. m. 1923, Mabel Dodge Sterne.
Jaime de Angulo (1887–1950), anthropologist and linguistic analyst of Indian languages; b. Paris; went to USA, 1905; M.D. from Johns Hopkins University, 1912; homesteaded in California near Carmel and lived there, 1916–48. He worked for Manuel Gamio in Oaxaca, September 1922–March 1923 on Mixe, Zapotec and other languages; worked with Jung in Zurich, 1923; wrote articles on Indian languages, a Taos grammar, Indian stories, etc. m. (1) 1910, Cary Fink of Kentucky; divorced, 1921; (2) 1923, Lucy ('Nancy') Freeland, anthropologist and linguist; divorced, 1943. See Gui de Angulo, *Jaime in Taos: The Taos Papers of Jaime de Angulo* (San Francisco, 1985) and 'Life of Jaime de Angulo' by D. H. Olmsted in *Achumawi Dictionary* (University of California Publications in Linguistics), xlv (1966), 1–6; see *Letters*, iv. 585 n. 2.

[2] 'True!'

[3] Willa Cather (1876–1947), American novelist. DHL had seen her when he was visiting New York (Brett 39–40 and Brett, *South Dakota Review* 12).

[4] See p. 87 n. 2.

[5] Walter Ufer (1876–1936), Chicago painter and member of the Taos Society of Artists; see *Letters*, iv. 344 and n. m. Mary Monrad Frederiksen.

[6] Mabel Luhan had given the ranch to her son John Evans 'several years' before; he named it 'The Flying Heart'. She persuaded him to trade it back, so she could give it to Frieda who later gave her the MS of *Sons and Lovers* in exchange (Letter 3152). On moving to the ranch DHL renamed it 'Lobo' ('wolf') after the mountain on which it is located (Letter 3122) and about 9 August 1924 started calling it 'Kiowa' (see Letter 3383 for his reason for this name) (Luhan 191, 192, 195; Letter 3191).

drop of moonshine to him. So sorry Mrs Secker had a bad go.[1] The young gentleman arrived rather stormily.

We are safe in Taos. Today blazing hot sun, and the birds very lively. Two days ago, deep soft snow. We still feel the altitude a bit – but are chirping up after that European winter. Frieda is growing lively again. When it doesn't snow, we go riding on horseback – Brett too. You know Dorothy Brett, Lord Esher's daughter came with us.[2] Off we go, on these mustang ponies. Fun! And I am writing short stories. But they are a bit Europe wintry and smitten. My soul isn't thawed out yet.

I had a letter from Molly Skinner, asking for a few alterations in *Boy in the Bush*. I copy them out and send them to you. If there is time, please make these little changes to please her. – And if you like, omit the last chapter, or the last two chapters even. I feel fed up about the world and its pruderies and its perpetual cold in the head. One must pile cowardice on cowardice, apparently. I wish you would write a little letter to

Miss M. L. Skinner, 'Leithdale', Darlington nr Perth, West Australia.

and tell her if you are making the alterations or not; – let her see I did ask you: – and give her all information about the book.

I hope you got that Magnus MS. from Murry. If you do decide to publish, you are free to make what omissions you like, both from my MS. and Magnus'.[3] Perhaps best change the name all through – to Maurice Gross or Maurice le Grand.[4] And change anybody else's name. – Let me know.

I don't think I shall get to Mexico till late autumn – which means I shall not finish 'Quetzalcoatl', the Mexican novel, this year.[5]

I do hope things are going well and happily, at Iver chiefly, also at 5 John.[6]

Yrs D. H. Lawrence

P.S. You will of course send Miss Skinner six copies of the book.

Alterations in *The Boy in the Bush*
(for Miss Skinner).

[1] Secker m. 1921, Caterina Maria ('Rina') (1896–1969), daughter of Luigi and Caterina Capellero whom DHL later met (see Letter 3542 and n. 2). Secker's son was born on 11 March 1924. [2] Reginald Baliol Brett (1852–1930), 2nd Viscount Esher. [3] Magnus'] yours

[4] Secker wrote to DHL on 25 April that there would be 'ample time' for DHL to see the proofs, and 'As to the names, my own idea would be in general to give the right initials with dashes, and to put the authors initials alone, M.M., on the title page. I think this would be very much better than manufacturing a fictitious name, and would help to preserve its appearance of truth' (Secker Letter-Book, UIll).

[5] DHL wrote the first version of 'Quetzalcoatl' May–June 1923 in Chapala, Mexico (published as *The Plumed Serpent*, 1926).

[6] Secker's home and business addresses respectively.

Omit.

Ch XX. the dog 'began to lick the scattered brains.'

Ch XI – 'At the Sacrament. This is my Body, he knew he never wanted to taste that Body, nor drink that Blood.'

Ch IX – 'Our Lady and her Blessed Son –'

Ch I. p. 4 – his trousers 'seemed as if they were slipping down'

p. 35. – 'in front of'

Miss Skinner would also like the last chapter, and if possible, the last two chapters, omitted. A moi, ça m'est égal. Je m'en fiche de ce monde craintif.[1]

DHL

Miss Skinner would like worked in at the end of Ch. XXIV, this refrain: 'And the changing, curious truth remained. He didn't want to love the family, but he loved them with an enduring love. He couldn't do without them: would be lost without them: Tom, and Lennie, and Monica. His individuality seemed merged in them, that part of his individuality that was human, and flesh that perisheth. He loathed loving them, their hands gripping and clinging and wringing his heart, but nevertheless, while he lived he would love them. He resented it, but he couldn't help it. He loved them. Even Jane – she was part of the family. He might ride away for a time. He might philander round other folk. But he would always come back to Monica and Tom and Lennie and Jane. They held him. But he held them: he was their master. They were his. They clung to him, and he could never cut adrift from them –'

Chap. XXIII – Monica should say, after she shook her head: 'It seems dreadful, dreadful – but I'm glad, deep down within me I'm glad he's gone. He was frightful to me, leaving me. No one knows the dreadfulness to a girl, facing the world with her trouble – facing it alone – he marrying that Mary Ann,[2] leering at me over his barrier of respectabilities – *I'm glad you killed him.* The thought of him alive, and leering, was unbearable – an unbearable torture'.[3]

---

[1] 'To me, it's all the same to me. I don't give a damn about the timid world.'

[2] Sarah Ann Ellis in *The Boy in the Bush.*

[3] Secker had posted the proofs to DHL on 3 April 1924 (Secker Letter-Book, UIll). DHL reconsidered Mollie Skinner's suggestions when he corrected the proofs, and substituted 'blood' for 'scattered brains'; eliminated the references to tasting the Body and drinking the Blood; substituted 'with very noble subjects' in the English first edition and deleted in the American; retained the references to trousers 'slipping down' and kept 'front' in 'And he felt as if the front of his body was scorched'; did not use the 'refrain' for chap. XXIV; and revised the passage in chap. XXIII. The last two chapters were retained. (The two-page list of alterations is at IEduc.)

3100. To Curtis Brown, 4 April 1924
Text: MS UT; Unpublished.

Taos. New Mexico. U.S.A.
4 April 1924

Dear Curtis Brown

I send you three stories –

'Jimmy and the Desperate Woman',

'The Last Laugh'

'The Border Line'.

Basil Blackwell can have whichever he wants, if he wants one. Probably 'The Last Laugh'.

Don't send any of these to the *Adelphi*, in any case.[1]

They won't be very popular – but I must work off some of the depression of that Europe.

It is sunny here, and one can ride one's pony in the sun across the sage. Anything to forget those disastrous cities.

I can't do anything about pictures for the *History* Book here, but I think I'll ask my sister-in-law in Munich. Meanwhile I'll ask Collins to send her a copy of the book.[2]

I want to go on doing stories – I hope cheerful ones now – for a while. Don't suppose I shall finish 'Quetzalcoatl' this year. Feel I had just as leave keep it back.

Best wishes.

D. H. Lawrence

I've sent copies of these stories to Barmby. Let him know if he is to hold one back – what Blackwell wants.

Curtis Brown,
6 Henrietta St. Covent Garden
London W.C.2.

[1] I.e. to Murry.

[2] Vere Henry Gratz Collins (1872–1966), Educational Books Manager of Oxford University Press, had encouraged DHL to write *Movements in European History* (1921). The Lawrences stayed briefly with Collins at 2 Hurst Close, Garden Suburb, Hampstead in December 1915. See *Letters*, ii. 482–3 and iii. 194 n. The Press wanted to publish an illustrated edition, and DHL asked Else Jaffe's help in finding suitable illustrations; see p. 29 n. 1.

3101. To Willard Johnson, [7 April 1924]

Text: MS YU; Unpublished.

Taos. New Mexico.
Monday

Dear Spoodle[1]

Why didn't you tell me how much I owe you for typing that story?[2] Please let me know.

And would you be so good as to send at the same time a ribbon for the Corona type-writer?

We went up to the ranch yesterday: very nice.[3] I think we shall move up there before long. – The madding crowd strives somewhat.[4]

Bynner says you went back like a rag – or a wisp of hay, or something equally rugged.[5] Sorry! Hope I didn't do anything to you.

Many regards from us both to Bynner.

DHL

Will you let us know if there is an important dance at San Felipe or at Santa Domingo at Easter.[6] If there is we'll come over.

Night

Your letter came tonight. Mabel says this shady-looking cheque is good. Brett didn't do the drawing – she only traced out my drawing with tracing paper, to save time.[7] Just leave it 'by D.H.L.', won't you. I don't think it's any

---

[1] Willard ('Spud' or 'Spoodle') Johnson (1897–1968), American journalist and editor; editor and co-founder of the *Laughing Horse*, 1922–39, to which DHL contributed. See *Letters*, iv. 316 n. 5.

[2] Probably 'The Last Laugh' which is typed more expertly and in a different style from 'Jimmy and the Desperate Woman'; that has the characteristics of Brett's typing (e.g. many errors and letters added by hand on right margin); both are in George Lazarus's collection. Brett remembered that DHL 'sent away' one story 'to be typewritten. – this was the one about me: he thought I would be angry and hurt. When I did read it, I thought it was an excellent portrait of me' (Brett, *South Dakota Review* 66). No typescript of 'The Border-Line' survives; see p. 19 n. 5.

[3] Lobo Ranch.

[4] Cf. Thomas Gray's 'Elegy Written in a Country Churchyard' (1751), l. 73 ['Far from the madding crowd's ignoble strife . . .'].

[5] To Santa Fe where Johnson and Harold ('Hal') Witter Bynner (1881–1968), American poet, lived. The Lawrences had spent their first night in New Mexico with them. See *Letters*, iv. 316 n. 4.

[6] The whole party attended the Santo (or San) Domingo spring corn dance on Wednesday 23 April (see Letters 3115ff).

[7] A sketch of a male and female Indian doing a corn dance as described in 'The Dance of the Sprouting Corn' (see p. 36 n. 2); it was reproduced in the special DHL issue of *Laughing Horse* (April 1926) and on the dust-jacket of Secker's *Mornings in Mexico* (1927). A more finished version with additional detail and pueblos in the background and entitled *The Corn Dance* was published along with the article in *Theatre Arts Monthly*.

good altering the London Letter.[1] Ida Rauh is very nice[2] – Jaime is a little fantastic, but it's his line.

3102. To Harriet Monroe, 8 April 1924

Text: TMSC NWU; cited in Harriet Monroe, 'D. H. Lawrence', *Poetry*, xxxvi (May 1930), 93.

Taos, New Mexico
8 April 1924

Dear Harriet Monroe:

Probably it's a long while since we were in Chicago – it seems only yesterday. It was awfully nice to see you and know you – I shall never forget the afternoon, that lake with a stripe of snow like a skunk's nose. It was best before the other people came – but I liked the young man and his wife very much: and Mrs. Freer.[3]

We find Taos very pleasant again – very beautiful – and the raging spirits somewhat soothed. My wife just calming down after the depressing swirl of Europe, and Miss Brett blissfully happy on an old horse.[4] Both sending you warm regards. I must say I am glad to be out here in the south-west of America – there is the pristine something, unbroken, unbreakable, and not to be got under even by us awful whites with our machines – for which I thank whatever gods there be. If you come this way come and see us. You can always have lots of room to yourself. Don't forget.

Many greetings to you.

D. H. Lawrence

3103. To Baroness Anna von Richthofen, [10 April 1924]

Text: MS UCB; PC v. [Indian Dance at Taos Pueblo]; Postmark, Ta[os] APR 11 1924; Unpublished.

Taos. New Mexico.
10 Apr

Wir sind wirklich so gern hier[5] – die Leute sind alle sehr nett, auch die Indier

[1] DHL wrote 'Dear Old Horse: A London Letter' in January after receiving the December 1923 issue of the *Laughing Horse* (see *Letters*, iv. 555); it was published in the May 1924 issue.

[2] Ida Rauh (1877–1970), American founder of Provincetown Players and outspoken feminist, actress and sculptress. m. 1911, Max Forrester Eastman (1883–1969); divorced 1922. She lived with Andrew Dasburg, 1922–8; see p. 159 n. 1. She and Dasburg were witnesses at Mabel Luhan's marriages to Maurice Sterne and Tony Luhan. DHL wrote the part of Michal in *David* for her. See obituary in *New York Times*, 12 March 1970, p. 41.

[3] Unidentified, but perhaps the young couple were those who, after dinner in a restaurant, took them 'to their attic studio, where we sit and wait for our train' (Brett 40–1).

[4] Bessie (Brett 46).

[5] DHL's correspondent is Frieda's mother, Baroness Anna von Richthofen (1851–1930). See *Letters*, i. 409.

freuen sich, dass wir wieder da sind. Und die Mabel ist ganz gut geworden, – für uns, nicht für Alle. Sie hat den Ranch an Frieda geschenkt – deine Tochter ist Guts-Besitzer, und sehr stolz – wir gehen nächsten Monat da-oben, um die Holzhäuser wieder aufzubauen – Siehst du diese Tänzern? Wir kennen alle. – Die *Brett* ist selig. Wie geht's dir? Ist der Frühling noch da? Hier noch nicht – aber heisse Sonne.

DHL

[We really love being here – people are all very nice, the Indians too are glad, that we're back. And Mabel has turned very good, – to us, not to everyone. She's presented Frieda with the Ranch – your daughter is lady-of-the-manor, and very proud – we're going up there next month, to build up the wooden houses – See these dancers? We know all of them. – The *Brett* is blissfully happy. How are you? Is it still spring there? Here not yet – but hot sun.

DHL]

3104. To Else Jaffe, [10 April 1924]

Text: MS Jeffrey; PC v. [Indians dancing at Taos Pueblo]; Postmark, [. . .]; Unpublished.

Taos. New Mexico.
10 April.

We[1] are really awfully glad to be back here, in the height and space. Everybody seems very nice – makes us very welcome – even the Indians. Snow is still on the hills, but the sun is hot, and we ride, and are busy with little things. Mabel has given Frieda that little ranch – F. quite pleased. We shall go up next month and build up the log houses a bit. Of course one can only live there the summer: but it is very lovely in summer. I don't suppose I shall get down to Mexico till late autumn, to work on my 'Quetzalcoatl' novel again.

DHL

3105. To Mark Gertler, [10 April 1924]

Text: MS SIU; PC v. [Indian dance]; Postmark, Ta[os] APR 11 1924; Unpublished.

Taos. New Mex.
10 Apr.

We've[2] not had a word from England since we left – send a line. It's awfully good to be here again – really – such a relief. Frieda is puffed up: she *owns* a ranch of 160 acres, with log cabins and pine trees. Brett is still in a state of bliss – rides like an amazon in a cowboy hat, on a huge old brown mare. But now

[1] DHL's correspondent is Frieda's elder sister, Else Jaffe (1874–1973). See *Letters*, i. 391 n. 2.

[2] DHL's correspondent is Mark Gertler (1892–1939), painter. He had been a friend of DHL's since autumn 1914 and knew Brett from the Slade. See *Letters*, ii. 214 n. 1.

she's going to buy a buckskin pony. You never saw sûch a thrilled female. All goes smoothly, so far.

DHL

3106. To Margaret King, [10 April 1924]
Text: MS Forster; PC v. [Indian children dancing]; Postmark, Tao[s] AP[R] 1[. . .] 1924; Unpublished.

Taos. New Mexico
10 April

No word from England[1] – how are you all? Did you get the rug I sent from New York? – It is very good to be out here again – such a relief, to be in the big spaces. How do you like the boy dancing – we were in the pueblo yesterday and a lad danced for us just like this – they learn young. Your Aunt Frieda has got a little ranch of her own.

DHL

3107. To John Clarke, [10 April 1924]
Text: Lawrence–Gelder 124.

Taos. New Mexico.
[10 April 1924][2]

We[3] are so glad to be back in the west – it is very nice – everybody pleased to see us, even the Indians, apparently. I simply can't stand the big cities any more. We haven't had a word from England since we left – how are you all?

3108. To Curtis Brown, 10 April 1924
Text: MS UT; Huxley 599–60.

Taos. New Mexico
10 April 1924

Dear Curtis Brown

This just come from Secker.[4] It's another of my literary mix-ups. Magnus was a man I knew in Italy. He committed suicide in Malta, after borrowing money from a nice and not rich Maltese whom I knew. Magnus left various MS., of not much value: one about his experiences in the Foreign Legion. In

[1] DHL's correspondent is Margaret Emily ('Peggy' or 'Peg') King (b. 1909), the older daughter of his elder sister Emily.
[2] Dated with reference to the contents of the two previous postcards.
[3] DHL's correspondent is John ('Jack') Lawrence Clarke (1915–42), the elder son of his younger sister Ada.
[4] See p. 16 n. 7. (DHL's letter was written below and around Secker's letter.).

order to get some money back for Michael Borg, the Maltese, I wrote a long memoir of Magnus, to go before the Legion book. I wanted very much to recover for Borg the eighty odd pounds Magnus borrowed.

Magnus left a wife – but the MSS. I think legally belong to Michael Borg.[1] Anyhow there is that debt, which I know of personally.

Would you write and ask *Michael Borg*, 34 Fuori la Mina, *Valletta*, Malta, if he will accept the 50% – or what he wants.

Ask Secker to let you see the MSS, if you are at all interested. It is interesting.

Ask Secker please to change Magnus' name – I have already suggested it to him: and to change all names, – I have no idea where Mrs Magnus is: I only know she had repudiated her husband before he died, and refused to pay any of his debts.

I don't know what to answer Secker about percentage, and especially about the American side. Will you settle it all? I suppose there won't be a great sale for the book, and I don't mind taking the ten per cent up to 2000. You judge if it is right.[2] But we must let Seltzer know. – Seltzer, by the way, had the MSS for nearly two years – and it was by the merest odd chance I said to Murry – who was reading it out of curiosity – *send it in to Secker*. You see Secker knew all the Florence and Capri part of it.

I asked Barmby to cable the acceptance of *Boy in Bush*. Secker will make Miss Skinner's alteration[s] – I asked him to: as far as he likes.

Secker can leave out anything he likes from my MS of Magnus, or from Magnus own.

Seltzer writing me – very hurt.

I hope you dont hate all this trouble.

D. H. Lawrence

[1] See *Letters*, iv. 178 and n. 2.

[2] Secker responded to Curtis Brown on 24 April 1924 (Secker Letter–Book, UIll):

> Many thanks for your letter about the Magnus Memoirs. As the English situation at least is clear, I will proceed to put the composition in hand. As to America, I feel in the circumstances that it would not be unfair for me to share to the extent of one-third in any profits arising from a separate copyright edition there. After all, this manuscript has been considered and turned down by many publishers over here, and presumably in America also, and it was chiefly due to Lawrence's telling me the whole story one day that I promised to consider the matter again. (I had already returned the manuscript to the author who sent it to me from Malta shortly before his death 1919). I have personally put in a good deal of work on the manuscript, and I do not think it is too much to say that had I not agreed to print it now, it would have been abandoned, and I think moreover that Lawrence understood at the time that I was expecting to participate in American profits. Apart from this point, I should be quite happy to leave all American negotiations in your hands, and I hope to hear that you do not think my claims unreasonable.
>
> Yours sincerely,

I am writing Michael Borg now. – Also to Secker to deal entirely with you.

I want you to let Barmby know at once about this *Magnus* thing, so he can settle as you think best with Seltzer.

DHL

I shan't get my Mexican novel[1] finished this year – shall stay the summer here, I think –

P.P.S. I wrote my sister-in-law in Munich to find me illustrations for *Movements in European History*, and to Vere Collins,[2] at the Oxford Press, to inform her of what he wants. They can communicate [. . .] direct. Seltzer writes he would like to pub. the new illustrated edition in America, when it is ready.[3]

DHL

3109. To Thomas Seltzer, 10 April 1924

Text: MS UT; Postmark, Taos APR 12 1924; Lacy, *Seltzer* 131–2.

Taos. New Mexico.
10 April 1924

Dear Thomas

I just heard from Secker he wants to publish the Magnus Memoir and the *Foreign Legion* thing this autumn – and he wants American rights; to sell sheets to America. Will you let Barmby know your wishes in the matter, and he'll communicate with Curtis Brown, who will arrange the whole affair for me.

I don't think the new edition of *Movements in European History* will be ready yet, but I have asked Curtis Brown to let the Oxford Press people know that you would like to do the book this side with illustrations, when it *is* ready.

I told you F[rieda] has got her little ranch here: and I think we shall stay till late autumn – therefore I shan't get the 'Quetzalcoatl' novel done this year. I don't feel much like working at anything just now. The winter was a bad one.

Some time at your leisure, would you send me that translation of *Max Havelaar*, that the man in Australia did – W. Siebenhaar.[4] I should like to go through it to see what there really is in it. The MS. is in the safe, I think.

Brett sent you a jacket design today.[5] I hope you like it – I do – and that it

[1] *The Plumed Serpent*. [2] See Letter 3100 and n. 2.

[3] *Movements in European History* has never been published in the USA.

[4] William Siebenhaar (1863–1937), b. Holland and emigrated to Western Australia in 1891, government official and writer. m. 1899, Lydia Bruce Everard. Siebenhaar published a translation of *Max Havelaar* (1860) by Multatuli (pseudonym for Eduard Douwes Dekker, 1820–87): see p. 320 n. 2. See *Letters*, iv. 240 n. 2.

[5] For *The Boy in the Bush* (reproduced Roberts 427); DHL modified Brett's design (see Letter

comes well in time. If you need to make any modifications in it, do just as you please.

Hope all goes well.

DHL

3110. To Michael Borg, 10 April 1924
Text: TMSC UT; Unpublished.

TAOS. New Mexico. U.S.A.
10th, April 1924

To Michael Borg. 34 Fuori la Mina. Valletta. Malta
Dear Michael Borg

I have just heard from my English publisher, Martin Secker, 5. John St. Adelphi, London, that he might publish Magnus' *Foreign Legion* book, with my Memoir, in the coming Autumn, if it can all be satisfactorily arranged. He doesn't want to pay any advance, but suggests that you and I divide the royalties between us. I have written to my agent,

Curtis Brown, 6 Henrietta St, Covent Garden, London W.C.2

to write and make all necessary arrangements with you. Curtis Brown is perhaps the best known Literary Agent in London, so you can put complete confidence in him. I don't know what will happen on the New York side – You know how hard Mountsier tried to place the M.S. over here, and failed. – Mountsier, by the way, had a bad nervous breakdown, and could not continue the work.[1] Curtis Brown does all my business transactions on this side too, through his New York Branch, which is managed by

A. W. Barmby, Curtis Brown Ltd. 116 West 39th St. New York City.

Now I hope we can at last settle this weary business. There was nothing to do but wait for an opportunity – and the opportunity at last is here. I am glad for your sake – because as you know, I only made this effort because of that debt of Magnus' to you.

I know you will make a straight and honest agreement with Curtis Brown. I am sending a line to Don Mauro.[2]

My wife joins me in kindest regards to yourself, also to Salomonee.[3]

Yours sincerely D. H. Lawrence[4]

3118). Both versions are unlocated. The drawing sent to Secker (Letter 3111) is DHL's and shows a man bowing to a kangaroo (UInd).

[1] Robert Mountsier (1888–1972), American journalist and DHL's literary agent in USA, 1921–3. See *Letters*, iii. 24–5 n. 4.

[2] Don Mauro Inguanez. (The letter has not been traced.)

[3] Walter Salomonee.

[4] There is a note in an unidentified hand at the top of the TMSC: 'Copy of letter to Michael Borg'.

3111. To Martin Secker, [10 April 1924]
Text: MS UInd; PC v. [Indians dancing at Taos Pueblo]; Secker 57.

Taos, New Mexico.[1]
10 April

Dear Secker

Here is a jacket-design for the *Boy in the Bush*, if it's not too late, and if you want it. I made it, and I think it's rather nice. – We are all enjoying being here – a bit remote. – The postcard is the Indians dancing in the pueblo here – they come with the drums and sing with us in the evening.

I enclose a list of *Boys*[2] – will you please send them out for me when the book is ready.

Hope all is well and happy at Iver – you're a new trinity now.

DHL

3112. William Siebenhaar, 10 April 1924
Text: TMSC NWU; Unpublished.

Taos, New Mexico.
10 April 1924.

Dear Mr. Siebenhaar,

Your letters and the *Western Mail* came on to me – very many thanks. We have fled west. We found Europe so depressing. But you, coming in new, will enjoy it: its past is *always* wonderful, let its present be what it may. I have heard from Miss Skinner, a bit scared by her new *Boy*. I expect Martin Secker will have the book out in May. It is between-seasons, but it doesn't do me any harm, so it ought not to affect the *Boy* himself. I will order a copy for you.

I don't forget *Max Havelaar*. But at the moment publishers are in despair, so I am keeping quiet about it. Heaven knows why book-selling should be in a bad way – but it is.

We are awfully glad to be back at the foot of the Rockies, on the desert: to smell the sage-brush, and hear the Indians' drums, and ride a pony once more. The real civilised world depresses me more and more: but then, I'm not ripe yet to bask in the past, which I do hope you will enjoy doing. It's a man's legitimate reward, when he's worked most of his years. I can see Mrs. Siebenhaar is enjoying Italy.

Best of wishes from us both,

D. H. Lawrence

[1] On some occasions (e.g. Letters 3217, 3220, 3227, 3230, 3236, 3251–3, 3255) DHL used a postcard or a photograph as a notecard; when no postmark is recorded, this practice should be assumed.

[2] The list of addresses is missing.

3113. To Thomas Seltzer, [18 April 1924]

Text: MS UT; Lacy, *Seltzer* 133.

Taos.
Good Friday

Dear Thomas

Will you send this man a photograph and that biographical book, if you think fit.[1]

Secker talks of deferring *Boy in the Bush* till Sept 1st. I am quite willing – I suppose you are.[2] Settle with Curtis Brown anyhow.

We want to go next week up to Frieda's ranch, with a workman, to build up the log houses. That will have to be done. Then we'll get a bit of furniture and spend the summer there – Deo volenté – Meanwhile all well here – very well, in fact. Only a bit more solitude one wants.

Deep snow yesterday.

DHL

[1] DHL's letter is written on the verso of Liljegren's, which reads:

Lund
31–3–24

Dear Sir,

I have been asked by Prof. Hans Hecht, of Gõttingen, to write a students' handbook of mod. Engl. literature. The work is to be illustrated, portraits of the most important authors inserted, etc. As you seem to me to be one of the most remarkable living Engl. novelists, I should like to ask you for a portrait & what information about your life and work you will care to give. If your publisher sends your next novel to me, I might review it here, as you are totally unknown in Sweden (which is a pity).

I am, dear Sir, yours very truly

S. B. Liljegren
Prof. Engl. Lit.
University of *Lund*. Sweden.

Sten Bodvar Liljegren (1885–1984), Swedish professor, author of books and articles on English and American literature, editor of *Litteris; an international critical review of the humanities* (Lund) and *Essays and Studies on American Language and Literature* (Upsala; Cambridge, Massachusetts), 1945– ; he did not publish the handbook. Hans Hecht (1876–1946), Professor at Göttingen, author of books on Robert Burns and a Medieval English literary handbook with L. L. Schücking, 1926–31 in six parts, etc.

The 'biographical book' may have been *D. H. Lawrence, An American Interpretation* by Herbert Jacob Seligmann (1891–1984), journalist and author, published by Seltzer on 28 February 1924. It included a 'Biographical Note', pp. 75–6, which quoted from Edwin Björkman's introduction to *The Widowing of Mrs. Holroyd* (New York, 1914) that covered DHL's life sketchily as far as the writing of *The White Peacock*.

[2] See p. 19 n. 4.

3114. To Curtis Brown, [20 April 1924]

Text: MS UT; Unpublished.

Taos.
Easter Sunday

Dear Curtis Brown

I send a little article – 'Indians and Entertainment'.[1] I sent the original typescript to Barmby, asking him to try the more serious magazines. – I don't mind where this goes in England – but it is a good study, for a heavier sort of periodical, perhaps.

I suppose it is as well if *Boy in the Bush* waits till Sept.

I'll send you more short things.

Yrs D. H. Lawrence

3115. To Mark Gertler, [23 April 1924]

Text: MS SIU; PC v. Deer-Dance San Juan. N M.; Postmark, Santa Fe APR 23 1924; cited in Moore, *Poste Restante* 79.

Santa Fe.
[23 April 1924]

We came down here for a few days, for the Indian dances.[2] They are great fun. You'd laugh to see Brett dancing à la Kate Greenaway[3] next a very wild savage with a tall feather in his hair. – I had your letter – hope you liked Italy. I will write. Kot and Murry have relapsed into disapproving silence – tant pis pour eux[4] – But you will write.

DHL

3116. To Catherine Carswell, [23 April 1924]

Text: MS YU; PC v. Deer-Dance San Juan. N M.; Postmark, Santa Fe APR 23 1924; cited in Moore, *Poste Restante* 79.

Santa Fe.
[23 April 1924]

We came down here for a day or two, to Indian dances. I like them very much.

[1] Published in *New York Times Magazine*, iv (26 October 1924), 3 and *Adelphi*, ii (November 1924), 494–507 (Roberts C126); collected in *Mornings in Mexico* (1927). DHL recorded in his diary that he sent the MS of this article along with others to Barmby on 30 September 1924 (Tedlock, *Lawrence MSS* 98).

[2] DHL wrote 'The Dance of the Sprouting Corn' soon after seeing the dances ('This is the Wednesday after Easter . . .'). It was published in *Theatre Arts Monthly*, viii (July 1924), 447–57, and *Adelphi* (August 1924) with DHL's drawing (see p. 27 n. 7) (Roberts C122).

[3] I.e. in a rather demure fashion, sometimes with arms flung up, as portrayed in illustrations by Catherine ('Kate') Greenaway (1846–1901).

[4] 'so much the worse for them'.

Had your letter – really too bad about that job.[1] There are great bothers too here, between the Indians and the government.[2] I feel one can't get far enough away from the world. F[rieda] sends love.

DHL

3117. To Margaret King, [23 April 1924]

Text: MS Needham; PC v. Santa Fe, New Mexico; Postmark, Santa Fe APR 23 1924; Unpublished.

Santa Fe.
Wed

– We came down here for a day or two to go to the Indian dances. Had your mother's letter – so glad you are in the new house, and enjoying it.[3] We are going up to Frieda's ranch next week –

DHL

3118. To Thomas Seltzer, 2 May 1924

Text: MS UT; Lacy, *Seltzer* 133.

Taos. New Mexico.
2 May 1924

Dear Thomas

I send you here the design for the book-jacket. I took Brett's design and worked it out in the two colours myself – think it is very effective, dont you?[4]

I am sending by the same post the duplicate of Secker's proofs for *The Boy in the Bush*. There are a few alterations – not much. I think I have eliminated to fit the insertions, so it won't mean any moving of the type.[5]

[1] Donald Carswell had given up his job on *The Times* for the Bar; 'that job' may have been a vacancy for a Lord Chancellor's Visitor for which he felt particularly well qualified since he was knowledgeable about mental health. But after being encouraged to apply, Carswell discovered that he lacked the requisite seniority at the Bar; there were many apologies from those who had virtually offered him the position.

[2] DHL is probably referring to the meeting on Good Friday 18 April 1924 at the Taos pueblo of the Indians and officials from the Bureau of Indian Affairs over the banning of religious dances; see 'O! Americans', especially ll. 110–53, composed, according to the poem (l. 105), on Easter Sunday and date stamped in Curtis Brown's office 28 May (MS Mills College, Oakland, California); it was published in *New Mexico Quarterly*, viii (May 1938), 75–81, and Vivian de Sola Pinto and Warren Roberts, *The Complete Poems of D. H. Lawrence* (1964), i. 774–80. See also Jaime de Angulo's account of the meeting in Gui de Angulo, *Jaime in Taos*, pp. 57–61.

[3] DHL's elder sister, Emily Una ('Pamela') King (1882–1962). m. 1904, Samuel Taylor King (1880–1965). The family had moved from 480 Main St, Carlton, Nottingham to 'Torestin', Brooklands Rd, Sneinton Hill, Nottingham.

[4] See Letter 3109 and n. 5.

[5] Presumably including changes made to accommodate Mollie Skinner's objections; see Letter 3099 and p. 25 n. 2.

We've had cold and snow again. But now it is soft, and on Monday we are going up to the ranch with a couple of Indians and a workman,[1] to start repairing the house. I feel like getting out there. I feel, more than I ever did, that I should like to be right away from the world.

We get on all right down here, however. Mabel is really very much changed – for the better, I think.

Hope all goes well.

Yrs DHL

3119. To Martin Secker, 2 May 1924

Text: MS UInd; Postmark, Taos MAY 3 1924; Unpublished.

Taos. New Mexico.
2 May 1924

Dear Secker

I send herewith the revised proofs of *Boy in the Bush*. There are a few alterations, but I think I've eliminated exactly to fit the insertions, so it won't mean any moving of the type. It you find it doesn't quite fit, you can alter a word or two.

As for the last chapter, I think myself it's all right. But if you'd care to leave it out – why, do it. If not, Miss Skinner must be content as it is.

We've had a sudden burst of cold weather and snow here – Now it is soft again, and we want to go up on Monday with a couple of Indians to Frieda's ranch, about 17 miles away. You knew she had a little ranch, 120 acres, at the foot of the mountains, mostly pine trees. It's pretty wild, and I think we shall enjoy it for the summer. But we shall have to build up the log house, which has rather fallen into disrepair. We shall be pretty busy up there.

Hope all goes well, with the family particularly, also with the business.

Frieda sends her regards to Rene and you.

Yrs D. H. Lawrence

I forget to say, they are asking about *Boy in the Bush* for the Insel Verlag, would like to see it at once, because they may publish it and *Kangaroo* in German, as companion books.[2] As soon as possible, will you please send a couple of copies of revised proofs to my sister-in-law:

Frau Dr. Else Jaffe, Konradstr. 16. *Munich*. Bavaria.

She would do the translation. Send it registered.[3]

[1] Included at various times: Trinidad Archuleta and his wife Rufina, Geronimo and his wife, John Concha, Pondo and Candido; DHL and Brett call the carpenter Richard while Mabel Luhan names him as 'Pablo Quintana' (Brett 80, Luhan 195). See Letter 3122.

[2] Insel Verlag published *The Rainbow* (1922) and *Sons and Lovers* (1925), both translated by Franz Franzius, and other of DHL's books in translation. Else Jaffe translated *The Boy*, but it was published by Deutsche Verlags-Anstalt in Stuttgart in 1925.

[3] Secker's reply of 23 May read (Secker Letter-Book, UIll):

3120. To William Hawk, [2 May 1924]
Text: MS UT; Postmark, Taos MAY 2 19[. . .]; Unpublished.

Taos.
Friday evening

Dear William[1]

We couldn't get up to the saw-mill with the car, but we asked the blacksmith to order from Aleris a load of lumber,[2] 2 × 4 and 1 × 10 or 1 × 8.

If anyone happens to be going to San Cristobal from Del Monte, I wish you'd send this order down again, to make sure the man has it. And tell him to deliver it at our little ranch on Tuesday, as we intend to go up on Monday, if the weather will let us.

– A load of 2 × 4 and of 1 × 10 or 1 × 8. I think Tony told the blacksmith ten dollars' worth, but it may as well be a wagon load.

We were so pleased to see the ranch again.[3] It still seems like a home.

Greet everybody.

Yrs D. H. Lawrence

3121. To Thomas Seltzer, 4 May 1924
Text: MS UT; Postmark, Taos MAY 5 1924; Lacy, *Seltzer* 134.

Taos. New Mexico
4 May 1924

Dear Thomas

We have packed up ready to go to the ranch tomorrow. We shall have to get letters via Del Monte, so the address will be

care Del Monte Ranch, *Questa*, New Mexico.

I am thinking of my income tax: I may as well pay the second half now. I believe Miss Kameny paid $43.47. Let me know if this is right, and I'll send a check to the Collector of Inland Revenue at Albuquerque.

Dear Lawrence

Many thanks for yours of May 2 and for the proofs of "The Boy" which I received at the same time. I am leaving the last chapters exactly as they stand, and the book has now gone to press as you returned it to me. It will not be long before this is completed and then I will post a copy to Dr Else Jaffe.

All well here and at home. We are now having some summer at last. I hope you are both enjoying the ranch. I am looking forward very much now to seeing proofs of the Magnus manuscript, and I expect to be posting these to you next week.

Yours

1 William Hawk (1891–1975) and his wife Rachel Woodman Hawk (b. 1898) ran a small dairy farm on his parent's ranch, near Lobo Ranch (Parmenter 256).

2 Possibly the same family as Frederico Alires (see Letters 3432 and n. 5 and 3437), but the correct form of the name is not known.

3 Del Monte Ranch owned by Alfred Decker Hawk (1862–1950) and his wife Lucy Moore Walton Hawk (1864–1942) who were the Lawrences' landlords (1922–3) during their winter there with Knud Merrild and Kai Götzsche. They were the parents of William, Betty Cottam and Bobbie Gillete. See Parmenter 269–71.

I shall be glad to be on the hills again, near the trees, now the warm weather has at last come. Bynner wants us to go down to Mexico, but I suppose we shall wait, now, for autumn.

Saluti DHL

3122. To Mabel Dodge Luhan, [12 May 1924]

Text: MS Brill; Luhan 197–8.

Lobo.
Monday[1]

Dear Mabel

Geronimo came up in a carriage – milordo! – so the coachman will bring you this note. – I do wish I'd thought to ask you if we could have the adobe tools for a week – we ought to begin dobying in the morning, and we want to begin cementing the chimney now but no trowels or tools.

Later we shall want whitewash – or alabastine or whatever it is – and white and turquoise paint – and brushes.

And a packet of tin-tacks and another pound of putty: hinges for cupboards – and screws.

These things whenever anything is coming up, on wheels.

Thundering like the devil, and fierce rain. Good you're in shelter. Ponies neighing, trees hissing, Richard scuttling.[2]

Candido is very nice – he enjoys doing things. We chinked the end room this morning, it is all ready to plaster. Now we want to build chimney – going to get sand as soon as rain holds off.

My article – 'Pan in America' – will, I think, have to have two parts.[3] I'll see if I can finish first half this evening, and send it to Spoodle to type, if he comes.

Remember the address is

Del Monte Ranch, Valdez. N. M.

was that what you gave the postwoman? we've had no mail.

Hope you're feeling better, and *very* comfortable, by way of contrast.

A rat + chipmunk + squirrel-widow – enlivened night.

DHL

[1] Dated with reference to the early stages of work on the cabins and DHL's not having received any post (see Letter 3124).

[2] Mabel Luhan describes Pablo Quintana (see p. 38 n. 1 for name discrepancy) as 'the dignified Mexican drunkard, who was an excellent carpenter' who came 'for a couple of weeks to make furniture and do the things that were hard for Lorenzo to manage' (Luhan 195). See also Letter 3125.

[3] The article exists in two MSS of 7 and 12 pp. (Roberts E300.5a and b); DHL rewrote it probably in June. The second, longer version was published in *Southwest Review* in January 1926 and collected in *Phoenix: The Posthumous Papers of D. H. Lawrence*, ed. Edward D. McDonald (New York, 1936), pp. 22–31.

And the loan of the little grindstone.

I wish Contentos[1] was sold – he spoils the other horses, and he'll never be good to ride any more.

3123. To Mabel Dodge Luhan, [12 May 1924]

Text: MS Brill; Luhan 198.

[Lobo]
Monday *Evening*

Like a fool, I let the man go without this letter.[2] Send it to post.

Ask Tony if anyone in the pueblo will let me have a sack of fine straw – almost chaff – for plaster. But dont bother about this – I'll manage with the rough, unless the other turns up easily.

More rain – but hot again.

Been a very busy day – very satisfactory.

DHL

3124. To Mabel Dodge Luhan, [14 May 1924]

Text: MS Brill; Luhan 199–201.

[Lobo]
[14 May 1924]

[Frieda Lawrence begins]

I looked for you to-day, a very perfect day – Sorry you felt so ill. I also did think the Lord wanted me higher up, but am better! I think Lawrence gasped at the idea of *another* house, no, lend us one of the others – Nice to get such a fat mail – We are looking forward to coming on Saturday – the change and getting away from the work – I lay in your hammock all afternoon in the sun[3] – My mother writes *sadly* that we are so far away! Well, Haime can keep *his* sanity all to himself![4] Last night we went for a beautiful walk and heard the Indians singing far away! Richard was *horrid* but has recovered[5] – I *like* the different attitude of the Indians towards work, not so efficient but a game and *life* in it, that's why adobe looks so pleasing.

Much love and get better.

F.

[1] One of Mabel Luhan's horses.

[2] The coachman (see preceding letter). It is on the same serrated paper as Letter 3122 and is also written in pencil.

[3] Mabel Luhan had hung 'a swinging bed between two trees' at her cabin on Lobo (p. 197).

[4] Jaime (or Xaime) de Angulo.

[5] Frieda's comment and DHL's 'Richard was rather tiresome for two days' were instigated according to Brett by Richard's arriving at the ranch one day 'roaring drunk' which was followed by 'two days of sodden drunken sleep' (Brett 80).

[Lawrence begins]

Lobo
Wed. evening

Dear Mabel

Your mail came – thank you for *Delight Makers* yesterday[1] – so sorry the pains – we felt uneasy about you. Best keep warm and still. Frieda too had pains today, and spent a good deal of the time in the camp hammock. She's better this evening. One has days of discouragement. – I wonder what Clarence will really be like![2] I think we shall like him. Jaime is simply an impertinent, through and through. No more of him, no matter what works or doesn't work inside him. I'd rather have heard from Ida. – I think the Spoodle is really nice, in the last issue. – I know the Brett is a terrible sloven – but don't bother. – Another letter from Murry – still putting up little catty defences – leaves me cold. Letter from Seltzer, saying business is still very bad, and I am to be careful with my money, not spend much. But the advice would sound better from a different source. – John Concha must have been mad with us all, to neglect those mares.[3] I feel mad with him. – I always like my three Indians – they try to do all they can for me, so nicely. The walls of Jericho (the log cabin) are re-built,[4] and chinked and chinked-plastered outside, and inside end room. But alas, lute is rifted,[5] they couldn't get on with the chimney, rocks were too lumpy, not flat enough. So I had to send Trinidad[6] for William's wagon with more straw, and we've started making adobe bricks – 34 made this late afternoon – look very nice, lying in rows in the field. It rained on them a bit, just to show that even a 'dobe is a naked dog. – Richard was rather tiresome for two days – I wished him anywhere but here – today he's 'good' again – Lamp-glass has just cracked. – I think the man's drawings are good – I don't

[1] *The Delight Makers* (New York, 1890) by Adolph Francis Alphonse Bandelier (1840–1914), pioneer American archaeologist. The novel is about the betrayal of the prehistoric New Mexico Pueblo Indians by their ruling class to the Navajos.

[2] Clarence E. Thompson, Harvard graduate and later screen writer. Protégé of Alice Sprague who sent him to Taos and Mabel Luhan. See also Nehls, ii. 516 nn. 12 and 13.

[3] John Concha (1877–1969), a Taos Pueblo Indian. Eanger Irving Couse (1866–1936), a Taos artist, used Concha as a model as a young man (Laura M. Bickerstaff, *Pioneer Artists of Taos*, Denver, 1955, p. 49). (Mabel Luhan gives his name as Juan, p. 195.) See *Letters*, iv. 325 and n. 2.

[4] The wall of the city of Jericho 'fell down flat' when the Israelites all gave 'a great shout' (Joshua vi. 20).

[5] '... The little rift within the lute' in 'Merlin and Vivien' of Tennyson's *Idylls of the King* (1859–85).

[6] There are photographs and paintings of Trinidad Archuleta, son of John Archuleta and Christina, Tony Luhan's sister, and his wife Rufina by Brett in her book opposite pp. 50, 68, etc. (see Illustrations for one of these). See Brett 50 and Brett, *South Dakota Review* 16. Trinidad was a famous dancer at the Taos pueblo (Joseph Foster, *D. H. Lawrence in Taos*, Albuquerque, 1972, p. ix). For Rufina, see p. 49 n. 3.

feel myself competent to do anything at all serious. – Don't talk of more houses – what with Jericho and Rattenheim,[1] I feel I'm deep in. But heaven knows what we'll do in the future. But for God's sake, let us be our best selves, and be friends. When we are our best selves, we *are* friends. – I haven't finished the article yet[2] – too many things to do, till late evening. But I had said the things you wrote about the Indians, differently. At present I feel a trifle discouraged, don't want to write. We shall be ready by 1.0 oclock Saturday to come down to Taos, but if the motor-car is any trouble, we will ride horseback.

DHL

Geronimo doesn't like to ride horseback – I said, if you sent the car, he could go down with us. He *arrived* in a little carriage. Tony might tell the man of the little carriage not to come, if Geronimo is going down in the car.

Candido says he'll stay the week-end all alone, and then go down to the Pueblo on Monday. – He might like his brother.

3125. To John Middleton Murry, 16 May 1924

Text: MS NYPL; cited in Murry, *New Adelphi* 456.

Del Monte Ranch. Questa, New Mexico
16 May 1924

Dear Jack

We learn from Brett that you are marrying a girl called Violet le Maistre, on the 20th of this month[3] – and I see by the calendar it is already the 16th. If you can settle down with her and be happy I am sure it is the best for you. Better, as you say, than wild-goose-chasing in other continents.[4] I hope you'll have a nice place in Dorset, and make friends with your own destiny. I'm sure you can, if you will, take the rest of your life peacefully, with a wife, a home, and probably children. Anyhow that's what I wish you – an acquiescent, peaceful happiness.

We are out on Frieda's ranch, with three Indians and a Mexican carpenter, building up the log cabin – the 3-room one. It has been neglected for some years. You would like making adobe and so on, and the camp at evening – but I think you'd not feel comfortable in your skin, for long, away from England. It's much better as it is – I am sure of that. I think by the end of next week the houses will be done. There's a two-room cabin where Mabel can come when she likes, and a one-roomer for Brett. We've got four horses in the clearing –

1 'Rats' home'. 2 'Pan in America'.

3 Murry married Violet le Maistre (d. 1931), an assistant on *Adelphi*, on 24 April 1924. His first wife was Katherine Mansfield (1888–1923), short story writer; see *Letters*, ii. 31 n. 5.

4 See p. 47 n. 1.

and spring is just here – the wild gooseberries all in flower, and an occasional humming-bird, many blue jays. But the vibration is so different, England is as unreal as a book one read long ago, *Tom Brown's Schooldays* or something of that.[1] Often, too, it is trying – one has to bear up hard against it. Then the altitude, about 8,600 ft, tells on one for a time. The sun is setting, the pines are red, the Indians are just starting drumming. All good luck to you.

DHL

3126. To Katharine Throssell, [16? May 1924]
Text: Katharine Prichard, 'Lawrence in Australia', *Meanjin*, ix (Summer 1950), 256.

[Lobo]
[16? May 1924][2]

No! I thought you were too feminine about *Kangaroo*. You'll probably like *Boy in the Bush* better.

3127. To William Hawk, [16? May 1924]
Text: MS UT; Unpublished.

[Lobo]
[16? May 1924][3]

Dear William

Got no stamps – will you put them on for me.

DHL

Hope the baby is better.[4]

3128. To William Hawk, [16? May 1924]
Text: MS UT; Unpublished.

[Lobo]
[16? May 1924][5]

Dear William

Thank you for the eggs – they were very welcome. We go down to Taos for the week-end tomorrow. Do you mind keeping track of stamps.

DHL

[1] By Thomas Hughes (1822–96); published in 1857.

[2] The card could have been written any time after the move to the ranch and prior to the publication of *Boy* late in August 1924; the earliest likely date is 16 May after DHL received his first post at the ranch.

[3] This and the following note cannot be dated with confidence: soon after the move to the ranch and the first heavy post is likely. Also this letter is on the same paper with serrated top edge as Letters 3122 and 3123.

[4] Walton Hawk, b. 18 September 1923; see *Letters*, iv. 524.

[5] See note on dating the preceding letter; this may follow up the request for stamps; also the reference to the trip to Taos makes 16 (or 29) May likely. This letter is written on the verso of the right half of a music programme from Paris.

3129. To Thomas Seltzer, 18 May 1924

Text: MS UT; Postmark, Taos MAY 20 1924; Lacy, *Seltzer* 135–7.

Del Monte Ranch. *Questa*, New Mexico.
18 May 1924

Dear Thomas

We have come down to Taos for the week-end, to rest, after a very strenuous fortnight up at the ranch. With three Indians and a Mexican carpenter we have built up the 3-room log cabin – and very good little house – and made adobes for the chimney. Now there's a thunder-storm – and my adobes will get wet – Tomorrow we are going back – on horseback – and I hope in the coming week to get the houses all finished, roofs shingled and all. Then we shall move into the 3-room cabin, Mabel can have the 2-room when she likes, and Brett will have a tiny one-roomer. We've got four horses in the clearing, and saddles – so we are set up. – You know the ranch is about 2 miles up from Del Monte, and a good deal wilder. I think we should enjoy it for the summer, and in the autumn, about October, go down to Mexico. – By the way I had a letter from Manuel Gamio – quite a famous man down there, head of the Anthropologist Department.[1] He sent me his book, and wants me to go and see him in Mexico. I shall be glad to do so. – I wish you would send him a couple of my books – perhaps *Kangaroo* and *Captain's Doll*. Do you think he would like those?

Señor Dr. Manuel Gamio, Dirección de Antropologiá,
Filomeno Mata 4, *Mexico. D.F.*

I must go down in the autumn, to finish 'Quetzalcoatl'. And I think Gamio will be a most useful man to discuss it with.

What are you settling about publishing the *Boy*? I hope you can arrange satisfactorily with Barmby. – I'm glad I've got some money in the bank, to fix up this ranch – but I'm being very economical.[2] Of course, once the *work* is done, we shall spend very little. – And naturally I don't write when I slave building the house – my arms feel so heavy, like a navvy's, though they look as thin as ever. And after riding over 20 miles yesterday, my legs feel a bit heavy too. – I hope later to be able to find someone who might work the ranch and make a *little* living out of it – it could easily be done – so that the place needn't be abandoned in the winter. – Taos is looking very lovely, full spring, plum-

[1] Manuel Gamio (1883–1960), distinguished Mexican archaeologist; Inspector General of Archaeological Monuments, 1913–16; Director of Archaeology, Department of Agriculture, 1917–24; Director of Rural Population, Department of Agriculture; and Director of the Instituto Indigenista Interamericano. Author of books on Mexican archaeology and rural life. In 1919 at San Juan Teotihuacán, 30 miles n. of Mexico City, he excavated a pyramid with sculptures of Quetzalcoatl and Tlaloc. The book DHL received was probably *Forjando Patria* (*Forging a Nation*, 1916). See Nehls, ii. 519–20 n. 51 and Parmenter 277–80.

[2] In a diary entry dated 6 June: 'Spent on building ranch up, $217.65 in wages, $195.00 Gerson & Santa Fe. & about $50.00 lumber & oddments' (Tedlock, *Lawrence MSS* 98).

blossom like wild snow up the trails, and green, green alfalfa, apple orchards in bloom, the dobe houses almost pink in the sun. It is almost arcadian. But of course, the under-spirit in this country is never arcady.

I'm sorry business is still bad – but hope you're pulling through all right. Greet Adele – I hope she's well and sporting.

DHL

Mabel is not at all well, in health, I think – so she is quiet and subdued, different – much nicer really.

By the way, when I get back to the ranch I'll post my second half of the *income tax* to Albuquerque, unless word from you prevents me. I'd rather pay it here.

3130. To Catherine Carswell, 18 May 1924

Text: MS YU; Postmark, [. . .] N. Mex. MAY 20 1924; Carswell 219–20.

Del Monte Ranch. *Questa.* New Mexico
18 May 1924

My dear Catherine

We have often spoken of you lately. I wonder what you are doing. We had your letter about your cottage and Don's job. That was mean, to take the job back again. You *do* have bad luck.

Did I tell you Mabel Luhan gave Frieda that little ranch – about 160 acres – up here in the skirts of the mountains. We have been up there the last fortnight working like the devil, with 3 Indians and a Mexican carpenter, building up the 3-room log cabin, which was falling down. We've done all the building, save the chimney – and we've made the adobe bricks for that. I hope in the coming week to finish everything, shingling the roofs of the other cabins too. There are two log cabins, a 3-roomer for us, a 2-roomer Mabel can have when she comes, a little one-roomer for Brett – and a nice log hay-house and corral. We have four horses in the clearing. It is very wild, with the pine-trees coming down the mountain – and the altitude, 8,600 ft. takes a bit of getting used to. But it is also very fine. – Now it is our own, so we can invite you to come. I hope you'll scrape the money together and come for a whole summer, perhaps next year, and try it. Anyway it would make a break, and there is something in looking out on to a new landscape altogether. – I think we shall stay till October, then go down to Mexico, where I must work at my novel. At present I don't write – don't want to – don't care. Things are all far away. I haven't seen a newspaper for two months, and cant bear to think of one. The world is as it is. I am as I am. We don't fit very well. – I never forget that fatal evening at the Café Royal.[1] That is what coming home means to me. Never again, pray the Lord.

We rode down here, Brett and I. Frieda lazy, came in the car. The spring down in the valley is so lovely, the wild plum everywhere white like snow, the cotton-wood trees all tender and plumy green, like happy ghosts, and the alfalfa fields a heavy dense green. Such a change, in two weeks. The apple orchards suddenly in bloom. Only the grey desert the same. – Now there is a thunderstorm, and I think of my adobes out there at the ranch. – We ride back tomorrow. – One doesn't talk any more about being happy – that is child's talk. But I do like having the big, unbroken spaces round me. There is something savage unbreakable in the spirit of place out here – the Indians drumming and yelling at our camp-fire at evening. – But they'll be wiped out too, I expect – schools and education will finish them. But not before the world falls.

Remember me to Don. Save up – and enjoy your cottage meanwhile.

Yrs DHL

3131. To Willard Johnson, [19 May 1924]
Text: MS YU; Unpublished.

[Lobo]
[19 May 1924][2]

We're at the ranch – finish this week-end, I hope – glad to see you.

DHL

3132. To Willard Johnson, [26 May 1924]
Text: MS YU; Unpublished.

Del Monte Ranch, Valdez. Taos County
Monday[3]

Dear Spoodle

We've been so busy up here – but we're in our house now. I didn't know what to say to you about Mabel and her suggestion – but you will be wise for

[1] On his last visit to England, at a dinner at the Café Royal to which DHL had invited some old friends, he asked them one by one to go with him to New Mexico to set up an ideal community (Brett and Murry said yes, and only Brett carried it through); see Carswell 205–13 and Brett 20–2.

[2] The letter is written on the back of an envelope which is addressed in an unknown hand and postmarked: [T]AO[S] May 20 (8 AM) 1924. DHL's postscript may have been added to someone else's letter subsequent to the departure from Taos on the 19th for the ranch. For finishing the house 'this week-end', cf. the two preceding letters.

[3] Dated with reference to the Lawrences' having moved into their cabin (cf. the two following letters) and Mabel Luhan's 'suggestion' (Letter 3133).

yourself.[1] We shall be pleased to see you here – in about a week more, we shall be tidy. Clarence is here,[2] and I think he's a nice fellow – not weak really, at all. Let me know how you're feeling.

The *Horse* is good.[3]

DHL

3133. To Witter Bynner, [26 May 1924]

Text: MS HU; Postmark, Ta[os] MAY 27 1924; cited in Bynner 250.

Del Monte Ranch. Valdez, Taos County.
Monday[4]

Dear Bynner

I didn't write – didn't know what to say, hate to interfere between you and Spoodle or anything like that. I'm rather glad he's being wise and wary[5] – no good going like a bull at a gate, anyhow.

We've *slaved* up here – but our house is nearly ready – we moved in on Saturday. In a little while, when we can make you a place to camp in, I hope you'll come and see us. Send a line.

DHL

3134. To Thomas Seltzer, [26 May 1924]

Text: MS UT; Lacy, *Seltzer* 137–8.

Del Monte Ranch, *Questa*. New Mexico
Monday

Dear Thomas

Will you please send a copy of *Psychoanalysis and the Unconscious*, and *The Captain's Doll* to

Dr. W. C. H. Osborne, Gisela-Strasse. 1. *München*, Germany.

He wants to translate *Fantasia*.[6]

We've moved in to our log cabin – great fun.

DHL

Saw your picture with your infant prodigy![7]

Thank you for paying my tax.

[1] Johnson was considering Mabel Luhan's offer to be her secretary; he later accepted and moved to Taos (Bynner 250).

[2] Mabel Luhan drove Thompson to Lobo on 24 May (according to Brett 92); they all made an excursion to Red River on Sunday the 25th; the Luhans and Thompson left Lobo most probably on the 27th after Mabel Luhan's crying fit (Brett 93–4, Luhan 205–7).

[3] The May issue (no. 10) of the *Laughing Horse* (which contained 'Dear Old Horse').

[4] Pencil note on MS in unidentified hand: 'Mailed 5/27/24'.

[5] Bynner 250 says this is a reference to Mabel Luhan's 'suggestion': see n. 1 above.

[6] The translation by Walter Carl Henry Osborne (1879–) was published in 1929 as *Spiel des Unbewussten* (Roberts D79).

[7] Seltzer had just published *Janitor's Boy and Other Poems* by Nathalia Clara Ruth Abarbanel (1913–) who wrote under the name Nathalia Crane. See Letter 3552 and p. 343 n. 2.

3135. To Mabel Dodge Luhan, [28 May 1924]

Text: MS Brill; Luhan 198–9.

[Lobo]
Wed. noon[1]

Dear Mabel

Sending this by Richard – he is just leaving – not quite finished shingling, but near enough.[2]

We will come down on Saturday if you wish it and if you send the car. Trinidad and Rufina[3] say they want to go down for the week-end – and in that case we can't leave Brett. But if they stay over Monday, Brett will stay here.

We have washed and painted the other house – looks a different place.[4] Thunder and lightning and deep hail – very cold. The devil's in it.

No news this end – nothing happened –

Hope you're feeling well.

DHL

3136. To Frederick Carter, 3 June 1924

Text: MS UT; Moore, *Intelligent Heart* 229–30.

Del Monte Ranch, *Questa*. New Mexico
3 June[5] 1924

Dear Carter[6]

Your letter this evening. I was glad to hear the *Beacon* news – never heard of the periodical.[7] The *Adelphi* does one no good.

I got an agent in New York to tackle my publisher, and the thing will be straightened out – but will take about a year. It wasn't nice.

My wife has got a little ranch up here – about 150 acres, in the mountain

[1] Dated on the assumption that there was a second weekend trip on 31 May–1 June to Taos as Brett suggests (pp. 94–5).

[2] 'The roof is being put on my [Brett's] house. The drunk Richard has emerged but by this time your patience is exhausted and you send him home for good. Candido finishes the shingles on my roof' (Brett 94).

[3] Trinidad's wife was, according to Mabel Luhan, 'soon called The Ruffian by Lorenzo, she was so hard to move, like a piece of heavy, carved oak-wood, obstinate and stolid, with shining eyes' (p. 195); see also p. 42 n. 6. But DHL called her 'Lufina' for a while in April 1925; see Letters 3385ff. and then Rufina (3395) or Ruffina (3401). (Blanche C. Grant in *Taos Indians*, Taos, 1925, records that Joe Archuleta and Rufina Romero were married in December 1922 and were the first Indians to use the wedding ring, p. 101.)

[4] The Luhans' cabin.

[5] June] May

[6] Frederick Carter (1883–1967), painter and etcher; he was interested in astrology and the occult. He and DHL had corresponded since December 1922. See *Letters*, iv. 365 n. 3.

[7] Part of Carter's *Dragon of the Alchemists* (published in book form, 1926) was printed in the *Beacon*, iii (June 1924), 526–34. The *Beacon*, which ran October 1921–June 1924, February–March 1925, was published by Blackwell in Oxford and devoted itself to 'three essential and inseparable things – Education, Religion and Art'. Contributors included Stanley Spencer, Gustav Holst, Julian Huxley, Richard Church and Rabindranath Tagore.

foot-slopes, mostly pine trees, but two clearings – not much water, though. We are about two miles up from DelMonte Ranch, get our mail there. It's a lonely spot here – beautiful scenery – altitude 8,500 ft. We have two little log houses and a tiny cabin. We have been a month working like niggers, building up this one house, which was falling down, and shingling the others. We had four Indians working on the job and a Mexican carpenter. The last Indians went down to Taos – 17 miles – today, and we are alone, save for a friend, Dorothy Brett, who paints – and is a daughter of Viscount Esher. – We have five horses[1] – ride down to Del Monte for milk and butter. I've just been having a struggle with three of the horses – they've gone wild, demons. Wish there was another man here to help, these times. It's a pity you haven't some money, to come and try the life here. You could have one of the houses, and Mrs Carter could start a little farm. Everything is all right, except the ditch to bring the water here from the canyon. But the winter is long and cold and lonely – we were at Del Monte last winter. – We have a spring, but it doesn't give enough water to irrigate. – I should rather like to see Mrs Carter tackle the place. – As for myself, I am a wandering soul. I want to go down to Old Mexico at the end of September, and my wife will go with me. It means abandoning this place, which is a pity. We should probably come back next April.

I haven't been doing much work since last autumn. The winter, and the visit to Europe, was curiously disheartening. Takes one some time to get over it.

As for the war, it changed me for ever. And after the war pushed the change further.

Shall be glad to see the *Beacon*. There is nothing new of mine – save a Pan story in that anthology of stories, *The New Decameron*[2] – and a story to come in the *Smart Set*.[3]

[1] Contentos, Cequa or Chiquita, Poppy, Azul and Bessie (Letters 3122, 3137 and 3147).

[2] Nancy Pearn wrote to DHL on 9 May 1924 (TMSC UT):

> Dear Mr. Lawrence,
>
> We have now definitely placed "THE LAST LAUGH" with "The New Decameron" at Twenty-Five Pounds, the understanding being that they have the British and American Book Rights in this story for two years from the date of publication, thereafter all rights to return to you.
>
> I am afraid, as you say, that there are very few possibilities so far as periodicals go for the other two stories, but you may rely on our taking advantage of any possible opening.
>
> The article "INDIANS AND ENTERTAINMENT" has just come to hand, and we are going to try it with the reviews.
>
> Yours sincerely,
>
> Cheque just come to hand is enclosed.

For 'The Last Laugh' see p. 20 n. 2.

[3] 'The Border-Line' in September 1924; see following letter and n. 5. It also appeared in *Hutchinson's Magazine* (see p. 57 n. 4) and was collected in *The Woman Who Rode Away*.

Warm regards to Mrs Carter, also to you.

Yrs D. H. Lawrence

3137. To Mabel Dodge Luhan, [4 June 1924]
Text: MS UT; Unpublished.

Lobo
Wed[1]

Dear Mabel

The chair reigns beside the cupboard, and looks very handsome.[2] I sit in it at evening. But I shall take the bar out. The rest is comfortable.

We wont come down at the week-end – seem so busy. And we are asking the Hawks up Sunday: so I suppose you won't want to come up for the week-end. Come any day, if you feel like it. – I'm sending you Gerson's list,[3] but if it's not to your mind to come up, Geronimo is coming on Monday with his wife to make the oven – the adobes are drying – and he'd bring the things if you'd be so good as to tell him. But if you feel like it do come. Brett is in her house. – The horses were demons yesterday – I caught Contentos, and fastened him to a tree with a thick rope. You should have seen him. All the devils! He broke the rope, and got loose. And the Chiquita leapt the boundary fence and was gone. But she came back. We must hobble Contentos, or shoot him – or shut him up.[4]

I've done one of the hardest days work in my life today – cleaning the well. All the foul mud of the Thames – and stank like hell. Now it's excavated and built in with stone, and the pipe sunk two feet deeper – Lord, this is the week we promised ourselves rest. I've still got to go to the Hawks' for milk – and it's 7.0 p.m. Wish we had a cow.

I hope you're well – no pains. As for wrestling with material, try a foul well. Greet Clarence.

DHL

That story 'The Border Line', of the woman who went to Germany, sold to the *Smart Set* for 175 dollars.[5]

[1] This letter precedes Letter 3145 where DHL says Geronimo failed to come.

[2] Mabel Luhan made DHL a chair which he called 'The Iron Maiden' (Luhan 202–3).

[3] Gerson Gusdorf (1869–1951), b. Germany, came to New Mexico in 1885, started 'Bond–McCarthy–Gusdorf' in 1905 with Frank Bond and John H. McCarthy, and then opened his own general store, known locally as 'Gerson Gusdorf'.

[4] Mabel Luhan had used 'the clearing of alfalfa fields' for their horses to graze. 'We had kept them there when we were not using them, and some we kept there all the time, the aging ones and the colts, and Lorenzo said they must stay right on.' Tony was 'extremely mad . . . when I confessed I'd given away the ranch and really had no more right to pasture our horses there or let the Indians go up and stay there when they were hunting' (Luhan 194–5, 203).

[5] DHL's diary entry for 6 June: 'Further 157.50 paid in by Curtis Brown from Smart Set for *The Border Line* story' (Tedlock, *Lawrence MSS* 98).

3138. To Mabel Dodge Luhan, [5 June 1924]

Text: MS Brill; Luhan 213–15.

Lobo.
Thursday[1]

Dear Mabel

Your letter about 'flow.' Anyhow, how can one *make* a flow, unless it comes? To me it seems you always want to force it, with your will. You can't just let it be. You want evident signs, and obvious tokens, and all that. On Saturday evening, you can't just let one be still, and let the flow be still. You want to 'do things' to me, and have me 'do things' to you. That isn't flow. I only wanted to sit still and be still on Saturday evening. Must I then exert myself to dance or to provide entertainment: I never ask you to exert yourself. I wish to heaven you would be quiet, and let the hours slip by. But you say it's not your nature. You'll say it is your nature to 'do things' to people, and have them 'do things' to you. That wearies me. Even you apply your *will* to your affection and your flow. And once my own *will* is aroused, it's worse than most people's. But I do assert that, primarily, I *don't* exert any will over people. And I *hate* the electric atmosphere of wills. You'll say it's because I just want my own will to predominate. It's not even that. It's that I want my will only to be a servant to the 'flow', the lion that attends Una, the virgin; or the angel with the bright sword, at the gate.[2] That's all I want my will to be. Not a rampaging Lucifer. But in you, even your affection is a subordinate part of your everlasting will, that which is strong in you.

If the problem is beyond solving, it is. Who knows. But there's the problem. How not to arouse these bristling wills of ours – they're in all of us the same – and admit a natural flow. The moment *one* exerts a will, the whole thing rouses in all the rest of us. And hell to pay.

And of course, it's so much easier to flow when one is *alone*, and the others

[1] This letter would have been written after a weekend visit to Taos; 22 May and 5 and 26 June are the possible dates. DHL reports that Mabel Luhan was 'quiet and subdued' (Letter 3129) during the first visit. Her placing of it suggests the 5 June date as does DHL's refusal to dance (see Luhan 210–13); the calm tone of Letters 3137 and 3139 and Mabel Luhan's mention of Alice Sprague argue against it. But after the weekend of 19–23 June (see p. 60 n. 3) when the dancing took place on Sunday, together with the breakdown in relations (Letter 3152) make the 26 June date unlikely. With reservations, the 5 June date has been accepted.

About 5 June, Brett records 'Frieda tells me that the letter you [DHL] received from Mabel the evening before, had thrown you into one of your terrific rages, and you had broken the red chair' (p. 97).

[2] The virgin Una (truth) protected by the lion (England) is from Book I of Edmund Spenser's *Faerie Queene* (1589–96). Angels with a 'flaming' sword guard the garden of Eden (Genesis iii. 24, AV).

are just thought about. As soon as two are together, it requires a great effort not to fall into a combat of wills. Even wrestling with one's material.

As for the apple-blossom picture,[1] the symbolism, the meaning, doesn't get me, so why should I bother about it.

DHL

Even with Brett, if you'd take your will off her, she'd be all right. But you wont. – It's no good *insisting* on 'flow'. The minute anybody insists, on anything, the flow is gone. And I *know* when the real flow is gone there is nothing left worth having. And perhaps I have a fatal little germ of hopelessness. Because, of course, your letters stop Frieda's flow, and her will starts up in a fury – as yours about Brett. And what then? Then my will is up in arms, and it's only a fight: useless all round.

I *know* that the only way to life at all, is to accept the invisible flow. And the flow should be manifold, different sorts, not exclusive. As soon as you try to make the flow *exclusive*, you've cut its root. Only one has to guard against false flow – which is *will* in disguise – like Lee Witt or Bynner.

3139. To Mabel Dodge Luhan, [6 June 1924]

Text: MS Brill; Unpublished.

[Lobo]
[6 June 1924][2]

Thanks for bringing the things. As a matter of fact, we were all sleeping an hour after the efforts, and you stole away so quietly.

If Tony sees Geronimo, ask him to get me about four pounds of rope, for halters, from Gersons – I've none left.

Glad you feel like riding – you must be better.

DHL

Sending your shawl.

[1] Unidentified, but see Letter 3130.

[2] Brett records that she and the Lawrences were sleeping when Mabel Luhan and Thompson 'arrive in the car with the provisions [cf. Letter 3137]. They come soundlessly over the field, creep in with the provisions, and drive soundlessly off' (p. 97). José is left with a note: 'He is to take Contentos, and the little mare, Cequa, down to Taos' (hence the need for more rope). The incidents are placed by Brett in early June.

José worked for Mabel Luhan and was described by her as 'our tattered Mexican' who looked after the animals and the fields (Luhan 176, Brett 45).

3140. To Witter Bynner, [7 June 1924]

Text: MS HU; Postmark, [. . .] JUN [. . .]; Huxley 611.

Del Monte Ranch. Valdez. Taos County
Saturday[1]

Dear Bynner

We've finished all our hard work – and the little guest-house is ready. If you and Spoodle would like to come up for a week, let us know, and come. I think we can manage to be good-tempered and aimiable for a while. And we can talk Mexico plans. I still feel very much drawn down there.

Only let us know a day or two ahead, then come. It is fresh up here, and not dusty. And as a rule, the wicked cease from troubling, and the weary are, thank goodness, more or less at rest again,[2] after 5 weeks slaving.

DHL

3141. To Mabel Dodge Luhan, [7 June 1924]

Text: MS Brill; Luhan 249.

[Lobo]
[7 June 1924]

Dear Mabel

We'll all soothe down a bit, then we'll come to Taos and see if we can't really get into a harmony. If everybody does his her[3] bit, I'm sure we can. Instead of being all wild like the horses. We'll all chew the cud of contemplation in our little corrals, then trot out for a reunion.

Anyhow the hard work is *really* done here – and as you say, it should be done with. Too great a strain when it lasts so long. Now we lift off[4] the strain.

Believe me, I *do* want us to be at peace together, all of us.

DHL

3142. To Curtis Brown, 7 June 1924

Text: MS UT; Huxley 603.

Del Monte Ranch. *Questa*, New Mexico.
7 June 1924

Dear Curtis Brown

I return the signed contract for the Magnus book. Michael Borg also wrote in a very friendly way – as he ought – saying he'd had a nervous breakdown. Another! – You will automatically pay him half the royalties.

[1] Dated with reference to '5 weeks slaving': Monday 9 June would be five weeks. Also cf. reference to having 'finished the hard work' in Letter 3142.

[2] Job iii. 17 ('There the wicked cease from troubling; and there the weary be at rest.').

[3] 'her' is written immediately above 'his'.

[4] MS reads 'of'.

I wish, if you have not done so, you would send a copy of the *Boy in the Bush* contract to

Miss. M. L. Skinner – *Darlington*, nr Perth. West Australia.

She is dying to see it. –

We've finished the hard work on the ranch here, and I'm hoping for a bit of leisure. I might even try a bit of my own work again.

I shall expect to hear from you from New York.

Yrs D. H. Lawrence

3143. To Idella Purnell, 9 June 1924

Text: MS UT; Nehls, ii. 350–1.

Del Monte Ranch. Valdez, Taos County–New Mex.
9 June 1924

Dear Idella[1]

We are up at this ranch – which now belongs to Frieda. – We have built up the houses – two – and it is quite nice – expect Bynner and the Spoodle next week. But I intend to come to Mexico in the autumn – I think in October – and I look forward very much to coming back. I have had a couple of letters from Manuel Gamio, the anthropologist in Mexico. He seems nice.

I think a good deal of Guadalajara and Chapala.[2] I *really* like it better there than here. But am pledged here for the summer.

I heard the tragedy of your motor-car. Alas, poor Dr Purnell!

Remember me to Percy Holm and Mrs Holm, and to Mrs Valliton,[3] and I hope it won't be very long before I'm having a sip of your Daddy's tequila.

Frieda sends greetings with mine.

D. H. Lawrence

Oh, do send Götzsche another couple of those *Palms* with his cover-jacket.[4] I never got those for him.

Are you still as much in love with the Muse.

[1] Idella Purnell (1901–82), American poet, lived in Guadalajara. She was a former student of Witter Bynner's at the University of California; 1923–30 she edited *Palms: A Magazine of Verse* to which DHL contributed. He met her in May 1923. See *Letters*, iv. 435 n. 2. She lived with her father, Dr George Edward Purnell (1863–1961), a dentist who had settled in Mexico in 1891.

[2] DHL lived at Calle Zaragoza 4, Chapala, 2 May–9 July 1923.

[3] Capt. Percy Grenville Holms, O.B.E., British Vice-Consul at Guadalajara (1908–15, 1919–33), and his wife were friends of the Purnells, as was Carnot K. Valiton. See Nehls, ii. 232, 498–9 n. 117 and 518 n. 25.

[4] Kai Guldbransen Götzsche (1886–), Danish painter, designed the cover for *Palms*, i, no. v (Christmas 1923). He had arrived in the USA in 1921 with Knud Merrild (1894–1954). DHL met them in Taos and invited them to winter with the Lawrences at Del Monte Ranch, 1922–3. See Merrild's *A Poet and Two Painters* (1938) and *Letters*, iv. 344 n. 1.

3144. To Martin Secker, 11 June 1924

Text: MS UInd; Postmark, Taos JUN 13 1924; Huxley 603–4.

Del Monte Ranch. *Questa*, New Mexico
11 June 1924

Dear Secker

I had your letter – am expecting the proofs of the Magnus book.[1]

Do a little thing for me, will you. Order *Punch*, for six months, to Mr. F. W. Gillett, at this address.[2] And order a couple of periodicals for me – not highbrow, not *London Mercury*; the best of the popular magazines, like the *Strand*, or *Hutchinsons*, or the *Bystander*. I haven't seen one for years, and I think it would be good for me to know *what* popularity is. – Order them for six months, will you, and send me the bill. I'll send you a cheque.

And if you have anything on your list, old or new, that you think we should like, send us something. There is nothing to read up here.

It's suddenly midsummer and blazing hot. I like it. I think Frieda would like to turn me into a western farmer. Mais non!

Grüsse[3] D. H. Lawrence

3145. To Mabel Dodge Luhan, [12 June 1924]

Text: MS Brill; Luhan 215–16.

Lobo.
Thursday[4]

Dear Mabel

Has your Mrs Sprague come?[5] If she has, do bring her up here to see us. – I wrote and asked Bynner and Spud to come for a week, to try how it is. – Soon I want to come to Taos too – but not for the week-end. Think it would be better *not* a week-end. Sundays are better away from civilisation. How are you? – Time passes quickly and quietly here – I ride every day, if only for the milk. –

[1] See p. 38 n. 3.

[2] Frederick W. ('Ted') Gillete, husband of Barbara ('Bobbie'), née Hawk (1904–76). See p. 39 n. 3. According to Brett and others, Gillete was 'a rich young man' (*South Dakota Review* 20); his uncle was Speaker of the House of Representatives. He came to Taos for his health and worked a summer with the Forest Service (hence, probably, his connection with the Hawks; see p. 57 n. 2). According to the address-book DHL started at Kiowa the Gilletes had two New York addresses, and they travelled extensively (see Letter 3247).

[3] 'But no! Greetings'.

[4] This letter precedes the visit to Taos 19–23 June when DHL met Alice Sprague and follows Letter 3137 where Geronimo was expected.

[5] Alice Louise Sprague, née Bragley. m. 1883, Carleton Sprague (1858–1916), editor. She was a friend of Mabel Luhan's from New York. She introduced Mabel to Maurice Sterne, who became her third husband, and sent Clarence Thompson to Taos. See Nehls, ii. 516–17 n. 13 and Luhan 208, 211.

Brett has walked off to Gallina to try for fish. – I began to write a story.[1] – Am getting used to this place and its spirit – then one likes it. – F[rieda] is dozing – she had a cold. I'm just riding down with this to catch the mail-man.

I hope you are well. Come and see us if you want to, but whatever you do, don't 'rattle up to the ranch and back.' As you say, no more of that. But it needn't *be* that.

Greet Tony and Clarence

DHL

Geronimo isnt a man of his word – he has never turned up to build the oven. – If you are coming I know you wont mind bringing the goods from Gersons. If you are not coming, Ted Gillett will bring the things up. Don't you bother in the slightest. – But come and see us.

I missed the mail – bad luck. Ted Gellett won't be going out again – he's gone today – but Louis Cottam will be coming here on Monday, he'd bring the things.[2]

3146. To Nancy Pearn, 18 June 1924

Text: MS UT; Unpublished.

Del Monte Ranch. *Questa*. New Mexico.
18 June 1924

Dear Miss Pearse[3]

Thank you for your letter telling me about 'The Border Line' story.[4] Good

[1] Either 'St. Mawr' or 'The Woman Who Rode Away', the sequence of writing cannot be established. See *St. Mawr and Other Stories*, ed. Brian Finney (Cambridge, 1983), pp. xxiv–xxv and the following letter.

[2] Louis Francis Cottam (b. 1892) was in the Forest Service from 1918; he was 'a fine man, quiet, with great integrity' (Brett, *South Dakota Review* 20). m. 1922, Elizabeth ('Betty') Moore Hawk (1902–71). See p. 39 n. 3. They had two children: Barbara (b. 1924) and Brooke (b. 1931).

[3] Annie ('Nancy') Ross Pearn (1892–1950), manager of the Magazine Department, Curtis Brown (London). DHL wrote to her as 'Miss Pearse' for several letters.

[4] Nancy Pearn wrote on 29 May (TMSC UT):

Dear Mr. Lawrence,

I am so glad on this sunshiny day – and you know London *can* have perfectly beautiful Spring days now and again – to be able to send over to you the good news that we have just placed "THE BORDER LINE" with ["] Hutchinsons Magazine", and have secured from them the price of Forty Pounds, the understanding being that they will not use the story until we have had time to try out the possibilities in the States, with a view to simultaneous publication on both sides.

We have also a letter from "The Adelphi" accepting with pleasure the article "THE DANCE OF THE SPROUTING CORN". They, also, are awaiting news from America before scheduling.

You will by now have heard that the Twenty-Five Pounds has been collected from Blackwell's for "THE LAST LAUGH".

With kind regards,

Yours sincerely,

news! You will have heard that the American dept. sold the same story to the *Smart Set* for $175.00. This leaves you with only one of those three difficult stories.[1]

I shall send you soon a couple more – one is finished, one is being done again.[2] They will both be *very* difficult to place. But never say die. It's more fun when the odds are heavy against one.

We are up here on a little ranch in the Rocky Mts, that belongs to my wife – with the desert stretching away below to the west. It's fine to look at, but not altogether so easy living in these wildish places. One feels dislocated sometimes. – But soon I hope you'll get the atmosphere of the place, in a story.

Is Mr Barmby in London? – Ask him why he never told me was going to England. Mrs McCord told me.

A hot day with a high wind, and a big forest fire burning across in the mountains. Pray heaven the wind wont bring it this way.

Yours sincerely D. H. Lawrence[3]

3147. To Thomas Seltzer, 19 June 1924

Text: MS UT; Postmark, Taos JUN 20 1924; Lacy, *Seltzer* 138.

Del Monte Ranch, Questa. New Mexico
19 June 1924

Dear Thomas

Will you please send a copy of *Sea and Sardinia* to Clarence Thompson, care Mrs Luhan. Taos. New Mex.

We are down in Taos for a day or two – hot weather, but windy and a big fire

[1] 'Jimmy and the Desperate Woman'; see p. 19 n. 5.

[2] Probably 'The Woman Who Rode Away' was 'finished', and 'St. Mawr' was 'being done again'; two MSS once existed for the latter. See preceding letter and p. 57 n. 1. Brett had started typing 'The Woman'; DHL had torn the MS from his 'copybook' by about 17 June (Brett 107).

[3] Nancy Pearn replied on 10 July (TMSC UT):

Dear Mr. Lawrence:

It was jolly to have your letter of June 18th, with the heading "Questa", which brought to mind my happy trip through that country two years ago.

I am so glad you are pleased with the news about "THE BORDER LINE". You may rest assured that our New York office keeps in touch with us all the time, thus making it possible to arrange for simultanous dates of publication.

I am now looking forward to receiving some more stories, in spite of your warning that they will be very difficult to place.

Mr. Barmby is due in London any day now. I will ask him why he kept his departure a secret. Perhaps he never thought you would be interested in knowing.

Kind regards,

Yours sincerely,

(Lida McCord worked for Curtis Browns.)

burning on the mountains – terrified lest it come this way. We get to be very fond of the ranch, the three of us alone, with three horses – ride every day. I was working at a couple of short stories – *The Smart Set* bought one called 'The Border Line' – *The New Decameron* another, for anthology – and the *Theatre Arts Monthly* has a little article of mine, with two little drawings of mine.[1] Dont know when they all appear. – There was a man here yesterday, George Creel – quite nice, not so very – said he'd give me a letter to Calles if I want it.[2] Manuel Gamio writes very friendlily from Mexico. – Clarence Thompson is a young New Yorker staying here – nice boy – and there is a Mrs Sprague – Always somebody at Mabels, when one descends from the hills.

I hope all goes well with you. It is high summer with a big moon – has Adele got a nice cottage? – We've got a Pips pup, 1 month, called Jerome, and Geronimo in Spanish.[3]

DHL

The Hawks had three horses struck dead by lightning 10 days ago: Laddie, and Shadow, and Blackie – all that we used to ride.

Tell Adele my mare is called Poppy, and F[rieda] has a grey horse, the Azul – Brett has old Bessie.

3148. To Willard Johnson, [21 June 1924]

Text: MS YU; Huxley 611.

Taos.
Sat.

Dear Spoodle

We have been down here a few days – go back this afternoon. Clarence is here, and Mrs Sprague – she's a nice elderly woman.

[1] 'The Dance of the Sprouting Corn' with illustrative sketch (see p. 27 n. 7); the other sketch was not used and is unidentified.

[2] George Edward Creel (1876–1953), American journalist and political leader; author of *Quatrains for Christ* (1907), *Wilson and the Issues* (1917), *Rebel at Large: Recollections of Fifty Crowded Years* (1947), etc. m. (1) Blanche Bates (1873–1941), 1912; (2) Alice May Rosseter, 1943.

According to Mabel Luhan, he 'was on his way to Mexico. He had been a sort of messenger from our President to the Mexican President at one time and he knew everyone down there'. So she arranged a meeting which was not a success; see Luhan 217–21. Creel was going to do research for a history of Mexico (published as *The People Next Door*, 1926), which he had decided to write after going as an emissary for President Woodrow Wilson in October 1920 to attempt to settle differences when Alvaro Obregón (1880–1928) was elected president (*Rebel at Large*, pp. 79–80).

[3] Pips was a French bull terrier, offspring of Mabel Luhan's Lorraine; she was also known as 'Bibbles' and 'Pipsey' (and several other names according to Merrild, *A Poet and Two Painters*, pp. 160–1). She spent the winter of 1922–3 with the Lawrences and party at Del Monte Ranch. Jerome and Alfred (Letter 3149) were renamed Roland and Oliver (see Letter 3150).

In all these complicated triangly businesses of inviting and not inviting and coming and not coming I feel a bit disconnected. But if you come to[1] the ranch and would like to stay a while and we feel it would be nice – why, let it be so. But let's let things evolve naturally of themselves, without plans or schemes or triangles vicious or otherwise. I'm tired of all that old stuff. I really am.

This sort of personal wingle-wangle has been worked to death. Let's drop it, and say *basta*![2]

Clarence has got the lease of this 2-storey house for Mabel's life-time, so we're taking out our things for him to move in.[3]

Greet Bynner. Tell him to roll our way when he feels like it, without afterthought.

DHL

3149. To Thomas Seltzer, 23 June 1924

Text: MS UT; Postmark, [. . .]; Lacy, *Seltzer*, 139, 140.

[Taos, New Mexico][4]
23 June 1924

Dear Thomas

Will you send a copy of *Birds Beasts* to

Mrs Alice B. Sprague, c/o Mrs Luhan, Taos. New Mexico.

We are just off back to the ranch, with 12 bottles of smuggled whiskey[5] and two of Bibble's pups – named Jerome and Alfred – and thunder brewing.

Wish us luck

DHL

3150. To Baroness Anna von Richthofen, 28 June 1924

Text: MS UCB; Frieda Lawrence 186–7.

Del Monte Ranch. *Questa*. New Mexico.
28 Juni 1924

Meine liebe Schwiegermutter

Seit so lange habe ich dir nicht geschrieben. Wir hatten aber hier so viel zu

[1] to] for [2] 'enough!'

[3] Mabel Luhan describes this visit at length: Thompson and Frieda danced together and went off for a late night walk; Mabel Luhan and DHL danced; Tony was somewhat inadvertently made angry; the next morning Thompson revealed to Mabel Luhan that Frieda 'says [DHL] has *told* her he will destroy you' which he is accomplishing gradually and DHL 'is determined to kill you [Mabel]'; and Thompson berated DHL 'You devil! I *know* you now!' for which as 'the hero of the moment' he got the 'Two-story House'; see Luhan 221–39. For a different version of the dancing partners see Brett 109. See also Introduction, pp. 4–5.

[4] Here and on several occasions later (e.g. Letters 3194 and 3211), DHL used paper headed 'Taos, New Mexico'.

[5] Although prohibition was over, Mabel Luhan said that liquor 'was difficult to get and not good when we got it' (p. 224).

thun; und auch ist meine Korrespondenzlust schwach. Ich weiss nicht warum: aber Worte und Sprache mir etwas langweilig geworden sind. Wir wissen so gut, ohne was zu sagen. Ich kenne dich, du kennst mich, so kann ich nicht mehr auf Papier reden.

Du weisst, die Frieda ist ganz stolz auf ihrem Ranch, und ihrem Pferd, der *Azul*. Er ist der Mann mit zwei Weiber, meine *Poppy*, die sehr scheu ist, aber schön: sorrel-farbe, und schnell; und dann die alte *Bessie*, Brett's altes Ross. Bessie ist auch rot – oder 'sorrel'. Jeden Abend gehen wir, alle drei, unten an Del Monte – nur 3 oder 3½ km. – durch Wald und über den Lobo-fluss. Du weisst, dieser Ort heisst Lobo: das meint *Wolf*, auf Spanisch. – Die Frieda spricht immer an seinem Azul: 'Ja, Azul, du bist ein guter Bub. Ja, mein Azul, geh' du vor, geh' dann. Jeh, hast du Angst, dummes Pferd? Es ist nur ein Stein, ein grosser weisser Stein. Dann warum Angst haben, Azul, mein Azul.' – So redet sie immer: weil sie ein Bisschen Angst, sie selber, hat. – Es gibt immer was zu thun. Ich habe zwei Geschichten – Erzählungen, meine ich – geschrieben. Jetzt machen wir ein Dach über der kleinen Verandah, vor der Küche-thüre – mit acht Säulchen, Pinienbäume, und Brettern oben [Frieda Lawrence deletes 'oben' and inserts 'drüber']: sehr nett. Es ist beinah fertig. – Du weisst auch wir haben einen Indischen Herd, aus Adobe gemacht. Er steht draussen, in der Nähe von der Küche-thüre: wie ein Bienenhaus gebaut:

[drawing].

Letzte Woche kam die Francesca, eine Indierin, die Dienstmagd ist, von Del Monte. Ich habe Brot gemacht, und wir haben Brot und Hühner im Herd gebacken: sehr gut ausgekommen. Wir können zwanzig Stück Brot in einer halben Stunde, im Herd backen. – Fünf Minuten oben von hier stehen noch die drei Zelte, und die Betten dabei. F. und ich haben da geschlafen, unter den grossen Sternen die hier niedrig auf den Bergen hangen. Kommt morgen, und ein sehr schönes graues Eichhorn läuft im [Frieda Lawrence corrects to 'in der'] Balsam-pinie und uns schimpft. Sonst in der Welt niemand – nur die grosse Wüste unten im Westen. – Wir gehen nicht viel nach Taos, und die Mabel kommt wenig hierher. Wir haben unseres eigenes Leben. Die Brett ist etwas Simpel, aber harmlos, und hilft immer gern.

Die Else schreibt, der Friedel kommt nach Amerika. Er soll wirklich hier kommen. Ich glaube die Else wird auch kommen: sie hat einen Willen zu Amerika. Gut auch. Aber das Leben in Amerika ist leer und dumm, leerer und dümmer wie bei uns. Ich meine das Stadtleben, und Dorfleben. Hier, wo man allein ist mit Bäumen und Bergen und Chipmanks und Wüste, kriegt man etwas aus der Luft; etwas wild und ungezähmt, grausam und stolz, schön und manchmal übel, das wirklich Amerika ist. Aber nicht das Amerika von den Weissen.

Kommt dein Geburtstag wieder, du alte Walküre. So reitest du auf deinem Geistross von Jahreszipfel zu Jahreszipfel, und guckst immer weiter in die Zukunft. Ich schick dir einen Cheque. Wie gerne wäre ich bei dir, um deine *Lebewohl* [Frieda Lawrence alters to '*Lebehoch*'] im guten Moselwein zu trinken. Hier giebt's keinen Wein und das schöne laute *Lebewohl* [Frieda Lawrence alters to '*Lebehoch*'] kann nicht zwischen die Pinien klingen. – Nächstes Jahr aber trinken wir zusammen, auf deinem Tag.

wiedersehen. DHL

Ich vergass, wir haben zwei kleine Bibbles-söhne: zwei Hündchen von unserem Pips. Sie sind sechs Wochen alt, heissen Roland und Oliver, und sind lustig, klein und fett und mit aufgehebten Fuss, wie Chinesiche Löwen.

[My dear Schwiegermutter

I've not written to you for so long. But we had so much to do here; and my desire to write is weak, too. I don't know why: but words and speech have become a bit boring to me. We understand so well, without saying anything. I know you, you know me, so there's nothing else I can communicate on paper.

As you know, Frieda is quite proud of her ranch, and of her horse, *Azul*. He's the husband with two wives, my *Poppy*, who is very shy, but beautiful: sorrel-coloured, and quick; and then old *Bessie*, Brett's old horse. Bessie is red too – or 'sorrel'. Every evening all three of us go down to Del Monte – only 3 or $3\frac{1}{2}$ km. – through woods and over the Lobo river. As you know, this place is called Lobo: which means *Wolf*, in Spanish. – Frieda is always talking to her Azul: 'Yes, Azul, you're a good boy. Yes, my Azul, on you go, go on then. Oh, are you scared, silly horse? It's only a stone – a big white stone. So why be scared, Azul, my Azul.' – That's how she always talks: because she's a bit scared herself. – There's always something to do. I've written two stories – short novels, I mean. Right now we're making a roof over the little verandah, in front of the kitchen-door – with eight little pillars, pine-trees, and boards on top: very nice. It's almost done. – You know, too, we have an Indian oven, made of adobe. It stands outside, near the kitchen-door: built like a bee-hive:

[drawing].

Last week Francesca came, an Indian woman who is a servant at Del Monte. I've made bread, and we've baked bread and chickens in the oven: turned out very well. We can bake twenty loaves of bread in half an hour in the oven. – Five minutes further up from here the three tents are still standing, with the beds beside them. F. and I have slept there, under the big stars that hang low on the mountains here. Morning comes, and a very lovely grey squirrel runs up the balsam pine and scolds us. No one else in the world – only the great desert below to the west. We don't go to Taos much, and Mabel rarely comes here. We have our own life. The Brett is a bit simple, but harmless, and always likes helping.

Else writes that Friedel is coming to America.[1] He really should come here. I think Else may come too: she has a will-to-America. All right. But life in America is empty and stupid, emptier and stupider than with us. I mean city-life and village-life. Here, where one is alone with trees and mountains and chipmunks and desert, one gets something out of the air: something wild and untamed, cruel and proud, beautiful and sometimes evil, that really is America. But not the America of the whites.

Here's your birthday come round again,[2] you old Valkyrie. On you ride on your steed-like spirit, from one year's peak to the next, always looking further into the future. I send you a cheque. How much I'd like to be with you, to drink your *Farewell* [Frieda Lawrence alters to '*Health*'] in good Moselle. Here there's no wine and the lovely loud *Farewell* [Frieda Lawrence alters to '*Health*'] cannot ring among the pine-trees. – But next year we'll drink together, on your birthday.

wiedersehen. DHL

I forgot, we have two small sons of Bibbles: two puppies from our Pips. They are six weeks old, called Roland and Oliver, and are gay, small and fat with paws up, like Chinese lions.]

3151. To Edward McDonald, 3 July 1924

Text: MS UT; Postmark, Questa JUL 5 1924; Moore 795.

Del Monte Ranch. *Questa*, New Mexico.
3 July 1924

Dear Professor McDonald[3]

I have your letter and the Cabell bibliography.[4] It's not exactly cold I feel, but a bit bewildered. But if people want bibliographies, and if you are willing

[1] Friedrich ('Friedel') Jaffe, (b. 1903), Else Jaffe's eldest child, came as an exchange student (see Letter 3214), spending the first term at St John's College, Annapolis and the second at Johns Hopkins, Baltimore. His area of study was 'political science but chiefly *America*' (letter to the eds. from Frederick Jeffrey). [2] On 14 July.

[3] Edward David McDonald (1883–1977), from Ohio, B.A. Indiana University, 1910; taught at several colleges; head of English Department, Drexel Institute of Technology, now Drexel University, 1919–54. Compiled *A Bibliography of the Writings of D. H. Lawrence* (Philadelphia, 1925) and *The Writings of D. H. Lawrence 1925–1930* (Philadelphia, 1931) edited *Phoenix: The Posthumous Papers of D. H. Lawrence*. Also produced bibliographies of Norman Douglas (1927) and Theodore Dreiser (1928) for the Centaur series. m. Marguerite Bartelle.

[4] *A Bibliography of the Writing of James Branch Cabell* compiled by Guy Holt (1892–1934), (Philadelphia, The Centaur Book Shop, 1924) with an introduction ('About These Books') by Cabell (1879–1958). It was the third volume in The Centaur Bibliographies of Modern American Authors Series, preceded by Hergesheimer and Stephen Crane (DHL's would be the sixth).

to take all those pains, *bueno*! I'll help as much as I can. But I'm not much good.

I will write you a little introduction, but tell me what kind of thing you would like me to say.[1] I don't really care a snap about first editions, or whether e's are upside-down or not. So I also have nothing really to say, in that line. Only I don't feel like saying it in as many words as Cabell does: haven't got the style.

But it *looks* a nice little book: affects me a bit as tables of logarithms used: and I got a certain thrill out of them.

Yours Sincerely D. H. Lawrence

Can I say how Mitchell Kennerley never gave me a sou for *Sons and Lovers* in America?[2] – I would like to get back at him: and surely a bibliophile would like to know that his Kennerley copy was a swindle.

DHL

3152. To Mabel Dodge Luhan, [3 July 1924]

Text: MS Brill; Luhan 241–2.

Lobito.
3 July.

Dear Mabel

Had your cards[3] – yes, we're all right up here – been making a Porch over the kitchen door.

Come and see us up here – if you can get any one to drive you to the lion's den. – Don't mention our coming down: I mean don't speak of it, don't even suggest it: I have a vision of Tony and Clarence, with set faces, departing an hour before the arrival: C. said that he and T. had so decided: and I haven't the heart to disturb the nest to that extent.[4]

But bring Mrs Sprague if you come – give her our regards anyhow.

And bring a bit of meat from Cummings,[5] and a few vegetables.

I hope you got the piano. Perhaps it will have strains to soothe – etc.

DHL

[1] DHL wrote 'Introduction to Bibliography' which was published under the title 'The Bad Side of Books' in McDonald's bibliography.

[2] A continuing complaint from 1913; see *Letters*, ii. 99 and iii. 74 n. 4.

[3] Mabel Luhan had promised not to see DHL again in order to get Thompson to pursue Tony who had left after the disastrous evening (see p. 60 n. 3), but she sent cards to DHL and Frieda when she and Tony went to Santa Fe overnight (Luhan 232, 241).

[4] 'Clarence had made [Tony] agree that if Lorenzo ever came back there [to Mabel's house], they two would leave together!' (Luhan 240).

[5] Albert A. Cummings (1865?–1934), Taos butcher. See Foster, *D. H. Lawrence in Taos*, p. 334.

[Frieda Lawrence begins]

My sister wrote that she sent off on the *6th* 3 packets of manuscript as 'insured', as she could make them![1] So look out for them, they are addressed to Taos to D.H.L. I hope theyll arrive safely and if it gives you a 100th part of the joy I get out of the ranch you will get quite a lot – The pups are very gay, we dont know which is nicer – at first we had to take a lot of care of them, they were so little to be without a mother – Yes, we have flourished – somebody 'the Drexel Institute' want to do a bibliography of L – We slept out one wonderful night with the stars entering into one and a most handsome squirrel very indignant in the morning – I suppose we have all calmed down again – I am still trying to find out *who* was Solomon's baby?[2] We ride every day – the porch is such a success –

All good things to all of you!

F.

I liked my card –

3153. To Witter Bynner, [3 July 1924]

Text: MS HU; Postmark, Questa JUL 3 1924; Huxley 612.

Del Monte Ranch. Valdez. Taos County
Friday[3]

Dear Bynner

All right. When you want to come up, let us know, and if you wish we'll arrange for you to come straight out here, without staying in Taos at all. We are very rarely down there, either. And there is no-one in the little guest cabin – nor likely to be. – I understand your feeling. I myself am sick to death of personalities and personalisms and tittle-tattle and threads back and forth, like a lot of ravelled knitting, and oneself the kitten trying to pick one's way out of it. Basta! to it all, and ten times basta.

We keep fairly cool up here – but you'll have more or less to *camp*, help with the chores and all that. You won't be particularly comfortable – and of course, society is strictly limited. But you can always depart when you've had enough, and in the meantime it's not bad. I will keep my irritatingness in bounds, I hope.

Frieda sends a bright Hello! – Brett a more stalky one.

DHL

[1] Else Jaffe was sending the MS of *Sons and Lovers*. (MS reads 'of of manuscript'.)

[2] Cf. 1 Kings iii. 16–28.

[3] Because of the postmark, this letter must have been written on 3 July (though 'Friday' was 4 July); also it must precede Letter 3154.

I rival the Spoodle in rags of paper.

Thank Spoodle for the blocks[1] – say when you're coming.[2]

3154. To Willard Johnson, 4 July 1924

Text: MS YU; Unpublished.

Del Monte Ranch, Valdez. Taos County
4 July 1924

Dear Spoodle

Thank you for the wood blocks – Brett has begun on one.

I dont have any strong feeling about a Lawrentian number of the *Horse* – certainly I don't want to do one all by myself.[3] But if you wish, I will help all I can – and you will put in just what you like. We'll talk about it when you come – which, I suppose, will be before long. When you come bring me a nice fat exercise book – you know, the sort I like to write in – such as we got in Guadalajara.[4]

Endless thunder here – wish Jove would put the bolt aside a bit.

We shall be glad to see you.

DHL

3155. To Rolf Gardiner, 4 July 1924

Text: MS Lazarus; Huxley 604–5.

Del Monte Ranch. *Questa*. New Mexico
4 July 1924

Dear Mr Gardiner[5]

I had your letter only last night. Duckworth's[6] knew I was in America. Curtis Brown, 6 Henrietta St. always has my address.

[1] Wood blocks for carving; see following letter. Brett may have been inspired by the many woodblock illustrations by local artists which were reproduced in the *Laughing Horse*.

[2] This postscript is on the back of the envelope.

[3] Issue no. 13 (April 1926) was devoted to DHL and included 'A Little Moonshine with Lemon', 'Mediterranean in January', 'Europe Versus America', 'Beyond the Rockies', 'Paris Letter' and Corn dance sketch (see p. 27 n. 7).

[4] DHL and Frieda were in Guadalajara late in April 1923 with Bynner and Johnson to meet Idella Purnell.

[5] Rolf Gardiner (1902–71), farmer, forester and pioneer of Land Service Camps for Youth in northern Europe after World War I. Graduated from St John's College, Cambridge, 1924. Founded Springhead Estate in Dorset, 1927, to realise DHL's vision; promoted husbandry and international exhanges. See Nehls, iii. 665–7 n. 60.

[6] Publisher of DHL's early books including *The Trespasser, Sons and Lover* and *The Prussian Officer*.

I would have done a notice of *Harbottle*, but now it is too late.[1] Anyhow I hope the book comes along. It will interest me.

Myself, I am sick of the farce of cosmic unity, or world unison. It may exist in the abstract – but not elsewhere. And we may all find some abstract ground to agree on. But as soon as it comes to experience, to passion, to desire, to feeling, we are different. And the great racial differences are insuperable. We may agree about abstract, yet practical ideas, like honesty, speaking the truth, and so on. And there it ends. – The spirit of place ultimately always triumphs. An American of pure English descent is different in all his reactions, from an Englishman.

To tell the truth, I am sick to death of the Jewish monotheistic string. It has become monomaniac. I prefer the pagan many gods, and the animistic vision. Here on this ranch at the foot of the Rockies, looking west over the desert, one just *knows* that all our Pale-face and Hebraic monotheistic insistence is a dead letter – the soul won't answer any more. Here, when we have the camp just above the cabin, under the hanging stars, and we sit with the Indians round the fire, and they sing till late into the night, and sometimes we all dance the Indian tread-dance – then what is it to me, world unison and peace and all that. I am essentially a fighter – to wish me peace is bad luck – except the fighter's peace. And I have known many things, that may never be unified: Ceylon, the Buddha temples, Australian bush, Mexico and Teotihuacan,[2] Sicily, London, New York, Paris, Munich – don't talk to me of unison. No more unison among man than among the wild animals – coyotes and chipmunks and porcupines and deer and rattlesnakes. They all live in these hills – in the unison of avoiding one another. As for 'willing' the world into shape – better chaos a thousand times than any 'perfect' world. – Why, you cant even have a 'perfect' camp on a Bucks common – Blarney!

To me, chaos doesn't matter so much as abstract, which is mechanical, order. To me, it is life to feel the white ideas and the 'oneness' crumbling into a thousand pieces, and all sorts of wonder coming through. It is painful – much more painful, and endured inwardly, than K[ibbo] K[ift] tests. But there it is. I hate 'oneness', its a mania.

And what do I care, really, about all that stuff. I am glad if White Fox and

[1] *Harbottle: A Modern Pilgrim's Progress From This World to That Which Is to Come* (1924) by John Gordon Hargrave (1894–), founder of 'Kibbo Kift, the Woodcraft Kindred' and in the 1930s leader of the Green Shirts, a Fascist-like movement, concerned with credit control. Gardiner followed his ideas of leadership and training. Hargrave was half Jewish. See Nehls, iii. 77–81. See also Letter 3190 and p. 93 n. 2.

[2] Teotihuacán ('The City of The Gods'), the most important city in pre-Columbian Central Mexico; it has a Quetzalcoatl temple. See *Letters*, iv. 417–18 and n.

his K K'ers have a good time.[1] Chacun a son goût,[2] – and let him keep it. I have mine, and it's different. I know there has to be a return to the older vision of life. But not for the sake of unison. And not done from the *will*. It needs some welling up of religious sources that have been shut down in us: a great *yielding*, rather than an act of will: a yielding to the darker, older unknown, and a reconciliation. Nothing bossy. Yet the natural mystery of power.

Anyhow don't bother. Accept what seems good to you, reject what seems repulsive; and don't feel condemned or over-implicated. To hell with stunts – when they cease to amuse.

Yrs D. H. Lawrence

3156. To Mabel Dodge Luhan, [7 July 1924]

Text: MS Brill; Unpublished.

Lobo.
Monday

Dear Mabel

Tony's nephew has just come for the mare Poppy. Pity no-one let me know he wanted her.[3] I could have looked out for another horse. – I want the boy to take Bessie too, but he doesn't want to – doesn't want to lead them both, I suppose. I will send her down the first opportunity.

I am writing to Gersons[4] to send me up a few things in a wagon; and shall ask him to send the wagon first to your house, to collect the trunks. There will be four: one of mine, two of Friedas, and one of Bretts: also a small leather suitcase of Frieda's.[5] I hope it won't be a trouble to you to have the things put on the wagon.

And let me know what there is here of yours I can send back on the wagon: get all this straightened out.

Best wishes from all

D. H. Lawrence

Frieda says she left things in a drawer – bottom of washstand. Would Maggie put them in the trunks and suitcase – nothing of Frieda's is locked. –

[1] Hargrave's title was 'White Fox, Headman K. K.' (Nehls, ii. 78).

[2] 'Everyone to his own taste'.

[3] 'Tony said: "I think we done enough for those Lawrences. I'm going to send for my mare. Better my nephew use her." He sent Fernando up to get her from the ranch, but I sent no letter as I had always done before. When the boy came back, he brought one of my horses, too, one of those I had lent Lorenzo, though I had not told him to do so' (Luhan 241). See also Brett 146.

[4] Gerson Gusdorf; the letter is unlocated.

[5] A reversal of previous arrangements according to Mabel Luhan: 'They were to keep on the Two-story House, leaving their trunks with their winter things in them along with most of their good clothes, for at the ranch they only needed corduroys and wash dresses' (p. 195).

So sorry to give you trouble. – There are also two coats of F's hanging in the cupboard.

DHL

3157. To Mabel Dodge Luhan, 7 July 1924
Text: MS Brill; Luhan 239.

Lobo.
7 July 1924

Dear Mabel

I am asking Gerson's man to deliver this note to you, as you may not have had my letters. – Will you please let the man put our trunks on his wagon: one of mine, two of Friedas, and a leather trunk of Bretts: also a brown leather suitcase of F's. Frieda says she left some things in a drawer upstairs: would you be so good as to let Maggie put them in the trunks or the suitcase. Nothing of Frieda's is shut up. Mine and Bretts are locked. I find we shall be needing bits of winter clothing, and other things we have left behind. And as I need things sent out on a wagon, this is a good opportunity to bring everything up. – The rain has practically ruined the road: otherwise, I know, you would have been out to see us. I wish you would send word by the man, if there is anything we can put on the wagon and send down to you.

Best regards from us all.

D. H. Lawrence

3158. To Mabel Dodge Luhan, [7 July 1924]
Text: MS Brill; Unpublished.

Lobo.
Monday

Dear Mabel

I sent you a note by Tony's nephew: but it looked so insecure in his pocket, I'm afraid he may lose it.

He came up for Poppy. You will probably be wanting Bessie too, so I will send her down at the first opportunity.

I wanted Gerson to send me up things in a wagon, so have asked him to send the man round to you with a note, so that he can put the trunks on the wagon and bring them up at the same time: one of mine, two of Friedas: one of Bretts: also a leather suitcase of Frieda's. F. left some things in a drawer, upstairs, and two coats in the cupboard. Would Maggie mind putting them in Frieda's trunks – or in the suitcase? I'm sorry to trouble you. But one wants a bit of winter underclothing again, it is quite cold: and we left those things in the trunks.

Terrific storms up here, and floods of water from the sky.[1] The road up from the Hondo looks impassable.

Tell me if you saw Mr Frayne about the taxes.[2] I want to go and see him when I come down.

Hope everything is going well with you all.

Yrs D. H. Lawrence

Please send a note by the man to say if there is anything I can send you down on the wagon.

DHL

3159. To Martin Secker, 7 July 1924
Text: MS UInd; Secker 58.

Del Monte Ranch. *Questa.* New Mexico
7 July 1924

Dear Secker

Here are the revised proofs of the Magnus Introduction – hope they haven't been too long travelling.[3]

Yrs DHL

1 DHL had been caught in a thunderstorm on Saturday 5 July on his way to Wayne's Farm – where he would get chickens and eggs – across the Hondo River. He had stayed under a bridge for an hour and a half sheltering from the rain (Brett 120). See Letters 3162 and 3175 and p. 73 n. 5.

2 Frayne was a lawyer, probably in Taos.

3 Secker wrote to DHL on 17 June (Secker Letter-Book, UIll):

Dear Lawrence

At last I am able to send you proofs of your Introduction to the "Foreign Legion", I have only made a few alterations, and one "cut" at the end, where you let yourself go on the subject of M.'s attitude towards certain things. Also, I have turned Don Martino into Don Bernardo. Will you please let me have these back as soon as you have had an opportunity of running through them.

I have heard disquieting news about Seltzer financial position, but I am relieved to think that you put your affairs in Curtis Brown's hands and I have no doubt that they were able to put your account in better shape. Indeed, this may have precipitated matters. As I expect you know, Curtis Brown is now in New York. Miss Skinner is now in London but I have not yet seen her. Unless there are good reasons for changing plans, I intend to publish "The Boy" on September 1 at the latest.

I hope all goes well with you and Mrs Lawrence. My uncle in Goslar writes in most despondent terms of the state of affairs there, noone apparently having any money at all. How is the Mexican book coming along? I shall be very interested to hear news of your work and plans.

Yours

3160. To Curtis Brown, 7 July 1924

Text: MS UT; Unpublished.

Del Monte Ranch. *Questa*, New Mexico
7 July 1924

Dear Curtis Brown,

I enclose MS. of a story 'The Woman Who Rode Away'.[1] I sent the other copy to New York. – Now good luck to it!

D. H. Lawrence

3161. To Mollie Skinner, 8 July 1924

Text: MS WAPL; Postmark, Valdez JUL 9 1924; Moore 797–8.

Del Monte Ranch, *Questa*. New Mexico
8 July 1924

Dear Miss Skinner

I was very much surprised to get your ship-board letter, and to know that by now you will be in London – I hope you will have a good time: and that you won't be disappointed at waiting until September 1st for *The Boy*. Secker sent me his advertisement leaflet: too bad that he leaves you out so much: it is not *my* wish, not a bit: just a publisher's attempt to use a known name and suppress an unknown one. I hope 'Lettie' meets with a warm reception. What do you say you'll call it? *Black Swans* sounds nice, to me.

I am sorry we shan't be seeing you. We are here on this ranch, which now belongs to my wife – it is fine and wild. But I want to go down to Old Mexico in the autumn, to finish a novel I began there.[2]

I have written you several letters since we have been back in America: they take so long. Also Seltzer is supposed to have sent you a hundred dollars advance on royalties, for *The Boy*. As soon as I had your letter, I wrote and asked him, if he had not sent the cheque to Australia, to send it to you in London. Anyhow I hope it will turn up. – If you need a few pounds, tell Curtis Brown, and they can always get you £25. or £30. advance from Martin Secker.

Be sure and let me know how you find London, and how 'Lettie' is received. I shall be very much interested to read her again.

I think *The Boy* will be translated at once into German.[3]

All good wishes to you from my wife and me.

Yours Sincerely D. H. Lawrence

[1] DHL must mean typescript: he sent the MS to Curtis Brown's New York office on 30 September 1924 (Tedlock, *Lawrence MSS* 98); see p. 136 n. 2. The story was published in *Dial*, lxxix (July–August 1925) and *Criterion* (July 1925, January 1926; see Roberts C131); it was collected in *The Woman Who Rode Away*; see also p. 481 n. 4.

[2] *The Plumed Serpent*.

[3] By Else Jaffe; see Letter 3119 and n. 2.

3162. To Mabel Dodge Luhan, [8 July 1924]
Text: MS Brill; Luhan 247–8.

[Taos, New Mexico]
[8 July 1924]

[Mabel Luhan begins]
Dear Lorenzo.
Can I send this to the Horse?[1]

Mabel

[Lawrence begins]

[Lobo]
Tuesday evening

Dear Mabel

Do as you like about the poem – 'Tocca a Lei'.[2]

Meat came this evening – many thanks. – In that same storm – Saturday – I sat under the Hondo bridge, holding Poppy – en route to the Waynes to get eggs.[3] But got so wet, went back.

I was very much annoyed when that boy – I didn't recognise him – suddenly arrived yesterday and demanded *Tony's two horses* – as if we had stolen them. However – poco me importa.[4]

Clarence's being mad or glad doesn't affect me. He is only a stranger. – And what has Tony to remember or to forget?

No, don't let's fix it – better not. Let them stay mad, and me go my own way – plum or poison-berry – non mi fa niente![5]

Basta! to all that nonsense.

We'll think of each other kindly, at a distance. The world is too full of mere people – like a forest of nettles and weeds.

I wrote and asked Gerson's to collect my trunks and send me up things. I waited for you to come, to arrange it. We really need the trunks. Do hope you won't mind being bothered.

No sign of MSS as yet – expect they'll come tomorrow. Come up and fetch yours, if you wish:[6] else I'll send it.

[1] 'Plum' with the subtitle '(Apologies to D. H. Lawrence)' was published in Luhan 244–6; see following Letter; it was not published in *Laughing Horse*. See also Brett 123 where she referred to the poem as 'Little Jack Horner'.

[2] 'It's your turn'.

[3] See p. 70 n. 1. The Waynes lived at the first farm after Upper Hondo (on the way to Desmontes).

[4] 'it matters little to me'.

[5] 'it doesn't bother me!'

[6] *Sons and Lovers*; see p. 23 n. 6.

F[rieda] wrote you, but we forgot to bring the letter down. She too in a peace-making, let's-fix-it mood.

But to me all this stuff of being mad and doing mean little things is just a bore. I say basta! bastissima!

Ciruela mystica[1]

am sending both puppies – it seems so cruel to have one alone, and leave it when we go for milk, and so on, while it's so small. They were re-named Roland and Oliver: the little one Roland. Probably you'll name them to your liking.

DHL[2]

3163. To Mabel Dodge Luhan, [10 July 1924]
Text: MS Brill; Luhan 248–9, 250.

[Lobo]
Thursday

Dear Mabel

Thank you for sending the things.

Would you like to hear all Clarence said to me? Pfui! – You have some admirable young men. – And ask Sara in detail for the 'queer talk' to the Hawks', do! – and see what she'll invent.[3]

And you know quite well there is no need for either Clarence or Tony to be 'mad'. It's pure bunk. But you always bring these things about. – Think I care about their madness?

However, I refuse myself to get 'mad.' – We'll remain friendly at a distance – or at least, I will.

I'd rather you didn't send out that poem, at least with my name on it.[4]

There is still another *brown* trunk of Frieda's down at your house. I'll send for it next time I order a wagon. – Am very sorry you had to send Tony's wagon. – Did you get the MSS you wanted?[5] The post office said you took them. – No, don't let's be 'mad', anyhow.

DHL

[1] 'enough! more than enough! Mystical plum' (correctly 'mística').

[2] The postscript is on the verso of an unfranked envelope which probably belongs with this letter. See Brett 153 on DHL's reason for getting rid of the puppies.

[3] Sara Parsons Higgins (b. 1901) (Luhan 248); see *Letters*, iv. 361 n. 1.

[4] 'Plum' (see preceding letter and n. 1).

[5] When the Luhans stopped in Valdez on 5 July the postmaster had a package for DHL addressed in care of Mabel Luhan; she extracted the MS of *Sons and Lovers*. They were caught there by a storm (see p. 70 n. 1) which made the roads to Lobo impassable (Luhan 243–4, 247).

[Frieda Lawrence begins][1]
Dear Mabel

A book arrived from you last night,[2] it's a godsend, we have no books, except your bible! – Do you like the pups? We have had such struggles with the horses, there's one nice new pony;[3] but last night Lawrence put turpentine on the fleabites of the horses and there *was* a circus! *Lots* of strawberries. The Ufers came one day,[4] said the MSS of Sons and Lovers, they had 'heard' I had given it you (they always hear so much) was worth at least $50,000, at least! Swinburne Hale told them!![5] It gave me a shock to think of it in terms of dollars – a bit of one's life! I have not got one of my trunks and the things in Clarence's house, in the bottom drawer of washstand, put them somewhere else in a box if they are in his way! I will come and get them some day! As to the destroying stuff,[6] it's all unreal and unwholesome *bunk* to me! Not true – as if I would let it happen! It's getting lovelier up here, red with flowers higher up where the young aspens are and a white lily! Come and have a cocktail sometime and don't let your men bunk!

Yours ever Frieda.

3164. To E. M. Forster, [14 July 1924]

Text: MS KCC; PC v. Indian Dance, San Ildefonso. N.M.; Postmark, Taos JUL 14 1924; Huxley 613.

Del Monte Ranch. *Questa. New Mexico*, USA
[14 July 1924]

Don't forget you are due to send me your novel, I want to read it.[7] Saw Murry's *Bou-oum* crit. – but even that is better than his *miaow* – anyhow, damn the universe and its echo[8] – je m'en fiche. On peut toujours s'en ficher, même de l'univers.[9]

DHL

1 Frieda's letter is unlocated; the text is from Luhan 250.
2 See Letter 3169 and n. 5.
3 Brett's pony Dan; see Brett 124 for her account of the effect of turpentine on the horses.
4 See Brett 123.
5 Swinburne Hale (1884–1937), American poet and lawyer; graduated from Harvard University, 1905. m. 1910, Beatrice Forbes-Robertson (1883–), lecturer and author. See Foster, *D. H. Lawrence in Taos*, pp. 58–60.
6 See p. 60 n. 3.
7 *A Passage to India* (June 1924) by Edward Morgan Forster (1879–1970), whom DHL had known since January 1915. See *Letters*, ii. 262.
8 In his review of *A Passage to India*, 'Bou-oum or Ou-boum?' (*Adelphi*, ii, July 1924, 150–3), Murry said: 'A cave of Marabar is the symbol of the universe for Mr. Forster: no wonder then that he should have waited so long before inviting an echo from it. He might almost as well have waited an eternity' (p. 151).
9 'I don't give a damn. One can always be indifferent, even to the universe.'

3165. To Earl Brewster, 15 July 1924

Text: MS UT; Brewster 75–6.

Del Monte Ranch. *Questa*, New Mexico.
15 July 1924

Dearl Earl[1]

We had your letter, and Achsah's – Capri seems so far away – so dim. I suppose it is the effect of this region.

Frieda is the proud owner of a little ranch here at the foot of the Rockies, among the trees, two miles above Del Monte. We look far out over the desert – far beyond Taos, which lies below, 17 miles away. We had four Indians and a Mexican, to build up the rather delapidated log cabins – now all is more or less ship-shape – and F. and I live in the 3-room cabin – nice big rooms – a friend, Dorothy Brett, a painter, who came with us from London – is in a tiny one-room cabin, and there is a 2-room cabin for visitors – when we get any. We have each our own horse, and ride down to Del Monte Ranch every day for mail and milk. It's our nearest point to the road. – I myself find a good deal of satisfaction living like this alone in this unbroken country, which still retains its aboriginal quality – and in doing for myself all I need – the women doing the women's part – That is, Frieda does it. But I make shelves and cupboards, and mend fences, bake bread in the Indian oven outside, and catch the horses. – I doubt if you would really like it. One has to be so much harder, and more cut off, out here. Either one stands on ones own feet, and holds one's own on the face of the land, or one is mysteriously pushed out. – America has really just the opposite vibration from Asia – here one *must* act, or wither: and in Asia, it seems to me, one *must* meditate. I prefer this, because it is harder. – But I think action – continual rushing round in motor-cars etc – can be much more silly than meditation.

I want to go down to Mexico City early in October. F. loves it here, but I hanker rather for old Mexico. And I have a novel half finished down there, which I want to get done this winter. Perhaps next year we may come round via China to India – have a standing invitation to friends in Darjeeling, far north, in the Hymalayas.[2] I shall let you know. – Meanwhile many greetings across the world, to you three.[3] We shall meet again – perhaps next year.

So a rivederci DHL

[1] Earl Henry Brewster (1878–1957) and Achsah Barlow Brewster (1878–1945), American painters. DHL met them on Capri in April 1921 and went to Ceylon at their invitation in 1922. See *Letters*, iii. 711 and n. 2.

[2] J. Elder Walker; see Letter 3171 and p. 80 n. 6.

[3] Including the Brewsters' daughter, Harwood (b. 1912).

3166. To Mabel Dodge Luhan, [16 July 1924]
Text: MS Brill; PC; Postmark, Taos JUL 16 1924; Unpublished.

[Lobo]
[16 July 1924]

Sorry I haven't Reed's poems[1] – have none of your books – isn't it in Clarence's house.

DHL

3167. To Mabel Dodge Luhan, [17 July 1924]
Text: MS Brill; Luhan 216.

[Lobo]
Thursday[2]

Dear Mabel

Many thanks for sending up the things. The saddle will do very nicely – only its *hard*. I'll send a cheque when I've got one – my book is empty. – We forgot to ask for Frieda's brown trunk: someday when you're coming alone in the car, and sitting in front, would you perhaps put it in the back. – The weather is calming – and the raspberries coming ripe – if you come up, we'll be quite quiet and peaceful. – F. has got the diarrhœa – seems a bit of an epidemic – so we won't come down this week-end.

Emilie's sister[3] came with the wagon – her husband – nice people – stayed the night.

They'll bring you the note.

DHL

3168. To Mabel Dodge Luhan, [17 July? 1924]
Text: MS Brill; Luhan 250.

[Lobo]
Thursday[4]

Dear Mabel

Yes, do come up. It's silly of us to be in a state of tension. – Only Sunday afternoon we're going out.

DHL

[1] Possibly *Tamburlaine and Other Poems* (1916) by John Reed (1887–1920), American journalist and sympathiser with the Bolshevist revolution, about which he wrote in *Ten Days That Shook the World* (1919); he had been Mabel Luhan's lover.

[2] This letter appears to be later than Letter 3163, but to precede the series of letters asking for a book of cheques (3176, 3183, 3184). Also DHL seems to have calmed down from the disastrous weekend in Taos in June (3162, 3163) and the sending of Tony's nephew to get the borrowed horse on 7 July.

[3] See p. 102 n. 3.

[4] It is impossible to date this note with certainty because there were several periods with varying 'tension' May–August 1924. 17 July as the date for a half-hearted attempt to begin reconciliation has been chosen since Mabel Luhan places it about then in her narrative.

3169. To E. M. Forster, 23 July 1924

Text: MS KCC; cited in P. N. Furbank, *E. M. Forster: A Life* (1978), ii. 124, 163.

Del Monte Ranch. *Questa*, New Mexico
23 July 1924

Dear EM

Your book came two days ago, and I have read it and think it very good.[1] The day of our white dominance is over, and no new day can come till this of ours has passed into night. Soit![2] I accept it. But one must go into the night ahead of it. So there you are. – I don't care about Bou-oum – nor all the universe. Only the dark ahead and the silence into which we haven't yet spoken our impertinent echoes. – You saying human relationships don't matter, then after all hingeing[3] your book on a very unsatisfactory friendship between two men! *Carito*![4] – After one's primary relation to the X – I don't know what to call it, but not God or the Universe – only human relations matters. But secondarily. There is that religious relationship first – and one is inarticulate about it.

Thank you for the book. I suddenly read three books in succession, as chance shuffled them this way – we hadn't a book to read, till 3 weeks ago. – *Beasts Men and Gods – Caste and Outcaste* – by a Brahmin, Mukerji[5] – and your book. Ahora sufficiente![6] – I won't read any more books for a spell, for my belly is full.

I think we stay here till October – Frieda now *owns* this little wild ranch – not I. – Then in October, I suppose, down to Old Mexico, to finish a novel, and see the gods again there. – One can go no farther than one's blood will carry one. But there are worlds beyond worlds, and some sort of trail.

Dear E.M. do you remember asking me, on the Downs in Sussex[7] – how I knew you were not dead – *if* I knew? – Quien sabe![8] One dies so many deaths, it too ceases to matter. – But there's not a soul in England says a word to me – save your whisper through the willow boughs.

DHL

[1] See Letter 3164 and n. 7.

[2] 'So be it!'

[3] 'is it hingeing?' was added between lines after several attempts to spell 'hinging'.

[4] 'Caro' in Italian means 'dear'; '–ito' is a Spanish diminutive. It is assumed that DHL intended the word to mean 'My dear man!' Cf. Letter 3256.

[5] *Beasts, Men and Gods* (New York, 1922) by Ferdinand Antoni Ossendowski (1876–1944) on which DHL had commented in February 1924 (see *Letters*, iv. 586). *Caste and Outcast* (1923), autobiography by Dhana–Gopàla Mukhopãdhyaya.

[6] 'Sufficient now!' (The correct spelling is 'suficiente'.)

[7] Forster visited the Lawrences 10–12 February 1915 when they were staying at Viola Meynell's cottage Greatham at Pulborough, Sussex.

[8] 'Who knows!'

3170. To Thomas Seltzer, 23 July 1924
Text: MS UT; Postmark, [. . .]JUL 25 1924; Lacy, *Seltzer* 140–1.

Del Monte Ranch, *Questa*, New Mexico
23 July 1924

Dear Thomas

I have your letter about the Magnus book, among other things. I really don't care very much what you do about that. When I did the proofs, it seemed to me interesting, but so very much passed into the past, and so very European. Maybe America wouldn't be interested. – Anyhow I *don't* think it's any good publishing my essay without the Magnus part. If you buy sheets from Secker, you can wait a bit about it, I suppose. Anyhow personally I don't care if the book is not published over here.[1]

By the way, did you send $100.00 to Miss Skinner. She is in London with the MS. of another novel: took a 3rd Class return, but luckily got a 1st Class passenger to nurse. If you didn't send her the hundred, I wish you would – to

Miss M. L. Skinner, c/o Agent. Gen. for West Australia, Australia House, Strand, London W.C.2.

If you want the *Boy* to wait till Sept. 1st, insist on it with Curtis Brown. Myself I don't see what difference it makes: but since Secker held you up, there's no need for you to fit in to a day. But I don't want it to be later than Sept 1st.[2]

I heard that you were in a low way financially. I hope it's not true, but fear it is. Yet I believe you can weather through. – I think you have made an inward mistake, between your gods. You say you are a sacrifice to the arts. I'm afraid it's an unwilling sacrifice. No Thomas. You wanted to be a big publisher, and to beat Knopf etc. But men must serve at the altar they're dedicated to. You're

[1] Knopf published *Memoirs of the Foreign Legion* in USA, which Secker favoured in his letter of 17 June 1924 to Knopf (Secker Letter-Book, UIll): 'I want to draw your attention to "Memoirs of the Foreign Legion", a set of proofs of which should be in Curtis Brown's hands by the time you receive this. He is undertaking the American negotiations and I have told him that inasmuch as my wishes count in the matter I should like you to have it.'

DHL had known Alfred Abraham Knopf (1892–1984) since December 1923 (see *Letters*, iv. 544).

[2] Secker published on 28 August. He wrote to Curtis Brown's office on 12 August (Secker Letter-Book):

> Thank you for your letter of the 9th. My last information about the American publication date of "The Boy in the Bush" was that Seltzer was issuing it on September 1 or perhaps a week earlier, so I then fixed Thursday August 28 as the date of English publication, and I cannot now very well alter it, still, I imagine that this is so close to Seltzer's date as to make no difference.
>
> Could you kindly enquire if in the event of Seltzer's deciding to purchase "Memoirs of the Foreign Legion" from me he would be willing to accept a bill falling due in six months from the date of shipment for the amount. I have had so much difficulty in collecting his account that I would prefer a definite arrangement.
>
> Yours sincerely

not born for success in the Knopf sense, any more than I am. I don't 'sacrifice' myself: but I do devote myself: and to something more than the arts. You began by so doing. You began to serve – and to serve, let us say, the arts. Then you wanted the arts to serve you, to make you a rich and prosperous publisher. So you sat down between two stools. And it is distasteful.

A man must follow his inner destiny. And it was your destiny to serve something – let us say the creative truth. That isn't the destiny of a Doran, let us say.[1] He makes the creative truth serve him, for money. Every man has his destiny. If you truly serve 'the arts', they won't let you down. They won't make you very rich, but they'll give you enough. Only a man has to devote himself. And your excursions into the popular field are only absurd.

We sit very quietly here. My adventure after all is the great adventure, which may be yours as well as mine. In early October I want to go down to Old Mexico, to finish 'Quetzalcoatl'. Meanwhile we live, circumstantially, from day to day, with the hills and the trees.

F[rieda] says she will write to Adele. I hope you do really like the summer cottage.

Yrs DHL

3171. To Martin Secker, 23 July 1924

Text: MS UInd; Postmark, Taos JUL 25 19[. . .]; cited in Huxley 605–6.

Del Monte Ranch, *Questa*, New Mexico
23 July 1924

Dear Secker

Thank you for the books. The American post is a thief – charged me 85 cents on one packet, 74 c. on the next. A couple of books! F[rieda] has already read Machen and Oliver Onions.[2] Why does Machen pity himself so much? A

[1] George H. Doran (1869–1956), American publisher; he was to have published *The Rainbow*, but decided not to. See *Letters*, ii. 417 n. 5.

[2] Secker had written on 26 June 1924 (Secker Letter-Book, UIll):

Dear Lawrence

Many thanks for yours. I have taken out a six-months subscription to Punch for Mr Gillett, and for yourself a similar one to The Weekly Edition of The Times (not the Lit. Sup.). Also to day I have posted to you the July Strand Magazine, Onions' "In Accordance with the Evidence" in the hope that you do not know it, as well as Machen's two autobiographical books "Far Off Things" and its sequel "Things Near & Far." Also, as the situation seems desperate, I shall from time to time post you Illustrated London News, Tatlers and such like, as well as occasional critical weeklies which reach me in great profusion.

Magnus proofs are on their way to you, and so is an advance copy of "The Boy" one of which latter I have sent to Dr Jaffe.

Best wishes to you both.

Yours

Secker had published the novel by Oliver Onions (1873–1961), *In Accordance with the Evidence*, in 1912. The autobiographical novels by Arthur Llewelyn Jones Machen (1863–1947), were published by Secker in 1922 and 1923 respectively; see *Letters*, i. 107.

la guerre comme à la guerre.[1] – The weekly *Times* also came: it seems on the whole such bunk. And the *Strand* Magazine terrible piffle. No, the periodical stuff is no go. The books are better. – When the Rimsky-Korsakoff memoirs are out, I should like to see them.[2] – And charge everything to me: that's the simplest.

I hear Miss Skinner is in London. Now be nice to her. I *know* she's hard up: wish you would advance her £25 or £30. on *The Boy* – unless she's *had* her advance on that. I hope her new novel is good. I read a beginning that I liked very much, but it went wrong. So she wrote it again. – If necessary, I must help her a bit. – Write and tell me what you think of *Black Swans* – her book.

Did you have the little pair of moccasins for the boy?[3] Hope they'll go on. You have to work them on like a glove, from the front: not pull them like a shoe.

We sit here very quietly – with the sun and the thunderstorms, the trees and the horses. I go on slowly with my second long-short story – a queer story.[4] Frieda of course admires her 'place' all the time. The flowers were all out – July is the month of rains. But already it's getting dry again, dry, dry. And the desert pale with dessication.

Seltzer says he thinks he doesn't want *The Boy in the Bush* to come out till 1st Sept. I suppose that makes no matter; to you. – I was surprised to see *Studies in Classic American Literature* – had no idea you were bringing it out at once.[5] Send a copy to E. M. Forster, will you: and one to

J. Elder Walker. 'Eddolver.' *Darjeeling*. North India.[6]

and to

E. H. Brewster: Torre Quattro Venti. *Capri*. (Napoli).

And when the *Boy in the Bush* comes, send copies to:

Mrs S. King. 'Torestin' – Brooklands Rd. Sneinton Hill. Nottingham.
Mrs. L. A. Clarke. Grosvenor Rd. Ripley, nr Derby.[7]
J. Elder Walker, 'Eddolver'. Darjeeling. N. India.

1 'It is as it is.'

2 *My Musical Life* by Nicholas Andreievich Rimsky-Korsakov (1844–1908); Secker published it in June 1924. See Letter 3220.

3 Adrian Secker.

4 'St. Mawr'.

5 Published in June 1924; Seltzer's edition had been published in August 1923.

6 John Elder Walker (1879–1957), b. in Scotland, an engineer with the East India Railway Company; he travelled on *R.M.S. Orsova*, with DHL, from Colombo to Perth, disembarking on 4 May 1922 (see *Letters*, iv. 235). m. Dolores Louisa Carlo Kuster, née Aguila (1867–1952), b. India. The Walkers were visiting Mrs Walker's daughter Vera and son-in-law Sydney Riley after the birth of their son in Melbourne, in 1922; they eventually retired and died there. (In the address book – located at UT – started at Kiowa Ranch, DHL gave Walker's address as 11 Yarra Grove, Hawthorn, near Melbourne.) 'Eddolver' was the Walkers' large three-storeyed house on a hill-side in Darjeeling.

7 Lettice Ada Clarke (1887–1948), DHL's younger sister; see *Letters*, i. 27.

W. Siebenhaar. c/o. C. Outram Esq. Silverleigh. Purley. Surrey.
E. M. Forster – Harnham. Monument Green. Weybridge.
Mrs. Catherine Carswell. 110 Heath St. Hampstead, NW3.
Mrs. Sophie Farbman. 5. Acacia Rd. St. Johns Wood. N.W.3.[1]
– and to me here, one copy.

Am reading *Passage to India*. It's good, but makes one wish a bomb would fall and end everything. Life is more interesting in its undercurrents than in its obvious: and E. M. does see people, people, and nothing but people: ad nauseam.

I hope all goes well. F: will be writing again. Thank you very much for all the trouble you took for me.

Yrs D. H. Lawrence

3172. To Witter Bynner, [24 July 1924]
Text: MS HU; Unpublished.

The Ranch
Thursday.[2]

Dear Bynner.

You sent me the wrong letter, didn't you? Anyhow, I suppose you'll be coming, and the little house is ready, and Mabel says she'll bring you up – so its all right –

Au revoir to you both

DHL

3173. To Willard Johnson, [24 July 1924]
Text: MS YU; Unpublished.

[Lobo]
Thursday

Dear Spoodle

The ranch seems as inaccessible to some people as the moon. – If ever you want to come straight up, I'll have a car or a wagon meet you: perhaps a wagon. – I'm sorry not to see you, but come next week, and tell Bynner to come.

DHL

[1] Sonia ('Sophia') Farbman, wife of a Russian journalist, Michael ('Grisha') Farbman (1880?–1933), with whom Kot lived at 5 Acacia Road, St John's Wood, known as 'the cave'. See *Letters*, ii. 570 n. 3.

[2] This and the letters following are dated on the basis of Johnson's trip to Lobo 30 July–7? August 1924.

3174. To Mabel Dodge Luhan, [28 July 1924]

Text: MS Brill; Luhan 253–4.

[Lobo]
Monday

Dear Mabel

This in a hurry. – If Hal and Spud are coming, would you give the list to Gersons. If Sabino is home,[1] would he bring the things in his wagon – if not, Gersons can hire a man.

When they come, would you bring some meat as usual –

I'll let you see my story when it's done – it goes very slow.

We should like to go to the Snake Dance.[2] But not on Aug 4th, because of the two journeys. And soon it will be time to go to Mexico.

Hope you get this tomorrow.

DHL[3]

3175. To Mabel Dodge Luhan, [28 July 1924]

Text: MS Brill; Luhan 199.

[Lobo]
Monday

Dear Mabel

Of course I forgot a bit of my list, in the rush: baking day too. If not too late, will you ask Gersons to send these things in the wagon. – And as you come, if you feel like it, will you call at Wayne's and bring me 3 doz eggs! It's the low cellar-like house, on the road between Seco and Hondo, about $\frac{1}{4}$ mile out of your way, when you come by the Whiskey Distilleries – about $\frac{1}{4}$ mile straight forward along the road to Hondo, where you leave it at that little sign 5 miles to Del Monte Ranch – the turning you take to bring you to the top of the Valdez canyon. – A long low white and black shanty on the right.

And would you mind asking the bank for a book of cheques for me.

Don't bother about the eggs unless it amuses you to see that place, with all its chickens.

DHL

[1] José's brother (Letter 3240).

[2] The Lawrences left on 13 August with the Luhans to go to Arizona for the Hopi snake dance. The 'two journeys' may refer to making two short trips for the various dances, instead of the fortnight jaunt they did make, or to a plan for another trip to Santo Domingo (Letter 3176).

[3] Written on the verso of an advertisement in the form of a letter from the Pacific Coast Shredded Wheat Company, Oakland, California.

3176. To Mabel Dodge Luhan, [29 July 1924]
Text: MS Brill; Luhan 223–4, 199.

[Lobo]
Tuesday

Dear Mabel

Did you get my letters ordering things from Gersons? Hope it's not a nuisance. – In the second letter – gone today – I asked for these few extra things.

Yes, come up, and for God's sake let's be peaceful – I hate my nerves being jolted: and strange people weary me[1] – only a sense of hospitality carries one through – and one becomes more and more estranged from strangers. – I think Spoodle can sleep in the barn – he won't mind, I'm sure – if you are in the guest-house.

Bring only a very little meat – the Hawks have killed a pig, we can eat some of that. And never mind about the eggs. – But do bring me a book of cheques, please from the Taos bank.

We'll talk about tripping when you come up.

A little too much thunder lately, in the sky. It wearies one. But not so badly as people.

DHL

[Frieda Lawrence begins]

Dear Mabel,

Thank you for photographs, letter, and books to-day, I scrubbed the guest-house for you – if Spud can stay a day or two order a camp-*mattress* for him – Bring him if you like and *Tony*. – The big[2] farm-house near New York sounds rather jolly.[3] Yes, I am *sure* you want to be alone. I die inside me if I don't. I want to come to San Domingo, just my days. I don't know if I will.

So we expect you. Bring Lorraine, if you like.

F.

[Lawrence continues]

extra things ordered in todays letter (by post to you)

[1] Mabel Luhan says the 'strange people' were George Creel and Blanche Bates's leading man (p. 223, 217); that meeting occurred on 19 June (Letter 3147). It is possible that DHL refers to the Hales and Foster; see Letter 3185 and n. 1.

[2] MS for Frieda's letter is missing from here on; the text is taken from Luhan 224.

[3] Mabel Luhan was 'feeling shattered of late' but wanted to come with Johnson to Lobo for 'a day or two', and she wrote to DHL that she had decided to rent Finney Farm at Croton-on-the-Hudson for the winter, where she had been before (Luhan 223).

20 lbs potatoes
1 tin bowl
1 lb putty
dressed lumber:
  2 planks 1 × 10
  3 planks ½ × 6″. or by 8″.[1]

3177. To Witter Bynner, [29 July 1924]

Text: MS HU; Postmark, Taos JUL 31 1924; Huxley 612–13.

Del Monte Ranch. *Valdez*
Tuesday.

Dear Bynner

All your three letters today – I'm sorry you are ill, and not coming. But do come – whenever you like – we'll have the house ready. We laughed a bit at the little fellow of gold[2] – but aimiably. We're all absurd, and it's better to be pleasantly so than poisonously so. – As for difficulties, *plus ça change* etc.[3]

But come up before you – or we – go far away. – I've not seen any of your poems or things about me.[4] I never care, so long as it isn't mean, what people say about me. I've really reached the point of realising that most people naturally dislike me – especially on second thoughts, they do. It's just part of the chemistry of life.

Spoodle may come tomorrow – quien sabe! It's a world of maybe's.

Yrs DHL

3178. To Norah Oliver, [30 July 1924]

Text: MS UT; PC v. [Indian on horse with mountains in background]; Postmark, Taos JUL 31 19[. . .]4; Unpublished.

Del Monte Ranch. *Questa*, New Mexico
30 July

Dear Spitzmans[5]

Your letter wandered along – we are here in the U.S.A. but going down to

[1] It is impossible to be certain whether the list belongs with this letter.

[2] Unidentified.

[3] 'The more things change' (the more they stay the same).

[4] E.g. 'Lorenzo', 'A Foreigner' and 'D. H. Lawrence' (Bynner 147–8, 182 and 325–7). The first and third were published in *Caravan* (New York, 1925), pp. 39, 40–4 (see Letter 3607 and n. 1), and 'A Foreigner' in *Indian Earth* (New York, 1929), p. 41; the latter was dedicated to DHL and was composed of a prologue and two sections, 'Chapala Poems' and 'Pueblo Dances'.

[5] Norah Doreen Oliver (1906–), born at Wood Green, Middlesex; DHL addressed his postcard to the home of her parents, Herbert James Oliver (a wholesale jewel-case maker) and Amy Florence Oliver, in Herne Hill, London. Her occupation and her connection with DHL are unknown, but they must have met in Mexico in Autumn 1923.

Mexico in October. My wife has a little ranch here, and we are living in the cabins – very good for summer, but the winter too cold, as we're 8500 ft up. – Götzsche is in New York – I'll tell him what you *don't* say.[1] Lawford, I suppose, is in Pachuca – I'll send him your fond remembrances.[2]

Yrs D. H. Lawrence

3179. To Ada Clarke, [30 July 1924]

Text: MS Clarke; PC v. [Taos Indians ready for ritual race]; Postmark, [Va]ldez JUL 31 1924; Lawrence–Gelder 126–7.

[Lobo]
30 July

Wonder why I have not heard from you – Did you get the Indian bracelet I sent for your birthday?[3] Emily wrote so I suppose nothing is wrong. There is nothing new here – Did you go to Wembley – I'll bet it's a wearisome place – too much of a good thing.[4] Did baby's moccasins fit him[5] – work them on like a glove.

DHL

The postcard is the Taos Indians ready for their race – a ritual race.

3180. To Nancy Pearn, 30 July 1924

Text: MS UT; Unpublished.

Del Monte Ranch, *Questa.* New Mexico
30 July 1924

Dear Miss Pearse

Yes, let the *Criterion* have that story 'Jimmy and the Desperate Woman' if

[1] Götzsche returned to New York to paint (Merrild, *A Poet and Two Painters*, pp. 350, 357–8).

[2] DHL met Evelyn Lawford in Mexico, and travelled with him to England in November 1923 (*Letters*, iv. 549). (DHL recorded his address as 33 Claverton St, Pimlico, SW (UCB address book), but this must have been the home of a relative (Miss Clara Annie Maud Green lived there 1909/10–1955), or possibly he boarded there.)

[3] On 16 June.

[4] The British Empire Exhibition at Wembley Park, London, opened 23 April 1924 and again in April 1925, was to promote empire unity and displayed products solely of the empire; it covered 216 acres and 27,000,000 people attended. (Mollie Skinner suggested to Secker that *The Boy in the Bush* 'might find a ready sale at the Wembley Exhibition', Secker to Manager, Publicity Dept, Offices Agent General for Australia, 19 September 1924; Secker Letter-Book, UIll.)

[5] Ada's younger son, William Herbert (b. 1923); he was called 'Bertie' (Letter 3349) as DHL had been as a child.

they want it.[1] I dont mind if they pay less. I don't suppose anybody else will accept it – or over here either. – I am just winding up 'St. Mawr', a story which has turned into a novelette nearly as long as 'The Captain's Doll'. But this isn't a good place to write in – one does too many other things: and too many thunderstorms.

Hope all goes well with you.

Yours Sincerely D. H. Lawrence

3181. To Edward McDonald, 31 July 1924

Text: MS UT; Postmark, Valdez JUL 31 1924; Moore 799–800.

Del Monte Ranch. *Questa*. New Mexico
31 July 1924

Dear Mr McDonald

I'm sure you know more about my published works than I know myself. – *The White Peacock* was my first book: and those 'Still Afternoon' poems in the *English Review*, my first appearance in 'good black print.'[2] There was a youthful story in the bad grey print of a provincial newspaper – under a nom de plume.[3] But thank God that has gone to glory in the absolute sense.

[1] Nancy Pearn had written on 14 July 1924 (TMSC UT):

Dear Mr. Lawrence,

The only likely place, as I see it, for "JIMMY AND THE DESPERATE WOMAN", is "The Criterion", a Quarterly Review which, as you probably know, is published by Cobden-Sanderson. Of course they cannot pay as much as a big monthly like "Hutchinson's", who, have, by the way, already seen and declined this story, but we hope to be able to get ten or twelve guineas out of them. "The Criterion" has a high standing among the "highbrows". We shall not release it here, of course, until we hear from New York.

Yours sincerely,

In her letter of 6 September, Nancy Pearn confirmed that *Criterion* would take the story and pay £18 'which will prove to you, knowing their limited finances, how keen they were to have this story' (TMSC UT).

It appeared in the October issue (iii, 15–42); it was not published in a periodical in USA. See also p. 270 n. 3.

[2] Five poems ('Dreams Old and Nascent' I and II; 'Baby Movements' I and II; 'Discipline'), under the general title 'A Still Afternoon' in *English Review*, iii (November 1909), 561–5; see *Letters*, i. 137.

[3] 'A Prelude' appeared in *Nottinghamshire Guardian*, 7 December 1907, under Jessie Chambers's name. The story was 'rediscovered' in 1949; see *Love Among the Haystacks and Other Stories*, ed. John Worthen (Cambridge, 1987), pp. xxiii–xxv.

The list of books horrifies me by its length: I'm sure they are all there (no, there's the history I remember later). I believe *The Widowing of Mrs Holroyd* appeared first in New York – Duckworth bought sheets from Kennerley:[1] and Seltzers *The Captains Doll*, did it synchronise with Secker's *England My England?*[2]

In the magazine stuff, there is the *Adelphi*, with several things: *Hutchinson's*: once, I believe, *The Strand*: and *Vanity Fair*: and Harriett Monroe's *Poetry*: – something in *The Athenæum* – London – in 1919: and *The Saturday Westminster* earlier than that.[3] – Then there are the stories in *The New Decameron* anthology, and in another anthology done by – I forget his name – Cournos: John Cournos.[4] – Also, you may like to know, – I forgot this too – The Oxford University Press has published a little text-book by me *Movements in European History* under the nom de plume *Lawrence H. Davison*. I believe they think of reprinting it, with pictures. And I believe it was published in 1920.[5] – It's a book I like, myself.

This is all I remember at the moment. Do write to me for anything you want.

Yours sincerely D. H. Lawrence

There's an essay with a drawing of mine in this month's *Theatre Arts Monthly*. N.Y.[6]

[1] Mitchell Kennerley published on 1 April 1914; Duckworth (from Kennerley's sheets) on 14 April.

[2] *The Captain's Doll* was published on 11 April 1923 while Secker's edition entitled *The Ladybird* had been published by 22 March. *England, My England* was published by Seltzer 24 October 1922 and Secker January 1924.

[3] *Adelphi* published stories, essays, translations and poems from September 1923; see Roberts C109, C111–13, C116–19, C121–2. *Hutchinson's Magazine* had 'The Fox' (November 1920) – DHL never could remember this (see Roberts C73.5) – and 'Fanny and Annie' (21 November 1921). *Strand* published 'Tickets Please' in April 1919. *Vanity Fair* published 'The Proper Study' under the title 'The Proper Study of Mankind' in January 1924, and 'On Being a Man' in June 1924; *Adelphi* published these two (December 1923, September 1924) and 'On Being Religious' (February 1924) and 'On Human Destiny' (March 1924). *Poetry* had published DHL since 1914 (see p. 15 n. 1); see Roberts C28, C29, C32, C35, C47, C59, C67, C99, C106, C115, C199. 'Whistling of Birds' appeared in *Athenæum* (11 April 1919) under the pseudonym 'Grantorto'. *Saturday Westminster Gazette* published poems, stories and essays 1912–13; see Roberts C11–13, C15–17, C20, C24, C26.

[4] 'The Wintry Peacock' in *The New Decameron III* (1922) and 'The Horse-Dealer's Daughter' in *The Best British Short Stories of 1923* (1924), ed. Edward J. O'Brien and John Cournos (see pp. 270 n. 3 and 410 n. 1).

[5] Published February 1921; to be published with illustrations in May 1925. See Roberts A17.

[6] 'The Dance of the Sprouting Corn'.

3182. To Amy Dawson Scott, 4 August 1924

Text: MS UT; Unpublished.

Del Monte Ranch, *Questa*, New Mexico, U.S.A.
4 August 1924

M. Scott. Esq

Dear Sir[1]

Thank you for the invitation to join the P.E.N. club. I shall be glad to do so, and enclose cheque for a guinea.

I wish, in return, you would give me a card to the Mexico City branch. I shall be going down there shortly.

I do think that artists – writers – are perhaps the only people who may be capable of imaginative international understanding.

Yours sincerely D. H. Lawrence

3183. To Clarence Thompson, [5 August 1924]

Text: MS SIU; Unpublished.

Del Monte Ranch. Valdez.
Tuesday

Dear Clarence

Thank you so much for the Tortoise – he's very shiny. When you come up, will you bring some meat: the pig lost its ice and went bad: Del Monte luck. – And please a packet of stamped envelopes – and a book of cheques from the bank – And if Gersons have any fruit – peaches or anything – and green vegetable.

I am still a rag – immure myself in my room and stay blank. Don't like being down.[2]

Spud will go, I suppose, towards the week-end.

If there is anything out of your sale you think I might like to buy, like the bubbly inkwell or anything, set a price and bring it me.

DHL

And I'll write in the *Sea and Sardinia* if you wish.

[1] Catherine Amy Dawson Scott (1865–1934), née Dawson, poet, novelist and editor. m. 1895, Horatio Francis Ninian Scott; divorced c. 1920. Early in World War I she founded Women's Defence Relief Corps to train women to take the jobs of men who had gone to war and the To-Morrow Club in 1917 to support and encourage young writers. In 1921 she founded P.E.N., the International Association of Poets, Playwrights, Editors, Essayists and Novelists to promote co-operation between writers all over the world; John Galsworthy was president of the English Centre, 1921–3 and the International P.E.N., 1923–33. See Marjorie Watts, *P.E.N. The Early Years 1921–1926* (Archive Press, 1971).

[2] About 2–3 August, DHL spat blood for two days according to Brett (139–41), and Dr T. P. Martin examined him.

3184. To Mabel Dodge Luhan, [5 August 1924]
Text: MS YU; Unpublished.

[Lobo]
[5 August 1924]

Dear Mabel

Got up a bit today, but still feel raggy with a sore chest and thick throat. We'd be jollier next week. Spoodle won't go till Bynner summons him – I suppose towards the week-end. – I solaced myself reading the second vol. of *Arabia Deserta*[1] – Gaspard said he'd give you back the first vol. – then bring it me.[2] It's the only thing I can read just now. Thank God it's so long. – I hope everything will turn out nice and we can go to Hopiland – would do me good, I believe.[3]

DHL

[Frieda Lawrence begins]

Dear Mabel,

Do pay us a visit; L[awrence] is better but still not well – I feel tired too, so come and see us but for your stay wait till next week, then we can ride and enjoy it! I am afraid it is dull for the Spud – Would you be so kind as to send to *Altmann's* New York[4] (I dont know the rest) for 3 wool and silk chemise vests, large size, white – and 3 pair white thin woollen knickers, mine are going and it's too cold for thin things –

It was so jolly to get Clarence's parcel – I love the tortoise and the lonely bird –

Love F –

Hope you are well!

3185. To Mabel Dodge Luhan, [7 August 1924]
Text: MS Brill; Luhan 255.

[Lobo]
Thursday

Dear Mabel

I was thinking, if the Younghunters would like to stay here while we go to the dance, they are very welcome.[5] – Or if they perhaps are going with us, the

[1] *Travels in Arabia Deserta* (1888, re-issued 1921) by Charles Montagu Doughty (1843–1926); see *Letters*, iv. 586 and n. 3.

[2] Leon Gaspard (1882–1964), Russian-born painter. His wife Evelyn (d. 1956), née Adell, was also a painter. See *Letters*, iv. 361 n. 4.

[3] See p. 82 n. 2.

[4] B. Altman & Co., Fifth Avenue, New York (founded in 1854).

[5] John ('Jack') Young-Hunter (1874–1955), Scottish-born portrait painter who settled in USA in 1913. His portraits included one of Mabel Luhan, 1936; he was noted also for his studies of American Indians, especially in *The Covered Wagon*. His land bordered Mabel Luhan's. m. (1) 1899, Mary Town Good (b. 1872), landscape and portrait painter; (2) 1921, Eva ('Eve') Renz Schroeer (1894?–1963). See his obituary in *New York Times* (10 August 1955), p. 25.

Gaspards. They seemed to like the place so much, perhaps they would enjoy a week here on their own. – Will you, if you feel like it, ask them. – I wish I'd asked you to bring me a good gargle for my throat: it hurts like billy-o! this evening. I should hate it if it kept me back.

The fishermen aren't home yet – nearly six. Afraid the dish of fish are still aswim. They have become a fable.

Thank you so much for the books and things and all the trouble we have given you: not to mention the terrible event of the broken Catellack:[1] done en route here or hence, alas!

DHL

3186. To Carlo Linati, 8 August 1924

Text: TMSC Bonsignore; Moore 800.

Del Monte Ranch. Questa. New Mexico, U.S.A.
August 8, 1924

Dear Signor Linati,[2]

Your letter reached me here. I am asking Martin Secker and Thomas Seltzer, my publishers, to send you the books you want.

I have lived a few years in Italy, and loved the country very much. I used to think the *Corriere della Sera* about the best paper in Europe. All the things that *Times* smothered over, it said fairly plainly. There is, indeed, a certain kind of Italian honesty which I like very much better than the English and American brand.

I shall be interested to see your article.[3] When you write, will you tell me if there are any good Italian books published lately?

Did you take *Lady into Fox* seriously?[4] I thought rather a childish *Jeu d'ésprit* for grown up nursery. Do you know E.M. Forsters work? He has just

[1] Probably Swinburne Hale's 'brand new Cadillac touring car', which after a heavy rain storm 'went throught a bridge' on the way back from Lobo. Hale, his sister Margaret and Joseph Foster 'had to abandon it and walk miles in the dark' (Foster, *D. H. Lawrence in Taos*, pp. 131, 144).

Margaret Hale (1891–1962), m. 1927, Joseph O'Kane Foster (1898–1985), writer.

[2] Carlo Linati (1878–1949), Italian critic, had written on Ezra Pound. He published an Italian translation of 'The Fox' and 'The Ladybird' in 1929 (Roberts D112). See *Letters*, iv. 232 and Giuseppe Gadda Conti, 'Una Lettera Inedita di D. H. Lawrence', *English Miscellany*, xix (1968), 335–8.

[3] 'Un esploratore di uomini', *Corriere della Sera* (Milan, 18 December 1924), 3. Linati's was a generally favourable article; he considered the poems to be DHL's best writings.

[4] The prize-winning novel (1923) by David ('Bunny') Garnett (1892–1981), novelist, editor and biographer; see *Letters*, i. 315 and iv. 575 and n. 2. Linati's translation *La Volpe* was published in 1929 by Casa Editrice Treves.

published *A Passage to India*. I think he is about the best of my contemporaries in England.

With best wishes

Yours very sincerely D. H. Lawrence

3187. To Martin Secker, 8 August 1924

Text: MS UInd; Postmark, Taos AUG 11 [. . .]; Secker 59.

Del Monte Ranch. *Questa*, New Mexico.
8 Aug 1924

Dear Secker

I am sending you Carlo Linati's letter, which you forwarded. Will you send him the books he wants: at least, *Lost Girl. Aaron's Rod. Women in Love. Fantasia. Studies in Classic Amer. Lit.* – and, if you like, *Sea and Sardinia*. But please yourself. And write him and tell him what you think he ought to know. – I am asking Seltzer to send *Sons and Lovers*, and *Rainbow*, if he has it ready.[1]

I got the copy of *The Boy*: very nice. Hope it is liked. Be sure and tell me about Miss Skinner and her new novel.[2] – Thank you so much for the papers etc you send.[3] Jack Squire is a suburban rat: but then, so are they all.[4] – I don't think Ted Gillett ever got *Punch*.[5] Do please ask them to send it for six months, and you pay the subscription, and charge it to me.

I've nearly got to the end of my second 'novelette' – a corker.[6] It's much better if I'm not *popular*: you'll get much more from me later.

We're going to Hopi Land – further west – about 4 days away – motoring – to see the Snake Dance.

Hope all is well. F[rieda] sends tanti saluti, and to Mrs Secker and the heir.

Yrs D. H. Lawrence[7]

[1] Seltzer published these 10 November 1923 and 1 November 1924 respectively.

[2] *Black Swans*.

[3] See p. 79 n. 2.

[4] (Sir) John Collings Squire (1884–1958), editor of the *London Mercury*; see *Letters*, ii. 204 n. 4. DHL may have been reacting to Squire's article (*London Mercury*, January 1924, 317–18) in which he regretted the philosophising in *Birds, Beasts and Flowers*, while praising the descriptions, and added: 'It may be prose; but it has a curious intensity.'

[5] See Letter 3144; Secker had written to the editor for a six-months' subscription on 26 June (Secker Letter-Book, UIll).

[6] 'St. Mawr'.

[7] Secker replied on 26 August (Secker Letter-Book, UIll):

Dear Lawrence

Many thanks for yours of the 8th. I am sending the books to C.Linati, including "Aaron's Rock". I cannot understand why Gillett has not received Punch, as I hold their receipt for a six months postal subscription as from June 26. I will make enquiries.

The first edition of 2000 "Boy" was quickly exhausted, and I reprinted 1000 before publication. Now I am on the point of printing another 1000. I think it will do well. But my best news is that you have finished another novelette, for I am looking forward most of all to another collection like "The Ladybird".

I will let you know how the Boy goes on.

Yours

3188. To Thomas Seltzer, 8 August 1924

Text: MS UT; Postmark, Taos AUG 13 1924; Lacy, *Seltzer* 142.

Del Monte Ranch. Questa. New Mexico
8 Aug. 1924

Dear Thomas

Carlo Linati – you remember he had an article on Verga in the *Dial*[1] – writes from Milan that he wants to do an article on me for the chief Italian newspaper – the *Corriere della Sera*. Of course he wants books given him. I asked Secker to send them – it is good publicity, I suppose. Only would you send *Sons and Lovers*, and, if it is ready, *The Rainbow*. You can write Linati and tell him anything you think he ought to know – that is, if you wish.

Sig. Carlo Linati. 33 Via Farini, *Milan*. Italy.

I had the covers of the *Boy* – very nice.[2] Tell me the day of publication: and send me a copy for myself. I already had a Secker copy. When are the *Little Novels of Sicily* coming?[3] I see it in your list. Send me a copy.

You knew that a Professor McDonald, at the Drexel Institute. Philadelphia, was doing a *Bibliography* of my books?

No Thomas, I don't think you are cut out as a Big Publisher. It's a bad race. Patience, tenacity, the long fight, the long hope, the inevitable victory – that's it.

We are going with Mabel to the Hopi Land – about 10 days – to see the Snake Dance. – And in early October to Mexico. The summer is passing. But it is very lovely here now.

I like the *Boy's* jacket.

Remember us to Adele. So glad you like the cottage and the country where you are.

Yrs DHL

3189. To Maud Drummond, 8 August 1924

Text: MS UT; Unpublished.

Del Monte Ranch, *Questa*, New Mexico
8 Aug 1924

Dear Miss Drummond[4]

My sister-in-law, Frau Dr Jaffe-Richthofen, writes to me from Munich that she cannot get any reply from you to her questions about the German translation of *The Boy in the Bush*. – She is now taking up the translation of my books into German seriously – and if the Insel Verlag release *The Boy* from

[1] 'Giovanni Verga and the Sicilian Novel', *Dial*, lxxi (August 1921), 150–2. Linati had compared Verga's realism to DHL's (p. 151).

[2] See p. 32 n. 5.

[3] See p. 20 n. 3.

[4] Annie Maud Drummond, secretary in Curtis Brown's office.

their hold, I think she can arrange very well with another publisher. Anyhow, will you please answer her.

I see Seltzer has announced the Verga stories, *Little Novels of Sicily* in his autumn list. Will you tell me please what Basíl Blackwell is doing with this book? He ought not to be behind Seltzer. Has he fixed a date?

The autumn is coming here – very lovely and clear after all the thunder. We are going away to the Hopi land, further west, to see the snake dance: am a little afraid of the heat down there. I expect we shall be away a couple of weeks. – Then in early October we must go down to Mexico – I must finish my 'Quetzalcoatl' novel.[1] – Soon I shall send you a novelette like *The Captain's Doll*.

Hope it is as sunny and nice in England now as here.

Yours Sincerely D. H. Lawrence

3190. To Rolf Gardiner, 9 August 1924

Text: MS Lazarus; Huxley 606–7.

Del Monte Ranch. *Questa*, New Mexico. U.S.A.
9 Aug 1924

Dear Rolf Gardiner

I thought *Harbottle* poor stuff: snivelling self-pity, exasperatedly smashing a few cheap parlor-ornaments, but leaving the house standing stuffy, suburban, sterile, smug, a nice little upholstered nest of essential cowardice. – White Fox, forsooth![2] White rat!

Bah! If ever you edit another paper, take up a hatchet, not a dummy teat of commiseration.[3] What we need is to smash a few big holes in European suburbanity, let in a little real fresh air. – Oh, words are action good enough, if they're the right words. But all this blasted snivel of hopelessness and self-pity and 'stars' and 'wind among the trees' and 'camp-fires'[4] – and

[1] *The Plumed Serpent*.

[2] See p. 67 n. 1. John Harbottle returned from the First World War to find his wife Rachel had left him; his two sons dead. In a state of depression and disorder he lived at his home 'Roselea' for some time, and then went on various journeys where he met an artist, a biologist, a spiritualist, a mystic, etc. on his 'mental pilgrimage' (p. 198). He decided that he should work for the 'New World under the New Duty based upon World Service and World Patriotism' (p. 344), but fell ill from appendicitis and died. For 'White Fox', see p. 68 n. 1.

[3] Gardiner took over a Cambridge undergraduate paper called *Youth* in 1923 and re-issued it in a new form as an 'international quarterly of young enterprise'; see Nehls, iii. 73–5. The first article in the October 1923 issue, 'Youth and Europe', is by Gardiner with an epigraph from DHL ('There is only one evil, to deny life'); the issue also contains a review of *Fantasia* by Camilla Coventry (pp. 32–5).

[4] Probably allusions to 'Anthropomorphic' by Gardiner, adapted from the German of Franz Werfel (*Youth*, ii, October 1923, pp. 26–7) and 'Nature Ritual and Ceremony' by 'John Hargrave (White Fox)' (pp. 5–10) in which he expounded on the merits of nature worship and the 'Wander-Camp Test'.

witanagemotery – shit! – Its courage we want, fresh air, and not suffused sentiments. Even the stars are stale, that way. If one is going to act, in words, one should go armed to the teeth, and fire carefully at the suburbanians – like Wells, White Fox, Barrie, Jack Squire – even Murry – all the lot.[1] Piff! – and down they go!

If it's going to be Youth, then let it be Youth on the war path, not wandervogeling[2] and piping imitation nature tunes to the taste of a cake of milk chocolate, and pitying itself and 'all other unfortunates'. To the rubbish heap with all unfortunates – A great *Merde!* to all latter-day Joan-of-Arcism.

God, God, God, if there *be* any youth in Europe, let them rally and kick the bottom of all this elderly bunk. Not snivel or feel hopeless. What's the good being hopeless, so long as one has a hob-nailed boot to kick with? *Down with the Poor in Spirit*![3] A war! But the subtlest, most intimate warfare. Smashing the face of what one *knows* is rotten.

Murry said to me last year: 'Come, only come, and do what you like with the *Adelphi*.' I came in December. He went green at my first article, and – wouldn't print it.[4] *No Lorenzo, you'll only make enemies.* – As if that weren't what I want. I hate this slime of all the world's my friend, my half friend, anyway I'm not going to make an enemy of him.

Well, here's to you and your bygone *Youth*.

D. H. Lawrence

3191. To Mabel Dodge Luhan, [9 August 1924]

Text: MS Brill; Luhan 254–5.

Kiowa – Lobo.
Sat.

Dear Mabel

Brett says she would rather stay up here in her little house while we are away (we had the soap and letter, many thanks) – so let someone suitable come up – if it's Indians, Geronimo and wife.[5] – Throat still sore, but not so bad. Hope Señor de Angulo y Mayo will *not* turn up.[6] – We'll be ready Wed. afternoon.

DHL

[1] DHL had known Sir James Barrie (1860–1937), dramatist and novelist, slightly; see *Letters*, ii. 120 and iii. 77. The *Adelphi* magazine is reviewed in the October 1923 issue of *Youth* (pp. 60–1), but Gardiner's lead article 'On Harbottle, Geometry and Tradition' in the Summer 1924 issue (ii, pp. 145–8) mentioned Wells and Joan of Arc (and DHL), so DHL may have been sent this issue also. (*Love Poems and Others* and *Birds, Beasts and Flowers* were reviewed by Gardiner under the title 'Precepts and Concepts' in the Spring 1924 issue, ii, pp. 131–2).

[2] Cf. 'Wandervögel and the New Education' by A. S. Neill (*Youth*, October 1923, pp. 28–31).

[3] Cf. Matthew v. 3.

[4] 'On Coming Home'; see *Letters*, iv. 549 n. 4 and *Reflections on the Death of a Porcupine and Other Essays*, ed. Michael Herbert (Cambridge, 1988), pp. xxxiii–xxxiv.

[5] Described by Brett as Geronimo's 'one-eyed wife' (p. 106).

[6] 'Mayo' was de Angulo's mother's maiden name.

Manuel and Albidia are at the Pueblo[1] – it would be very good if they would stay up in the little house while we are away – will you ask them? They are not due at Del Monte till Thursday, but they might be persuaded to come Wed afternoon to us, so Brett won't be alone: otherwise she can sleep at Del Monte a night.

There is everything in the little house that Manuel and Albidia would want – bedding and everything.

The flowers are lovely –

We'll be ready Wed. afternoon.[2]

3192. To Mollie Skinner, 10 August 1924

Text: MS WAPL; Postmark, Taos AUG 13 1924; Moore 801.

Del Monte Ranch. *Questa*, New Mexico.
10 Aug 1924

Dear Miss Skinner

I had a copy of *The Boy* from Secker: looks very nice. Seltzer will distribute for you six complimentary copies in America – or anywhere – if you send him addresses. We did the American jacket between us[3] – rather nice. –

I want to hear more of your London experiences, and how 'Letty' is looking. –

Seltzer wrote that he sent you some time ago a cheque for $100.00 to Australia. Hope you get it safely. – And I hope you'll shortly get £10. from Curtis Brown for German translation of *The Boy*. It's already being done.

Let me know how you have fared, and if you had a good time.

Yrs D. H. Lawrence[4]

3193. To Mabel Dodge Luhan, [10 August 1924]

Text: MS Brill; Unpublished

[Kiowa]
Sunday

Dear Mabel

On Wednesday, would you bring

10 lbs sugar[5]

[1] Manuel who did carpentering work for Mabel Luhan, and Albidia Marcus, her maid who had worked for John Young-Hunter (*Reviewing the Years*, New York, 1963, p. 87). Maurice Sterne did a head of her (Mabel Dodge Luhan, *Edge of Taos Desert*, New York, 1937, p. 229). In the event two Indian women, Rafalita and Anna, stayed with Brett (p. 147), and see p. 101 n. 1.

[2] All postscripts are on the envelope.

[3] DHL and Brett; see p. 32 n. 5.

[4] DHL addressed the letter c/o Australia House in London; it was re-addressed there and forwarded to Stourport. Cf. Letter 3232.

[5] For making raspberry jam; see p. 101 n. 1.

2[1] bottles Listerine

A bit of meat for Brett.

The Listerine is a gargle stuff, and I owe some to Rachel.

Always bothering you! – Throat a bit better – I gargle and rub it and ointment it like the devil.

DHL

3194. To Hon. Dorothy Brett, [13 August 1924]

Text: MS UCin; Postmark, Taos AUG 14 1924; Irvine, Brett 36.

[Taos, New Mexico]
[13 August 1924]

Dear Brett –

Mabel sent up meat with Ted Gillette, but not sugar, I think. You can ask them to bring that.

In case Geronimo comes to *work* a day or two, I want him first to mend the *corral* – support the roof where its falling – then throw back the earth near the oven – where I began – and the earth behind the kitchen window – then dig the earth back at the well, so we can put the barrel directly under the mouth of the pipe, and dispense with that tin gutter, which won't be safe for the horses – they push it aside – when we are[2] away. – But Geronimo may not come to work – Tell him I'd like him to help me a week when he's free.

Just off.

DHL

3195. To Else Jaffe, [14 August 1924]

Text: MS Jeffrey; PC v. San Ildefonso, N.M.; Postmark, Santa Fe AUG 14 1924; Frieda Lawrence 185.

Santa Fe
[14 August 1924]

– We are motoring with Mabel Luhan to the Hopi Country – hotter down here. Curtis Brown wrote they were arranging with you for *Boy in the Bush* – hope everything is satisfactory. And what a pity Baltimore is so far.[3]

DHL

3196. To Martin Secker, [14 August 1924]

Text: MS UInd; PC v. Pueblo of Santa Clara, N. Mex.; Postmark, Santa Fe AUG 14 1924; Unpublished.

Sante Fe
[14 August 1924]

– We are going motoring about 10 days to the Hopi Country – hot down here –

[1] 2] 3 tins mustard [2] are] are n't [3] Where Friedel Jaffe was to stay.

but good to get down again for a spell from the high altitude. – Send a copy of Magnus[1] to Mrs Mabel Luhan. Taos. will you – and one to me.

DHL

3197. To Mark Gertler, [14 August 1924]

Text: MS SIU; PC v. Baking Bread, Santa Fe, New Mexico; Postmark, Santa Fe AUG 14 1924; cited in Moore, *Poste Restante* 79.

Santa Fe

[14 August 1924]

– We are motoring about ten days to the Hopi Country, and Brett, with two Indians, is minding the ranch. – By the way, I saw a letter of yours to her which seemed to suggest I had repeated to her your conversation with me – I had not – nor hinted it even. – Hope your troubles are righting themselves.

DHL

3198. To Catherine Carswell, [14 August 1924]

Text: MS YU; PC v. San Ildefonso, N.M.; Postmark, Santa Fe AUG 14 1924; Unpublished.

Santa Fe.

[14 August 1924]

Glad you are settled in the country[2] – we are motoring to the Hopi land with Mabel Sterne. I ordered the new-coming books for you from Secker – hope you get them – Alas Ivy![3]

DHL

3199. To Hon. Dorothy Brett, [14 August 1924]

Text: MS UCin; Postmark, Santa Fe AUG 14 1924; Irvine, Brett 36–7.

[Hotel De Vargas, Santa Fe, New Mexico][4]

Thursday

Dear Brett

We got all the way here last night – tired. I went about your telephone bit: he says the ear-piece is all right, only where you've stripped the wire it makes a short circuit, and will need new wires, which he will get from Denver. – The best thing is if you can send your machine down at once, the man says he himself was deaf and has used an ear phone – that probably there is a loose

[1] *Memoirs of the Foreign Legion.*

[2] See p. 19 n. 1.

[3] Ivy Teresa Litvinov, née Low (1889–1977), novelist and friend of Catherine Carswell. m. 1916, Maxim Litvinov (1876–1951). She met DHL in 1914 and was now living in Russia. See also Letter 3565 and n. 5.

[4] Written on headed paper.

connection merely, in the machine. So if Ted Gillett could bring the machine down to Taos, the stage would deliver it to this address, and we, on our return journey, would pick it up and bring it home. This man seems sensible. I think he is Mr. Sloan himself.

The Sloan Electric Co. 307 San Francisco St. *Santa Fe.*

The lower altitude feels good, but even this little town seems smelly. Throat a bit better. Hope all goes well with you at the ranch.

DHL

I left the ear-piece with the man, to have new wires.

Remember the post address to this side (south) is *Valdez.* Not Questa.

3200. To Ada Clarke, [14 August 1914]

Text: MS Clarke; PC v. Corn Husking, San Juan Pueblo. N. Mex.; Postmark, Santa Fe AUG 14 1924; Unpublished.

[Santa Fe]
17 Aug.

We are motoring with Mabel Sterne for about ten days – still haven't heard from you – and about Oct 1st we shall be leaving the ranch, for Old Mexico.

Love to you all.

DHL

3201. To Hon. Dorothy Brett, [15 August 1924]

Text: MS UCin; PC v. Pueblo Indian Corn Dance Ceremony; Postmark, New La[guna] [. . .]; Irvine, Brett 37.

Laguna –
Friday

We got here last night – go on today to Gallup – not too hot – only the car wearies one.

DHL

3202. To William Hawk, [15 August 1924]

Text: MS UT; PC v. Hopi Snake Priest Entering Snake Kiva, Oraibi, Arizona; Postmark, New Laguna AUG 15 1924; Unpublished.

Laguna
Friday morning.

Getting on very well so far – it has rained a great deal down here, so not hot or dusty – and luckily fine again now – going on today to Gallup.

DHL

3203. To Adele Seltzer, [15 August 1924]

Text: MS UT; PC v. Hopi Snake Dance, Arizona; Postmark, New Lag[una] AUG 15 1924: Lacy, *Seltzer* 143.

Laguna.
Friday

F[rieda] and I are going with Mabel and Tony to the Hopi country in Arizona to see the snake dance – hot down here, but I like it – only the motor car always wearies one.

DHL

3204. To Clarence Thompson, [15 August 1924]

Text: MS UT; PC v. Hopi Snake Priest Entering Snake Kiva, Oraibi, Arizona; Postmark, New L[aguna] AUG 15 1924; Unpublished.

Laguna.
Friday morning

Got here last night – smooth sailing – setting off now for Gallup – not hot, has rained a good deal down here. Suppose you are not en route.

DHL

3205. To John Middleton Murry, [16 August 1924]

Text: MS NYPL; PC v. Kiva of Ancient Cliff Dwellers, in Ceremonial Cave, Rito de los Frijoles Canyon, New Mexico; Postmark, [. . .]; Unpublished.

Laguna.
16 Aug

We are motoring with Mabel to the Hopi Country in Arizona to see the snake dance – hot – but interesting desert and mesas – Brett stays at home to mind the ranch, with two Indians. Hope all goes well with you.

DHL

3206. To Thomas Seltzer, [16 August 1924]

Text: MS UT PC v. Chili (Red Pepper) Drying in Front of Adobe Home, New Mexico; Postmark, Saint Michaels AUG 16 1924; Lacy, *Seltzer* 143.

St. Michaels.
16 Aug

Stayed a night here with the Days,[1] on the Navajo Reservation – awfully nice.

[1] According to Mabel Luhan Sam Day had arrived fifty years before and started a trading post; 'his wiry little old wife' – a Yankee – 'knew how to make a home in the wilderness'; see Mabel's detailed description of the family pp. 259–62. Mrs Day hinted that she received copies of books from other writers who had come through and DHL thought *The Lost Girl* would be 'sufficiently blameless' (p. 261).

– Will you send me a copy of *The Lost Girl* to the ranch: I suppose we shall be back there in nine or ten days: we left Brett at home.

DHL

3207. To Emily King, [18 August 1924]

Text: MS Needham; PC v. Pueblo Indians, Rehearsing for the Deer Dance; Postmark, New [Laguna] [. . .]1924; Unpublished.

Laguna.
18 Aug

We are motoring with Mabel Luhan to the Hopi Country in Arizona, to the snake dance – hot – and a bit tiring. I ordered you a couple of copies of *The Theatre Arts* – with an article[1] and drawing of mine – Give one copy to Ada. Why haven't I heard from her.

DHL

3208. To Willard Johnson, [20 August 1924]

Text: MS YU; PC v. Hopi Snake Priest Entering Snake Kiva, Oraibi, Arizona; Postmark, Albu[querque] AUG 22 1924; Unpublished.

Chin Lee, Arizona
— Wed

Saw dance on Monday – interesting rather than beautiful – coming crookedly back – may be in Santa Fe Saturday or Sunday – Cañon de Chelly today – *pas grande chose* – on to Gallup tomorrow. See you and Bynner in Santa Fe.

DHL

3209. To Emily King, [20 August 1924]

Text: MS Needham; PC v. Hopi Snake Priest Entering Snake Kiva, Oraibi, Arizona; Postmark, Albuq[uerque] AUG 22 1924; Unpublished.

Chin Lee. Arizona
20 Aug

We saw the snake dances on Monday – priests dancing with live rattle snakes in their mouths – weird rather than beautiful. Now we are in the Navajo country where your rug came from – big desert country, hot, with sand blowing in the wind – Hope we'll get home in a few days – the motor car wearies me, though it's a big heavy one. But no roads – just wild trails.

DHL

[1] 'The Dance of the Sprouting Corn'.

3210. To Hon. Dorothy Brett, [20 August 1924]

Text: MS UCin; PC v. Hopi Snake Priest Entering Snake Kiva, Oraibi, Arizona; Postmark, Albu[querque] AUG 22 1924; Irvine, Brett 37.

Chin Lee, Arizona.
Wed

We saw the snake dance at Hotevilla on Monday – very interesting but not beautiful – expect to get to Gallup tomorrow – doubt if we shall be in Taos before Sunday or Monday. I had a bad time with throat and ear – it got worse – but thank goodness is better again. – Weather has favoured us, but I weary of the motor car.

DHL[1]

[1] Brett wrote to DHL on 15–17 August (MS YU) (he wrote 'Just Back from the Snake Dance' on the back of the first two pages of it):

Kiowa
Friday =

Dear Lawrence =
Dear Frieda =

I am sitting in your porch eating breakfast. What cheek you will say, how dare she – well . . she dares = Chippy is sitting on a log opposite to me cleaning his or her whiskers, how shall we ever know?

I have not been afraid in the usual way – of animals or men, but in other ways I have been troubled. I suppose it is always so when one is alone facing oneself = & lately I have been obsessed with the idea that perhaps I am "sometimes more than deaf". that perhaps the slow poison that has destroyed my ears is creeping slowly up into my brain = unnoticeably to me = Yet inside I know that I am not such a dumb dud = I put up, against my deafness, a fierce fight = & I try & keep it off others, the knowing what an effort it is for other people, hampers me & holds me silent = & also a queer shyness I have = & revolt. These last two days have been cold and stormy – last night the sky was dark & sinister – dark with black rain falling & between the two storms a band of greenish orange light & a howling fierce wind as if all the devils and witches were riding the sky – one storm went over Taos, the other round our hill at the back – & the two storms & the storm in myself seemed to break together with a final tearing crash – And when I went out across to my little house, the moon was sailing across a clear starry sky & I felt calm too = So after two days one rose again with a brilliant hot sun & smooth sky =

Well – I went to the Blacksmith = the young dude accompanying me – on the old white horse – He salutes nobly every one he meets, he used his spurs on that tame old horse till it pranced along on five legs instead of four – in agony of mind & body = I was furious – He wants to buy Dan – but we mus'nt let him – He is'nt fit to have a horse = Rachel is wild at having to lend him horses = The Blacksmith I found surrounded by myriads of children = The old fierce father, women – children – The dude went prancing off for a further ride while I sat in the shed = The blacksmith suddenly asked me if you had lost a book – He's found a coverless sodden book & it was called Blue or Yellow River! I managed to start home without the dude, he caught me up though, with a flourish – but later on over the fence appeared the pale face of Gellett – looking for the cows = he took the dude's horse & left him to foot it home, while I went on to escape a storm & found Bobby dyeing her khaki breeches a beautiful burnt sienna!

Yesterday I was to go up to Lobo with Rachel but she could'nt come – would I ride with Jim Johnson & Perkins – I agreed to a short morning ride & took them a round = Somehow its no use – I *am* different. The December before last my third eye opened very suddenly – & the manner of its opening was strange – & from that moment I have felt an Ishmael among the

3211. To Mabel Dodge Luhan, [23 August 1924]

Text: MS Brill; Luhan 268.

[Taos, New Mexico]
Sat. evening

Dear Mabel

Too late to telegraph. We met Eve leaving[1] – met her in the stage at Velarde. Clarence is packed, and thinks to go Tuesday. Saw the Jaimes: Jaime is Jaime – the wife seems nice.[2] For the rest, all quiet. Emilie complains of pains in her shoulders[3] – I gave her the *baume*. I think we shall go up tomorrow morning – Sunday – if I can get my Gersons goods.

For the rest, everything quiet here.

I'm glad I made the trip – the only really bad thing was that ear of mine, and I felt real sick that part of the time. I liked the rest of it.

Perkins & dudes = So, inwardly raging I trailed them around & showed them my wonderful tree & felt I had betrayed it, it really seemed to shrink from them = Oh, that third eye – it made Dunning think I belonged to some mysterious, rare people – he wouldn't tell me what people or anything about them – & insisted on my getting the date of my birth & the hour – etc – to find my stars = I did – & my stars let me down badly! to Dunnings discomfort =

The Adelphi has arrived – your Corn Dance – thank heaven. & apparently you and Murry have been heavily attacked by the Spectator "Oh! Mr Porter" = Murry replies – honestly & sincerely – but if it had been me – I would have taken your name in vain & beaten their spineless backs with you = Yes – there is Christ in Heaven & D. H. Lawrence on Earth – so look out you miserable blighters & counted ten cheerfully over their dirty corpses = when you come back you must tell me about Rudolph Steiner =

Rafalita & Anna & I, have been this morning picking raspberries – they are now prone in their house from exhaustion only half of them picked – we go up again tomorrow & I must beg – borrow or steal sugar = trees have been blown down up there last evening = I am also having a lot of wood cut up = for the stove & fireplace = I hope they are happy =

I am wondering how you have got on = Has it been "lots of fun". or are you both terribly hot & tired = I am anxious for you after your being ill = It may have helped you on the other hand it may not. & I think of you constantly plodding across the Desert in a cloud of sand = & you've left your glasses = oh dear = And the apples on the hat have melted = & dripped on to your hair Frieda =

Sunday. Yesterday I went for a 20 mile ride = oh! such a ride = I was asked to accompany William & those congealed women up to the [MS incomplete]

I have used used this soft paper like a hanky & only written on one side, so that you can blow your nose in it without getting inky & bury it in the sand. When you bring back my ear machine will you carry it as if it were Rachel's baby – even more tenderly = or else it will get broken again – & don't let it come up in the Stage.

[1] Eve Young-Hunter, secretary to Mabel Luhan (see p. 89 n. 5).

[2] Nancy de Angulo; they brought their son Alvar (1924–33).

[3] In *Altitude*, written in the summer of 1924, Emilia is Mabel Luhan's cook (*The Complete Plays of D. H. Lawrence*, 1965). Brett remembered her as the 'Mexican cook, Amelia' (p. 44).

I'll write a sketch for the *Theatre Arts*, and draw one too if I can: not for the *Horse* to laugh at.[1]

DHL

We all liked the baby – Johns – so much.[2]

3212. To Edward McDonald, 24 August 1924

Text: MS UT; Postmark, Valdez AUG 26 1924; *Centaur* 37–8.

[Kiowa]

24 Aug 1924.

[3][1. Has 'The Crown', which appeared in *The Signature* ever been reprinted?]
No.[4]

[2. 'Adolph' (*Dial*, Sept. 1920, and *The New Keepsake*) has not, so far as I remember, been used elsewhere. Is this right? I have always liked 'Adolph' a lot.]
No – 'Adolf' has not been used elsewhere.[5]

[3. 'Reality of Peace'. Four parts (*Eng*[*lish*] *Rev*[*iew*] May–Aug, 1917). I do not recall this material in any other place. Should I have?]
No! but in the *Athenaeum* – London – when Murry was editing it – I

[1] Mabel Luhan's response to 'Just Back from the Snake Dance', written 22 August, had been:

When we reached Santa Fe, I flung myself on the bed in the De Vargas Hotel and lay in a dark mood of disgust until the hour came for sleep and I roused myself to go into the Lawrences' room to say good night. Lorenzo handed me a few sheets covered with his small, clear writing, and I read it standing beside the bureau; and then, without a word, laid it down and, saying good night, left them.

He had written a dreary terre à terre account of the long road to the Hopi village and of the dance, a mere realistic recital that might have been done by a tired, disgruntled business man. It had no vision, no insight, no appreciation of any kind. I grew inwardly colder and more aloof towards Lorenzo. I had not taken him to the Snake Dance to have him describe it in this fashion. Disappointed and incensed, I decided to let them go on without me and I remained behind for a few days in Santa Fe at Alice's house.

Before I left them – as I stood frozenly, saying good-bye at the roadside – Lawrence pushed through the wall that had grown up between us and said:

'I know you didn't like that article of mine. I'll try and do another one.' (Luhan 267–8)

'Just Back from the Snake Dance – Tired Out' was published in *Laughing Horse* (September 1924), 26–9. DHL wrote 'The Hopi Snake Dance' on 26 August (see p. 110 n. 3); it was published in *Theatre Arts Monthly*, viii (December 1924), 836–60 and *Adelphi* (January–February 1925) (Roberts C127) and collected in *Mornings in Mexico*.

[2] John Ganson Evans (1902–78), writer and sociologist, Mabel Luhan's son. m. (1) 1922, Alice ('Corbinetta') Oliver Henderson (1907–88); divorced 1932/3; (2) 1933, Claire Spencer, novelist. The baby was Natalie Sarah (8 January 1924–1971).

[3] The questions, in square brackets, are in McDonald's handwriting.

[4] It appeared serially in the three numbers of *Signature* (4 October, 18 October and 1 November 1915).

[5] 'Adolf' appeared in *The New Keepsake for the Year 1921* (1920).

think in 1918 – appeared an article that belonged to this series.[1] J.M. Murry could tell you, if it matters at all –

The Adelphi – 18 York Buildings, Adelphi, W.C.2.

[4. 'Love' (*Engl. Rev.* Jan. 1918). Did you use this in any other place?]
No! (at least I can't remember having done so. I'd utterly forgotten these little essays.)

[5. Same question for 'Life' (*Engl. Rev.* Feb. 1918).]
No.

[6. 'Two Principles' (*Engl. Rev.* June, 1919), which was No. 8 of the 'Classic Studies' papers to appear in *Engl. Rev.*, is not, unless my memory tricks me, used *per se* in book. Is this right?]
Yes. The *Studies in Classic Amer. Literature* are all very much altered, in book form, from the *English Review* form.[2]

[7. 'Rex' (*Dial*, Feb, 1921) only printing?]
Yes. But a man wants to put it in a Dog Anthology. – Curtis Brown, my agent – 116 W. 39th St – has track of it.[3]

[8. Of the three things in *The Ladybird*, only 'The Fox', according to my record, appeared serially, that in the *Dial*.[4] Right?]
Right.

But there was a first (not very good) story, called 'The Thimble', appeared in some out of the way American magazine – can't remember its name – would rather like 'The Thimble' to disappear into oblivion – but confess to it.[5] I think I could find out the magazine, if it matters at all. The poetess Hilda Aldington, who writes under her initials H.D. (Hilda Doolittle)[6] – she came from Philadelphia – Prof. Doolittle[7] – I believe – she could tell you.

[9. Didn't you print more of *Sea and Sardinia* serially than the two *Dial* things: 'As Far As Palermo',[8] and 'Cagliari'? It's rotten that this book

[1] 'Whistling of Birds'; see p. 87 n. 3.

[2] The *English Review* versions were collected in *The Symbolic Meaning*, ed. Armin Arnold (Arundel, 1962).

[3] It was published in *Stories from The Dial* (New York) in August 1924. The 'Dog Anthology' has not been traced.

[4] June–August 1922. 'The Captain's Doll' never appeared serially.

[5] *Seven Arts*, i (March 1917), 435–48. 'The Thimble' was rewritten as 'The Ladybird'.

[6] Hilda Doolittle (1886–1961) had published Imagist poems in anthologies and journals since 1913; DHL had known her since 1914. m. Richard Aldington (1892–1962), poet, novelist and biographer, in 1913 and separated 1919. See *Letters*, ii. 203 and iii. 31; and p. 426 n. 2.

[7] Charles Leander Doolittle (1843–1919), Professor of Astronomy and Mathematics at LeHigh University, 1875–95; Professor of Astronomy at University of Pennsylvania in Philadelphia, 1895–1912. m. (1) 1866, Martha Cloyes Farrand (d. 1875); (2) 1882, Helen Eugenia Wolle.

[8] McDonald wrote 'Palmero'.

apparently didn't sell over here. Stupid asses! Have the English had more sense about it? Secker made a beautiful book of it.]
Only the two *Dial* bits. – I think Secker sold more than Seltzer did.

Thank you for writing about the MSS. I'll see to it. I'm very careless. My wife just gave the MS of *Sons and Lovers* away. I don't believe Seltzer will have *Movements* ready this autumn. Ask him to keep it quiet as possible. If you cant get one of the first printing in America, write to Humphrey Milford in London and tell him I want him to send you a copy.[1]

DHL

3213. To Thomas Seltzer, 26 August 1924
Text: MS UT; Postmark, Valdez AUG 26 1924; Lacy, *Seltzer* 143–4.

Del Monte Ranch. *Questa*, New Mexico
26 Aug 1924

Dear Thomas

We got back from that trip last night: rather tired. I'm not really fond of 'tripping', and I hate sitting in a motor-car.

When I said Frieda had this ranch from Mabel Lujan as a gift, I ought to have said that Frieda, in return, made Mabel a gift of the MS. of *Sons and Lovers*. The ranch was worth only about a thousand dollars: Mabel had paid twelve hundred for it, and had let it go to ruin for six years. Swinburne Hale and others at Taos cry out on me for a fool: said why didn't I pay the $1000 and keep the MS. – But we like the ranch, anyhow.

Only all this expostulation about the *Sons and Lovers* MS. makes me feel I ought to be more careful of the rest of my MSS. You have them all in safe deposit in my name, haven't you? – I wish you would arrange it that Barmby has access to the safe deposit, so he can put in all the MSS as I send them to him, and keep track of everything. Let us arrange this as soon as possible, so that it's done before I go to Mexico.

And before I go to Mexico, I should like you to put some more money to my account, as I shall need a fairly large letter of credit to take with me.

I am trying hard to find someone to live at the ranch during the winter. I am afraid, if we just shut it up, the Mexicans will break in and make a smash.

I wish you would send a copy of *Psychoanalysis and the Unconscious* and a copy of *Fantasia* to

[1] Humphrey Milford (1877–1952), Publisher to the University of Oxford since 1913. See *Letters*, iii. 326.

Clarence Thompson, The Harvard Club, 27 West 44th St. New York. And will you send to me here, please, a copy of *Birds Beasts*, for Swinburne Hale.

We shan't take very much luggage down to Mexico this time: leave everything here, and make this our centre.

Is *The Boy* out yet? I do hope he will do well, and you'll have a good autumn.

Yrs DHL

3214. To Clarence Thompson, 27 August 1924

Text: MS (Photocopy) UCLA; Postmark, Questa AUG 30 1924; Moore 804–5.

Del Monte Ranch. *Questa*, New Mexico
27 Aug 1924 Wednesday

Dear Clarence

We had a telegram from Frieda's nephew Friedel Jaffe, who has just arrived in New York from Munich to go to an American University. He is a nice boy of 21. Would you care to see him and tell him about Taos (not beneath the surface) and about the ranch. Frieda would like it if you would. He is c/o The Institute of International Education – 522 Fifth Avenue, New York.

I guess you are on your way back west. I am so tired after that Hopi-trip, I don't know what to do with myself. – No sign, thank heaven, from below. – I burned that hideous Indian doll – seriously set fire to her. She was too ugly.

I forgot to pay you for the curtain stuff – remembered only the bed and pillars.[1] Probably this ten dollars is too little.

I asked Seltzer to send you *Psychoanalysis and the Unconscious* and *Fantasia*.

Good luck to you and your new work. I feel it's a new phase altogether. The old idols put in the kitchen stove, like that doll.

Let us know how you get on.

DHL

[1] The four twisted pillars (see Letters 3240 and 3257) were intended for the porch to be built over DHL's door (Letter 3219 and sketch); two were used (Letter 3257). Mabel Luhan says the kitchen porch was supported on 'some carved posts which poor Clarence had intended for *his* house' (pp. 195–6), but the kitchen porch had eight pillars (Letter 3150).

3215. To Clarence Thompson, [28 August 1924]

Text: MS UT; Postmark, [. . .]AUG 28 1924; Unpublished.

Del Monte Ranch. Questa, N. Mex
Thursday

Dear Clarence

Mabel talks – writes in a note[1] – of coming east at this week-end, to see 'an aunt who is dying, and Bobby Jones'[2] – Absit omen![3]

By the way, do you know Mary Foote, whose saddle I've got?[4] If you do, I wish you'd ask her if she'd let me buy her saddle and bridle. I dont suppose she'll ever come for it, and it's too bad for me to go on using it all the time.

Yes, I do feel bad that the summer was spoilt (had your letter). But let's hope it was like having one's appendix out: not possible twice.

Yrs DHL

Remember me warmly to Mrs Sprague.

3216. To Mabel Dodge Luhan, [28 August 1924]

Text: TMS and MS Brill; Unpublished.

[Frieda Lawrence begins][5]

Del Monte Ranch, Valdez, New Mexico
28 August 1924

Mr Edgar Miller[6]

Sir,

Mrs Lujan[7] sent on your letter about Lucy and her Complaint. It seems to me a dirty little thing to do, on Lucy's part. Why didn't she *say* to Mrs Lujan that she wanted more money?

My husband and I were in another house and had nothing to do with the paying on this occasion. But I should be very sorry to think we sponged at all

[1] DHL wrote 'talks' and then added 'writes in a note' above it without deleting the original word. Mabel Luhan did not return to Taos before going to New York.

[2] The aunt was probably one of her mother's three sisters. Robert ('Bobby') Edmond Jones (1887–1954), American stage-designer for theatre, ballets and operas, and later for films; producer, from 1925 principally at Greenwich Village Playhouse, New York; he staged the first performance of several plays by Eugene O'Neill. He wrote *The Dramatic Imagination* (1941). A friend of Mabel Luhan's from the time of her first marriage. m. 1933, Margaret Huston Carrington (d. 1942). See obituary in *New York Times* (27 November 1954), p. 13.

[3] 'May there be no ill omen in that!'

[4] Mary Foote (1872–1968), American painter. Her portrait of Mabel Luhan (c. 1915 at Villa Curonia) is in National Portrait Gallery, Washington. See *New York Historical Society Quarterly*, lxi (July–October 1977), nos. 3–4

[5] Frieda's letter is typed (probably by Brett); DHL signed it.

[6] Unidentified.

[7] 'Lujan' was the original spelling; see *Letters*, iv. 518 n. 4.

on your poor Indians. Please allow me to send my cheque for the five dollars. But also allow me to suggest that you should advise your 'poor Indians' to make their complaints directly, and on the spot, and not to seem falsely pleased when they are discontented.

Yours faithfully Frieda Lawrence
(Mrs D H Lawrence)

[Lawrence begins]

Thursday

Dear Mabel

These are the letters sent today.[1] What canaille! Ever more canaille! – I put $5. in F's letter. Easiest, and best way to snub that fellow.

Rush for post. Let us know about your going east.

DHL

Ask Tony to ask Geronimo if he is coming up Monday for a week's work will you.

[1] The following letter (TMS Brill) was typed on the same machine as Frieda's letter and was signed in DHL's hand:

27 August 1924

Mr Edgar Miller
Dear Sir

In answer to your letter of the 20th. inst, regarding Lucy's 'Complaint', let me make you a statement of services received from Lucy and her husband.

We camped outside Lucy's house on the bit of waste ground. *Our own provisions* were cooked on Lucy's stove: we had paid her fifty cents for an armful of fuel. She gave us, of her own food, a loaf of bread and a dish of mutton. Besides this, she washed dishes for us, and for me she washed two dresses, two chemises and a pair of stockings. The husband carried water for us, that was all.

Lucy had from me five dollars in silver, for herself: she seemed pleased. Twice we gave her dollar for the child, and once twenty-five cents. This makes $7.25. I bought a silver buckle from the husband for three dollars. And they all seemed quite satisfied.

It seems to me the family was sufficiently paid. As far as the 'only complaint' goes, this is certainly the only mean breach of hospitality I have met among the Indians.

If you have anything further to communicate, I shall be glad to take up the matter with Mrs Nina Otero Warren, Supervisor of Pueblos, of Santa Fe.

Yours faithfully Mabel Lujan

Maria Adelina ('Nina') Emelia Otero-Warren (1881–1965), county superintendent of schools 1917–29; at various times she served as liaison officer with the Pueblo Land Board and inspector of Indian Service in the Department of the Interior. (See obituary in Santa Fe *New Mexican*, 4 January 1965.)

3217. To John Middleton Murry, [30 August 1924]

Text: MS NYPL; PC v. Hopi Snake Priest Entering Snake Kiva, Oraibi, Arizona; cited in Murry, *New Adelphi* 456.

Del Monte Ranch. *Questa*, New Mexico.
30 Aug

Dear Jack

I'm sending Curtis Brown my article on the 'Hopi Snake Dance'.[1] No doubt it's too long for you – but read it, anyhow, as it defines somewhat my position.

That trip to the Hopi Country was interesting, but tiring, so far in a motor-car. The Navajo Country is very attractive – all wild, with great red cliffs bluffing up. Good country to ride through, one day. The Navajos themselves real wild nomads: alas, they speak practically no English, and no Spanish. But strange, the intense religious life they keep up in those round huts. This animistic religion is the only live one ours is a corpse of a religion.

I think we go down to Mexico in about five weeks.

DHL

3218. To Nancy Pearn, 30 August 1924

Text: MS UT; Unpublished.

Del Monte Ranch. *Questa*, New Mexico
30 Aug. 1924

Dear Miss Pearse

I wish I knew what *Hutchinsons* wanted to cut from 'The Woman Who Rode Away' – and how much. I don't quite fancy having my stories cut: they aren't like articles. But if you can guarantee the cut is small and not significant, I agree. – Only, why can't they make a bit of a break, and publish the story complete?[2]

[1] See p. 103 n. 1.

[2] Nancy Pearn had written on 12 August 1924 (TMSC UT):

Dear Mr. Lawrence:

I was a little scared when I realised the length of the new story – between twelve and thirteen thousand words – of "THE WOMAN WHO RODE AWAY", and sure enough the first thing that Hutchinson's, who had asked for the first offer, said was: "We like it immensely, but simply cannot use it at its present length", so they want us to ask you if you will be so good as to give them permission to cut some of the beginning, in order to bring the length nearer to their average. The editor thinks that, cut in such a way, the intrinsic part of the story would not suffer, and hopes very much you will see no objection to giving him the required permission. We could, if you wished, arrange for Hutchinson's to send you proofs, although, in the event of this story being placed in America and scheduled for an early date, the delay might be prejudicial to the arrangement of simultaneous issue.

If you are prepared to accept Hutchinson's proposal, we can secure £40 for British serial rights. They w[oul]d publish the story in their new monthly mag. "Woman".

Yours sincerely,

I am sending you the article: 'The Hopi Snake Dance'. If you offer this to Murry for the *Adelphi*, tell him not to cut it, even though it's long.

I enclose a letter from Brussels. Will your foreign dept. see to it? Or is it your job as it is periodical stuff? I wrote the man, 'Yes'.[1]

Did you see Miss Skinner when she came to your office? I'm so afraid you weren't very nice to her. Ask Miss Drummond.

I value my 'Hopi Snake Dance' article rather highly, so if nobody wants it as it is, let them go without it.

Yours sincerely D. H. Lawrence[2]

3219. To Margaret King, 31 August 1924

Text: MS Needham; cited in V. de S. Pinto, 'D. H. Lawrence: Letter-Writer and Craftsman in Verse', *Renaissance and Modern Studies*, i (1957), 8–9.

Del Monte Ranch. Questa. New Mexico
31 August 1924

My dear Peg

We got back from the Hopi Country last Monday – I'll probably write an article on the dance.[3] But how I hate long distance trips in motor-car – so tiring! We went about a thousand miles altogether.

You ask me what we grow on the ranch: Nothing. There is a big clearing, on which the old owners used to grow alfalfa, and we call it the alfalfa field (it's a sort of clover, alfalfa, blue, grows tall and thick). Forty years ago a man came out looking for gold, and squatted here. There was some gold in the mountains. Then he got poor, and a man called McClure had the place. He had 500

[1] Both the enclosure and DHL's reply are missing.

[2] Sonia K. Chapter, the assistant manager of the Periodical Department, replied on 22 September 1924 (TMSC UT):

Dear Mr. Lawrence,

In Miss Pearn's absence on holiday I am replying to your letter of 30th August.

Hutchinson's finally decided that they wanted to cut "THE WOMAN WHO RODE AWAY" a good deal more than you would like – in fact they said "drastically" so they returned the MS and we are going ahead elsewhere.

In the meantime we have heard from our New York Office that they have sold the story to the Dial but they are not likely to publish for some months.

We have sent "THE HOPI SNAKE DANCE" on to the Adelphi, who have just taken "INDIANS AND ENTERTAINMENT", with your instructions with regard to cutting. Our Foreign Department are dealing with the letter you enclosed.

Yours very truly

[3] The notebook in which 'The Hopi Snake Dance' is the first item is dated '26 August 1924' which suggests DHL began writing it that day; the second item, 'Introduction to Bibliography' is dated 1 September. Also DHL had written to Nancy Pearn the day before (30 August) that 'I am sending' the Hopi piece (see preceding letter).

white goats here, raised alfalfa, and let his goats feed wild in the mountains. But the water supply is too bad, and we are too far from anywhere. So he gave up. Mabel Luhan bought the place for $1200 six years ago, and let it go to rack and ruin.[1] Now she traded it to Frieda for the MS. of *Sons and Lovers*. Every one is very mad with me for giving that MS. The ranch was worth only about $1000, and the MS of *Sons and Lovers* worth three or four thousand – so everybody says. But I don't care.

I'll draw you a little plan of the place:

[sketch of ranch]

We have only one little spring of water – pure water – that will fill a pail in about 3 minutes: it runs the same summer and winter. If we want to grow anything, we must water, irrigate. Maclure used to bring the water in a made ditch, over deep places by wooden[2] runnel bridges, for nearly 3 miles: from the Gallina Canyon. Then, from the house canyon, he brought it down two miles. It's very difficult, though, in a dry country with dry gravelly soil. You can't bring much flow, so far: and in summer very often none. So we leave the ranch quite wild – only theres abundant feed for the five horses. And if we wanted to take the trouble, we could bring the water here as Maclure did, and have a little farm. – There's quite a lot of land, really – it say 160 acres, but it takes a terrible long time to go round the fence, through the wild forest. – We got lots of wild strawberries – and we still get gallons of wild raspberries, up our own little canyon, where no soul ever goes. If we ride two miles, we can get no farther. Beyond, all savage, unbroken mountains.

We get our things from Taos – 17 miles – either by wagon or when someone is coming in a car. Our road is no road – a breaking through the forest – but people come to see us. Every evening, just after tea, we saddle up and ride down to Del Monte Ranch, for the milk, butter, eggs, and letters. The old trail passes this gate, and the mailman, on horseback, leaves all the mail in a box nailed on a tree. Usually we get back just at dark. Yesterday we rode down to San Cristobal, where there is a cross-roads, a blacksmith, and a tiny village with no shop no anything, save the blacksmith – only a handful of Mexicans who speak Spanish – we went to get Frieda's grey horse – the Azul – shod. They call him in Spanish el Azul – the Blue. – During the day there's always plenty to do – chopping wood, carrying water – and our own work: some times we all paint pictures. Next week the Indian Geronimo is coming up to help me mend the corral, and build a porch over my door, and fix the spring for the

[1] Cf. the account given in *St. Mawr*, ed. Finney, pp. 140–5.
[2] MS reads 'a wooden'.

winter, with a big trough where the horses can drink. I want a Mexican to come and live here while we are away: to keep the place from going wild, squirrels and bushy-tailed pack-rats from coming in, and to see the water doesn't freeze for the horses. It gets very cold, and snow often knee deep. Sometimes, for a day or two, no getting away from the ranch.

There, I hope that's all you want to know.

I hope your exam went well. – As for Wembley, I don't a bit want to go there.[1] But London can be fascinating.

So glad you like your new house: we had the photographs. I must send you some photographs of here.

I haven't heard from your Aunt Ada at Ripley for so long. Is anything wrong there?

Love to you all.

DHL

The autumn is coming, very lovely. The alfalfa field is all mauve and gold, with dark michaelmas daisies and wild sunflowers. I send a pound each for you and Joan.[2]

3220. To Martin Secker, 31 August 1924

Text: MS UInd; PC v. Snug as a Bug in a Rug. Pueblo Indian Papoose; Secker 60.

Del Monte Ranch. *Questa*, New Mexico
31 Aug 1924

Dear Secker

Thank you very much for the Rimsky Korsakoff Memoirs: Frieda is deep in them. I didn't complain of surcharge *postage*, but of these theiving customs.[3]

[1] See p. 85 n. 4.

[2] Joan Frieda King (b. 1920), the younger daughter of DHL's sister, Emily.

[3] (DHL's inability to spell 'thieving/thief' is frequently confirmed by the MS of *The Plumed Serpent.*) DHL was replying to Secker's letter of 13 August (Secker Letter-Book, UIll):

Dear Lawrence

Many thanks for yours of July 23, which reached us a week ago. I am sorry you had to pay those postal charges on the books, and hope it was not due to under-stamping at this end, as we are usually careful about such matters. I will send no more "popular" magazines. The Times will stop at the end of the subscription, and at least it contains pictures to look at. I will continue to send The Illustrated London News unless you tell me not to, and occasional critical articles which although they are filled with a lot of solemn nonsense, sometimes contain an article worth reading.

I am publishing "The Boy" on August 28, Seltzer I understand doing so on September 1. I fixed this date because my previous advice from Curtis Brown was that Seltzer's date was September 1 or very probably a fortnight earlier. I did not see Miss Skinner, and do not know whether she is still in London. But in any case a substantial cheque for the subscription sales will go to Curtis Brown on publication day. I feel decidedly hopeful about the book. I will let you

They charged one dollar nine cents customs duty on this one book: about 5/-. It's disgusting. I think the only thing is to write inside them: From M.S. to D.H.L. or something, and destroy any possible commercial value.

I'm sorry about Miss Skinner and her new novel, she'd be so disappointed. But I don't think I want to re-write another. Good to have sold 1000 copies of *The Boy* to Australia! – I'll ask Seltzer if he's coming out with *The Rainbow*. He's sent me no sheets so far. – Perhaps I'd better make a few alterations on the original English copy. I don't know why I feel at all eager for this book to re-appear. – Did you ask about that *Punch* for F.W. Gillett? – I suppose we'll be going down to Mexico in about five weeks' time.

We got back from that trip to the Hopi Country last Monday – I hate long distances in a motor-car.

Yrs DHL

3221. To Ada Clarke, 31 August 1924
Text: MS Clarke; cited in Lawrence–Gelder 127–9.

Del Monte Ranch. *Questa*, New Mexico.
31 August 1924

My dear Sister

I haven't heard for you for months – nor if you got your birthday present, nor the little shoes for baby – nothing. Have your letters gone lost?

We were away a fortnight motoring to the Hopi Country: I had promised an article on the Snake Dance. The Navajo Country is very wild and strange – real old savage America. But there are too many motorcars now in the world. And long trips in motor car weary me to death.

know the what the English subscription amounts to, and I have just succeeded in selling an edition of 1000 to Australia (Robertson & Mullens).

Curtis Brown sent in Miss Skinner's manuscript "Black Swans", but as it was, it was quite hopeless and I fear nothing can be done with it as it stands. We did not imagine that you would wish to spend the time in re-writing another work, but if so, of course, that is another matter.

The proofs of "The Memoirs" arrived safely, and I have now sent them to Press. I gathered from Doug[las]'s letter to Curtis Brown that he would have no objections of any kind to make, and if there is any need to consult Don Martino I imagine that you will have written. I do not see myself that there is anything he can take exception to. I am arranging to bring this out in October and there again I feel very hopeful of showing some satisfactory returns.

I see by the way that Seltzer is bringing out a new edition of "The Rainbow" this autumn, if you could let me have a set of revised proofs I should be very glad to add the title to your list at any time. Unless your new novel was to appear in January or February next I could publish it then. I have attended to your complimentary copies of "Classic American Literature" and "The Boy".

I hope you are both having a good summer. All is quite well at home, and we hope it will not be too long before you are both able to pay us a visit there.

Yours

You'll be getting *The Boy in the Bush* this week. It will amuse you. Poor Molly Skinner came to England from West Australia – so excited – by steerage – and bringing the MS. of another novel: *Black Swans*. Alas, Martin Secker writes me that *Black Swans* is quite useless for publication as it stands. And I doubt if I want to re-write another book, and re-create it, as I did *The Boy*. I'm sorry for Molly Skinner, her hopes dashed. – Jack, in the *Boy*, was her brother[1] – she was a general's daughter, went to Australia with her mother, an Australian, 20 years ago. I suppose she's about forty or forty-two. – They're poor now. – However, she'll be getting £60 or £70 this week, from *The Boy*.

Here the time slips by. I have got a new black horse Aaron – he is very handsome, and I like him very much. He only cost $35.00 – about £8. – a saddle costs twice as much. But horses are cheap here, now there are so many motor cars. Bretts Dan, a pony, only cost $15. – not £4. And he's a handsome little fellow. But F[rieda]'s horse – the grey – the Azul we call him – was fifty dollars.

I suppose we shall be here five or six weeks still, then I must go to Mexico to finish my 'Quetzalcoatl' novel. I've not done a novel this year – nor much small stuff – so not earned much. But I have plenty, as Seltzer very slowly pays up. I keep a thousand dollars in hand if I can, now. He owes me a good bit yet. – Did you get the little 'Corn Dance' article I sent via Emily, and my drawing in it?

Mabel Luhan talks of going to New York for the winter. Alas, she has antagonised nearly everybody – and she and Tony, the Indian, hardly get on at all. Everybody asks how much longer it will last. For myself, I don't know or care. Poor Mabel, she has been so spoilt, she makes her own life a torment at last. We all keep friendly, without too much closeness.

The autumn is coming here – we are so high. The summer has many thunderstorms – down on Del Monte they had three horses killed, in June, by one flash. But autumn is clear and blue, hot days, cold nights with great stars settling on the mountains. Now the big clearing in front of the house is really amethyst, with dark-coloured Michaelmas daisies, not very tall, and great gold patches of wild sunflower. But it's really a hard country, not a soft flowery country, though we've had endless strange, rather fascinating flowers up here, at this height.

How are you all? I'm sure Emily would have said if anything was wrong. Baby must be thinking of toddling now. – And how is father?[2] – I send him £10. – If ever you want anything for him, extra, only let me know. – I was so

[1] John ('Jack') Russell Skinner (1881–1925), whom DHL had met briefly at Leithdale; see also Letter 3467 and n. 2.

[2] John Arthur Lawrence (1846–1924), a retired miner; see Letter 3234.

sorry about Florrie Cooper.[1] Curious how often one thinks of them. I only hope Gertie keeps well.[2] She is really right not to care: caring would only help to send her the same way.

Send us a line – we've not been able to understand this long silence – even a postcard lets one know that all is well.

Love from us both to you all.

DHL

3222. To Harriet Monroe, 3 September 1924

Text: TMSC NWU; cited in Monroe, *Poetry*, xxvi. 94.

Del Monte Ranch, Valdez, New Mexico.
3 Sept 1924

Dear Harriet Monroe

I had your letter *last night* – had just heard you were likely to be at the fiesta in Santa Fé. You are sure to see somebody there who will tell you about us. We are here, about seventeen miles north of Taos, on a little ranch of my wife's, paid for by the MS. of *Sons and Lovers*. I wish you would come up and see us. Mabel Luhan has gone to New York for the moment, or she would drive you up. But Swinburne Hale no doubt would bring you, he knows the way. And we should be glad to see you, all of us.

The mail is very slow – I hope this will reach you. Let us know what you are doing.

Yours, D. H. Lawrence

3223. To Edith Isaacs, 6 September 1924

Text: MS WHist; Huxley 613.

Del Monte Ranch, *Questa*, New Mexico.
6 Sept. 1924

Dear Miss Isaacs[3]

Thank you for your letter.

I did an essay on 'The Hopi Snake Dance': and feel rather deeply about the said essay. But no doubt it is far too long and far too speculative for your magazine. I don't want to cut it down at all: not for anybody. But if you wish I will try to write a little purely descriptive essay such as the 'Corn Dance' one. – Mrs Lujan can lend you pictures.

[1] An older sister (1879/80–1924) of Frances and Gertrude (next note); she died from tuberculosis on 28 July.

[2] Gertrude ('Grit') Cooper (1885–1942), a childhood friend of DHL's at Lynn Croft, Eastwood. Since 1919 she had lived with his sister, Ada Clarke; see *Letters*, i. 23.

[3] Edith Juliet Isaacs (1878–1956), née Rich, editor of several periodicals, including *Theatre Arts Monthly*, 1924–46 and author of several books on the American theatre. m. 1904, Lewis Montefiore Isaacs (d. 1944).

If, by the way, she calls in your office, and you have that 'Hopi Dance' MS. from Curtis Brown – I told Mrs McCord to send it you – and if Mrs Lujan would like to read it, please let her do so.

I hope my wife and I may meet you, and all the *Theatre Art*-ists, one day.

Yours Sincerely D. H. Lawrence

3224. To E. M. Forster, 10 September 1924
Text: MS KCC; Unpublished.

Del Monte Ranch. *Questa*, New Mexico
10 Sept 1924

Dear E. M.

You asked me if I found 'individuals' out of England, since I don't find'em in. No, I don't But one does find a great strange spirit of place, and a different race-impulse out here. It seems much bigger, with open gaps that go away into the unknown. England's tight to me like a box.

I sent Curtis Brown an article last week 'The Hopi Snake Dance'. I should like you to read it. I asked Murry to read it, though it will be too long for his *Adelphi*. Just borrow the MS. from Murry, if you care to, then let me know what impression you get. – I suppose you read the little 'Dance of the Sprouting Corn' in the Aug. *Adelphi*.

The Boy in the Bush is only half mine. – Anyhow the adventure, even in a far country, is really *inside*, not out.

We go down to Mexico early in October. Meanwhile this address is always safe.

Yrs. D. H. Lawrence

3225. To Edward McDonald, 10 September 1924
Text: MS UT; *Centaur* 13.

Del Monte Ranch. *Questa*. New Mexico
10 Sept 1924

Dear Mr McDonald

I send you this little 'Introduction' for the bibliography.[1] If you think it is in any way unsuitable, tell me, and I'll alter it. I don't mind a bit.

We are going down to Mexico City early in October, so I'd like to get all my things cleared up before I go.

Best wishes D. H. Lawrence

[1] Written 1 September; see pp. 64 n. 1 and 110 n. 3.

3226. To Herbert Milne, 12 September 1924

Text: MS BL; Postmark, Taos SEP 16 1924; Unpublished.

Del Monte Ranch. *Questa*, New Mexico. U.S.A.
12 Sept. 1924

Dear Milne[1]

I hesitate to approach you with a request, but Brett says you won't mind.

You know – or you don't – the Oxford University Press brought out a sort of High School history text-book, four years ago, called *Movements in European History* – and they gave me a pseudonym, *Lawrence H. Davison*, because they were afraid of my own name. Now they aren't. Now they want it. They want to bring out a new edition of the book, with an added chapter,[2] and with *illustrations*. They keep writing to me to suggest illustrations. And how can I? They don't hang on the boughs of pine-trees at the foot of the Rocky Mountains. I thought, since you were in the British Museum, that imposing place, you might fairly easily be able to lay your hand on a few pictures – wood-cuts or heaven knows what – that might be good to put before the eyes of the rising generation. Something the Oxford Press would be allowed to print. If you think it's possible, would you communicate with Vere H. Collins. Oxford University Press. Amen House. Warwick Square, London E.C.4. He's in charge of the thing. He'll send you a copy of the book and all information.

I feel guilty, making this attack on your time and attention: but if it's a trouble, just don't take any notice.

We have been up here on this ranch now five months: it is so far from Hampstead and the Thursday evenings. One day when you've all changed your minds, I hope you'll come here, and let's have a few Monday Mornings instead of Thursday evenings. – Brett paints a bit – shoots rabbits and pack-rats – fishes and doesn't catch 'em – rides her horse Ambrose – and seems very well.

You must really come out one day and have a little tiny house on this place too. Would you care to? – for a summer?

We're going down to Mexico next month (Deo Volenti) – for winter warmth – this is 8000 ft up, gets deep snow – and to finish a novel I began a year ago.

If there's anything I can do for you, I'd be glad to do it.

Yours D. H. Lawrence

[1] Herbert John Mansfield Milne (1888–1965), graduated Cambridge, 1912; classical scholar on the staff of the British Museum; edited *The Codex Alexandrine* (1909–), *Catalogue of literary papyri in the British Museum* (1927), etc.

[2] The Epilogue was completed by 28 September (Letter 3245); it was not published until 1972, in an edition of *Movements* by Oxford University Press.

3227. To Nancy Pearn, 12 September 1924

Text: MS Lazarus; PC v. Pueblo Indians Singing (Part of Corn Dance Ceremony) San Domingo, New Mexico; Unpublished.

Del Monte Ranch, Questa, New Mexico
12 Sept 1924

Dear Miss Pearse

Here's a little article I did for the *Saturday Review* – New York. Just show it to Murry to tease him – then do as you please.[1]

It's autumn here – snow on the mountain again, but calm sunny days, very lovely. – We go down to Mexico next month, to finish the novel. The novelette 'St. Mawr' is nearly typed out.

Yrs D. H. Lawrence

3228. To Bobbie Gillete, [12 September? 1924]

Text: MS Chavez; Unpublished.

[Kiowa]
Friday[2]

Dear Bobbie

I didn't forget your poems: only I never could find you anywhere near alone, and didn't like to talk of them before people.

I like 'Married Young' very much: and 'Semper Idem'. You are best when you do a moment of real experience, quite simply: something you distinctly felt. When, as in 'Horseback' or 'Pas Vrai', you do a vague, unrealised emotion, or something you *think* you feel yourself or that somebody else will feel, it's not so good. Frieda likes 'Horseback'. But I think it isn't quite true: some element in it that makes it banal: been done before. 'Horse of flame' is a bit of a cliché: so is 'the sweet earth' and 'nostrils belching smoke'. And when a poem has ready-made phrases in it, it can't be quite sincere. You haven't got at the real spark of your own feeling. – 'Reality' is the worst of the poems, in my opinion: *really* banal. After all, it's vulgar to run to a *rainbow* for a pot of gold. A rainbow gives one so much: why want money from it. – What do you *actually* want from the rainbow? – Make your poem out of that. – The same with the mountains poem as with 'Horseback': the emotion is too generalised, not specifically you. – 'God! beauty hurts so!' – that is really cliché. It's been

[1] Sonia Chapter answered DHL's letter on 2 October (TMSC UT): 'As Miss Pearn is now away on holiday I am writing to thank you for your article, "CLIMBING DOWN PISGAH", which we have sent on to Mr. Murry'. The essay was published posthumously in *Phoenix*.

[2] The date is uncertain; the letter could have been written at almost any time after DHL's move to the ranch on 5 May. September is chosen because on 14th DHL mentions his sore throat to both Emily King and Mabel Luhan, combined with evidence of his affection for the Gilletes and gratitude for their friendship in Letter 3247.

in dozens of poems. It isn't quite what you, in your own distinct individual you, mean – It is general. But poetry is only second-rate when it's made out of general, generalised feelings, that anybody might have and might express in the same ready-made way. I think the little 'Song' is pretty, I like its rhythm, though the sentiment is a wee bit cheap. – 'Pas Vrai' is, as the title says, not true. I don't think a man ever feels that way at that time. He'd have to be a very unpleasant man. Though a man may easily feel that way when he's angry or thwarted, and not revelling at all in red lips.

Have you got any more poems? If you have, let me see them. I think those two, 'Married Young' and 'Semper Idem', and perhaps 'Sangre de Cristo' and 'Song', you might send to Harriett Monroe, to *Poetry* – 232 East Erie St. Chicago and tell her I said I thought she'd like to see them: and say who you are.[1]

I put the little titles for references. You alter them of course to your own feeling.

I'll come tonight to dinner: my miserable throat hurts. But I'll have a talk with you whenever you find a free moment.

D. H. Lawrence

3229. To Edward McDonald, 13 September 1924

Text: MS UT; Postmark, Questa SEP 16 1924; *Centaur* 13–15.

Del Monte Ranch. *Questa*. New Mexico
13 Sept 1924

Dear Professor McDonald

I sent you yesterday the little preface to the *Bibliography*, and want you to tell me if it's what you require.

The things in the *Westminster* will, I think, be in the *Saturday Westminster*, in Miss Royd Smith's day[2] – one article, or more, that afterwards went into *Twilight in Italy*, and must have appeared in 1913 or 1914.[3] Ask Murry if he remembers. He was a contributor then.

I never saw Heineman's *White Peacock* in a red binding: but he might have done a colonial edition in red.[4] I have got a colonial *Rainbow* which I found in

[1] None of Bobbie Gillete's poems appeared in *Poetry*.

[2] Naomi Gwladys Royde Smith (d. 1964), writer and literary editor of *Westminster Gazette*, 1916–22. m. 1926, Ernest Milton (see also p. 470 n. 1).

[3] 'Christs in the Tirol', *Saturday Westminster Gazette* (22 March 1913), collected as 'The Crucifix Across the Mountains', but other travel essays and stories and poems appeared there (see p. 87 n. 3).

[4] Heinemann's colonial issue had tan covers (Roberts A1c); no copy in red is known.

Perth library West Australia and bought back for 5/-: bound in *brown*.[1] They've got another, too.

I'll write to Secker myself about the unexpurgated *Lost Girl* and ask if he can't send me a copy.

I'd clean forgotten I ever signed any *Bays*. You ask Amy Lowell, tell her I told you.[2] She's quite nice. – I'll write and ask Cyril Beaumont, if you like.[3] He's got a list of my 'Collectors.' Let me know.

The Oxford Press are doing a new edition of *Movements in European History* and want illustrations and an epilogue. The epilogue, all right. But they are pestering[4] me here to suggest what illustrations they shall use – they want about a dozen. And do old woodcuts and such grow like leaves on Rocky Mountain pine trees! – I suppose you don't know off-hand where one could find a few suitable things that the Oxford Press might reproduce? – They're an incompetent show, if ever there was one.[5] But pleasant with it.

Let me know if I can do anything for you.

Tell Mrs McDonald that poor Molly Skinner – she is 'Jack's' sister, now about 40 – Jack's antecedents, general and all, are real – came steerage to London from Perth W.A. in her excitement over *The Boy* – and everybody snubs her, and she has no money – I suppose Secker must have paid her £50 or so by now – we go halves – and treats her as if she'd no right to exist. It's too bad. I met her in W. Australia – she showed me a MS then – no good, but queer – I said write a straightforward record of Australia. A year later the MS of *The Boy* fell on me in Mexico – It was full of material, but disjointed, disconnected, all wrong: somehow one couldn't read it. I think her MS. is with Seltzer – one day you must read it. So not to disappoint her I set about and re-wrote the whole thing, every word. But the material *is* hers, and she should get her dues. Now she came pelting to London with a new novel *Black Swans*, full of great hopes of being an authoress by herself – and Secker says it's no good –

[1] Methuen's colonial issue had brown covers; see Roberts A7b and p. 21 for history.

[2] DHL had had trouble posting the signature sheets for the thirty signed copies on vellum from Capri in January 1920 because of a postal strike (*Letters*, iii. 238 n. 2, 462). *Bay* was published in November 1919 by Beaumont after considerable delay and with many mistakes (leaving out poems and the dedication, etc.; see pp. 465, 469). Amy Lowell was sent a copy (p. 475).

[3] Cyril William Beaumont (1891–1976), bookseller and publisher; published DHL's *Bay*; ran the Beaumont Press, 1917–31, specialising in the work of contemporary writers; he was himself an authority on the theatre and classical ballet. See *Letters*, iii. 212 n.

[4] MS reads 'they pestering'.

[5] one] won

there, that's that. The *Times Literary Supplement* called her Mister[1] – but I'll send you her last letter. I must get Murry to praise her.

That is for Mrs McDonald. E. M. Forster wrote he didn't like the *Boy* so much as the others. Do you like his work?

Yrs D. H. Lawrence

3230. To John Middleton Murry, 13 September 1924

Text: MS NYPL; PC v. Corn Dance, Pueblo of San Domingo, N. Mex.; Moore 807.

Questa, New Mexico.
13 Sept 1924

Dear Jack

If you do a review of *The*[2] *Boy in the Bush*, please praise Molly Skinner, say the *material* is hers, I only re-cast it – she's down because people seem to want to tell her she shouldn't exist in the connection, and it's not fair. – I wrote to your Milne at the British Museum to ask if he could suggest illustrations for the new edition of *Movements in European History*, for the Oxford Press. They pester me – and what can I do out here? I feel it was rather cheek to bother Milne – but ask him if he minds, and let me know, will you. – It's lovely autumn here – so beautiful and far. Pity you couldn't *step* over. – We are going down to Mexico in October – I suppose Brett too. The birds are all coming down from the mountains – I feel like going south too – always want to go south. But I think Frieda rather hates leaving her ranch. Brett shoots rabbits – cottontails they call them here.

DHL

3231. To Martin Secker, 13 September 1924

Text: MS UInd; Postmark, Questa SEP 1[. . .]192[. . .]; Secker 60–1.

Del Monte Ranch. Questa. New Mexico
13 Sept 1924

Dear Secker

The *Punches* arrive: thank you very much. I look at the *Times* weekly and my heart sinks weekly: it all seems so fatuous. – The *Times Sup*. review amuses me. *The Boy* might be popular. – I *do* wish they mentioned Miss Skinner's share and praised it. I *do* wish people were nice to her. Are you sure her *Black Swans* wasn't good? Why not? She seemed so depressed, and no wonder.

Yes, the novelette 'St. Mawr' is finished and Brett is typing it out. It's good

[1] *The Times Literary Supplement* reviewer mentioned 'Mr. M. L. Skinner' at the beginning and then closed: 'Whatever Mr. Skinner's share in [the novel] may be, the best and the worst are the best and the worst of Mr. Lawrence. And the best is Mr. Lawrence's very best' (28 August 1924, p. 523).

[2] *The*] Molly

– a bit bitter – takes place in England, then moves to this ranch – some beautiful creation of this locale and landscape here – But thank god I don't have to write it again. It took it out of me. The longish story 'The Woman Who Rode Away' might go with it. Hutchinsons want to cut that story and print it in *Woman*, Curtis Browns tell me. 'St. Mawr' must be more than 30,000 words. 'The Woman Who Rode Away' about 15,000.

Professor E. D. McDonald. The Drexel Institute, *Philadelphia*. Pa. – who is doing a very thorough bibliography of me, wants very much to know if any of the unexpurgated *Lost Girl*s went out, and if he can get a copy – Because a London dealer advertises a copy of the unexpurgated novel for sale. McDonald has written for it, but is very much afraid he might not get it. If you have one, do send it him.

And did you ever see Heinemann's *White Peacock* bound in red? Was there a colonial edition, do you know?

Lovely autumn here now, very lovely. But I feel like going south soon. I always want to go south.

Frieda asks, How is Mrs Secker, and why no word from her.

Yrs D. H. Lawrence[1]

[1] Secker's response was (Secker Letter-Book, UIll):

October 9 1924

Dear Lawrence

Many thanks for yours of Sept 13. The facts about "The Lost Girl" for Professor E.D.McDonald are as follows. When the book was being subscribed, it was found necessary in order to secure for it Library circulation to make small verbal amendments in two places, so two cancel pages were printed and inserted in a number of copies. Later on, when the Library demand had ceased, these cancel pages were ignored, and all subsequent binding orders present the book as originally issued. It was a mere temporary expedient undertaken for a special purpose. I could not say whether "The White Peacock" was ever bound in red cloth: I have never seen one, nor do I know whether a Colonial edition was ever issued.

Now let me give you some good news. Some months ago Curtis Brown told me that he had failed to place an Australian edition of "Kangaroo", and asked me to see what I could do in the matter. I approached Robertson & Mullens through their London manager, suggesting that they should not only take an edition of the obvious book "Kangaroo", but also consider the question of importing editions of all your past works of fiction. Yesterday I heard that they will do this, taking 500 copies of all the books with the exception of "England, My England" of which they will take 250 only, on the ground of its being short stories. It is not so much the immediate returns which makes this so satisfactory, but it gives you at once an entire fresh public. I think there is no doubt that they will continue to import these old titles, and I think we can count on an initial order of 1000 for future books. "The Boy" goes on very steadily, and Australia has repeated 500, making so far 1500 in all. I do not think it will stop at that. Too early yet to say anything definite about M.M., but all aspects are propitious.

I am delighted to hear about "St Mawr". I hope that this with "The Woman" and one more may make an early volume.

I will write again directly I have any fresh news to report.

Yours

This is misremembered about *The Lost Girl*; the small number of surviving copies with the original, unexpurgated text indicate that Secker did not revert to the unaltered text; see *The Lost Girl*, ed. John Worthen (Cambridge, 1981), pp. xxxix–xl, liii.

3232. To Mollie Skinner, 13 September 1924
Text: Moore 807.

Del Monte Ranch, Questa
13 September 1924

Dear Molly Skinner:

Your letter from Stourport[1] today – I saw the *Times* review: it's too bad they leave you out: and it's not my fault, I assure you. I do hope *Black Swans* is going well. Get the opinion of somebody competent. Write to Mrs Catherine Carswell, 110 Heath St, Hampstead, N. W. 3. She is our very good friend, and wrote two good novels.[2] She is in the country – but write to her and meet her. She can help you probably. She understands publishers and so on. – Do you take notice what cowardly reviewers say about me – *quelle canaille*! If I'd listened to reviewers I shouldn't exist. – We are all well – leave for Mexico proper in October. – Didn't you get a good cheque from Curtis Brown? Secker said he paid one in. I think if you press Curtis Brown, he will get you an *advance* from Secker. Do it. And I hope you have Seltzer's $100.00. Best wishes to you from us both.

[1] She wrote as follows (MS UT):

Agent General Western Australia, Strand, London
28th. Aug. 1924

Dear Mr Lawrence.

Your letter (Aug 10th) came this morning like a drop of water to a thirsty 'Jack'.

I am boarding at "Wendy" Cottage Stourport, in Worcestershire with relations of Miss Beakbanes while I work up "Black Swans" It wanted it. Its nearly done. Curtis Brown is away. But I must believe in myself I suppose, and hammer it in somewhere. Curtis Brown's Private Secretary tried it with Secker but they wouldn't have it. My London experiences are all misted in the gloom of not having enough cash to open the gates of freedom from anxiety! I learnt long ago how to open the gates of 'exclusiveness'. I can *get in* anywhere – but I can't stay. Not that I want to. I'm like Tom. '*Lets git*'.

Your letter came first thing and I went to breakfast and picked up the Times Supplement and read that! – they seem to like it! Leaves me rather out of it – 'Mister' too – but all I think of, is the extraordinary chance that made you interested in my attempts to express the 'divine Spark' – as you call it!

You have been most kind and generous, *the* most kind & generous soul in the world, and I've got to forgive you for those end chapters – because they are yours. And I do think you have *brought* it all *out* like a magician. May I dedicate Black Swans to you, if I get it taken?

My very kindest love to Mrs. Lawrence. and everything good to her Ranch!

I will send and ask Secker to send those copies of The Boy to Australia: Thank you.

The real Jack – you may be interested to hear – is still swotting on his mine at Bullfinch[?], Southern X, W.A.

Kindest regards

From Yours v. sincerely. M. L. Skinner

[2] *Open the Door!* (1920) and *The Camomile* (1922). See *Letters*, ii. 187–9 and iii. 58, 173.

3233. To Amy Dawson Scott, 13 September 1924

Text: MS UT; Unpublished.

Del Monte Ranch. *Questa*, New Mexico.
13 Sept 1924

Dear Mrs Scott

Thank you for your letter and the P.E.N. card of introduction. My wife and I are going down to Mexico in October, when I hope to meet Señor Estrada and give a hand, if I can, to the P.E.N. activities down there:[1] though dinners I don't care for.

Yours Sincerely D. H. Lawrence

3234. To Emily King, 14 September 1924

Text: MS Lazarus; Unpublished.

Del Monte Ranch. Questa. New Mexico
14 Sept 1924

My dear Pamela

I had your cablegram last night about father. It was the last thing I expected, Ada had just written he was as well as ever. – It is better to be gone than lingering on half helpless and half alive. But it upsets one, nevertheless: makes a strange break.

When did he die – what date?[2] The cablegram did not say. And when did you bury him. I hope it didn't rain. And really, I thank God I wasn't there at the funeral. No, no more of that.

I send you ten pounds to help with the black – if you wear it. It's bad to put children into black, in my opinion. I sent Ada £10. for him, a fortnight ago: and send her another £10. now, for expenses. If there is anything else, you must let me know.

And if you want help for Peg – if she wants to go to some other school or anything – only tell me.

We shall be going down to Mexico in October. The high altitude and the thin cold air changing now to autumn have given me a sore chest and throat

[1] Genaro Estrada (1887–1937), Mexican diplomat and writer; Under Secretary of Foreign Affairs (Relaciones Exteriores) in 1924, published *Poetas Nuevas de Mexico* (1916), *Pero Galín* (1926), etc.; president of Mexican branch of P.E.N. See Nehls, ii. 520 n. 52 and Parmenter 7, 17.

[2] 10 September 1924; see Letter 3256.

which doesn't get better quickly, so I shan't be sorry to go. We shall either shut up the ranch or get a couple of Mexicans to live here.

Frieda sends love to you all, with mine.

DHL

3235. To Mabel Dodge Luhan, 14 September 1924
Text: MS Brill; Luhan 271–2.

Del Monte Ranch. *Questa*, New Mexico.
14 Sept 1924

Dear Mabel

I had your letter about Brill last night.[1] I knew it was very much as he said: that there was a fatal disconnection, and that it was passing beyond your control. I am glad you are going to put yourself into a doctor's hands. Because you have now to submit to authority, and to a certain measure of control from outside. And except to an authority like a recognised doctor's, you would never have submitted.

The thing to do is to try, try, try to discipline and control yourself. And to remember that, even if all the people in the world go negative and futile, and you yourself have stuck to something which is more than all people or any people, the real thing which is beyond anybody's malevolent reach, then you yourself will never feel negative nor empty. One should discipline oneself never to do things which one's own self disapproves of – and then one can't go to pieces. But it will be hard for you to get over your disintegrative reaction towards people and circumstances – everything. As you say, you went that way so long ago.

We shall be going down to Mexico in October. My chest and throat stay sore, I want to go south. I don't want to go east for the winter: no. For this winter you must fight this thing out more or less by yourself. It is your job.

I don't know if this will reach you – but send it to the club on chance.

DHL

[Frieda Lawrence begins]

I wrote to a nephew[2] to come and see you but I daresay he wont be in time – At first you sounded quite gay and now this last letter! I have felt myself like a

[1] Dr Abraham Arden Brill (1874–1948), b. Austria, psychiatrist. Studied at New York and Columbia Universities; assistant physician in psychiatry clinic in Zurich. He was chief of the psychiatry clinic, assistant professor in psychiatry at the Post-Graduate Medical School, Columbia, and held several similar posts at New York University; author of books on psychiatry and translator of Jung. See Nehls, ii. 517 n. 15.

[2] Friedel Jaffe.

tiger with a steady suppressed growl going on inside me! Just things in general! And yet it's so lovely up here now, let us know when you come back and tell us all your news!

Get better –

I wont bother you with vests!

F –

3236. To Ada Clarke, [14 September 1924]

Text: MS Clarke; PC v. Pueblo of San Felipi; Unpublished.

[Kiowa]
[14 September 1924]

I had sent £10. for father before I had the cable: then £10. more. Let me know if you have received this: and also, *how much* the funeral expenses are, and I will send more money. I would like to pay half of everything, so that George[1] and Pamela needn't have to find much. They haven't got much. Be sure and let me know. – I have been able to wring some money out of Seltzer through my agent – about $3000 dollars altogether, this year. If I can get it like this, bit by bit, I don't mind at all. My fear is that he may go bankrupt. But even then I have money in England. – Did you have to make a new grave for father – all separate?[2] – I hate to think of that Eastwood cemetery. I hate to think of Eastwood anyhow. Next time, you must come out here and see us: better than my coming back.

DHL

3237. To Alfred Decker Hawk, 15 September 1924

Text: MS ColU; Paul Delany, ed., 'D. H. Lawrence: Twelve Letters', *DHL Review*, ii (Fall 1969), 201.

Del Monte Ranch, Valdez
15 Sept 1924

Dear Mr Hawk

I wonder[3] if you would lend me your type-writer for a couple of days? Mine has just gone wrong, when there is a last bit of work to finish and send away in a hurry:[4] oh tiresomeness of all machinery.

[1] DHL's eldest brother, George Arthur Lawrence (1876–1967); see *Letters*, i. 135 n. 1.

[2] DHL's anxiety here and in Letter 3251 was unfounded; Arthur Lawrence was buried in the family grave, and his name appears on the gravestone immediately below his wife's.

[3] wonder] would

[4] According to Brett, Frieda had attempted to clean the typewriter: 'She boiled it . . . It never moved again. Just died in its tracks' (Parmenter 169). There was a change of typewriter at p. 148 of the 'St. Mawr' typescript (in the Lazarus collection).

William says you are coming home next month, so we shall see you and Mrs Hawk before we leave. I feel you are our *real* neighbours.

Yours very sincerely D. H. Lawrence

Mr Hawk says would you bring the typewriter if you come, please, Betty.

DHL

3238. To Willard Johnson, 15 September 1924
Text: MS YU; Unpublished.

Del Monte Ranch. Valdez.
15 Sept 1924

Dear Spoodle

The beastly typewriter broke just when there is a bit of work to finish quick. Can one get this part renewed – the machine is a Corona No 3. – and this is the bit that jumps up and down.

When are you coming? Bring your typewriter along, will you?

Horse came, and amused me.[1]

This in a hurry to get down and catch mailman.

Greet Bynner – tell him not to hide his face from us altogether – really!

DHL

No news of Brett's machine!!!!!![2]

3239. To Robert Mountsier, 18 September 1924
Text: MS Smith; Unpublished.

Del Monte Ranch. *Questa*, New Mexico
18 Sept 1924

Dear Mountsier

Will you be so good as to hand over to Mr A. W. Barmby, Curtis Brown's manager in New York all the manuscripts and papers I left in your keeping. Barmby is taking charge of everything for me, and I want to see if I can get straight at last.

We are having the struggle with Seltzer that you warned me about. You were right and I was wrong about him. And here we are! – Do you remember what MSS. of mine Seltzer had?

[1] No. 11 (September 1924) with 'Just Back from the Snake Dance – Tired Out'.
[2] Her listening device.

We intend to go down to Mexico in October, so that I can finish the novel I have two-thirds done. What about your Taos book?[1]

Hope all goes well with you.

Yrs D. H. Lawrence[2]

3240. To Willard Johnson, [18 September 1924]

Text: MS YU; Unpublished.

Del Monte Ranch. *Valdez*
Thursday evening

Dear Spoodle

Just got your letter from Taos. We had yours from Santa Fe only on Tuesday – I wrote to Santa Fe – and I sent a note to Ralph Myers[3] to ask him to catch you in Taos as you passed and ask you to come out on a wagon, and bring the 4 twisted pillars and the old wooden bedstead from Mabel's stable – I bought them from Clarence. Perhaps Sabino, Josè's brother, would bring you on a wagon – if not, Gerson will find you a man. I want these things out – so its

[1] Apparently never published.

[2] This letter was sent to Mountsier by Barmby who wrote as follows on 26 September 1924 (TMS UT):

> I am attaching herewith a letter from Mr. D. H. Lawrence who asks me to get in touch with you to see which of his manuscripts you have. We are taking charge of all Mr. Lawrence's manuscripts and have collected various ones from Seltzer, so if you would be good enough to let us know which you have, we will arrange to have them collected.
>
> Sincerely yours

For his part, Mountsier replied to DHL on 29 September 1924 (TMSC UT) as follows:

> What you have written fails to take up the matter in full in accordance with the agreement you made with me when I was in Taos and which, at your request, I copied into a letter to you. According to this agreement you were to pay me ten per cent. commission on the royalties *for* 1923 received from Seltzer. This sum, whatever it is, less a balance of some twenty dollars, is still due me.
>
> Regarding this you wrote me last winter that no matter what you had written you meant only the royalties received during 1923, and that that settled the matter. But you wrote me you would take the matter up with me later.
>
> I am considering this whole affair from the attitude which you chose to adopt toward me early in 1923. If you choose again to consider my work with contracts and manuscripts for a period extending even beyond 1923 and for time and trouble taken in 1921 and 1922 with getting under your control books for which I received not a cent of commission, the agreement which you chose to make in so far as paying me a ten per cent. commission on the royalties for 1923 was not unfair to yourself.
>
> You say that you wish to get your affairs straight at last, and for months I have wished to have the whole matter settled and ended so far as I am concerned.
>
> I thank you for your kind wishes.
>
> Sincerely yours,

[3] Ralph Myers (1885–1948), Taos painter. See *Letters*, iv. 422 n. 2.

my wagon. Come as soon as you can – Have you heard of Bretts machine – When does Mabel get back from New York? Really this week-end?

DHL

3241. To Mabel Dodge Luhan, [19 September 1924]
Text: MS Brill; Luhan 272–4.

Kiowa
– Friday evening

Dear Mabel

I found your letter this evening: and here's the answer:

1. Yes, one has to smash up one's old self and get a new one *with* a new skin (slow work).
2. One *must* kick bunk when one sees it; hence one *must* be a destructive force. You have hurt yourself, often, by letting the bunk get by and *then* kicking at random, and getting the victims below the belt. You *must* discriminate sufficiently and say: That's *bunk*! Kick it! – not kick in the wrong place.
3. One does talk too much – and one shouldn't. I speak for myself as well. – Though I don't think it matters terribly, unless one deliberately makes bad mischief – which happened this summer, in *talk*.
4. About Tony – I'm afraid you and Clarence *caused* him to take a violent prejudice against me, that time. I really have nothing against him: except that it is foolish even at the worst to be swayed too much. – About his relation to you, yours to him, I would never venture *seriously* to judge. (You really shouldn't mind the things one says casually – only the things one says really, having considered.) I do think you have a terrible lot of the collective self in you. I do think this helps to split you rather badly in your *private* self. I do think there is a good deal of subtle feminine sort of *épatez le bourgeois* in you: sometimes crude. I think this encroaches into your better relations, with men especially – that is, with Tony. It's a very difficult and tiresome thing, the mass self: and perhaps far stronger than you allow. Always allow for it in yourself:[1] then you can get your own feet of your *own* self, and make your *real* decision – You wouldn't please me at all by giving up Tony. I believe in seeing a thing through. If you care for him and believe he cares for you, stick to him tight. But do, do be careful of your mass self: Don't parade him – dont *épatez le bourgeois*

[1] Someone heavily crossed out several lines which are also omitted from Mabel Luhan's book: here about eleven words are lost of which the last are apparently 'him happier'; in the following five lines, below, 'You wouldn't . . . tight. But' and 'Don't parade . . . with him' were also crossed out, but have been recovered.

with him: be very very careful to preserve your real, private feelings from your mass feelings. In this instance, your mass feelings will ruin you if you let them. – And don't, through a sort of feminine egotism, want Tony to live too much through you. You know how bad that is. – It is a pity you ever made Tony jealous of me: it caused a bad confusion in his feelings, which he won't easily be able to straighten out. Because, as you know, he was not naturally jealous of me: his *instinct* knew better.

5. I wish there could be a change. I wish that old built-up self in you, and in the whole world, could give place to a new alive self. But it's difficult, and *slow*. And perhaps the only thing that will really help one through a great change is discipline, one's own deep, self-discovered discipline, the first 'angel with a sword'.

To your P.S. – You need have no split between Tony and me: never: if you stick to what is *real* in your feelings in each direction. Your real feelings in the two directions won't cause any disharmony. – But *dont* try to transfer to Tony feelings that don't belong to him: admit all the limitations, simply. And never again try to transfer to me feelings that are not *real* for me. Admit the limitations here too.

Try, above all things to be still and to contain yourself. You always want to rush into action. Realise that a certain kind of stillness is the most perfect form of action, like a seed can wait. One's action ought to come out of an achieved stillness: not be a mere rushing on.

DHL[1]

[1] Mabel Luhan replied (MS Brill):

Taos, New Mexico
Sunday.

Dear Lorenzo –

Please donot get impatient with me for asking so many questions but what is so queer is that I seem to know quite clearly for other people & am absolutely blank for my self. For instance you wrote me I must learn to discipline and control my self severely. I am ready to if I knew in what way. Do you mean I should begin to serve the concrete? Such as to get up deliberately in the morning & begin to deliberately *make* my self *do* things? Such as house work? You know my tendency is to lie in bed & muse or half-think, & try to reach my own centre – or try to meditate; then to get up and dress with a great economy of attention – (a genius for short cuts well accomplished!), hurry down stairs & give everybody a few *orders of things to do*. Then to muse around some more – talk some maybe – offering bright ideas to any one around of what *they* should *do* – write some letters – do an errand – eat – Then muse until the churning energy in me is beating me wild – & I decide to go & *walk* somewhere to get rid of it. . . . . You know the kind of days.

Doing things is a kind of agony for some reason. As you knew, just to decide to hang up those grapes with you whom I like to be *with* made a subtle peculiar pain run along my nerves. I suppose you don't know what this is like? So is that what you mean? I should force my self into it, hating it?

Now I'm going to tell you. There is something that takes this away – this uneasiness in action. There are two things.

One is being in love. Then everything is glorious & easy & a pleasure. I am efficient – doing things easily. But it's silly for me to think of being in that condition, though not impossible ever! I mean I call it being in love but it is merely a kind of flow that is accomplished by somehow getting my life tube in allignment with some one else's & having *their* life-flow run into my tube & *run my machinery*. This is what many people call being in love. It is a kind of vampirism. I can live at top strength if I get some one else's life in alignment with mine. I know the answer to that, though. "The Kingdom of *Life* is *within*" –

The other thing that releases me from this gummed up state is *writing*. If I can over come the terrible resistance & inertia that seizes me before I begin – if I can once get started & know I want to say something – it comes. Then I am off – in a good running pace. And *after* having done some writing, everything is different. The room I sit in seems to be beneficent & the light bathes one in a mild peaceful glow. All the misery & tug & pull are gone. Then I can *do* anything. Easily. Or I can walk out into the street & take an *objective* interest in *anything*. Feel pleasant. And the negative criticism is gone. Every thing is in a mild glow. Living isn't a mess and a struggle & the beating blood in side doesn't beat at one any more. It goes along like a river at the same tempo as the sun.

But the terrible inertia to overcome in order to *start* writing! Also I can only write *for* someone & you are positively the only audience I care to say anything to. Besides the inertia I always remember your words – "I shall never consider you a writer or even a knower." And these words paralyze me except for occasional letters or poems or parodies that *are* letters.

But one thing I have found out this morning. Life in action, in *doing* things, or experiencing activity outside one – is only possible as a *secondary* thing. There must be some *primary* thing to *use one* before one can even take a walk without agony of continence. Do you understand? If one lets oneself off in the vampire love – or rather starts – the movement by someone else's presence – then one can *bear* to wash dishes without absolutely groaning & cursing.

Or if one can do some writing for someone – then after it, the world appears – mild, sober, lovely or interesting. At least one isn't *pinioned*.

Now both you & Brill feel *I* have to do all the work this winter. With guidance I have to *do* the thing, whatever it is.

Can you tell me *what* this thing literally is? Finding myself? I believe I've been a kind of were-wolfess.

What kind of control & discipline did you mean? *Would writing do* as a cure & a help? Shall I try to start a life history or something? Save this letter if you think it would help Brill. Its so hard for me to formulate things – maybe it would aid him.

– Yrs, M. L.

P.S. Now you see Tony *per se* gives me the sense of *zest* in life – in doing things – sometimes. But so much spoils it. I suppose we must admit our different cultures – our surface lives – have taken different directions. So that there is practically nothing for us to unavoidably *do* together. For he likes mexican dances & I don't. He likes the simple movements of life, like the plaza life & I don't.

And there is little we can talk about of *current* life. About general essentials & the eternities – we are in agreement & can speak together about them.

If we sit in a room, it is in silence. We do not afford each other an outlet, yet we both feel reality in each other, & thro' each other.

I do not *try* to make him live thro' me as you say I do, but I *wish* he did – that we both could. I try to – for when he is at the table I know I enjoy my food better. When there are only the others there – they are only pale shadows to me. When he has come in at midnight from a dance – I sleep better. If I wake up & find he has not come in & is not sleeping next my room, I am in a panic of terror lest something has happened to him. He is my security for living. My whole personal life. Have I got to give up the wish for a personal life? Have we *all* go[t] to give it up?

M. L.

3242. To Willard Johnson, [21 September 1924]
Text: MS YU; Unpublished.

Del Monte Ranch, *Valdez*. N. Mex.
Sunday

Dear Spoodle

You might possibly come back with Ted Gillett. If you do, will you *please* not forget the Brett's listening machine. She sent it to Sloan's, but he didn't do it, so John Evans was going to take it to another man. Ask John about it, will you. And save the remainder of Brett's hearing and of my throat.

[Frieda Lawrence begins]

Dear Spud (but you have a new name and I dont remember it)

I did *love* the photographs could we have them enlarged? and have several? I have'nt taken any more, you take them so much better, we will wait for you – Sorry Bynner is not coming!

Glad to see you –

Frieda

3243. To Idella Purnell, 21 September 1924
Text: MS UT; Nehls, ii. 361.

Del Monte Ranch, *Valdez*, New Mexico
21 Sept 1924

Dear Idella

The summer is gone, and autumn is here, and it is time, as you say, to be turning south. But the days are still very lovely – sunny and silent. So we shall stay on two or three weeks – not more: then come down to Mexico City. I think we shall stay a while in the *Capital*, and make plans there for the next move.

Spud is coming up here today from Taos – Bynner has gone to California for a while. He (Hal) says he'll pay us a flying visit before we depart. – Mabel Lujan is going to winter near New York, to be in touch with doctors, as she is not well. And there we are, the lot of us.

How is Dr Purnell? I look forward to seeing you both again.

a rivederci D. H. Lawrence

3244. To Edward McDonald, 24 September 1924
Text: MS UT; PC v. Hopi Indian Pueblo, Oraibi, Arizona; Postmark, Taos SEP 25 1924; *Centaur* 15.

Del Monte Ranch. Questa. New Mexico
24 Sept. 1924

Dear Dr McDonald

Glad the introduction will do. Do you mean you want a sort of title for it?

Call it: 'The Bad Side of Books' – or anything else you like! – We leave in two weeks time – Deo Volente. – It really must have been a terrible sweat for you, doing that bibliography. It's a mystery to me why people do things, most things. – I'll send my Mexican address – but

c/o The British Consulate, 1. Av. Madero. Mexico D.F.

is always good.

I like the Centaur as a symbol:[1] would like to write a centaur story: but can't in these white countries, where the lower half of man is an autombile, not a horse. – I just finished a novelette 'St. Mawr' – more or less a horse story. I wanted it to be a centaur story – but – la mala suerte[2] – impossible.

D. H. Lawrence

3245. To Edward McDonald, [28 September 1924]

Text: MS UT; Postmark, Ta[os] [. . .] 19[. . .]; *Centaur* 15–16.

Del Monte Ranch. *Questa*, New Mexico.
Sunday

Dear Mr McDonald

Thank you so much for the pictures. I like the little 'German Knight in armour' and things like that extremely[3] – and I think it would be great fun to put four or so on a page for full-page illustration, as you suggest. I should be very glad if you could send me more, for the other chapters – but I hate to trespass on your time. – I am sending these pictures on to the Oxford Press now – with an Epilogue which they asked for, but which will make them hesitate. – In a couple of days time I will send you the copy of *Memoirs of the Foreign Legion*, which Secker just sent me: unless it gets too dirty with people reading it and leaving it under the trees.

I don't suppose I shall get away[4] – for Mexico – till about October 12th. or 14th. But the nights freeze already up here, and I simply disbelieve in cold, snow, Nordic stuff altogether.

Yrs D. H. Lawrence

3246. To Baroness Anna von Richthofen, [29 September 1924]

Text: MS UT; Unpublished.

[Frieda Lawrence begins]

[Taos, New Mexico][5]
den 29. X 24

Liebe mère,

Endlich geht das Packet ab – 2 Gemälde, ein Beutel, eine Decke, ein kleiner

[1] The Centaur Book Shop of Philadelphia was to publish McDonald's *Bibliography*; see p. 176 n. 2

[2] 'Bad luck' ('la' is not idiomatic usage).

[3] It was not used; see Letter 3441.

[4] away] to

[5] Written on headed paper; as are the two following letters.

Teppich, ein weiss und blaues Tischtuch zum herschenken! Heute ist San Hieronimo und Fiesta – und Wettrennen der jungen Indianer bemalt und mit Federn besteckt – Ich schicke Dir diese Briefe, Barby *verlobt*, so vergeht die Zeit! In 14 Tagen oder so gehen wir nach Mexico, es zieht Lawrence hin, mir tut's leid schon zu gehen! Ich wollte Du könntest sehen, wie schön es ist – Im Haus bist Du so vertreten – Mit Kissen und Deckle – und Arbeitssack! Und in diesem Land bewundern sie alles von Dir gemachte – Lawrence trägt nur Deine Schlipse – geht's Dir gut – Sage Nusch ich denke oft an sie und möchte ihr die längsten Briefe schreiben, es ist aber immer so *viel* los, sie müssen eben einmal kommen – Von Mexiko hoffe ich dann zu kommen. Lawrence sieht so gut aus, ich bin dünner geworden vom Reiten, aber ich fürchte die Dicke überholt mich wieder, wenn ich nicht mehr reite – von Friedel so nette Briefe! Es geht ihm gut. Jener Seltzer ist Lawr noch so viel Geld schuldig, es ist recht ärgerlich. Sagt er hat's nicht und bringt doch so viele Bücher heraus – die Berge werden gelb und rot und eine Herbstpracht hier, ich habe mich in dies Land hier hineingewachsen. Bald besucht Dich Else, Du wirst froh sein sie so nah zu haben im Winter.

Alles Gute

Deine Tochter Frieda

[Lawrence begins]

Grüsse Grüsse Schwiegermutter – St. Hieronymus Feste hier in Taos – wir bleiben nur zwei Tage. – Schicken dir heut' die zwei Bilder: auch einen Bett-decke, und einen ganz kleinen Navaho Decke – letzten von Amerika. Bleib wohl.

DHL

[Frieda Lawrence begins]

[Dear mère,

The parcel is finally going off – 2 paintings, a bag, a blanket, a small carpet, a white and blue tablecloth to give away! Today is San Hieronymus's day and fiesta[1] – and races for the young Indians, painted and decorated with feathers – I send you these letters, Barby *engaged*, how time flies![2] In a fortnight or so we go to Mexico, it draws Lawrence there, I'm sorry to go so soon! I wish you could see how beautiful it is – You are really a presence in the house – With

[1] The San Geronimo fiesta, a celebration of the harvest, took place at the Taos Pueblo. DHL had attended in 1922 (see *Letters*, iv. 316).

[2] Frieda's youngest child, Barbara Joy Weekley (b. 1904) had become engaged to an Irishman, Henry MacElwee. See also Letters 3349 and 3535.

cushions and little cloth – and workbag! And in this country they admire everything you've made – Lawrence wears only your ties – are you well – Tell Nusch I often think of her and would like to write her the longest letters, but there's so *much* happening, they will just have to come – I hope to come on from Mexico. Lawrence looks so good, I've grown thinner from riding, but I'm afraid fatness is going to overtake me again, when I'm no longer riding – such nice letters from Friedel! He's well. That Seltzer still owes Lawr so much money, it's really irritating. Says he hasn't got it and still brings so many books out – the mountains are turning yellow and red and a splendid autumn here, I've grown part of this country here. Else visits you soon, you'll be glad to have her so near in the winter.

All the best

Your daughter Frieda

[Lawrence begins]

Greeting Greetings Schwiegermutter – Feast of St. Hieronymus here in Taos – we only stay two days. – Sending you today the two pictures: a blanket too, and a really tiny Navaho blanket – last of America. Keep well.

DHL]

3247. To Earl and Achsah Brewster, 30 September 1924

Text: MS UT; Brewster 76–7.

Del Monte Ranch. Questa. New Mexico
30 Sept 1924

Dear Earl and Achsah

I haven't heard from you: did you get my letter? – I ordered for you from Secker a copy of *Boy in the Bush* and of *Memoirs of the Foreign Legion*. Did you get them?

A very young couple – Ted Gillett and his wife Bobbie – our only neighbours out here – Mr Hawk, Bobbie's father, owns the Del Monte Ranch, where we ride for milk and mail – are coming to Europe – rather shyly – and may land in Naples. If they do, will you look after them, for my sake? They have been very good to us. Pilot them into a pleasant *not* expensive hotel and help them to have a nice time – please.

We intend to go down to Mexico in a fortnight's time – but letters to the above address will follow us straight down. Write to us. And you must come really and see us out here – it's such lovely country – or in Mexico.

Yrs D. H. Lawrence

3248. To Curtis Brown, 30 September 1924

Text: MS UT; Huxley 614.

[Taos, New Mexico]
30 Sept 1924

Dear Curtis Brown

I am sending you today the MS. of the novelette 'St. Mawr', which I have finished this summer. It works out more than 60,000 words I believe. With 'The Woman Who Rode Away' – and another story of out here that I am doing, called 'The Princess', it will make a book.[1] – If anyone wants to do 'St Mawr' serially, they can cut it all they like, so long as the book form is complete. – If you think it better, 'St. Mawr' can be called 'Two Ladies and a Horse'.

The Oxford Press apparently are going ahead with *Movements in European History* in the illustrated edition. They asked me for an 'Epilogue'. Here it is. Will you hand it over to them. And perhaps you had better make a new contract for this new edition, what do you think? – I am writing them direct about illustrations.

We think to leave in a fortnight's time. Write to me either

c/o The British Consulate, 1. Av. Madero, *Mexico D. F.*

or else via Barmby. All Mexican letters come through New York. – I am so bothered about Seltzer, who doesn't pay me. Otherwise all well.

Yrs D. H. Lawrence[2]

3249. To Vere Collins, [30 September 1924]

Text: TMS OUP; D. H. Lawrence, *Movements in European History* (Oxford, 1971), p. xiii.

[Taos, New Mexico]
[30 September 1924]

Dear Collins,

I sent an Epilogue for *Movements* to Curtis Brown. If you don't like it, don't use it. Or if you want to omit any part of it, do so.[3]

[1] Brett had gone to Columbine Lake with Bill Hawk and the 'dudes' on 16 August, and her description (see pp. 101–2) had inspired DHL to go (with her and Bill and Rachel Hawk), probably late in August. This lake is the setting for 'The Princess' (see Brett 149–52); Brett was the model for the title character.

Gui de Angulo identifies the story that Mabel Luhan said Jaime de Angulo read to them in April 1924 as 'The Witch' (de Angulo, *Jaime in Taos*, pp. 9, 99; Luhan 186); it may have served as a source for 'The Princess', and is published in de Angulo, pp. 101–29.

[2] DHL records in his diary for 30 September: 'Sent to Barmby (Curtis Brown) – *St. Mawr*: also MSS of the same, & of *Woman who Rode Away. Last Laugh. Jimmy & the Desperate Woman Border Line. Dance of the Sprouting Corn. Indians & Entertainment*. Sent other copy of St Mawr to Curtis Brown London: & to Oxford Press epilogue for Movements in European History: & some illustrations for same. – Going down to Taos for San Geronimo –' (Tedlock, *Lawrence MSS* 98–9, corrected from MS).

[3] The extract exists as a quotation – headed 'Extract from letter from Lawrence 30 Sept.' – given

3250. To Baroness Anna von Richthofen, 2 October 1924
Text: MS UCB; Frieda Lawrence 188–9.

Del Monte Ranch. *Questa*. New Mexico
2 October 1924

Meine liebe Schwiegermutter

Wir sind wieder zu Haus – Gott sei Dank. Wenn man drei Tage mit Leuten gesessen hat, ist man satt, hat man genug. Doch wollen wir nächste woche weg: ein Paar Tage in Taos bleiben, dann nach Mexico. Du sollst mir schreiben:

c/o. British Consulate, 1. Aven. Madero, *Mexico. D.F.*

bis ich dir eine neue Adresse schicke. Die Brett reist mit: wir wissen nicht was sie anders machen könnte, und können sie nicht hier allein lassen. – Ich geh' sehr gern nach Mexiko: weiss nicht warum, aber ich möchte immer süd-wärts reisen. Hier ist es auch schon kalt, besonders in der Nacht. Die Sonne kommt nicht [Frieda Lawrence interjects: über] die Berge hinüber bis ½ 8: dann wird es warm. Und dann stehen die Pferde stein-still, von Kälte benommen, mittel im Alfalfa-feld, sich wieder in der Sonnen-wärme ein-weichend.[1] Meistens ist die Sonne heiss wie Juli: aber heute gibt's Wolken.

Hoffentlich bekommst du dein Paket mit Decke und Bilder. Du wirst dich darüber erfreuen, sicher. – Ich schicke dir zehn Pfund für Holz. Du sollst dich gut und warm behalten.

Hier schliessen wir alles zu. Die guten Sachen, Silber, Decken, Bilder, Betten, nehmen wir auf Wagen herunter nach Del Monte, an[2] die gute William und Rachel. Del Monte gehört, weisst du, an Mr. Hawk, der Vater von William. Die alten haben ein ziemlich grosses Haus, aber reisen viel, nach California u s w. Die Jungen, William mit seiner Frau Rachel und das ein-Jährige Kind, wohnen im Log-cabin wo wohnten wir, vor zwei Jahren. Da machen Sie Butter und besorgen Kühe und Hühne. Jeden Abend reiten wir herunter, um Milch und Post von William zu holen. Er bringt die Briefe immer vom Post-kasten hinauf. Rachel und William werden alles gut für uns behalten und besorgen. Montag kommt ein Mr Murray, Arbeiter, um Fensterläden zu machen. Wir lassen die Pferde hier bleiben, bis Dezember, wann kommt der grosse Schnee. Dann holt sie der William nach Del Monte herunter (nur 2½ km), und futtert sie jeden Tag mit Alfalfa. So bis Frühling, wann wir wieder-kommen.

Ich weiss nicht wie lange wir in Mexiko City bleiben wollen. Ich möchte

in a memorandum dated 26 November 1924 from Collins to the Secretary of the Clarendon Press, Oxford. The original MS has not survived. Collins' memo continues: 'Mr Milford says at present we will do nothing, but when the n[ew]/e[dition] is published we will send him the £10 in advance of royalties, and I will write to him to explain it was unusable.' See Introduction to *Movements in European History*, ed. Philip Crumpton (Cambridge, 1989), pp. xxix–xxx.

[1] ein-weichend] sich [2] an] zu

wieder südwärts gehen, nach Oaxaca, wo wohnen Maya Indier und Zapotekas. Da ist es immer warm: auch heiss. Und da möchte ich meinen Roman fertig bringen.

Hier sind die Bergen gold mit Aspen und Cotton-wood Bäume, und rot mit Scrub-oak, kleinen Aiken [Frieda Lawrence corrects to Eichen]: wunderschön. Tannen und Fichten aber beinah schwartz. Ein schöner Moment! Wird aber nicht dauern.

Wiedersehen, schwiegermutter. Kommt Winter wieder für alle alten Damen, leider!

DHL

[My dear Schwiegermutter

We're home again – thank God. When one's been sitting with people for three days, one's fed up, one's had enough. But next week we want to go away: stay a couple of days in Taos, then on to Mexico. You should write to me:

c/o. British Consulate, 1. Aven. Madero, *Mexico. D.F.*

until I send you a new address. Brett is travelling with us: we don't know what else she could do, and we can't leave her here by herself. – I'm glad to be going to Mexico: don't know why, but I always want to travel southwards. Here it is already cold, too, especially at night. The sun doesn't come [Frieda Lawrence interjects: up] over the mountains until 7.30: then it turns warm. And then the horses stand stock-still, numbed with cold, in the middle of the alfalfa-field, soaking themselves again in the sun-warmth. Mostly the sun is hot like July: but today it's cloudy.

I hope you got your parcel with blanket and pictures. You'll like them, I'm sure. – I send you ten pounds for wood. You've got to keep yourself nice and warm.

Here we're shutting everything up. We're taking the good things, silver, rugs, pictures, beds, on the wagon down to Del Monte, to good William and Rachel. Del Monte belongs, you know, to Mr. Hawk, William's father. The old people have a biggish house, but travel a lot, to California etc. The young ones, William and his wife Rachel and the one-year-old child, live in the log-cabin where we stayed two years ago. They make butter there and look after cows and chickens. Every evening we ride down, to get milk and post from William. He always brings the letters up from the post-box. Rachel and William will keep and take good care of everything for us. Monday, a Mr Murray, workman, comes to make shutters.[1] We're letting all the horses stay

[1] Scott Murray, handyman, 'an obliging workman with a team of horses' who lived in San Cristobal (Parmenter 271).

here, till December, when the big snow comes. Then William takes them down to Del Monte (only $2\frac{1}{2}$ km), and feeds them with alfalfa every day. And so on till spring, when we come back again.

I don't know how long we want to stay in Mexico City. I want to go southwards again, to Oaxaca, where the Maya Indians and the Zapotecs live. There it's always warm: even hot. And there I'd like to finish my novel.

Here the mountains are gold with aspens and cotton-wood trees, and red with scrub-oak, little oaks: wonderful. Firs and spruce, though, almost black. A beautiful moment! But won't last.

Wiedersehen, schwiegermutter. Winter returns for all old ladies, unfortunately!

DHL]

3251. To Emily King, 2 October 1924

Text: MS Needham; PC v. Corn Dance, Pueblo of San Domingo, N. Mex; Unpublished.

Del Monte Ranch.
2 Oct. 1924

My dear Pamela.

We were at Taos for the San Geronimo fiesta – found your letter when we came back – Didn't you bury father with my mother? Wasn't there room?

I sent you ten pounds and Ada altogether twenty. If you want anything more, let me know. My agent, with a great struggle, has just got me another $1000 from Seltzer – and I have now some money again in England.[1]

We are leaving here next week – stay a bit in Taos – then on to Mexico.

c/o The British Consulate, 1. Aven. Madero. Mexico. D.F.

will find me, till I send an address. – It's a pity Peg's honors won't get her Matric. exemption – and she'll have to get Matric. Though I hate exams. and exam. fiends. – You remember I promised to help with her education. Let me know definitely what are the plans for her for next year.

DHL

3252. To Margaret King, [2 October 1924]

Text: MS Needham; PC v. How Navajo Rugs Are Made; Unpublished.

[Kiowa]
2. Oct.

My dear Peg.

Bad luck about those honors. But except that you do want to go on for a

[1] On 20 October, DHL recorded that he had $2285.21 in his Chase National Bank and £303.00 in his English bank accounts (Tedlock, *Lawrence MSS* 99).

degree, I don't care. I don't care for those smart exam-fiends who are so clever and so irritating.

Did you get my letter about the ranch? It seems long since I sent it.

It seems to me there is no such desperate hurry about your getting matric. You don't want your degree till you are nineteen or twenty – you can take Matric next June. What's the hurry. I told your mother I would help with your education. Why don't you send me a notion of what you want: how much school costs and will cost, and all that. Send a little plan of the future, what you will require for the next three years or so, and we'll fix it up.

We leave here next week – it's freezing every night now, but usually, hot days. How is Joan?

Love DHL

3253. To Thomas Seltzer, 2 October 1924

Text: MS UT; PC v. Fisher's Peak and Trinidad, Colorado; Postmark, Valdez OCT 3 1924; Lacy, *Seltzer* 145.

Del Monte Ranch, Questa. New Mexico
2 Oct 1924

Dear Thomas

I wish you would send a copy of *Touch and Go* and *Widowing of Mrs Holroyd* to

Carlo Linati, *Camerlata* (Como). Italy.

He says he would like to see if he could translate one for the theatre.

We leave here next week: stay a day or two in Taos: then on to Mexico. I will send you an address. But

c/o The British Consulate, 1. Aven Madero, Mexico DF.

will find me.

Is *The Boy in the Bush* out? Why didn't you send me just one copy? Have you sent out my six – or five – copies as I asked? – I am glad you could pay some more money in to Curtis Brown: now I can travel with a more easy mind.

Yrs D. H. Lawrence

3254. To Martin Secker, 2 October 1924

Text: MS UInd; Postmark, Valdez OCT 3 1924; Secker 61–2.

Del Monte Ranch. *Questa*, New Mexico
2 Oct 1924

Dear Secker

We are leaving here next week. If you write, address me

c/o Curtis Brown Ltd, 116 West 39th. St. New York City.
The letters come straight down from New York to Mexico.

Did you send any books to Carlo Linati. I enclose his second letter.[1] If there is anything of mine he wants, let him have it.

And you sent out copies of *The Boy* for me, didn't you? My sisters write they have received none. You have the list of addresses? Send my sisters also a copy of *Memoirs of the Foreign Legion*, will you. It is

Mrs Clarke. Grosvenor Rd. *Ripley nr. Derby*

and

Mrs King. 16 Brooklands Rd. Sneinton Hill, *Nottingham*

– Miss Skinner seems very piqued that *The Boy* is reviewed as *my* work. I wish they attended to her more.

I have sent the novelette 'St. Mawr' to Curtis Brown. Perhaps a better title is 'Two Ladies and a Horse'. Do you think?

We were awfully upset to hear of Gilbert certified insane.[2] Do you think he had fair play?

It was very good of you to send us papers all the summer. Those were our only connection with the 'public' England.

'St. Mawr' came out over 60,000 words: long. It would make a smallish book: or a complete one, with that other story 'The Woman who Rode Away': which Hutchinson's are using, I think – cutting it a bit – in *Woman*: – and with a third story I am doing 'The Princess'. All three have some of this country in them.

If you want me in a hurry,

The British Consulate. 1. Aven. Madero. Mexico D.F.

will find me always.

Magnus' book looks like a Church hymnal:[3] *Ora pro nobis*.[4] Did you send it to Michael Borg and to Don Mauro? I should like Mary Cannan to have a copy[5] – and Catherine Carswell. 110 Heath St. N.W.3.

Yrs D. H. Lawrence

[1] The letter is unlocated.

[2] Gilbert Cannan (1884–1955), novelist and playwright. His mental health had deteriorated over several years; when he was certified he was a patient in Priory Hospital, Roehampton. See n. 5 below and *Letters*, ii. 208.

[3] It had black cloth boards with gold lettering (Roberts B14).

[4] 'Pray for us.'

[5] Mary Cannan, née Ansell (1867–1950), m. (1) (Sir) James Barrie, (2) 1910, Gilbert Cannan. Mary Cannan was a neighbour and became a friend of the Lawrences when they lived near Chesham, Bucks., in 1914–15; their friendship had been renewed in Capri and then in Sicily, in early 1920.

3255. To Ada Clarke, [2 October 1924]
Text: MS Clarke; PC v. Pueblo Indian Corn Dance Ceremony; Unpublished.

Del Monte Ranch
– 2 Oct.

My dear Sister

Your letter yesterday about father: it does upset one.

We leave here next week for Taos on our way to Mexico. Write
c/o British Consulate, 1. Av. Madero, *Mexico. D.F.*
– until I send an address.

I hope you got *Boy in the Bush* from Secker: also *Memoirs of the Foreign Legion*, with my introduction – I asked him long ago to send them, but have now reminded him again.

The nights are already very cold here – but the days hot. I feel like going south, though. – No, don't send things here – one has to pay so much duty, and I don't need anything.

Love. DHL

3256. To John Middleton Murry, 3 October 1924
Text: MS NYPL; Huxley 614–16.

Del Monte Ranch, *Questa*, New Mexico
3 October 1924

Dear Jack

We had your letter. I am glad you have a good time on the Dorset coast, with Violet.[1] But don't you become the 'mossy stone'– unless, of course, you want to.[2] And perhaps you will find fulfilment in a baby.[3] Myself, I am not for postponing to the next generation – and so ad infinitum. Frieda says every woman hopes her *baby* will become the Messiah. It takes a man, not a baby. – I'm afraid there'll be.no more Son Saviours. One was almost too much, in my opinion.

I'm glad you like the Hopi Dance article. All races have one root, once one gets there. Many stems from one root: the stems never to commingle or 'understand' one another. I agree Forster doesn't 'understand' his Hindu. And India to him is just negative: because he doesn't go down to the root to

[1] At The Old Coastguard Station, Chesil Beach, near Abbotsbury, Dorset which Murry had bought in April 1924 (John Carswell, *Lives and Letters*, 1978, pp. 204–5).

[2] Wordsworth, 'She dwelt among the untrodden ways' (1800), ll. 5–6: 'A violet by a mossy stone/ Half hidden from the eye!'

[3] See Letter 3516 and n. 5.

meet it. But the *Passage to India* interested me very much. At least the repudiation of our white bunk is genuine, sincere, and pretty thorough, it seems to me. Negative, yes. But King Charles *must* have his head off. Homage to the headsman.

We are leaving here next week. There was a flurry of wild snow in the air yesterday, and the nights are icy. But now, at ten oclock in the morning, to look across the desert at the mountains you'd think June morning was shining. Frieda is washing in the porch: Brett is probably stalking a rabbit with a 22-gun: I am looking out of the kitchen door at the far blue mountains, and the gap, the tiny gate that leads down into the canyon and away to Santa Fe. And in ten days time we shall be going south – to Mexico. The high thin air gets my chest, bronchially. It's *very* good for the lungs, but fierce for tender bronchi.

We shall never 'drop in on one another' again: the ways go wide apart. Sometimes I regret that you didn't take me at what I am, last Christmas: and come here and take a different footing. But apparently you did what was in you: and I what is in me, I do it. – As for Kot, there is just nothing to say. It is absurd, but there it is. The ultimate son of Moses pining for heavy tablets. I believe the old Moses wouldn't have valued the famous tablets if they hadn't been ponderous, and millstones round everybody's neck. It's just Hebraic. And now the tablets are to be papier mâché. Pfui! carito! it's all bunk: heavy, uninspired bunk. Che lo sia![1] – Kangaroo was never Kot. Frieda was on the wrong track.[2] And now Kot is sodden.

– Despedida, despedida
Eran fuentes de dolores –[3]

The country here is very lovely at the moment, aspens high on the mountains like a fleece of gold. Ubi est ille Jason?[4] The scrub oak is dark red, and the wild birds are coming down to the desert. It is time to go south. – Did I tell you my father died on Sept. 10th., the day before my birthday. – The autumn always gets me badly, as it breaks into colours. I want to go south, where there is no autumn, where the cold doesn't crouch over one like a snow-leopard waiting to pounce. The heart of the North is dead, and the fingers of cold are corpse

[1] 'Who knows!' ['Chi . . .'].
[2] An identification Frieda continued to make; see her letter to Richard Aldington, 20 November 1948 in *Frieda Lawrence and her Circle: Letters from, to and about Frieda Lawrence*, ed. Harry T. Moore and Dale B. Montague (1981), p. 89.
[3] ' – Bid farewell, farewell/They were fountains of sorrow –'.
[4] 'Where is that Jason?'

fingers. There is no more hope northwards, and the salt of its inspiration is the tingling of the viaticum on the tongue.

Sounds as if I was imitating an Ossianic lament.[1]

You can get me in Mexico

c/o The British Consulate, Av. Madero #1. Mexico. D. F.

But I want to go south again, to Oaxaca, to the Zapotecas and the Maya. Quien sabe, si se puede![2]

Adios DHL

3257. To Clarence Thompson, 5 October 1924

Text: MS UT; Postmark, Valdez OCT 7 1924: Moore 812–13.

Del Monte Ranch. *Questa*, New Mexico.
5 October 1924

Dear Clarence

We are in the throes of packing up, to go down to Mexico. I expect to leave this ranch on Saturday – stay two days at Taos – then go on to El Paso. I will send you an address from Mexico: or

c/o The British Consulate. 1. Av. Madero. Mexico D.F.

will always find me.

We went down to Taos for two days, for the San Geronimo fiesta. I know that it is no use keeping up strained or violent relationships. In myself I remain the same. But, for the rest, one must free oneself from any violent feelings in these matters, and go one's way quietly, and free, beyond it all.

We have built a porch over my door, and used two of your twisted pillars. They look very nice. Frieda is reserving the other two for a room she wants to build for herself.

By now you will have begun your work. I hope you will like it and that it will satisfy you. The best thing is to work and to have peace with oneself, and within oneself. Enough of frictional reactions.

I am glad to go away, too. To go right away and forget, and perhaps get a bit of a new beat in my heart, in Mexico. One gets badly hurt. But so long as one is not damaged, it doesn't matter much.

[1] Ossian was a legendary Gaelic bard, third century AD. In the 1760s James MacPherson published poems which he falsely claimed were Ossian's. See 'The Princess' in *St. Mawr*, ed. Finney, 159:15–17.

[2] 'Who knows, if one can!'

We stayed the two nights in your house: dismal it felt, too. And with Mabel's permission we brought away your paint-brushes and materials. Frieda has already painted a picture with them.

Aur revoir! Clarence. The thing to do is to surmount the whole misery, and be beyond it and at peace.

F. says she wants to write and thank you for your effort on her nephew's behalf.

Yrs D. H. Lawrence

3258. To Robert Mountsier, 5 October 1924

Text: MS Smith; Postmark, [. . .] OCT 7 1924; Unpublished.

Del Monte Ranch. *Questa*. New Mexico
5 October 1924

Dear Mountsier

You choose to take an offensive tone in your letter.

I said the money I received from Seltzer in 1923, and not the money I received in 1924.[1] I meant it too.

You put moreover a deliberate mis-statement in your letter. You say that the commission of 10% on royalties from Seltzer in 1923 is *still owing to you*, less some twenty dollars. Do you want deliberately to tell a lie? I have two receipts from you, for your commission which I paid in April and October 1923. – And Seltzer has *still* not completed the payment on the October 1923 statement. On the statement of April 1924 I have received as yet nothing from him.

I must once more ask you, therefore, to hand over to Mr Barmby all Manuscripts and papers of mine you have in your possession. They are not in any sense your property. And what name does one give to a man who deliberately detains property not his own?

[1] DHL had carried on extensive correspondence early in 1923 to settle accounts with Mountsier; the payment was delayed until late October (*Letters*, iv. 521) when DHL had received the statement for autumn royalties from Seltzer. But Mountsier had claimed a 'third and last payment' in December which DHL refused to pay (p. 550). For the particular letter to which DHL is referring, see p. 128 n. 2.

Kindly address any further communication c/o Mr Barmby.

Yours faithfully D. H. Lawrence[1]

3259. To Curtis Brown, 8 October 1924

Text: MS UT; Huxley 616–17.

Del Monte Ranch. *Questa*, New Mexico
8 Oct. 1924.

Dear Curtis Brown

We are packing up to leave here on Saturday – 11th. I suppose we shall stay a day or two in Taos[2] then on to Mexico City. It is time to go. Last evening came a deep six inches of snow, that is thawing slowly today. It is very early,

[1] A handwritten note on the verso of the envelope reads:

Dear Bob;
I want to read your book about Taos when it is published
Hope you are well

Sincerely Bill Hawk.

Mountsier replied to DHL on 8 November 1924 (TMSC UT):

Dear Lawrence,

I have shown to Mr. Barmby your letter of March 3, 1923, in which you wrote: "Will you write that you are satisfied if I pay you ten per-cent of all my receipts from Seltzer for this current year? There will probably be very little from any other source. And will you promise to send me back all MSS and papers belonging to me as soon as you go east."

On December 24, 1923, you wrote from London, after I had written you regarding a third and last payment, covering receipts or royalties for the second half of 1923: "I don't understand that. I thought I said clearly a tenth of the money I received in spring and autumn, 1923, from Seltzer. That was what I meant. And that I have given you." I sent you receipts for the payments of ten per cent. commission on royalties received by you from Seltzer for the periods July–December, 1922, and January–June, 1923.

My letters of January 11 and September 29, of this year, referred to the unpaid instalment of ten per cent on royalties from Seltzer for the period July–December, 1923, which I consider due on the basis of what you wrote – you wrote *for*, not *during*.

I also wish to point out that in your letter of October 5, 1924, you accuse me of deliberately lying and of adopting an offensive tone. You cannot prove either by my letters to you. At no time during my relations with you as your representative in this country nor since their termination in January, 1923, have I adopted an offensive attitude toward you despite certain actions and words on your part.

Although you may not admit it now, you know that, for the two years and more I was acting as your business representative in the United States at your request and for what you chose to pay me, everything I did was in your interest, and that, in view of the comparatively small payments of 1921–1922 and despite your payment of my fare to and from Taos, for a trip made to save you the trouble, not to mention saving you from Seltzer, the payment in question will not remunerate me for all the work I did for you in connection with "The Trespasser," held by Duffield, "The Rainbow" and other books held by Huebsch, "Sons and Lovers," held by Kennerley, and work with the contracts and typescripts of five of your books published since June, 1923 – for all of which you know that to date I have received nothing.

Yours truly, Robert Mountsier

[2] Taos] Mexico City

and summer will more or less come back, but it is the first real stroke from the paw of winter. Besides I want to go. I always do want to go South, though here is lovely.

I sent you last week the typescript of 'St. Mawr' – a long novelette. This week-end I will send you 'The Princess'. It is being typed now. I guess it is 15,000 words. With 'The Woman Who Rode Away' and 'St. Mawr' it will easily make a book of three novelettes. But not gay, alas. I enclose herewith the agreements with the Deutsche Verlagsanstalt.[1] Keep my copy for me.

I'm glad you saw Seltzer. I'm sure he's in a bad way, poor devil: though he did help to bring it on himself, trying to be a big publisher when God cut him out a little one; if not tiny.

I wonder if you had a nice time in America. *Innerlich*, one usually has a tough time here, I think, though *äusserlich* it's all right.

I liked Barmby very much, and all your people in London are awfully nice. But I do wonder how you make such big outfits pay. I'm afraid I don't help much, that way.

Yrs D. H. Lawrence

3260. To Catherine Carswell, 8 October 1924

Text: MS YU; Postmark, Questa OCT 10 1924; Carswell 221.

Del Monte Ranch. *Questa*, New Mexico
8 October 1924

Dear Catherine

A long time since I wrote you, because I lost your address. Anyhow I'm glad you are in the country with a place of your own.[2]

We are packing up to leave here. Last night came the first snow: six deep inches. Today it's thawing dismally. It's very early for snow. And no doubt the Indian summer will come back. But it's a blow. – The horses have come up, very *miserably*, want to be ridden. Well, I shall have to ride down for the milk.

If the roads are passable, we shall go down to Taos on Saturday, stay a day or two, then go down to Mexico City. My spirit always wants to go south – Perhaps one feels a bit of hope down there. Anyhow the white civilisation makes me feel worse every day. Brett will go down with us. But if we take a house, she must take a little place of her own. Not be too close. Here she has a little one-room cabin to herself. There is a 2-room guesthouse: and still a third sort of little log barn we can make into a little house. It's so much easier that way.

The summer has gone. It was very beautiful up here. We worked hard, and

[1] See p. 38 n. 2.

[2] See p. 19 n. 1.

spent very little money. And we had the place all to ourselves, and our horses the same. It was good to be alone and responsible. But also it is very *hard* living up against these savage Rockies. The savage things are a bit gruesome, and they try to down one. – But far better they than the white disintegration. – I did a long novelette – about 60,000 words – about 2 women and a horse – 'St Mawr'. But it may be called 'Two Women and a Horse'. And two shorter novelettes, about 15000 words: 'The Woman Who Rode Away' and 'The Princess'. 'St. Mawr' ends here. They are all about this country more or less. I believe Hutchinsons are doing 'The Woman Who Rode Away' in their *Woman* (but cut down). They are all sad. After all, they're true to what is.

Seltzer still hovers on the brink of bankruptcy, and keeps me on the edge of the same. But by being careful we manage to have two thousand dollars to go to Mexico with.

I don't suppose we shall be back till end of April. Snow comes so late. I wonder if you'll be able to get over. I believe it would be just as cheap to come Hamburg – Amerika line Plymouth to Vera Cruz – Mexico. Maybe cheaper. But we'll see.

I loathe winter. They gas about the Nordic races, over here, but I believe they're dead, dead, dead. I hate all that comes from the north.

Poor Don, hope he has work, and that John Patrick flourishes. I ordered *Boy in the Bush* for you from Secker and also *Memoirs of the Foreign Legion*. I hope you had both.

The house is half dismantled: we are fastening the place up and leaving it. The snow is dropping wet off the pine-trees, the desert seems decomposing in the distance – Ugh! I must catch Aaron, my black horse, and ride down in the slush under those snow-dripping trees. Ugh! – But it's all in a lifetime.

F[rieda] sends her love, with many good wishes from us both.

D. H. Lawrence

3261. To Nancy Pearn, 8 October 1924

Text: MS UT; Unpublished.

Del Monte Ranch. *Questa*. New Mexico
8 October 1924

Dear Miss Pearn

I sent the 'St. Mawr' novelette – and now am sending 'The Princess'. Again she's 15,000 words, alas. But with 'The Woman Who Rode Away', this makes three novelettes for a book, which is what Secker wanted. Whether he'll want them when he sees them, who knows. But he may want to publish them in the spring.[1] In that case, if no-one else wants 'The Woman Who Rode' at her full length, Hutchinson's can have her and cut her short, if they like, and *if you think it wise to offer it again*. – If the things are coming out whole in book form *soon*, then the magazines can please themselves what they do: the devil take them: they can cut as they please.[2]

We leave here on Saturday. The first snow has fallen. Address me c/o Mr Barmby, I think that's best. Thank Miss Chapter for her letter. – I hope you had a good holiday. Where?

We shall be in Mexico City by the 20th of the month, I suppose c/o The British Consulate. 1. Av. Madero. Mexico D.F. – if ever there is a hurry.

Best wishes.

Yrs D. H. Lawrence

3262. To William Hawk, [11 October 1924]

Text: MS UT; Postmark, [. . .] OCT 13 1924; Unpublished.

[Taos, New Mexico][3]
Sat

Dear William

The vet left Taos some time ago – may be back in three weeks. – – Shall send an Indian to fetch the Azul down to Taos to be looked at.

Think we shall leave Thursday.

Thank you so much for everything.

D. H. Lawrence

Writing in post office.

3263. To Emily King, [13 October 1924]

Text: MS Needham; PC v. [Indians Dancing]; Postmark, Taos OCT 14 1924; Unpublished.

Taos
13 Oct.

We've left the ranch – stay here two more days – expect to be in Mexico by the 20th.

DHL

[1] Secker published *St. Mawr Together with The Princess* on 14 May 1925; Knopf published *St. Mawr* on its own on 5 June.

[2] See p. 109 n. 2.

[3] Written on headed paper.

3264. To John Middleton Murry, [13 October 1924]
Text: MS NYPL; PC v. Hopi Snake Dance, Arizona; Postmark, Taos OCT 14 1924; Unpublished.

Taos.
13 Oct.

– We leave Taos on Wed. – expect to be in Mexico City by the 20th. – If you publish the 'Snake Dance' article will you send copies to my sisters:

Mrs L.A Clarke. Grosvenor Rd. Ripley nr Derby
Mrs S. King. 16 Brooklands Rd, Sneinton Hill, *Nottingham*.

Hot weather again here, and very lovely: F[rieda] weeping to leave her ranch. But the snow will come again.

DHL

3265. To Edward McDonald, 15 October 1924
Text: MS UT; Postmark, Taos OCT 16 1924; *Centaur* 16.

[Taos, New Mexico][1]
Wednesday. 15 Oct 1924

Dear Professor McDonald

I will send you that book today – rather smudgy, but as the people have left it.[2] We leave here tomorrow for Santa Fe – expect we shall be in Mexico City by the 21st. – It has turned warm again here – but you can't tell when the snow will pounce down again. It's the 7,000 ft. altitude.

The Oxford Press cabled me that they had fixed the illustrations and to hurry the Epilogue. Well, they'll get it. Thank you so much for all the trouble you took.

Taos m'agace les nerfs.[3]

D. H. Lawrence

3266. To Mabel Dodge Luhan, [16 October 1924]
Text: MS Brill; PC; Luhan 279.

[Santa Fe]
[16 October 1924]

Dear Mabel –

It was a lovely drive: very beautiful, and about 22 miles further – Bynner comes Saturday. Spud is hesitating – one of the 'is lost' sort. I don't think he'll come with the car. We shall get away if possible today – if not, we shall have to stay till Sunday, as we'd get no Visas if we arrived El Paso Sunday. – If you

[1] Written on headed paper.
[2] *Memoirs of the Foreign Legion*: see Letter 3245.
[3] 'Taos gets on my nerves.'

want to write your apologia pro vita sua[1] – do it as honestly as you can – and if it's got the right thing in it, I can help you with it once it's done. You haven't enough restraint in you for creative writing, but you can make a document. Only *dont* go at it too slap-dash – makes it unreal. – Eliz. was a good girl.[2]

DHL

3267. To Mark Gertler, [18 October 1924]

Text: MS SIU; PC v. Kiva of Ancient Cliff Dwellers, in Ceremonial Cave, Rito de los Frijoles Canyon, New Mexico; Postmark, Santa Fe OCT 18 1924; Unpublished.

Santa Fe
18 Oct.

Thanks for your letter – glad you are well – we leave here for Mexico tomorrow – will write from there.

DHL

3268. To John Middleton Murry, [18 October 1924]

Text: MS NYPL; PC v. Chili (Red Pepper) Drying in front of Adobe Home, New Mexico; Postmark, Santa Fe OCT 18 1924; Unpublished.

Santa Fe.
18 Oct.

We go on tomorrow to El Paso – very lovely autumn down here. Shall be in Mexico City (D. V.) by the 23rd.

DHL

3269. To Witter Bynner and Willard Johnson, [19 October 1924]

Text: MS YU; Unpublished.

[Santa Fe][3]
[19 October 1924]

Banged and thumped at 9:45 – house of the dead – sorry not to see you – Tony suddenly in a rush – Spoodle, write and let me know about the winter, and if you want that little article[4] – Bynner, are you coming to see us?

DHL

[1] The title of Cardinal Newman's autobiographical work (1864).

[2] Elizabeth (b. c. 1907) was Mabel Luhan's foster daughter; she suffered from arrested development. (This sentence was crossed out, and not printed in Luhan.)

[3] This letter is written on the back of a Hotel de Vargas envelope which is addressed to Bynner and Johnson in an unknown hand.

[4] Possibly 'Climbing Down Pisgah' (see Letter 3227 and n. 1).

3270. To Catherine Carswell, 20 October 1924

Text: MS YU; PC v. Plaza de Gallos. Cuidad Juarez, Mexico, View of a Cock Pit during an interesting moment; Postmark, El Paso OCT [. . .] 1924; cited in Moore, *Poste Restante* 81.

El Paso
20 Oct 1924

Don't know if I've remembered your address properly. – We cross into Mexico this morning – hot down here.[1]

Saluti. DHL

3271. To William Hawk, [20 October 1924]

Text: MS UT; PC v. Drawing the Threads in Mexico; Postmark, El Paso OCT [. . .] 1924; Unpublished.

El Paso.
20 Oct.

We cross the border this morning – stayed to see Bynner in Santa Fe. Hagenbeck's circus in town here[2] – just saw the procession – very nice.

DHL

3272. To Hon. Dorothy Brett, [23 October 1924]

Text: MS UCin; Irvine, Brett 37.

[Hotel Regis, Mexico D. F.][3]
[23 October 1924]
9.20.

Rattled for you in vain. We are going down to breakfast – be back in about an hour or less.

DHL

3273. To Baroness Anna von Richthofen, [24 October 1924]

Text: MS Jeffrey; PC v. Constitution Square and Cathedral, Mexico D.F.; Postmark, Mexico 24 OCT [. . .]924; Unpublished.

Hotel Monte Carlo. Av. Uruguay, Mexico. D. F.
24 Okt

Sind wieder hier im alten hotel – die Leute sehr freundlich und gut. Wir

[1] See Brett 159–60 on passport complications.

[2] Founded in Hamburg, Germany, in 1887 by Carl Hagenbeck; sold in 1905–6 to Benjamin E. Wallace (1848–1921); by 1921 it was run by the American Circus Company.

[3] Written on headed paper. When Brett and the Lawrences arrived in Mexico City after midnight, they stayed at the Hotel Regis, but DHL took a 'violent dislike' to it (Brett 162), and they moved to the Hotel Monte Carlo later the same day (23 October): 'The proprietor welcomes you warmly and we are given the best rooms.' This changing replicated the Lawrences' experience in March 1923: they moved from the Regis (which faced Avenida Juárez) to the Monte Carlo, run by an Italian family named Fortes, and stayed over a month; see *Letters*, iv. 414.

bleiben hier ein Paar wochen, dann will ich nach Oaxaca gehen – südwärts. Vielleicht bleiben wir der Winter da. – Etwas unsicher ist das Land – besser aber da unter. Leb wohl.

DHL

[Are back here in the old hotel – the people very friendly and good. We're staying here a couple of weeks, then I want to to Oaxaca – southwards. Perhaps we spend the winter there. – The country is a bit unsettled – but better down there. Farewell.

DHL]

3274. To Witter Bynner, [24 October 1924]
Text: MS HU; PC v. Tiger. Aztec Sculpture, Mexico; Huxley 618–19.

Hotel Monte Carlo. Av. Uruguay, Mexico D.F.
Friday

We got in after midnight on Wed. – train so late – journey otherwise uneventful, and not unpleasant. – You can buy tickets and book pullman now in El Paso station – much easier. But the food in the Pullman the same swindle. There has been a good deal of rain here – country looks nice, and it's almost chilly. The capital is shabby and depressed – no business doing – no money – everybody rather depressed – not a very nice feeling in the town. I think we shall go in a fortnight to Oaxaca. The English Vice Consul has a brother a priest in the Cathedral Chapter there and he would sponsor us![1] Ye Gods! But the man says it's very nice down there, and a perfect climate. If we stay, whatever will Idella say! – The Montecarlo is *almost* unchanged, but not many guests. We chose to go upstairs – Brett in your old room, we in the one inside, where the monkey, the parrot, and the Chihuahua dog abode. With a bowl of candied fruit, a flask of chianti, those coloured majolica cups and tea, we only need you two to push back the clock.[2] They're *very* nice to us in the hotel.

DHL

Somerset Maugham is here.[3]

[1] See Letters 3304 and p. 177 n. 2 and 3338 and n. 8.
[2] Bynner and Johnson had joined the Lawrences for most of their initial stay in Mexico in Spring 1923.
[3] William Somerset Maugham (1874–1965), novelist and playwright. (See *Letters*, iii. 505, 566.)

3275. To Emily King, [24 October 1924]

Text: MS Needham; PC v. Church of Guadalupe, Mexico; Postmark, Mexico D.F. 24 OCT 1924; Unpublished.

Hotel Monte Carlo. Av. Uruguay, Mexico D. F.
24 Oct

Arrived quite safely – things still unsettled down here, and the city depressed, nobody doing business. I expect in a fortnight we shall go south to Oaxaca, and perhaps stay the winter there.

Love DHL

3276. To John Middleton Murry, [24 October 1924]

Text: MS NYPL; PC v. National Museum, Mexico, D.F.; Postmark, Mexico D.F. 24 OCT 1924; Moore 815.

Hotel Monte Carlo. Av. Uruguay, Mexico D. F.
24 *Oct.*

Had quite a good journey down here – found your letter saying you may lecture in America. *When*? – I think we shall go down to Oaxaca, in the south, in about a fortnight – perhaps stay the winter there. – Things are still unsettled – mistrust – and no business doing – a depression in the city. – Somerset Maugham is here – suppose we'll see him.

DHL

3277. To William Hawk, [24 October 1924]

Text: MS UT; PC v. Constitution Square and Cathedral, Mexico D.F.; Postmark, Mexico D.F. 24 OCT 192[. . .]; Unpublished.

Hotel Monte Carlo. Av. Uruguay. Mexico D. F
Friday

We got to Mexico all right – train very late. Things said to be unsettled – no business doing, the city a bit depressed. But I think we shall go south to Oaxaca in about a fortnight. I wonder what it's like at the ranch now. Send us a line.

DHL

Many thanks for sending on the letters.

3278. To Zelia Nuttall, 24 October 1924

Text: MS Forster; Moore 815.

Hotel MonteCarlo, Av. Uruguay, Mexico D. F.
24 Oct 1924

Dear Mrs Nuttall[1]

My wife and I and a friend, Dorothy Brett, Lord Esher's daughter – are here again for a little while. We may go down to Oaxaca for the winter. But should like to see you again before we go. Will you lunch with us in town, at Sanborn's[2] or where you like? Or shall we come to tea in Coyoacan?[3]

Greetings from my wife and myself.

Yours sincerely D. H. Lawrence

3279. To Willard Johnson, [25 October 1924]

Text: MS YU; Huxley 619–20.

Monte Carlo Hotel. Av. Uruguay. Mexico D.F.
Sat

Dear Spoodle

I suddenly remember I promised Mr Hawk at Del Monte Ranch, *Valdez* – a typewriter ribbon for a Smith Premier typewriter: and I clean forgot it. If you can find one in Santa Fe, do please send it him with my compliments, and tell me how much it is.

Mrs Nuttall came to lunch today – full of news about the murdered Mrs Evans etc.[4] They expect more messes here – not revolutions, because nobody has any money to make one. But the place feels depressed. – Willie Maugham telegraphed me: he's gone to Cuernavaca, 'to work'. Damn his eyes and his work. – Gamio is in Yucatan with the Carnegie Institute excavators – at Chichen Itá – digging up the dead instead of looking after the living.[5] Have just written to Genaro Estrada, of the P.E.N. Club here. Will let you know

1 Zelia Maria Magdalena Nuttall (1857–1933), American archaeologist and author specialising in ancient and colonial history of Mexico. Her *Fundamental Principles of Old and New World Civilizations* (1901) was one source of DHL's *The Plumed Serpent*, in which she appears as Mrs Norris. DHL had met her on his first trip to Mexico; see *Letters*, iv. 421 and n. and Nehls, ii. 495–6 n. 87.

2 A well-known eating place, located in the House of Tiles on Avenida Madero.

3 Zelia Nuttall's house in Coyoacán, a southern suburb, had belonged originally to Pedro de Alvarado (1495?–1541), conquistador and lieutenant of Cortes.

4 Rosalie Evans, an American, died 2 August 1924 in defending her hacienda which she refused to surrender to the agrarian reform followers of Obregón who were attempting to confiscate it; see Parmenter 6–7.

5 The Carnegie Institution of Washington and the Department of Education of the University of Mexico were jointly carrying on excavations in Yucatán: including the finding of a Mayan altar at Chichen Itza (*New York Times*, 16 January and 15 March 1925, pp. 3 and II. 3).

what he's like when I've seen him. But expect nothing of this lousy city. – I feel they're all a bit of a fraud, with their self-seeking bolshevism. – The Brit. Consul very attentive – the Vice – has a brother a priest in the Chapter at Oaxaca. I think we shall go down there in a week's time: D. V. and all well. – They say the next revolution begins *on Monday*.[1] – We lunch tomorrow in Coyoacán, and dine in Tlalpam.[2] Good for us. – But I *really* feel cynical about these 'patriots' and 'socialists' down here. It's a mess. – Tube-roses on the table very strong smelling. F[rieda] got a sneezing cold. Making after dinner tea, with ess. peppermint, on the spirit-lamp. Bought Mrs Nuttall a door-knob to match, in the volador.[3] Very nice sarapes around: very nice: 16 pesos. Bought none yet, but have my eye on a fine white one, with brown markings. – This city no go. – For $50. got 101.50 pesos.

Vale DHL

3280. To Alfred Decker Hawk, 29 October 1924

Text: MS UT; Unpublished.

Hotel Monte Carlo. Av. Uruguay, Mexico D.F.
29 Oct. 1924

Dear Mr Hawk

I clean forgot that typewriter ribbon in Sante Fe: but I wrote and asked Spud Johnson to send it you.

Now I want to bother you again. In that green iron trunk is an envelope with the deeds of the ranch, and mixed among the ranch papers is a deed of a piece of land Mabel Lujan bought in Mill Valley, California. Now she would like to sell this bit of land in Mill Valley to Witter Bynner, who is suddenly crazy to have a home of his own. Would you be so good as to send the deed to him: Witter Bynner. Box 1061. Santa Fe, by registered mail. I think you have the key of the trunk. If not, a duplicate hangs in the green cupboard in my room, at the ranch: at the side. – But I am sure you have the key. – And William will keep a list of all the expenses.

It has been cold here, and we've both had *grippe*: and wished ourselves back at the ranch. It isn't so very nice in Mexico City now: everything depressed, nobody doing any business, everybody on the qui vive, uncertain as to what will happen when Calles gets in.[4] And nearly everybody with influenza colds. – The ranch is *much* nicer, really. If it's not icy up there.

[1] Cf. Letter 3290 and n. 2.

[2] With (Sir) Norman King (1880–1963), British Consul-General, 1920–6, and painter, who lived at Allende #24, Tlalpam; see Letter 3355 and *Letters*, iv. 534 and n. 4.

[3] The Volador was a Mexico City market which specialised in used hardware (letter to the eds. from Ross Parmenter).

[4] Plutarco Elías Calles (1877–1945) was inaugurated on 1 December 1924; he was president until 1928.

Next week we are going south to Oaxaca, where it is certainly warmer and probably more humanly agreeable. Meanwhile one sniffs and sneezes and goes out to dinner and drinks more drinks than one ever wants to drink, and wishes one hadn't. Altogether I don't like cities: and once more I realise it.

Remember us warmly to Mrs Hawk. If we don't like Oaxaca, I shall feel like walking straight back to New Mexico. Except that one ought to stay somewhere warm for the winter.

And thank you very much for all your kindness.

Yours Sincerely D. H. Lawrence

I shall be looking for news from you or from William.

3281. To Witter Bynner, 29 October 1924

Text: MS HU; Postmark, Mexico D.F. 29 OCT 1924; Huxley 620–1.

Hotel Monte Carlo, Av. Monte Carlo. Mexico D.F.
29 Oct 1924

Dear Bynner

Your letter to Frieda today about the deed. I think it's there all right, among the other deeds in the green iron trunk down at Del Monte, and I've written to Mr Hawk asking him to send it you at once, registered, to Box 1061.[1]

So you may buy that bit of land? A la guerre comme à la guerre.

We've both had terrible colds like the one I had in Puebla. And if it's merely Mexico City, it's *not* worth coming for. Chilly, reeking with influenza, and in bad spirits, the town. I think we go down to Oaxaca on Monday. – Somerset Maugham left for Cuernavaca the day we got in – but apparently he too is no loss. Disagreeable, with no fun left in him, and terrified for fear he won't be able to do his next great book, with a vivid Mexican background, before Christmas.[2] – A narrow-gutted 'artist' with a stutter.

We lunched with the venerable Mrs Nuttall: who has been nine months in California, without, apparently, bringing forth. But she was nice, and gave us lots of flowers. Dinner at Coyoacan, and drank Absinthe, gin, bouilly, Chablis, Beaune, port, and whiskey from beginning to end of an evening, and was not comforted.[3] – Genaro Estrada of the PEN club called on me – fat and bourgeois but nice – and I'm in for a supper at the Oriental Café on Friday evening, to meet the P.E.N.s.[4] Don't like the thought of it one bit.

[1] See preceding letter.

[2] Maugham published no such volume.

[3] Cf. Psalms lxxvii. 2; Isaiah liv. 11; Mathew ii. 18.

[4] The dinner was in honour of DHL with a printed folder that was both an invitation and programme. Those attending included Luis Quintanilla (see Letter 3289 and n. 1), Eduardo Villaseñor and Genaro Fernández MacGregor (the main speaker); see Parmenter 7–9. See Brett's and Frieda's accounts of DHL's description (Brett 163–4, Frieda Lawrence 162–3).

The Café Oriental was 'a modest downtown restaurant that specialized in chop suey' (Parmenter 7).

Want to get away into the country and be by myself.

Hope Spoodle is FINE!

Give many salutes to Mrs Hughes from us.[1]

Let me know if you get the deed all right: and then, if you *do* it.

DHL

Did Idella's parcel ever turn up? – Is it there, maybe addressed to *me*! – Oh that little silk frock![2]

3282. To Mabel Dodge Luhan, 29 October 1924

Text: MS Brill; Luhan 279–80.

Hotel Monte Carlo. Av. Uruguay. Mexico D. F.
29 Oct 1924

Dear Mabel

Your cable last night, and your note with Bynners today. I have written to Mr Hawk to send the Mill Valley deed to Bynner at once. It's in the green iron trunk down at Del Monte.

We've both had flue colds: everybody in this damned city coughing and sneezing: it's been very chilly: snow low down on Popocatepetl.[3] And the town uneasy and depressed: as if the bottom had fallen out of the barrel. Don't like it.

We think to leave for Oaxaca on Monday. Gamio is reported to be in Yucatan: but I don't care where he is. Somerset Maugham sent me a telegram: he left for Cuernavaca the day we came. But apparently he too is no loss: a bit sour and full of nerves and fidgets lest he shouldn't produce a Magnum opus with a Mexican background before Christmas. – As if he could fail!!

Don't talk to me about plays – the very word makes me swear. At the minute there's not a play-word in me,[4] and I'd rather be in New Mexico. If we don't like Oaxaca we shall probably toddle back. If I'm going to waste my sweetness on the desert air,[5] I'll damned well choose my desert. But pazienza!

Best write

c/o The Brit. Consulate, 2 Av. Madero. (not 1), Mexico D.F.

If I can sit still in Oaxaca, I shall probably pull off a play. But quien sabe!

[1] Christine Hughes, from Santa Fe, a friend of Ida Rauh and a woman with literary interests. She and her daughter visited Italy in December 1926 and renewed their acquaintance with the Lawrences (see, e.g. Letter 3931).

[2] See Letters 3283, 3320 and 3365.

[3] Popocatepetl and Ixtaccihuatl are twin volcanoes, s.e. of Mexico City.

[4] The allusion is to *David*; see Letter 3284.

[5] Gray, 'Elegy Written in a Country Churchyard', l. 56 ['waste its . . .'].

Wonder what happened to the Azul. I'll write and ask Dassburg.[1]
And how is Finney Farm?

DHL

3283. To Idella Purnell, 30 October 1924

Text: MS UT; Nehls, ii. 368.

Hotel MonteCarlo. Av. Uruguay, Mexico D.F.
30 Oct 1924

Dear Idella

I telegraphed to your mother about your parcel and got an answer[2] – a letter – saying she was just *sewing* the silk dress. Anyhow it never arrived, in Santa Fe.

We've been here a few days, with bad colds. Don't like it.

I've promised to go down and look at Oaxaca next week. Probably shan't like that. But I will let you know.

Everybody in this city sneezing and spitting. Hateful to be one of them.

I'll write from Oaxaca. F[rieda] sends regards.

DHL

3284. To Andrew Dasburg, 30 October 1924

Text: MS SyrU; Unpublished.

Hotel Monte Carlo. Av. Uruguay, Mexico. D. F.
30 Oct 1924

Dear Dassburg

I wish you'd write and tell me how my horse – the grey one – the Azul – is. You remember we had him brought down to Mabel's because he had a running place in his jaw. John Dunn was going to look at him:[3] and Louis Cottam was going to bring over the proper vet. from the road camp, early in November. Ask José or Tony how he is, please. And I'll send what money there is to pay.

So far, I'm a bit bored with Mexico. All this city has done is to give Frieda

[1] Andrew Michael Dasburg (1887–1979), American painter, b. Paris; painted *Absence of Mabel Dodge* (1913) and was an early modernist influence in Taos. m. (1) Grace Mott Johnson (1882–1967), sculptor, 1909; divorced, 1922; (2) Nancy Lane, 1928; divorced, 1932; (3) Marina Wister, daughter of Owen Wister, author of *The Virginian*, 1933; separated, 1945. See Nehls, ii. 487–8 n. 40, obituary in *New York Times* (14 August 1979), 15 and Van Deren Coke, *Andrew Dasburg* (Albuquerque, 1979).

[2] Idella Carrie Purnell, née Bragg (1876–?1929), b. Iowa, studied at the University of Texas, then went to Mexico with her parents. m. 1896, George Purnell. They had three children: Idella, Frances-Lee and Ralph. (See also Letters 3317 and 3365.)

[3] John Harris Dunn (1857–1954), stage driver from Taos to Taos Junction.

and me both the grippe, so that I've spent my whole time wiping my nose, and cursing. The city seems stupid and rather dreary, under the circumstances. As a matter of fact I believe it *is* rather stupid and dreary, apart from circumstances. It's very uneasy, no business doing, a great lack of confidence, and a consequent minginess. But next week we intend to go south where it's warmer, and wholesomer: to Oaxaca.

This is the only hotel that begins to be cheap. It's *not* got baths in bedrooms, or any plumbing de luxe, but it's clean, and you can have a room and food for about two dollars American, per day. So best note it. Unless you insist on plumbing.

Somerset Maugham moved down to Cuernavaca the day we arrived. But he too sounds mingy: in an agony to get to work on some real Mexican stuff. God help him. I shan't think of doing anything till we settle somewhere. – Send me a line will you – they'll forward letters from here.

Yrs D. H. Lawrence

Tell Ida the play is not dead, but sleeping.[1] – Wish I was.

3285. To Edward McDonald, 1 November 1924

Text: MS UT; Postmark, Mexico D.F. 1 NOV 24; *Centaur* 16–17.

Hotel Monte Carlo. Av. Uruguay. Mexico D. F.
1 Nov. 1924

Dear Dr McDonald

I heard from Secker today.[2] He said, for the sake of the libraries, two cancel pages were inserted in the *Lost Girl*. As soon as the library demand had ceased, the cancel pages were ignored, and the original printing bound. He doesn't say how many went out with cancel pages – I suppose a thousand or so.

Did you get the copy of the *Memoirs of the Foreign Legion*, which I sent you from Taos?

I think next week we shall go down to Oaxaca. But the best address is

c/o The British Consulate. 2. Av. Madero, Mexico D.F.

Mexico is a bit uneasy and depressed – and I got the bad cold that inhabits this town as a genius loci. Huitzilopochtli ousted.[3] – Yet down here something comes free in one, which the U. S. A keeps tied up.

Best wishes D. H. Lawrence

[1] Cf. Mark v. 39. [2] See p. 122 n. 1.

[3] The Aztec god of war, also of sun and of fire and sacrifices; he led the Aztec migration to Mexico City. DHL used his name and attributes in *The Plumed Serpent*.

3286. To Curtis Brown, 6 November 1924
Text: MS UT; Unpublished.

c/o The British Consulate. Av. Madero #2. Mexico D.F.
6 Nov. 1924

Dear Curtis Brown

Your letter of Oct 16th. – I feel a bit out of patience with Seltzer: he's been so furtive with me. And I'm sure he'll never do much good with me any more. But I leave it to you and Barmby to decide whether to go to Knopf with a book of mine, or not.

As for 'St. Mawr', I don't mind a bit whether it is published as a book by itself, or with the two other stories:[1] just as you and the publishers prefer. – I suppose you received the MS. of 'The Princess'?

It's good news about Australia.[2] Little by little the circle widens, and once it has opened, I don't think it will contract again.

It's uneasy and a bit tense down here: they are all on the qui vive about Calles coming in. But I don't suppose anything very bad will happen. We intend to go down on Saturday – day after tomorrow – to Oaxaca, in the south. It should be peaceful there, and perhaps I can do my Mexican novel, which is a good deal on my mind.

We lunched with Somerset Maugham yesterday. As an individual, I don't care for him. He hates Mexico, and is going away, to Yucatan and Guatemala. I am already tired of hotel and people.

Yrs D. H. Lawrence

[1] See p. 149 n. 1.

[2] Curtis Brown passed to DHL the information in Secker's letter of 16 October (Secker Letter-Book, UIll):

Dear Curtis Brown

I have some quite good news to report on the general D.H.Lawrence situation. Some months ago, partly at your instigation, I approached the London manager of Messrs Robertson & Mullens of Australia, not only with the idea of their taking up an edition of "Kangaroo", but suggesting at the same time that they should import editions of all the Lawrence fiction which I publish, five other titles. The negotiations with Melbourne were naturally of a protracted nature, but the upshot is that they have now agreed to the proposal, taking 500 copies of each book with the exception of "England, My England", of which they only order 250 on the ground of its being a collection of short stories. This gives Lawrence an entirely new public in Australia, and I think we can count in the future of selling them 1000 copies of each new book. In addition I have received a repeat order for 500 "Boy in the Bush", and an initial order of 1000 "Memoirs of the Foreign Legion", from the same firm. These arrangements are only just formally concluded and I hasten to let you know.

Lawrence writes that he has sent you a sixty thousand word story called "St Mawr". Possibly with the story which I believe Hutchinsons are printing somewhere there is the material here for a spring book.

Yours sincerely

3287. To Emily King, [7 November 1924]

Text: MS Needham; PC v. Visitors Attending Great Religious Festival, Pueblo of Taos, New Mexico; Postmark, Mexico D.F. 7 NOV 1924; Unpublished.

Mexico
7 No[*v*]

We are going down to Oaxaca tomorrow – I will write from there.

DHL

3288. To John Middleton Murry, [7 November 1924]

Text: MS NYPL; PC v. La Piramide, S. Juan Teotihucan, Mex; Postmark, Mex[ico] D.[F.] 7[. . .]; Unpublished.

Mexico
7 Nov.

We are going down to Oaxaca tomorrow – lunched with Somerset Maugham yesterday – sehr unsympatisch. He doesn't like Mexico – says the people are unfriendly. One gets what one gives. Will send an address.

DHL

3289. To Luis Quintanilla, [11 November 1924]

Text: MS Subun-So Book Store; Nehls, ii. 375–6.

Hotel Francia. *Oaxaca*
Tuesday

Dear Quintanilla[1]

We got here all right Sunday night: a very amusing journey: by the Ferrocarril Mexicano to Esperanza, then a wild little railway (2 hrs) to Tehuacan: slept the night there in a very nice Hotel Mexico: came on on Sunday, a wild queer lonely journey in a steep gorge.[2] Oaxaca is a very quiet little town,[3] with small but proud Indians – Zapotecas. The climate is perfect

[1] Luis Siegfried Quintanilla (1900–80), Mexican poet and diplomat; born and educated in Paris; Professor of English at the University of Mexico, 1923–5, and worked in the protocol division of Foreign Affairs. He was a member of the group of poets and artists called Los Estridentistas ('The Strident Ones'). m. 1923, Ruth Stallsmith (1903–), 'his gay American wife' (Brett 163). Estrada had asked Quintanilla to look after the Lawrence party after the P.E.N. dinner, and he took DHL to breakfast at Sanborn's and to meet Edward Weston. See Nehls, ii. 368–70, 520–1 n. 57 and Parmenter 8–9.

[2] Esperanza is the junction of the main British-built and owned Mexican Railway from Mexico City to Veracruz, opened 1873, and the branch line connecting with the Ferrocarril Mexicano del Sur, a narrow-gauge railway from Pueblo to Oaxaca – which DHL rode from Tehuacán to Oaxaca – built 1888–92. The gorge is Tomellín Canyon. (See Parmenter xxvi, 4, 53, 334.) For another description of this trip (in reverse) see 'The Flying-Fish' in *St. Mawr*, ed. Finney, pp. 213–16, and see also Brett's description, pp. 166–9.

[3] town] hotel

– cotton dresses, yet not too hot. – It is very peaceful, and has a remote beauty of its own. The Hotel Francia *very* pleasant[1] – such good amusing food – 4 pesos a day for everything. We want to go out to Mitla and Tule and Ejutla[2] – but will wait a bit, and if you come we'll all go together. There are two rivers,[3] but I've only seen one, with naked Indians soaping their heads in mid-stream. I shall bathe. There are no Fifis nor Lagartitos[4] – and the Indians go about in white cotton – they don't make them wear proper trousers as in most towns – – I think we shall move soon into a house with a patio, – stay here ten days or so more – and Miss Brett stay in the hotel.

The advantages of Chapala are, of course, the Lake, bathing, and the short journey. But this isn't touristy at all – quite, quite real, and lovely country around, where we can ride. A man has already promised to lend me a good Texas saddle. And we can go down to Ejutla and look at silver-mines, with the same man.[5]

Only, once more, Chapala is much more a proper holiday resort.

The journey costs 12.00 to Esperanza, 2.70 thence to Tehuacan, and then 12.50 on to Oaxaca. Leave Mexico 7.05 am – leave Esperanza 2.30 p. m. – arr. Tehuacan 4.30. Leave Tehuacan 10.30 a. m. – arrive Oaxaca about 7.0 p. m. Very nice people on the train, and wonderful scenery. really.

But if you want to feel you are on a *regular* holiday, go to Chapala. I'd hate you to come here and feel disappointed.

Many greetings to you both, and to JANE,[6] from us all.

Yrs D. H. Lawrence

Take a bit of lunch, perhaps, from Tehuacan, as you don't get food till 2.15. at Tomellin. – The little train is very *dusty* – wear old clothes as possible. But it's not too hot.

[1] Hotel Francia, named after its original French owners who built it in the 1890s, was run by Doña María Jarquin de Monros, Catalonian, widow of Juan Monros. See Parmenter 2 and Brett 170, 209. (Parmenter includes a photograph of her, plate 43.)

[2] Mitla, 26 miles down the s.e. arm of the valley, famous for tombs and ruined palaces; Santa María del Tule, an enormous tree; Ejutla, 50 miles s., jumping-off place for mines. See Brett 183–4 and Parmenter 17, 172–5.

[3] Atoyac and Jalatlaco Rivers (Parmenter 17).

[4] Quintanilla explained: '*Lagartijo* means lizard. That is how the play-boys of pre-revolutionary Mexico were called: Lizards, because these aristocratic society play-boys would spend their time leaning against the walls of fashionable stores on Madero Street (then called "Plateros") to take the sun and have a good look at the beautiful *señoritas* going by. Later on the *lagartijos* were called *Fifis*, a French name meaning nothing in particular. Some of them can still be found in Mexico City today, although the species is rapidly disappearing' (Nehls, ii. 522 n. 66).

[5] Donald Gazley Miller (1888–1953), American miner and engineer, in Oaxaca 1923–7, and neighbour at Avenida Pino Suarez; he took the Lawrence party to Mitla (see Brett 175, 182–3 and Parmenter 4, 17, 171, 177, 355 n. 1).

[6] Quintanilla's daughter, b. 1924.

3290. To William Hawk, 14 November 1924

Text: MS UT; Postmark, Oaxaca [. . .] NOV [. . .]; Moore, *Intelligent Heart* 334–5.

Hotel Francia. *Oaxaca.* Mexico
14 Novem 1924

Dear William

Your letter came today. Thank you so much for riding round and looking after the place. When I think of it, I wish I was back.

We got down here on Sunday night: it takes two days from Mexico City, though it's not so very far. Oaxaca is a little town, about 30,000, alone in the south, with a perfect climate. The market is full of roses and violets, the gardens are all flowers. Every day is perfectly sunny, a bit hot at midday. The natives are mostly Zapotec Indians, small, but very straight and alert and alive: really very nice. There is a big market humming like a bee-hive, where one can buy anything, from roses to horse-shoes. I wish we could send you some of the pottery, such beautiful colours, and costs nothing. But the last lot I sent got smashed. This is where they make the serapes like the one with the eagle that hung on the wall: and the little men stalk about in them, looking very showy. – The governor is an Indian from the hills. I called on him in the palace!!![1] – But everywhere the government is very Labour – and somehow one doesn't feel very solid. There are so many wild Indians who don't know anything about anything, except that they are told that every 'rich' man is an enemy. – There may be a bad bust-up in Mexico City: and again, everything may go off quietly.[2] But I don't like the feeling. If only it wasn't winter, we'd come back to the ranch tomorrow. I feel so weary of *people* – people, people, people, and all such bunk, somehow, with politics and self-assertiveness. – As it is, we shall probably take a house here for a month or two. Thank goodness my chest and throat are better, since we are here in this soft warm air. I want to get them sound this winter, and next year stay on much later at the ranch.

I will write to Taos about the Azul – get Tony to send him up if he has been attended to. Louis Cottam was going to have the road-vet. look at him, early this month. – I would rather he were up at Del Monte with his pals.

Brett lost Toby, and has had the tin-smith make her a substitute, shaped

[1] Isaac M. Ibarra (1888–1972), governor of the State of Oaxaca after Manuel García Vigil (b. 1882), was assassinated for seceding in April 1924; he was in office until Onofre Jiménez (1888–) was inaugurated on 1 December 1924, Ibarra was a Zapotec Indian from the Sierra de Juárez mountains; slim, spectacled and moustached; a self-educated ex-mine mechanic who became a General in the Oaxacan army and federal senator; and friendly to foreigners. See Parmenter xx–xxvii, 18–19 and plate 5. (Estrada had written to the Governor to ask him to look after the Lawrence party, p. 17.)

The Palacio Municipal, neo-Renaissance, was the state capitol building.

[2] General Angel Flores (1883–1926) was to lead a revolt which was scheduled to take place on 23 November; it did not come off (Parmenter 11).

like a funnel:[1] much excitement among the natives when she uses it. Her machine also works very fitfully, so that her ears are out of luck. – Frieda of course pines for her ranch, and the freedom. So really do I.

This letter, of course, is for Rachel as well.

Remember us all warmly to your mother and father, also to your son, and to Miss Wemyss,[2] and to the horses.

Yrs D. H. Lawrence

3291. To Curtis Brown, 14 November 1924

Text: MS UT; Huxley 621.

Hotel Francia. *Oaxaca*, Mexico
14 Nov. 1924.

Dear Curtis Brown

I got the Blackwell agreement last night, and return it herewith.[3] Better anyhow for Blackwell to set the book up himself.– I am glad Cape is doing *Mastro-don Gesualdo*.[4]

Barmby has fixed up with Knopf for *Memoirs of a Foreign Legion*. Adele Seltzer – spouse of Thomas – will say as I heard her say before: The English are all treacherous. But Jews are all Judases, and that's how Judas always talks, of other people's treachery. Basta!

I think we shall stay here a month or two – rent a house. This address will be good, though. Oaxaca is a little town in the south of Mexico – about 5,000 ft up – with a perfect climate: sun and roses. At the moment the country around is quiet, so we shall be able to ride out and about a bit: though everybody is of course scared as to what will happen next, and any day may bring a so-called revolution. I called on the governor of the State – mon Dieu!

[1] Maruca Monros Jarquín, daughter of the hotel proprietress, took Brett to a native tinsmith who made a replacement (Parmenter 13). See also Letter 3343.

[2] Walton Hawk, the son; and Timsy Wemyss, the cat (see Letter 3465).

[3] For *Little Novels of Sicily*.

[4] DHL had translated *Mastro-don Gesualdo* (1889) by Verga in January–March 1922. It had been published by Seltzer on 13 October 1923. Secker did not see the book until 16 September 1924 (Secker Letter-Book, UIll); he turned it down:

> Dear Curtis Brown
>
> I have now considered "Maestro-Don Gesualdo" very carefully, and feel very dubious indeed about its prospects of appeal to the English public. It is only the slight Lawrence interest in his being associated as translator which would carry it, and that being so I do not think I could undertake to set it up in this country. In the circumstances I think I will decline it, as I wish to have no further business relations with Seltzer, such as would be involved in the purchase of sheets.
>
> Yours sincerely

Jonathan Cape published the first English issue from Seltzer sheets in March 1925; see Roberts A28.

We met Somerset Maugham in Mexico City. He hates it here: has gone to Yucatan. He'll hate it there. I didn't like him. A bit rancid.

I hope I'll get my novel done this winter.

Yrs D. H. Lawrence

3292. To Emily King, 15 November 1924

Text: MS Lazarus; Unpublished.

Hotel Francia. *Oaxaca*, Mexico.
15 Novem. 1924

My dear Pamela.

We've been down here a week: only about 250 miles south of Mexico City, but it takes two days to get here, at twelve miles an hour pottering along on the little narrow railway, through the loneliest country you can imagine. Only about forty passengers – two little coaches – and twenty soldiers to guard us. There are always bandits, and so-called rebels – always attacking somebody or other, in the country. But the town is safe.

The climate here is perfect, just like midsummer, with a bright sun in a perfect blue sky every day, and roses and hibiscus flowers in full bloom. For a penny or two one buys big bunches of really handsome roses. The Indians are Zapotecas, small, but very erect and rather fierce. They weave blankets and make very jolly pottery, and come in wild from the hills to sell them. I will send you a Oaxaca blanket if the post is safe enough – which is doubtful. – No, don't ever send me things to the U S A or here – the duty is ridiculous. – We know nearly everybody in Oaxaca already (you pronounce it Wa-há-ka – the x in Spanish always a strong h – this for Peg's benefit). I called on the governor in the Palace. He was an Indian from the hills. It is all the most absurd sort of socialism you can imagine – and very unsettled.

Next week we shall move into a house – F[rieda] and I.[1] Brett will stay on in the hotel. One gets tired of being always with other people. And I suppose we shall stay here till about March, then begin to move north. I do wish the ranch wasn't so high – it got my chest rather badly. Here it is about 5,000 feet – which is just right.

I want if I can to finish my Mexican novel this winter – though it takes one a little time to adjust oneself.

[1] For descriptions of the house at Avenida Pino Suarez #43 and its surroundings see Brett 173–4 and Parmenter 29–30.

I haven't heard from any of you – suppose it's the mail which doesn't come. But I guess everything is all right.

Love to all from us both.

DHL

x

x x Joan's kisses

x

This address is safe.[1]

3293. To John Middleton Murry, 15 November 1924

Text: MS NYPL; cited in Murry, *New Adelphi* 457.

Hotel Francia, *Oaxaca*, Mexico:
15 Novem 1924

Dear Jack

We've been down here a week now – wiggled for two days on a little railway through the lonely, forbidding country. It's only 250 miles south of Mexico City, at that. Oaxaca (you pronounce it Wa-há-ka) is a little town about 30,000, in a wide valley with mountains round, lonely and a bit lost. It's not far from both coasts, but there's no railway. You can ride in 4 or 5 days, either to the Pacific or the Atlantic – if you don't get shot. The country is always unsettled. They've spread such an absurd sort of socialism everywhere – and these little Zapotec Indians are quite fierce. I called on the Governor of the State, in the Palace. He is an Indian from the hills, but like a little Mexican lawyer: quite nice. Only it's all just crazy. Tomorrow he asked me to go out to the opening of a road into the hills.[2] The road isn't begun yet. That's why *we* open it. And during the picnic, of course he may get shot.

It's the chief market today – such a babel and a hubbub of unwashed wild people – heaps of roses and hibiscus flowers, blankets, very nice wild pottery, cakes, birds, vegetables, and awful things to eat – including squashed fried locust-beetles. F[rieda] and I bought pots and blankets – we shall move into a house next week, and are collecting bits of furniture from various people.[3] It's the house of an Englishman who was born here, and who is a priest in the

[1] Written next to the hotel address.

[2] See Parmenter 21, 23 for an account of the opening of the completed section of the road to Teotitlán del Valle (DHL did not attend), which was part of the proposed highway to Sierra de Juárez.

[3] From the Kulls who were leaving Oaxaca shortly (see p. 174 n. 2) and from G. William and Emma (née von Violand) Thompson, friends of Edward Rickards. The Thompsons owned a large house; he was a partner in a mine at Taviche; and she was the daughter of an aristocratic Austrian political refugee. See Parmenter 15–16, 30–1.

Cathedral chapter.[1] Brett will stay on in the hotel – the proprietress is Spanish, and very nice.

But everything is so shaky and really so confused. The Indians are queer little savages, and awful agitators [. . .] pump bits of socialism over them and make everything just a mess. It's really a sort of chaos. And I suppose American intervention will become inevitable – you know, socialism is a dud. It makes just a muck of people: and especially of savages. And 70% of these people are real savages, quite as much as they were 300 years ago. The Spanish-Mexican population just rots on top of the black savage mass. And socialism here is a farce of farces: except very dangerous.

Well, I shall try and finish my 'Quetzalcoatl' novel this winter – see what comes of it. The world give me the gruesomes, the more I see it. That is, the world of people. This country is so lovely, the sky is perfect, blue and hot every day, and flowers rapidly following flowers. They are cutting the sugar-cane, and hauling it in in the old ox-wagons, slowly. But the grass-slopes are already dry and fawn coloured, the unventured hills are already like an illusion, standing round inhuman.

No mail here yet – let us know how you all are.

DHL

This address is good.

3294. To Ada Clarke, 15 November 1924

Text: MS Clarke; cited in Lawrence–Gelder 129–30.

Hotel Francia. *Oaxaca*, Mexico.
15 Nov. 1924

My dear Sister

We got down here all right – there is always a certain risk in Mexico, especially on a little narrow railway that winds for hours and hours in a gorge. This is a little town, lonely, way in the south, with little rather fierce Zapotec Indians. The climate is lovely: just like midsummer, cloudless sun all day, and roses and tropical flowers in full bloom. My chest had got very raw, up at the ranch: that very high altitude. That's why we had to come south so soon. Already it's nearly healed up. – The altitude here is just about 5,000 feet. – They are always expecting more revolutions: it's the most unsettled country, and the most foolish, politically, on the face of the earth. But I don't suppose anything will happen to affect us seriously.

Next week F[rieda] and I are going into a house, we get so weary of hotels, though this is very nice. But Brett will stay on here in the hotel.

[1] See Letter 3304 and p. 177 n. 2.

We've not had any letters yet – I don't know if any have gone astray. The post is more or less a risk, anyhow, so don't think of sending anything out here. Nor to the United States either – except some little thing worth half a crown. Because the U.S.A. makes me pay a dollar duty even on a book – that is 4/6. Ridiculous.

The winter is so lovely here, I hope the country will stay quiet. Otherwise we shan't be able easily to get out. But we should leave by the early spring – March – anyhow.

I wonder how you have got on with your house. How thrilled you will be when you move in?[1] If the post is safe, I will send you a Oaxaca blanket – very brilliant and amusing.

My agent has started to leave Seltzer – he is not giving him the *Memoirs of the Foreign Legion*. Poor Thomas will squeal, but then he's deserved it. Let me know if you got the books from Secker.

One feels far away here. – I want to get my Mexican novel finished, if I can.

Hope all goes well. Love from us both.

DHL

This address is safe.[2]

3295. To Alfred Decker Hawk, 17 November 1924

Text: MS (Photocopy) HU; Unpublished.

Hotel[3] Francia. *Oaxaca*. Oax.
17 Novem. 1924

Dear Mr Hawk

Thank you so much for troubling with the mail. – But please don't send on any more books, I have such a fuss with them here. – I heard from the post-mistress in Taos there are four small parcels for me there, so I have written her asking her to forward them on to you, for you to keep for me. You might one day look into them and tell me what they are.

We are moving into a house tomorrow, but Miss Brett is staying on in this hotel, and this address is always good. I hope I shall be able to get a bit of work done before I move again – but really am sorry we left the ranch so soon, since your weather has been so good. This climate is perfect, but I miss the freedom.

Did you find that deed for Witter Bynner? – Keep a list of the expenses, and I will pay it whenever you send it.

And many thanks for your kindness.

Yours Sincerely D. H. Lawrence

[1] On Gee Street, Ripley.

[2] Written next to the hotel address.

[3] Hotel] Del Monte

Don't send on anything but letters – I have such a struggle to get the other things out of the post here.

DHL

3296. To John Middleton Murry, 17 November 1924

Text: MS NYPL; Huxley 623–4.

Hotel Francia. *Oaxaca*. Oax. Mexico.
17 Novem 1924.

Dear Jack

I sent you a letter two days ago, and yesterday came the little yellow cry from your liver. You were bound to hate Kot, and he you, after a while: though I don't suppose the hate is mortal, on either side. The *Adelphi* was bound to dwindle: though why not fatten it up a bit.[1] Why in the name of hell didn't you rouse up a bit, last January, and put a bit of gunpowder in your stuff, and fire a shot or two. But you preferred to be soft, and to go on stirring your own finger in your own vitals. If it's any good, to you or anybody, all right! But if it's no good, what the hell! – It seems to me, the telephone-book magazine, and the pale yellow *cri de l'âme*[2] are equally out of date. Spunk is what one wants, not introspective sentiment. The last is your vice. You rot your own manhood at the roots, with it. But apparently it's what you want.

The article you wearily mention is the 'Snake Dance' article, I suppose. If you really cared about it, I'd tell Curtis Brown to let you have it at the price you can afford to pay. But if you don't really care, what's the good.

Sometimes the American Continent gets on my nerves, and I wish I'd come to Sicily or south Spain for the winter. But as it is, I suppose we shall stay a few months here, since we're moving into a house tomorrow. But if I still feel put out by the vibration of this rather malevolent continent, I'll sail from Vera Cruz and spend my last dollars trying the mushiness of Europe once more, for a while. It's a fool's world, anyhow, and people bore me stiffer and stiffer. – Fancy even a Zapotec Indian, when he becomes governor, is only a fellow in a Sunday Suit grinning and scheming. People never never never change: that's the calamity. Always the same mush.

But it's no good. Either you go on wheeling a wheelbarrow and lecturing at

[1] The *Adelphi* was in crisis: circulation had fallen; there was not enough money to pay Kot's salary; and Kot was unhappy that Murry used the magazine as a personal forum. Murry offered to sell *Adelphi* to Kot for £200; when Kot accepted, Murry stated he would not contribute articles and then withdrew his offer (Carswell, *Lives and Letters*, pp. 205–8).

[2] 'cry of the soul' (i.e. the *Adelphi* in its pale yellow paper cover).

Cambridge[1] and going softer and softer inside, or you make a hard fight with yourself, pull yourself up, harden yourself, throw your feelings down the drain and face the world as a fighter. – You wont, though.

Yrs DHL

3297. To Mollie Skinner, 17 November 1924

Text: MS WAPL; Postmark, [. . .]; Skinner 151.

Hotel Francia. *Oaxaca*. Oax. Mexico.
17 Nov 1924

Dear Mollie Skinner

I'm glad Jonathan Cape is going to do *Black Swans*, and even that Edward Garnett roars at you to make you do it better. He was a very good friend of mine, old Edward.[2]

The Boy seems to be doing very well over here, though they say business is bad in the U.S.A. Anyhow Seltzer seems pleased.

We are here way down in the south of Mexico, with brilliant sunshine every day, and warm. My wife and I are moving into a house, to stay a few months if we like it, and if I can get on with the novel I have a good deal written. But I get a bit tired of the American continent after a certain time: it is so hard and jolting, and I want to go away. Sometimes I feel very much like going to West Australia again, and going way down to the south coast, where the sands are white and the big trees stand up to the sea. I feel very much attracted that way. Do you think I should like it?

I shall be so glad to see *Black Swans* sailing out with folded wings. Send it me as soon as it is out, so that I can see what you've done with it, and how you have come on.

Greetings from my wife and me.

D. H. Lawrence

3298. To Clarence Thompson, 17 November 1924

Text: MS UT; Postmark, [. . .]; Moore 820–1.

Hotel Francia. *Oaxaca*. Oax.
17 Nov. 1924

Dear Clarence

You shouldn't let my doings bother you, anyhow: but *especially* my doings

[1] References to Murry's gardening activities (F. A. Lea, *The Life of John Middleton Murry*, 1959, p. 125), and to the Clark Lectures he gave at Cambridge in the summer of 1924 which were expanded into *Keats and Shakespeare* (see Letter 3516 and n. 3).

[2] Edward Garnett (1868–1937), critic, essayist and dramatist; DHL's close friend and mentor in his early years as an author; see *Letters*, i. 297. A letter to Mollie Skinner from Garnett, 29 November 1924, with 5pp. of notes on *Black Swans* is at WAPL.

as reported from certain quarters.[1] Why has that any weight with you? – In me there is no change, and never will be: only surface adaptations. And I trust even those won't much longer be necessary. But in this life, one has to make a certain number of surface adaptations, or one would wear oneself out.

I am glad you like your work. It's the main thing. All that other stuff one can, and should, forget: dismiss it out of oneself. Why be ridden by anything, even a night-mare. One is[2] stronger than one's nightmares.

We are way down here in the south of Mexico – marvellous sunshine every day, but rather stupid people. F[rieda] and I are moving into a house tomorrow, but Brett will stay on in the hotel. I suppose we shall be here a month or two: though I'm wishing I'd gone to Europe instead of coming here. Sometimes I hanker for the Mediterranean, and long to get away from the American continent altogether. However, I'll try first if I can get any work done. If I can't, I shall sail.

And then the year will end, and it will be a New Year, and I hope to heaven the trails of the old won't go smearing over on to the new. Really one ought to be able to get a fresh start.

Frieda wears her best frocks, but doesn't really enjoy it. Brett lost Toby, and had the tin-smith make her another, like a gramophone horn: the delighted astonishment of these little Indian natives! I called on the governor in the Palace: he was an Indian from the hills, and is an Indian in a sunday suit! Dio benedetto![3] What a fool's world altogether!

Greetings from us all D. H. Lawrence

[Frieda Lawrence begins]
Dear Clarence!

I thought of you hard on the first of October, and am very glad you like the work! It is wild down here and makes one believe in morals, life becomes such an untidy show without – Thank you so much about Friedel – he is homesick! It's such a lovely sun, the people gave us feasts in Mexico City – but a little goes a long way! There really is need for your rose coloured trousers in the world.[4]

I do enjoy the exquisite bits you gave me –
With all good luck to you!

Love Frieda

excuse pencil, I am writing in the patio –

[1] Probably Mabel Luhan, who had also gone to New York, for the winter.
[2] is] of [3] 'Blessed be God!'
[4] Brett recalled his 'pink corduroy pants' (*South Dakota Review* 15), and in *Altitude* the character Clarence enters '*in rose-coloured trousers and much jewellery*'.

3299. To Curtis Brown, 17 November 1924

Text: MS UT; Unpublished.

Hotel Francia. *Oaxaca*, Oax. Mexico.
17 Novem 1924

Dear Curtis Brown

As I said before, I don't mind if 'St. Mawr' appears as a complete book.

As for a title, it seems all right to me: 'Two Ladies and a Horse'. But if Secker wants 'Lou and a Bay Horse' or 'St. Mawr and the Witts' or 'Madam on the High Horse' – he can choose.[1]

I heard from Middleton Murry, that he cant afford the price you ask for the article 'The Hopi Snake Dance'. If he *really* wants that article, you might let him have it at his own price, as he says he has it in print. If his *Adelphi* is going to live.

I wish you could send a copy of that article to my sister-in-law, Frau Dr Else Jaffe: She translated the 'Corn Dance' article for the *Neue Merkur*, which is perhaps the best monthly in Germany, and it was very much liked.[2] They might be glad of 'The Snake Dance'. Whatever money comes from the periodical things in Germany, I let my sister-in-law keep it. So charge any expenses to me, please.

Secker was mean to send *you* those copies of the *The Boy in the Bush*. I sent him half a dozen addresses, and asked him to mail the copies for me. Now I

[1] Curtis Brown had obviously told DHL about the reaction to 'St. Mawr' conveyed in Secker's letter of 24 October (Secker Letter-Book, UIll):

Dear Curtis Brown

I am about half way through "St Mawr" and I think it is very good indeed. I now quite agree with you that it would be a pity to include any other material which would otherwise be available for another collection of stories in the future, and I will therefore produce this as a full-length novel. I think Lawrence should be asked to suggest a third alternative title, for "Two Ladies and a Horse" seems to me a little clumsy. I am now returning you the typescript, as you wish.

Yours sincerely

On 8 December Secker again wrote to Curtis Brown (Secker Letter-Book):

Dear Curtis Brown

Many thanks for yours of the 6th. I have now come to think that after all "St Mawr" would be the best title for the new Lawrence book. All the other titles which have been mentioned seem to me to suggest too much a magazine short story. I think we might decide on "St Mawr", which will probably have the advantage of meeting the author's preference in the matter.

As far as I know all copies of "The Boy in the Bush" have been dispatched according to instructions. We have also posted copies of the "Foreign Legion" to Michael Borg and to the Monastery at Montecassino.

Yours sincerely

[2] 'Der Tanz vom sprießenden Korn' by D. H. Lawrence, trans. Else Jaffe (*Der Neue Merkur*, viii, October 1924, 104–10). The second section of chap. XXIV of *The Boy in the Bush* also appeared there as 'Jack im Busch; Ein Kapitel aus einem australischen Roman' (viii, June 1925, 793–813).

have to pay duty in the USA. duty in Mexico, and have a struggle to get things out of the post, here. Don't please send me books to Mexico.

Lovely climate here. We're moving into a house, and I hope to finish my novel. But politically it's a mess, this country.

Yrs D. H. Lawrence

3300. To Ida Rauh, 17 November 1924
Text: MS UT; Postmark, Oaxaca 17 NOV 24; Unpublished.

Hotel Francia. *Oaxaca.* Oax.
17 Nov. 1924

Dear Ida

We have been down here a week. In two days F[rieda] and I are going into a house, and then I shall really sit down to the play:[1] and make it either Aztec or Jewish – King David or Moses: or else Montezuma. But I want it to be as *little* of a costume play as possible: only the *people*, not the so-called romance. I hope I'll be able to do it. At the moment I feel out of sorts, and a bit sick of the American continent, wishing I had gone to South Italy or Spain. Sometimes a longing for Europe comes over one: America seems to have such *hard* elbows digging into one. Nevertheless I suppose we shall stay here a month or two: unless we feel very sick of it, and sail from Vera Cruz to Spain.

I'll really have a shot at the play. But don't count on it very much. I may not manage it, and if I do, probably no-one will like it. However – never say die.

Brett lost Toby, and had the tin-smith make her another, like a gramophone horn, with a pipe-fitting for the bend. We contemplate painting it in and out with dazzling colours, to fetch the sound in.

I wrote to Andrew in Taos, but am afraid he'd be gone. I thought he was staying longer than you.

It's wonderful sunny weather here – that's one thing. But I've got a revulsion from this continent, want to take a ship. A train's no good.

Yrs D. H. Lawrence

3301. To Hon. Dorothy Brett, [20 November 1924]
Text: MS UCin; Irvine, Brett 38.

Ave. Pino Suarez. #43.
Thursday

Dear Brett

Here is the book and Mrs Kuhl's two baskets, with a note for her asking her to tea, tomorrow.[2] *Send over baskets and note by the Hotel porter.*

[1] *Noah's Flood* or *David*; see Letters 3362 and n. and 3378 and n. 2.

[2] Carola Kull (1886–1966), Lithuanian, amateur artist, and Hermann Kull (1889–1967), Swiss dentist (trained in USA) were in Oaxaca, 1922–February 1925; see Letter 3329. See Parmenter xxv, 65–82 and Brett 187, 189.

Can you ask the chambermaid for our washing – la ropa limpia de mis amigos[1] – and give it to Rosalino, who will bring this.[2] We expect you to tea.

DHL

The bit of stuff is for Mrs Kull.

3302. To Edward McDonald, 20 November 1924

Text: MS UT; Postmark, Oaxaca 20 NOV 24; Moore 822–3.

Aven. Pino Suarez #43, *Oaxaca.* (Oax.), Mexico
20 Nov 1924

Dear Mr McDonald

Movements was first issued in blue.[3] Somebody walked off with my one copy in Taos, or I'd have sent it you. But that always happens to me.

That print on the cover of *Tortoises* was found by Robert Mountsier – 417 West 118th St – New York: who was being my agent at the time. I understood it was a complete print, yet the view is surely Hiroshige's.[4] Mountsier would tell you.

I never knew Heinemann printed *White Peacock* from American plates.[5] Wonder why. – You know a story about him? – You know his wife went off with D'Annunzio, and after she'd gone he had a public auction of her underclothing, garters, knickers and all, he being, I imagine, auctioneer.[6] – Such is a publisher. – And Methuen, who wept about the *Rainbow*, is, I am told, real publisher of the Villiers Street pornographic stuff.[7]

I'm ashamed to think of 28 books. For heavens sake don't try to make it more.

Seltzer will never advertise *The Boy*. He hasn't a cent. Heaven knows how he holds on at all.

[1] 'my friends' clean clothes'.

[2] Rosalino, a Zapotec, born c. 1904 in Santa María Zoogochí, in the Sierra de Juárez. See Parmenter 84–5; Brett 175, 178–80, 195; Rosalino is featured in 'Corasmin and the Parrots', 'The Mozo' and 'Walk to Huayapa', collected in *Mornings in Mexico* (1927).

[3] The first impression was issued both in light-brown and blue bindings; see Roberts A17.

[4] It is a complete print, *Mannen Bridge* (Fukagawa Mannen-bashi), no. 51 of *100 Views of Edo* (*Meisho Edo Hyakkei*) (Tokyo, c. 1856–9) by Andō Hiroshige (1797–1858): in the foreground, a turtle, for sale, is suspended in a window with Mount Fuji seen across the river.

[5] See Introduction to *The White Peacock*, ed. Andrew Robertson (Cambridge, 1983), pp. xxxi, xxxv–xxxvi.

[6] William Heinemann (1863–1920), publisher, m. 1899, Donna Magda Stuart Sindici, author, whose first novel *Via Lucis* (1898) Heinemann published; divorced 1904. Heinemann's friends denied the story of the auction (Moore 823); his wife translated D'Annunzio's *Il Fuoco* as *The Flame of Life* (Heinemann, 1900) under the pseudonym 'Kassandra Vivaria'.

[7] Villiers Street (which runs from the Strand to the embankment near Charing Cross station) was reputedly the haunt of dubious booksellers and publishers. Methuen had no connection with it or its alleged activities.

A man Edward Weston just took a good photograph of me in Mexico City.[1] But I don't care what Mason takes.[2] – By the way, if you see him, do give him this address. I suppose we shall be here three months anyhow.

Oaxaca is a little lonely town way in the south, with a perfect climate, and mule cars that run every half hour – tram cars – and little strutting Zapotec Indians. The house has a patio with big trees, and great empty rooms. We camp on the verandah. But at the moment I don't feel up to anything – as if the world had sort of come to an end. As you feel about politics. – Perhaps it has.

Anyhow, I'll lie low a bit, and get my pecker up. – Myself, I don't know American slang, and I'm sure pecker isn't improper in English.[3] If it is, tant mieux.[4]

Yrs D. H. Lawrence

3303. To Ada Clarke, [21 November 1924]

Text: MS Clarke; Photograph [Street scene with mule carts]; Postmark, Oax[aca] [. . .]; cited in Lawrence–Gelder 124.

Ave. Pino Suarez #43. *Oaxaca*. Oax.
21 Nov.

We are in the house, very nice and peaceful: but Brett is staying on in the hotel. I am getting busy again, too. It is a wonderful climate, brilliant sun all day long: and a nice little easy town. – I had a little letter from you. My mother-in-law is

Frau Baronin von Richthofen. Ludwig-Wilhelmstift, *Baden-Baden*.

Else writes that she too – F[rieda]'s mother – seems to be failing a bit. Perhaps it is the winter.

DHL

3304. To Baroness Anna von Richthofen, 22 November 1924

Text: MS Jeffrey; PC v. [Lawrences in Mexican street]; Frieda Lawrence *Nur Der Wind . . .* (Berlin, 1936), p. 235.

Avenida Pino Suarez #43. *Oaxaca* (Oax.), Mexico
22 Nov. 1924

Liebe Schwiegermutter

Siehst du die zwei Kinder, in einer Oaxaca-strasse. Die Frieda lasst sagen,

[1] Quintanilla took DHL to meet Edward Henry Weston (1886–1957) on Sunday 2 November, and Weston asked DHL to sit for him which he did on 4 November (in two poses; see Letter 3321). See Nehls, ii. 521 n. 62.

[2] Harold Trump Mason (1893–1983), proprietor of the Centaur Bookshop, Philadelphia, founded in 1921. He also founded the Centaur Press which published the Centaur Bibliographies Series. m. (1) Ann Brakely (1892–1963); (2) Doris Duval.

[3] 'Pecker' means 'courage, resolution', chiefly in the phrase 'to keep one's pecker up', but it later acquired the USA slang meaning of 'penis'.

[4] 'so much the better'.

sie sieht dicker aus, wie die wirklichkeit. Doch fängt sie weniger Brot und Kuchen an zu fressen.

Ich gebe dir die Haus-addresse. Wir sind schon ganz zu-heim – haben grossen Zimmer mit sehr wenigen Möbel, ein herrlichen Verandah mit Tisch und Rocking-chairs, wo wir essen, ein sehr schonen Patio, inneres Garten, mit riesen-grossen Bäume, Kaffee-pflanzen, hibiscus blumen, poinsettias – sehr schön. Haben auch ein Dienst-junger der heisst *Rosalino*, eine alte Frau *Natividad*, zwei Jungen, die heissen *Maria de Jesus* und *Maria del Carmen*. Das Haus gehört an einem Engländer, hier geboren – er ist Catholischer Pfarrer, im Dom – und heisst Padre Eduardo Rickards – sehr nett – er wohnt im anderen Flügel. – Im Orangen-baum sitzen jetzt zwei Papagein, und schreien *Perro*! Oh *Perro*! *Perro*! (meint *Hund*!) – und dann bellen wie das Hündchen das liegt unter meinem Tisch – er schämt sich furchtbar, vor den Papaginen und ihren *Imitation*. Sie *jappen* ganz und gar wie er, der Corasmin, jappt, und er kann es nicht mehr ausdauern. – Wir waren heut Morgen im Markt – der Rosalino geht hinten mit grossem Korb. – haben 4 Enten, viele schöne Töpfe gekauft. Markt is Samstags voller wilden Indier von den Bergen. Gieb die andere Karten an Else, bitte.

D.H.L.

Frieda hasste ihr Bild, hat eine andere Karte auf-geklebt, dass du es nicht sehen sollst!

[Dear Schwiegermutter

You see the two children, in a street in Oaxaca. Frieda asks me to say, she looks fatter than she really is. But she is starting to guzzle less bread and cake.

I give you the house address. We are already quite at home – have big rooms with very little furniture, a splendid verandah with table and rocking-chairs, where we eat, a very lovely patio, enclosed garden with gigantic trees, coffee-plants, hibiscus flowers, poinsettias – very beautiful. We also have a servant-boy who is called *Rosalino*, an old woman *Natividad*,[1] two youngsters who are called *Maria de Jesus* and *Maria del Carmen*. The house belongs to an Englishman, born here – he is a Catholic parish priest, in the cathedral – and is called Father Eduardo Rickards – very nice – he lives in the other wing.[2] – There are two parrots now sitting in the orange-tree, shrieking *Perro*! Oh

[1] Natividad was Edward Rickards' cook.

[2] Edward Arden Rickards (1879–1941), b. Oaxaca, son of Constantine Rickards, Scottish merchant and miner, and Jane Arden, daughter of a Protestant minister. Studied for Roman Catholic ministry at Oscott College, near Birmingham; had been secretary-treasurer to Archbishop Eulogio Gregorio Gillow y Zavalza (1841–1922) and priest of La Merced; arrested in 1926 and lived for months with his brother Constantine (see p. 198 n. 8) in Mexico City. See Parmenter 25–43.

Perro! *Perro*! (means *dog*!) – and then they bark like the little dog that lies under my table – he is horribly embarrassed by the parrots and their *imitation*. They *yap* just in the way that he, Corasmin, yaps, and he can't bear it any longer.[1] – We were in the market this morning – Rosalino follows with a large basket. – We have bought 4 ducks, lots of nice pots. On Saturdays the market is full of wild Indians from the mountains. Give Else the other cards, please.[2]

DHL

Frieda hated her picture, has stuck another card on, so that you don't see it!]

3305. To Joan King, [22 November 1924]

Text: MS Needham; PC v. [Mexican boy ploughing with oxen]; Unpublished.

[Av. Pino Suarez #43, Oaxaca]
[22 November 1924]

Dear Joan

This is a boy ploughing with big oxen and a wooden plough. – We've got two parrots in the garden that call Perro! Perro! (dog!) and then they bark exactly like the little white dog Corasmin. He gets so mad, he goes and lies under the trees, and the parrots go on shrieking after him Perro! Perro! Oh Perro! – yap – yap – yap! He can't bear it. – That's how parrots are.

x x x DHL

3306. To Margaret King, [22 November 1924]

Text: MS Forster; PC v. [Mexicans with heaps of sugar-cane]; Unpublished.

Av. Pino Suarez #43, Oaxaca. (Oax), Mexico.
[22 November 1924]

Dear Peg

This is sugarcane they have brought in from the fields to crush. They also sell lengths for the natives to chew. This is just how the natives look – the men in white calico and big hats and serapes (blankets) and the women in full starched skirts and rebozos (their shawls). Mostly they speak Spanish, but the men from the hills only speak Zapotec or Mixtec – Indian. Our boy, Rosalino, is a Zapotec – it's taken him two years to learn the bit of Spanish he knows. The cook is called Natividad and her two daughters, Maria de Jesus and Maria del Carmen.

DHL

[1] Corasmín was Edward Rickards' much loved dog (described as a pug and poodle mixture). See Parmenter 30 and 'Corasmin and the Parrots'. [2] DHL's 'Note on Miss M. L. Skinner'.

3307. To Achsah Brewster, [22 November 1924]

Text: MS UT; Photograph [Lawrences, Fr. Rickards and Corasmin in their garden]; Brewster 71.

[Av. Pino Suarez #43, Oaxaca]
[22 November 1924]

Dear Achsah

We had your letter yesterday – Capri sounds gay. Harwood must be growing a big girl. One day you must come and paint Mexico – it is very 'different' – This is F[rieda] and me in the garden, with the Padre who owns the house, and the dog *Corasmin* and the parrots. I hope you got the Magnus book.[1] F. sends love.

DHL

3308. To Emily King, [29 November 1924]

Text: MS Needham; Photograph [Street scene in Oaxaca]; Unpublished.

Aven. Pino Suarez #43. Oaxaca. (Oax), Mexico
29 Novem

My dear Pamela

Brett takes the pictures – these are not very good, but some which are being developed are better. We are settled in our house for a month or two – it's an old house with big high empty rooms, and an inner garden (a patio) with big trees, and orange trees and lemon and hibiscus and roses. The flowers are all out now – the rainy season ended in September – and it will be dry now till May. I am working again.[2] The sunshine is brilliant every day, all day long – but not too hot except at noon. We already know all the foreigners – Americans I mean – here. But it's a sleepy little town.

Love DHL

3309. To Curtis Brown, 29 November 1924

Text: MS UT; Photograph [Oaxacan street scene]; Unpublished.

Avenida Pino Suarez #43, *Oaxaca.* (Oax). Mexico.
29 Novem 1924

Dear Curtis Brown

We are settled in this house for the moment – perhaps better use this address. – Had your note about the *Movements in European History.* Seltzer *advertised* the book – but was far from setting it up, so I asked Barmby to tell

[1] *Memoirs of the Foreign Legion.*

[2] DHL began working on the second version of *The Plumed Serpent* on 19 November, according to the date in the first notebook.

him to leave the matter in abeyance. – As far as I am concerned, the Oxford Press are welcome to control the American sale of the book. Anything, I am tempted to think, rather than Seltzer.

Yrs D. H. Lawrence

One of Miss Brett's attempts at photographing a Oaxaca street![1]

3310. To Hon. Dorothy Brett, [December? 1924]

Text: MS UCin; Irvine, Brett 38.

[Av. Pino Suarez #43, Oaxaca]
[December? 1924][2]

Dear Brett

Here is Rosalino for the book – I have to send a note, or he's too shy to ask.

DHL

3311. To Richard Cobden-Sanderson, 1 December 1924

Text: MS UT; Unpublished.

Av. Pino Suarez #43. *Oaxaca*. (Oax.), Mexico
1 Dec. 1924

Dear Cobden-Sanderson[3]

The copy of *The Criterion* wandered in today[4] – the first time I have seen the production. I like Mr. Bain's '1789' very much: the spirit of the thing.[5] I feel inclined to cry aloud: Thank heaven somebody else feels that way. And I like that about Newman, though the style is a bit misty.[6]

[1] Although no letters from DHL to Curtis Brown survive for December 1924, or to Nancy Pearn from 8 October 1924 to April 1925, letters from her to DHL do. She told him on 7 November that they were offering 'The Princess', 'The Woman Who Rode Away' and 'St. Mawr' but without much hope of success; on 13 December that *Criterion* would run 'The Woman Who Rode Away' in two parts and pay about £20 (*Dial* had already accepted it); and on 3 February 1925 that 'The Princess' would appear in April and May issues of the *Calendar* ('£3.3.0 a thous[and] – approx. 17,000 words') (TMSC UT). See also p. 331 n. 1.

[2] This note cannot be dated precisely; it could have been written any time between 19 November 1924 and 18 January 1925.

[3] Richard ('Dickie') Cobden-Sanderson (1884–1964), publisher, was the publisher of *The Criterion: A Quarterly Review*, 1922–5; it was edited by T. S. Eliot, 1922–39 under various titles. (Cobden-Sanderson was the son of Thomas James Cobden-Sanderson (1840–1922), bookbinder and printer, which explains why DHL addressed the envelope to 'T'.)

[4] The issue for October 1924 (see Letter 3180 and p. 86 n. 1).

[5] Francis William Bain (1863–1940), author, wrote thirteen volumes of Indian stories, 1913–20; '1789' (*Criterion*, iii. 43–71) closed with the recommendation that to judge the revolutionaries, one must examine what they did rather than what they said.

[6] 'The Experience of Newman' (pp. 84–102), by Ramon Fernandez (1894–1944), author of books on Molière, Gide, etc., had been translated by Richard Aldington; the article was collected in *Messages, première série* (Paris, 1926).

Anyhow I am so relieved that *The Criterion* has got some guts, and isnt another *Adelphi* or *London Mercury*. I hope you'll print me again, and that I may meet you when I come to London.

Yours Sincerely D. H. Lawrence

3312. to Emily King, [4 December 1924]

Text: MS Needham; Photograph [Lawrences in Mercado de Industria]; Unpublished.

Aven Pino Suarez, OAXACA (Oax), Mexico
4 Decem.

My Dear Pamela

F[rieda] and I. and the boy Rosalino shopping in the market – he carries the basket. Usually Natividad, the woman servant goes – but sometimes we. – I send you three pounds – one for you, one for Joan, one for Peg – for Christmas – and hope you'll have a good time. – It stays the same here – hot and sunny. –

Love DHL

3313. To Ada Clarke, [5 December 1924]

Text: MS Clarke; Photograph [Lawrences in Mercado de Industria]; Unpublished.

Av. Pino Suarez #43, *Oaxaca* (Oax), Mexico
5 Dec

My dear Sister

The boy with the basket is the servant, Rosalino – this is the market. I have got you such a handsome serape, with the gods on it – but hesitate to send it by post. – Enclose a pound each for Jack and Bertie to buy themselves something for Christmas. – Hot sunny weather here.

Love and a good Christmas.

DHL

3314. To Hon. Dorothy Brett, [7 December 1924]

Text: MS UCin; Irvine, Brett 38.

[Av. Pino Suarez #43, Oaxaca]
[7 December 1924][1]

Rosalino for the book – Father Rickards said rebels had broken our railway bridge, but no word in the *Mercurio*.

DHL

[1] A breakdown in railway service occurred on 5 December 1924 when two bridges were burned; the trains were operating again by 7 December as reported in *Mercurio* (Parmenter 94). Brett associates this note with the day that they went to see *The Thief of Baghdad* (pp. 188–9), at Teatro Luis Mier y Teran on 7 December (Parmenter 177).

3315. To William Hawk, [7 December 1924]

Text: MS UT; Photograph [Exterior of Hotel, La Sorpresa, at Mitla]; Unpublished.

Av. Pino Suarez #43. *Oaxaca.* (Oax), Mexico
Sunday

Dear William

This is outside the Hotel at Mitla, where the ruins are. If you look in the picture you'll see a white hat – me. We motored out there – $3\frac{1}{2}$ hours to do 33 miles – and supposed to be good time.[1] Oh roads! I was battered and shattered. – It's hot here, and I go about in sandals, barefoot, – there was a scorpion on the floor this morning. – 'Rebels' burnt the bridge on the railway a few days ago, but it's mended, so the train comes again. *Have you seen the Azul*? Poor old thing, I shan't be happy till I know you've got him safe. – We want to send a parcel of the pots from here. – If a parcel of books comes – *The Boy in the Bush* or *The Memoirs of the Foreign Legion*, send me a copy of each here, please, so that I can give them to people.[2] It seems a long way from the ranch. – and still further from Christmas, in this heat. Glad you are all prospering.

Yrs D. H. Lawrence

3316. To Luis Quintanilla, [7 December 1924]

Text: MS Subun-So Book Store; Photograph [Lawrences, José García and Ambrosio Quero at Mitla]; Nehls, ii. 384–5.

Aven. Pino Suarez #43. *Oaxaca*, Oax
Sunday

Dear Quintanilla

I was sorry you couldn't come down, but glad to hear of Pesos 20 per diem. Sounds almost as good as an engine-driver – I think in many ways you are a born diplomat – who knows, you may save Mexico yet.[3] She needs a bit of saving: even along with Calles' nice words. Personally, I believe he means them. But it's a far cry to Lochaber.[4]

We are settled in half the Rickards house – the English Vice Consul – the brother here is a *padre* in the Cathedral *Mitra*[5] – but a nice man. Of course we know *all* the Americans: there are no English. I am working at my novel,[6] which is just beginning to digest its own gall and wormwood. Saluti cordiali to Señor Estrada – I am almost afraid to write his name, in view of the 'strained relations' and Mexican national sensitiveness. But risk it. – The picture is

[1] Donald Miller drove them to Mitla, probably on 30 November (Parmenter 171–2).

[2] DHL signed a copy of *Memoirs* for Carola Kull, and dated it 14 January 1925 (Parmenter 80).

[3] See p. 195 n. 1.

[4] 'There is still much to be done about it', proverbial Scottish saying.

[5] The semi-detached building on the n.e. corner of the cathedral where cathedral business is conducted (Parmenter 33).

[6] *The Plumed Serpent*.

Mitla: top of my head. Miss Brett has taken to photography. The other man is José Garcia whom I think you know.[1] – All good wishes to M. le diplomate – and to Madame – and Jeanne, not of Arc.[2]

D. H. Lawrence

3317. To Alfred Decker Hawk, [7 December 1924]

Text: MS Chavez; Photograph [Lawrences, Fr. Rickards and Corasmin in their garden]; Unpublished.

Av. Pino Suarez #43. *Oaxaca*. (Oax), Mexico
Sunday[3]

Dear Mr Hawk

Just had your letter – thank you so much for seeing to the things. The parcels are absurd: they were for a girl Idella Purnell, from her mother in Berkeley – Idella is in Guadalajara. I asked Mrs P. to send the things to *Santa Fe*, and I'd take them into Mexico: she sent them, late to Taos! Oh people! – We are in a house – a big old house of some English people who had mines here 50 years ago – the Padre in the picture is the only one left here: Father Rickards. He's in the cathedral here – and very nice. The dog is Corasmin. And can you see the parrots. They yell *Perro*! *Perro*! and then bark so exactly like Corasmin that he nearly dies of embarrassment. – We know all the Americans, and have to fight to avoid tennis etc. It is hot summer weather, full of flowers. I am busy with my novel. Miss Brett took to photography. She is staying on in the hotel. But her Spanish is still a minus quantity.

– All good wishes. D. H. Lawrence

3318. To Earl Brewster, 9 December 1924

Text: MS UT; Photograph [Oaxacan street scene]; Brewster 77–8.

Avenida Pino Suarez #43. *Oaxaca* (Oax), Mexico
9 Decem. 1924

Dear Earl

Thank you so much for promising to look after the Gilletts a bit. Probably by this time they are in Italy. – We have taken a house down here for the winter. It's a lovely climate, hot and sunny, roses and hibiscus and bananas, but not tropical heat. The town is isolated away in the south. In the mountains round,

[1] José García, b. Oaxaca, caretaker of mines and friendly to Americans (Parmenter 173). (Quintanilla did not know him.) His name was used in *The Plumed Serpent*. (Also in the photograph is Ambrosio Quero, the eldest son of the owner of La Sorpresa, who was their guide, Parmenter 174–5.)

[2] Jane Quintanilla; see Nehls, ii. 522 n. 79.

[3] Sunday is accepted despite DHL's remark in Letter 3320 that he had heard about Idella Purnell's parcel only the day before (i.e. 9 December).

the Zapotec and Mixtec Indians, little wild people, but sympatico. You would like it for a time: but not long. I don't believe you would ever like the inner hardness, the sort of iron backbone that is the real characteristic of America. And don't ever think of trying to settle in Santa Fe – Capri is *much* better, really. I would rather live in Capri than in Santa Fe. – But some time, come and see us. And some time, come and look at this dark, dangerous Mexico. It is perhaps the antithesis of India, on the same plane. – I have a bit of a longing for Italy. I would have liked to walk with you in Calabria.[1] Perhaps in the spring we will sail to Naples: and perhaps then we can walk in Calabria or the Abruzzi. One needs a *rest* after America: the hardness, the *resistance* of all things to all things, inwardly, tires one. – Hope you had the Magnus book.

DHL

3319. To Martin Secker, [9 December 1924]

Text: MS UInd; Photograph [Lawrences in Mercado de Industria]; Postmark, Oax. [. . .]; Secker 53–4.

Aven. Pino Suarez #43. *Oaxaca* (Oax.), Mexico.
9 Decem. 1923

Dear Secker

We are settled in a house down here, and I am doing my Mexico book. This is a marvellous climate – roses, bananas, lilies – the madonna lilies wild on the mountains – The little town of Oaxaca is lonely, away in the south and miles from anywhere except the Indian villages of the hills. I like it: it gives me something. When one once gets over the peculiar resistance Mexico offers always. The boy in the picture is our mozo Rosalino – marketing with us. Frieda wants to come to Europe in the spring to see her mother and children: don't quite know if we shall manage it. – I was glad to hear about the Australia sales. How is everything going with you. Did you send *Boy in the Bush* to my two sisters? They keep on complaining. And did you send the Magnus book to E. H. Brewster, Torre Quattro Venti, *Capri*. Do if you haven't so far, – I wonder what Douglas thought of it. Have you heard?[2] – Are Mrs Secker and

[1] Brewster, accompanied by Antonio, who worked for the family at Quattro Venti, left on 25 September 1924; they went to San Paolo, Calabria, then to Cosenza and San Giovanni in Fiori, Crotone and Xatanzaro, returning early in October to Naples.

[2] George Norman Douglas (1868–1952), novelist and essayist, whom DHL first met when Douglas was Assistant Editor of the *English Review* in 1913 (see *Letters*, ii. 31 and n. 4). He had settled in Italy and Capri. DHL portrayed him as James Argyle in *Aaron's Rod*.

Douglas wrote to Secker in October 1924: 'If you expect a 2nd edition, I might also write an introduction (little memoir): say 4000 words' (Mark Holloway, *Norman Douglas*, 1976, p. 331), and Secker replied on 24 October 1924 (Secker Letter-Book, UIll): 'I have posted you a copy of the Foreign Legion. I have just reprinted the book but I should be delighted if you could write a supplementary memoir of 4000 words or so, as you suggest. I will include it in the next printing,

the little Secker going gaily? – Is there further news of Gilbert Cannan. – I seem to hear nothing from London at all. Send me what news there is.

Yrs D. H. Lawrence

3320. To Witter Bynner, [10 December 1924]

Text: MS HU; Photograph [Lawrences in Mercado Benito Juárez Maza]; Huxley 624–5.

Av. Pino Suarez #43. *Oaxaca.* (Oax.)
10 Dec.

Dear Bynner

Thank you for your letter and the poem: makes me wish I had seen that Buffalo dance.[1] Dassburg said you were probably going to the Calles inauguration, so half expected to hear of you or from you in La Capital. – Idella's parcel, I heard yesterday only, went to Taos, was sent to Del Monte, and is enshrined in the green iron trunk. If ever you are really coming to Mexico, do, please, write to Mr A. D. Hawk, Del Monte Ranch, Questa (or Valdez) – and let him send you the parcel. I feel a bit stuck with it. – I have not heard from Spud. – We are here in a house – perfect climate this place – attractive quiet little town. Brett is in the hotel. Heaven knows what we shall do in the spring – Frieda is sniffing Europe-wards once more: her mother and children. If we go, it will be from Vera Cruz. But will let you know.

Yrs DHL

Brett has taken to photography.

3321. To Edward Weston, [19 December 1924]

Text: TMSC UT; Nehls, ii. 387.

Av. Pino Suarez #43. Oaxaca. Oax.
[19 December 1924][2]

Dear Mr Weston

Thank you very much for the photographs. I like them very much: think I like the one with the chin up better than the other looking down: but like[3] both of them. I would write to *Vanity Fair* myself, but have clean forgotten the editors name:[4] and I had lunch with him in the spring. But I am doing one or

at the same time making any reasonable payment you suggest for the use of this.' Douglas defended Magnus in *D. H. Lawrence and Maurice Magnus: A Plea for Better Manners* (Florence, 1924, and released in England on 21 January 1925).

[1] 'A Buffalo Dance (*Santo Domingo*)' in Bynner's *Indian Earth*, pp. 66–71.

[2] Dated with reference to the next letter.

[3] TMSC reads 'like like'.

[4] Francis Welch ('Frank') Crowninshield (1872–1947), editor of *Vanity Fair*, 1914–35; wrote satirical and critical articles for magazines.

two little articles which will probably suit *Vanity Fair*.[1] Next week I shall send them to my agent, AW Barmby of Curtis Brown Ltd. 116 West 39th st. New York, and tell him about the portrait too. He would look after it if you like. And I'll tell my English agent, Curtis Brown. 6 Henrietta St. Covent Garden. London W.C.2, to approach one of the big London illustrated periodicals, if you like. You write to Barmby and to Curtis Brown, if you feel so inclined. It seems to me you have reached the point where you should go in for a bit of publicity. *Vanity Fair* might like some of your less startling nude studies, if you could stand seeing them reproduced and ruined.

Let me know if I can help you in any way. Tackle the world, its a rather stupid bull, to be taken by the horns, not dodged.

Greet the Signora.[2] Let me know when you leave. Those two addresses of my agent are always good. Wish I had a copy of *Aaron's Rod* to send you. There is supposed to be a parcel of my books on its way to me, but it must have fallen into somebody's pocket.

Yours D. H. Lawrence

3322. To Luis Quintanilla, 19 December 1924

Text: MS Subun-So Book Store; Nehls, ii. 388.

Av. Pino Suarez #43. *Oaxaca*. Oax
19 Dec 1924

Dear Quintanilla

I had the portraits from Edward Weston: they are very good, I think. I want him to get them published, in New York *Vanity Fair* and in London, perhaps the *Sphere*. They like to have a bit of text too. Why don't you do a little article on Mexico D.F. – and me thrown in – and Weston thrown in – for *Vanity Fair*. Sounds as if I wanted to get publicity for myself, but it's not that. *Vanity Fair* knows me already very well. But it would be quite nice for me, and good for Weston, because they ought to know a wee bit about him, when the photograph is published. It's time he tackled the world. And then you, with your Paris-Post-bellum amusing style, you could very successfully do little articles – two or three thousand words – for a paper like *Vanity Fair*, which everybody

[1] 'Mornings in Mexico. Friday Morning' (published as 'Corasmin and the Parrots'), 'Mornings in Mexico. Saturday Morning' ('Market Day'), 'Mornings in Mexico. Sunday Morning' ('Walk to Huayapa') and 'Mornings in Mexico. Monday Morning' ('The Mozo'). For periodical publication see p. 432 n. 2 and Letter 3899 and n. 2; all were collected in *Mornings in Mexico*.

[2] Tina Modotti, Italian photographer; Weston's mistress: they had lived in Mexico since August 1923.

reads. Little amusing articles, even on Calles etc – to hurt nobody. Why don't you do that? I think I can get them accepted all right. Do the P.E.N. Club a bit funnily. And the mother of Jane can help you, she'll know what to put in. Don't say you're used up by the FOREIGN OFFICE, that's too farcical.[1]

Yours D. H. Lawrence

3323. To Alfred Decker Hawk, 20 December 1924
Text: MS UT; Unpublished.

Aven. Pino Suarez #43. *Oaxaca.* (Oax)
20 Dec. 1924

Dear Mr Hawk

I am sending you this letter of the man Frayne, because I don't trust him very much, and I know he is Mabel Lujan's creature. It annoys me rather to be paying John Evans' taxes and fines,[2] but I'd rather do that than write them letters about it. And I don't really want to correspond with this Frayne. I don't trust him. – You know all about paying the taxes. Would you mind sending in this cheque for me, if you think it is all right? Or better, I'll make the cheque out to you, the balance to go to expenses, and perhaps you would be so good as to pay the taxes with your cheque. – I don't see why the taxes for 1921 should have been $38.60, and for 1924 $59.05. Is that right, do you think?[3]

I am very mistrustful of Mabel Lujan too. Do you think those deeds are all right?

I'll send Frayne word that you are fixing up the taxes for me, if you will be so good. I should feel so much surer.

Please forgive me for bothering you. Tell William I am glad he fetched the four horses.

Remember us kindly to Mrs Hawk.

Yours Sincerely D. H. Lawrence[4]

[1] Quintanilla took DHL's suggestion: see Letter 3332 and n. 1.
[2] On Kiowa Ranch, formerly owned by Evans. [3] See Letter 3354.
[4] Possibly accompanying this letter was a note (MS Chavez) from Frieda written on the verso of a photograph (as used for Letters 3312, 3313 and 3319):

Dear Mrs Hawk!

My best Xmas wishes, though it does not feel like Xmas here at all – You see us here shopping in the market, the boy with the basket is our servant – You never carry things here, not like *our* ranch life! We are looking forward to seeing you in the spring!

Yours sincerely Frieda Lawrence

3324. To Winchell Bóttern, [20 December 1924]

Text: MS UT; Photograph [An Indian and dog]; Unpublished.

Aven. Pino Suarez #43. *Oaxaca* (Oax), Mexico.
20 Dec

Dear Mr Bóttern[1]

I'm sorry about that book – but I can't remember in the least what was done with it.[2] I am almost sure I did *not* take it away from L[os] A[ngeles]. Have you asked Götzsche and Merrild? Götzsche perhaps has it. I *know* I never had it at all in my possession in Mexico last year. – If it doesn't turn up, do let me know if I can get you another copy. – Many congratulations on the baby girl: I am sure you are proud of her.[3] Remember me to Merrild. I hope he is doing well.

Yours Sincerely D. H. Lawrence

3325. To Anna Bóttern, [20 December 1924]

Text: MS UT; Photograph [Oaxacan street scene]; Unpublished.

[Av. Pino Suarez #43, Oaxaca]
[20 December 1924]

Dear Mrs Bóttern

How nice of you to have a daughter: I can see you're as proud as punch. I'm sure we shall come through L[os] A[ngeles] one day, then I shall be interested to see if she'll pull my nose or my beard: sure to be one or the other. – Why don't you translate 'The Fox', if you'd like to?[4] I'm not sure whether they're doing it in Swedish or not. My agent is

A.W. Barmby – Curtis Brown Ltd. 116 West 39th. St. New York City

he will arrange anything you want. – We are way down here for the winter – my wife and I in a rambling old house. It's a marvellous climate, all hot sun and cool nights. – I often laugh when I think of *Aida* and the interrupted supper in your flat.[5]

Regards from my wife and me.

D. H. Lawrence

[1] J. Winchell Bóttern, a Danish painter, and his wife Anna (née Grabow), were friends of Merrild and Götzsche in Los Angeles; see *Letters*, iv. 507 and n. 1.

[2] Unidentified.

[3] Simone (1924–); see Letter 3387.

[4] She did not translate any of DHL's works.

[5] The Bótterns, Merrild, Götzsche and DHL went to *Aida* at the Hollywood Bowl in September 1923; during the subsequent late meal in the Bótterns' room, the landlady came in twice because of the noise and laughter (Merrild, *A Poet and Two Painters*, pp. 321–2).

3326. To Edith Isaacs, 20 December 1924

Text: MS WHist; Photographs [Oaxacan street scenes]; Unpublished.

Aven. Pino Suarez #43, OAXACA. (Oax), Mexico[1]
20 Dec. 1924

Dear Miss Isaacs

Thank you for your letter. I wanted so much to see the article gaily appearing in the *Theatre Arts*, but no sign yet of the books. I hope they will come along. Did you really send them? Would you forward a copy to

Frau Baronin von Richthofen, Ludwig-Wilhelmstift, *Baden Baden*, Germany.

and one to

E. M. Forster, 'Harnham', Monument Green, *Weybridge*, near London. England

and two copies to my sister

Mrs L. A. Clarke, Grosvenor Rd, *Ripley* nr Derby, England.

My sister-in-law will want to translate the article into German. The 'Corn Dance' one came in the *Neue Merkur*. – I feel a qualm at the thought of your paying so much.

There are said to be interesting dances in the Indian villages here, at Christmas. I shall see. But they wont be anything like the Pueblo Indian ceremonies: not nearly so good. There's nothing in the world like the dances in New Mexico.

I am still hoping the copies of the *Theatre Arts* which you sent me will turn up.

Send me a *bill* for these others.

Yours Sincerely. D. H. Lawrence

3327. To Lady Cynthia Asquith, 23 December 1924

Text: MS UT; Unpublished.

Av. Pino Suarex #43. *Oaxaca*. (Oax.) Mexico
23 Dec. 1924

Your[2] note this morning – we are wintering here in the hot sun, where we can live out of doors. We may come to England in the spring, when I hope we shall see you. Or we may go straight up to New Mexico, where Frieda is now the

[1] Two photographs (the same as Letters 3303 and 3318) used as notecards.

[2] DHL's correspondent, Lady Cynthia Asquith (1887–1960), née Charteris, met DHL in July 1913 (see *Letters*, ii. 48); they frequently exhanged letters thereafter. Her husband, Herbert ('Beb') Asquith (1881–1947), the son of the former Prime Minister, Herbert Henry Asquith (1852–1928), was a barrister and also a poet and novelist.

proud owner of a little wild ranch at the foot of the Rocky Mountains, 8,500 feet up. We don't grow anything – only have four horses to ride: severely simple life. But now it's snow there.

I haven't got a single book of my own. I asked for a couple to be sent. When they arrive, I'll autograph one and let you have it, though it will be too late for your bazaar. However, it'll do for the next.

Remember me to Herbert Asquith. Merry Christmas to you from us both.

Yrs D. H. Lawrence

3328. To Mollie Skinner, [3 January 1925]
Text: MS WAPL; Postmark, Oaxaca 15 ENE 25; Unpublished.

[Frieda Lawrence begins]

Oaxaca Mexico
3.1.25

Dear Miss Skinner,

A happy new Year to you! I have written you many letters in the spirit only, when one was finished, another one was ready, so they were never born in the flesh! I am very glad your Black Swans are going to appear – *Dont* let the critics worry you, Lawrence *never* reads their criticism only I get mad occasionally – This is to welcome you in Australia, you will have the other half of life again, that you dont get in London – I hope one day you will come and see us at the ranch, I love it – This is a strange country, quite fantastic in its wild politics or no politics, but you will read it in Lawr's next novel, I like it by far the best! London to me is a wilderness and rabble, but just a few people! You will be on the sea now – we may go to Europe before long!

All good luck to you and the 'swans'!

Yours Frieda Lawrence

[Lawrence begins]

Dear Miss Skinner

I had your note about an introduction to *Swans*: and I wrote one.[1] But then I decided – and I'm sure I'm right – that you'd be better *without* an introduction by me. Critics would only be dragging me in all over everything again. – We may get to London in March, then I'll see Garnett.

Yrs DHL

[1] DHL probably wrote 'Preface to *Black Swans*' on 24 December 1924 ('Tonight is Christmas Eve'); it was first published in *Phoenix II: Uncollected, Unpublished and Other Prose Works by D. H. Lawrence*, ed. Warren Roberts and Harry T. Moore (1968).

3329. To William Hawk, 6 January 1925
Text: MS UT; Unpublished.

Av. Pino Suarez #43. *Oaxaca.* Oax. Mexico
6 Jan. 1925.

Dear William

We've got a parcel of pots and little things packed up for you and Rachel since before Christmas, and never got it off yet. The post is such a weariness and struggle here, and they keep on *losing* the things sent me from New York; so that one gets disheartened. Here one sits at the end of this thread of a narrow-gauge railway, and if that snaps – nothingness! It *is* queer and forlorn down here. – This morning Brett went riding horseback with the dentist and his wife[1] – Swiss – and she came home almost in tears, for the ranch. I never saw her so depressed. – It's so queer here, never free, never quite safe, always a feeling of being hemmed in, and shut down. I get sick of it myself: feel I shall bust. The ranch is *far* better. – But then there is the brilliant hot sun all day long and every day, and the mountains standing up dark and bluish from the yellow, blazing valley bed. – But the people are so curious and sombre and unfree inside themselves. Freedom is a gift inside one's own soul, you can't have it if it isn't in you. And it's not in the Mexicans.

Frieda wants to go and see her mother, too. Her sister writes that she seems to be failing – the mother. I hope not. We hear from her: and she is always lamenting that we are in Mexico, wanting us to go to Germany. I suppose it means we shall have to go, for a little while. I ought to go to London. So probably we shall sail for England from Vera Cruz in February. Brett doesn't want to go. She's afraid she couldn't afford it, and couldn't get back to the ranch this summer. Her heart is set on the ranch, and her 'little Ambrose', as she calls that aimiable pumpkin on four pins (don't tell her I said so). Therefore probably you'll hear from her soon, saying she's wending her way north, to Del Monte. She could stay in one of your houses till we get back, couldn't she?[2]

Is there any Taos news? I hear from nobody – Deo gratias![3] Has Tony gone east to join the redoubtable Mabel?[4] Witter Bynner went, and then Spud Johnson: so I wonder if Tony took his blanket and his two neat pigtails along too. Yo no voy![5]

I'm glad you fetched down the horses. Frieda is always moaning about the Azul's jaw. Did he have his tooth out, poor devil? How is everybody? – the

[1] The Kulls.
[2] This is the first hint of trouble over Brett (Frieda to DHL: 'I want the Brett to go away', Frieda Lawrence 165). See Brett 199–207.
[3] 'Thanks be to God!'
[4] See Letter 3383.
[5] 'I'm not going!'

baby, this cold (the newspapers say) weather? The wind blows a bit of a chill down here, which is supposed to indicate snow in the north. – In Mexico City there is a bad influenza going round. – But I guess it's really quite nice at Del Monte. – Hope Rachel is feeling brisk and cheerful, and that Miss Wemyss has not bitten the pup's nose off by now. What a cat she will be when we see her again! – Yes, it will be good to smell the cows in the corral once more – though at this moment the patio is reeking with the scent of some sweet tropical flower. Damn tropical flowers, anyhow.

Ask your father if he got my letter and cheque, about those taxes.

Best of good wishes to you all, for the New Year:

and au revoir.

Yrs D. H. Lawrence

Send $25.00 towards the horses: but nail Brett for 'little Ambrose' and still littler Dan.

3330. To Hon. Dorothy Brett, [9 January 1925]

Text: MS UCin; Moore 836–7.

[Av. Pino Suarez #43, Oaxaca]
Friday evening[1]

Dear Brett

The simplest thing perhaps is to write, as one can't shout everything.

You, Frieda and I don't make a happy combination now. The best is that we should prepare to separate: that you should go your own way. I am not angry: except that I hate 'situations', and feel humiliated by them. We can all remain decent and friendly, and go the simplest, quietest way about the parting, without stirring up a lot of emotions that only do harm. Stirred-up emotions lead to hate.

The thing to do is to think out quietly and simply, the best steps. But believe me, there will be no more ease between the three of us. Better you take your own way in life. Not this closeness, which causes a strain.

I am grateful for the things you have done for me. But we must stand apart.

Yrs D. H. Lawrence

[1] Dated to allow time for Brett to make plans for her journey (see Letters 3334, 3335, 3338, 3339); her own account suggests a much shorter time span (p. 205).

3331. To Curtis Brown, 10 January 1925
Text: MS UT; Huxley 625.

Av. Pino Suarez #43. *Oaxaca.* Oax.
10 Jan. 1925.

Dear Curtis Brown

Will you tell this woman she can do as she likes as far as I am concerned. You do as you think really best. I don't quite see why Secker rakes in two guineas, by himself.[1]

I am sending you four articles – 'Mornings in Mexico' – nice and short – via Barmby. By the way, The Contemporary Magazine – Cobden Sanderson's quarterly[2] – say they would like something of me in every issue, and I like them, so will you let them have any little thing they want. – Did Barmby send you a copy of *The Theatre Arts*: with my 'Hopi Snake Dance' article? – I am getting ahead with the Mexican novel. If heaven is with me, I should finish it this month. I had a good deal done from last year. – It will probably make you open your eyes – or close them: but I like it very much indeed. – If I finish by the end of the month, then about 2nd February we shall go to Mexico City, to see about a ship. My wife feels she must see her mother, and my father died, and my sisters keep worrying to see me. So perhaps we'll be in England by March.

I wired Barmby to proceed with Knopf for the next book. – Secker is good

[1] DHL's letter is written in the margins of Susan Miles's letter (TMS UT):

19 Woburn Square, W.C. 1.
December 16th. 1924.

Dear Sir,

I am compiling an anthology of passages, in prose and verse, on Youth, to be published next year by John Lane and should be glad if you would allow me to use the following extract from *The Boy in the Bush*: p.190. "Lennie came riding........p.191. slept all night." and p.198. "Dr. Rackett said *he thought it a wise plan, and further* that if.......p.200. these old men".

I should like to omit the words which I have underlined; and I should like to print the extracts under the title "Lennie", numbering them (i) and (ii).

I have written to Martin Secker and have been told that I may use the passages on payment of Two Guineas, if you will give your permission. I very much hope that you will agree.

Yours faithfully, Susan Miles

To D.H.Lawrence, Esq. c/o Curtis Brown, Ltd. 6 Henrietta St. W.C.2.

Susan Miles was the pseudonym of Ursula (Wyllie) Roberts (1887–1975); selections from chap. XII, entitled 'Lennie' appeared in the 'Take Pity Upon Youth' section of *An Anthology of Youth in Verse and Prose*, chosen by Susan Miles (John Lane, 1925), pp. 301–7.

The two guineas were to be sent to Curtis Brown and the fee split (Curtis Brown to S. Miles, 4 February 1925; TMSC UT); and Secker to Curtis Brown, 3 February 1925 (Secker Letter-Book, UIll).

[2] I.e. *Criterion.*

at changing his mind![1] I think we shall have to leave him less margin. – As for Seltzer, if only he'd have been open and simple with me, I'd have borne with him through anything. But a furtive little flea who hides his hand from me as if I was going to fleece him – whether fleas have hands and fleece or not – why – Basta!

Yrs. D. H. Lawrence

3332. To Luis Quintanilla, 10 January 1925

Text: MS Subun-So Book Store; Nehls, ii. 388–9.

Pino Suarez #43. *Oaxaca*. Oax.
10 Jan. 1925

Dear Quintanilla

Did you get the photographs? I signed and sent them back.

And the little article came. I was a bit sad, because *it* was sad and rather bitter: in fact very: with *undigested* spleen. Is that how you really feel about them? I doubt if they'd print it, because the touch isn't light enough. I'm

[1] Secker wrote to Curtis Brown on 8 December 1924 (Secker Letter-Book, UIll):

Dear Curtis Brown

I have been thinking over the question of the length of "St Mawr". I calculated when the typescript was in my hands that it did not run to much more than 50,000 words, and as there are no chapters or breaks of any kind in the text there is no possibility of giving it any appearance of greater length. Now if set in the same style as "England, My England" (and I am anxious not to depart from the uniform page and setting in which I have kept all the Lawrence fiction so far), I do not think that it will make a book of more than 160 pages or so, for which obviously I cannot charge 7/6.

The next point is that up to the present I think I am right in saying that it was the collection of three novelettes, called in this country "The Ladybird" which sold better than anything else. The book received remarkable notices, and it is a form which suits Lawrence. I do not know what extra material there is available at the moment, but I feel very strongly that the best way to treat "St Mawr" is to make it the first story in a collection of three, or possibly of only two, if the length of this latter is fairly substantial.

Will you kindly think over the question in the light of these representations. It would be far better to wait a little if necessary and let the Lawrence public have full measure than to publish a very short book and cause disappointment. It is quite probable that Lawrence is even now half way through another of these novelettes, in which case its inclusion need cause little delay.

Yours sincerely

and on 13 December (Secker Letter-Book, UIll):

Dear Curtis Brown

D.H.Lawrence

Many thanks for yours of the 10th. I think it would be a good plan to include "The Princess" in the volume "St Mawr", and I can then make it an ordinary 7/6 book which I am sure will be the most satisfactory course. I expect you will know by the end of January about the serial possibilities of both, and if you could let me have them then I could fix on March publication, subject of course to Knopf's plans.

Yours sincerely

afraid I had to go scribbling on your MS. – By the way, type on one side only, for literary MSS.

I couldn't help writing out your little article again.[1] I'll get it typed, and send it you. You could, you know, easily write these little sketches. Only it means *conquering* your own sadness and heaviness inside first, and being able to laugh at it all, if only on the wrong side of your face.

My wife wants to go to Germany to her mother. Probably at the end of the month we shall come up to Mexico to arrange a ship, and sail in February. – But then, should see you and Jane and Janes mother.

Till then, adios! D. H. Lawrence

3333. To Edith Isaacs, 10 January 1925

Text: MS WHist; Huxley 626.

Av. Pino Suarez #43. *Oaxaca.* Oax.
10 Jan. 1925

Dear Miss Isaacs

The two copies of *Theatre Arts* have come: thank you very much. I must say it's a *very* attractive production, and amazingly without printer's errors. Makes one believe it *can* be done. – Yes, I like my 'Hopi Dance' extremely, in appearance. I'd rather see it in *Theatre Arts* than in among the ads. of those great and profitable periodicals that have so much space and so little room for anything. – There's never a dance down here. They're terribly un-dancy, these Zapotec and Mixtec Indians. But when I see something that might do for you, I'll have a whack at it and send it along.

The first copies you sent me have disappeared, I am afraid, for ever: along with various books, contracts etc. The mail is letting me down.

Many thanks to you.

Yours Sincerely D. H. Lawrence

3334. To Emily King, 12 January 1925

Text: MS Needham; PC v. [a Mexican pottery]; Unpublished.

Pino Suarez #43. Oaxaca
12 Jan. 1925

My dear Pamela

Glad you had that *Boy in the Bush* at last – Christmas and New Year gone – very quiet here, save for crackers. – I think we shall go up to Mexico City the

[1] Quintanilla wrote 'Mexico, Why Not?' about the American tourists whom he guided around as part of his government job; it was dated 30 December 1924. DHL's version was published as 'See Mexico After, by Luis Q' in *Phoenix*. See Parmenter 143–5, 148.

first week in Feb. and see about ships. Probably F[rieda] and I will land in England some time in March or early April. Brett wants to go straight back to Del Monte, so I suppose she'll do so. Quite hot here – Feb. will be very hot.

Hope you are all well and busy.

Love DHL

The view is a little pottery here in Oaxaca.

3335. To Luis Quintanilla, 12 January 1925

Text: MS Subun-So Book Store; Nehls, ii. 389–90.

Av. Pino Suarez #43, *Oaxaca*, Oax
12 Jan 1925

Dear Quintanilla

I send you your little article, which I'm sorry I went scribbling on: and also mine. You mustn't take offence at anything I say: because of course I don't mean any. – I find even my article barely covers its rancour, *rancor*, and is a bit bewildering. There must be a terrible bitterness somewhere deep down between the U.S.A. and Mexico, covered up. When one touches it, it scares one, and startles one. — But just put my little article in the fire, if you don't like it. – Or if you like it, send it to *Vanity Fair* or some paper, and see if they'll print it over Luis Q.[1] I doubt if they will. It'll make them too uneasy. But fun to try them.

I have done a lot of my novel again – I had the biggest part done last year. It is good, but scares me a bit, also.

We think to come up to Mexico the first days in February, and probably sail for England on the 20th. Feb., from Vera Cruz. I don't feel very easy in my skin, in Mexico this time. Perhaps I ought to go home for a bit.

Miss Brett doesn't want to go to England – wants to go straight back to our ranch in New Mexico – and leave any time now. If she arrives in Mexico City, will you and your wife look after her a bit. Ask Mrs Quintanilla if she will. And if you hear of anybody nice with whom Miss Brett might travel up to El Paso, tell me, will you. I don't like to think of her going alone.

The little article is yours to do as you like with, entirely. Perhaps best just make an autodafe.

It's lovely and warm now here. What is it, makes one want to go away?

Best of wishes to you. D. H. Lawrence

[1] Years later Quintanilla recalled the difference between his spontaneous piece and DHL's 'polished' version: 'I never tried to place the Lawrence version because I did not agree with everything in it' (Parmenter 148).

3336. To Ada Clarke, 12 January 1925

Text: MS Clarke; PC v. [Huts and Mexicans at Mitla]; Lawrence–Gelder 130–1.

Pino Suarez #43. Oaxaca
12 Jan 1925

My dear Sister

I had your letter yesterday. – We shall probably come to England – F[rieda] and I – end of March or in April. I think we shall go up to Mexico City the first week in Feb. – so don't write here. – I've been very busy – wish I had got this novel done. Brett isn't coming to England – going to Del Monte – pining for the horses and the freedom. But it will be cold then.

love DHL

Ordered copies of *Theatre Arts* with 'Hopi Snake Dance' article for you and Pamela.

Mitla – huts and natives.

3337. To Amy Lowell, 16 January 1925

Text: MS HU; S. Foster Damon, *Amy Lowell: A Chronicle* (New York, 1935), pp. 669–70.

Av. Pino Suarez #43. *Oaxaca* (Oax), Mexico
16 Jan 1925.

Dear Amy[1]

Thank you for your letter and the little cheque.[2]

We were the summer in New Mexico – you know Frieda is now the proud possessor of a little ranch there, up in the mountains, about 17 miles from Taos. But we came down here end of October, because of the cold. It got my chest a bit: or the altitude: 8,500 ft. I expect we shall go back there in the summer: like it very much: come and see us one day.

But about March I think we shall go to England and Germany, for a month or two. Frieda's mother is very old, and keeps wanting her to go home. And my father died, and my sisters keep wanting to see me. – Probably we shall be in London when you are.[3] If so, I hope to see you again: it was 1914, and Richard was not yet a soldier[4] – You can always find me

c/o Curtis Brown. 6 Henrietta St, Covent Garden. W.C. 2.

[1] Amy Lowell (1874–1925), American Imagist poet. DHL met her in 1914 and corresponded with her frequently. See *Letters*, ii. 203 n. 2.

[2] She wrote on 31 December 1924 (Damon, *Amy Lowell*, pp. 467–9) and enclosed a 'cheque for the February and August statements' which were both very small because *Some Imagist Poets*, the anthologies for 1915–17 to which DHL had contributed, with exception of six copies of the 1917 volume, were now out of print and the royalties 'for two cents a time will disappear'.

[3] Amy Lowell planned to leave on 15 April 1925 for a lecture tour in England (Damon, *Amy Lowell*, p. 667).

[4] Richard and Hilda Aldington and the Lawrences were guests at a dinner party given by Amy Lowell at the Berkeley Hotel, London, on 13 August 1914 (*Letters*, ii. 207 n. 3).

He's in the telephone book: is a literary agent.

I should like very much to have *Keats*.[1] Am as a matter of fact rather fond of fat two-vol books with letters in them and all that.

Did my 'Quetzalcoatl' novel down here. It scares me a bit. But it's nearly done.

I wonder where I should ask you to send me the *Keats* book. Perhaps best c/o Curtis Brown and *to await arrival*. Tell them to mark it that, please. Then perhaps I'll review it in London. A threat! – But I should like to have it. – And if you tell either Thomas Seltzer or Martin Secker to give you the *Boy in the Bush* from me, they'll do it at once.

It's awful to have such a bad time with your health.[2]

I never said I knew all America: or all about it.[3] God forbid! and keep on forbidding!

One day, perhaps, we may be aimiable to one another for half an hour in your Brooklyn Garden.[4] If pansies are out – Jusqu' alors![5] – or no, till London again.

Yrs D. H. Lawrence

Frieda sends saluti e ricordi.[6]

Remember us to Mrs Russell.[7]

DHL

3338. To Constantine Rickards, [16 January 1925]

Text: MS Forster; Unpublished.

Oaxaca. Oax.
16 Jan. 1924

Dear Mr Rickards[8]

Many thanks for sending the mail. I enclose a little cheque for stamps.

Miss Brett thinks of leaving on Monday, arrive Mexico Tuesday morning,

1 Amy Lowell's *John Keats*, 2 vols, was published on 10 February 1925 (Damon, *Amy Lowell*, p. 671).

2 She had written; 'your energy amazes me. My many operations took a great deal of my energy away' (ibid., p. 668).

3 She had read *Studies in Classic American Literature* and 'found not a little divergence of view': until DHL had seen the whole of America he had not seen it at all 'you dear prejudiced soul' (ibid., p. 669).

4 DHL probably had in mind her home in Brookline, Massachusetts.

5 'Until then!'

6 'greetings and remembrances'.

7 Ada (Dwyer) Russell (1863–), Amy Lowell's life-long friend and companion.

8 Constantine G. Rickards (1876–1950), lawyer and British Vice-Consul in Oaxaca and Mexico City, 1910–43; interested in archaeology and wrote *The Ruins of Mexico* (1910). m. Adela Durán, daughter of a Mexican general in the bodyguard of Porfirio Díaz (1830–1915) (Parmenter 27, 38 and Nehls, ii. 365–6). Brother of Edward Rickards; see Letter 3304 and p. 177 n. 2.

on her way to New Mexico. – She never heard a word of that miserable listening machine of hers, from the man in Vera Cruz.[1] Best get it sent, if possible, straight to Mexico City, for her to take along. Though you must be as sick of the sound of it as I am.

I expect we shall be up in La Capital the first week in February, when I shall come to thank you.

Father Rickards still hasn't got rid of his cough. Otherwise all quiet,

Yours sincerely D. H. Lawrence

3339. Ida Rauh, 16 January 1925

Text: MS UT; Postmark, Oaxaca 16 ENE 25; Unpublished.

Av. Pino Suarez #43. *Oaxaca.* Oax.
16 Jan. 1925

Dear Ida

You are back in Santa Fe.

I went on with my 'Quetzalcoatl' novel down here: nearly done: extraordinary book: probably they'll have my head off for it.

I could take a wonderful and terrible play out of it, if I dared. *I dare do all that may become a man*, said somebody.[2] It's the becoming – But I shall not forget that play. It's rankling somewhere.

Brett leaves here Monday, going to Del Monte Ranch – staying awhile en route in Mexico City. I'll tell her to let you know when she comes to Santa Fe. Just look after her a little bit, will you? I don't like her travelling all that way alone: mais les femmes seront toujours seules.

We stay here a bit. Then, end of February or early March, to England – Germany – peut être le paradis. Plus on voyage, plus on n'arrive pas.[3]

But I expect we'll be back at the ranch by June. – Quien sabe.

Best wishes to Andrew. Best wishes to you and the boy:[4] sure he's better in New Mexico.

As for the stage – on it or off it, it's the same old show.

Yrs D. H. Lawrence

If you see Mrs Hughes, remember me to her. She was very nice to us.

As for the gay troubadour, Hal – and the troubadour triste, Spud – 'they sing beneath another cover now –'.[5]

[1] Mr Drake (Letter 3345). [2] *Macbeth* I. vii. 46.

[3] 'but women will always be alone . . . perhaps paradise. The more one travels, the more one doesn't arrive.' [4] Her son, Daniel Eastman (1913/4–69). [5] Unidentified.

3340. To Hon. Dorothy Brett, [20 January 1925]

Text: MS UCin; Photograph [Mexican man and boys]; Irvine, Brett 39.

Av. Pino Suarez #43. Oaxaca. Oax
Tuesday 20 Jan.

Dear Brett

A letter from Miss Hughes:[1] she is in the Hotel de Genêve[2] – you remember we went there, where the old woman spoke to us – and is just up from an attack of grippe – going directly to Cuernavaca. You'd better call and see her at the Genêve. – Cold here today, and cloudy. Expect you have got the *norte* blowing in Mexico. – Do you remember what we did with the long, long letter from the man who wanted to come to the ranch? – His wife wrote today, really indignant that I had ignored him.[3] a very funny letter. Wish I had the other to compare.

DHL

3341. To Carlo Linati, 22 January 1925

Text: MS Neville; Moore 826–7.

Avenida Pino Suarez #43. *Oaxaca*, (Oax), Mexico.
22 Jan. 1925

Dear Carlo Linati

The *Corriere della Sera* with your article on me, wandered in today.[4] It makes me laugh a bit. I never knew I was so *frenetico*. You leave me quite out of breath about myself. Well well, in a world so anxious for outside tidiness, the critics will tidy me up, so I needn't bother.[5] Myself, I don't care a button for neat works of art. But you read too much of me at once, I think. – And again, I can't help laughing, your article seems such a breathless series of explosions. Do I really seem like that? – all you say?

I have been busy down here in Mexico doing a novel I began last year: it's nearly done. I dread to think of it's going out into the world. I call it 'Quetzalcoatl'.

But really, Signor Linati, do you think that books should be sort of toys,

[1] Rosalind Hughes (1881–1976), secretary from California, in Oaxaca on holiday 14 October–26 December 1924 at the Hotel Francia. According to her, DHL wrote at least twice to ask her to look after Brett in Mexico City (Parmenter 2, 194, 213).

[2] According to Parmenter (letter to the editors), the hotel was Edwardian, old-fashioned and comfortable, used by academics and New England spinsters.

[3] Kyle and Mary Crichton; see Letter 3462.

[4] See p. 90 n. 3.

[5] Linati presents DHL as a writer whose imaginative intensity exceeds his capacity for thematic and structural control.

nicely built up of observations and sensations, all finished and complete? – I don't. To me, even Synge, whom I admire very much indeed, is a bit too rounded off and, as it were, put on the shelf to be looked at.[1] I can't bear art that you can walk round and admire. A book should be either a bandit or a rebel or a man in a crowd. People should either run for their lives, or come under the colours, or say *how do you do?* I hate the actor and audience business. An author should be in among the crowd, kicking their shins or cheering them on to some mischief or merriment – That rather cheap seat in the gods where one sits with fellows like Anatole France[2] and benignly looks down on the foibles, follies, and frenzies of so-called fellow-men, just annoys me. After all, the world is *not* a stage – not to me: nor a theatre: nor a show-house of any sort. And art, especially novels, are not little theatres where the reader sits aloft and watches – like a god with a twenty-Lira ticket[3] – and sighs, commiserates, condones and smiles. – That's what you want a book to be: because it leaves you so safe and so superior, with your two-dollar ticket to the show. And that's what my books are not and never will be. You need not complain that I don't subject the intensity of my vision – or whatever it is – to some vast and imposing rhythm – by which you mean, isolate it on to a stage so that you can look down on it like a god who has got a ticket to the show. I never will: and you will never have that satisfaction from me. Stick to Synge, Anatole France, Sophocles:[4] they will never kick the footlights even. But whoever reads me will be in the thick of the scrimmage, and if he doesn't like it – if he wants a safe seat in the audience – let him read somebody else.

I think my wife and I will come to Europe in the spring. If we come through Milan I will let you know. Anyhow we leave here in February. If you have anything to write me, will you address me

c/o Curtis Brown, 6. Henrietta St. Covent Garden. London. W.C. 2.
England.

Thank you for the article, and all the interest you took in my works. – I feel like coming to Italy again.

Yours sincerely. D. H. Lawrence

[1] For DHL's early familiarity with plays by John Millington Synge (1871–1909), see *Letters*, i. 142, 183, 260–1.

[2] DHL liked *L'Ile des Pingouins* (1908) by Anatole France (pseudonym of François Anatole Thibault) (1844–1924) in 1909 (*Letters*, i. 104), but was extremely critical of *Le Petit Pierre* (1918) and called France 'a very graceful piffler' in April 1919 (ibid., iii. 348–50).

[3] I.e. in an exceedingly expensive seat (gallery tickets were about 2 Lire, first-row boxes about 18).

[4] For DHL's regard for Sophocles, see *Letters*, i. 261, 525 and n. 1.

3342. To Hon. Dorothy Brett, [23 January 1925]
Text: MS UCin; Postmark, Oax[aca] 23 E[. . .]; Irvine, Brett 39–40.

[Frieda Lawrence begins]

Oaxaca
Friday

Dear Brett,

Your squirrel sat this morning in the sun in the Doña Maria's window![1] We had a letter from the man who wanted to come to the ranch – The *wife* wrote this time, so funny and *cross* – *Why* was L[awrence] going to miss this chance of meeting this great man! – *Are'nt* they funny! And he was using his *capital* for the journey and did L object that they had a hunting lodge! [Lawrence substitutes 'Seat' for 'lodge', and interjects: (I think she meant in the saddle!)] Lawrence is seedy but getting better, well you must be exhausted after such a work like the novel – I said to my mother, it had grown out of the soil of this country like a cactus – L said they showed him two letters from Murry to you, does the lost sheep want to come home to the fold by any chance?[2] I have got to go to Kull for my teeth, beastly and expensive – They cant sell the furniture, Mr Thompson is suspected of a dark damsel and the Aikins dont get on[3] – That's the gossip – I wont say anything about deeper things, I dont know where I am – L is recovering, has a dread of Mexico, we may go from Plymouth either straight to Devonshire or France or Spain – People all speak very kindly about you – Not that you care – A nice letter from old Hawk about that ranch business – And my Ma delighted with the last photos – I drank only milk again the day you left – measuring my 'lost' waist!! – Hope all your plans will be successful – We are getting restless too –

Yours ever F.

[Lawrence begins]

Nothing new here – We'll go our little ways quietly with as few feelings as possible – I'm so sick of feelings – as for arguments, *nada*! – They sent on your machine – such a *crate* – huge! – Mr Hawk wrote deep snow at the ranch. Guess it's melted by now. I feel like shifting – but dont want to hang round in hotels. – Sorry you dont care for 'Isabel'[4] – but you wouldn't care for the

[1] Brett had bought 'a baby squirrel and a cage' which must have been left with the hotel proprietress, María Jarquin de Monros (Brett 191).

[2] See following two letters.

[3] Colonel Albert D. Akin (1870–1956), American mining engineer and co-owner with G. William Thompson of a mine; stayed in Oaxaca at the Hotel Francia, 1923–6. m. Jean Harmon (1898–1969), his second wife, 1923; she helped to nurse DHL in February 1925 (Parmenter xxiii, xxv, 2, 75, 361).

[4] On Avenida San Salvador #68; see Parmenter 255.

MonteCarlo by yourself. I guess we shall go back there – Natividad now smitten down with the flu.

Let us know how you are getting on.

DHL

We bought two mountain lion skins – nice – wish you could have taken one to the ranch.

3343. To Hon. Dorothy Brett, [26 January 1925]

Text: MS UT; Postmark, Oaxaca 26 ENE 25; Huxley 626–8.

Av. Pino Suarez #43. Oaxaca. Oax.
Monday morning

Dear Brett

Your letter with Murry's enclosed this morning. They make me sick in the pit of my stomach: the cold, cold, insect-like ugliness of it. – I shall avoid meeting Murry.

If Mexico City is so unpleasant we shall probably stay here an extra week or fortnight, and go straight to Vera Cruz. I don't like the sound of it. – You are right, I think, about King.

And a word about friendship. Friendship between a man and a woman, as a thing of first importance to either, is impossible: and I know it. We are creatures of two halves, spiritual and sensual – and each half is as important as the other. Any relation based on the one half – say the delicate spiritual half alone – *inevitably* brings revulsion and betrayal. It is halfness, or partness, which causes Judas. Your friendship for Murry was spiritual – you dragged sex in – and he hated you.[1] He'd have hated you anyhow. The halfness of your friendship I also hate. And between you and me there is no sensual correspondence.

You make the horrid mistake of trying to put your sex into a spiritual relation. Old nuns and saints used to do it, but it soon caused rottenness. Now it is half-rotten to start with.

When Maruca[2] *likes* a man and marries him, she is not so wrong. Love is chiefly bunk: an over-exaggeration of the spiritual and individualistic and analytic side. If she likes the man, and he is a man, then better than if she loved him. Each will leave aside some of that hateful *personal* insistence on imaginary perfect satisfaction, which is part of the inevitable bunk of love, and if

[1] Brett and Murry had been in love since 1920 but were lovers for less than a year in 1923 after the death of his wife Katherine Mansfield (Sean Hignett, *Brett: From Bloomsbury to New Mexico, A Biography*, 1984, pp. 109–15, 133–42).

[2] Maruca Monros Jarquin.

they meet as mere male and female, *kindly*, in their marriage, they will make roots, not weedy flowers of a love-match. If ever you can marry a man feeling *kindly* towards him, and knowing he feels kindly to you, do it, and throw love after Murry. If you can marry in a spirit of kindliness, with the criticism and the ecstasy both sunk into abeyance, do it. As for Toronto, I don't think you have any *warm* feeling at all for him[1] – I know your Captain Seeley:[2] there is a kind of little warm flame that shakes with life in his blue eyes: and that is more worth having than all the high-flown stuff. – And he is quite right to leave his door open. Why do you jeer? You're not superior to sex, and you never will be. Only too often you are inferior to it. – You like the excitation of sex in the eye, sex in the head. It is an evil and destructive thing. Know from your Captain that a bit of warm flame of life is worth all the spiritualness and delicacy and Christlikeness on this miserable globe. – No Brett, I do *not* want your friendship, till you have a full relation somewhere, a *kindly* relation of both halves, not *in part*, as all your friendships have been. That which is in part is in itself a betrayal. Your 'friendship' for me betrays the essential man and male that I am, and makes me ill. – Yes, you make me ill, by dragging at one half at the expense of the other half. I am so much better now you have gone. – I refuse any more of this 'delicate friendship' business, because it damages one's wholeness.

Nevertheless I don't feel unkindly to you. In your one half you are loyal enough. But the very halfness makes your loyalty fatal.

So sit under your tree, or by your fire, and try, try, try to get a real kindliness and a wholeness. – You were really horrid even with William: and no man forgives it you, even on another man's account.

Know, know that this 'delicate' halfness *makes* evil. Put away all that virginal stuff. – Don't still go looking for men with strange eyes, who know life from A to Z. Maybe they do, missing out all the rest of the letters, like the meat from the empty egg-shell. Look for a little flame of warm kindness. It's more than the Alpha and the Omega. And respect the bit of warm kindliness there is in people – even William and Rachel. And try and be *whole*, not that unreal half thing your brothers hated you for,[3] and that all men hate you for, even I. –

1 Frank Prewett ('Toronto') (1893–1962), Canadian-born poet and protégé of Lady Ottoline Morrell to whom Brett had been attached in 1919 (Hignett, *Brett*, p. 102); he married after the First World War and again during the Second. See 'Introduction' by Robert Graves in *The Collected Poems of Frank Prewett* (1964), pp. vii–viii.

2 Brett wrote to Ruth Quintanilla on 24 February 1930 (TMSC UT): 'Do you remember that odd sea Captain in my hotel!!'

3 Oliver Sylvain Baliol Brett (1881–1963), 3rd Viscount Esher, 1930; president of the British Drama League; and Maurice Vyner Baliol Brett (1882–1934), Assistant Keeper and Librarian to London Museum, 1919–34.

Try and recover your wholeness, that is all. *Then* friendship is possible, in the kindliness of one's heart.

Yrs DHL

Remember I think Christ was profoundly, disastrously wrong.

3344. To John Middleton Murry, 28 January 1925

Text: MS NYPL; Huxley 628–9.

Av. Pino Suarez #43. *Oaxaca.* (Oax)
28 Jan. 1925.

Dear Jack

Brett sent on your letters. That seems to be an absolutely prize sewer-mess, of your old 'group.'[1] – Pray read my story in the *Criterion.*[2] I doubt if Kot would be so kind to you, as to assert its 'truth'. Doesn't he know *all* the real truth? – much more suitable to his purposes. – Please dont 'defend' me to H. M. Tomlinson or to anybody else.[3] As for your Tomlinson, I have seen him about five minutes: can't imagine why you should have to defend me in his precious eyes.

Mon cher, c'est canaillerie pûre et simple. Je m'en fiche[4] – without feeling pious about it.

You remember that charming dinner at the Café Royal that night? You remember saying: I love you Lorenzo, but I won't promise not to betray you.? – Well, you *can't* betray me, and that's all there is to that. Ergo, just leave off loving me. Let's wipe off all that Judas–Jesus slime.

Remember, you have betrayed everything and everybody up to now. It may have been your destiny. – But in Kot you met a more ancient Judas than yourself. There are degrees within degrees of initiation into the Judas trick. You're not half way on yet. Even Kot is miles ahead of you. It's a case of Sauve-toi.[5] Judas was a Jew, and you're not quite that, yet.

All I want to say is, don't think you can either love me or betray me. Learn that I am not lovable: hence not betrayable.

[1] The 'group' was composed of Murry, Kot, H. M. Tomlinson and his brother Philip, and John William Navin Sullivan (1886–1937), reviewer for *The Times*, musician and scientist (Carswell, *Lives and Letters*, p. 205).

[2] 'Jimmy and the Desperate Woman': Jimmy is modelled on Murry. (Despite his marriage in April, Murry, according to Brett, was having an affair – for which there is circumstantial evidence only, Parmenter 268.)

[3] Henry Major Tomlinson (1873–1958), author of travel books, novelist and professional journalist; friend of Murry since 1917, contributed to *Adelphi* and objected to excerpts of *Fantasia of the Unconscious* in *Adelphi*. m. 1898, Florence Margaret Hammond. See also Letter 3886 and n. 1.

[4] 'My dear, it is dishonesty pure and simple. I don't give a damn'.

[5] 'Save yourself'.

Frieda and I may come to England in the spring. But I shall not want to see anybody except just my sisters and my agent. – Last time was once too many.

One day, perhaps, you and I may meet as men. Up to now, it has all been slush. Best drop that Christ stuff: it's putrescence.

We leave here in a fortnight: where for, I am not quite sure.

Yrs DHL

3345. To Hon. Dorothy Brett, [28 January 1925]

Text: MS UCin; Postmark, Oaxaca 28 ENE 25; Moore 830

Av. Pino Suarez #43. Oaxaca. Oax.
Wednesday.

Dear Brett

Don't send me any more Murry letters. The smell of that London stink I want no more in my nostrils. I have written Murry also to that effect.

I will write to the Drake man at Vera Cruz about that machine: though it does bore me. – The box was sent to you at the Isabel hotel. You should have it by now. Much best unpack the machine[1] and put it in your trunk.

I am tired to death of all the indecencies of intimacies. I want to be left alone, decently. There must be a complete new attitude. And till then, silence about all this stuff.

DHL

3346. To Martin Secker, 29 January 1925

Text: MS UInd; Postmark, Oaxaca 29 ENE 25; Secker 62.

Oaxaca.
29 Jan. 1925

Dear Secker

We were glad to hear from you: but all sounds horribly damp and damped down.

We leave here next week – for Mexico City. I think we shall probably be in England for a short time, end of March or in April. Then I shall see you.

You know Knopf is publishing *St Mawr*: and they want to do it alone.[2] I too

[1] machine] trunk

[2] See p. 194 n. 1. Secker wrote to Knopf on 29 January 1925 (Secker Letter-Book, UIll):

Dear Mr Knopf

Many thanks for your letter of the 18[?]th about D.H.Lawrence, on whose entry into your list I congratulate you most warmly.

First of all, about the contents of the "St Mawr" volume. Curtis Brown represented your wishes in the matter of the book over here containing the title story only, but while I considered it very carefully I decided I could not very well alter my decision to include "The Princess", as a make-weight to bring up the volume to the requisite length to range with his other works in

would prefer it to come by itself, even if it is a little book. Sometimes it is good to put out a little book. And it's not a good idea to put 'The Princess' at the end, I feel.

I have finished 'Quetzalcoatl' – or at least, am in the last chapter. It is a long novel. I feel, at the bottom of my heart, I'd rather not have it published at all. But anyhow, it isn't tomorrow.

Hope everything is cheering up.

Yrs D. H. Lawrence

3347. To Curtis Brown, 29 January 1925

Text: MS UT; Unpublished.

Oaxaca.
29 Jan. 1925

Dear Curtis Brown

We leave here next week – for Mexico City. After that I am not quite sure. So better not write till you hear. We shall probably be in England by end of March. I will let you know.

Barmby sent the Knopf agreement for *St Mawr*. I too would rather this story were published by itself, although it is short.

I have done my 'Quetzalcoatl'. I haven't tried, as you suggested I might, to be a second Anatole France. I shouldn't even be flattered to be the *first* Anatole France – though he was[1] a nice old man. I am afraid, sales or no sales, I prefer the colour of my own flag. However, I shall bring 'Quetzalcoatl' along.

Jusqu' alors.

Yrs D. H. Lawrence

fiction. Without altering the entire format and printing in different type it would have been impossible for "St Mawr" alone to reach even 200 pages. As there are now six or seven Lawrence titles in a uniform style you will appreciate the undesirability of a change.

Now as to date of publication. I cannot afford to miss the spring season with the book, and to postpone until June would be most unwise, that month and July being the very worst in the year. I am willing to alter my plans and not publish until May, and perhaps on your side you may find it possible to advance your date a little. There would be an additional reason for clearing the decks early if as I imagine may well be the case, Lawrence has already finished his long Mexican novel. If this is so, would it not be possible for us to get into step and arrange to publish this simultaneously in January next? The third week in that month is in my opinion one of the best times for a good new novel, certainly in this country, and presumably also with you.

Yours sincerely

Alfred A. Knopf Esq

Duplicate proofs of *St Mawr* will be sent to Lawrence very shortly

Secker persisted in wanting to include 'The Princess' despite its being accepted for serial publication (Secker to Curtis Brown, 4 February 1925, Secker Letter-Book).

[1] was] is (France d. 13 October 1924).

3348. To Alfred Decker Hawk, 30 January 1925

Text: MS Lazarus; Moore, *Intelligent Heart* 337–8.

Oaxaca.
30 Jan 1925.

Dear Mr Hawk

Thank you a thousand times for seeing to those taxes for me.

We leave here next week, for Mexico City. Miss Brett has already departed. I suppose soon you'll be seeing her at the ranch. – We are going to Europe for a while: my wife wants to see her mother, who complains she will not see us again. Probably we shall sail on the 20th. Feb. – to England. I want to be back at the ranch by June at latest, to fix up that *water*. – It seems a bit of a waste of life and money, to trail off to Europe again so soon. But I suppose it's in one's destiny.

I am wondering very much how deep the snow is, and how Miss Brett will stand the cold. But if she goes into the Danes' cottage,[1] it is so sunny, and warm with a fire.

Tell William I will write to him tomorrow and send some money for the horses. I forgot last time.

I look forward, really, to being back and *out of the world*. One does get sick of people – endless, endless strangers and people one doesn't want to be bothered about. And this autumn we won't hurry away. I don't see why we can't stay on till Christmas. – It will be so nice to have you and Mrs Hawk for responsible neighbours, so I needn't feel the father in Lobo.

We had a jolly letter from Bobbie in Capri – she seemed to enjoy it. One day you'll be setting off with Mrs Hawk for a trip.

My wife sends many greetings to you and Mrs Hawk, so do I.

Yours sincerely D. H. Lawrence

Remember me to Scott Murray when you see him.

The address in Mexico

c/o The British Consulate, Av. Madero #2. Mexico D.F.

3349. To Ada Clarke, 30 January 1925

Text: MS Clarke; Unpublished.

Oaxaca.
30 Jan. 1925

My dear Sister

The photograph of father came today.[2] It's very nice: I see a good deal of myself in it.

[1] Merrild and Götzsche.

[2] See Keith Sagar, *The Life of D. H. Lawrence* (1980), p. 170, for the photograph; it was taken at the back of Ada Clarke's house in Grosvenor Road, Ripley.

We leave here next week, for Mexico City. I am not sure how long we shall be there. But probably by the end of March we shall be in England – or early in April. So don't write till I send an address.

I am sending you now your sarape: a big and very fine one: and in the parcel a puma-skin for Emily. – You will hang the blanket in a hall or a smoking-room: or if it's too startling for the house, then in the shop. They're quite unique in the world, these Oaxaca sarapes: Oaxaca you pronounce Wa-há-ka: like tomato.

Glad you had such a gay time at Christmas. Here it was very quiet. – I hope the house is getting on, so I can see it ready. But surely it will be ready by April – and the flowers coming out too.

Brett has gone off to the ranch, to look after it till we get back. We ought to be there at least by June, to bring down the water from the Gallina canyon, for irrigating.

It's quite hot here: but shade is cool. We had a little earthquake.[1] I feel like a breath of the sea – I mean I would like to breathe the sea again. Mexico is dry, dry, dry as bath brick. Frieda wants to see her mother – and her daughter Barby, who has got engaged to an Irishman.[2]

So Bertie II is already talking! Wonder what sort of a *pronunciamiento* he'll make, in his day.

I'll let you know the moves.

DHL

3350. To Constantine Rickards, [30 January 1925]

Text: MS Forster; Unpublished.

Oaxaca.

31 Jan. 1925. Friday.[3]

Dear Mr Rickards

Thank you for the letter forwarded. – We leave here next week – arrive in Mexico City about Thursday, I suppose. Then look for a ship. – I wish there was such a thing in the world as a good Cargo boat that might take my wife and me and loiter with us to Yucatan or Jamaica or somewhere. I'm not very anxious to arrive in England till spring comes. – But I suppose nice Cargo boats have disappeared off the face of the waters.[4] Do you know anything about them?

[1] DHL had been suffering from influenza and then he (and Frieda) got 'malaria' (but see p. 210 n. 3): 'While he was so ill an earthquake happened into the bargain . . . I felt ill and feverish and Lawrence so ill in the next room . . .' (Frieda Lawrence 166). The earthquake was too small to be recorded (Parmenter 39).

[2] See p. 134 n. 2.

[3] Friday was 30 January.

[4] Cf. Genesis i. 2; vii. 18.

All very quiet in Oaxaca: very pleasant: but I feel now like moving again. Would like to smell the sea, too.

Hasta luego[1] D. H. Lawrence

3351. To Constantine Rickards, [4 February 1925]
Text: MS Forster; Unpublished.

Oaxaca
4 Feb.

Dear Mr Rickards

I said we'd come to Mexico this week – but man proposes –[2]

The tail-end of my influenza got tangled up with a bit of malaria in my inside – very unpleasant. But with quinine injections, much better already. I suppose we shall come up next week – about the 12th. – and look for ships. I don't suppose there'll be any mail worth forwarding.

Yrs D. H. Lawrence

3352. To Hon. Dorothy Brett, [5 February 1925]
Text: MS UCin; Postmark, Oaxaca 5 FEB 25; Moore 831.

Oaxaca.
Thursday

Dear Brett

You hear how my flu remains got tangled up with *malaria*: these houses have malaria mosquitoes from that little river. So I am still in bed – having quinine injections shoved into me.[3] But hope to be up Sunday, and get away from Oaxaca next week. I hate the place – a let-down. The doctor – a Mexican[4] – says the *race* is exhausted – But the novel is finished. – I almost envy you the

[1] 'Goodbye' (literally, 'until soon').

[2] 'Man proposes but God disposes', from Thomas à Kempis (1380–1471), *Imitatio Christi*, I. xix. 2.

[3] Frieda had written to Brett the day before, postmarked 4 February (MS UCin):

Wednesday

Dear Brett,

Lawrence has been so ill – Malaria, Influenza, Inflammation of the bowels – But yesterday he turned for the better, to-day he is out of the wood – But my word it has been a struggle! Hope you are all right – No news, otherwise – I think we shall catch that boat on the 20th, but L wont be fit to travel for another ten days –

Love to you –

Write F.

See also the letter to Brett, 20 February 1925, in Irvine, Brett 42.

[4] Dr José E. Larumbe (1883–1956), director of the Hospital Militar; he treated foreigners in Oaxaca (Parmenter 318).

ranch – even the snow: the log fires, the cosy evenings with the lamp, the home-made bread and the feeling that one's blood isn't being sullied. – Guess I've had malaria since December.[1] I had it in Ceylon. – I've very little desire to stay in England: but the sea, and the change will be good. And after all, one can so easily cross the Atlantic, again.

Go quietly and simply at El Paso and they won't bother you. If they charge duty on the things, I'll pay.

I think even of Santa Fe with pleasant feelings, after here: wouldn't mind if I was in the De Vargas.[2] – You'll only be a *month* earlier than last year.

Remember me to everybody.

DHL

The address

AWBarmby, Curtis Brown Ltd, 116 West 39th St, New York City.

3353. To Hon. Dorothy Brett, [7 February 1925]

Text: MS UT; Telegram, Oaxaca FEB 7 1925; Unpublished.

Oaxaca. Oax
7 Feb

Dorothy Brett,
Hotel Isabel. San Salvador núm. 68 sesenta y ocho –
Much better bon voyage.

Lawrence.

3354. To William Hawk, 7 February 1925

Text: MS UT; Postmark, Oaxaca 11 FEB 25; cited in Moore, *Intelligent Heart* 338.

Oaxaca.
7 Feb 1925

Dear William

I send you thirty dollars towards the horses: your father said he'd give you the remainder from the hundred for the taxes. I would have sent before but my cheque-book was nearly empty. Now I've got a new one.

Miss Brett is leaving Mexico City tomorrow, for El Paso. I hope she'll have a good journey. See she pays you for Dan and 'little Ambrose.' We think she'll be happy in the Danes' cottage.

I have been steadily out of luck this trip down here: don't think I shall ever come to Mexico again while I live. I wondered why I wasn't well down here –

[1] DHL must have had a recurrence of his Ceylon infection: Oaxaca is too high for the malarial mosquito but typhoid fever was endemic (Parmenter 318).

[2] The hotel where the Lawrences and the Luhans stayed at the beginning and end of the Hopi snake dance trip and the Lawrences and Brett on their way to Mexico (Letters 3199, 3269).

thought it was the remains of the old flu – and so it was, but with malaria. This place is full of malaria. I've had the doctor and heavy quinine injections, and feel a rag: but much better. We hope to get away some time next week, to Mexico City – and sail for England from Vera Cruz the 20th (D.V.!!)

– I hope the *Azul* is better – and that it's nice at the ranch now. Did Rachel get her basket of pots sent by parcel post? – sent some weeks ago. How is Rachel? – weary of the winter. – Brett will be arriving with a lot of bits of stuff.

Your father's note this morning about the double assessment of the ranch for 1923. – I am infinitely obliged to him for all his trouble. – Wonder if Rachel will let you wear your black and white blanket? – guess she'll put it on the floor.

Well, I'll never come down here again. Hope we'll get back by May, see you again and start a human life.

Remember us very warmly to Rachel, Walton, Miss Weems.

Yrs D. H. Lawrence

3355. To Hon. Dorothy Brett, 15 February 1925

Text: MS UCin; Postmark, Oaxaca 13 FE[. . .]; Irvine, Brett 41.

c/o The British Consulate. Av Madero #2, Mexico D.F.
15 Feb. 1925

Dear Brett

We had your cabelgram from El Paso – hope the journey was pleasant.

We are in the *Francia* at Oaxaca – I was moved down yesterday.[1] That malaria got me badly – I can hardly stand. But I hope, very much, we can get away to Mexico in a week's time, out of the malarial area. – The doctor said that bad cases of malaria were spread from that Soldiers hospital on the Llano – that one near us – when *bad* cases of pernicious paludismo are brought up from the low countries! Nice for other folks! – and that childrens playground.

Am glad to be in the Francia – feel safer.

King asked us to stay at Tlalpam – we may do so, till we sail – which will now, I trust, be on March 10th. I've got a few more days in bed here yet.

I sent $14.30. to the man Drake at Veracruz for you: the cheque you sent me got torn up while I was ill – so you can pay those dollars for me some time, to William or somebody. I wish I was anywhere rather than in Mexico, at the moment. I'm sure even snow will look nice. Let us know how everything is at Del Monte – write c/o King. – F[rieda] has got a bit of malaria too – You were lucky to escape.

[1] Clyde Wilson (1903–), son of Robert Wilson who was a miner and mine manager at Taviche, drove DHL to the Hotel Francia – DHL had to be moved by stretcher – and later drove the Lawrences to the railway station (Parmenter 2–3, 326, 341).

Col Akin was hit in the leg by a bullet while playing tennis.[1]

The Kulls are unheard of – ten days gone into that awful fever-country.[2]

DHL

Poor Gertler! – perhaps it is the best for him.[3]

3356. To Thomas Seltzer, 15 February 1925

Text: MS UT; Postmark, Oaxaca 19 FEB 25; Lacy, *Seltzer* 145–8.

c/o The British Consulate. Av. Madero #2. Mexico D. F.
15 Feb 1925

Dear Seltzer

Yes, I agreed at last with Barmby that he should offer the short novel *St. Mawr* to Knopf. It seemed better all round: in the end even better for you. – But that does not mean I shall never offer you anything more. I am not so very sure that one exclusive publisher is wisest. Let us see how things work out: and if Knopf does one book, why should you not do another, if you wish to?

We hope to sail in about a fortnight's time to England, though I am not sure how long we shall stay. – Curtis Brown's address finds me.

Yrs D. H. Lawrence

3357. To Curtis Brown, 15 February 1925

Text: MS UT; Huxley 629–30.

c/o The British Consulate. Av. Madero #2. Mexico D. F.
15 Feb 1925

Dear Curtis Brown

Am still in Oaxaca – but was moved down to the hotel yesterday – Been having the devil of a time with malaria – think it's got under. – That comes of hot winter sun! – I *hope* and pray we can get up to Mexico City in a week's time, out of the malarial areas. – With luck we should sail for England from Veracruz on March 10th – land in England about March 25th. I shall bring the MS. of 'Quetzalcoatl' with me, and you can get it typed out for me – then I can go over it. It is finished.

Had a long cablegram from Seltzer – *Is it true you are going to Knopf? etc.* I replied that *St. Mawr* was offered to Knopf, but that I didn't see why, in the future, we couldn't offer another novel to Seltzer, if all goes well. And I mean that. I don't quite believe that it is good for me to be monopolised by one

[1] See Irvine, Brett 104 n. 24.

[2] They went to the Costa Chica to provide dental services for plantation workers (Parmenter 67).

[3] See Letter 3365. Gertler was engaged to a Jewish girl, Phyllis Wilkinson in late 1924; the engagement was subsequently broken off (see John Woodeson, *Mark Gertler: Biography of a Painter, 1892–1939*, 1972, pp. 293–4).

publisher in each country. I think two publishers stimulate the sales much better than one. For example, a more popular publisher than Secker would, I believe, handle a little novel like *St. Mawr* much better than Secker. I believe you think it wisest to put all one's works into the hands of one publisher – but seriously, I don't agree. One becomes like a special sort of medicine. – But we will talk this over when I see you. – Hold my mail for me.

I hope Secker has agreed to publish *St Mawr* alone, without 'The Princess'. I wrote him I preferred that.

Yrs D. H. Lawrence

3358. To Emily King, 25 February 1925

Text: MS Lazarus; Unpublished.

Tehuacan (Puebla).
25 Feby 1925

My dear Pamela

We have got away from Oaxaca – I was tied down by flue and malaria: am simply green! That's what tropics and high altitudes do for you. F[rieda] has got a bit of flue also, and is very depressed. – We go on tonight to Mexico City, but thank heaven there is a Pullman, one can sleep through the night. We shall probably stay in Mexico City till a boat sails from Veracruz to England – some three weeks ahead. It's a nuisance to have to wait so long, but most things in these countries are a nuisance. We land, I suppose, in Plymouth, and we may stay down in Devonshire a month or so, by the sea, while we're there. – I tried to post you a puma skin, but the post office returned it. They are fools. We shall bring it along. – Tell Peg I had her letter – am glad she got her exemption.[1] I think she'll prefer secondary teaching – elementary is no joke. But I'll write when I feel a bit more solid.

Love to you all.

DHL

3359. To Hon. Dorothy Brett, [27 February 1925]

Text: MS UCin; Postmark, Mexico D.F. 27 FEB 1925; Irvine, Brett 43–4.

Mexico D. F.
Friday

Dear Brett

We got here yesterday – shaken sicker by that pullman from Tehuacan. Staying in the Imperial Hotel, top floor, sunny (but it's all cloudy today) – with bathroom and electric heater – too feeble to rough it. F[rieda] is sick, and

[1] Her Matriculation Exemption.

eats nothing – I am pale green and no longer fat. Apparently there's not a ship to England till March 17th – awful to wait here all that time. There might be a Dutch boat. We got to the Consulate today – had your wire – doctors say I must go down to sea-level as soon as possible – I get thinner and thinner. – Imagine all that wild winter at the ranch! – We're seeing nobody here. I feel like lying very low for a while, in Devonshire, by the sea. We'll see how it works.

The basket for F's mother is very pretty.

The Americans in Oaxaca were *so* kind, when I was ill.[1]

Will let you know what we do next.

DHL

[Frieda Lawrence begins]

Dear Brett,

I am glad you are having a good time and that everybody is nice with you – Thank you for the present you left for my mother – Let's all take a new turn – We are all tired to sickness and death of all these little personal relations – The gods must come back into us and into life – Lots of gods – And who gets the biggest egg does'nt matter, at present I feel like little ones – L. has *Malaria* really and I have a scrap too, my nose is *too* thin, I dont like it – I had better stay fat! We still dont know *where* to go – London is no go anyhow –

L got your drawing book is sending it!

You are a society bird!

Yours F.

I feel so relieved as if we had all made a move *on*! and out of sickness into health and bigger spaces!

3360. To Baroness Anna von Richthofen, [1 March 1925]

Text: MS UT; Unpublished.

[Frieda Lawrence begins]

Hotel Imperial, Mexico

[Lawrence interjects: 1n März] *Sonntag*

Liebe mère,

Hier sind wir sehr elegant mit eignem Wohn-und Badezimmer – ich endlich und Gott sei Dank im Bett und bedient – Lawr viel besser nach einer *grässlichen* Reise aus jenem Höllenland – Wir verhalten uns mäuslestaad im Winkel drin – Am 17. geht unser Schiff Hamburg Amerika Linie Holsana

[1] Jean Akin helped Frieda with the nursing. Others were Norman W. and Geraldine Taylor, Canadian and American respectively, and Ethel R. Doctor (1892–1978), American, all Presbyterian missionaries; as well as the Thompsons, Donald Miller and the Wilsons. See Parmenter 325–6.

[Lawrence corrects to *Rio Bravo*] über Havanna nach *Plymouth*. Da *Seeluft* gut für Malaria ist, wollen wir ein Haus nehmen so in der Salcombe Gegend – denk, wenn Du da noch einmal auftreten könntest – Plymouth ist nah von Salcombe – Auf dem Schiff haben wir jeder eine hübsche Kabine – Ach, Anna, ich habe eine Fegfeuerzeit hinter mir, aber *hinter* mir – Jetzt wieder *voran* – L schläft – das ärgste war die seelische Niedergeschlagenheit und die *Nerven*, es war zum verzweifeln – Es war als ob er nicht mehr leben könnte noch wollte – Von Friedel einen netten Brief, es ist nur zu seiner Ehre dass er Amerika nicht mag – Im wunderschönen Monat Mai kommen wir dann zu Dir – Wenn wir wohler sind – und es warm ist – Die Ranch kann ich vermieten – an Willa Cather – Denk, wenn mir Lorenzo gestorben wär, trotz allem schweren, es wäre nicht denkbar für mich –

Deine Tochter Frieda

[Lawrence begins]

Ja, Schwiegermutter, man stirbt nicht so leicht. Jetzt springt die Frieda auf, will grüne Seide kaufen, für einen Rock.

Wir fahren 17n Marz aus Veracruz auf Schiff *Rio Bravo*, vom Hamburg–Amerika Linie: kommen an Plymouth 3n April oder 4n.

[Frieda Lawrence begins]

[Dear mère,

Here we are very elegant with our own living- and bathroom – at last, thank God, I'm in bed and waited on – Lawr much better after a *dreadful* journey from that hell of a country – We keep quiet as mice in the corner – On the 17th our ship Hamburg Amerika Line Holsana [Lawrence corrects to *Rio Bravo*] leaves for Plymouth, via Havana. Since *sea air* is good for malaria, we want to take a house somewhere in the Salcombe area – suppose you could once more set foot there – Plymouth is near Salcombe – On the boat we each have a nice cabin – Oh, Anna, a time of purgatory lies behind me, but *behind* me – Now *forwards* once again – L is asleep – the worst was the emotional depression and the *nerves*, it drove one to despair – It was as if he couldn't or wouldn't live on – A nice letter from Friedel, it's only to his credit that he doesn't like America – In the wonderful month of May, then, we come to you – When we're better – and it's warm – I can let the ranch – to Willa Cather – Think, if I'd lost Lorenzo, in spite of all the difficulties, it would be unthinkable for me –

Your daughter Frieda

[Lawrence begins]

Yes, Schwiegermutter, one doesn't die so easily. Now Frieda is leaping up, wants to buy green silk for a skirt.

We travel 17th March from Veracruz on the *Rio Bravo*, of the Hamburg–Amerika Line: arrive in Plymouth the 3rd April or the 4th.]

3361. To Curtis Brown, 2 March 1925

Text: MS UT; Huxley 630.

Imperial Hotel. Mexico D.F.
2nd March 1925

Dear Curtis Brown

Well anyhow we've got out of the Valley of Oaxaca: I was so ill down there, with malaria and flu.

We are due to sail on the Hamburg–Amerika boat *Rio Bravo* from Veracruz on the 17th – land in Plymouth about April 3rd. I think we shall stay down in Devonshire for a while, to get strong: doctors say I must be by the sea: too much altitude in these places. If there is anything urgent, a letter would get me on board the *Rio Bravo* at Plymouth: but there won't be: and I'll write you at once. I'll bring the 'Quetzalcoatl' MS. along, and have it typed in England.

Yrs, auf wiedersehen D. H. Lawrence

3362. To Ida Rauh, 3 March 1925

Text: MS UT; Postmark, Mexico D. F. [. . .] MAR 25; Unpublished.

c/o The British Consulate, Av Madero #2. Mexico D. F.
3 March 1925

Dear Ida

I had your letters, and today your telegram. We got up here last Thursday – simply shattered: but are pulling ourselves together. My malaria and grippe got me very badly in my inside, there'd soon be no more me, but my shoes. Am still taking beastly quinine. The doctors say we must go to sea-level for some months to shake off the effects. Even here the altitude is very bad. We are sailing to England on the 17th – in two weeks' time: on the 15th we go down to Veracruz. In England we shall stay quiet a bit by the sea. And probably by June we shall be back at the ranch: if the money holds out. I hope you'll come and see us there. – I've got a very attractive scheme worked out for a play: Noah, and his three sons, his wife and sons' wives, in the decadent world: then he begins to build the ark: and the drama of the sons, Shem, Ham, Japhet, – in my idea they still belong to the old demi-god order – and their wives – faced with the world and the end of the world: and the jeering-jazzing sort of people of the world, and the sort of democracy of decadence in it: the contrast of the demi-gods adhering to a greater order: and the wives wavering between the two: and the ark gradually rising among the jeering: I would write you the part of the wife of Japhet (they've got no names in the Bible the women) – wonder if I'll feel enough strength to do it![1] But oh, what about the actors! – Remember me to Andrew.

DHL

The address in England
c/o Curtis Brown, 6 Henrietta St. *London* W.C.2.

3363. To Hon. Dorothy Brett, [3 March 1925]
Text: MS Subun-So Book Store; Nehls, ii. 396.

[Frieda Lawrence begins]

Hotel Imperial, Mexico City
Tuesday 3. March

Dear Brett,

My mother will love her basket, it was nice of you – and the little cloth! We are better and the Lord be praised – I was ill with fever that the soles of my feet peeled! and always knowing that L[awrence] was *worse* – He looked like the shadow of a white rose-leaf! But now we are enjoying the getting better – Yes, would'nt it be fun to arrive at the ranch but altitude is poison for malaria, it needs the sea – The Hawks are good people! Lord, how you must enjoy the great space and loneliness – I do hope in a few months we come back; if not, shall I let the ranch to *Willa Cather* and for rent let her pay for the irrigation ditch? – We have our berths for the 17 – Arrive Plymouth second of April – go to Lynmouth or some sea-side – *No* people for me, they only do one harm and you know my attitude to them – We have seen nobody but King, he has rather a mean face – And the Azul after the mares you bet you!! Is Tony with Mabel? – We have two rooms high up and our own bath and W. C. Fancy so much snow at the ranch –

Love F.

Use anything of the ranch things you like!

[Lawrence begins]

We sail on the *Rio Bravo* from Veracruz two weeks today – leave here, I suppose, Sunday week: land in Plymouth about April 3rd, and stay in

[1] *Noah's Flood* exists in a pencil MS in the notebook which DHL started with 'The Hopi Snake Dance' (see p. 110 n. 3). It has two scenes; DHL revised the first scene in a later MS (published in *Phoenix*).

Devonshire. I feel I never want to see another soul, except very casually. – Strike of tram-cars here.[1] We are mostly in our rooms: see *nobody*, really. One envies you the space and freedom: but I must go to sea-level for a bit.

DHL

Our ship sails March 17th: I have already booked cabins.

3364. To Idella Purnell, 3 March 1925

Text: MS UT; cited in Bynner 252.

Imperial Hotel. Mexico D.F
3 March 1925

Dear Idella

I have just got your letter. The parcels went to the ranch – Bynner said he was coming to Mexico in March, and I asked him to be *sure* to bring them. Now I doubt if he'll come. He is due back in Santa Fe very shortly. I am writing at once to the ranch to have the things sent to you, save the hats. You write Hal, to Santa Fe – he still may come: to bring you the hats.

We both got malaria so badly in Oaxaca, we can hardly crawl. I never knew the town was reeking with malaria, till I had it myself and was in bed a month. We struggled up here last week – and are sailing for England on the 17th – just two weeks today. This time I *really* want to get back to Europe, for this sickness has taken all the energy out of me. – We had much better have come to Chapala, but Frieda didn't want to. She now hates Mexico: and I no longer like it.

It's amusing to hear of your speculations.[2] Don't plunge very deep – I wouldn't trust anything here. And believe me, Guadalajara is about the best place in this damned republic.

I hope you'll get your things soon. If there's a bit of delay, it may be because there's six feet of snow up at Del Monte, and the mail may have difficulty getting out. Then these wretched customs here.

Remember me warmly to Dr Purnell.

Souvenirs. D. H. Lawrence

3365. To Hon. Dorothy Brett, [3 March 1925]

Text: MS UCin; Postmark, Mexico D.F. 4 MAR 1925; Irvine Brett, 45–6.

[Imperial Hotel, Mexico D. F.]
3 March. – evening

Dear Brett

Mr Hawk has two parcels of clothes and hats that I was to take to Idella

[1] The street-car strike began on 1 March; by the 8th, the strikers demanded (unsuccessfully) that George Conway (see p. 228 n. 1), then managing director of the Mexican Light and Power Company, be expelled from Mexico.

[2] See Letters 3392 and 3442 and n. 2.

Purnell, and which that old fool of a Mrs Purnell sent to Taos when I told her Santa Fe. Idella writes she wants the things, especially the *dress*, very badly. She doesn't want the hats in any hurry. Would you please pack up the dress, dress-length and such etceteras and post them to

Miss Idella Purnell. Galeana #150, *Guadalajara*, (Jal.), Mexico.

I don't think I'd send the hats or the face-cream. Make it as easy as possible. Mr Hawk will help you.

I sent you off a final parcel of *batteries* the other day – hope they'll arrive all right. You'll be set up in ear-goods.

We have our ups and downs with this fever, but gradually get stronger. Really, I curse them all, for not having warned us. Because one simply can't get this malaria out of one's blood. One doses oneself sick with quinine, and leaves off to be prostrate with fever.

I have just seen King at his office – I feel so uninterested in everybody. Nobody else has discovered us, till there is a message from Quintanilla this evening. How the hell did he know we were here? And I thought he was in Guatemala or heaven. I simply *cant* see people and make talk.

Hope all goes well at Del Monte. Use anything you want out of the trunks.

DHL

The address in London is

c/o Curtis Brown, 6. Henrietta St. London W.C.2.

– he'll send me all my mail.

No, I only meant poor Gertler, marrying a little Jew wife. But Frieda says I ought to say wise Gertler, happy Gertler – so I hold my tongue.

3366. To Luis Quintanilla, [3 March 1925]

Text: MS Subun-So Book Store; Nehls, ii. 396.

Hotel Imperial.
3 March

Dear Quintanilla

They gave me your note this evening. I went and got malaria, plus grippe, so badly in Oaxaca, that I was a month in bed and can still hardly crawl through the days. My wife got it too. We were lying absolutely low, here, not having the energy for a thing. But come in and see us: we're almost always stuck here.

We are sailing to England on the 17th – two weeks today – and till that time, struggling through the days with some difficulty, feeling done in by this dirty sickness.

I thought you had gone to Guatemala, Washington, or Pekin: are you sure you've not?

Kindest regards from us both to Mrs Quintanilla. We'll muster up courage in a few days to have our teas in Sanborn's, shall we?

Yrs D. H. Lawrence

3367. To Thomas Seltzer, 5 March 1925

Text: MS UT; Postmark, Mexico D.F. 7 MAR 1925; Lacy, *Seltzer* 148.

Imperial Hotel, Mexico D.F.
5 March 1925

Dear Seltzer

I've been so sick with malaria – thought I'd die. We sail for England on the 17th, from Veracruz – get there 3rd April. –

Will you send to

Señor Genaro Estrada, Secretaria de Relaciones Exteriores, Mexico D.F. a copy of Seligman's book on me[1] – Estrada is under-secretary for foreign affairs, and wants to write a critique on me.

Yrs D. H. Lawrence

3368. To Emily King, [11 March 1925]

Text: MS Lazarus; Unpublished.

Hotel Imperial, Mexico D F.
11 March

Dear Pamela

Another blow. After various examinations and blood tests, the doctor[2] won't let me take a sea voyage nor go to England. He says I must stay in Mexico in the sun, or return to the ranch. So we shall go back to the ranch as soon as I can travel: am still in bed here. Write to me to Del Monte Ranch, *Questa*, New Mexico. – I shall go there as soon as possible. He says I *must* stay in the sun. – But it's a blow.

Love DHL

3369. To Alfred Decker Hawk, 11 March 1925

Text: MS ColU; Moore, *Intelligent Heart* 338.

Hotel Imperial. Mexico D.F.
11th March 1925

Dear Mr Hawk

The doctor has made an analysis of blood and so forth, and says I had *much*

[1] See Letter 3113 and n. 1.

[2] Dr Sidney Ulfelder (1875–), American, head of surgery at the American hospital (Parmenter 354). Quintanilla said that Ulfelder told him – and Frieda – that DHL had tuberculosis (Nehls, ii. 396). See Frieda Lawrence 166–7.

better come to the ranch, that the sea-voyage will shake me and bring on fever, and England will not be good for me. He insists on our coming to New Mexico: and thank goodness, there is Del Monte to come to. Could you get the apple orchard cottage ready for us? We shall leave (D. V.) next week – perhaps the 17th, when the ship was due to sail – and arrive somewhere about the 21st. I am so glad to be able to come straight to Mrs Hawk and you, and to William and Rachel, and Del Monte. It is really the only home one has got.

Tell Miss Brett. Tell her to prepare for us. We want to have a happy, friendly time, all of us.

Au revoir D. H. Lawrence

3370. To Hon. Dorothy Brett, 11 March 1925

Text: MS UCin; Postmark, Mexico D.F. 11[. . .]; Moore 832.

Hotel Imperial, Mexico D F.
11 March 1925

Dear Brett

The doctor says I must *not* go to England nor take a sea-voyage at present, but the ranch is where we ought to be. – So help Mr Hawk to get ready for us – the apple orchard cottage – we hope to arrive by 21st or 23rd. And let us pray to the gods to keep us all quiet and kindly to one another, *all* of us. We *can* do it, if we will.

DHL

[Frieda Lawrence begins]

I am really *glad* to come back, delighted – It has been a time!

F.[1]

[1] Frieda wrote again to Brett about 19 March (MS UCin):

Hotel Imperial, Mexico

Dear Brett,

So we are coming, starting the end of next week – Stay 2 or 3 days in Santa Fé do some shopping – The doctor says in a year Lawr's lungs should be quite cured, but he must *not* write and become a vegetable – And Brett, it would be better if you will stay at the Dane's cottage, I think it would be a strain if you came to our ranch, both for L and me; You will be more helpful, if you want to help down at the ranch, we must get a nice couple it wont be easy to find, Lawr wants a man to work with; I am glad to come but I hate not to have seen the children and my mother – Lawrence had taken a decided turn for good, it was time – And I want to give all my strength to his recovery, he must'nt paint or any thing – And you see, Brett, both to Lawr and me you *are* a guest and a friend, any thing else was just your idea – but never a *fact*, it is *bad* – and you are all so good in your *consciousness* but you see a lot of things you also are that you dont know of, there is a strangled self in you that does all sorts of things you never know – And I know that your living with us took the unconscious ease and glamour out of my life – I always later on felt you waiting and watching and I hated it – *That* is'nt what I want – Let us be simple friends and relase all that other soul stuff – And it is'nt that I want myself the adoration you give to

3371. To Idella Purnell, [11 March 1925]
Text: MS UT; Bynner 252–3.

Hotel Imperial, Mexico D F
11 March

Dear Idella

The doctor has kept me in bed since Friday – blood tests etc – *insists* we must not go to England, but that we return to New Mexico. So we give in. – If possible we'll leave next week for Santa Fe. I'm sorry not to have seen you and your father – am still in bed here – and a perfect rag.

I do hope you are better. I didn't know you'd left the Consulate: are you glad.[1]

We'll meet on a happier day than this.

Yrs D. H. Lawrence

3372. To Curtis Brown, [11 March 1925]
Text: MS UT; Huxley 630.

Hotel Imperial. Mexico D.F.
11 March

Dear Curtis Brown

Still in bed here. Doctor made all sorts of examinations, blood tests etc: says I must *not* risk a sea-voyage nor the English climate, for some months: must stay in the sun, either here, or go to the ranch. So as soon as I can travel we shall go to the ranch. Write me there

Del Monte Ranch. *Questa*, New Mexico.

This is rather a blow, indeed. It's been a series of blows lately.

Yrs D. H. Lawrence

3373. To Ida Rauh, [11 March 1925]
Text: MS UT; Postmark, Mexico D.F. 11 MAR 25; Unpublished.

Mexico D.F. Hotel Imperial
11 March.

Dear Ida

The doctor *insists* that I ought to go to New Mexico, to the ranch, *not* risk a sea-voyage nor the English climate, yet. So we give in. If possible, we leave here next week for El Paso: and we may be in Santa Fe by the 20th. I'm very

Lawrence, it would stifle me – It makes everything tight round me and Lawr feels the same – and surely that silly, poky little house cant in itself mean much to you – anyhow I could'nt have you there again – You will hate me for this, but I also have my life to live and the responsibility

Yours F.

[1] She had been working as a secretary in the American consulate at Guadalajara.

shaky, so shall have to stay pretty quiet. But shall be glad to see you and Andrew and the boys.[1] – Oh, I've been so knocked out – and after all these blood tests and things, I give in.

Au revoir, then D. H. Lawrence

3374. To Curtis Brown, 16 March 1925

Text: MS UT; Unpublished.

Mexico.
16 March 1925

Dear Curtis Brown

Herewith the Oxford Press agreements.[2] I told you the doctor wont let me come to England at present. We leave for the ranch in a few days time. Write me there. – I am feeling better.

Yrs D. H. Lawrence

3375. To Alfred Decker Hawk, [19 March 1925]

Text: MS ColU; cited in Moore, *Poste Restante* 82–3.

Hotel Imperial. Mexico D. F.
Thursday. 19 March

Dear Mr Hawk.

The doctor has kept me on a little longer here: but we shall leave on Monday for El Paso, or at latest, on Tuesday: that is the 24th. So we should be in Santa Fe by 27th. I will let you know – and will telegraph the day we are to arrive in Taos, so if you send me a letter to the post office, or c/o Walter Ufer, I will have everything brought up that you may want to order in Taos, as we shall want a wagon for the luggage.

I am feeling much better, therefore seeing too many people. I shall be glad to see Del Monte again, and you all, the Montañeses.

Don't forget to send a list to Taos of the things you need – or, quickly, a list to Santa Fe, care of Mrs Andrew Dassburg, of anything I can bring you from that town.

Please tell Miss Brett, and Saludos! to everybody.

D. H. Lawrence

[1] Daniel Eastman and Alfred Dasburg (1913–), son of Dasburg and his first wife.
[2] For the illustrated edition of *Movements in European History*.

3376. To Idella Purnell, [19 March 1925]

Text: MS UT; Bynner 253.

Hotel Imperial. Mexico
Thursday

Dear Idella

The doctor put me in bed again, and kept me there: threat of pneumonia. Now I'm up and about. The ship has gone – but doctor says I *must not* go to England now: so we're going to ranch – Del Monte Ranch, Valdez. New Mexico.

This time, *nothing* has gone right.

Let's hope for the next time.

If you come to the U.S., come and see us at the ranch – really.

Yrs D. H. Lawrence

3377. To Luis and Ruth Quintanilla, [19 March 1925]

Text: MS Subun-So Book Store; Nehls, ii. 397.

[Frieda Lawrence begins]

Hotel Imperial
Thursday

Dear Mrs Quintanilla,

Gramond[1] came and said Jane was ill – I am so sorry – That's why we have'nt heard from you both – Do ring up and say how she is – It will upset your plans but it's really better than if she had fallen ill on the voyage[2] – O dear, I really cannot bear anybody being ill any more and a baby ill is heartrending, I hope she is better already –

Our love to you both Frieda Lawrence

[Lawrence begins]

Dear Quintanilla

We were very much distressed to hear Jane was ill. I hope it's not bad, and that Mrs Quintanilla will be able to sail. Really, there is a doom on us all in Mexico: best for us to depart. – We are due to leave on Tuesday morning: I am finished with the doctor thank God. – Let us know how it is: we don't go out till about 11.0: and if we can do anything for you in *any* way, anywhere, let us know.

D. H. Lawrence

[1] Perhaps Stuart E. Grummon (1901–60), secretary to the US embassy; the Lawrences had met him in Oaxaca (Parmenter 79). As the daughter of an American mother, Jane Quintanilla would be a matter of concern to him.

[2] Ruth Quintanilla had been planning to take her daughter to the USA (Parmenter 149–50).

3378. To Ida Rauh, [19 March 1925]

Text: MS UT; Postmark, Mexico D.F. 19 MAR 25; Unpublished.

Hotel Imperial. Mexico D. F.
Thursday 19[1]th. March

Dear Ida

The doctor kept us a bit longer. We leave *definitely* on Monday – 23rd – or Tuesday – 24th: so we should be in Santa Fe by 26th or 27th.

I began a play[2] which, poco a poco,[3] will, I think, come to what I want: and you want.

We'll go to De Vargas and ring you up.

Greet Andrew.

DHL

But don't tell people we are coming – I don't want to see them.

3379. To Martin Secker, [20–3 March 1925]

Text: MS UInd; Postmark, Mexico D.F. 23 [. . .] 25; Secker 51–2.

Mexico D. F.
20 March

Dear Secker

We are done in after all, I got so ill with my malaria etc, the doctor wouldn't let me sail: says I mustn't go to England before end of summer. So we're going back to the ranch – leave next Tuesday. The address as before

Del Monte Ranch, *Questa*, New Mexico.

It will be cold for a while longer yet, but the sun will be good. We both feel disappointed, having counted on an English spring. But after all, perhaps the sure sun over here is better than the hypothetical sun over there.

Send me just one copy of *St Mawr* to the ranch, will you – and the rest: to my sisters, one each to Mrs Clarke and Mrs King – a copy to

E M. Forster, 'Harnham', Monument Green, Weybridge

– and one to

Catherine Carswell, Hawthorn Cottage. Gt. Kingshill, High Wycombe, Bucks

and one to

J.M.Murry, The Old Coast Guard Station, *Abbotsbury*, Dorset.

I wonder if the *Adelphi* has really died. Do hope you'll have a nice summer.

Yrs D. H. Lawrence

[1] 19] 18

[2] *Noah's Flood*, or possibly, *David*; DHL had finished six scenes of the latter by 14 April (Letter 3394).

[3] 'slowly'.

March 23rd

The proofs of *St Mawr* came – I am returning them today. Apparently you didn't include 'Princess' after all.[1] – We leave in two days time.

DHL

3380. To Emily King, [23 March 1925]

Text: MS Needham; PC v. El Popócatepetl; Postmark, [. . .]; Unpublished.

Mexico D.F.
Monday 23 March.

We have booked berths in the Pullman to leave Wednesday – so we should be in Santa Fe by Saturday, on a through journey. I managed to send your puma skin today, to Ada's – after a struggle. I am feeling much better – and everybody here is very nice to us. – It is your birthday[2] – I had thought we should be home for it. But we'll come later in the summer when I am quite solid again.

Love to all. DHL

3381. To Ida Rauh, [23 March 1925]

Text: MS UT; PC v. Amecameca, Arrieros; Postmark, Mexico D.F. 23 MAR 25; Unpublished.

Mexico D.F.
– Monday 23 March

We have booked berths on the Pullman for Wednesday morning, so we ought to arrive in Santa Fe Saturday morning – shall go to the De Vargas. Hope the weather will be decent up there. – This last week have had quite a good time, going out: such a relief to have one's life back.

Hasta luego! DHL

3382. To Alfred Decker Hawk, [29 March 1925]

Text: MS UT; cited in Moore, *Poste Restante* 83.

De Vargas. Santa Fe
Sunday

Dear Mr Hawk

We got here this afternoon: I think we shall come up on Tuesday, with Mr and Mrs Dassburg. They will drive us straight up to Del Monte: so we should

[1] Secker sent DHL proofs of *St. Mawr* about 24 February 1925; Secker did not see 'The Princess' until he received proofs of the *Calendar of Modern Letters* at the beginning of March (Secker to Knopf and Curtis Brown, 6 and 3 March 1925; Secker Letter-Book, UIll).

[2] On 21 March.

be with you on Tuesday afternoon. Could you, do you think, give the Dassburgs a bed for the night? We will help Mrs Hawk.

So sick of travelling – shall be so glad to settle.

Au revoir to all D. H. Lawrence

tell Miss Brett not to bother to come down to Taos – car will be full.

3383. To Emily King, [31 March 1925]

Text: MS Lazarus; Unpublished.

Santa Fe.
31 March

My dear Pamela

We got here on Sunday – the journey seemed long and wearisome. But it is good to be here: everybody very friendly, the sun so clear and the air so fine and pure. It will soon make one well. There is no snow, save on the mountains, and the peach-trees are coming into bloom. But of course Del Monte is higher. The Dassburgs are motoring us up today – they are artist friends. It takes rather long, 90 miles of desert and mountain road – but it's very lovely. I really like this country better than any landscape I know – the desert and mountain together. – Mabel Lujan is still in New York with Tony – Witter Bynner got back two days ago. Everybody seems to have spent a rather hard winter.

We shall stay a month or so down at Del Monte, before we move up to our ranch: Kiowa ranch we call ours: because the Kiowa Indians used to camp on the hill on which the ranch stands. – It will be good to have a real country life: the space, and silence, and the horses. Brett is at Del Monte. She will stay on there: not move up with us to our ranch this summer.

But we were disappointed not to see the spring in England. But I hope we can come in the autumn all the same. I feel rather a hankering after England – perhaps because I was ill, then one wants to come home.

I hope you are all feeling well and happy. Write to me to Del Monte.

Love to you all. DHL

3384. To Anne Conway, 2 April 1925

Text: MS Booth; Postmark, [. . .] APR 2 1925; Moore, *Intelligent Heart* 339.

Del Monte Ranch. *Valdez*, Taos County. *New Mexico*
2 April 1925.

My Dear Mrs Conway[1]

We got here yesterday – mountains snowy, wind wild and cold, but bright

[1] Anne Elizabeth Conway, née Tawse (1881–1962), b. Scotland. m. 1908, George Robert Graham Conway (1873–1951), resident engineer for Aberdeen, 1898–1907; chief engineer of

sun. I'm not altogether here yet: bits of me still on the way, like luggage following. We're staying with our neighbours for a while.

The Emigration people in El Paso – the Americans – were most insulting and hateful. Before you grumble at the Mexicans, as the worst ever, try this sort of American. *Canaille* of the most bottom-doggy order, and filthy with insolence.[1]

The basket of food was a great consolation on the journey, especially the fruit. We ate *all* the pie: not at all like invalids. The people in the Pullman dreary: and in the drawing-room a Mexican family with seven children. – Never come via El Paso, if you can help it.

I still have a lurking hankering for Europe. I think at the end of the summer, we shall both sail.

Thank you so much for being so kind to us. Tell Conway I hope his troubles are smoothing out. – Really, Mexico City is not so bad, you know: when one finds one's own countrymen still sterling. (Even the 'bad old woman', don't you think?)

Write us a line – tell us the news: whether Joseph has yet changed his many-coloured coat, etc.[2] – and about Luz y Fuerza – and millefleures.[3]

Yrs D. H. Lawrence

3385. To Amy Lowell, 6 April 1925

Text: MS HU; Damon, *Amy Lowell*, pp. 696–7.

Del Monte Ranch. *Questa*, New Mexico
6 April 1925

Dear Amy

I have so often wondered if you are sitting in London, in the Berkeley, maybe:[4] and see where we are. I got malaria in Oaxaca: then grippe: then a typhoid inside: was so sick, I wearied of the day. Struggled to Mexico City,

British Columbia Electric Railway in Vancouver, Canada, 1912–16; managing director from 1916, and from 1927 president of Mexican Light and Power Co. and Mexican Tramways Co. till 1947 and 1942 respectively. Conway was an avid collector of Spanish colonial documents (Parmenter 164). The Conways befriended the Lawrences in Mexico City; DHL's signature and that of 'Frieda Lawrence née von Richthofen' appear in Anne Conway's Guest Book – 'March 18. '25. Lunch.' See also p. 219 n. 1.

[1] DHL never forgot the humiliation he endured; see his letter to Maria Cristina Chambers, 19 January 1929.

[2] The Mexican counterpart to the Biblical Joseph (cf. Genesis xxxvii. 3) is unidentified.

[3] 'Light and Power – and a thousand flowers'.

[4] Amy Lowell had had to cancel her trip to England; she had a hernia attack on 10 April and continued in poor health until 12 May when she died from a stroke (Damon, *Amy Lowell*, pp. 699, 701). Her secretary wrote to DHL on 22 April about her health: see *The Letters of D. H. Lawrence & Amy Lowell 1914–1925*, ed. E. Claire Healey and Keith Cushman (Santa Barbara, 1985), p. 127.

was put to bed again for three weeks – then packed off up here. We had booked our passages to England, but the doctor said I *must* stay in the sun, he wouldn't be answerable for me if I went on the sea, and to England. So we came here. The Emigration Authorities at El Paso treated us as Emigrants and nearly killed me a second time: this after the consul and the Embassy people in Mexico – the Americans – had been most kind, doing things to make it easier for us. They only made it harder. The Emigration Dept is Dept of Labour, and you taste the Bolshevist method at its crudest.

However – after two days fight we got through – and yesterday got to our little ranch. There is snow behind the house, and sky threatening snow. But usually it's brilliantly sunny. And the log fire is warm. And the Indian Trinidad is chopping wood under the pine tree, and his wife Lufina,[1] in her wide white boots, is shuffling carrying water. I begin to feel better: though still feel I don't care whether it's day or night.

I saw notices of your Keats book. Pity after all I didn't ask you to send the promised copy here: I could have wandered in it now. But I'll write to Curtis Brown. And I'll send you a copy of my little novel *St Mawr*.

I managed to finish my Mexican novel 'Quetzalcoatl' in Mexico: the very day I went down, as if shot in the intestines. But I daren't even look at the outside of the MS. It cost one so much: and I wish I could eat all the lotus that ever budded, and drink up Lethe to the source. Talk about dull opiates[2] – one wants something that'll go into the very soul.

Send a line to say where you are and how you are liking it. If you come west, come and see us. I hope to get to Europe in the autumn.

Frieda is happy arranging her house.

Souvenirs! D. H. Lawrence

3386. To Edward McDonald, 6 April 1925

Text: MS UT; Postmark, Valdez APR 8 1925; *Centaur* 17–18.

Del Monte Ranch. *Questa*, New Mexico
6 April 1925

Dear Dr McDonald

We are back here: I got your letter today: we arrived in this house yesterday. I was ill in Oaxaca – got malaria – with grippe – and typhoid – a mere wreck. Struggled to Mexico City, was put to bed for three weeks again – and the doctor sent me here to recover, though I wanted to go to England, and we had booked passages. This explains my not having written, my not having thanked

[1] I.e. Rufina; see p. 49 n. 3.

[2] Keats, 'Ode to a Nightingale' (1819), l. 3.

you for the Havelock Ellis book[1] – (though he's a bit soft and *fungoid*) – and all the other sins of omission. – We'll stay here the summer now.

I shall be pleased to get the bibliography, though it frightens me to think of seeing my 'works' arrayed against me.

Norman Douglas is really terrible. He despised Magnus and used him badly: wouldn't give him a *sou*: said most scandalous things of him: and Magnus was very bitter about it. Moreover Douglas sent me a letter telling me to do as I liked about that MS., and to say what I liked in an introduction. Add to this that the facts about Magnus were much worse than I put them – and that the facts about Douglas no man would dare to print – and there we are. *Really*, one should avoid immoral people, whose *souls* are immoral. – Tomlinson – I saw him last year and he was most amiable – is mad, I suppose, because I said the *Adelphi* magazine was slop: Murry's part, anyhow. But then Tomlinson is a sort of failure in himself.

They can all go their own way to Hell. They'll arrive there soon enough without my damning them.

I haven't seen 'The Princess', but will ask for it.[2] And I'll send you a copy of *St. Mawr*.

Yrs D. H. Lawrence

3387. To Anna Bóttern, 6 April 1925

Text: MS UT; Postmark, Val[de]z APR 8 1925; Unpublished.

Del Monte Ranch. *Valdez*, New Mexico
6 April 1925

Dear Mrs Böttern

I had your letter today. I was awfully sick with malaria and typhoid in Oaxaca: struggled to Mexico City. was in bed another month, and the doctor sent me back here to recover, when I wanted to go to Europe. – Here it is still cold, but sunny. The Indian Trinidad is chopping wood in the yard,[3] and Lufina, his wife, is helping my wife in the kitchen: we only got back yesterday, but it seems as if we'd never gone away. I have written to Götzsche to tell him he can come for the summer if he cares to: but perhaps he's making money at some *job*. – What, by the way, is Merrild doing for a living? And does he earn a *good* living? And will he marry the bobbed hair?

I was sorry about that book of your husband's. Did he write to Götzsche about it?

[1] Perhaps *The Dance of Life* (Boston and New York, 1923; 1925) or *Impressions and Comments, third (and final) series, 1920–1923* (Boston and New York, 1924) by Havelock Ellis (1859–1939).

[2] In *Calendar of Modern Letters*.

[3] yard] kitchen

As for the translation, I expect the letter was handed on from New York to the London office, and they're slow. Perhaps they wouldn't want to give consent for the translation of just the one story – 'The Fox': they'd want the book complete with 'The Captain's Doll' and the 'Lady Bird'. But I don't know. I'll write to London myself, and ask them to write to you at once. They may have sold Swedish translation rights: does that mean Denmark too.

My wife is glad to be back in her own place: though today it threatens to snow!

Best wishes to you three. I suppose Simone is a Fatherland in herself.

Yrs D. H. Lawrence

3388. To Curtis Brown, 6 April 1925
Text: MS Forster; Moore 834.

Del Monte Ranch. *Questa*, New Mexico.
6 April 1925

Dear Curtis Brown

We got back on to our own ranch yesterday. Today it threatens to snow: but with a good log fire, I don't care. The Indian is chopping wood in the yard, and his wife is helping Mrs Lawrence to get tidy – everything all right. I'm still not much good, but shall soon pick up.

I wish you'd have sent to me *The Calendar* copies that contain 'The Princess'. I should like to see it.

A Danish woman, friend of ours, is pining to translate *The Captain's Doll* novelettes into Danish. I wish you'd send her a line to say if she can go ahead.[1]

Mrs Anna W. Bottern, 1810 Walton Avenue, *Los Angeles*, (Calif.).

I hear Norman Douglas attacks me on behalf of Magnus. Rather disgusting, when one knows what N. D. is: and how he treated M., wouldn't give him a sou; and when I have a letter from Douglas telling me to do what I liked and say what I liked about that MS: and when one knows how bitter Magnus was about Douglas, at the end. And when one knows how much worse the *whole* facts were, than those I give. – However, canaille will be canaille.

Let me know how everything goes.

Yrs D. H. Lawrence

3389. To Ida Rauh, 6 April 1925
Text: MS UT; Postmark, Valdez APR 8 1925; Unpublished.

Del Monte Ranch. *Valdez*, New Mex.
6 April 1925

Dear Ida

We came up to our own house yesterday. We've got Trinidad (Tony's

[1] See Letter 3325 and n. 4.

nephew) and his wife Lufina to look after us. Today it's cloudy, and threatens snow, but there's peace and a warm fire. Frieda is very happy, on her own ground again. As for me, I am only half awake, and not very keen on coming wide awake just yet.

The Hawks are still rather in a muddle. Brett is staying on down there, but talks of going into one of the small cabins – We heard Tony was back in Santa Fe, and the newspaper says 'Spud expected.'

I was awfully sorry you went back in that whirlwind, with the earth rising up and enveloping you like a grave. Hope it had no bad effects. It wasn't much of a trip for you and Andrew. I'm so sorry. Later I hope you'll come here: when it no longer threatens snow.

I'll go on with the play when the spirit moves me; I hope soon. Anyhow it's a real thing to me, in a world of unrealities.

F. greets you both, so do I.

D. H. Lawrence

3390. To Hon. Dorothy Brett, [7 April 1925]
Text: MS UCin; Irvine, Brett 47–8.

[Frieda Lawrence begins]

[Kiowa]
[7 April 1925][1]

Dear Brett,

It looks like snow. Lawrence is sleeping quite a lot of the time – *If* you dont go to Taos to-morrow come to tea at 4 o/clock – If you do, come to supper if you are not too late or tired, or come Thursday to lunch – We are very still and peaceful, it is incredible, I felt there would *never* be any more peace – Now it's snowing – Timsy the cat knew the place as if she had never left and was so excited, caught a mouse in the chilly dawn, Trinidad and Ruffina seem happy and useful – Lawrence need'nt do a thing and I am developping into a 'chef' – I will give you an example of my 'chefferie' when you come –

Soon you must get into your apple orchard – Ruffina and Trinidad can help.

Yours F –

The meat is very good –

[Lawrence begins]
Dear Brett –

Ask Mrs Hawk what she makes the dog-food of, will you: because Trinidad

[1] Dated with reference to the possibility of snow; see Letters 3385, 3388 and 3389.

has brought two lean and silly hound-pups, and I don't know what to put between their ribs. Perhaps Mrs Hawk might let me have a bit of meal for them: We've got fat. – We've no yeast for bread. I asked Rachel if she could lend us some – ask Trinidad if he's got it. Looks as if you wouldn't get to Taos tomorrow.

Don't bother to get stove-piping or any big things, if they will be a nuisance. – William might lend us the pack-saddle, and Trinidad could bring everything on Azul.

3391. To Hon. Dorothy Brett, [11 April 1925]

Text: MS UCin; cited in Huxley 631.

Kiowa
Saturday.[1]

Dear Brett

There's not much to say – and it's no good saying much.

I don't believe Frieda would ever feel friendly towards you, again – ever. And that means friction and nothing else.

You are, you know, a born separator. Even without knowing that you do it, you set people against one another. It is instinctive with you. If you are friendly with one, you make that one unfriendly to the others: no matter who it is. It's just a natural process with you. – But it usually turns everybody into an enemy, at last. – It's no use your talking about friendship. I know you have done many things for us, like making the dandy beer and bringing eggs. On that side, your friendship is good. But the spirit, the flow, is always towards separating. Most of us, myself included, are a good deal that way. But it's useless, in the end. Among three people, always two against one.

It's no good our trying to get on together – it won't happen. Myself, I have lost all desire for intense or intimate friendship. Acquaintance is enough. It will be best when we go our separate ways. – A life in common is an illusion, when the instinct is always to divide, to separate individuals and set them one against the other. And this seems to be the ruling instinct, unacknowledged. Unite with the one, against the other. And it's no good.

Yrs DHL[2]

[1] This letter cannot be dated precisely; it may have been written after Brett first visited Kiowa on 8 or 9 April, or at a later date.

[2] Irvine, Brett prints four undated notes from Frieda to Brett (nos. 29, 31–3, pp. 47–50); no. 29 (MS UCin) serves as an example:

Dear Brett,

No, dont come this afternoon, Lawrence is not fit for explanation – And there are'nt any – I offered you being a *distant* friend but you want to be an intimate one – You and I have *never* been

3392. To Idella Purnell, 12 April 1925
Text: MS UT; Bynner 253.

Del Monte Ranch. *Valdez*, New Mexico
12 April 1925

Dear Idella

We have got back to our own ranch. Your letter came. You know, we had booked berths to England from Veracruz, and the doctor wouldn't let us go. Said we must come here and stay in the quiet and cool and sun. I should really have liked to see your place in the barranca: but the Lord disposes! Wish we'd never gone to Oaxaca.

We saw Bynner in Santa Fe: he talks of Mexico – Chapala – in May or June: and Spud writes from New York, that, though he won't *accompany* Hal, he will probably follow later. We shall stay on here, I expect till late autumn. Perhaps you will pass this way: it's near, from El Paso. I think for the winter itself we shall go to Europe. I've got a bit of a Heimweh – a nostalgia – for Europe – though that may be only because I have been ill.

The ranch is very beautiful, now in the April sunshine: and very clean, having emerged from under three feet of snow. But the winds come sometimes very cold, with a flurry of snow: so of course I got a chill and was in bed again. It is unlike me to keep on being sick, and I hate it. But I hope this is the last set-back.

I'll send you my new little novel *St Mawr* when it comes out – next month.

Remember me to Dr Purnell. How I regret we didn't come to Guadalajara to drink anise with him, instead of going to that beastly Oaxaca.

Frieda sends her regards, with mine.

Yrs D. H. Lawrence

3393. To Zelia Nuttall, 12 April 1925
Text: MS Forster; Moore 834–5.

Del Monte Ranch. *Valdez*, New Mexico
12 April 1925

Dear Mrs Nuttall

We have come up to our own little ranch: very lovely now in the sunshine, but cold winds can come, with flurries of snow, so of course I had to take cold once more. However, I think it's not much. Lying on the porch this warm afternoon, with the pine-trees round, and the desert away below, and the

friends what *I* call friends – no we never could be and I go mad, when you bully me here on my own ground, where surely I may have or not have people as I choose – Your attitude towards me I have always resented – I wish you no ill, but dont want you in my life

F –

Sangre de Cristo mountains with their snow pale and bluish blocking the way beyond, it seems already far to Coyoacán. Here the grass is only just moving green out of the sere earth, and the hairy, pale mauve anemones that the Indians call Owl flowers stand strange and alone among the dead pine needles, under the wintry trees. Extraordinary how the place seems *seared* with winter: almost cauterised. And so winter-cleaned, from under three feet of snow.

My wife is happy, being on her own place again, and I am just gathering myself together, the last bits of me, as it were, struggling in from the long journey. Miss Brett has got a little house on our neighbour's ranch, and is thrilled through and through by her nice sorrel horse, Prince.

I am waiting for a parcel of books from New York, to send you the poems I promised you.[1] It should be here in a day or two.

We haven't started the pigeons yet: but I'm going to talk it all over with the carpenter. He will make the proper houses.

We think with such pleasure of the Casa Alvarado and of your kindness and hospitality;[2] and of all the flowers in the garden.

Herzliche Grüsse,[3] from my wife and from me.

Sincerely D. H. Lawrence

3394. To Ida Rauh, [14 April 1925]
Text: MS UT; Unpublished.

Del Monte Ranch. *Valdez*, New Mexico
Tuesday

Dear Ida

The vegetables and bit of Roquefort came today: very many thanks: also the Pantanberge.[4] I see no bill: so send $10.00 – and if there is any balance, keep it till we want something else. If I owe you more, tell me.

We are sunny and warm, in our own house. But it *was* cold – the wind – so of course I got a chill, and am still half in bed. But feel stronger.

I have done six scenes of the play. Myself I like it very much. But it's nearly all *men*. You may not like Michal, but I think she'll interest you. Today I shall give the MS so far to Brett, she will begin typing, and when she's ready, I'll send you a copy – even though it's only six scenes – and you can see what you think of it: also I shall be very glad of Andrew's opinion. But don't say

[1] See Letter 3403.

[2] See p. 155 n. 3. Frieda wrote to Zelia Nuttall on 19 March 1925 accepting an invitation for lunch on Saturday the 21st (MS Forster).

[3] 'Cordial greetings'.

[4] According to a letter of 30 October 1927 to Emily King, DHL took it for his bronchials 'to harden the tissue and make it resist chills. I take the French *Solution Pantanberge* – which is creosote and chalk, unsweetened'.

anything to anybody else. When it's a bit further on, you and Andrew must come up, and we'll talk everything over. (No acts – only about 12 scenes, one after the other.)

Brett says will you send her that puzzle-book: also a type-writer ribbon – Remington portable *ribbon* (not a whole machine) – red and black – or only black. *I pay for it.*

Nina Witt suddenly appeared with Tony: Nina thrilled at getting a divorce from Lee, and going back post-haste to New York to marry Leonard Rucker[1] – aged 40 – bachelor – very dark – Scotch descent from South – Kentucky – poor parents – or poorish – ran away from home when young – spent his life adventuring – was an interpreter in France during war – has been a prize-fighter – can overthrow Japs at jiu-jitsu – knows men from A to Z. (pronounce Zee) – is at present a sort of psychological examiner in the Y.M.C.A. to find out what men's 'gifts' really are – and admires my 'works.' – But Nina is thrilled, and he may be really rather interesting. – Do know him? – Tony was rather offensive: hope he won't come here any more. – Spud wrote from Finney Farm: sort of HellO! – Clarence returning with Mabel and going to build a house on Mabel's land (Tony says). – I told Spud[2] I didn't want anybody to come here uninvited.

Hope you weren't agonised by that ride home. Let us know how you all are.

DHL

3395. To Baroness Anna von Richthofen, 15 April 1925

Text: MSS UCB and Jeffrey; Frieda Lawrence 190–1.

Del Monte Ranch. *Questa*, New Mexico
15 April 1925

Meine liebe Schwiegermutter

Heute kamen deine Briefe. Und du warst auf dem Merkur? Ja, du bist jünger wie ich.

Wir sind schon eine Woche auf unserem Ranch. Wir haben alles fest und wohl gefunden: nichts zerstört, nichts kaput: nur haben die Mäusle den Stuhl Mabel Lujan's gefunden, und die Wolle aufgefressen. Sicher sind sie vergifted. – Im zweiten Haus haben wir zwei junge Indier, Mann und Frau, Trinidad und Rufina. Die Rufina ist kurz und dick und zwanzig, wackelt wie eine Ente in weissen Indier Hoch-schuhen. Der Trinidad ist keusch wie ein Mädel, in seinem zwei Haarzöpfen. Aber die beide sind sehr nett, arbeiten nicht zum Schwitzen, machen alles was wir wollen. Wir haben immer noch die drei Pferde; sie bleiben aber darunter bei den Hawks, auf Del Monte, bis Gras

[1] Nothing came of it. [2] Spud] Tony

und Alfalfa etwas gewachsen sind. – Wir hatten drei kalte Tage – der Wind kann eiskalt kommen. Ich wieder erkältet. Aber jetzt ist das Wetter mild und warm, sehr schön, und Frühling in der Luft. Alles war sehr rein geputzt, auf dem Land, heraus von ein Meter-Schnee gekommen. Jetzt stehen die ersten Anemone Blumen, wie Crocus gebaut, aber etwas grösser und stolzer und haarig, auf brauntotem Boden unter den Tannen. Alles ist aber wieder sehr trocken, das Grass ist kaum gekommen, doch kann nicht mehr wachsen. Wir warten wieder auf Schnee oder Regen. – Die Brett bleibt auch unten auf Del Monte, in einem Häusle allein, in der nähe von den Alten[1] Hawks. Sie wollte hierauf kommen, die Frieda sagte aber nein. Wir sind dann nur zwei Weisse und zwei Rote (mehr gelb-braun) am Gut. Der Trinidad holt Milch und Butter und Eier von Del Monte – ich liege in der Sonne – die Frieda ist wieder zufrieden, als Gutsbesitzerin.

Der Friedel soll in Mai kommen: schreibt selig. Wahrscheinlich kehrt er wieder in's Vaterland, am Ende des Sommers. Wir meinen, in September, auch nach England und Deutschland zu kommen. Aber der Herrgott herrscht.

Wir kaufen ein Wagen, und der Trinidad soll Kutscher werden. Dieses Jahr arbeite ich nicht: bin bös, dass ich so krank war.

Die Mabel ist noch in New York. Aber Freitag kam der Tony – hässlich wie ein Pfannkuchen – mit der Nina Witt: eine Mabel-freundin, sehr reich, der [Frieda Lawrence corrects to 'die'] mit einem Lump, Lee Witt, in Taos verheiratet war. Nun aber lässt sie sich – oder er sich – scheiden, und sie will sofort einen anderen verheiraten. Sie hat wie ein Ziegchen getanzt und geskippt: und hat 45 [Frieda Lawrence corrects to '47'] Jahre. Sie sind alle verrückt. Man sagt, die Nina hat acht Millionen. Sie sieht wie eine arme Schullehrerin aus.

Morgen geht die Frieda im Auto mit Betty Hawk nach Taos, um wieder einzukaufen. Wir sind sehr nett und warm hier, und haben alles was man braucht.

Gut dass du Freunde bei dir hast.

Ich schicke ein bisschen Stecknadelgeld.

Ich schreibe sofort am Inselverlag.

Wiedersehen DHL

Bös ist die Frieda, sie schenkt ein Paar Jahre an der arme Nina.[2] Diese hat am neuen Mann schon gesagt, sie möchte ein Baby kriegen. Aus 47 Jahre kommen Kinder nicht mehr.

[1] MS Jeffrey begins here.

[2] DHL drew a line from Frieda's alteration of Nina Witt's age ('45' to '47') to the postscript.

[My dear Schwiegermutter

Your letters came today. And you were up the Merkur?[1] Yes, you are younger than I.

We've already been a week on our ranch. We found everything nice and tight: nothing destroyed, nothing broken: only the mice found Mabel Lujan's chair, and ate the wool. No doubt they're poisoned. – In the second house we have two young Indians, husband and wife, Trinidad and Rufina. Rufina is short and fat and twenty, waddles like a duck in tall white Indian boots. Trinidad is chaste as a girl, with his two plaits. But both are very nice, don't sweat over their work, do everything we want. We've still got the three horses; they stay down with the Hawks though, at Del Monte, till the grass and alfalfa have grown a bit. – We had three cold days – the wind can get ice-cold. I've got a chill again. But now the weather is mild and warm, very beautiful, and spring in the air. Everything on the land came very clean and pure out of a metre of snow. Now the first anemone flowers are standing up, shaped like crocus, but a little bigger and prouder and hairy, on dead-brown earth under the pines. But everything is very dry again, the grass has hardly appeared, yet can't grow any higher. We wait for snow or rain again. – Brett stays down below at Del Monte, in a little house by herself, near the old Hawks. She wanted to come up here, but Frieda said no. So we're just two whites and two reds (yellow-brown, rather) on the estate. Trinidad fetches milk and butter and eggs from Del Monte – I lie in the sun – Frieda is happy again, as lady-of-the-manor.

Friedel should come in May: writes very happily. He probably goes back to the Fatherland, at the end of the summer. We too mean to come to England and Germany in September. But the Lord will prevail.

We're buying a buggy, and Trinidad will turn coachman. I don't work this year: am cross, that I was so ill.

Mabel is still in New York. But on Friday came Tony – ugly as a pancake – with Nina Witt: a friend of Mabel, very rich, who has been married to a blackguard in Taos, Lee Witt. But now she wants – or he wants – a divorce, and she means to marry someone else immediately. She's danced and skipped like a little goat: and is 45 [Frieda Lawrence corrects to '47']. They're all mad. People say Nina has eight million. She looks like a poor school-teacher.

Tomorrow Frieda is going by car to Taos with Betty Hawk, to shop again. We're very nice and warm here, and have everything one needs.

Good that you have friends with you.

I send you a little pin-money.

I'll write to the Inselverlag at once.

Wiedersehen DHL

[1] Mercurius (670 m.) is the highest mountain near Baden-Baden.

Frieda is wicked, she makes poor Nina a present of a couple more years. The latter has already told the new man she wants to have a baby. Children no longer come from 47 years olds.]

3396. To Curtis Brown, 15 April 1925

Text: MS UT; Huxley 631–2.

Del Monte Ranch. *Questa*, New Mexico
15 April 1925

Dear Curtis Brown

I get so nagged at about Douglas' pamphlet on me and Magnus, that I send you here Douglas' letter to me on the business. I really think it ought to be printed: though I don't care much.[1] Use your discretion. But please preserve D's letter.

I bothered about that MS. only for the sake of those two Maltese.[2] From 1921 to 1924 I tried to get the thing published. The New York publisher[3] wanted to publish my introduction, alone, as an essay, without the *Legion* MS. I refused, and waited.

Having written half the book, surely half the proceeds are due to me.

As for Douglas' co-writing – it's a literary turn: Besides, Magnus re-wrote the *whole* thing, after I talked with him in Montecassino. I really sweated to get that fellow money, and Douglas wouldn't give him a cent.

I get more and more bored with my fellow-men.

Yrs D. H. Lawrence

3397. To Harold Mason, 17 April 1925

Text: MS UN; *Centaur* 18–19.

Del Monte Ranch. *Questa*. New Mexico
17 April 1925.

Dear Mr Mason

Yes, if you wish it, I think a little book of uncollected essays might be nice.[4] Those you mention: and the essays that appeared last year in *The Adelphi* and

[1] The letter of 26 December 1921 quoted in part in Letter 3623; see also Letter 3400.

[2] Borg and Inguanez. [3] Seltzer.

[4] This became *Reflections on the Death of a Porcupine and Other Essays*, published by the Centaur Press on 7 December 1925. None of the essays mentioned here was included. See Introduction to *Reflections*, ed. Herbert, pp. xix–xli.

in the New York *Vanity Fair*: like 'On being a Man' – 'On Being Religious' – Or the two essays on Indian dances, that have appeared in the *Theatre Arts* Magazine.[1] – Though perhaps the American things are best kept apart. You would have to settle the business terms with A.W. Barmby, of Curtis Brown Ltd. 116 West 39th Street, New York. – But I will tell him to agree to the terms you consider fair.

Please do send my copies of the autobiography here:[2] except, would you kindly send one direct to Barmby, to New York, and one direct to Curtis Brown. 6 Henrietta St. Covent Garden. London W.C. 2. – The remaining copies to me. – It is rather a struggle getting things mailed, out here.

I hope you'll enjoy Europe. We had booked our passages from VeraCruz, but the doctor wouldn't let me sail. But I think we shall go in the autumn – to England and Germany, then South. – And it is lovely here now. Sometimes, when one isn't well, the *hardness* of the American continent makes one feel bruised.

Yours Sincerely D. H. Lawrence[3]

[1] See p. 87 n. 3; the 'Indian dances' essays were 'The Dance of the Sprouting Corn' and 'The Hopi Snake Dance'.

[2] I.e. McDonald's *Bibliography*.

[3] David Jester, Jr, Mason's junior partner, replied as follows from the Centaur Book Shop, 18 May 1925 (TMSC Mason):

Dear Mr. Lawrence

Please accept my apologies for not having answered sooner your letter of 17 April, which arrived the day before Mr. Mason's departure for England.

To do a book of your essays will give us a great amount of pleasure. I have written Mr. Barmby stating the book will be an Autumn publication, and that we prefer not to speak of terms until we know the approximate cost of the book. And this knowledge we will hardly possess until later in the Summer.

In the meantime, largely guided by Dr. McDonald, we will make a tentative table of contents, which will be sent you for your approval. Would it be possible for you to supply us with at least one essay which has not appeared previously in magazine form?

The Bibliography will be ready within the next fortnight. We shall be careful to send copies to Mr. Curtis Brown of London, and to Mr. Barmby. I hope you will be pleased with the finished product. Dr. McDonald has taken infinite pains and has compiled, I believe, an accurate and interesting bibliography.

Finally, I wish to express my admiration for your introduction to the Foreign Legion book, an opportunity which has not hitherto presented itself. I have finished also the third installment of THE PRINCESS in the Calendar. It seems to me the long short story, a story the length of THE PRINCESS and LADYBIRD, is an excellent medium of artistic expression. At any rate you have used it admirably.

Yours faithfully,

3398. To Nancy Pearn, 17 April 1925

Text: MS UT; Huxley 632.

Del Monte Ranch. *Questa*, New Mexico
17 April 1925

Dear Miss Pearn

Thank you for your letter.[1] – We were disappointed not to come to England: but, D.V., shall come in the autumn. And I am so thankful to be feeling better. I thought sometimes I was never going to get out of Mexico, what with malaria, and a typhoid condition inside, and flu making my chest go wrong. However, we are on our own ranch, and though I feel still shaky – must lie down most of the time – I am rapidly getting better. It's lovely spring weather up here, but very dry: though there was deep snow for some months. We've got an Indian and his wife to do for us: it is good to be quite quiet.

You've done awfully well with those difficult stories. 'The Princess' and 'Mornings in Mexico' are still wandering this side.

I'm not so very keen on giving those sketches to Murry.[2] It seems to me, it's always *his* friends who make attacks on me – like Tomlinson:[3] and so often I can see Murry's words coming out against me, through people who frequent him. I don't like that kind of friendship. But you use your own judgment.

I wish I did some nice popular little stories. We'll see how the summer goes with me. I feel it will be a long time before I do another novel.

Yours D. H. Lawrence

[1] Nancy Pearn had written on 1 April 1925 (TMSC UT):

> Dear Mr. Lawrence
>
> I am so very sorry to hear the reason of your non-arrival in England. We had so looked forward to seeing you again, and hope that you will soon be able to persuade your doctor that a sea voyage would be just the thing for you.
>
> I have written to Mr. Barmby asking him about dates for "MORNINGS IN MEXICO", three of which, namely, "CORASMIN AND THE PARROTS", THE MOZO, and "WALK TO HUAYAPA", the "Adelphi" wishes to use. Middleton Murry can only pay at the rate of Half a Guinea per page, but I gather you want us to let him have contributions from time to time.
>
> I enclose a letter which has just arrived from Mr Murry, which I took the liberty of opening thinking it might concern the articles in question.
>
> Yours sincerely,

The letter from Murry is missing. (There is another hiatus in the letters to Nancy Pearn, until 13 October 1925, Letter 3506)

[2] Acknowledging this letter on 8 May (TMSC UT) Nancy Pearn promised to 'bear in mind what you say about "The Adelphi" in future, and rather than put Murry first will see that he is left to the bottom of the list unless he later turns into a good boy'.

[3] 'D. H. Lawrence and Norman Douglas', *Weekly Westminster*, iii (n.s.) (14 February 1925), 472. Tomlinson had not read DHL's 'Introduction' to the *Memoirs*, but stated: 'I would not accept the evidence of a popular novelist about the soul of a cocoanut.' By contrast he considered Douglas's *Plea for Better Manners* a 'rare and lively book' which he would read again; the author 'know[s] the weight and swiftness of the English language'. Tomlinson challenged DHL 'to explain, at least, who appointed him to be the biographer of Maurice Magnus'.

3399. To Hermann Piehler, 17 April 1925

Text: TMSC NWU; Huxley 633.

Del Monte Ranch. *Questa.* New Mexico, U.S.A.
17 April 1925.

Dear Sir,[1]

I received your letter only last night.

The scene of my Nottingham–Derby novels all centres round Eastwood, Notts. (where I was born): and whoever stands on Walker Street, Eastwood, will see the whole landscape of *Sons and Lovers* before him: Underwood in front, the hills of Derbyshire on the left, the woods and hills of Annesley on the right. The road from Nottingham by Watnall, Moorgreen, up to Underwood and on to Annesley (Byron's Annesley)[2] – gives you all the landscape of *The White Peacock*, Miriam's farm in *Sons and Lovers*, and the home of the Crich family, and Willey Water, in *Women in Love*.

The Rainbow is Ilkeston and Cossall, near Ilkeston, moving to Eastwood. And Hermione, in *Women in Love*, is supposed to live not far from Cromford. The short stories are Ripley, Wirksworth, Stoney Middleton, Via Gellia ('The Wintry Peacock').[3] *The Lost Girl* begins in Eastwood – the cinematograph show being in Langley Mill.

I hope this will meet your requirements.

Yours faithfully D. H. Lawrence

3400. To Blanche Knopf, 18 April 1925

Text: MS UT; Unpublished.

Del Monte Ranch. *Questa*, New Mexico
18 April 1925

Dear Mrs Knopf[4]

Thank you for sending the books.[5] I haven't got them yet, but look forward to their coming.

I'm sending Barmby a little article – as he asked me – for your *Borzoi* almanach.[6] – I'm sick of being nagged at by small dogs, and now I'll throw a

1 Hermann Augustine Piehler (1888–) revised many travel books, including Baedeker's, and wrote a series 'for everyman', e.g. *England for Everyman*, in the 1930s.

2 Byron was supposed to have courted Mary Chaworth, heiress of the Annesley family, at Annesley Park; see *The White Peacock*, ed. Andrew Robertson (Cambridge, 1983), p. 70 and note on 70:7.

3 Stoney (or Stony) Middleton is a village about 15 miles n. of Middleton-by-Wirksworth where DHL lived May 1918–April 1919. For Via Gellia see *Letters*, iii. 232.

4 Blanche Knopf, née Wolf (1894–1966). m. 1916, Alfred Knopf. She was Vice President, 1921–57, and President, 1957–66, of her husband's company and director of Random House Inc., 1960–6.

5 See Letter 3421.

6 'Accumulated Mail' in *The Borzoi 1925* (published by Knopf), pp. 119–28.

few stones in their teeth. Goodbye to tolerance. People only insult one when one is decent, so the one thing to do is to turn round and kick them when they get too close to one's heels. – Barmby too has an exact copy of a letter from Norman Douglas to me, in 1921, about the *Foreign Legion* MS. I think it would come very *à propos* in the 1925 Almanach. Anyhow read it. – Douglas is frightfully hypocritical in his doddering degeneracy. And Magnus was a thousand times worse than I showed him.

I didn't correct the *St. Mawr* proofs very well – felt too sick. Am better. – But there were only typographical errors, a clerk can find them.[1] I didn't know you wanted a revised set of *Secker* proofs.[2]

Yours D. H. Lawrence

3401. To Emily King, 21 April 1925

Text: MS Lazarus; Moore 839.

Del Monte Ranch, *Questa*, New Mexico
21 April 1925

My dear Pamela

Your letter came – Yes, I was awfully sick: malaria, typhoid condition inside, and chest going wrong. Am much better – but must be careful all summer – lie down a great deal. – When the wild cold winds come, I just go to bed. In the wonderful sunny days – they are six out of seven – I potter about and lie on a camp bed on the porch. I don't work yet, Trinidad and his wife Ruffina – the Indians – do most things for us. – We have brought up two horses – and bought a buggy – it stands by the barn. Trinidad drives it in style.

Now they are busy, away at the Gallina canyon, about two miles off, building a little dam and putting in pipes, to get the water out of the canyon into our irrigation ditch, which winds round the hills to the house. – It's rather an expense. But we must have water on the land. The spring has been so dry, the grass is already burnt up, and the alfalfa doesn't move. Today it threatens to snow. Monday was a hot, blazing sunny day. So it changes. Everybody wishes it would rain or snow. But of course, today the men are working at the Gallina, with cement, that will spoil if it snows much, or freezes. – Frieda's nephew Friedel Jaffe – Else's son – who has been this year an exchange student at an American university, is coming in May, for the summer – then he'll go back to Germany. – We want to come to Europe in the autumn. – Brett is staying down on Del Monte. – You will soon get *St. Mawr* from Martin Secker: it's

[1] A set of Secker's proofs (auctioned at Sotheby's on 18 December 1985) had just over 20 small corrections.

[2] Secker to Knopf, 6 March 1925; 'About ten days ago I posted to [DHL] sets of proofs of "St. Mawr", asking him to forward on corrected set to you' (Secker Letter-Book, UIll).

supposed to be out in May. – I'm really better – but had a bad turn. – I've got a new publisher over here: Knopf – a Jew again – but *rich* and enterprising – seems very nice. – Seltzer is staggering, staggering. – I send £5. for you and the children.

Love from us both. DHL

One day you will come and spend a summer here.

3402. To Mollie Skinner, 21 April 1925

Text: MS WAPL; Postmark, Questa APR 24 1[. . .]; Moore 839–40.

Del Monte Ranch. *Questa*, New Mexico
21 April 1925

Dear Mollie Skinner

Your letter of 26th Feb. today. We were thinking about you, and wondering about *Black Swans*. I'm looking forward to reading it soon. When is it due?[1] I'm sure it's best for it to appear absolutely without any connection with me. That way you'll exist in yourself and by yourself, for the tribe. I'll write an introduction to your third novel, if you like.[2] – It's time we should be getting statements of sales for the *Boy*. – It's always a long time before the money comes in: but it will come.

I'll send you my new novel *St. Mawr* when I get it: or I'll ask Secker to post it direct. It is due in May.

You know, we got back here two weeks ago. I was awfully ill in Mexico – thought I was never going to get out: malaria, typhoid condition inside, and chest going wrong with flu. Still have a cough and have to stay a good deal in bed. But glad to be back on our own ranch. We have a young Indian couple, Trinidad and his wife Ruffina, looking after us. It has been hot and sunny – but today cold and crumbling snow, and I'm in bed. –

Don't bother about critics and immediate returns – Writing, essentially, is its own reward. If it's a joy – and a pain – to you, struggling and producing a book – then go ahead, and never mind the rest. Write when there comes a certain passion upon you, and revise in a later, warier, but still sympathetic mood.

I got my novel 'Quetzalcoatl' done in Mexico: at a tremendous cost to myself. Feel I don't want ever to see it again. Loathe the thought of having to go over it and prune and correct, in typescript.

I expect we shall be here all summer. We want to go to Europe in

[1] Cape published it in July 1925 (reviewed in *TLS*, 16 July 1925, p. 478).

[2] Mollie Skinner wrote several more novels (*Tucker Sees India*, 1937; *W.X.–Corporal Smith*, 1941; etc.) and a book of short stories (*Men Are We*, 1927); and there are some unpublished novels at WAPL, but none has an introduction by DHL.

September. – You won't be happy in that little cottage on the creek-slope, unless you work. – Why not write your *mother's* novel?

Yrs D. H. Lawrence

3403. To Zelia Nuttall, 21 April 1925

Text: MS Forster; Moore 838–9.

Del Monte Ranch. *Valdez*, New Mexico
21 April 1925

My dear Mrs Nuttall

I am sending you a copy of *Birds Beasts and Flowers* today: probably you won't like them. But some you will. – We made the cover-design between us:[1] fun it was.

I've lost my address-book with all the addresses: very crippling. Out of my memory, I sent Mrs Hogarth a book to Liverpool #90.[2] Is that right? If not, Mrs Hogarth can recover the book from the post office. Would you mind giving her her letter?

I am a good deal better. The days are mostly hot and sunny, but they can be fiendish, with a grey stone-cold wind that blows out of some frozen hell. So I went to bed once more, with fever. But I am better. We brought up two of the horses, and the new-painted buggy, and our two Indians, Trinidad and Ruffina, trot out with us. We look such a bundly Mexican outfit. For the rest, I don't do much: but slowly wade my way through the sandy wastes of Doughty's *Arabia Deserta*. I read it on and on and on, without quite knowing why. – Trinidad brought up Miss Wemyss, our cat, in a sack. She was our kitten last autumn. She emerged from her sack trembling and ruffled with a cat's farouche dismay. Then she began to creep round very slowly, and remember. – And suddenly, after half an hour, she exploded from under the bed in fireworks of friskiness. She had suddenly remembered *everything*. – The horses knew us too, perfectly. Nice!

Very best regards from us both. D. H. Lawrence

[1] Merrild and DHL for the Seltzer edition. (DHL inscribed the copy for Zelia Nuttall, 'remembering the pleasant hours of the Casa Alvarado'; it is now in the collection of W. Forster.)

[2] Mrs J. H. Hogarth, Liverpool #90, Mexico D. F. is given in DHL's address books (UCB; UT). Zelia Nuttall wrote on this letter: 'Mrs. Hogarth & her husband, leading members of the British Colony, not only invited the Lawrence's to their house but took them on several excursions in their motor car & entertained them generously.' Mr Hogarth headed the (British) United Shoe & Leather Co.; the Hogarths were close friends of the Conways.

3404. To Basil Blackwell, 21 April 1925

Text: MS Subun-So Book Store; Unpublished.

Del Monte Ranch. *Questa*, New Mexico
21 April 1925

Dear Basil Blackwell[1]

I have just received from Seltzer his half-dozen copies of *Little Novels of Sicily*. That makes me wonder if you have your edition ready. And if you have, would you be so kind as to send out for me my six copies. If they are posted to me here, I shall have to pay a large duty on them, and have a great job to get them at all. – I shall take the liberty of giving you the addresses, and leave it to your kindness.

1. Mrs L. A. Clarke, Grosvenor Rd. *Ripley* (Derby)
1. Mrs S. King, 16 Brooklands Rd. Sneinton Hill, *Nottingham*
1. Mrs Catherine Carswell, Hawthorn Cottage, Gt Kingshill, High Wycombe, *Bucks.*
1. Frau Baronin von Richthofen, Ludwig-Wilhelmstift, *Baden-Baden, Germany*
1. Miss Barbara Weekley, 49 Harvard Rd, *Chiswick. W.*
1. Mr E H Brewster, Torre Quattro Venti. *Capri* (Napoli), Italy.

If there is anything I can do for you, let me know.

Yours sincerely D. H. Lawrence[2]

3405. To Alfred Decker Hawk, [ante 30 April 1925]

Text: MS UT; Unpublished.

[Kiowa]
[ante 30 April 1925][3]

Dear Mr Hawk

When Murray does come, I will say nothing. – But he can unscrew the long lengths of this old iron pipe, so it can be put on the wagon for you. – And don't talk of paying me for it – there is so little – and it's really no use to me. But we'll hunt up the joints. I can only find two taps – should be three.

Yours D. H. Lawrence

[1] (Sir) Basil Henry Blackwell (1889–1984), chairman of Basil Blackwell and Mott Ltd (publishers), 1922–69 and of B. H. Blackwell Ltd (booksellers), 1924–69. See Letter 3096 and p. 20 n. 3.

[2] See Letter 3427 and n. 2.

[3] This and the following letter are dated to form a sequence with Letters 3406, 3408 and 3409.

3406. To Alfred Decker Hawk, [30 April 1925]
Text: MS UT; Unpublished.

[Kiowa]
Thursday

Dear Mr Hawk

Did you want the cement immediately? – if so I'll send the two bags down tomorrow, and get more from Hondo.

Will you please send me the milk-etc. bill.

There are two brass taps and a few lengths of piping, I will send down to you, if you have any use for them. They are no use to me.

Yrs D. H. Lawrence

3407. To Andrew Dasburg, [1 May 1925]
Text: MS SyrU; Unpublished.

Del Monte Ranch. *Valdez*, New Mexico
Friday

Dear Andrew

I do hope Ida isn't ill: let us know. – Brett got the type-writer ribbon: for which many thanks. Therefore Ida must have got my letter and the cheque for all the goods. – I am better, but the cold winds do get my bronchi, and then I just stay in bed. We have got men laying pipes in the Gallina canyon to bring the water for the land: a job. I get out there afternoons when fine: two miles. But still am not much good to anybody but myself. The play is well on: $\frac{2}{3}$ done, easily. Brett is slowly typing. I do want you and Ida to see[1] it and say what you think: I hope you'll make stage sketches, really, for your part.

Let us know how you are.

Yrs D. H. Lawrence

3408. To Alfred Decker Hawk, 3 May 1925
Text: MS UT; Unpublished.

[Kiowa]
Sunday. 3 May 1925

Dear Mr Hawk

I would hate to have any unpleasant feeling between the two houses. – I know the pipes would have cost me very much more if I had had to buy them

[1] see] think

new. Only I hoped they wouldn't come to quite so much, because Seltzer just doesn't pay me my money. – Of course I agreed to your price for the pipes, so please let it stay at that. And please send me the bill for horses and milk and all the things, or I shall just feel uneasy.

Let us say no more about it. And let me send the balance for the pipes a little later, when I've got a bit more credit in the bank.

Yours Sincerely D. H. Lawrence

3409. To Alfred Decker Hawk, [4 May 1925]

Text: MS UT; Unpublished.

Kiowa.
Monday

Dear Mr Hawk

I am much too like you in temperament not to know what it means, suddenly to feel blazing mad. I'm awfully sorry, and would rather have paid for the pipes twice over. – Murray didn't talk against you: he only said it was more than he'd figured. He really doesn't talk against you, as far as I've ever heard. – It's usually I who go flaring up at a wrong moment, and regret it afterwards. – But I'm sure we shall always remain friends.

I send you the letter I wrote last night.

Frances[1] and Ruffina didn't come: they stayed to dance the evening woman's dance: they *may* come today. Trinidad came alone in the buggy.

Our regards to Mrs Hawk. I'm afraid we men sit in the same boat, and our wives get a laugh at us when they see the water chopping.

Yrs D. H. Lawrence

3410. To Alfred Knopf, [4 May 1925]

Text: Moore 840–1.

Kiowa Ranch
4 May 1925

Dear Knopf:

Many thanks for the advance on royalties Barmby told me of. Willa Cather wrote that she suggested it. Irritating that one should need an advance, at this late hour!

[1] Along with Albidia Marcus (see Letter 3191 and p. 95 n. 1), Frances had worked for John Young-Hunter.

Barmby was in a sort of panic at the title 'Quetzalcoatl'. Must one really discard such a fascinating word? – And use its translation: 'Feathered Snake': or more luscious, *The Plumed Serpent*. – Or 'Men in Big Hats' (doesn't fit). I can't think of anything because 'Quetzalcoatl' has been stuck in my mind for two years.

Miss Brett has done a quite beautiful design for a jacket, of Mexicans in big hats: has some real Mexican quality in it. I hope you'll like it and be able to use it.[1] But we must find a title.

Thank Mrs Knopf for the books: they came.

3411. To Ida Rauh, [7 May 1925]
Text: MS UT; Unpublished.

[Kiowa]
Thursday

Dear Ida

So sorry you were ill. – I am much better. – I finished the play today. – We shall be pleased to see you – I think Brett will quite like putting you up. – Bring me another bottle of Pantanberge from the drug-store, please: or better bring two bottles. – Frieda wrote to Mrs Hughes,[2] via Bynner, about some plants. Those two might appear for a night. – Can you bring a box of type-writing paper – they have only the foolscap sort, so long, Brett has to cut the ends off. – Do hope you'll like the play. – If Mrs Hughes was coming, she might bring you straight up, without stopping in Taos.

DHL

Can you find out from the vet. when he is coming to Taos?

[Frieda Lawrence begins]
Dear Ida,

Yes, do come, should Bynner and Mrs Hughes come too bring plenty of food – by that I mean fresh vegetables and a leg of lamb and a tongue –

I like the play very much –

Yrs Frieda

I think Mical is a good role and for you!

[1] Knopf used it for *The Plumed Serpent* (see the reproduction, Roberts 427).
[2] Christine Hughes.

3412. To Blanche Knopf, 9 May 1925

Text: MS UT; Unpublished.

c/o Del Monte Ranch, *Questa*. New Mexico
9 May 1925

Dear Mrs Knopf

I am glad you like my article for your almanach.[1] Will you please put in this bit, which I forgot: it is from a 'serious' English weekly.[2]

'But Oh,[3] my other anonymous little critic, what shall I say to thee? *Mr Lawrence's horses are all mares or stallions.*

Honi soit qui mal y pense,[4] my dear. Though I'm sure the critic is a gentleman (I daren't say *man*) and not a lady.

Little critics' horses (sic) are all geldings.'

Please put this in.

Yrs D. H. Lawrence

3413. To Alfred Decker Hawk, [10 May 1925]

Text: MS UT; Unpublished.

[Kiowa]
Sunday night

Dear Mr Hawk

The Indians arrived so late, Frances stayed the night here.

Trinidad brought along another boy, who can work on the ditch tomorrow. So if Onofre comes up with Murray, that is enough. –

The water should be through the pipes by noon tomorrow. When the ditch is done, I hope you and Mrs Hawk will come up, and we can have a festival of the waters. – Perhaps on Thursday! – The ditch will take two or three days more.

Yrs DHL

[1] Blanche Knopf wrote on 2 May 1925 (TMSC UT):

Dear Mr. Lawrence,

Your article for THE BORZOI is just in and most excellent. Thanks for getting it to us so very promptly. I have read it with a great deal of interest and am sure it will strike terror into a good many people. The Norman Douglas letter is interesting too, and I am glad to have it.

I hope you are feeling a good deal better now, than you were when I last heard about you.

The ST. MAWR proofs did very well and all that had to be done was done by you.

With kindest regards,

Yours sincerely, Mrs. Alfred A. Knopf.

[2] The source is unidentified; Blanche Knopf was uncertain how to include the quotation in 'Accumulated Mail' (see Letter 3421 and n. 1); but it was included (see *Reflections*, ed. Herbert, pp. xlviii–xlix, 244).

[3] But Oh,] But what Oh,

[4] 'Evil be to him who thinks evil'.

3414. To Ida Rauh, [10 May 1925]

Text: MS UT; Postmark, Taos MAY 11 1925; Unpublished.

c/o Del Monte Ranch, *Valdez.* N. Mex.
Sunday. 9 May 1925

Dear Ida

We are wondering why we haven't heard from you. Brett wrote you she'd be pleased to have you in her cabin, and I put in a note. Didn't you get it? – We were expecting you this week-end.

I told you the play is finished, and a good deal is typed out. We might have some fun with it, when you come.

Bring me, please, two more bottles of that Pantanberge Solution, and a packet of type-writing paper – the ordinary squarish sort. And let us know when you can come. – We expect Frieda's nephew, Friedel Jaffe, on the 19th. – but I think he's coming over from Raton.[1] – Before he comes, we have a spare bed, if you happen to come with Mrs Hughes.

I wonder what you'll think of the play – but anyhow it will be amusing to read, amongst us.

Is Andrew back? If he is, he'll bring you, and he can have the bed in the tiny cabin. A motor-car can run up easily, now, between Del Monte and here – in about fifteen minutes.

Anyhow we'll arrange everything when we know you are coming.

Yrs D. H. Lawrence

3415. To Dr Anton Kippenberg, 12 May 1925

Text: MS GSArchiv; Unpublished.

Del Monte Ranch, *Questa.* New Mexico, U.S.A.
12 May 1925

Dear Dr Kippenberg[2]

I have asked Curtis Brown, of 6. Henrietta St. London W.C.2. – to send you copies of four little sketches of mine called 'Mornings in Mexico'. They were written in the winter when I was down in Oaxaca.

If you care for any one of them, will you please use it for this year's Almanach – whichever one you like. The other three, perhaps you will be so good as to post them to Frau Dr Else Jaffe – per Adr. Frau von Richthofen. Or if you have other use for them, let me know. I suppose we shall be here, at this address, until September. Then we intend to come to England.

Yours Sincerely D. H. Lawrence

[1] Friedel Jaffe came by rail to Raton, and crossed the Sangre de Cristo mountains in some passing vehicle, to Taos where he was met by DHL and Trinidad.

[2] Dr Anton Kippenberg (1874–1950) was the head of Insel Verlag, Leipzig; see p. 38 n. 2.

Elsa Weekley, c. 1932

Barbara Weekley, c. 1922

Nancy Pearn, c. 1922

Dorothy Brett, c. 1925

Trinidad and Rufina Archuleta, from a painting by Brett

Ida Rauh

Alfred Decker and Lucy Hawk, with Ring, c. 1915

Rachel Hawk, Betty Cottam, Bobbie Hawk (later Gillete), William Hawk, Ted Gillete and Louis Cottam, 1921

Lydia and William Siebenhaar

Edward McDonald, c. 1929, from a portrait by Harry Kidd

Luis Quintanilla, 1924

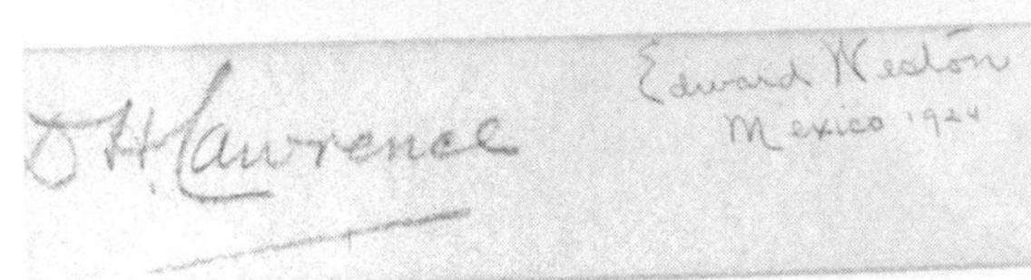

D. H. Lawrence, 4 November 1924, from a photograph by Edward Weston

George Conway

Edward Rickards

Harold T. Mason, from a photograph by Barrie Unrath

Alfred Knopf, 1924

Blanche Knopf, c. 1920s, from a photograph by G. Maillard Kesslere

Carl Seelig, c. 1925

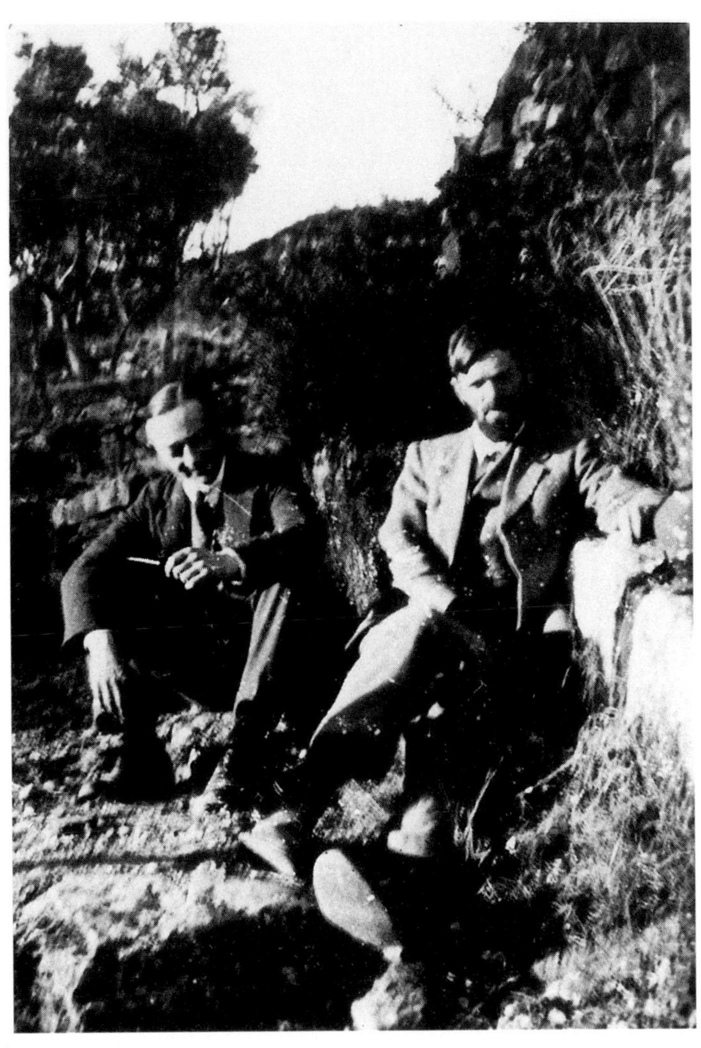

Martin Secker and D. H. Lawrence, Spotorno, January 1926

Rina Secker and Frieda Lawrence, Spotorno, January 1926

Harwood Brewster, Brett, Achsah and Earl Brewster and Lawrence, Capri, from a photograph in *Eve*, 31 March 1926

Elfie and Joseph Rosebery

Arthur Gair Wilkinson

Charles Lahr, 1927, from *Head Study* by Jacob Kramer

This in answer to the letter from Frau Katharine Kippenberg, which I received today.

3416. To Thomas Seltzer, 13 May 1925

Text: MS UTul; Postmark, Taos MAY 15 1925; Lacy, *Seltzer* 148–51.

c/o Del Monte Ranch. *Questa*. New Mexico
13 May 1925

Dear Seltzer

I had your book about the dinner yesterday,[1] and your letter today. We have been back some weeks. I was very ill in Mexico, and the doctors wouldn't let me sail for Europe. But now I am much better: and hope to get to England in the autumn – Meanwhile I am just 'ranching.'

In answer to your letter, I cannot promise to give you all my future books, to publish. The next novel, the one I finished in Oaxaca, is already promised to Knopf. I cannot withdraw. I would not have withdrawn from you, if you had showed me confidence for confidence. But you didn't. – Now, as to the future, I know nothing and can promise nothing. We will let time work out its own solution.

Will you tell your clerk to put *Questa*, not *Taos*, for my address.

And I do hope things will really brighten for you.

Yrs D. H. Lawrence

3417. To Hon. Dorothy Brett, [15? May 1925]

Text: MS Harvey; *Sunstone Review*, v (1976), 40.

[Kiowa]
[15? May 1925][1]

Dear Brett

We thought it would be best if you drive straight to *your* house, tomorrow, and we come down about six and get fires going and the beginnings of a meal, and be there to meet you. Then Ida will have her things there.

If you ride Prince up in the morning, I can ride him down again.

Murray says Rachel had her baby – a girl – on Tuesday morning.[2] Doing well. Thank heaven –

DHL

[1] An 86-page pamphlet titled *Thomas Seltzer: The First Five Years* included letters from many (but not DHL) who could not attend the dinner on 16 April 1925 to mark Seltzer's five years as publisher. See G. Thomas Tanselle, 'The Thomas Seltzer Imprint', *Papers of the Bibliographical Society of America*, lviii (1964), 380.

[2] Shirley Glenn Hawk, b. 12 May 1925; this letter was written a few days later.

Murray arrived!! – So he is putting a stone foundation to your little collapsing ho[use.][1]

3418. To Eduardo Rendón, 21 May 1925

Text: MS McGuire; cited in Moore, *Intelligent Heart* 341–2

Del Monte Ranch, *Valdez.* Taos County, New Mexico
21 May 1925

Dear Rendón[2]

Only today I got the copy of *BirdsBeasts and Flowers* which I ordered for you. Hope you'll get it safely. It's the last book of poems of mine – and vers libre. Some earlier ones are 'enchainé' – I suppose that's the opposite of 'libre' – and since you're an aesthete, probably you'd like those better. But I like these.

The summer has come on the ranch – hot days. I go about with a hoe, irrigating – and for the time being am rancherito y nada mas.[3] They have sent me the typescript of my Mexican novel – I did so want to call it 'Quetzalcoatl', but they all went into a panic – and they want the translation – *The Plumed Serpent* – I suppose they'll have to have it – but sounds to me rather millinery. They urge me to go over the MS., but I feel still that I can't look at it. It smells too much of Oaxaca, which I hated so much because I was so ill. – Altogether I think of Mexico with a sort of nausea: not the friends, but the country itself. It gave me a bad turn that time: doubt if I ever shall come again. – But if I can rouse myself to go over that MS., I'll get the publisher to set it up in type, and then I'll sent you a proof. The book won't be out till early 1926.

Thank goodness I am much better – but don't quite forget yet my shakiness. We have an Indian and his wife on the ranch to work for us – but really I feel I never want to see an Indian or an 'aborigineee' or anything in the savage line again.

Ask Mrs Conway why she never wrote me in answer to my letter. If she'd done so I'd have sent her a book.

I sent Mrs Nuttall these *BirdsBeasts*, also: wonder *very* much what effect they will have on her.

Remember me to Mrs Rendon – Miss Brett also sends remembrances. Hope all goes well with you. – My wife's nephew is staying with us, and my head is full of German, for a change. What a bore other languages are!

Molti saluti[4] D. H. Lawrence

[1] MS torn.

[2] Eduardo Bolio Rendón (1886–1980), English-educated Mexican, amateur architect and dealer in rare books and MSS; intellectual who argued with DHL about religion in Mexico; and friend of the Conways (Parmenter 223, 313–14).

[3] 'little rancher and nothing more'.

[4] 'Many greetings'.

3419. To Henry Mathews, 21 May 1925

Text: MS UTul; Postmark, Va[ldez] MAY 23 1925; Huxley 633–4.

Del Monte Ranch, *Questa*. New Mexico
21 May 1925

Dear Sir[1]

In answer to your letter of April 25th, which I have received only today, I wish to say that in my preface to the *Memoirs of the Foreign Legion* there is nothing but the exact truth: as far as any human being can write the exact truth. As for Maurice Magnus' MS, it is certainly authentic – I went over it with him in the monastery of Montecassino, there is no possibility of any fraud. As for his precise truthfulness, I would not answer. Yet I don't think he lied in this memoir. – He wanted to call it 'Dregs.' – Norman Douglas – who is the N. D. of the Florence episode in my introduction – wrote a sort of little pamphlet defending Magnus – and reproaching me. You can get it it London. But Douglas would not question any of the *facts* of the book – he only thinks I am hard on M. M. But in *life*, Douglas was much harder on him – very much.

Yours faithfully D. H. Lawrence

3420. To David Jester, 23 May 1925

Text: MS UT; *Centaur* 19.

Del Monte Ranch, *Questa*. New Mexico
23 May 1925

Dear Mr Jester

I told Barmby to hunt out for you the six little articles called 'The Crown' – written for *The Signature*.[2] I think the MS is there, in a safe in New York. Two of these were never published. Would you like them? If so, urge Barmby to root out that little roll of MS, and I'll look at the essays: I've not seen them since 1915: nor, I suppose, has anybody. But E.M. Forster said he liked them best of all my small things – and Dr McDonald liked them. – Remember me to him. – If you want something else, I'll see what there is. Let me know.

Secker is printing 'The Princess' along with 'St Mawr' – but Knopf isn't. – I wrote three, 'Princess', 'The Woman Who Rode Away' and 'St. Mawr' for one book. But 'St Mawr' got a bit long. The *Dial* is printing 'The Woman Who Rode Away' – in June.[3] But the *Dial* bores me.

Yrs D. H. Lawrence

[1] Henry Willard Mathews (1875–1939), a Yale graduate, was on the staff of the General Reference Department of Boston Public Library, 1920–38.

[2] See Letter 3212 and p. 103 n. 4.

[3] It appeared in the July and August issues; see p. 71 n. 1.

3421. To Blanche Knopf, [23 May 1925]
Text: MS UT; Unpublished.

Del Monte Ranch, *Questa*. New Mexico
Saturday 23 May

Dear Mrs Knopf

I return the article at once. The insert goes very nicely where you put it.[1]

Thank you very much for sending *Mistress of Husaby*. It's really better than *Tree of the Volkungs*. But both interested me. And the middle part of *Harvest in Poland* very good – at the Lelewel house. But the satanism and spiritism addled.[2]

Tell your clerk, please that the address is *Questa* and not *Taos*.

We'll agree to call the Mexican novel – *The Plumed Serpent* – though it sounds like a certain sort of 'lady in a hat.' – I'll try and bring myself to revise the MS – though I still hate the sight of it.

Yrs D. H. Lawrence

3422. To Curtis Brown, 26 May 1925
Text: MS UT; Huxley 634.

Del Monte Ranch, *Questa*, New Mexico
26 May 1925

Dear Curtis Brown

Your letter, and Secker's about the Douglas letter.[3]

I don't want to bother any more about that business: neither pamphlets nor articles. When I was feeling sick, I felt sore. Now I am better, I don't care what Douglas or anybody else says or pamphletises. They can all go their own way to oblivion, and if Secker doesn't re-print *The Foreign Legion*, I don't care a bit.

[1] Blanche Knopf wrote on 15 May 1925 (TMSC UT): 'Certainly, I am including the addition for THE BORZOI article. It sounds amusing to me. However, just where do you want it placed in the article?' She replied to DHL's letter of 23 May on 1 June (TMSC UT):

Dear Mr. Lawrence,

Thanks for sending back the article. I want to get one thing straight with you and that is, whether you wish to include the Norman Douglas letter in this article and if so can you let me have a duplicate copy of it as the one you sent was badly torn. Please set me straight on this before we go to press.

Fine! I think THE PLUMED SERPENT an exceedingly good title and I hope you will be getting the manuscript to us soon.

With regards and good wishes,

Yours sincerely,

[2] *The Mistress of Husaby* by Sigrid Undset (1882–1949), Danish novelist, trans. Charles Archer; *The Tree of the Folkungs* by Karl Gustaf Verner von Heidenstam (1859–1940), Swedish novelist, trans. Arthur G. Chater; *Harvest in Poland* by Geoffrey Pomeroy Dennis (1892–1963), novelist and essayist. The first was published on 15 May and the latter two on 10 April 1925 by Knopf.

[3] Both are unlocated.

I'm sure you'll agree with me about this. I think public 'controversies' *infra dig.*, anyhow.

I did a play – a Bible play – *David* – which I'll send you when it's typed out. But I don't care about having it published.

Yrs D. H. Lawrence

3423. To Questa Postmaster, 27 May 1925
Text: MS UT; Unpublished.

c/o Del Monte Ranch
27 May 1925

The Postmaster. *Questa*

Dear Sir[1]

I have not yet received the registered letter of which you notified me last Saturday, though I sent a letter by return, asking you please to put the letter and receipt slip in Mr Hawk's bag. I wish you could let me have the letter at once, as it may contain business I need to attend to.

With thanks for your courtesy.

Yours truly D. H. Lawrence

3424. To Emily King, [30 May 1925]
Text: MS Lazarus; Moore 841–2.

Kiowa Ranch. c/o Del Monte Ranch, *Questa*. N. Mexico
Saturday 30 May

My dear Pamela

I had your letter yesterday: am thinking that by now Ada should have received the parcel from Mexico with the puma skin for you. Hope it won't go lost.

We are getting on well here. I am much better – almost my normal self again. But I have to beware of the very hot sun, and of the sudden cold.

We have been on our own ranch all the time: only stayed down on Del Monte five days. But Brett is down there, in a house of her own. The water from the Gallina is for here: it runs gaily past the gate, though the stream isn't very big now. It is a terribly dry spring – everything burnt up. I go out every morning to the field, to turn the water over a new patch. So the long 15-acre field is very green, but the ranges are dry as dry sand, and nothing hardly grows. Only the wild strawberries are flowering full, and the wild gooseberries were thick with blossoms, and little flocks of humming birds came for them. –

[1] Unidentified.

We are now building a new corral for the four horses – and we are having a black cow on Monday[1] – and we've got white hens and brown ones, and a white cock – and Trinidad caught a little wild rabbit, which is alive and very cheerful. That's all the stock: except for Rufina's sister and two little Indian tots with black eyes. The sister has only got an unknown Indian name, and speaks nothing but Indian. – We made a garden, and the things are coming up. We have to turn the stream on the garden, in dozens of tiny channels, to irrigate it. And the nights sometimes are still very cold. – Trinidad saw a deer just behind the houses, last week. But I don't want him to shoot it.

I hope you will come one day and spend the summer: we will manage it, when we are all a bit richer.

By now you will have got a copy of *St. Mawr*: and there is a description of the ranch in that.

Glad you've got another dog. Heaven knows what is best for Peg: I *hated* teaching.

Here is the kiss for Joan x
x

Love DHL

Frieda's nephew Friedel Jaffe is here – quite a nice boy of 21.

3425. To Ada Clarke, 30 May 1925

Text: MS Clarke; cited in Lawrence–Gelder 132–3.

Kiowa Ranch, c/o Del Monte Ranch, *Questa*, New Mexico
30 May 1925

My dear Sister

I had your letter – You must be feeling awfully set up, with your new house! I do hope the blanket will arrive safely, that I posted for you in Mexico City. You really ought to have it by now.

The flowers in your garden sound wonderful: especially the auriculas and polyanthus. I like them so much. Here, it is so terribly dry, there are no flowers yet, save the scarlet and yellow wild columbines – they are nice. Our little garden seeds – nasturtium, sweet-pea, etc – are only an inch high. The nights are cold: then the sun by day can be blazing hot. And it is so dry, my little stream that we bring from the Gallina is half dry. I have to turn it over the garden, and over the alfalfa field, bit by bit: irrigating. That's my job. Then we're building a new little corral, for the horses and the black cow – she is coming up on Monday. Then Rufina has got her sister here, another Indian,

[1] To be called 'Susan'.

and they are 'dobeying the houses – plastering them outside with a sort of golden-brown mud – they look pretty. It is done every spring. We have chickens too – white leghorns, and common brown Mexican hens. The Indian sister has two little black eyed Indian children. And Friedel Jaffe, Frieda's nephew is here. Quite a nice boy. So altogether we are a bunch: takes some feeding. – Today Trinidad and Ruffina have gone down to Taos in the buggy and two horses, to buy the supplies. They won't come back till tomorrow. I am much better – almost myself again. I don't work as hard as last year – though there's always something to be done. – When the corral is finished[1] and the barn re-roofed, we shall slack off. – I hope one summer you'll come and see it all, and learn to ride a horse. –

I suppose you've got *St. Mawr* – the end of that is a picture of this ranch.

I'm glad the children thrive. – But when one reads of unemployment in England, one wonders, when you are so very busy.[2] – So glad Gertie is better. Remember me to Eddie.[3]

Love. DHL

3426. To Witter Bynner, [31 May 1925]
Text: MS (Photocopy) Kimball; Bynner 256.

[Frieda Lawrence begins]

Kiowa, Del Monte, Taos
[31 May 1925]

Dear Hal Bynner,

Quite out of the blue your little parcel was handed me and when I saw the new cigarettebox, I thought you had sent me som[e] specially good ones, but no – inside was the lovely jade[4] – I am making myself a green linen dress for it – So many thanks – I like the thin animal on top – I hope your play will be a success[5] and do come up some time the middle of June or after – We have got 9 chickens, an irrigation ditch that looks like a brook, to-morrow comes a black cow – Lawrence is much better – It's *raining!* We have also 4 grown up Indians and 2 little ones. Embarras de richesse!!

I am enclosing a letter to Mrs Hughes.

Yours gleefully with my jade Frieda

[1] MS reads 'finish'.
[2] Unemployment was regularly treated in the newspapers at this time, e.g. see leaders in *The Times* for 15 May and 29 June 1925.
[3] Ada's husband, William Edwin Clarke (1896–1964), tailor. m. 1913. See *Letters*, i. 174n.
[4] Bynner had brought Frieda a necklace from China (p. 256).
[5] *Cake* (1926), a play in verse 'some aspects of which were said to be a satire on Mabel Lujan' (Bynner 336). For DHL's response to the play, see his letter to Bynner, 13 April 1928.

[Lawrence begins]
Dear Bynner

Thanks for sending the poem: I had seen it in *Palms*: thought it good.[1] – Run up and see us before you go south –

Yrs DHL

3427. To Curtis Brown, [c. 1 June 1925]
Text: MS UT; Unpublished.

[Kiowa]
[c. 1 June 1925][2]

Dear Curtis Brown

Dont know why Blackwell sent this to me – tell him it's your show.

Yrs DHL

– Put the cheque to my account please, and charge me the percentage.

3428. To Blanche Knopf, 5 June 1925
Text: MS UT; Unpublished.

Del Monte Ranch, *Questa*, New Mexico
5 June 1925

Dear Mrs Knopf

No, don't use the Norman Douglas letter at all, please.[3] I felt sore at him for a while, but now prefer to forget him and all that stuff.

I went through the 'Quetzalcoatl' MS – will do a few things to it, and send it on. After all, I hate giving it out to be published. It is different from my other books: and to me, the one that means most to me. If Knopf thinks better to put it aside for some time, I shall be a bit relieved. Then I might do a third long story, to go with 'The Princess' and 'The Woman Who Rode Away' – (now appearing in *The Dial*) – for next spring.

But we will see.

Yours Sincerely D. H. Lawrence

[1] Probably one of Bynner's two poems in the Christmas issue of *Palms*: 'Earth-balm' or 'Following', ii (Christmas 1924), 133–4.

[2] DHL wrote on Blackwell's letter; his own is dated accordingly. Blackwell wrote:

May 22nd 1925

Dear Mr Lawrence,

I must apologise for taking so long to answer your last letter. I have, however, sent out the six copies to the addresses you give. I have much pleasure in enclosing a small cheque for advance royalty subscribed before publication.

Wishing the book every success,

Yours very truly,

The letter was signed, on behalf of Basil Blackwell, by his partner (Sir) Adrian Spear Mott (1889–1964). See Letter 3404 and n. 1.

[3] See p. 256 n. 1.

3429. To Idella Purnell, [5 June 1925]

Text: MS UT; PC v. Chili (Red Pepper) Drying in Front of Adobe Home, New Mexico; cited in Bynner 254.

c/o Del Monte Ranch. Questa. N.M.
5 June.

Dear Idella

I got the *St. Mawr* copies two days ago – send you one now – perhaps it will amuse you. I wonder how you'll like Los Angeles – you'll get more interest than in Guad[alajara]. We sit tight here on the ranch. I find in myself very little inclination to move, for the moment. There's rather a nice Danish woman and man you might like to know:

Mrs Anna Winchell Bóttern, 1810 Walton Avenue. Los Angeles.

She talks of translating *The Captain's Doll* into Danish. You might send her a note if you'd care to see her. – Haven't seen anybody from Santa Fe – or even Taos – since we are here – Bynner may run up. Ask your father to ask Robles Gil how many pesos I have left in their bank – and I can give you a cheque for a subscription or two – or should it be dollars now? – I hope you'll have a good time in California – tell us how it is. Frieda sends remembrances.

DHL

3430. To Dr Trigant Burrow, 6 June 1925

Text: MS (Photocopy) HU; Huxley 634–5.

c/o Del Monte Ranch. *Questa*, New Mexico
6 June 1925

Dear Dr Burrow[1]

I found your letter and the two reprints when I got back here.[2] I am in entire

[1] Dr Trigant Burrow (1875–1950), b. Virginia, psychoanalyst and writer; M. D., University of Virginia, 1899; Ph. D., Johns Hopkins University, 1910. Studied in Zurich with Jung, 1910; clinical psychiatrist, Johns Hopkins Hospital, 1911–27; founder of American Psychoanalytic Assocation, 1911, president 1925–6; directed Lifwynn Foundation for Laboratory Research in Analytic and Social Psychiatry. m. 1904, Emily Sherwood Bryan. See Nehls, iii. 678–80 n. 213.

[2] Burrow's letter of 28 January 1925 (Nehls, iii. 680) read:

Dear Mr. Lawrence:

You were so good as to be interested in some earlier writings of mine and I have thought many times to write you of my appreciation and to say how much I have enjoyed your own delightful essays on psychoanalysis. Knowing your feeling for the subject I am prompted to send you reprints of two recent papers of mine. They are part of a larger thesis that is the outcome of intensive research of the last years with groups of students involving the social reactions of "the unconscious." I had hoped that this work would have found its way to publication, but it is evident that American publishers are very chary of scientific trends whose basis lacks the accustomed precedents.

I should be very glad if these essays may be of interest to you. With appreciations and good wishes,

Very sincerely yours,

One paper was 'Social Images versus Reality', *Journal of Abnormal Psychology and Social Psychology*, xix (1924), 230–5, and the other probably was 'A Relative Concept of Consciousness: An Analysis of Consciousness in its Ethnic Origin', *Psychoanalytic Review*, xii (January 1925), 1–15.

sympathy with your idea of social images. In fact, I feel myself that the Jewish consciousness is now composed entirely of social images: there is no new-starting 'reality' left. Nothing springs alive and new from the blood. All is a chemical re-action, analysis and decomposition and re-precipitation of social images. It is what happens to all old races. They lose the faculty for real experience, and go on decomposing their test-tubes-full of social images. – One fights and fights for that living something which stirs way down in the blood, and *creates* consciousness. But the world won't have it. To the present human mind, everything is ready-made, and since the sun cannot be new, there can be nothing new under the sun.[1] – But to me, the sun, like the rest of the cosmos, is alive, and therefore not ready-made at all.

I don't wonder you haven't got your book published.[2] Those *Unconscious* things of mine hardly sell at all, and only arouse dislike.[3] I'm not going to bother any more about that side of things. People are too dead, and too conceited. *Man is the measure of the universe.*[4] Let him be it: idiotic foot-rule which even then is *nothing*. In my opinion, one can never *know*: and never-never *understand*. One can but swim, like a trout in a quick stream. As for the stones that sit tight and think they *know*, permanently – they are only swimming very slowly in a much slower stream – stupidly.

Yrs D. H. Lawrence

3431. To George Conway, 10 June 1925

Text: MS Moore; Moore, *Intelligent Heart* 341–2.

c/o Del Monte Ranch, *Valdez*. New Mexico
10 June 1925

Dear Conway

We had Mrs Conway's letter today – so glad to hear all the gossip, so sad to hear of the rising sea of troubles. But I had, and have, a bad feeling about this Mexico of just now. Thank the Lord I am out of it. – So you went to Toronto! I

[1] Ecclesiastes i. 9 ['there is no new thing under . . .'].

[2] *The Social Basis of Consciousness* was published in 1927, and DHL reviewed it; see his letter to Burrow, 3 August 1927. Burrow on 12 July 1927 said 'it was first written some four years ago' (Nehls, iii. 682), and the first footnote to 'A Relative Concept' (see note above) states that this article was a chapter of a larger thesis about 'the outcome of a practical experiment in group or social analysis' (p. 1).

[3] *Psychoanalysis and the Unconscious* and *Fantasia of the Unconscious*.

[4] Conflation of Protagoras' 'Man is the measure of all things' (Plato, *Theaetetus*, c. 368 BC) and 'He gave man speech, and speech created thought,/ Which is the measure of the universe' (Shelley, *Prometheus Unbound*, 1819, II. iv. 73–4).

once looked across that lake which is there – without much desire to sail over. There are so many places in the world that, thank God, one need not go to.

We sit here on our own little ranch, up to the eyes in doing nothing. I spent all the golden evening riding through the timber hunting the lost cow: and when at last I got her into corral, I felt more like killing her than milking her. Meanwhile my wife was going round and round the fowl-barn, trying to drive in the four new Rhode-Island-Red hens, which refused to go to roost. Our two Indians have gone down to Taos.

But after all, I'd rather hunt the cow through the timber, though I swear myself black in the face, than try to 'push the business on' in Mexico. You really have my sympathy, with all those morons and morones.

I don't do any work since we are here – except milk the black-eyed Susan and irrigate the field – when there's any water. I never felt less literary. But I've revised the MS. of my Mexican novel – which I wanted to call 'Quetzalcoatl'. But the publishers wept at the sound of it: and pleaded for a translation: *The Plumed Serpent*. Mrs Conway will say it means the lady of Coyoacan, with a feathered hat:[1] but I don't care. I think it sounds a bit silly – *The Plumed Serpent*. But *je m' en fiche*.

I hear from people in Philadelphia: they seem *really* to like Hergesheimer out there: say he really *is* a real person: books or not.[2] So that Mrs Conway neednt, I think, have any qualms, if she feels like fluttering through his domains.

It's been blowy and rather cold here: *very* dry, dry to dessication: and summer only started yesterday. I expect autumn will set in tomorrow. We're too high – over 8000 ft. I am about my normal self again – but shall never forgive Mexico, especially Oaxaca, for having done me in. I shudder even when I look at the little MS. you gave me, and think of that beastly Santo Domingo church, with its awful priests and the back-yard with a well-ful of baby's bones.[3] Quoth the raven: *Nevermore*.[4] But this *Nevermore* is a thankful, cheerful chirrup, like a gay blackbird. Nevermore need I look on Mexico – but

[1] I.e. Zelia Nuttall.

[2] Joseph Hergesheimer (1880–1954), novelist and short story writer, e.g. *The Lay Anthony* (1914), *Java Head* (1919). DHL would have heard about him from the Centaur Press people; they had published a bibliography of his writings (see p. 63 n. 4).

[3] Part of the monastic complex of Santo Domingo was used as a barracks, and soldiers searching for treasure discovered a passage twenty feet long by almost five feet wide and covered four feet deep with children's bones, generally assumed to be those of illegitimate offspring of the Dominican friars driven out in 1859 when monasteries were abolished. Col. Akin was alerted by General Ibarra and took photographs on 13 August 1924 in the secret room (Parmenter 164–5). The 'little MS.' is unidentified (ibid. 347–8).

[4] In Edgar Allan Poe's *The Raven* (1844).

especially Oaxaca. – Yet my 'Quetzalcoatl' novel lies nearer my heart than any other work of mine. I shall send you a copy next year – D.V.

I hope you are having a bit of peace with Gage and your other MSS.[1] Really, the world isn't worth one's effort. Here, thank God, not many people come – and I have only once been out of the gates of the two ranches, ours and Del Monte, since we came from Mexico.

I was glad to hear from Mrs Conway – was afraid she might be unwell, she didn't seem over-robust. We shall stay on here, I suppose, till September or October: then to Europe. We might even see Mrs Conway over there: London or Paris. That would be fun. If ever you go to Winnipeg, or some such place, do stop off and see us here.[2]

I'll send Mrs Conway another book – pleasant and untroublesome, with pictures.[3] We both, my wife and I, remember so gratefully how kind you were to us, coming to the station – and the basket! We still have it – the basket with the purple band.

Au revoir D. H. Lawrence

3432. To Alfred Decker Hawk, [c. 16 June 1925]

Text: MS UT; Unpublished.

[Kiowa]
[c. 16 June 1925][4]

Dear Mr Hawk

Mr Murray borrowed these tools: many thanks for the loan of them. There is also a shovel of yours, but the boy is far down the field with it.[5] I'll send it tomorrow.

Will you please give Trinidad the other buggy-seat.

Yrs D. H. Lawrence

[1] Unidentified. Conway collected MSS; he took a particular interest in materials relating to the activities of Englishmen brought to trial in the Inquisition in the sixteenth century; and had published an article on Gage: 'Un inglés en México: Tomás Gage (1597–1656)', *Ethnos* (Mexico), i (1922), 228–35. [2] See pp. 228–9 n. 1.

[3] Likely *Sea and Sardinia*, illus. by Jan Juta (b. 1897), South African painter (see *Letters*, iv. 24 n. 4).

[4] The tools would have been returned after the work on the irrigation pipes or the corral was completed and before Trinidad left on 18 June.

[5] Frederico Alires, a young Mexican from San Cristobal who worked for DHL (see Letters 3434 and 3437); see Letter 3120 and n. 2. He died a few years later from sheep tick fever (Brett, *South Dakota Review* 68).

3433. To Hon. Dorothy Brett, [17 June 1925]

Text: MS UT; Unpublished.

[Kiowa]
Wed[1]

Trinidad is going to San Cristobal. – Do come to supper – glad the play is done.

Do we go to Hot Springs tomorrow?

DHL

3434. To Baroness Anna von Richthofen, 18 June 1925

Text: MS Jeffrey; Frieda Lawrence, *Nur Der Wind*, pp. 238–9.

Del Monte Ranch. *Questa*, New Mexico
18 Juni 1925

Meine liebe Schwiegermutter

Gleich kriegst du wieder einen Geburtstag: was für eine schöne Reihe Geburtstagen hast du! Und herum gehst wie eine Backfisch, Merkursteigend und Waldkaffeefressend, in neuen Röcken! Und hier sitzen wir armen Bauernleute, müssen Kuh Milchen und Hühne besorgen. Die Frieda macht zwei Pfund Butter in der Woche!! Heute kriegen wir schon acht Eier!!! Die Black-Eyed Susan, die Kuh, war wieder durch die Zaune herausgeflogen, der Friedel aber, mit dem Mexicaner Frederico, schnell auf ihrem Schwanz, hat sie wieder eingebracht. Jetzt fresst sie, schwarzes Tier, zu einem grossen Holzstück gebunden. Die Indianer sind weg: Schmutzfinken alle. Morgen geht der Friedel mit dem jungen Mexicaner Fred, nach Taos, im Wagen: Friedel sagt immer, auf Englisch, wägon – *in the weygon*! Doch spricht er gut Englisch. Er sagt er will in August nach Deutschland kommen – am 8n von New York fort. Wir werden später kommen, in September.

Und geht die Nusch in Kniekurzen Röcklein. Ich bin der Moses der Familie, und will sie schimpfen. Es muss ganz lustig sein, in Baden. Hier ist es *zu* trocken. Die wilde Erdbeeren sind ausgetrocknet ehe sie reif werden können, und mein Feld geht in Pulver. Ich habe etwas Heimweh nach Europa. Doch ist dieses Leben sehr gesund, ich bin wirklich viel stärker. Ich hätte aber sehr gern die Englischen Wiesen sehen, eh' sie gemäht sind, und Kirschen in Deutschland essen, und Weintrauben in Italien. Ich meine, nächstes Jahr kommen wir nicht wieder nach Amerika. Vielleicht will der Arbeiter Murray hier auf dem Ranch wohnen, und alles besorgen. – Meine Schwester in Ripley hat ein grosses neues Haus gebaut, und ist *sehr* stolz. Gott sei dank, ich habe

[1] Trinidad was sent away and Brett had finished typing *David* by 18 June 1925; see Letter 3436. At the time of this letter, though the play was typed, Trinidad had not been dismissed: hence Wednesday 17 June is conjectured.

kein grosses neues Haus mir um Hals gebunden, wie Susan an ihrem Holzstück. Man kann nicht mehr sagen: ich bin ein Fremdling überall, sonst 'überall bin ich zu Haus.' Es ist vielleicht noch schlimmer – wie findst du, Schwiegermutter?

Grüsse an Alle. Lebe wohl! Und wann wir kommen, werden wir Moselwein trinken, und stille Herbsttage geniessen.

dein Schwiegersohn DHL

[My dear Schwiegermutter

You're about to have another birthday; what a lovely row of birthdays you've got! And you go about like a teenager, climbing up the Merkur and guzzling in the Coffee House in the wood, in new skirts! And here we sit, poor peasants, having to milk the cow and look after the chickens. Frieda makes two pounds of butter a week!! Today we got as many as eight eggs!!! Black-Eyed Susan, the cow, flew off through the fences once again, but Friedel, along with the Mexican Frederico, quickly on her tail, brought her back in again. Now she's grazing, black animal, tied to a large lump of wood. The Indians have gone: filthy beggars all of them.[1] Tomorrow Friedel goes to Taos in the buggy with the young Mexican Fred: Friedel always says, in English, wagon – *in the weygon*! But he speaks good English. He says he wants to come to Germany in August – leaving New York on the 8th. We'll come later, in September.

And does Nusch go around in knee-length little skirts.[2] I am the Moses of the family, and want to scold her. It must be quite jolly in Baden. Here it is *too* dry. The wild strawberries are dried up before they can get ripe, and my field turns to powder. I'm a bit homesick for Europe. But this life is very healthy, I'm genuinely much stronger. I'd really love, though, to see English meadows before they're mown, and to eat cherries in Germany, and grapes in Italy. I think next year we won't come back to America. Murray, the workman, may want to live here on the ranch, and look after everything. – My sister in Ripley has built a big new house and is *very* proud. Thank God I've not tied a big new house around my neck, like Susan with her lump of wood. One can no longer say: I'm a stranger everywhere, only 'everywhere I'm at home.' That's perhaps even worse – what do you think, Schwiegermutter?

[1] According to Brett 'Frieda has flown out at Trinidad's wife', who left in tears, and DHL requested that if she went, she was not to come back. Trinidad went with her, perhaps on 10 June (Letter 3431), he returned about 13 June. DHL must have hired Alires about this time (Letters 3432). By 18 June 'Frieda has sent Trinidad away . . . Trinidad does not understand. He looks bewildered and a bit injured' (Brett 218–19, 224).

[2] Frieda's younger sister, Helene Johanna Mathilde ('Nusch') Krug, née von Richthofen (1882–1971), m. (1) 1900, Max von Schreibershofen (1864–1944); divorced 1923; (2) 1923, Emil Krug (1870–1944). Her children were Anita (b. 1901) and Hadubrand (b. 1905).

Greetings to everyone. Goodbye! And when we come, we'll drink Moselle, and enjoy quiet autumn days.

your son-in-law DHL]

3435. To Martin Secker, 18 June 1925

Text: MS UInd; Postmark, Tao[s] JUN 20 1925; Secker 62–3.

Del Monte Ranch. *Questa*, New Mexico
18 June 1925

Dear Secker

I never thanked you for the copy of *St Mawr* which came safely. I hope it does well. The *Times Supplement* review was quite good.[1]

I have just revised the MS. of the Mexican novel – which *I* call 'Quetzalcoatl'. Knopf of course was horrified: so I had to translate the word, for him: *The Plumed Serpent*. He likes that very much. I hope you do. It is a longish novel – 100 thousand or a little more. It won't be easily popular, but in my opinion it is my most important thing so far. I will send this revised MS to New York, to Curtis Brown, and when they've made all the alterations in the duplicate, I'll tell them to let you see it. If it impresses you, I wish you could set

[1] Secker wrote to Curtis Brown on 28 May 1925 (Secker Letter-book UIll):

Dear Curtis Brown

Many thanks for your friendly letter of the 26th enclosing the contract for "St Mawr" which I am returning duly signed. Naturally I am delighted that this should carry with it a further option on a novel, and it is most kind of you to have inserted the clause. Although nothing is needed to stimulate my interest, or the attention I give to Lawrence's work, it is at the same time very encouraging to feel that I enjoy your confidence and his. May these pleasant relations continue for long.

Next autumn, or possibly in January, I am launching a new series of copyright books, in a pocket size, under the general title of The New Adelphi Library. The price will be 3/6 a volume, and of course, the titles will be reset for their appearance in this new form. I believe the sales will be steady and continuous. What I wished to include of Lawrence's was the story "The Captain's Doll" from "The Ladybird", in my opinion one of the most remarkable things he has written. I wrote to him merely to ask whether he would have any objection to this story appearing in the series, saying that I would discuss terms with you as soon as he had agreed. I am proposing to pay a royalty of 10% on the first 2000 copies, then 15%, which I think is fair, with payment on publication for the subscription royalties. If you agree to this, all that should be necessary, I think, would be a letter to this effect, which can be attached to the existing "Ladybird" contract.

I am pleased with the "St Mawr" notice in the Literary Supplement today, and I shall send it to Lawrence. He does not see press-notices, so I use my discretion in the matter. I may say that I send him very few for most of them are liable to cause a rush of blood to the head. But this one is intelligent and perceptive, and he will like it.

Yours sincerely

The *TLS* review was the only favourable notice in the British press at that time; see *St. Mawr*, ed. Finney, pp. xxxvii–xxxviii. The anonymous reviewer praised DHL's perceptions as expressed in the 'living symbols' of the horse and his evocation of the New Mexican landscape.

up in galley form fairly soon, because I should very much like to show a set of proofs to a Mexican friend in Mexico City, to have his opinion, which I should value very much.[1] Do you think you might do that? – You would publish the book, I suppose, in the spring.

We are busy on our ranch just ranching – have brought a stream of water from the Gallina Canyon – and built a new corral. We have the four horses and a buggy, in which Frieda sometimes sails out, driven by the Indian Trinidad. I milk the cow – black-eyed Susan – and F. collects the eggs. Sounds idyllic, but the cow escapes into the mountains, we hunt her on horseback and curse her blacker than she is: an eagle strikes one of the best hens: a skunk fetches the eggs: the half wild cows break in on the pasture, that is drying up as dry as pepper – no rain, no rain, no rain. It's tough country. We hope to come to England in the autumn.

I hope all goes well with you, and with Mrs Secker and the son. Somehow it seems far, this summer, to London – farther than ever. Tell me any news and remember me to anybody who cares.

Yrs D. H. Lawrence

3436. To Ida Rauh, 18 June 1925

Text: MS UT; Unpublished.

Del Monte Ranch, *Valdez*, New Mexico
18 June 1925

Dear Ida

Glad you are revived.

Here is the last of the play. I sent my other two MSS. to my agent: one for London. But Barmby, my agent himself, is in England – so are the Knopfs. So probably an indefinite delay. No me hace.[2]

The stream at the gate runs until 2.0 in the afternoon. Then the sun has sucked it up. It is very dry here. We have a cow, Black-eyed Susan, whom I milk morning and evening – I seem to be forever milking. We have pulled down the old corral, and made a new smaller one out of the old lumber. Also re-roofed the barn. We have sent the Indians away – too[3] much of a Schweinerei[4] – Now the lesser house is the dairy – all cleaned up and nice. We make about 2 pounds of butter per week: F[rieda] does it. But today already 8 eggs.

I hear Spud is to manage the Indian Trading Concern. I think it will be a good thing for him.

Friedel, F's nephew, is here – till mid or end of July.

[1] Rendón, and also Conway; see Letters 3418 and 3465.
[2] 'It makes no difference to me.'
[3] Indians . . . too] Indias . . . two
[4] 'Mess'.

Come with Andrew and see us before you go east. There is a bed now. F. sends greetings.

D. H. Lawrence

3437. To Hon. Dorothy Brett, [19 June 1925]

Text: MS Harvey; Unpublished.

[Kiowa]
Friday[1]

Dear Brett

I pay the boy – Fred Alires – two dollars a day. He brought me two chickens from San Cristobal – at a dollar each: poor chickens, and it's too much. – I say the people can take 1.50 or have the chickens back. – If they want the birds back, let me know: and then pay the boy only 50 cents, as the 1.50 is on his cheque.

DHL

3438. To Catherine Carswell, 20 June 1925

Text: MS YU; Carswell 222, 223–4, 229.

Del Monte Ranch. *Questa*, New Mexico
20 June 1925

My dear Catherine

I was so ill down in Mexico in Oaxaca – with malaria, flue, and tropical fever – I thought I'd never see daylight. So everything slipped. But we got back here about ten weeks ago, and I am beginning to be myself again. But it was no joke. – As far as prosperity goes – I have left Seltzer, who hangs, like a creaking gate, long: and gone to Knopf, who is a better business man. But of course I still have to live on what is squeezed out of poor Seltzer.

We've been busy here – brought a stream of water from the Gallina Canyon – about two miles – to irrigate the field. But it's so dry, for all that. The water just disappears. We have a black cow, whom I milk every morning and evening – and Frieda collects the eggs – about eight a day – from the eleven hens. Frieda's nephew Friedel Jaffe is staying the summer with us – he helps. We had an Indian and wife to do for us, till last week; then we sent them away. 'Savages' are a burden. So a Mexican boy comes up to help: and even him one has to pay two dollars a day: supposed to be very cheap labour.

Lovely to think of cherry trees in bloom: here the country is too savage, somehow, for such softness. I get a bit of a heimweh for Europe. We shall come in the autumn – D. V. – and winter somewhere warm.

[1] Alires had arrived before Trinidad left (Letters 3432 and 3434), and Alires and Friedel Jaffe were to go to Taos on 19 June (3434); for payment, see also the following letter.

Who is the other boy you have with you? One of Goldring's boys?[1] I don't know.

Glad you liked *St Mawr*. In Mexico I finished my Mexican novel. It's very different. But I think most of it. – Pity you don't do any writing.

All good wishes from us both to you and the boy and Don.

Yrs D. H. Lawrence

3439. To Curtis Brown, [23 June 1925]

Text: MS Forster; Huxley 636–7.

Del Monte Ranch: *Questa*. New Mexico
23 June 1923

Dear Curtis Brown

I had your radiogram last night – it took three days by post, from the air station here in New Mexico.[2]

I seem to remember that O'Brien does a sort of anthology of short stories each year, but whether English or American publishing I don't know. – I had thought, that perhaps I would do a third long story, to go with 'The Woman Who Rode Away' and 'The Princess', and make a vol. for America. – But perhaps it would be better to leave it to you to decide. If this O'Brien concern is a good one, and you think it best to let him have 'The Princess', then agree with him. Anyhow 'The Princess' is used for England, already.[3]

I expect by this time you have the MS. of the play *David*. It is a good play, and for the theatre. Someone ought to do it.

I think next week I'll send the MS. of *The Plumed Serpent* ('Quetzalcoatl'), my Mexican novel, to the New York office, asking them to make the

[1] Brendan Hugh McBride Goldring (1918–42), son of Douglas Goldring, novelist and playwright whom DHL had met in 1919 (see *Letters*, iii. 371 n. 3). Hugh and John Carswell went to school together for a term in France during the spring of 1925 and spent the summer holiday together.

[2] A copy of it reads (TMSC UT):

20th. June. 1925.

LAWRENCE DEL MONTE RANCH QUESTA MEXICO

MAY O'BRIEN HAVE PRINCESS FOR BEST BRITISH SHORT STORIES WRITING CURTIS BROWN

[3] Secker objected to the inclusion of 'The Princess'; P. P. Howe wrote to Nancy Pearn on 9 July 1925: 'His view is that the story is an integral part of a volume which has been too recently published to make the procedure advisable' (Secker Letter-Book, UIll). Nancy Pearn wrote to DHL on 15 July 1925 (TMSC UT) that she had arranged for 'Jimmy and the Desperate Woman' to be included in *The Best British Short Stories of 1925*, ed. Edward J. O'Brien and John Cournos, (published 17 October 1925), pp. 88–114.(For the 1926 volume, see p. 481 n. 4.) See also p. 86 n. 1 and Letter 3181 and n. 4.

Edward Joseph Harrington O'Brien (1890–1941), American author and editor (see *Letters*, iv. 296 n.).

corrections on the duplicate and forward a copy to you at once. I consider this my most important novel, so far. Will you show it to Secker. Perhaps he might set it up soon, if he likes it, in galleys. I should like very much to show it to a Mexican friend, in Mexico City, and have his opinion, before it is finally printed. I'm a bit afraid to send the MS. down there.

When is Barmby coming back to New York?

Knopf advertises that I shall henceforth publish exclusively with him. He's not justified in so doing. – Seltzer writes an expostulation. – I never made any 'exclusive' promise to Knopf, and I don't think Barmby ever did.[1]

Yrs D. H. Lawrence

3440. To David Jester, 29 June 1925

Text: MS UT; *Centaur* 21.

Del Monte Ranch. *Questa*, New Mexico
29 June 1925

Dear Mr Jester

The bibliographies have come. They are very nice: almost nicer done than *any* of my own books. I like them very much. As for Dr McDonald, he leaves me speechless, I feel I have lived in such a state of ignorance of my own fate. What labours! I hope to heaven it will be worth it to him.

I am sending you here a little article on 'The Novel', as you asked me, for the small book of essays.[2] Let me know if it is too antiseptic for you. I think it's amusing.

I really am pleased with the bibliography. Almost it makes me feel important.

Yrs D. H. Lawrence

3441. To Edward McDonald, 29 June 1925

Text: MS UT; Postmark, Questa JUL 1 1925; *Centaur* 19–20.

Del Monte Ranch. *Questa. New Mexico*
29 June 1925

Dear Dr McDonald

The bibliographies came on Saturday evening, and created quite a sensa-

[1] In *Publisher's Weekly* for 6 June 1925, Knopf had advertised: '*A new publishing connection* D. H. Lawrence *permanently joins the Borzoi list with the publication of his latest novel* ST. MAWR . . . Mr. Lawrence's work will henceforth appear exclusively under the Borzoi imprint' (cvii, p. 1864). A similar announcement appeared in the issue of 13 June (p. 1920).

[2] For the history of its alterations and publication in *Reflections on the Death of a Porcupine*, see *Study of Thomas Hardy and Other Essays*, ed. Bruce Steele (Cambridge, 1985), pp. xlvii–xlix.

tion on the ranch. I like both the books very much indeed: to look at and to touch.[1] And all the work you have put in, into the inside, abashes me. It seems to me wonderfully complete, and *alive*: marvellous to make a bibliography lively. I have got the signed copy No. 2., and it shall be a *Vade Mecum*, quite invaluable to me, who keep so little track of my things.

I am sending Mr Jester a little article on 'The Novel', which my wife says is too much. But it's what I genuinely feel, and *how* I feel, so what's the odds. Anyhow it can be altered if necessary.

Somebody sent me the first sheet of the *N[ew] Y[ork] Tribune* with Stuart P. Sherman's article on me. It amused me rather. But a beard is a thing that cultivates itself: if you'll let it. I must get the second leaf, and see what he says about *St. Mawr*.[2] They pretend it's one of my best things: it isn't. But it's easy for them. My novel that I did in Mexico – which I called 'Quetzalcoatl', but which poor Knopf, fainting over, got me to translate into *The Plumed Serpent*; – this I consider my chief novel so far. Thank the Lord it won't be published till next year, at least.

We are due to go to Europe for[3] the winter – and I want to go. America is so eternally and everlastingly tough: very good for one, for a bit; but after too long, it makes one feel leathery in one's soul. Continual leathery resistance all the time. Mexico more so. I think it's time I was softened down a bit, with a little oil of Europe.

I'll send you a copy of the new *Movements*, with the pictures. They are nice pictures. The Oxford Press people were too conceited to use yours: chosen in America. I did them an Epilogue which they were frightened to use. It was for the future rather than the past. But why shouldn't a history book reach both ways! – Apparently they're cancelling that picture of Boston – Milk St. – and putting in a view of Boston from the sea.[4] So this may make another bibliographical item.

Now I'll hunt my aimiable but wayward cow, Susan, who disappears into

[1] What the second book might be is uncertain, possibly the fifth volume in the Centaur series, *A Bibliography of Carl Van Vechten* by Scott Cunningham (1924).

[2] 'Lawrence Cultivates His Beard' by Stuart Pratt Sherman (1881–1926), American literary critic, in *New York Herald Tribune Books* (14 June 1925), 1–3. See *Letters*, iv. 355 n. 4 and 499. Sherman commented at length on symbolism in *St. Mawr* and called it 'mordantly satirical'. See *D. H. Lawrence: The Critical Heritage*, ed. R. P. Draper, (1970), pp. 250–7. See also Letter 3446.

[3] for] to

[4] The Old South Church in Boston was mistakenly identified as the place where Patrick Henry made his 'Give me liberty or give me death' speech; it was replaced by a view of Boston harbour (Roberts A17b).

the timber and stands block still like invisibility itself, while I walk past her and on and on. She's a black blossom.

Yrs D. H. Lawrence

3442. To Idella Purnell, 29 June 1925
Text: MS UT; Bynner 254–5.

Del Monte Ranch. *Valdez,*[1] New Mexico
29[2] June 1925

Dear Idella

I'm glad you like *St Mawr*. Did you see Stuart P. Sherman in the *N[ew] Y[ork] Tribune*, on me and my beard. As if my beard didn't cultivate itself! It is merely that I refuse to extinguish it.

The 10,000 acres of yours really sound fascinating. But heaven knows about the 'colony.'[3] Artists and 'live people' are usually most lively hating one another. But try it and see. Anything's worth a try.

We are due to go to Europe for the winter. I feel, a little relief from the American Continent will be good for me. But I have been inoculated with Mexico: who knows when it will fetch me back. When it does, I shall write post haste to you and your Daddy, to know if I can come to the ranch. No more Oaxacas for me. I loved Chapala, Guadalajara, Jalisco, much the best: and I do wish we had come there again. But never mind. We shall see what we shall see.

Frieda was asking me to ask you if, by chance, you have that little book of poems *Bay* – from which you printed some bits in *Palms*.[4] The one copy we had in Chapala was the only one – and F's. But I am almost certain you brought it me back. It has disappeared.

Your letters are getting a Californian note to them: a certain cheery look-into-the-future with-bright-eyes touch. I suppose that's why you want to go back to Guad, where the future doesn't really exist. When we came down to Guad. two years ago, Götzsche and I, we came from California – Los Angeles. I wonder how I'll come next time.

But I feel you're enjoying yourself in L. A.

Yrs D. H. Lawrence[5]

1 *Valdez*] *Questa* 2 29] 26

3 'Dr. Purnell had had at this time a chance to buy an extensive tract of beautiful wild acreage with waterfall and marble quarries not too far from Guadalajara', and Idella Purnell considered founding an artists' colony there (Bynner 254).

4 'Four Poems' ('Bombardment', 'After the Opera', 'The Little Town at Evening' and 'Last Hours'), in *Palms*, ii (Christmas 1924), 146–9. It may have been returned to her; see Bynner 255.

5 Idella Purnell wrote on the letter: 'tiger leaping thro forest for Bøtterns' (and several names).

3443. To William Hawk, [July? 1925]

Text: MS UT; Unpublished.

[Kiowa]
[July? 1925][1]

Dear William

Can you let us have butter – and more eggs when there are any. There are 3 cows and calf feeding round here – do you know whose they are?

DHL

3444. To Alfred Knopf, 1 July 1925

Text: Moore 845–6.

Del Monte Ranch, Questa
1 July 1925

Dear Knopf

I heard from Curtis Brown today that he had sent you the MS. of my play *David*. I wanted you and Mrs Knopf to see it. But really, I don't want it published, unless it is produced. Curtis Brown thinks it would be better if it appeared first as 'literature.' Myself, I am a bit tired of plays that are only literature. If a man is writing 'literature,' why choose the form of a play? And if he's writing a play, he surely intends it for the theatre. Anyhow I wrote this play for the theatre, and I want the theatre people to see it first. Curtis Brown says it is full of long speeches that call for a whole company of Forbes-Robertsons.[2] There might be a whole company of even better men. I believe there might be found Jews or Italians or Spaniards or Celts to do the thing properly: not Teutons or Scandinavians or Nordics: it's not in their blood – as a rule. And if the speeches are too long – well, they can be made shorter if necessary. But my God, there's many a *nigger* would play Saul better than Forbes-Robertson could do it. And I'd prefer the nigger. Or men and women from that Jewish theatre.[3] – Curtis Brown says it is not a 'popular' play. But damn it, how does he know even that? Playgoing isn't the same as reading. Reading in itself is highbrow. But give the 'populace' in the theatre something with a bit of sincere good-feeling in it, and they'll respond. If you do it properly.

I hope you are enjoying Europe: I think it's about time I went back.

[1] This note cannot be dated; it may have been written after Susan was acquired, and Brett's account (p. 226) relates the circumstances DHL describes to the middle of Friedel Jaffe's visit.

[2] Sir Johnston Forbes-Robertson (1853–1937), famous actor (his last professional appearance had been at Harvard in 1916).

[3] Probably the Theatre Guild; see Letter 3447.

3445. To Ida Rauh, 2 July 1925

Text: MS UT; Postmark, Taos JUL 6 1925; Unpublished.

c/o Del Monte Ranch. *Valdez*, New Mexico
2 July 1925

Dear Ida

I sent you the last scenes of the play two weeks ago, but haven't heard if you've received them. And already I am asking you for the MS. back. Would you mind sending it to me here, as Frieda is set on translating it into German.[1]

I heard from my agent: he is thrilled by the play, says it will need very careful placing, and wants me to let Knopf publish it at once. To the last, I don't feel very willing. However, we shall see.

I am glad you are better – hope all goes well with you.

Yrs D. H. Lawrence

3446. To Stuart Sherman, 11 July 1925

Text: MS UIll; Moore 846.

Del Monte Ranch. *Questa*. New Mexico
11 July 1925

Dear Mr Sherman

I was amused by your article on me and my beard. But it isn't a beard needs 'cultivating'. It's a clean chin man has to work over.

But I like to know what you say, because you do care about the deeper implication in a novel. Damn 'holiday reading'! They take even Dostoevsky to the sea-side now, and eat a horn of ice-cream while they read him:[2] now that life is 'one long holiday.' My God, give me a few unholydays, then!

I have thought many times it would be good to review a novel from the standpoint of what I call morality: what I feel to be essentially moral. Now and then review a book plainly. – I will do it for your paper if you like.[3]

To pave the way – and have some stones to pull up and throw at the reader's head – I did two little articles: 'Art and Morality' and 'Morality and the Novel'.[4] If you care to ask my agent, Curtis Brown, for them, you can have them if you like.

[1] A 254-page MS of the German translation by Frieda exists, and a corrected typescript which DHL typed and revised in June 1926 (UCB); see Letter 3729.

[2] Sherman believed one theme in *St. Mawr* is DHL's 'own profound revulsion from polite tea-table literature' and compared his effect on readers to that exercised by Hardy and Dostoievsky. (Draper, *The Critical Heritage*, pp. 252, 257).

[3] The offer was not taken up, but see Letter 3550.

[4] Written at the same time as 'The Novel'; see Letter 3440 and n. 2. They were published in the *Calendar of Modern Letters* ii (November 1925), 171–7 and ii (December 1925), 269–74 respectively; collected in *Study of Thomas Hardy*, ed. Steele, pp. 163–76.

The point was easier to see in painting, to start with. But it wouldn't be so very out of the way, in a literary paper.

I didn't care for the comparison with *Trionfo della Morte*. D'Annunzio is a sensationalist, nearly always in bad taste, as in that rolling over the edge.[1]

Yours Sincerely D. H. Lawrence

3447. To Ida Rauh, [13 July 1925]

Text: MS UT; Postmark, [. . .] 13 1925; Unpublished.

Del Monte Ranch. Valdez. N. Mex
Monday

Dear Ida

Have just got the MS. Many thanks. Frieda is already immersed in her translation. I have written to Curtis Brown, to send a copy of the play to the Guild Theatre.[2] If he hasn't a copy in New York now – he ought to have – I'll send him this one.

I thought you weren't very much interested: and that you'd have much preferred a more personal play, about a woman. Probably you would – and naturally. But I myself am a bit tired of[3] personal plays, 'about a woman.' Time we all sank our personalities a bit, in something bigger.

Frieda's nephew, Friedel Jaffe, is leaving on Saturday, and should arrive in Santa Fe on Monday next, on the stage. He will stay a night at the Fonda,[4] and go on to Denver next morning. If you would care to see him in the evening – Monday – he'd no doubt be glad, as he doesn't know anybody in Santa Fe. But don't go out of your way.

[1] *Trionfo della Morte* (Milan, 1894) by Gabriele D'Annunzio (1863–1938), Italian poet, novelist and dramatist. DHL had seen one of his plays in 1913 and 'rather enjoyed it – fearful melodrama' (*Letters*, i. 505), and had read *Trionfo* by 1916 (ibid., iii. 43).

Sherman wrote: 'In *The Triumph of Death*, for example, D'Annunzio worked out for middle-aged people, a generation ago, the entire course of exactly such passions as rage through *The Rainbow* and *Women in Love* . . . And [D'Annunzio's] book ends with the appropriate mortal consummation of sex-antagonism: [the aristocrat and his peasant mistress] roll fighting over a precipice in a last embrace' (Draper, *The Critical Heritage*, pp. 254–5).

[2] The Theatre Guild was founded in 1918 by former members of the Washington Square Players who were unhappy with the commercialism in the theatre and wanted to produce contemporary work; it was successful and had its own building on West 52nd Street which opened 13 April 1925. DHL had been given the name of Philip Moeller (1880–1958), a founder and the stage director (UT address book). Ida Rauh's letter to Moeller had been forwarded to Florence, Italy; he replied on 12 June that the Guild Theatre would be delighted to consider the play (TMS UT).

[3] of] about

[4] La Fonda Hotel on the main square in Taos.

Margaret Hale came up yesterday, with Doctor Light.[1] Miss Cather didn't seem popular: steam-roller effect.

Brett caught seventeen fish in the Hondo river, tell Andrew.

I'll let you know as soon as I hear anything from New York. Still hope you'll tackle Michal.

Yrs D. H. Lawrence

3448. To Emily King, 14 July 1925
Text: MS Lazarus; Moore 847–8.

Del Monte Ranch, *Questa*, New Mexico
14 July 1925

My dear Pamela

It's full hot summer now, and I wanted to send you just a little money, for if you go away to the seaside. Will you be going in August, or when?

We have decided to go to New York about the middle of September, and stay about a fortnight – come to England at the end of the month. It can still be lovely in October – Then towards the end of October we must go to BadenBaden: Frieda's mother harps so on our coming. She wants us to give this place up, and not come back to America – Perhaps we shall spend all next year in Europe: we'll see how we feel.

Friedel is leaving next Saturday – some friends are motoring him down to Taos:[2] he'll stay just a night in Santa Fe. The students – the exchange students – are only allowed to stay twelve months in this paradisal country, into which all the wild beasts of Europe are clamoring to get. It's amazing, the simple frenzy people have, to come to America – Friedel simply hated his time in the east, in this country. Here of course it's very different – not the U.S A. at all. Myself, I hate the real U.S.A., Chicago and New York and all that. I feel very much drawn to the Mediterranean again: we may winter in Sicily.

It's a very quiet life here – I've never been down to Taos since we arrived: don't want to go. Am not very keen on seeing people: prefer to be alone on the ranch. That's the best of it, one really can be alone. – There's no change here – except it's very hot today. We rode down to San Cristobal to get Ambrose shod, this morning – there is a little wayside blacksmith in the valley. I

[1] Dr Gertrude Underhill Light (1871–1960), M.D. from Johns Hopkins University School of Medicine, 1898, practised medicine in New Mexico; she was a close friend of Joseph Foster and Margaret Hale. She is included in the painting *Ourselves and Taos Neighbors* (1937) by Ernest Leonard Blumenschein (1874–1960), which is reproduced in Lois Palken Rudnick, *Mabel Dodge Luhan: New Woman, New Worlds* (Albuquerque, 1984), p. 322.

[2] Margaret Hale and Ruth Swaine, wife of Frank T. Swaine, architect, who lived near Rancho de Taos and in the 1920s was the proprietress of La Cumbre Guest House (Brett 239; Foster, *D. H. Lawrence in Taos*, pp. 147–8; Nehls, ii. 520 n. 125).

noticed, riding through the timber, the porcupines are gnawing the tops of the pine-trees. I saw a huge one with all his bristles up, the other evening, just in front of the house. Wish I'd killed him. – And I heard Aaron squealing and running to corral – he's my black horse, very nice – and I found he'd got a little bunch of porcupine quills in his nose. Had to pull them out one by one with the pliers, and he hated it. But they weren't very big ones.

When Friedel has gone we shall be alone. But I really like that best. When there's any work to be done, I get a man up from San Cristobal. Brett is still down at Del Monte. Today she's gone fishing – The other day, she caught 17 trout in the Hondo – but most of them were small. We made a supper of them, though.

I don't suppose Joan will ever *love* her school – why should she? – They have brought out a new edition of my history, with pictures in – very nice. I'll send one.

Love DHL

3449. To Ada Clarke, 14 July 1925

Text: MS Clarke; Unpublished.

Del Monte Ranch. *Questa*, New Mexico
14 July 1925

My dear Sister

The photographs of the house are very nice: it's really a pretty house. I'm sure you'll feel quite different, having plenty of space and light and air, and a garden. We expect to come to England at the end of September – it's a bit late, but it can still be beautiful then. And I don't want to shut this place up again too soon, after having so much done to it this year. –

I expect we shall stay in New York a fortnight or so: and some time in October, towards the end, go to BadenBaden: Frieda's mother simply fixes her mind on our coming. For the cold months, we might go to Sicily: and perhaps stay in Europe all next summer: we will see. I feel I've about had my whack of America, for this time. Frieda of course wants to have her girls to stay with her: I don't know where. We'll just see, when we get over to Europe.

Friedel is going on Saturday – he has to leave the country in August, as the students are only allowed to stay twelve months. One would think the place was Paradise, the way it's hedged in. But Friedel will be glad to get back to Germany – he hated the time he spent in the east – New York – Maryland. I would hate to have to stay long in the U.S.A. too – anywhere but here, which is so different, and Mexican really.

There's nothing new on the ranch: except it's very hot. But the thunder-storms come rolling over the mountains, this month. It's been such a dry year, there are no wild strawberries, and I doubt there'll be no wild raspberries. There were so many last year. One of the hens persisted in being broody, so we let her sit just seven eggs. They're due to hatch tomorrow or Wednesday. Susan, the cow, behaves herself now, and no longer escapes away into the timber, and has to be hunted on horseback. I milk her, so it keeps me tied to the ranch. But I don't care – I've no desire to go out, I hate motoring these long distances here.

It's just like Aunt Ada to sprain her ankle at the crucial moment: I have half an idea, it's to draw all the attention to herself.[1]

Is Gertie with you in the new house? Are you still sending Jackie to school in Ripley? Is old Mr Clarke full of admiration for the new house?[2] Is old Mr Gillett still alive?[3] Has Willie Hopkin married again?[4] I can hardly imagine what Mrs Limb will be like, now.[5] Must be fifteen years since I saw her. Tell me the news of them all – if there is any.

Love. DHL

3450. To David Jester, 15 July 1925

Text: MS UT; *Centaur* 21–2.

Del Monte Ranch. *Questa*, New Mexico
15 July 1925

Dear Mr Jester

The Preface to the *History* was an epilogue – I haven't got a copy here – the only one went to London. I dont know how it would fit in a book of essays.

But if you could send me a few of the essays, like the one on 'Love', I think I would rather revise them a good deal: perhaps re-write them.[6] That would amuse me just now. I don't very much want to re-publish half-baked sort of stuff. I'd like to make a complete little book, with more or less a central idea, an organic thing. How many words do you want, by the way? – We could *pretend*

[1] Ada Rose Krenkow, née Beardsall (1868–1944), DHL's maternal aunt. m. Fritz Johann Heinrich Krenkow (1872–1953). See *Letters*, i. 77 n. and iii. 267 n. 5.

[2] Ada Clarke's father-in-law, William Clarke (1856?–1929); he had a tailor's shop in Ripley.

[3] Possibly father of Thomas Gillott (1886–1913), artist; see *Letters*, i. 278 n. 4.

[4] William ('Willie') Edward Hopkin, m. (1) Sarah ('Sallie') Annie Potter (1867–1922); (2) 17 September 1925, Olive Lizzie Slack (1895–1988). Willie and Sallie were among DHL's closest friends in Eastwood and played a prominent part in its political and intellectual life. *See Letters*, i. 3, 176 n. 2.

[5] Mrs Limb was the mother of Emmeline (close friend of Ada Clarke) and Mabel (1886–1909), childhood friend of DHL's, and the wife of William T. Limb (1858–1928). See *Letters*, i. 35 n. 4 and 85 n. 1.

[6] See Letter 3212; some of the ideas in 'Love' and 'Life' were developed in '......Love Was Once a Little Boy' which was included in the *Reflections* volume. See *Reflections*, ed. Herbert, pp. 331–46.

it was the old essays. But I don't like those volumes of oddments men bring out. Real oddments should remain odd, and uncollected.

If you let me know quickly, I can perhaps get the thing done before we leave in September.

Those old essays are too didactic – essays are no good outside a mood, a humour.

Yrs D. H. Lawrence[1]

3451. To Willard Johnson, [17 July 1925]

Text: MS YU; Unpublished.

Del Monte Ranch. *Valdez*, N. Mex.
Friday evening.

Dear Spud

Your letter came this evening. Friedel leaves in the morning: he is staying the week-end out at Margaret Hale's place,[2] and coming into Santa Fe by the stage on Monday (D. V. to all this). I guess he will hand you this note himself, together with the book for Mrs Hughes. Please give it to her, and tell her we still hope to see her. The invitation holds good: bona fide.

Willa has a will of her own.[3] It's usually the other person that's the wisp. Brett calls her the steam-roller. Frieda says she likes her. Now figure it out.

[1] Jester replied on 21 July 1925 (TMSC Mason):

Dear Mr. Lawrence,

The essays have been gathered together for some time, but we wanted to send them to you in a decent form. They are now in the process of being typed – the ones clipped from magazines, and the two in manuscript, THE CROWN and THE NOVEL. The double spacing afforded by the typewriter will make them much easier for you to revise or correct. The entire lot should go forth to you by the end of the week.

The number of words we can use is indefinite and flexible. Personally, I should like to see a rather full book, and strongly urge you not to eliminate any part of THE CROWN, which is long in itself, and altogether splendid. And of course we must retain the essay on the novel.

You are right when you speak of unity. The book must be an organic thing. But everything will be left to you, and we will print whatever you finally elect. Then there is the matter of a title, upon which we will ask you to decide.

You really can't rush things too much, as we are very anxious to publish the book in the early Autumn. It will be quite an event in our lives, I can assure you.

Yours faithfully,

[2] Margaret Hale and Foster lived on a ruined ranch near Ranchos de Taos (Foster, *D. H. Lawrence in Taos*, p. 9).

[3] Willa Cather had visited Taos in 1912; she came in 1925 to do research for *Death Comes for the Archbishop* (1927) and stayed with Mary Austin and Mabel Luhan. She went up to Kiowa Ranch (Letter 3454) and later sent DHL her favourite book *The Song of the Lark* (1915) (Nehls, ii. 414).

I am very well: really much better than I was last summer.

We expect to leave in September – go to Europe.

I've no desire to be in Chapala have you?[1]

I think Ida doesn't try to interfere with one's inside – which is saying a lot. But are you still looking for La Belle Dame Sans Merci?

Is the horse still laughing?[2] on which side of his face?

Yrs DHL

3452. To Ida Rauh, [24 July 1925]
Text: MS UT; Unpublished.

Del Monte Ranch, Valdez, N.Mex
Friday

Dear Ida

Your letter today. So sorry you aren't feeling well. But you will feel better.

I can't understand about the play. More than a week ago I heard from my agents, that they had just received my third copy of *David* and were sending it that day to the Theatre Guild.

I'll telegraph as soon as I can get a telegram down to Taos.

Meanwhile I wish you'd write to the Theatre Guild people and tell them that Curtis Brown. 116 West 39th. St. – had orders to give the MS to them long ago, and explain.

Damn agents and their delays!

Brett was down in Taos this morning and saw Tony in Gersons: so they must have been back early, if he was in Gerson's Friday morning.

We expect Spud and Christine Hughes tomorrow: hope they'll be able to get up.

I'll let you know as soon as ever I hear anything. Get well!

D. H. Lawrence

3453. To Ida Rauh, 26 July 1925
Text: MS UT; Postmark, Valdez JUL 29 1925; Unpublished.

Del Monte Ranch. Valdez. N. Mex
26 July 1925

Dear Ida

Thanks for having Friedel to dinner. We had a post-card from Raton: the

[1] With Bynner. [2] I.e. *Laughing Horse*.

train had to go back, and wait a night, because a bridge had gone down in a cloud-burst. Had some heavy rains here too.

I understand your feelings about the play, but don't approve of them: that is, I don't approve of your feeling old. It is only when one *lets go* that one feels old: or is old. You're not old. – I am waiting for further news from New York.

We expected Spud and Christine Hughes this week-end, but they didn't turn up. I suppose something prevented them.

Seems already a bit like autumn, and there is a feeling of going away in the air. Yet I suppose we shall stay on another six weeks. Let us know when you are coming up. And remember us both to Andrew and Dan.

Yrs D. H. Lawrence

3454. To Earl and Achsah Brewster, 29 July 1925
Text: MS UT; Brewster 81–2.

Del Monte Ranch. *Questa*, New Mexico.
29 July 1925

Dear Earl and Achsah

I had a letter yesterday from my landlord in Oaxaca,[1] and he said, a registered letter arrived for me, from Capri, but that the post people would neither let him sign for it, nor would they forward it, but insisted on sending it back to where it came from. So if it is thrown back at you, know that it is because the Mexican post officials are more tiresome far than the Italians at their worst.

We have been here since May. I was so ill in Oaxaca: malaria and complications: thought I'd never get out. However, I'm about my usual self now – Frieda and I are alone – I milk the cow, Frieda looks after the chickens, and we both manage the four horses. Sometimes I drive the buggy, but usually we get an Indian or a Mexican. It's the kind of life I like for summer: but the winter would be too stiff. Dorothy Brett is staying down on our neighbour's ranch: she comes up most days. – We think of coming to Europe in the autumn: first to England, then Paris, then BadenBaden, then Italy. So I hope with some confidence to see you: perhaps in November. Let me know where you'll be. We shall be here till mid-September, I suppose. My agents address always get me, anyhow:

[1] Edward Rickards.

Curtis Brown. 6 Henrietta St. London W.C. 2.
or for America –
Curtis Brown Ltd. 116 West 39th St. New York.

Brett thinks she might like to winter in Capri. She is a painter, very deaf, about as old as I am, has a modest but sufficient income, and is daughter of Viscount Esher. If she comes, I'll give her a letter to you, shall I?

Willa Cather was staying in Taos: came up to see us. I must say, she is a bit heavy-footed: but she has strength.

Write and say how you are, and send news. And au revoir: a rivederci. Harwood will be Miss Brewster before we see her again, unless we hurry.

Souvenirs! D. H. Lawrence

3455. To Curtis Brown, 31 July 1925
Text: Huxley 637–8.

Del Monte Ranch, Questa, New Mexico.
31 July, 1925.

Dear Curtis Brown, –

I'm glad you are sweating after agriculture rather than literature, for a bit. It's more fun. My pursuit of both, out here, is spasmodic: but I put the salt on the tail of the agricultural bird occasionally. Anyhow, I milk my black cow Susan at 6.0 a.m. and after tea in the evening: and I irrigate when the water's running: and I see to the rather small garden: and I chop wood. In fact, my wife and I are quite alone on this ranch now. But I get a Mexican or Indian when there's any real work to do – heavy. And sometimes, in state, I set off with my wife and Hon. Dorothy Brett in the spring wagon, to go and shop the few things one can buy in Arroyo[1] Hondo, ten miles off. We look a real old outfit, but the two horses are quite nice.

Pity you are leaving so early. We are due to arrive in New York about Sept. 15th: sail about the 30th. So I shall see you in London (D.V.). I'll really bring myself to meet a few people in New York: at least, I say so now.

To-day I sent off the third copy of the play.[2]

Hope you and Mrs Brown are having a good time.[3]

Yrs., D. H. Lawrence

[1] Huxley reads 'Arrozo'. [2] This contradicts Letter 3452.

[3] Albert and Caroline Curtis Brown were on holiday in New York State (Nancy Pearn to DHL, 15 July 1925, TMSC UT).

3456. To David Jester, 12 August 1925

Text: MS UTul; Unpublished.

Del Monte Ranch, *Questa*, New Mexico
12 Aug 1925

Dear Mr Jester

I got the package of MSS.[1] Many thanks. I will send you the complete thing in a few days: 'Crown' first, and then all the other stuff, I suppose, new. I will call it, if you don't mind, after one of the longest essays:

Reflections on the Death of a Porcupine and Other Essays.

I wrote a little introductory note to 'The Crown'.[2] – I'll get as near 45,000 words as possible.

Secker very much wanted a book for the autumn: but I think we won't give him this: just let it be published by your Centaur, which is just the right steed. I am glad to be doing this book, really, *not* through a 'public channel'. I feel you are half private: which suits me better.

As for the MS, if he cares to have it, give 'The Crown' to Dr McDonald[3] (because I promised him a copy of the history, and he's got one) – and do you keep that of the novel, if it's any use to you.

I expect we shall be in New York about Sept 15th – to stay a couple of weeks, on our way to England. If you or Mr. Mason or Dr McDonald are in town, let me know.

Yrs D. H. Lawrence

[1] DHL was responding to Jester's letter, 28 July 1925 (TMSC Mason):

Dear Mr. Lawrence,

Here are the essays. You will note a few are not typed, but we found it a longer task than we anticipated and felt they should reach you without further delay.

I intended adding a post-script to my last letter, asking you if we should return the manuscript of THE CROWN to Mr. Barmby. In the meantime, it is quite secure in the safe, together with the manuscript of THE NOVEL. Please let us know what should be done with the two manuscripts as they are rather on our minds.

Mr. Mason returned from Europe last week. He shares fully my enthusiasm about THE NOVEL and my belief that not the least enjoyment will be watching the reviews. We are both fresh from THE CROWN, having read it aloud together in order to detect possible mistakes in the typed copy. The essay becomes finer each time it is read, and we feel that THE CROWN, in its entirety, should be the leading essay in the book. THE CROWN is about 22,000 words, and there can be 48,000 without making too large a volume.

It has just been arranged for the Centaur Press to publish a small, limited, edition of Coppard's poems. So now we will have three books for the Autumn. Yours faithfully,

[2] 'The Crown' and 'Note to The Crown' were included in *Reflections*.

[3] The first three sections of 'The Crown' are typescript with corrections and comments in McDonald's hand (some are signed by him); the fourth, fifth and sixth sections are apparently the 1915 autograph MS (see Letter 3420); all are now at UT.

3457. To Willard Johnson, [12 August 1925]
Text: MS YU; Unpublished.

Del Monte Ranch. *Valdez*, New Mexico
Wed.[1]

Dear Spud

Had yours and also Mrs Hughes' today. Sorry you weren't well: and Mrs Hughes too. We expected you both week-ends: got Brett's little house for you. – But come when you can: it doesn't make any difference. We are here – Susan the cow keeps me fixed. We expect to leave for New York about Sept 12th – time goes so quickly.

Many thanks for looking after Friedel Jaffe: he has sailed. In Chicago they picked his pocket, left him with railway ticket and 15 cents: he had to travel 24 hours on 15 cents; then he got to his University and got a cheque cashed. Just like him!

Hope you and Mrs Hughes are both all right now. – How is Bynner? Tell Ida Rauh we'll be expecting her up.

Yrs D. H. Lawrence

3458. To Martin Secker, 13 August 1925
Text: MS UInd; Postmark, [. . .] AUG 14 1925; Secker 63.

Del Monte Ranch, *Questa*, New Mexico.
13 Aug 1925

Dear Secker

I had a telegram from Curtis Brown that you are willing to publish *David* in autumn. I don't want it published yet. I want to try the theatres first. I want Curtis Brown's to try the theatres in London, *quite seriously*. I myself got into touch with the New York *Theatre Guild* about it. You might tell this to Curtis Browns.[2]

[1] Dated with reference to the letter following which also announces DHL's departure date as 12 September.

[2] Secker had written to Michael Joseph of Curtis Brown on 10 August 1925 (Secker Letter-Book, UIll):

Dear Mr Joseph

I have now read D.H.Lawrence's play "David", and with great interest. I do not see that its prior appearance in book form will do anything to prejudice its chances in the theatre (one can quote the case of "Hassan" as an example), and I should like to bring it out in the course of this coming autumn, if matters can be arranged. It would be better to do that, I think, than to defer it to the spring, since there is already the new Lawrence novel provisionally fixed for one of the early months of next year. As to terms, I would suggest 6/- as the published price, a royalty of 15%, and a cheque on publication to cover the accrued royalties to date. If I could put the composition in hand at once, I would send Lawrence proofs in slip form to work on, and if he returned them to me promptly it should be possible to publish by November 1 or so.

Yours sincerely

Thanks for saying you'll print *The Plumed Serpent* at once.[1] Has C. B. sent you the MS. from New York?[2] They've had it some time.

We expect to leave here Sept 12 – stay about two weeks in New York – reach England first week in October.[3] Then I shall see you. Don't suppose I shall stay long in England. – Frieda says your son is a little Secker. –

St. Mawr a bit disappointing. The Bloomsbury highbrows hated it.[4] Glad they did. Don't send any more of my books to E.M Forster – done with him as with most people. Vogue la galère.[5]

A Frenchwoman is translating *Birds Beasts and Flowers*.[6] Wonder if she'll put it over.

a rivederci D. H. Lawrence

3459. To Curtis Brown, 14 August 1925

Text: MS UT; Unpublished.

Del Monte Ranch. *Questa*, New Mexico.
14 August 1925

Dear Curtis Brown

I mislaid this list of typescripts.[7] Will you please destroy the ones I crossed out, and be so good as to keep the others for me till I come.

We leave this ranch Sept. 10th. and expect to arrive in England about the first week in October. I shall come in to the office as soon as I am in London.

I had the cablegram about *David*. I don't want the play *published* until it has been considered by any possible *producer*. The Theatre Guild in New York are now reading it. I wish you would try in London for a chance of *production*, before there is any thought of publication.

Yours sincerely D. H. Lawrence

After receiving Letter 3458 from DHL, Secker wrote to Joseph on 28 August 1925:

Dear Mr Joseph

I have just had a letter from Lawrence in which he states that he definitely does not wish the play "David" published just yet, but for you to continue your efforts with the managers. I am therefore returning to you the typescript. Lawrence also says that he expects to reach these shores on October 12.

Yours sincerely

[1] Secker had written to Joseph on 30 July 1925 (Secker Letter-Book, UIll):

Dear Mr Joseph

Many thanks for sending me the typescript of the new Lawrence novel "The Plumed Serpent", which I plan to publish early next year on a date to be mutually agreed with Mr Knopf. I have just had a letter from the author, asking me to have the book set up in slip, so that he may work on the proofs, and I am therefore putting the work in hand forthwith . . .

[2] New York] London

[3] MS reads 'September'.

[4] See p. 267 n. 1. Raymond Mortimer (1895–1980), in *Vogue*, was the only reviewer who could be associated with 'Bloomsbury'.

[5] 'Come what may.'

[6] Gabrielle Desgrand; see Letters 3700 and 3577.

[7] The list is missing.

3460. To Eduardo Rendón, 17 August 1925

Text: MS McGuire; Unpublished.

Del Monte Ranch. Valdez, New Mexico
17 Aug 1925

Dear Rendon

You didn't tell me if you got the copy of *Birds Beasts and Flowers* which I sent you.

I heard from Conway – he has gone to England: we may meet in London.[1] We leave this ranch about Sept 10th. – and expect to be in England the first week in October. My address there will be

c/o Curtis Brown Ltd. 6 Henrietta St. Covent Garden, London W.C. 2.

But I don't suppose we – or I – shall stay long in my native land. I expect to go south – Italy, or Sicily, or Egypt – for the winter.

My English publisher Martin Secker says he will print the 'Quetzalcoatl' novel at once. When I get to England I will send you a set of proofs, if you would like to read it, and if you will promise me please not to talk about the book at all, to anybody – only tell me what you think of it. It will not appear till next spring, publicly.

I had a press cutting from a man called Valle[2] – in Mexico City – about the *Verdadero Woodrow Wilson*, by David Lawrence. I think in Mexico they are convinced I wrote that article. But I am never David – always D.H. – and I find that the said David is a fairly well-known journalist, Washington Correspondent.[3] So much for my double.

Miss Brett leaves about the[4]

3461. To Helmuth von Erffa, 18 August 1925

Text: MS (Photocopy) in Earl Tannenbaum, ed., *D. H. Lawrence: An Exhibition of First Editions . . . Manuscripts, Paintings, Letters, and Miscellany at Southern Illinois University Library, April, 1958* (Carbondale, 1958).

Del Monte Ranch. *Questa*, New Mexico
18 Aug 1925

Mr Helmuth N. Erffa. NewYork

Dear Sir[5]

I had your letter today, about translating into German my story: 'The Woman Who Rode Away'.

[1] DHL gave Conway's addresses as c/o Canadian & General Finance Co, 3 London Wall Bldgs, EC and c/o Col. Dawson. 50 Forest Rd. Aberdeen (UT address book).

[2] Possibly Rafael Heliodoro Valle, writer and dealer in rare books; he was later Ambassador for the Honduras to the USA.

[3] *True Story of Woodrow Wilson* (1924) by David Lawrence (1883–1973), Washington correspondent for *New York Evening Post*, 1916–19; president of Consolidated Press Association, 1919–33.

[4] MS incomplete.

[5] Helmuth Hartmann von Erffa (1900–79), b. Lüneberg, Germany; student at Bauhaus, 1921–2; emigrated to USA, 1923; graduate of Harvard and Princeton. Later Professor and Chairman of the Art Departments at Swarthmore College and Rutgers University.

As far as I am concerned, you have my consent to translate this *Novelle*. But will you please make any definite arrangements with my agents:

Curtis Brown Ltd. Foreign Dept. – 6 Henrietta St. *London W.C.2.* England.

The Insel Verlag has already published two of my novels – *Romane* – in German:[1] and the *Neue Merkur* has published some smaller things.[2] I don't know whether the *Neue Rundschau* is acquainted with my work.[3] – Anyhow, please make any arrangements necessary, with Curtis Brown.

I think myself Germany might like 'The Woman Who Rode Away'. I have finished a novel about Mexico, which Knopf will publish next year in New York: and probably the *Insel Verlag* will publish in German.[4] This story will make a good forerunner.

Yours Sincerely D. H. Lawrence

3462. To Kyle Crichton, 19 August 1925
Text: MS Crichton; Nehls, ii. 420–1.

Del Monte Ranch. *Valdez*, New Mexico
19 Aug. 1925

Dear Mr Crichton[5]

Thank you for your letter, and the magazines.[6] – I read the New Mexico article: poor painters! They apparently *have* to hawk their wares for six months in the year, in this country: like the primitive tin-smith. I suppose it's the country. A la guerre comme à la guerre.

I didn't know *Time* existed: in all its vulgarity. – I would never kick my cow. But if Tiberius wished the public had only one head, so that he could cut it off,[7] I wish it had just one posterior, that I could kick. Never my good and decent cow.

[1] It later published Else Jaffe's translation as *Die Frau, die davonritt*, with 'England, My England', 'The Princess', 'The Fox', 'Glad Ghosts', 'The Border-Line' (1928). See also p. 38 n. 2 and Letter 3534.

[2] See Letter 3299 and n. 2.

[3] *Die Neue Rundschau* published some of DHL's letters posthumously; see Roberts C210 and C217.5.

[4] In 1932, trans. Georg Goyert (1884–) (Roberts D86).

[5] Kyle Samuel Crichton (1896–1960), American journalist and author; editor of *New Masses* (pseudonym Robert Forsythe) and *Collier's Weekly*, 1933–49. m. 1922, Mary ('Mae') C. Collier (1889–1969). They were living in Albuquerque because he had tuberculosis. For his account of their meeting, see Nehls, ii. 410–19; see also 'D. H. Lawrence Lives at the Top of the World – A Kindly Lion in a New Mexican Lair' in *New York World* (11October 1925), III, 4.

[6] Crichton published an article in the *New York World* on the Navaho Indians (Nehls, ii. 410); *Time* had a review of *St. Mawr*, 'Primal: A Burning Bay Stallion Incarnates Lawrentian Purity', v (29 June 1925), 13 and a letter from an outraged reader, Cassandra O. Phelps of Hobson, Montana ('Lawrence Scorned', vi, 20 July 1925, 25–6).

[7] Usually attributed to Caligula ['Would that the Roman people had but one neck']. Cf. DHL's *Movements in European History*, ed. Crumpton, p. 14.

I think it's even more awful to have the public loving one, than hating one.

The kind of love-intimacy, put-your-head-on-his-shoulder touch, that they assume in their print, is worst of all.

For all that, I don't care if you do your article for that newspaper, when I'm in Europe – so long as it doesnt appear before mid-October. When I'm gone, I don't mind what's said, good or bad. My actual ears mind.

I shall be glad to get your novel – I might even review it, if you should wish.[1]

Remember us to Mrs Crichton. So sorry your trip went bust. But what man with any stomach drinks moonshine? – I suppose it was moonshine. – Oh Mrs Crichton, why didn't you pour the moonshine into the desert air, where it belongs?

Yrs D. H. Lawrence

c/o Curtis Brown always finds me. We leave Sept 10th.

Didn't know this paper was grimy – the other side isn't. – It's the saddlebag. – Please excuse it.

3463. To Catherine Carswell, 24 August 1925

Text: MS YU; Postmark, Santa Fe AUG 24 1925; cited in Carswell 224.

Del Monte Ranch. *Questa*, New Mexico
24 August 1925

Dear Catherine

That was good hopeful news, about the Channel Isles.[2] I do hope it goes through all right: it would be a change for you, and a real mercy for Don to have a good sound work that interested him. We are running to the end of our stay here – leave about Sept 10th. I suppose we shall be in England in early October. If you are in Guernsey, it would be great fun to come and see you, on the way to France. Frieda talks of staying some time in England, seeing her children. But I dread the tightness and stuffiness of England – feel I shan't be able to breathe. But I may like it better this time. I expect I shall suffer a bit anyhow, being shut up in houses and towns, after being so free here. – I am as well as ever I was – but malaria comes back in very hot sun, or any malaria conditions. – I think it would be splendid for J[ohn] P[atrick] – fils, not père – a magistrate is a J. P., is he? – to be in Guernsey and get a sort of look-out into the world.

But we'll see you in one place or another, in October.

Yrs D. H. Lawrence

[1] Crichton's first published book was *Law and Order, Ltd.; The Rousing Life of Elfego Baca of New Mexico* (Santa Fe, 1928), but see also p. 293 n. 1.

[2] A magistracy in Guernsey; Catherine and John went with Donald Carswell for an interview, 'full of optimism', but he was not appointed (letter to eds. from John Carswell).

3464. To Martin Secker, 25 August 1925

Text: MS UInd; Postmark, [. . .] AUG 26 1925; Secker 64.

Del Monte Ranch. *Questa*, New Mex.
25 Aug 1925

Dear Secker

I forgot to tell you that some people called *The Centaur Press* – of Philadelphia – who did a bibliography of me – asked me to let them publish a little vol. of uncollected essays. I sent them the prepared MS. last week. I didn't care for the old essays, so they are all new, except the first, called 'The Crown' – which appeared in that scrap of a magazine I once did with Murry, called *The Signature*.

The new book makes about fifty thousand words – I'm calling it:

Reflections on the Death of a Porcupine and Other Essays

– They're essays written here, and the porc: was one I shot here.[1]

The Centaur Press do rather elegant books, for collectors. They want to get the *Porcupine* out this autumn, as soon as possible.

I don't know if you'd like to publish this little collection: please yourself entirely. But if you would, you can let me know:

c/o Curtis Brown. 116 West 39th St. New York City –

– and you can write to the Centaur people too, if you wish:

Harold T. Mason. The Centaur Book Shop, 1224 Chancellor St.
Philadelphia Pa.

Don't feel under any constraint about it, though. I don't care whether the *Porc.* appears in England, or not.[2]

Yrs D. H. Lawrence

3465. To Anne Conway, 28 August 1925

Text: MS Moore; Moore, *Intelligent Heart* 343.

Del Monte Ranch, *Questa*, New Mexico
28 August 1925

Dear Mrs Conway

I'm glad to think of you on Deeside – more wholesome there, than that gruesome Mexico. I put the bit of white heather in my hat, needing a bit of luck. We'll see what happens. True, you sent the sprig to my wife: but whatever else married people share and don't share, their luck is one.

[1] See Brett 244; Mabel Luhan claimed it was Tony's shooting of a porcupine that inspired the essay (pp. 203–4).

[2] Secker wrote to Mason and to DHL on 8 September 1925 (Secker Letter-Book, UIll), but negotiations were not successful. The volume did not appear under Secker's imprint until 1934, but 475 copies of the Centaur Press's edition were especially prepared for distribution in England and sold by Simpkin, Marshall, Hamilton, Kent and Co; see Roberts A32.

I'm sure you had a good time with the Hergesheimers – especially the house. I hear there's a book about it, coming.[1] Glad I don't have to write a book about my house – it wouldn't be four pages – the house is a log hut with never a treasure in it, save my precious self.

I heard from Conway just as he was leaving Mexico. That 'America Loca' poem about gets it: and Conway's translation is good.

But I feel I want to get out of America Loca for a while: I believe it sends *everybody* a bit loco. We leave here Sept 10th – expect to be in England by first week in October. Send me a line:

c/o Curtis Brown. 6 Henrietta St. Covent Garden, W.C.2.

And if possible, let us have dinner together somewhere. – I hope I shall be able to let Conway see a set of proofs of the 'Quetzalcoatl' novel: shall value his opinion: and yours too; if you'll give it. But you always are so modest in expressing yourself.

We've just sat tight and considered the lily all summer.[2] I am quite well. It grieves me to leave my horses, and my cow Susan, and the cat Timsy Wemyss, and the white cock Moses – and the place. Next time you pass, call here at this ranch instead of at Hergesheimer's house: it's very wonderful country.

My wife sends her greetings to you both, and hopes we may meet in a little while – so do I.

Yrs D. H. Lawrence

3466. To Mollie Skinner, 28 August 1925
Text: MS WAPL; Moore 850.

Del Monte Ranch. *Questa*, New Mexico
28 Aug. 1925

Dear Mollie Skinner

I am glad you are safe with Miss Beakbane at 'Leithdale'[3] – you will have enough things to do, and sunshine and space, and time to write. I wish I could be at Leithdale myself, for a few months. My wife loved it there, so did I.

The summer has gone by here, so quickly. I am quite well again, in the mountains with my horses, and the cow Susan. We are leaving for New York on Sept 10th. I am sorry to go. Yet it is good, not to stay too much alone, and not to be too long in America. This is a heavy, stubborn sort of continent,

[1] *From an Old House* (New York: Knopf, 1925), an autobiographical narrative about the history and rebuilding of the Hergesheimers' Dower House (started 1712) in West Chester, Pennsylvania.

[2] Matthew vi. 28 ('Consider the lilies of the field, . . .').

[3] Ellen ('Nellie') Beakbane, a Quaker, ran the guesthouse 'Leithdale' with her friend Mollie Skinner.

without much élan, no natural joy. – I suppose we shall be in England for the month of October, then go south, to the Mediterranean.

I have been waiting all summer for *Black Swans*. What is Cape doing? I'll look him up when I get to London, and see. And if the book is out, I'll get it and review it for one of the monthlies, if I can.[1] I'll have a try, when I'm in London.

Over here, things aren't very good. Seltzer is nearly bankrupt, and only pays me small doles, out of all he owes me. I've had nothing for *Boy in the Bush*, at all. But I suppose it will come. Anyhow I'll see they send you a few dollars, when any are squeezed out of Seltzer. We have no luck.

How's your new novel going? – Mine is being held over to Spring 1926. It's called *The Plumed Serpent*: it's the Mexican book. I'm glad it's not coming immediately. I get so weary of the public, it's smallness and fatuity.

I wonder if there's anything you'd like particularly to read? If there is, tell me, and I'll send it you from London. c/o Curtis Brown always finds me there: 6 Henrietta St. W. C. 2.

I shall look for word from you in London. Never bother about publishers and public; one goes one's own way, bit by bit. My wife sends her regards –

Yrs D. H. Lawrence

3467. To Mollie Skinner, [29 August 1925]

Text: MS WAPL; Postmark, [. . .] AUG 29 1925; Huxley 638–9.

Del Monte Ranch. *Questa*. New Mexico
28 August 1925

Dear Mollie Skinner

I sent you a letter yesterday, and last night came yours telling that your brother was dead.[2] He had no luck: one could see in his face, that he never would have luck. Perhaps it's really true, lucky in money, unlucky in love. But as a matter of fact, I believe he really never *wanted* to make good. At the bottom of his soul, he preferred to drift penniless through the world. I think if I had to choose, myself, between being a Duke of Portland, or having a million sterling and forced to live up to it, I'd rather, far, far rather be a penniless tramp. There is deep inside one a revolt against the fixed thing, fixed society, fixed money, fixed homes, even fixed love. I believe that was what ailed your brother: he couldn't bear the social fixture of everything. It's what ails me too.

And after all, he lived his life and had his mates wherever he went. What

[1] DHL did not review it.

[2] Jack Skinner died 14 July 1925.

more does a man want? So many old bourgeois people live on and on, and *can't* die, because they have never been in life at all. Death's not sad, when one has lived.

And that again is what I think about writing a novel: one can live so intensely with one's characters and the experience, one creates or records, it is a life in itself, far better than the vulgar thing people *call* life, jazzing and motoring and so on. No, every day I live I feel more disgust at the thing these Americans call life. Ten times better die penniless on a gold-field.

But be sure of my sympathy.

D. H. Lawrence

3468. To Alfred Decker Hawk, [30 August 1925]

Text: MS ColU; Delany, *DHL Review*, ii. 202–3.

[Kiowa]
Sunday

Dear Mr Hawk

I wanted to thank you before for your letter – but you were out on Friday.

We think to leave on the 10th September – I hope you and Mrs Hawk will come up and see us before we go. And I should be glad if you would keep a few things for us, like last year. William said he would look after the horses, as he did before.

I am sorry we are going so soon – Next year we must have some picnics and good times.

Yours sincerely D. H. Lawrence

3469. To Kyle Crichton, 31 August 1925

Text: MS Crichton; Nehls, ii. 421–2.

Del Monte Ranch. *Valdez*, New Mexico
31 August 1925

Dear Crichton

I read your story at once and will say my say at once – I can't typewrite.[1]

You are too journalistic, too much concerned with facts. You don't concern yourself with the *human inside* at all, only with the insides of steel works. It's

[1] Crichton explained: 'It concerned a young fellow (obviously myself) who had come from the coal mines, had worked in the steel works, and was relieved at getting back to the mines.' The story was never published, but a reader's report on 'The Tipple' suggests the story may have developed into a book (Lida McCord, Curtis Brown of New York, to Crichton, 5 March 1928, MS Crichton). (Crichton was the son of a coal miner.) See Nehls, ii. 526 n. 128.

the sort of consciousness the working man has: but at the same time, he's got a passionate sub-conscious. And it's this *sub-conscious* which makes the story: otherwise you have journalism. Now you want to be an artist, so you've got to use the artist's faculty of making the sub-conscious conscious. Take your Andy, a boy as blank as most American boys – who, to my mind, are far blanker than English or Scotch boys. It's the atmosphere of unending materialism does it. – But take your Andy, and look *under* his blankness: under his cheery-o! and all that, look for his hidden wistfulness, his absolutely shut-off passion, his queer, uncanny American isolation and stoicism, the fantasy of himself to himself – and give the same story in terms of these, not of his mechanical upper self. Your story is good *record*, and excellent for conveying fact. But where the living feeling should be, it's blank: blank as the ordinary American is.

Only the feeling is there – else the boy wouldnt possibly cry at the sight of a coal-mine again.

You've got the germ of a good, *novel* story: though pretty hard to work out. It might take a small novel to do it.

What was there in the mines that held the boy's feelings? The darkness, the mystery, the otherworldness, the peculiar camaraderie, the sort of naked intimacy: men as gods in the underworld, or as elementals. Create *that* in a picture.

Then, with just a bit of alteration, vivify that middle-part (the best) of your story: *steel*. Give the mystery, the cruelty, the deathliness of steel, as against the comparative softness, silkiness, naturalness of coal. Throw in that Alice as a symbol of the human ego striving in its vanity, superficial: but the man's soul really magnetised by steel, by coal, as two opposing master-elements: carbon versus iron, c and f.

When we get inside ourselves, and away from the vanity of the ego – Alice and smart clothes – then things are symbols. Coal is a symbol of something in the soul, old and dark and silky and natural, and matrix of fire: and steel is symbol of something else in the soul, hard and death-dealing, cutting, hurting, annihilating the living tissue forever. You've got to allow yourself to be, in some measure, the mystic that your real self *is*, under all the American efficiency and smartness of the ego – before you can be an artist.

Well, you'll be bored by this. – I wonder if you'd care for Paris: should say *not*. Either try Italy and the sun, or a Devonshire village. It's your visionary *soul* you need thawing out. – I can perhaps help you if you do go to Europe. All good wishes from us all to Mrs Crichton and you.

D. H. Lawrence

3470. To Joseph Foster, [5 September 1925]

Text: MS Foster; Postmark, [. . .] 1925; Unpublished.

[Kiowa]
Saturday

Dear Joe

I should have answered sooner, but waited to see if we'd go by Denver or not. I think, now, we shall – from Questa. It will be fun, trying another route.

Thank you so much for the invitation. Do hope Margaret Hale is all right. I think myself she wants a bit of lower altitude.

I shall come in, I expect, with Wm. Hawk in his Flivver one day early in the week – not later than Wednesday – and shall try to come out to you with the books: if not, leave them at Gersons. But will try and pop out for a farewell.

Kindest remembrances D. H. Lawrence

3471. To Edward McDonald, 7 September 1925

Text: MS UT; Postmark, Taos SEP 9 1925; *Centaur* 22.

Del Monte Ranch. *Questa*. N. Mex
7 Sept 1925

Dear Dr McDonald

Your letter this evening. Take it for granted I am wrong: I have nothing but merest memory to go on. Perhaps Mr Mason will be so good as to change the four, and make it three.[1] I know there were some *Signatures* never sold: so I suppose Murry will be selling them off. He will give me my share.

I have not heard at all from The Centaur, neither Mr Mason nor Mr Jester, so was just wondering if the MSS of the essays had gone lost. However, they must be there, with the Centaur.

We leave here next Thursday 10th – so shall be in New York by the 14th. Do come and see us if you are also in town. I expect we shall sail by the end of the month.

Maybe the Centaurs didn't care for the essays. I hope they won't feel under any obligation to publish them: not the slightest.

Hoping then to see you in New York, with Mrs McDonald if she is with you,

Yours sincerely D. H. Lawrence

By the way, the people of the Barnes Foundation sent me their little

[1] In the 'Note to The Crown' DHL had first written 'The helpless little brown magazine appeared four times . . .' but he changed this to 'three'; in typescript he reverted to 'four'; see Letter 3212 and p. 103 n. 4.

publication twice: I thought it had a pretty sound attitude to art.[1] If the Centaur does the *Porcupine*, I'd like to send the Barnes people a copy.

DHL

3472. To Emily King, 8 September 1925

Text: MS King; Photograph [DHL and Walton Hawk on horseback]; Unpublished.

Questa. N. Mex.
8th[2] Sept 1925

My Dear Pamela

We leave here on Thursday – in two days' time – shall be in New York on the 14th, all going well. Stay there about two weeks, then to England.

Love DHL

That's our neighbour's little boy – Walton Hawk, with me on Azul.

3473. To Martin Secker, 8 September 1925

Text: MS UInd; Photograph [DHL on horseback]; Postmark, Taos SEP 8 1925; Secker 64.

Del Monte Ranch
8 Sept. 1925

Dear Secker

We leave in two days' time – and shall be in England, I expect, by early October. If you happen to know of any little apartment in town that we could rent for a month, let me know, will you? –

c/o Curtis Brown. 116 W. 39th St,

– if there's time for that. – Just a little small place, preferably right in town.

Yrs D. H. Lawrence

3474. To Ada Clarke, 8 September 1925

Text: MS Clarke; Photograph [Lawrences with Timsy Weymss]; Unpublished.

Questa. New Mexico
8 Sept 1925

My dear Sister

We leave here in two days' time – go by Denver. It is lovely autumn, pity to go. I expect we shall stay about two weeks in New York, and be in England, as I said, early in October.

So au revoir DHL

[1] Either the Barnes Foundation's *Journal* (first issue, April 1925) or *An Approach to Art* by Mary Mullen (1875–), with fifty illustrations (78pp.) (Merion: The Barnes Foundation, 1923). The Foundation was an art school and museum in Merion, Pennsylvania, established 1922 by Dr Albert Coombs Barnes (1872–1951), American drug manufacturer, to house his collection and provide free instruction in art appreciation. (Barnes's own book *Art in Painting* was published in 1925, but was not 'little': it comprised 530pp.)

[2] 8th] 7th

That's me and Timsy, the cat, and F[rieda] in the doorway – in case you can't recognise us.

3475. To Margaret King, [11 September 1925]

Text: MS Needham; PC v. Bears in City Park Zoo, Denver; Postmark, Denv[er] [. . .] 12 1925; Unpublished.

Denver
11 Sept

On our way to New York – shall be there by Monday.

DHL

3476. To Hon. Dorothy Brett, [11 September 1925]

Text: MS UCin; PC v. Bears in City Park Zoo, Denver; Postmark, Denve[r] [. . .] 11 1925; Irvine, Brett 50.

[Denver]
Friday morning

leave here this morning for Chicago – I think you'd better go from Santa Fe or from *Raton* – there's such a lot of fuss changing lines this way – and 3 hours to wait in Blanca,[1] at night, with snow frozen on the streets – but the little hotel is warm. You try that trip to Raton – but be sure to write for reservations.

DHL

3477. To Curtis Brown, 14 September 1925

Text: MS UT; Unpublished.

71 Washington Place, New York
14 Sept 1925

Dear Curtis Brown

Herewith the signed agreement of *The Plumed Serpent.*[2]

[1] Blanca, Colorado, 50 miles due n. of Questa.

[2] Martin Secker had written to Curtis Brown's on 24 August 1925 (Secker Letter-Book, UIll):

Dear Mr Joseph

I have much pleasure in sending herewith the contract for "The Plumed Serpent", and shall look forward to receiving the counterpart with the author's signature in due course. In connection with the stipulated payment of £125 on receipt of this, would you think it unreasonable if I asked for a slight indulgency. As you know, I have agreed to defer publication until Knopf can fix his date, and at the moment it would not appear that this can in any event be earlier than February next. I am only just now beginning to send slip proofs to the author, and I understand that until he has worked on these he will not be sending the book to Knopf. If we could compromise in the matter I will undertake to send the cheque in November, but I would like to leave the matter entirely to Lawrence, and if for any reason he is counting on immediate payment, this shall be forthcoming.

There is no news yet, I suppose, about "David". As promised, I am enclosing Lawrence's general royalty account, with cheque in settlement.

Yours sincerely

We got to New York last night – shall go in to the office tomorrow to see what's happening to the play etc.

Tell Secker not to bother about the £125 advance on the *Serpent* just now, if he doesn't want to: though I wish Stern would get a bit of money out of Seltzer.

Till I see you in London.

Yrs D. H. Lawrence

3478. To Hon. Dorothy Brett, [15 September 1925]

Text: MS UCin; Postmark, New York SEP 16 1925; Moore 853.

c/o Mrs Nina Witt. 71. Washington Place, New York City
Tuesday. 15th Sept.

Dear Brett

We got here at 5.30 Sunday evening – which is pretty quick. We caught the connection in one hour at Chicago, as the train from Denver goes into the same station as the New York Central, so you don't have to cross the city. – But I think you'd be happier on the Santa Fe: and the Parmelee Transfer Co. takes you straight across the town in their bus, to the other station. – It was raining and steamy steamy hot – but now is grey and cool – not bad. – I feel I have nothing *at all* to do with this city – or any other city. Shall be glad to get away – I hope we can sail 26th. – I asked Nina, and she said you could come and stay here. Remember it's just off Washington *Square*, where nearly all the 5th Avenue buses stop – on the *west* side of the square. – It's quite a pleasant smallish arty house, with a negro cook Albertina. – If I were you, I wouldn't stay long here. I'll ask about Italian ships and let you know, so you can plan your departure. New York is useless. – We saw Barmby: he's gone dead since last year – not nice. I got no news from him – but should know something definite tomorrow. We went to the Grenwich Village theatre and saw a play about tramps – hoboes – amusing, but nothing.[1] I'll let you know what news I get of my play: being here, one expects nothing. – No sign of Ida.

If you happen to see any mail for me, send it

c/o Curtis Brown. 6 Henrietta St. Covent Garden. London W.C.2.

– I feel we shall soon be gone from here.

Of course one is a fool to leave the ranch. But perhaps Europe will be good for us, for the Winter.

Perhaps the simplest way for you to carry money to Italy, would be for you to take $100.00 – worth of Traveller's Checks – either from the American Express Co., or from your bank. Leave the rest in the bank.

[1] *Outside Looking In* by Maxwell Anderson (1888–1959) opened on 7 September 1925 at Greenwich Theatre; it was a dramatisation of *Beggars of Life* (1924) by Jim Tully (1891–1947).

One leaves off living when one gets inside a city – I just refrain from thinking about the Azul and Timsy and Moses and all of them.

à la guerre comme à la guerre.

I'll get Nina to write you a note of definite invitation.

Yrs D. H. Lawrence

no sign of your machine.

Remember us to Rachel and William – and to Mr and Mrs Hawk.

3479. To Hon. Dorothy Brett, [17 September 1925]

Text: MS UCin; Postmark, [. . .] 1925; Irvine, Brett 50–1.

71. Washington Place. New York City
Thursday

Dear Brett

I looked in at Cook's about sailings to Naples. The best seemed to be the Lloyd Triestino boat on the Consulich line, the *Presidente Wilson* – sailing Oct 6th. and calling at Boston, Azores, Lisbon, Naples – and going on to Patras, Ragusa, Trieste – which is near Venice. The First Class fare, all that long way – about 22 days at sea – is $209.00 – the same whether you go to Naples or to Trieste. Barmby went on this boat, and said it was good. It's 16 days to Naples.

Or you can go on a bigger line – The Navigazione Italiana – calling only at Palermo, in Sicily – on Oct 3rd or Oct 24th – at $250 first class. $135 second. – on these boats I think you could travel second. Then the Lloyd Sabaudo have the *Conte Verde* on Oct 10th – direct to Naples – rates about the same as the Navigazione Italiana – and you can go 2nd Class. All these ships are Italian – or, on the Consulich line, originally Austrian. Not many people travelling now.

Thomas Cook's office is 585 Fifth Av.

I think we shall sail next Monday night – 21st – to Southampton. I don't care for it here, want to get to sea. Had a telegram from Ida – she's not here yet. If I were you I think I wouldn't stay with Nina, unless she writes to you herself, and sounds a bit cordial. Write to Ida,

c/o Miss Florence Rauh,[1] 12 East 8th St, New York City

– and stay a couple of days in some little hotel. What's the odds, for two days or so. You've not much to do. Get your berth at Cooks – then go down with your passport, on the Overhead Railway – the Elevated – to the Battery, *down* town – and in the huge Customs House Building, get your permit to sail – you take your passport – but[2] before that, get your Italian Visa from the Italian Consul

[1] Ida Rauh's sister. [2] but] &

– 20 East 22nd St. – not so *very* far from Cooks. You can do it all in three days, easily. Your bank is also down town nearly at the Battery.

They're deciding about the play today – but I'm almost sure they won't do it.[1]

Poor Ida, I'm afraid she's doomed to more disappointment.

Frieda says she'll wear the shawl the winter and then bring it back to you – it's *very* pretty.[2]

Bah! – it's much better to stay on the ranch, and not even *try* these cities. I hate it here really, though everybody is quite nice.

I believe even England will be better.

DHL

you take off 10% for winter prices.[3]

3480. To Edward McDonald, [17 September 1925]

Text: MS UT; Postmark, [. . .] Sta. N. Y. SEP [. . .] 1925; *Centaur* 23.

c/o Mrs Witt. 71. Washington Place. (Spring 4114)
Thursday[4]

Dear Dr McDonald

Glad to hear that you and Mrs McDonald will be in town.

I'm not quite sure of our hostess' arrangements here – so shall we call, my

[1] The Theatre Guild did not produce *David*.

[2] Frieda wrote to Brett on 18 September 1925 (MS UCin):

New York
Friday

Dear Brett,

The shawl is mended, I ll wear it to-night with the Philadelphia Centaur people – It *was* nice of you to give it me and I ll wear it but I feel it's your possession and must return to you – I *am* dazed but less so – Seltzers horrid and finished – I went to lunch with them taking the attitude they would pay us if they *could*, but no, she almost hit me in the eye – We are the low money grubbers – Small beer! Knopf's in the *Heckscher* building – Rather nice, she pretty elegant, he expensive, heavy uninspired but honest – New York in a negative state, no news of the play – I feel as if Lawrence were beginning all over again – As Thomas said, the Lawrence *myth* is dead." He meant it spitefully – but no "myths" for me. The ranch seems floating in another sphere – Life has stopped for the moment – Barmby prosperous and disillusioned – People dont believe in *anything* – Love to Rachel. Lawr already does nt look so well!

F –

Nina's girl charming!

Knopf had moved his offices to the Heckscher Building on Fifty-seventh Street in 1924 (*Publisher's Weekly*, cv, 23 February 1924, 601–2). For 'Nina's girl', see Letter 3483 and n. 3.

[3] The postscript is written on a torn sheet from Cook's guide giving the lines and sailing dates to Mediterranean ports.

[4] Thursday] Friday

wife and I, and see you at the Algonquin tomorrow – Friday?[1] Will you ring up when you get this? – we shall be at Alfred Knopf's office for a time, round about 4.0 o'clock – otherwise I think you can get us here.

Saluti! D. H. Lawrence

3481. To Irita van Doren, 18 September 1925
Text: MS LC; Unpublished.

71. Washington Place. New York City
c/o Mrs Witt.
18 Sept 1925

Dear Mrs Van Doren[2]

My wife and I are passing through New York on our way to England – sail Monday. I got your letter – many thanks. Alfred Knopf just gave me three books, which will all interest me.

The Origins of Prohibition. John A. Krout[3]
Said the Fisherman: Marmaduke Pickthall[4]
Hadrian The Seventh Frederick Baron Corvo.[5]

Will you tell me if you would care for a review of any of these, from me. The telephone here is Spring 4114: if that will not be troubling you too far.

Gilbert Frankau sounds so funny in himself, that one could hardly be funny about him.[6]

Best wishes D. H. Lawrence

[1] The Lawrences met the McDonalds and the Masons on Friday 18 September at the Algonquin Hotel; the party went on to Madame Petite Pas Rest (see Marguerite Bartelle McDonald, 'An Evening with the Lawrences', *DHL Review*, v, Spring 1972, 63–6).

[2] Irita van Doren, née Bradford (1891–1966), American editor. Associate editor of *New York Herald Tribune Books*, 1924–6; literary editor of *New York Herald Tribune*, 1926–63. m. 1912, Carl Clinton van Doren (1885–1950), American editor and critic; professor at Columbia, 1911–34, and literary editor of *Nation*, 1919–22, and *Century*, 1922–5; divorced 1936.

[3] *The Origins of Prohibition* (Knopf, 1925) by (Dr) John Allen Krout (1896–1979). See Letter 3550; DHL's review appeared in *New York Herald Tribune Books*, 21 January 1926.

[4] *Saïd the Fisherman* by Marmaduke William Pickthall (1875–1936), first published in England and USA in 1903 and reissued in Knopf's Blue Jade Library in 1925. See Letters 3512 and 3513; DHL's review appeared in *New York Herald Tribune Books*, 27 December 1925 and was reprinted in *Adelphi*, iv (January 1927), 436–40.

[5] *Hadrian the Seventh* by Frederick William Serafino Austin Lewis Mary Rolfe (pseudonym, Baron Corvo) (1860–1913), published in England in 1904; first American publication in Knopf's Blue Jade Library, 1925. See Letter 3513; DHL's review appeared in *Adelphi* (December 1925), 502–6.

[6] Gilbert Frankau (1884–1952), novelist; author of *One of Us* (1914), *Peter Jackson, Cigar Merchant* (1919), *The Love Story of Aliette Brunton* (1922), etc. In 1924 he was impressed by Italian Fascism and spoke for the extreme right. (See obituary in *The Times*, 5 November 1952, p. 10.)

3482. To Bessie Freeman, [21 September 1925]

Text: MS UNYB; cited in Moore, *Poste Restante* 83.

c/o Nina Witt. 71. Washington Place, N. Y. C.
21 Sept

Dear Bessie Freeman[1]

Got your letter this afternoon, and we sail tonight – Too bad! Hope we may see you in the spring, when we come back – we're sailing to England, but I expect we shall winter in England.

We talked about you – and with Alice Sprague too. Should have liked to see you. Remember me to your brother and to Mrs Wilkeson.[2]

Yrs D. H. Lawrence

Frieda sends warm regards.

3483. To Hon. Dorothy Brett, [21 September 1925]

Text: MS UCin; Irvine, Brett 52–3.

71 Washington Place, Washington Square.
Monday 21 Sept

Dear Brett

We sail tonight, at midnight – this city is a weariness beyond expression – so nerve-jumpy, and steamy hot.

I just had a note from the Ear-phone people to say your machine is *mended*, charge $25.00. I am not going to fetch it, as people are coming in now and we must leave tonight – And it's no good bringing it to Nina's. Don't stay with Nina – she doesn't really want anybody. But the daughter, Marion Bull,[3] would like to see you, and would help you getting about. – I hope you've written to Ida. She will get you an hotel. If not, just go to the Brevoort, in Fifth Avenue, near here – or to the Algonquin in 44th St. I think you'll have no trouble with anything – they make no fuss giving a sailing permit.

c/o Curtis Brown. 6 Henrietta St. W.C. 2.

or

Martin Secker. 5 John St. Adelphi

always finds us in England.

I feel now I rather want to go for a bit, to England.

[1] Elizabeth ('Bessie') Wilkeson Freeman (1876–1951), a close friend of Mabel Luhan's since their girlhoods in Buffalo. DHL met her through Mabel Luhan and, in August 1923, visited her in Buffalo. m. (1) John Knox Freeman; (2) 1934, Chauncey J. Hamlin (1881–1963).

[2] Her brother may have been Paul (see *Letters*, iv. 333 and n. 1) and Mrs Wilkeson her mother.

[3] Marion Bull (1906–), daughter of Nina Witt by her first marriage. DHL wrote to her on 8 November 1927 when he heard of her marriage to Hamilton Eames. Nina Witt's other children were Katherine, and Harry (see Letter 3488).

Be sure and remember us to William and Rachel, and to Mr and Mrs Hawk – it's rather a rush.

DHL

3484. To Blanche Knopf, 21 September 1925

Text: MS UT; Unpublished.

71 Washington Place.
21 Sept 1925

Dear Mrs Knopf

Here are the proofs, before we sail.[1]

I am glad I know you and Knopf – it feels like having something safe behind me – a feeling I've never had before, in America.

As for the people, they'll buy me again, soon.

c/o Martin Secker will always find me.

Saluti buonissimi[2] D. H. Lawrence

3485. To Ida Rauh, 21 September 1925

Text: MS UT; Unpublished.

c/o Mrs Nina Witt. 71. Washington Place, New York City
21[3] Sept 1925 – Monday

Dear Ida

We sail this evening for England. – And no word still from the Theatre Guild – damn them. – New York not very nice – I hope you won't be disappointed in it. – Irene Lewisohn came here, and I liked her.[4] – We went to

[1] Blanche Knopf acknowledged the proofs of 'Accumulated Mail' on 22 September 1925 (TMSC UT):

Dear Mr. Lawrence,

Thanks for sending the proofs back so promptly. I assure you too it was the greatest pleasure meeting you and Mrs. Lawrence and my only regret was that we had so little time together. I assure you that we will do everything possible that there is to do – which I think is a good deal.

I do hope that you both have the best kind of a visit and am looking forward with keen enthusiasm to your return here in the early Spring.

With regards and very good wishes,

Sincerely yours,

[2] 'Very warm greetings'.

[3] 21] 19

[4] Irene Lewisohn (d. 1944), with her sister Alice, built and endowed the Neighborhood Playhouse, 1915, which produced ballets and new plays, first with amateurs and, by 1925, with professionals; later founder and director of Neighborhood Playhouse School of the Theatre and president of the Museum of Costume Art. (See obituary in *New York Times*, 5 April 1944, p. 19.)

Mrs Hare's place on Long Island – it's quite a lovely place, and they were *really* very kind.[1]

You have Curtis Browns address 116 West 39th St. – manager A.W. Barmby. In England

c/o Martin Secker. 5 John St. Adelphi. London W.C. 2

will always get me.

Good luck to you. D. H. Lawrence

3486. To Baroness Anna von Richthofen, 23 September 1925

Text: MS UCB; Frieda Lawrence 192.

S. S. Resolute[2]
23 Sept 1925.

Meine liebe Schwiegermutter

This is the second day at sea – very nice, with blue running water and a fresh wind. I am quite glad to be out of that America for a time; it's so tough and wearing, with the iron springs poking out through the padding. We shall be in England in five more days – I think we shall take a house by the sea for a while, so Frieda can have her children to stay with her.[3] And I must go to my sisters, and see their new houses. And then we must hurry off to BadenBaden, before winter sets in.

I don't feel myself very American: no, I am still a European.

It seems a long time since we heard from you – I hope it's a nice autumn. In New York it was horrid, hot and sticky.

Save me a few good Schwarzwald apples, and a bottle of Kirschwasser, and a few leaves on the trees, and a few alten Damen[4] in the Stift to call me Herr Doktor when I'm not one, and a hand at whist with you and my kurzröckigen Schwägerin, and a jubiläum in the Stiftsköniginkammer.[5] The prodigal children come home, vom Schwein gibt's kein mehr, nur vom Kalb.[6]

à bientôt!
auf baldigen Wiedersehn!
hasta luego![7]
till I see you!

DHL

[1] Elizabeth ('Betty') Hare, née Sage (1878–1948); b. Brooklyn, lived at Pidgeon Hill, Huntington, Long Island. m. (1) Walter L. Goodwin; (2) 1916, Meredith Hare (1870–1932), lawyer. She was a visitor to Taos and had a house in Santa Fe; generous in helping artists, founder of Colorado Springs Fine Art Center. See Brett, *South Dakota Review* 42 and obituary in *New York Times* (23 August 1948), 17.

[2] For this letter – together with the following five – DHL used the ship's notepaper.

[3] Charles Montague (1900–82), Elsa Agnes Frieda (1902–85) and Barbara Weekley.

[4] 'Black Forest apples . . . bottle of Kirsch . . . a few old ladies'.

[5] 'my short-skirted sister-in-law, and an anniversary in the Stift's Queen's Chamber'.

[6] 'there's no pork left, only veal'.

[7] 'see you soon' – in French, German and Spanish.

3487. To Earl and Achsah Brewster, 27 September 1925
Text: MS UT; Brewster 82–3.

S. S. Resolute
27 Sept 1925

Dear Earl and Achsah

Here we are, nearing Europe once more. We land in Southampton next Wednesday – the 30th. – I suppose we shall stay in England a month or so, then begin to move south – so probably shall see you before so very long. Send me a line to say if you are staying in Capri – I am so looking forward to the Mediterranean. Write me

c/o Curtis Brown, 6 Henrietta St, London W. C. 2.

I don't know exactly when Miss Brett will sail for[1] Naples – she wants to come early in October. I'm so afraid I forgot to give her a letter to you. She is a painter, and you would like her. I shall send a letter now and try to get her.

This Atlantic is an unsympathetic ocean: one never sees so much as a friendly fish.

Oh Achsah, we had your letter and the photographs of child and puppy.[2] What a big child, and little puppy! But she's Mademoiselle now, with a vengeance, no more Missy to be seen.

It will be real fun, meeting her and all of you again.

Souvenirs D. H. Lawrence

3488. To William and Rachel Hawk, [27 September 1925]
Text: MS UT; Postmark, London SEP 30 1925; Moore, *Intelligent Heart* 343–4.

S. S. Resolute
Sunday 27 Sept

Dear William and Rachel

Here it is Sunday afternoon – everybody very bored – nothing happening, except a rather fresh wind, the sea a bit choppy, outdoors just a bit too cold. We get in to Southampton on Wednesday morning, and glad shall I be to see land. There are very few people on board, and most of those are Germans or people from somewhere Russia way, speaking a language never heard before. We've had pretty good weather – went on board last Monday night, and sailed at 1 a. m. Queer to be slipping down the Hudson at midnight, past all the pier lights. It seems now such a long while ago. Though the weather has been pretty good, I had one awful day, blind with a headache. It was when we ran into a warm fog, so suppose it was the old malaria popping up.

I didn't care for New York – it was steamy hot. I had to run about and see people: the two little Seltzer's dangling by a single thread, over the verge of

[1] for] from

[2] For the photograph see *DHL Review*, xvii (Fall 1984), 203.

bankruptcy, and nobody a bit sorry for them. The new publishers, the Knopfs, are set up in great style, in their offices on Fifth Avenue – deep carpets, and sylphs in a shred of black satin and a shred of brilliant undergarment darting by. But the Knopfs seem really sound and reliable: am afraid the Seltzers had too many 'feelings.' Adele said dramatically to Frieda: 'All I want is to pay OUR debts and DIE'. Death is a debt we all pay: the dollars are another matter.

Nina is as busy as ever re-integrating other people – It was a pleasant house near Washington Square, but of course they were building a huge new 15-storey place next door, so all day long the noise of battle rolled. – The child, Marion Bull, is a handsome girl of eighteen and very nice indeed: trying to go on the stage, and the stagey people being very catty to her. I[1] rather hope she won't go on the stage, it might spoil her. – The boy Harry wasn't yet back in New York.[2] – That woman Mrs Hare sent a car and fetched us to their place on Long Island: beautiful place. But in proudly showing me her bees, she went and got stung just under the eye, and a more extraordinary hostess in an elegant house I never saw, as the afternoon wore on and the swelling swelled and swelled. It was too bad: she was very kind to us. – The nicest thing was when some people motored us out at night to the shore on Long Island, and we made a huge fire of driftwood, and toasted mutton chops, with nothing in sight but sand and the foam in the dark.

I lie and think of the ranch: it seems so far far away: – these beastly journeys, how I hate them! I'm going to stop it, though, this continual shifting.

How is Miss Wemyss: not still fighting her mother, I hope – like Brett at forty? Send me a line with news of you all:

c/o Curtis Brown. 6 Henrietta St. London. W. C. 2.

I do feel, I don't know what I'm doing on board this ship.

au revoir and remembrances D. H. Lawrence

3489. To Hon. Dorothy Brett, [28 September 1925]

Text: MS UCin; Irvine, Brett 53.

S. S. Resolute
Monday 28 Sept.

My dear Brett

Only two days more – we come to Southampton on Wed. morning. It has

[1] I] It

[2] Harry Adsit Bull Jr (1905–54) was a Harvard undergraduate. He became Assistant Editor of *International Studio Magazine*, 1928–31; later he was Editor of *Town and Country*, 1935–47. (See obituary in *New York Times*, 12 December 1954.)

been a smooth crossing, and quite a good boat. But one day I had the worst headache ever.

There aren't many people travelling, only 28 in this 2nd Class. But I feel horribly shut up – caged – in this small space. *Don't* go second on a small boat – be sure you get enough promenade room, it becomes unbearable, after a few days, when there isn't enough room to walk about.

I forgot to give you a letter to the Brewsters, so will enclose one in this.[1] You will need to know somebody there.

I'm not making any plans at all – see how things work out. Nothing nice at all happened in New York. I left about $30 in the bank: but Seltzer telephoned he was *going* to deposit some more! No word of the play.

On the whole, I am glad to be going out of America for a time: I feel like Europe.

You have the address:

c/o Curtis Brown. 6 Henrietta St. W.C.2.

We shall wonder what you are doing. Frieda much admired in the shawl. You will have got my letter telling you your machine is mended, so I didn't fetch it from the shop. You'll have ears in New York.

DHL

3490. To Kyle Crichton, [28 September 1925]

Text: MS Crichton; Nehls, ii. 425–6.

S. S. Resolute
Monday 28 Sept

Dear Crichton

I had your letter just before we left the ranch: now in two days we land in England. It has been quite a good crossing, even, for the Atlantic, comparatively sunny. But this is a dismal kind of ocean: it always affects me as the grave of Atlantis.

I have been thinking of what you say about not having had the courage to be a creative writer. It seems to me that may be true – America, of all countries, kills that courage, simply because it sees no value in the really creative effort, whereas it esteems, more highly than any other country, the journalistic effort: it loves a thrill or a sensation, but loathes to be in any way *moved*, inwardly affected so that a new vital adjustment is necessary. Americans are enormously adaptible: perhaps because inwardly they are not adjusted at all to their environment. They are never American as a chipmunk is, or as an Indian is: only as a Ford car or as[2] the Woolworth building.[3]

[1] It is missing; see Letter 3491.

[2] MS reads 'a'.

[3] In 1925 the world's highest building.

That's why it seems to me impossible almost, to be purely a creative writer in America: everybody compromises with journalism and commerce. Hawthorne and Melville and Whitman reached a point of imaginative or visionary adjustment to America, which, it seems to me, is again entirely lost, abandoned: because you can't adjust yourself vitally, inwardly, to a rather scaring world, and at the same time, get ahead.

So, with you, and these years of work behind you, the old habit, you'd find it awfully hard. But I don't see why you shouldn't dig down in yourself till you get out of sight of your street self, and there, little by little, get out the hidden stuff. All the things an American never allows himself to feel, much less to think. I always think there is, way down in most American men, a weird little imprisoned man-gnome with a grey beard and a child's quickness, which knows, knows so finally, imprisoned inside the man-mountain, while the man-mountain goes on so lively and cheery-o! – without knowing a thing. Till the little sprite ceases to live, and then the man-mountain begins to collapse. I don't see why, with a patient effort, you shouldn't bit by bit get down what the sprite in you says: even though the man-mountain has to work at a job. It is all a question of getting yourself focussed.

But heavens! I dont want to preach at you.

I guess we shall stay a month or so in England, but c/o Curtis Brown. 6 Henrietta St. London W.C.2 – that will always find me.

My wife sends remembrances to Mrs Crichton – hope the children keep gay and sturdy.

Regards to you both D. H. Lawrence

3491. To Ida Rauh, 28 September 1925
Text: MS UT; Postmark, London SEP 30 1925; Unpublished.

SS Resolute.
28 Sept 1925

My dear Ida

Will you give the enclosed to Brett – if you read my note to her you'll see how we are.

Frankly, there didnt seem much for me in New York. I hope you'll get more out of it. Maybe through Irene Lewisohn. She seemed to me to have a certain clear nice quality. I like her. I wish those Theatre Guild people weren't so damned week-endy – damn them. And my agents aren't so very much good either. If you have any sudden bright idea, then go and make A.W.Barmby do anything necessary. He is Curtis Brown's manager, at 116 W. 39th. – I met a girl playing heroine, now, in *Desire Under the Elms* – Helen Freeman.[1] She was a clear-cut thing, and seemed to know chalk from cheese, and I liked her. You might get to know her: via Alice Sprague or one of those.

And if you get bored in New York, try Europe for a bit. But I hope you'll get some satisfactory work. Nina Witt's girl Marion Bull is finding it very difficult to get on to the stage. She's a nice girl, very: quite straight and simple.

If there's anything I can do, let me know, won't you.

Yrs D. H. Lawrence

3492. To Catherine Carswell, [30 September 1925]

Text: MS YU; Unpublished.

[Garland's Hotel, Suffolk Street, Pall Mall, S.W.1.][2]
Wed[3]

Dear Catherine

Here for the moment. We'll come up to Hampstead tomorrow afternoon if you will be at home – about 4:0. If you'll be out, send a message or telephone, will you. We are in the side house, room No 3.

Au revoir D. H. Lawrence

3493. To Emily King, 1 October 1925

Text: MS Lazarus; Unpublished.

[Garland's Hotel, Suffolk Street, Pall Mall, S.W.1.]
1st October 1925

My dear Pamela

We had a good crossing, and got in here last night. I suppose we shall stay a week here, see a few people – Frieda seeing her children. Then we shall come up to stay with you and Ada.

We haven't decided how long we'll remain in England: perhaps take a house by the sea for a month: and after that go to Germany. We'll see.

Au revoir, then – and love. DHL

[1] Helen Freeman, American actress, was playing Abbie Putnam in Eugene O'Neill's *Desire Under the Elms* (1924) at Daly's Sixty-third Street Theatre in September 1925. She had written, produced, financed and acted in *The Great Way* at Park Theatre in 1921, was on the original board of the Theatre Guild and had acted in their first two plays. See *New York Times* (27 September 1925), VII, 2.

[2] For this and succeeding letters DHL used the hotel's headed notepaper.

[3] Written immediately on arrival at Garland's and before DHL realised that the Carswells were not in Hampstead but near High Wycombe, Bucks (cf. Letter 3501).

3494. To John Middleton Murry, [1 October 1925]

Text: MS NYPL; J. M. Murry, *The Reminiscences of D. H. Lawrence* (1933), p. 197.

[Garland's Hotel, Suffolk Street, Pall Mall, S.W.1.]
1 Oct 1924

Dear Jack

Frieda and I landed last night – Brett stayed behind in America – I suppose we shall be here a week – then go to my sister's, and perhaps take a house by the sea in Lincolnshire for a month – after that, the Mediterranean.

Let us know where and how you are, and if you'll be in Town.

DHL

3495. To Catherine Carswell, 1 October 1925

Text: MS YU; Unpublished.

[Garland's Hotel, Suffolk Street, Pall Mall, S.W.1.]
1 Oct 1925

Dear Catherine

We landed yesterday – stay here a week, then go the Midlands. I had no word from you at Curtis Browns, so wonder if you are in Sark.

Let us know.

DHL

3496. To Catherine Carswell, [2 October 1925]

Text: MS YU; Unpublished.

[Garland's Hotel, Suffolk Street, Pall Mall, S.W.1.]
Friday

Dear Catherine

Just had your letter. We may come on *Sunday*, and return early Monday morning, if that would do. – I'll telegraph tomorrow.

DHL

3497. To Nancy Pearn, [5? October 1925]

Text: MS Lazarus; Unpublished.

[6 Henrietta St, W.C.2]
[5? October 1925][1]

Dear Miss Pearn

You're not in! – I'll gladly write in the book. – We are probably going to the

[1] This note (left for Nancy Pearn at Curtis Brown's office) was written on a working-day very close to the Lawrences' expected departure for the Midlands on Wednesday 7 October 1925.

Midlands on Wed. afternoon – too bad for the *Calendar*?[1] I'll call in tomorrow morning:

D. H. Lawrence

3498. To John Middleton Murry, 6 October 1925
Text: MS NYPL; Huxley 639.

[Garland's Hotel, Suffolk Street, Pall Mall, S.W.1.]
6 Oct 1925

Dear Jack

We're going up to my sister tomorrow:

c/o Mrs W. E. Clarke. Ripley (Derby)

so shan't be able to come down immediately, but when we come south again, in about a month's time, then we can come and see you, if you are not in town. I expect we shall stay a month or so by the sea in Lincs.

I still feel queer and foreign here, but look on with wonder instead of exasperation, this time. It's like being inside an aquarium, the people all fishes swimming on end. No doubt about it, England is the most fantastic *Alice-in-Wonderland* country.

We shall go to the Mediterranean for the winter – I've an idea Ragusa, on the Adriatic, might be nice: real peasants still.

I hear poor Gertler is in a sanatorium.[2] Have seen the Carswells and Eders,[3] but no more of the old crowd – not Kot.

Hope you're all well and cheerful in the old Coastguard Station.[4]

Yrs DHL

3499. To Alfred Decker and Lucy Hawk, 7 October 1925
Text: MS Lazarus; Moore, *Intelligent Heart* 345–6.

[Garland's Hotel, Suffolk Street, Pall Mall, S.W.1.]
7 Oct 1925

Dear Mr and Mrs Hawk

I've been in my native land eight days now, and it's not very cheering: rather foggy, with very feeble attempts at sun: and the people very depressed.

[1] Nancy Pearn had told DHL in her letter, 3 October 1925 (TMSC UT) that the editor of the *Calendar of Modern Letters*, Edgell Rickword (see Letter 3912 and n. 2) hoped to see him on either 8 or 12 October.

[2] Gertler suffered from tuberculosis and was in the Mundesley Sanatorium, Norfolk, for several months from September 1925. He wrote to Kot, 8 October 1925, to say that he had no desire to see DHL (*Mark Gertler: Selected Letters*, ed. Noel Carrington, 1965, p. 218).

[3] Dr Montagu David Eder (1865–1936), an early Freudian psychoanalyst (see *Letters*, ii. 258 n. 2), and his wife Edith (née Low) had known the Lawrences for over 10 years.

[4] See Letter 3256 and n. 1.

There's a million and a quarter unemployed, receiving that wretched dole: and you can't get a man to do an odd job, anywhere. My publisher, down in the country, has 16 acres of good thick hay still standing, because he can't get it cut. He told the farmer he could have it for the cutting: the farmer said that, although there were eight unemployed men in the tiny village, he couldn't get a man anywhere to to do a weeks work. If the unemployed work for a week, they go off the list of the dole, and they find it so hard to get on again, it's safer not to work. So there's a terrible feeling everywhere: and London is more expensive than New York, and the spending is enormous. They look for a revolution of some sort: I don't quite see anything violent, but added to fog, it's horribly depressing.

We are going today up to the Midlands, to stay with my sisters. I don't suppose we shall be in England more than another fortnight – then go to Germany, to my wife's mother, and on to Italy.

It's a pity, really, to leave the peaceful ranch, and the horses, and the sun. But there, one's native land has a sort of hopeless attraction, when one is away.

We haven't heard from anybody in New Mexico since we are here. I am wondering if Brett has set forth yet.

And in the short rush in New York, we never called at the hotel to see if Ted and Bobbie were there – But I expect they weren't.

My wife sends warm greetings – I believe she wishes she were back. But the winter is here.

With remembrances and best wishes.

Yours Sincerely D. H. Lawrence

3500. To Martin Secker, [7 October 1925]

Text: MS UInd; PC; Postmark, London OCT 7 1925; Secker 55.

Garlands Hotel
Wed.

Dear Secker

It was so nice, seeing Bridgefoot.

Would you send a copy of the *Foreign Legion* book to

Wm. G. Lengel, 153 Queen Victoria St. E. C. 4.[1]

He wants me to do something in that line for his *Cosmopolitan* – but how can I?

DHL

[1] William Charles Lengel (d. 1965), American journalist; editor of *Smart Set* and associate editor of *Cosmopolitan*.

3501. To Hon. Dorothy Brett, 8 October 1925

Text: MS UCin; Postmark, London OCT 8 1925; Moore 858.

[Garland's Hotel, Suffolk Street, Pall Mall, S.W.1.]
8 Oct. 1925

Dear Brett

We've been eight days in the old hotel – which is just the same.[1] It's rather foggy, and gives me a cough.

I wrote Murry we are here. He wants us to go down to Dorset. But he's got the Dunnings next door.[2] And he's got Jesus badly, and nastily.[3] The *Nation* compares Murry, in detail, to Mr Pecksniff.[4] Anyhow it all sounds sloppy and nasty: I shan't go down.

You were quite right not to come to England: it's much worse than when I was here last time, almost gruesome. Gertler is in a sanatorium in Norfolk. Kot I've heard nothing of. Cath. Carswell is buried alive in a hole of a horrid little cottage in damp and dismal Bucks. There's no *life* in anybody. And at the same time, London is so expensive, it makes one's hair stand on end.

We are going up to the Midlands to my sisters today. We thought of taking a house for a month at the seaside near, for a month. But I know I couldn't stand it. So I expect we shall leave in a fortnight, for BadenBaden, and then go to Italy.

Compton Mackenzie and his wife, Faith Mackenzie were here to lunch.[5] Faith is going to Capri for the winter. She says she will look for you, and help you all she can. She seems to me reliable and nice – so you won't feel lonely.

We haven't heard a word from you, except that one little letter to Nina's – so I don't know where to address you. Frieda says you are still at the ranch. But I'll get Ida to post this on. Meanwhile,

c/o Curtis Brown, 6 Henrietta St. W. C. 2.

will always find me.

[1] The Lawrences had stayed at Garland's in February–March 1924 (see *Letters*, iv. 592–9).

[2] Mr and Mrs Millar Dunning, close friends of Murry. (Murry's other neighbours were the Tomlinsons; see Letter 3344 and n. 3.)

[3] He began work for his *Life of Jesus* (1926) at Abbotsbury.

[4] In a review of Murry's *To the Unknown God* (1924) – in *Nation and Athenæum*, 29 November 1924, p. 331 – Leonard Woolf complained about Murry's imprecision of thought but devoted special attention to his style: 'I found that Mr Murry's literary style was indistinguishable from that of one of the most famous characters' in *Martin Chuzzlewit*. Woolf then mixed sentences from Murry and Pecksniff, challenging the reader to distinguish them. (The review is reprinted in Woolf's *Essays on Literature, History, Politics etc*, 1927, pp. 240–4.)

[5] (Sir) Edward Montague Compton Mackenzie (1883–1972), novelist, and his wife Faith (1888–1960), biographer, had first met the Lawrences in August 1914; their friendship flourished best in Capri, early in 1920.

I'll go up and pack my trunk once more. But I'm getting *sick* of this travelling business.

Send us a line – we keep wondering about you.

Yrs D. H. Lawrence

3502. To Carl Seelig, 9 October 1925

Text: MS UCLA; cited in Armin Arnold, 'In the Footsteps of D. H. Lawrence in Switzerland: Some New Biographical Material', *Texas Studies in Literature and Language*, iii (Summer 1961), 188.

c/o Martin Secker, 5 John St. Adelphi, *London W. C. 2*
9 October 1925

Dear Mr Seelig[1]

I had your letter only today, as we arrived in England from America a few days ago.

Yes, the Russian novelists have meant a great deal to me – but Hamsun not so much.[2]

I found here a translation of *The Rainbow* and of *The Boy in the Bush*. I will send them to you. The Insel Verlag is now doing a translation of *Women in Love*.[3] This, with *The Rainbow* and *Sons and Lovers*, I like best of my books.

The last three years my wife and I have been in America: in Mexico and the United States. We have a little ranch in New Mexico: I expect we shall go back there in the spring. – I don't like politics at all: dont believe in them.

As for myself – *Sons and Lovers* is more or less autobiographical. But I am now forty years old.

I knew the Lake of Lucerne before the war: it can be very lovely. – In about a fortnight's time, my wife and I are going to BadenBaden, to see my Schwiegermutter. The address there is:

per adr. Frau Baronin von Richthofen, Ludwig-Wilhelmstift, *Baden Baden*.

I suppose we shall stay about two weeks: then go south, to Italy or Sicily, for the winter. I should like very much to call and see you on the way down. Will you let me know if it will be convenient for you?

Yours very Sincerely D. H. Lawrence

[1] Karl ('Carl') Wilhelm Seelig (1894–1962), Swiss journalist and editor; critic of literature, theatre and film. Trans. Swift's *Gulliver's Travels*, introd. by Hermann Hesse (Zurich, 1955). m. (1) 1921, Maria Margareta Deutsch (1898–); divorced 1928; (2) 1933, Martha Rosalie Suter (1892–).

[2] Knut Hamsun (1859–1952), Norwegian novelist best known for the novel translated as *Hunger* (1890).

[3] The translator was Thesi Mutzenbecher (Insel Verlag, 1927); see also p. 558 n. 3. See also p. 38. n. 2.

3503. To Martin Secker, [9 October 1925]

Text: MS UInd; Postmark, Nottingham OCT 9 1925; Secker 65.

c/o Mrs S. King. 16 Brooklands Rd, Sneinton Hill. Nottingham
Friday

Dear Secker

Of course I'm in bed with a cold, the moment I come here.

Could you send me that monograph by Shane Leslie on Frederick Rolfe, as soon as possible?[1] I am doing the review on *Hadrian The Seventh*, and should like a few facts. I'll send you the novel when I've done: I believe it would interest you.

A letter from a Swiss publisher, very enthusiastic about the German translations of me.

We give up the thought of taking a house in England: stay with my sisters till about the 20th, then go south.

It's melancholy up here too – but I don't smell much communism.

Remember us to Adrian the numberless, and Rina, and also salutations to Mrs Lamont.[2]

Yrs D. H. Lawrence

3504. To Catherine Carswell, [13 October 1925]

Text: MS YU; cited in Moore, *Intelligent Heart* 346.

c/o Mrs W. E. Clarke, Gee St. Ripley near Derby
Tuesday

My dear Catherine

I read *The Natural Man* and thought it very good indeed.[3] It's a pity it doesn't have a trifle more definite a conclusion – I don't mean ending merely. One hates war-books, reads them a bit under protest, and demands some sort of definite attitude afterwards: else one just can't stand it. But I think the actual *war* is exceedingly well done. Sometimes there ought to have been a bit whiter, intenser flame, I think. The Paris episode so easily becomes merely feeble and ridiculous, unless there is shown some *positive* feeling on the man's

[1] Presumably a reference to Shane Leslie's account in the *London Mercury* (1923) which was enlarged as the introduction to Corvo's *In his Own Image* (1924 edn). See also Letter 3506 and n. 1.

[2] Lucy Lamont, née Smart (1859–1953), widow of Thomas Reynolds Lamont (1826–98), Scottish genre painter and watercolourist. She had befriended Secker for over twenty years. He lived with her and her sister, Mercy Smart, at Bridgefoot, Iver, before his marriage in 1921 (at which she was a witness) and for several years after it.

[3] *The Natural Man* (Grant Richards, July 1924), a vivid war-novel by Catherine Carswell's younger brother, George Gordon MacFarlane (1885–1949), under his pseudonym Patrick Miller (see *Letters*, iii. 146 n. 4). The book was not published in USA.

part: not just diffidence. Diffidence, somehow, doesn't altogether meet the demands. The same often: a deliberate sort of diffidence and 'don't care', a numbness which is a sort of paralysis slowly creeping over the affective system. It takes away from the punch of the book: as if there were not quite enough powder in the cartridge. – But it's good, very good creation of the war. – Should have had a different title, in my opinion. One wonders very much what the next book will be like. – Grant Richards isn't much good as a publisher, is he?

We're going to Ripley tomorrow. The weather's awful, and we simply hate it up here. Frieda wants to go to London on Saturday – I may stay a couple of days longer. Probably we shall neither of us get to town till Monday.

It might be rather nice to stay in Gordons flat for a week, before we leave England.[1] That would be next week. Is it feasible, do you think? And already I've lost the address, found it again! – Of course we'd pay a rent.

I wonder if *The Natural Man* is done in America.

I'll send you a Midland pork pie from Ripley: they are good.

Anyhow we'll see you next week.

Oh Lord! let me pay when you're hard up! – what's the odds anyhow!

Oh how it wearies me here.

Greet Don and the young cyclist.

DHL

Have written direct to Gordon, to 12 Cardigan Rd.

3505. To Gordon MacFarlane, [13 October 1925]

Text: MS Carswell; Unpublished.

c/o Mrs W. E. Clarke, *Ripley* near Derby
Tuesday

Dear Gordon Macfarlane

Catherine gave me *The Natural Man* to read. I think it's extremely good of the war: the best I've read. I will talk with you about it, when we meet, if you like.

Do you think Frieda and I might stay in your Gower St. flat next week? I expect we shall get back in town on Monday. But if it's a nuisance, don't bother. We might stay seven days, then Paris.

Ugh! I hate it, the rain and dark and dismalness here.

My wife sends greetings, and to Mrs Macfarlane,[2] with mine.

Yrs D. H. Lawrence

[1] They stayed in MacFarlane's flat at 73 Gower Street, WC1, 22–9 October.

[2] Née Nancy ('Nannie') Niemeyer (d. 1942).

If we can come, we pay a rent: passed nem. con. Never knew you'd got a book! Is it out in America?

3506. To Nancy Pearn, [13 October 1925]

Text: MS UT; Unpublished.

c/o Mrs W. E. Clarke, *Ripley* near Derby
Tuesday

Dear Miss Pearn

I promised this review to the *New York Herald–Tribune*.[1] Would you please have it typed for me, and send a copy to Barmby, for Mrs Carl Van Doran, of the *N. Y. Tribune* – and if anybody likes to use the review in England, they're welcome.

Awfully dull and depressing weather here. I expect we shall be back in a week, and go straight to Paris. I'll let you know.

Best wishes. D. H. Lawrence

3507. To Catherine Carswell, [15 October 1925]

Text: MS YU; Unpublished.

c/o Mrs W.E. Clarke, Ripley near Derby
Thursday

My dear Catherine

Hope the pie will be good –

I'll let you know when we leave here.

DHL

3508. To Gordon MacFarlane, [16 October 1925]

Text: MS Carswell; cited in Moore, *Poste Restante* 84.

c/o Mrs W.E. Clarke, *Ripley*, Derby
Friday

Dear Gordon Macfarlane

Thanks for your letter – I don't think we shall get to London till Wednesday or even Thursday. – If you get a let, don't think of us. If not, we'd like the flat for at least a week. But I've lost the Gower St. number, and am not sure even if this Richmond one is right.

Haste! D. H. Lawrence

Expect we shall be here till Wednesday.

[1] Probably the review of Corvo's *Hadrian the Seventh* (cf. Letter 3503) which was intended for the *New York Herald Tribune Books* (see Letter 3513), but see Letter 3481 and n. 5.

3509. To Martin Secker, [16 October 1925]

Text: MS UInd; Postmark, Nottingham OCT 16 1925; Huxley 639–40.

c/o Mrs W. E. Clarke. *Ripley*, Derby
Friday

Dear Secker

Oh dear! the next to the last galley of 'Quetzalcoatl' is missing: galley 156.[1] Could you send it me at once? I think we shall stay here till next Wednesday.

I still say, this is the most important of all my novels. But I hate sending it out into the world.

Been motoring all over my well-known Derbyshire: one of the most interesting counties in England. But I can't look at the body of my past, the spirit seems to have flown.

In the proofs, the word *serape* is spelt half the time *sarape*. Both ways are correct, it's an Indian word. But ought one to stick to one form. God knows why I changed. I began sarape, wrote serape for thirty or forty galleys, then went back to sarape. Bore!

I'll come in to your office soon as we get back.

Greet all at Bridgefoot!

Tell the man, very nice man, in your office, I *do* mean what Ramón means – for all of us.[2]

Wiedersehen. D. H. Lawrence

3510. To Catherine Carswell, [17 October 1925]

Text: MS YU; Postmark, [Ripl]ey [. . .] OC 25; cited in Carswell 229.

c/o Mrs W.E.Clarke. Gee St. *Ripley*. Derby
Sat.

My dear Catherine

Had a wire from Gordon, asking us to Gower St. I'm so afraid he'll be expecting us Monday, though I wrote him last night – to 12 Cardigan Rd. Richmond – saying we think of staying here till Wed. – or even Thursday. But he is away, so may not get the letter.

And have I his address right? Like a fool, I have *again* mislaid the letter. And what is the number of Gower St? Is it 73?

I don't think we'll be later than Thursday, getting to town: and we'd be there most probably by lunch: so *do* come to tea.

The pie was a poor one, I'm afraid. When the maid came back, she said she had sent the biggest they had in the shop: but I'm afraid it was hardly worth sending.

[1] This galley is missing from one of the surviving sets of proofs: see Roberts E313h.

[2] A letter from Secker to Knopf (see p. 320 n. 1) suggests that 'the man' was P. P. Howe.

This time Don must get that job.

I'm weary of past things – like one's home regions – and dont want to look at them.

So sorry to bother you about the address.

Comparative opulence here – *comparative*, of course – judging by old home standards. I liked the old better, *then*: but don't want it back.

Au revoir to you three – I think it's nicer for J[ohn] P[atrick] to be able to buy himself little things he wants.

DHL

3511. To Alfred Stieglitz, 20 October 1925

Text: MS YU; Postmark, [. . .] 20 OC 25; Unpublished.

c/o Curtis Brown, 6 Henrietta St, London W.C. 2
20 Oct 1925

Dear Alfred Stieglitz[1]

Had your note today. I was in New York in September, and should have liked to see you: also to see Georgia O'Keefe, and some of her things. I hope when I come through – in the spring D. V. – I may see you then, and the cloud 'snapshots', your equivalents as you call them.

If I can remember, I'll have the Centaur Bookshop of Philadelphia send you my *Reflections on the Death of a Porcupine*: I know you'd like them.

I shall write to you when I come to New York next.

Yours D. H. Lawrence

3512. To Nancy Pearn, 20 October 1925

Text: MS UT; Unpublished.

c/o Mrs W.E. Clarke, Ripley (Derby)
20 Oct 1925

Dear Miss Pearn

I send you another little review for the *New York Tribune*.[2] Will you be so good as to have it typed, and charged to me, – and send it to New York. Hope it's not a bore.

We expect to be back in London on *Thursday afternoon*. I think we shall stay in Gordon Macfarlane's flat, 73 Gower Street: for a week or so, then go to Paris.

[1] Alfred Stieglitz (1864–1946), distinguished American photographer who had congratulated DHL on his *Studies in Classic American Literature* in September 1923 (*Letters*, iv. 499 and n. 2). Georgia O'Keefe (1887–1986), American modernist painter whose work was first exhibited in Stieglitz's avant-garde '291' Gallery, in 1916; she became his second wife in 1928.

[2] Of Pickthall's *Saïd the Fisherman* (see Letter 3481 and n. 4).

We've motored all over my native Derbyshire since we are here. It's a very interesting county.

If you want me to see anybody, fix it up, will you.

Yours D. H. Lawrence

3513. To Alfred and Blanche Knopf, 20 October 1925

Text: Moore 860–1.

Ripley, Derby
20 October 1925

Dear Knopf and Mrs Knopf:

I've sent the proofs of the *Plumed Serpent* back to Secker, so you should have a revised set very soon now.[1]

Will you please put under the title, on the title page, 'Quetzalcoatl' – so it is obvious that *The Plumed Serpent* is a translation.

THE PLUMED SERPENT
(QUETZALCOATL)

Another thing is the word *serape*: which is spelt so often *sarape*, that I simply didn't face altering it. Both ways are correct: it's an Indian word for a blanket that you wear: but *serape* is now commoner. God knows why I changed from one to the other. If you think it matters, tell the printers to set the one form, will you?

I still think it is my most important novel: never mind the weary public. It too has got to grow up. But my 'Quetzalcoatl' novel will stand a lot of wear.

I have sent reviews of *Hadrian VII* and of *Säid the Fisherman* to the *Tribune*. Hope they suit. I liked these two books very much. Very nice the Blue Jade Library. Would you care to put into it the Dutch masterpiece – or semi-masterpiece, it's no better than *Hadrian* – *Max Havelaar*. A man I know did a new translation, and asked me to write him an introduction.[2]

[1] Secker posted the proofs on 23 October as is clear from his letter to Knopf of that date (Secker Letter-Book, UIll):

Dear Knopf

I have posted to you today by registered post the whole of the slip proofs of "The Plumed Serpent" corrected by the author, so that your printers will now be able to go straight ahead. There is no occasion for Lawrence to see revises. I have not read the work in detail, but Howe has done so, and from what he has told me and from my own excursions into the text I feel I have a good idea of the work. I agree with you that it cannot be popular, but it is a book to which Lawrence himself attaches great importance, as I can well understand. Its Mexican setting should help it in America. Personally, I want Lawrence to write a long book in the "Lost Girl" vein, and as tactfully as I can I am suggesting that. I am seeing a good deal of him just now, and his plans for the immediate future are quite unfixed, but he wants to start a new book very soon, moving to Italy to do so.

Do you think you will be able to fix a date in January for publication?

Yours sincerely

[2] DHL wrote an introduction in May 1926; Siebenhaar's translation was published by Knopf in January 1927 in his Blue Jade Library (Roberts B21).

I'm going to do a review now of *Origins of Prohibition*.[1] – I don't think much of *Jezebel Pettyfer*: a bit spurious. And the Mencken *Americana* is already done. If you want me to do anything else that's not been done – *Life of Henri Brulard* – or the *Diaboliques* – or *Cook's Voyages*[2] – I like them all – they're worth a review too – would you ask Mrs Carl Van Doren at the *N. Y. Tribune*? I think my two reviews are rather nice.

It's pretty awful weather here. My God! this country isn't an isle in the sea, it's under the sea, and the people are all marine specimens. Drive me mad. But they're chirping up a bit about trade. Hope it's not a false dawn. There's no *kick* in the people: they're about as active as seaweed.

We're in Derbyshire at the moment, but going back to town. Expect we shall be in Paris by first week in November: and I think we shall go down to Ragusa, Dalmatia, for the winter: see if it's nice. Anything for space, and sun.

The Seckers in their red house lie anchored forever in the mist.

If you see Mark Wiseman, tell him we've been twice at the *Peacock* and he's remembered very smilingly there.[3]

But my native land seems to be turning to liquid.

Hope all flourishes: no more black eyes.

3514. To Joseph Foster, [26 October 1925]

Text: MS Foster; PC v. [London street-scene]; Postmark, London OCT 2[. . .] 25; Foster, *D. H. Lawrence in Taos*, p. 287.

[73 Gower St. W.C. 1.]
26 Oct.

How are you all! It pours with rain here, so we're fleeing south. Send a line sometime – c/o Curtis Brown, 6 Henrietta St. London W.C. 1.

D. H. Lawrence

3515. To Margaret King, [26 October 1925]

Text: MS Needham; PC v. London. St Paul's from Bankside; Postmark, [Lo]ndon OCT 26 [. . .]; Unpublished.

73 Gower St. W.C. 1.
Monday

We plan to leave here on Thursday afternoon – direct to Baden Baden – I

[1] See Letter 3481 and n. 3.

[2] The works referred to are: Haldane Macfall, *The Wooings of Jezebel Pettyfer* (1898; Knopf reissued 1925); H. L. Mencken, ed. *Americana 1925* (Knopf, 1925); Stendhal, *The Life of Henri Brulard*, trans. Catherine A. Phillips (Knopf, 1925); Jules Amédée Barbey D'Auréuilly, *Les Diaboliques*, trans. Ernest Boyd (Knopf, 1925); James Cook, *Voyages of Discovery*, ed. John Barrow (Knopf, 1925).

[3] 'The Peacock' is a well-known hotel in Rowsley, about 6 miles n.w. of Matlock, Derbyshire. Wiseman has not been identified.

don't want to be in Paris in pouring rain. – Was so nice to see you all – but keep alert.

Love. DHL

3516. To John Middleton Murry, [26 October 1925]
Text: MS NYPL; Huxley 640.

73 Gower St. W.C. 1.
Monday

Dear Jack

We gave up the idea of staying in England – We leave for BadenBaden on Thursday.

Could you come up on Wednesday – Come here, we'll see about a room for you. And I'll make no arrangements with Anybody for Wednesday.

I met The Constant Nymph and Rose Macaulay on Friday!![1] Also Wm Gerhardi: he's nice: said he was coming here tomorrow afternoon.[2] You might meet him. – Was in the Oxford Press this morning. Humphrey Milford said he liked your Keats book very much:[3] but not the *Adelphi* – Must you really write about Jesus? Jesus becomes more unsympatisch to me, the longer I live: crosses and nails and tears and all that stuff! I think he showed us into a nice cul de sac. But there – ! – England just depresses me, like a long funeral. But I cease to quarrel. No good kicking against the pricks.[4]

Greetings to your wife and the child,[5] from us both. DHL

3517. To Earl Brewster, 26 October 1925
Text: MS UT; Brewster 83–4.

London.
26 Oct 1925

Dear Earl

We leave for *BadenBaden* on Thursday. This climate is unbearable. I expect we shall stay a fortnight with my mother-in-law

Frau Baronin von Richthofen, Ludwig-Wilhelmstift, *BadenBaden*, Germany

[1] DHL is referring to Margaret Moore Kennedy (1896–1967) by the title of her popular novel, *The Constant Nymph* (1924). Emilie Rose Macaulay (1881–1958), well-known novelist, had recently published her satire, *Orphan Island* (1924).

[2] William Alexander Gerhardie (formerly spelt 'Gerhardi') (1895–1977), novelist and critic. He had published *Futility: A Novel on Russian Themes* (1922); *Anton Chehov: A Critical Study* (1923); *The Polyglots: A Novel* (1925). For Gerhardie's account of the meeting see Nehls, iii. 10–14.

[3] Murry's *Keats and Shakespeare* was published by Oxford University Press in August 1925. For Milford see p. 105 n. 1.

[4] Cf. Acts ix. 5 (AV).

[5] Katherine Murry, b. 19 April 1925.

– then come on south. Friends want us to stay on the Italian Riviera for a time – I'm not sure. – What are your plans? Let me know.

Miss Brett said she was sailing on 24th Oct from New York, and would stay in Capri in the Hotel Webster. Look her up if you hear nothing of her, will you?

I don't feel I'm going to sit still all winter – I feel like going to Dalmatia – Ragusa, Spalato – and to Montenegro – and perhaps the Isles of Greece. I'd love that. What do you say? – Achsah, what do *you* say?

au revoir D. H. Lawrence

3518. To Edward McDonald, [26 October 1925]

Text: MS UT; PC v. The Tower of London; Postmark, London OCT 26 1925; *Centaur* 23.

c/o Curtis Brown. 6 Henrietta St, London W.C.1.
26 Oct.

Dear Dr McDonald

No, don't think of coming to England these days, it's too depressing: rain, bad trade, general gloom. We're fleeing to the Mediterranean on Thursday. I'm sure one is far better off in Philadelphia.

It was a very great pleasure meeting you and Mrs McDonald – hope we shall see you when we come back. I've done proofs of my Mexico novel: nobody will like it, but I think it's my most important. – Not a word of the *Porcupine*! – If ever I can do anything for you, *only tell me* – (Mrs McDonald, *you* tell me).

D. H. Lawrence

3519. To Martin Secker, [26 October 1925]

Text: MS UInd; Postmark, London OCT 2[. . .] 1925; Secker 66.

73 Gower St, W.C. 1.
Monday

Dear Secker

Will you bring me, tomorrow, a copy of *Women in Love* and one of *Memoirs of the Foreign Legion* – hope you won't mind carrying them.

And would you send to my sister

Mrs S. King. 16 Brooklands Rd, Sneinton Hill, Nottingham

a copy of

Women in Love
Fantasia
and *Psychoanalysis and the Uncon*

I think we shall leave Thursday afternoon.

Au revoir DHL

3520. To Ada Clarke, [26 October 1925]
Text: MS Clarke; Unpublished.

73 Gower St. W.C. 1.
Monday

My dear Sister

The suit has just come, and looks very handsome. Frieda is jealous, it is so nice: the flannel trousers too. Awfully nice of Eddie to do it for me.

I too felt very depressed, coming back to London. If only this climate were not so accursed, with a pall of smoke hanging over the perpetual funeral of the sun, we could have a house in Derbyshire and be jolly. But I always cough – so what's the good.

It's pouring with rain here now, and dark as death.

I think we shall leave on Thursday afternoon, and go direct, Ostend Brussells Strassburg. I am weary of these cities – don't want to see Paris in the rain.

We met Margaret Kennedy (*The Constant Nymph*) – and Rose Macaulay and Wm Gerhardi the other day. They didn't make much impression on me. Yesterday we lunched with Cynthia and Herbert Asquith – rather sad – and a feeling of failure. She is now turning to literature, and trying to write. God knows what the result will be. She's done a children's book already – I've not read it yet.[1]

I was at the Oxford University Press today, and ordered you a copy of the *History*. Apparently they are doing well with it. The Irish Free State have ordered it as a text book: but on condition we take out every word of praise of Martin Luther, and any suggestion that any Pope may have erred.[2] Fools! But I don't care. Herbert Asquith says the present Duke of Rutland wants to go and live at Haddon Hall: is even getting it ready. He's Cynthia's brother in law.[3] If they do it, we'll make Cynthia ask us there, just to see how they do it.

I'll look for some toys for Bertram in BadenBaden – I simply haven't the heart to go into these shops.

Oh, the parcel was here when we arrived, and a great treasure. I duly take

[1] *The Flying Carpet* had been published in September 1925.

[2] The censoring of *Movements in European History* for the Irish edition (September 1926) was undertaken by Patrick O'Daly (1874–1932), a director of the Educational Company of Ireland. DHL probably collected from OUP the copy of the illustrated edn of *Movements* (May 1925) which had been marked by O'Daly and which DHL later referred to as 'mauled' (Letter 3543). (For the full story of the Irish edn see Philip Crumpton, 'D. H. Lawrence's "mauled history": The Irish Edition of *Movements in European History*', *DHL Review*, xiii (Summer 1980), 105–18.)

[3] John Henry, 9th Duke of Rutland (1886–1940) succeeded to the title on 8 May 1925; one of the family seats is Haddon Hall, 6 miles n.w. of Matlock. The Duke's sister was the widow of Hugo Lord Elcho (1884–1916), Lady Cynthia's brother.

the malt. And so many people had a bit of the fowl, and blessed Gertie's midnight labours.

We'll be back in the spring, then we can really stay.

Love DHL

They said at Curtis Browns they forwarded a cablegram to me to Ripley, last Thursday – but no sign of it! Yet all the other letters came!

3521. To Catherine Carswell, [26 October 1925]

Text: MS YU; PC v. London: Law Courts; Postmark, [. . .] OCT 2[. . .] 25; Unpublished.

[73 Gower St. W.C. 1.]
Monday

No, we are quite all right in this little flat – so *much* more free than in an hotel. Gordon and Nancy are coming to supper tonight. We think to leave 2.0 p. m Thursday. What time will you be in?

DHL

3522. To Irita van Doren, 27 October 1925

Text: MS LC; Unpublished.

c/o Curtis Brown. 6 Henrietta St, London W.C.1.
27 Oct 1925

Dear Mrs Van Doren

I sent two reviews, of *Hadrian The Seventh* and *Säid the Fisherman*. Now I'm doing one of *Origins of Prohibition*. Hope those I sent are more or less what you want. Tell me, will you? Has anyone done for you Oliver Onion's *Whom God Hath Sundered*? I just read it. I'll do that for you, if you wish.[1] And if anything comes in, that you'd like me to review, send it along. It amuses me, this winter, to leave my own books alone, and go for other men's.

My wife and I leave England tomorrow: expect we shall winter in Italy.

Hope all goes well with your family. Say Howdy to Carl van Doren from me – and greet Dr Sherman when you see him.

Sincerely D. H. Lawrence

3523. To Emily King, 27 October 1925

Text: MS Lazarus; Unpublished.

Frau Baronin von Richthofen, Ludwig-Wilhelmstift, *BadenBaden*, Germany
27 Oct. 1925

My dear Pamela

Your letter just come. Of course those school people won't want to let Peg

[1] Secker published Onions' trilogy in October 1925; no review of it by DHL ever appeared.

out of their clutches. A B.A. and a B.Sc. are not much good, except for a teacher. But I don't know anything about a commercial degree. I should be tempted anyway to take Peg from Mundella.[1] We'll hope she won't have to earn her living all her life. And if she's going to marry, then she'd better start to live and move a bit. Study is bad for her, making her slow, and physically stupid. I wouldn't let her cram, not for another day.

We leave on Thursday, direct to BadenBaden. I don't like big cities. We've seen a lot of people this week: now I've had enough.

And you ought to give a good heave, to get out of that Carlton shop. It's time you all spat on your hands, and took a fresh grip on life. You're going inert, which is no good.

Au revoir, then, till Spring. DHL

3524. To Hon Dorothy Brett, 28 October 1925

Text: MS UCin; Postmark, London OCT 29 1925; Irvine, Brett 54–5.

73 Gower St. W.C. 1.
28 Oct 1925

Dear Brett

We leave tomorrow for BadenBaden – it was all fixed up when I got your cable. But what can have made you come to England? – your passport was all right.

Murry is here this evening, much quieter, he seems: really settled down with his wife and child in Dorset: with the Dunnings next door. I don't think it's much good your seeing him. He's going back tomorrow.

Shall you go on to Capri? The Brewsters, and Faith Mackenzie, Compton Mackenzie's wife, are both expecting you there. We may stay on the Italian Riviera for a while: Frieda wants to have her children there, not too far. Better, I think, for you to go to Capri.

I'm glad to be leaving England – find it oppressive. If you needed a tiny flat for a week or two, probably you could have this, though it's not very nice – from Gordon Macfarlane – 2 guineas a week, and a good cook-charwoman.

There's no news. But write to BadenBaden to tell us what happened in New York. The address is

c/o Frau von Richthofen, Ludwig-Wilhelmstift, *BadenBaden*, Germany.

We met a few people – The Constant Nymph, and Rose Macaulay, Wm Gerhardi – but nothing that makes any difference – nothing to matter at all. Not much point in being here.

Send a line to BadenBaden.

DHL

[1] Her Grammar School in Nottingham.

3525. To Martin Secker, [30 October 1925]

Text: MS UInd; Postmark, Baden-Baden 30.10.25; Secker 66.

c/o Frau von Richthofen, Ludwig-Wilhelmstift,[1] *BadenBaden*
Friday

Dear Secker

Got here all right – but had to motor from Strasburg – Cooks told me the connections all wrong.

I went and left my nice new felt hat at 73 Gower St. If Rina is bringing a hatbox, I wish she'd put it in. It's been worn a few times. The woman at 73 is Mrs Woodhouse – I'll write her. And if you could send your boy for it, I'd be glad.

Im sorry to bother you, really – but you're so goodnatured about these things.

Grüsse DHL

If Rina's *not* bringing a hatbox, tell her not to bother at all.

3526. To Carl Seelig, [31 October 1925]

Text: MS SIU; Unpublished.

per Adr Frau Baronin von Richthofen, Ludwig Wilhelmstift,
BadenBaden
31 Novem 1925

Dear Carl Seelig

Please forgive the pencil – my pen is dry, and ink is still to seek.

We got here yesterday – lovely sunny Schwarzwald autumn – but always like something one remembers in a dream, not quite actual or present. I think we shall stay two weeks, then set off south. Will you be at home then? – that is, about Thursday, 12th November? – Myself, I ought to have gone to Paris: but I dreaded another large city, in the rain of autumn.

Many thanks for the books: the *Jahreszeiten* is *very* attractive, print and woodcuts and all – and I'm reading the poems.[2]

I send a passport photograph of myself:[3] but you'd know us anyhow – my beard.

Best wishes. D. H. Lawrence

[1] c/o Frau . . . Wilhelmstift] Hotel Eden

[2] Seelig sent his own compilation, *Die Jahreszeiten im Spiegel Schweizerischer Volkssprüche* (Zurich, 1925).

[3] According to Seelig (in *Neue Zürcher Zeitung*, 23 May 1957) DHL wrote on the reverse of the photograph: 'more or less'.

3527. To Emily King, [31 October 1925]

Text: MS Needham; PC v. [Scene by a lake]; Postmark, Baden-Baden 1.11.25; Unpublished.

BadenBaden.
Sat

We motored here from Strasburg yesterday – Frieda's mother looking older, moving much slower – otherwise everything about the same, very quiet, rather poor.

DHL

3528. To John Middleton Murry, [31 October 1925]

Text: MS NYPL; Huxley 641.

c/o Frau von Richthofen, LudwigWilhelmstift, *BadenBaden*
Sat 31 Oct

Dear Jack

I'm sorry I missed you – I hurried straight to the house, on the obvious way. I had such a nice bag of fruit for you to take home, with fresh figs and dates and Carlsbad plums. But perhaps you'd have hated carrying it, so heavy.

Just the same here – very quiet and unemerged: my mother-in-law older, noticeably. I make my bows and play whist with old Excellenzen: *Aber Excellenzchen*! cries my mother-in-law. Titles still in full swing here, but nothing else. No foreigners. Shades of Edward VII and Russian princes. The Rhine villages untouched and lovely: we had to motor from Strassburg: and the peasants still peasants, with a bit of that eternal earth-to-earth quality that is so lost in England. Rather like a still sleep, with frail dreams.

I read your November *Adelphi*.[1] Don't you see, there still *has* to be a Creator? Jesus is not the Creator, even of himself. And we have to go on being created. By the Creator. – More important to me than Jesus. – But of course God-the-Father, the Dieu-Père, is a bore. Jesus is as far as one can go with god, anthropomorphically. After that, no more anthropos.

Perhaps I'll write you a little article.

Regards to your wife, and to the baby. DHL

We're in the Hotel Eden – once really grand, now we only pay 9/6 a day, for food and all – each – and huge room with bathroom. Try the Schwarzwald one day.

[1] It contained Murry's article, 'A Simple Creed'.

3529. To Harold Mason, 2 November 1925

Text: MS (Photocopy) UT; *Centaur* 24–5.

c/o Frau Baronin von Richthofen, Ludwig Wilhelmstift, *Baden Baden*, Germany
2 Novem 1925

Dear Mason

I have fled again from my native land: it seems to me sunk in damp and gloom, beyond all bearing. Here we are only a bit better: visiting my wife's mother. Talk about departed grandeur, that's Baden! with the departure so terribly positive, one doesn't know what to do. I spend my time running away into the hills and the Black Forest, and coming home to talk aimiabilities (can't even spell the damn word, hate it so) and play whist with ancient Barons, Baronesses, Counts and Excellencies. I can hardly believe my own ears when I hear myself saying (in German, of course) – But, Excellence, those are trumps! Seems to me I need a life-belt.

We leave, pray god, about the 12th – stay a day or two with a man in Lucerne,[1] then to Italy. McDonald says he wants to go to England for a year. For heavens sake, prevent him: it's dismal plus.

Barmby wrote you had fixed up with him about the *Porcupine*, and expects it to be out end of this month. Fine!!! – as the Americans say so often. Did you ever write to Secker, or didn't you want to, about proofs? Ça m'est égal![2] I put a list of people to whom I want you to send a copy of the *Porcupine*, please. Hope it's not troubling you too much. Don't send *me* a copy till I send you a sure address.

Remember us warmly to the winzige gnädige Frau.[3]

Grüsse D. H. Lawrence

Mrs L. A. Clarke. Gee St. *Ripley* (Derby), England.
Mrs. S. King. 16 Brooklands Rd. Sneinton Hill, *Nottingham* (England)
John Middleton Murry. The Old Coastguard Station, *Abbotsbury*. Dorset.
Hon. Dorothy Brett. c/o The Viscount Esher, The Roman Camp. Callander. Perthshire, Scotland
Miss Barbara Low.[4] 13 Guilford St. London W.C. 1.

[1] Carl Seelig. [2] 'It's all the same to me!' [3] 'tiny lady'.

[4] Barbara Low (1877–1955) had known DHL since 1915 (see *Letters*, ii. 279). She was a pioneer in psychoanalysis in England; during March 1921 DHL briefly considered her as his London literary agent until he decided to employ Curtis Brown (see ibid., iii. 684, 699).

3530. To Catherine Carswell, [2 November 1925]

Text: MS YU; PC v. H. Hoffmann, Schwarzwaldferie; Postmark, Baden-Baden 2.11.25.; cited in Carswell 230–1.

c/o Frau von Richthofen. LudwigWilhelmstift
2 Nov.

Had a quick journey here – but no trains across the Rhine from Strasburg, so had to come by motor. Cooks were all wrong about trains. My mother-in-law looking older, slower, but still very lively, walks uphill to us in our hotel. She asks for news of you. – We shall stay about ten days longer. This place is unbelievably quiet and deserted – really deserted. Nobody comes any more: it's nothing but ghosts, from the Turgenev period.

DHL

3531. To Mabel Dodge Luhan, 2 November 1925

Text: MS Brill; Luhan 289.

c/o Frau Baronin von Richthofen, Ludwig Wilhelmstift, *Baden Baden*, Germany
2 Nov 1925

Dear Mabel

I have just got your letter. We are moving on to Italy in about two weeks' time, expect to winter there. When we get a settled address, I will write to Havelock Ellis, if you wish, for your M.S. Then I will write to you what I think of it, as far as I can; and if you really wish it.

Frieda's mother seems really older, than two years ago. But she still is brisk. This place is quiet as death.

I didn't care much for New York, the eight days we were there this time. Seemed stale.

This morning I was up at the Altes Schloss, looking over the Rhine valley: where we'd motored across, from Strassburg. Queer thing, to have a past!

Grüsse D. H. Lawrence

3532. To Gertrude Cooper, [2 November 1925]

Text: MS Clarke; PC v. Baden-Baden . . . Nach einem Original von H. Hoffmann; Postmark, Baden-Baden 2.11.25.; Unpublished.

BadenBaden.
2 Novem.

Had your letter just as we left: don't you be doing things for other people all the time, as you did for us. – I want to send some toys for Bertram, there are such amusing things here. But this place is more deserted every time we come: really terrible. The great places just stand empty. – It's a bit misty, but not cold, and I go off alone into the hills, through the woods. Wish you could all pop over – it's lovely really, old castles, and the Rhine in the distance.

Love. DHL

3533. To Nancy Pearn, 2 November 1925
Text: MS UT; Unpublished.

c/o Frau Baronin von Richthofen, Ludwig Wilhelmstift, *BadenBaden*, Germany
2 Nov. 1925.

Dear Miss Pearn

Could you please get the copies of *The Calendar* and *The Criterion* containing 'The Princess' and 'The Woman Who Rode Away'; and send them to my sister-in-law:

Frau Dr Jaffé-Richthofen, Bismarkstr 17, *Heidelberg*, Germany

She wants to translate them into German.[1]

We shall be here another ten days, I suppose. See me playing whist with old Baronesses, Countesses and Excellencies, and behaving like the sweetest house-spaniel. My God, I couldn't keep it up for long.

Would you please ask Miss Barnes, or whoever it is forwards my mail, to be so very kind as to dab on the extra stamps necessary for 'abroad.' My poor old Schwiegermutter has to have the postman up every time, to pay him the excess.

I want, *really*, to do some short things, the moment we are settled.

Sincerely D. H. Lawrence

I enclose remains of my English stamps – will you please put Jonathan Cape's address on the letter.[2]

3534. To Dr Anton Kippenberg, 2 November 1925
Text: MS GSArchiv; Unpublished.

per Adr. Frau von Richthofen, Ludwig-Wilhelmstift, *BadenBaden*.
2 Novem. 1925

Dear Dr Kippenberg

My wife and I are in BadenBaden for a couple of weeks. I found my copy of the *Almanach* here at my mother-in-law's: amusing, the 'Rosalino' article, in German.[3] I wish you would let your clerks send me two more copies.

[1] 'The Princess' had been published in the *Calendar of Modern Letters* March–May 1925 (Roberts C128–30); for the publication of 'The Woman Who Rode Away' see p. 71 n. 1. See also p. 288 n. 1.

[2] The letter to Cape is missing.

[3] The translation (by Franz Franzius) of 'The Mozo' (Roberts C151) appeared in *Insel Almanach für das Jahr 1926* (Leipzig: Insel-Verlag, [1925]), pp. 103–19.

My sister-in-law, Frau Dr Jaffe, would so much like to translate my new novel. I think she did *The Boy in the Bush* very well indeed. She knows me, and, it seems to me, she gets my rhythm so well: perhaps a little lighter, quicker than Herr Franzius.[1] – The new novel: *The Plumed Serpent* ('Quetzalcoatl') – appears in England in February. It is about Mexico. To me, it is perhaps my most important novel, so far; but it will not be popular, and I don't know if you will care for it. But anyhow my sister-in-law would like to translate it. Will you please tell me how you feel about that? If you wish, I will ask Martin Secker to send you a set of proofs at once.

I am glad you are going ahead with the translations, the Insel Verlag is always a pride and a pleasure.

With best wishes D. H. Lawrence

3535. To Hon. Dorothy Brett, 4 November 1925

Text: MS UCin; Moore 863–4.

c/o Frau Baronin von Richthofen, Ludwig-Wilhelmstift, *Baden Baden*
4 Novem 1925

Dear Brett

So you are back in the old milieu![2] Hope it's not so bad after all. I can't imagine *what* was wrong with your passport: it seemed to me all right.

I found England very damp and dreary: there's something about it, some sort of funking the issue, that I can't stand. The Constant Nymph was quite nice, but nothing. Gerhardi came to see me for an hour, and stayed seven hours. I like him, but nothing further: not worth while going on with. Murry came, and was very quiet, and quite nice, but nothing between us. He's slowly burying himself, and hates to be disturbed. Can't bear to be away for a day from Abbotsbury. His Keats book is quite good: of course a golden image of himself, except he never wrote 'Endymion', and is so much the wiser. I didn't see Kot: felt I couldn't stand any more. Went to Cynthia Asquith's – more sense of failure. – By the way, the letter you sent me to forward to Catherine Carswell inexplicably disappeared, so never got sent. I'm so sorry. Her address, if you want it, is *Hawthorn Cottage, Great Kingshill. High Wycombe. Bucks.* She is very poor, Don still has no work. My sisters were very nice: we stayed two weeks in the Midlands, and I coughed like the devil, with the filthy air. Frieda saw her children: Barby, the young one, engaged to an absolute nothingness of a fellow, 35, would-be-artist, born failure, sponge on a womans emotions. Now she's breaking it off: it's too ridiculous. Elsa, the elder, doing a job and quite bouncy. – Privately, I can't stand Frieda's children. They have a

[1] See p. 38 n. 2 and also Letter 3867.

[2] Brett was staying in Mayfair with her brother Oliver.

sort of suburban bounce and *suffisance* which puts me off. When they appear, I shall disappear. The boy kept his loftiness to the Vic[toria] and Albert Museum, and soon, very probably, will sit in one of the glass cases, as a specimen of the perfect young Englishmen.

Here I am stunned with hearing old ladies talk German, and having to talk back, and having to play whist with ancient Baronesses, Countesses and Excellencies. I have behaved very well so far, but am getting restive. We are due to leave on the 12th – tomorrow week: probably stay a day or two in Lucerne, to see a man there, then to the Riviera. Martin Secker's wife lives (her family) in Spotorno, she's just gone there, and we shall probably fix up for a while somewhere in that region: don't know yet. – The Brewsters and Compton Mackenzie's wife, Faith Mackenzie, are expecting you in Capri. I don't know what we shall do in the long run. – I don't at present want to go back to America, even to the ranch: feel more like drifting east. But we'll see. – I'm glad you liked New York, and profited by it. More than I can say for myself. Glad you didn't go to the Witts, though the girl is nice. – I ordered your copy of the *Porcupine* c/o your father. Secker is doing 250 copies of *David* at 2 guineas – will send you one.[1] That Miss Lewisohn was still considering the play, when Barmby wrote last. I don't care a damn. Feel like going my way for a bit, and sending the rest to Hell. Hot and moist here, but fine country, and I walk off alone. Train will probably be cheaper than boat, to Naples. Go to Thomas Cook in Ludgate Circus. I feel awfully annoyed with Aaron. It is probably a porcupine quill worked in: something of that: no good trusting to William. – This address always finds us, till I send another.

DHL

It is just possible you might be cured by Hypnosis but it's risky. If you like you can ask Dr Eder. 2 Harley Place. Marylebone Rd. – He knows all about those things, and is a friend of mine, a *nice* man, not a liar. He's poor, pay him a little fee: but he'll do you for nothing if you tell him it's from me. Look up the address in the telephone book: but I think I'm right.

3536. To Carl Seelig, [6 November 1925]

Text: MS SIU; Moore 864.

c/o Frau Baronin von Richthofen, Ludwig-Wilhelmstift, *BadenBaden*
Saturday 6 Novem.

Dear Carl Seelig

That is very nice of you and of Frau Seelig, to say you will meet us at

[1] Secker's limited edn of *David: A Play* (actually of 500 copies) was published in March 1926 at 15/-(Roberts A34). Secker had offered to produce an edn of 'anything between 500 copies at 21/- and 250 at 42/-' (letter to Curtis Brown, 30 October 1925, Secker Letter-Book, UIll).

Lucerne. We propose to leave here at 10.16 on Thursday morning, arriving at Lucerne at 4.45 the same afternoon. Perhaps you will look in the Swiss Fahrplan, to see if this is correct.

My German is pretty bad, but it will do. There is no need to bother with English.

I wonder how serious the Italian trouble is.[1] We want to go down to the Italian Riviera for the winter. – So we can leave our big luggage at the station in Lucerne, and go on to Italy by the Gotthardt I suppose – on Friday or Saturday.

But it is great fun stopping off in Switzerland to see you: and I love the VierwaldstätterSee.

Grüsse D. H. Lawrence

3537. To Curtis Brown, 10 November 1925

Text: MS UT; Unpublished.

per Adr Frau Baronin von Richthofen, Ludwig Wilhelmstift, *BadenBaden*
10 Nov. 1925

Dear Curtis Brown

We leave here tomorrow – stay a day or two in Lucerne – then down to the Italian Riviera. The address there is

Hotel Miramare, *Spotorno* (Genova), Italy.

Mrs Secker has her parents there. She is with them now, writes that it is sunny and warm, and that there is a pleasant house for us to rent, if we want it. So that sounds all right. If you come out in January, I suppose we shall still be in Spotorno.

Please see that my mail is forwarded now to Italy – as soon as I have a fixed address, I will try and save you the trouble of sending it on.

Au revoir, then. D. H. Lawrence

3538. To Martin Secker, [10 November 1925]

Text: MS UInd; PC; Postmark, Baden-[Ba]den 10 11 [. . .]; Secker 66.

BadenBaden.
Wed.

We leave here tomorrow – stay a day or two in Lucerne – then to Spotorno.

[1] The previous day, 5 November, an alleged plot by an Italian general to assassinate Mussolini in Rome during the Armistice-day celebrations had been uncovered by the police.

Had a letter from R[ina] – she knows of a house. Did you get a letter from me, bothering you about a hat?

The address will be Spotorno now.

DHL

3539. To Hon. Dorothy Brett, [11 November 1925]

Text: MS UCin; PC v. [Trees and undergrowth]; Postmark, Baden-Baden 11.11.25.; Irvine, Brett 56.

BadenBaden.
Wed.

We leave tomorrow – stay in Lucerne a day or two – then the address for the time being is Hotel Miramare. *Spotorno* (Genova). It's on the Riviera Ponente and you'll pass it in the train. Don't know how long we'll be there – but probably till New Year. – Am sending you Murry on Keats – quite good, in the die-away line.

Will write to Capri.

DHL

Frieda is bobbed, permanently waved, fluffed and thc leopard hasn't changed his spots.

DHL

[Frieda Lawrence begins]

I have short hair! 'fancy' myself –

F.[1]

3540. To William Hawk, [11 November 1925]

Text: MS UT; PC v. [A Forest Scene]; Postmark, Baden-Baden 11 11.25; Unpublished.

BadenBaden
11 Nov

We leave here tomorrow – haven't seen Brett yet. – We sent a parcel with a few toys etc for the children – hope they arrive all right – keep them for Christmas – How's the ranch? – have you shut the water off yet? – Still rain here. But have hopes of Italy. Remember us to everybody.

DHL

[1] Frieda wrote on the verso of the postcard.

3541. To Martin Secker, [12 November 1925]

Text: MS UInd; PC v. Baden-Baden; Postmark, Baden-Baden 12 11 25; Secker 67.

BadenBaden.
Thursday

Just running to the train – thanks for the letter. Call the last chapter just *Here!*[1] Nice proof of *David.*

DHL

Ought we to send same title to Knopf? If so, you do it, will you?

3542. To Curtis Brown, 16 November 1925

Text: MS UT; Huxley 641–2.

c/o Signor Capellero. Villa Maria, *Spotorno* (Genova), Riviera Ponente. Italy[2]
16 Novem 1925.

Dear Curtis Brown

We got here yesterday – it's lovely and sunny, with a blue sea, and I'm sitting out on the balcony just above the sands, to write. Switzerland was horrid – I don't like Switzerland anyhow – in slow rain and snow. – We shall find ourselves a villa here, I think, for the time.

I am enclosing Secker's agreement for *David.*

I had your letter with copy of Knopf's this morning. I know Knopf doesn't like limited editions – and he also likes to be important. But it doesn't seem to me to matter vastly. Secker gets all the first edition sales, even if he doesn't sell sheets. And anyhow, in the sunshine, one cares so very much less.

Yrs D. H. Lawrence

3543. To Vere Collins, [17 November 1925]

Text: MS SIU; Moore, *Intelligent Heart* 347–8.

presso Sigr Capellero. Villa Maria, *Spotorno.* (Genova), Italy.
17 Nov.

Dear Collins

I'm sending the mauled *History* by this mail.[3] When I went through it, I was half infuriated, and half amused. But if I'd had to go through it, personally, and make the decision merely from myself, I'd have sent those Irish b–s seven times to hell, before I'd have moved a single iota at their pencil stroke. – But do me a favour. Please keep this particular marked copy for me, will you, when you are through with it. Send it to me back here, if you can. It will always serve to stimulate my bile, and to remind me of the glory of the human race.

[1] Chap. XXVII of *The Plumed Serpent* had lacked a title in MS, typescript and proof.

[2] DHL was using the address of Rina Secker's father, Luigi Capellero, until he had one of his own.

[3] See Letter 3520 and n. 2.

Here it's sunny. We're in hotel for a bit – probably shall look for a house for the winter here, though the village doesnt amount to much. But if the sun shines on the Mediterranean, that's a lot.

I read the volume of essays – rather soft meat – sort of chopped up eggy mess you feed young gaping goslings on.[1] My God, where are the *men* in England now? The place is one howling nursery.

Murry's *Keats* was quite good – many thanks – but oh heaven, so die-away, the text might be: Oh lap up Shakspeare till you've cleaned the dish, and you may hope to swoon into raptures and die an early but beautiful death at 25. – I'm sick to death of this maudlin twaddle – and England's rotten with it. Why doesn't somebody finally and loudly say Shit! to it all!

Well – hasta otra vez.[2] D. H. Lawrence

3544. To Emily King, [18 November 1925]

Text: MS Lazarus; Unpublished.

Villa Bernarda. *Spotorno* (Genova), Italy
18 November

My dear Sister

We got here last Sunday – now have taken the Villa Bernarda until end of March.[3] The village isn't at all exciting, but we've had some good sunny days, with blue sea – and the house stands high above the little town, and has a big vineyard garden. I think we shall like it. The worst is the wind: it's very rough. I hope next month it will be quieter. But anyhow it's much better than the damp darkness of England.

We went motoring in Switzerland – icy cold – I hated it, and got a cold.

Have you made the final decision about Peggy? –[4]

I'll write when we are more settled.

love DHL

3545. To John Middleton Murry, 19 November 1925

Text: MS NYPL; Murry, *New Adelphi* 459.

Villa Bernarda. *Spotorno* (Genova)
19 Novem. 1925

Dear Jack

We've taken a house here till April – above the village and the sea – big

[1] Perhaps *Selected Modern English Essays* ('Mark Rutherford' to Middleton Murry) published by OUP in February 1925.
[2] 'till next time.'
[3] At the prompting of Rina Secker the Lawrences rented the villa from Angelo Ravagli (1891–1976) whom Frieda married in 1950 (having lived with him since 1933). See Letter 3559.
[4] See Letter 3523.

vineyard garden, and castle ruins – nice – you know the kind of thing. The village isn't anything to stare at, but there's the sea, and good walks in the hills.

I heard from Brett. She has got to Capri.

Did I tell you about a Dr McDonald, of Philadelphia, who did my bibliography. He's really nice – like a Canadian farmer, and quiet, and with energy. He is English Professor at the Drexel Institutue, Philadelphia, and he'd like to change his place, *for a year*, with an English professor – You know those school people – do you know anyone who would like the change? McDonald specialises in Elizabethan pamphlets – he's another for the Elizabethans: a very sound man, you'd surely like him.

I think you and Violet would like this place all right. Noli, the next village, was[1] a mediaeval republic of fisherman, and quite a gem in its way. But too past to live in. I prefer the frayed edges, like here.

The Villa Bernarda is a three-decker – or a four decker, with the contadino in the deeps – you could have bedroom and kitchen for yourselves, if you like – we rent the whole house – or there is this inn, the Albergo Ligure.

Saluti DHL

3546. To Hon. Dorothy Brett, [19 November 1925]

Text: MS UCin; Postmark, Spotorno 19.11 25; Moore 865–6.

Villa Bernarda. *Spotorno* (Genova)
Thursday

Dear Brett

We had your telegram yesterday evening. – the cold in the head – if I read the wire properly – is universal. We were motoring in icy Switzerland – hated it – and got colds in the head, to stop a clock.

We've taken the Villa Bernarda till March, and paid £25. sterling on the nail. We move in on Monday. The village is not much to brag about – but the hills are fine and wild, and the villa is above the houses, and has a big vineyard garden. If it won't be cold, it will be all right. I wish to heaven they'd put fireplaces in these houses.

I sent you Murry's book to the Hotel Webster.

Just had a letter from Rachel – seems cold and stormy there too: 'the same old treadmill' – she calls it.

Ask Brewster what he is doing, if they are really leaving Quattro Venti: all the news.[2]

[1] was] is

[2] The Brewsters had lived in Torre dei Quattro Venti, on Capri, when they first met the Lawrences in April 1921.

And remember us to them warmly: also to Mrs Mackenzie.

Saluti! DHL

Did I tell you Secker is printing *David* – limited edition, 250 copies.

3547. To Lady Cynthia Asquith, [19 November 1925]
Text: MS UT; Unpublished.

Villa Bernarda, Spotorno. Prov di Genova
Thursday

Taken a house here till end of March – it's nice when the sun shines.

Thought you a bit cross when we saw you last.

I'll do a story if the right wind blows – and let you have it by Christmas, Deo Volenti.[1]

Have you asked Oliver Onions to do you one? Some of his *Widdershins* stories very good.[2] You can get him

c/o Secker, 5 John St. Adelphi

– unless you have him up your sleeve.

Here's luck! DHL

Curtis Brown – 6 Henrietta St – will make you terms all right – quite aimiable – when the tale is writ.

3548. To Carl Seelig, [19 November 1925]
Text: MS SIU; Unpublished.

Villa Bernarda. *Spotorno* (Genova)
Thursday

Dear Carl Seelig

We have found ourselves a house here, on the hill above the village, with a big garden of vines – quite nice. But I wish there was a fireplace. We move in next Monday. There is plenty of room, so if you would like to come and stay a while, let me know, and we will have a room ready.

This village is not much of a show – but the sea is nice, there are good walks in the hills, and we had two days of brilliant sun. It is better than England and Germany, anyhow.

I ought to have thanked you sooner, for being so very kind and hospitable in Kastanienbaum. I am glad we came. Now you must pay us a visit, down here: and we can learn Russian, in preparation for the trip in the spring.

Remember me very kindly to Mrs Seelig – also to Herr Haas and to the Frau

[1] See Letter 3633 and n. 1.
[2] Secker had published the volume in 1911.

Doctor.[1] I do hope they will all come along one day, in the car. We have taken the house till April.

Saluti cordiali D. H. Lawrence

3549. To Martin Secker, [20 November 1925]
Text: MS UInd; Postmark, Spotor[no] 20.11 25; Secker 67.

Villa Bernarda. *Spotorno*, Prov di Genova
Friday

Dear Secker

I enclose a letter for the *Times*, since you want it.[2] For myself, I'm sick of that stuff. – I left the original of Douglas' letter at the ranch – but you will have a copy: or Curtis Brown will. – You know you may not print the Douglas letter entire – it is his property. – Will you go through my letter, and leave out what is best left out, and put in what needs to be put in. Make it all right. Make it shorter.

That seems early for the *Serpent*.[3] Knopf wails at the length: *My, but it's a long book, that*. Soit!

We've taken this villa, move in on Monday. It's just under the castle – the garden goes to the castle itself. It's nice – only hope it won't be cold. – I've got a cold, motoring in beastly Switzerland, and feel cross.

Will you send proofs of *David*, as you said. And will you send a copy of the *Serpent* to

Dr Anton Kippenberg, Insel Verlag. *Leipsig*. Kurzestrasse

as soon as it's out.

[1] Unidentified.

[2] Secker's letter to Curtis Brown, 23 November 1925 (Secker Letter-Book, UIll), clarifies DHL's remark. Secker was reacting to the publication in October 1925 of Norman Douglas's *Experiments* which included 'D. H. Lawrence and Maurice Magnus: A Plea for Better Manners' (cf. p. 184 n. 2). After commenting on the contract for *David* and the American edn of *Reflections on the Death of a Porcupine*, Secker continued:

> When I saw that Norman Douglas had given his attack on Lawrence the widest publicity by including it in his new book "Experiments", I thought Lawrence ought not to remain silent any longer and allow the case to go against him by default. I therefore wrote and suggested that he should send a letter to The Times Literary Supplement on the subject. I am glad to say that he has sent me a very good letter which I am to forward, but I have to obtain from you the text, or as much of it as he quoted to you, of that letter which Douglas wrote to him.

No communication from DHL appeared in *TLS*; see Letter 3623 for the letter which was later sent to the *New Statesman*.

[3] Secker was keen to publish as early in 1926 as possible; he had told Knopf and Curtis Brown so (Secker Letter-Book, UIll, 23 October and 10 November 1925). He published on 21 January 1926, Knopf on 5 February.

And will you send a copy of the Magnus *Memoirs* and a copy of *Birds Beasts* to

Carl Seelig. *Kastanienbaum* bei *Lucerne*. Switzerland.

Rina's got a little cold too – the boy flourishes. It's been chill and very windy – thank heaven, the sun is here again. Hope we'll all have a nice time at Christmas.

au revoir D. H. Lawrence

3550. To Nancy Pearn, 21 November 1925

Text: MS UT; Tedlock, *Lawrence MSS* 255.

Villa Bernarda. *Spotorno*. Prov. di Genova, Italy
21 Novem 1925

Dear Miss Pearn

We've taken a villa here till end of March, so perhaps we shall sit still a bit. I'm not crazy about the Riviera, as the Americans say, but the sun shines and the sea is blue, so for the moment, basta!

I promised this review ages ago, to the *New-York Herald-Tribune*.[1] Have it typed, and send it in for me, will you please? Pardon the trouble.

Lady Cynthia Asquith, an old friend of ours, is collecting a book of Ghost Stories. If the spirit moves, I'll have a shot at one, and send it along to you. I'm not going to start another novel. And if you have wind of a nice ghost story, you might let Lady Cynthia know.

Saluti D. H. Lawrence[2]

3551. To Blanche Knopf, 23 November 1925

Text: MS UT; Unpublished.

Villa Bernarda. *Spotorno*, Prov. di Genova, Italy
23 Novem 1925.

Dear Mrs Knopf

We have settled ourselves here, in a villa above the sea, till end of March. It's a nice old house sticking up from the little hill, under the castle, just above the village and the sea. The sun shines, the eternal Mediterranean is blue and young, the last leaves are falling from the vines in the garden. The peasant

[1] The review was of Krout's *Origins of Prohibition* (see Letter 3481 and n. 3). Above the title of the review he wrote: 'to Miss Pearn – letter at end.'

[2] Nancy Pearn replied on 30 November 1925 (TMSC UT):

I know Lady Cynthia Asquith and am aware of her activities. Before promising anything on behalf of our clients, we have told her she must let us have a quotation as to price, for frankly we don't see why a publisher should benefit by getting material by big names in this indirect way, and paying much less than his competitors would be obliged to pay . . .

people are nice, I've got my little stock of red and white wine – from the garden of this house – we eat fried chicken and pasta and smell rosemary and basilica in the cooking once more – and somebody's always roasting coffee – and the oranges are already yellow on the orange trees. It's Italy, the same forever, whether it's Mussolini or Octavian Augustus. In America one talks about Europe being old: in Italy, which is always a bit childish, one is horrorstruck by America's agedness. So it is.

I hear our little friend, Seltzer, is on the carpet again. It's awful, why doesn't he bow himself off the publishing stage, before it's too late.

And I hear that *The Plumed Serpent* will be out in early January. Your husband staggers under the length of the novel. A la guerre comme à la guerre. *St. Mawr* was too short. It's a pity one has to work, to write from one's deep inside. I'm not going to do it any more. Tisn't worth it. – I'm putting a list of people I want you to send the *Serpent* to.[1] Will you do it, please?

The sun is going to sink. I wish winter didn't have such short days.

Hope all goes well with you.

Saluti cordiali – from us both D. H. Lawrence

3552. To Hon. Dorothy Brett, [25 November 1925]

Text: MS UCin; Postmark, Spotorno 27.11 25; Moore 867–9.

Villa Bernarda. *Spotorno*, Prov. di Genova
Wednesday

Dear Brett

You've got the real doldrums. But one always feels bad, the first few days when one comes to Italy. It's sunny here, and the sun is hot: but *very* windy. – Our colds have cleared away, and I'm just taking things quietly.

I heard from Barmby that Knopf is using your cover design for *The Plumed Serpent*,[2] and has already paid $50–, and you can have the fifty dollars any time you write to Curtis Brown, 6 Henrietta St. Covent Garden, W.C. 2. – I ordered a copy of the book to you, to Hotel Webster. But if you tell them at the post office, they'll deliver it to you anywhere. It should arrive second week in January. I also ordered a copy direct to your father, to Callander, because I know you'll want him to see the design. Please tell him *you* ordered it. – The copy of *The Porcupine* should reach Scotland soon.

They must have rooked you pretty badly, over cabs etc. They would if they could, the swine. Everything is really pretty cheap. Forty Lire is less than two dollars: and a room alone at the De Vargas is $3.50. – We've paid twenty five

[1] The list is missing.

[2] Knopf used it on the dust-jacket: 'white paper printed in black and red with drawing of Mexican figures with large hats' (Roberts A33; reproduced on p. 427).

pounds for this house – which is quite enough. But it's got lots of room, a huge vineyard garden, and we're high over the sea. It's nice, but blowy. There is a contadino Giovanni downstairs, who runs for us.[1] And the sea is mostly blue. It's quite good to lie low in. And living is very cheap: we ought to manage on five shillings a day. I want to economise, as Seltzer is hardly held together by a safety pin: and he has my five thousand dollars. Barmby wrote that Nathalie Crane, the infant poetess[2] – you remember her photograph, with Thomas – is now suing Thomas for not paying her her royalties, and he is cutting a sorry figure in court. Beastly!

Frieda expects her daughter Barby this week, or next: and her elder daughter at Christmas. Possibly my sister will come in January: and Murry, and Frieda's sister from Berlin. It was no good going far down to Capri, if we are to have these visitors: which seems to be the point of our stay here.

But in the spring I should like to come south: in February, maybe. I should like to see spring once more in Sicily, so would Frieda: it is so lovely. We might all make some sort of excursion, with light luggage: perhaps to Amalfi and Paestum (where I've never stopped) – and Sicily. – I wish we weren't always poor. I wanted to go to Dalmatia and the Isles of Greece. Why doesn't anybody ever have a yacht, and sail the coasts of the Mediterranean – Greece, and Constantinople, and Damascus, and Jaffa, and Egypt, and Tunis and Morocco – or at least Algiers. How nice it would be! Why do beastly people like Nina Witt have the millions.

There is something I like very much about the Mediterranean: it relaxes one, after the tension of America. Wait a bit till you get used to it, and you'll like it too. – But after a while, it always sets me longing to wander, to do a sort of Iliad. But even if all of us, and Earl and Aschsah, put our money together, we'd never afford a little ship, which is so much the best for this sea of many shores. You see, one need never sail for more than a night, then there's somewhere else to land at, if one likes.

Ma basta! Non usciamo mai fuori della bisogna dei soldi.[3]

Do you really feel like typing? I'll send you a few little things. – Spud wrote: Mabel is in New York for a month,[4] and Tony in California. He (Spud) is getting ready his number of the Lawrence *Laughing Horse*.[5] I know it will be awful: che lo sia![6] That Kyle Crichton,[7] from Albuquerque, did an article on

[1] For a fuller description of Giovanni Rossi see Letter 3568.

[2] Her volume of poems, *Janitor's Boy* (see Letter 3134 and n. 7) had been very favourably reviewed; it reached its 8th printing by December 1925.

[3] 'But enough! We'll never be in a position not to need money.'

[4] month] fortnight

[5] Published in April 1926. (DHL added the explanatory 'Spud' interlinearly and without brackets.)

[6] 'so be it!'

[7] Crichton] Crighton

us at the ranch: I haven't seen it. – William is selling all his cattle, and asks, do I want him to keep me any. I suppose I want a cow and calf: but God knows when I'll go back. – As for Kot, Murry, Milne and the rest – well, I only saw Murry, and what was the good of that? Let the dead bury their dead.[1]

I'm enclosing two little MSS. – one for Spud.[2] Make one carbon copy, will you? And count the thousands, and I'll pay the current rate, 1/- per 1000, 3d for carbon.

DHL

The people here – peasants – are awfully nice – it's sort of like old times: they bring us fish, and carcioffi. – Why don't you have a room, as we did, at the top of the Palazzo Ferraro, and just go out for your chief meal?[3]

Tell Earl and Achsah I am writing.

[Frieda Lawrence begins]

We are in a house and I am doing the chores again, all the jolly Italian cooking – There's an old Giovanni, last year he was dying one night the doctor said, but in the middle of the night he felt 'such a hunger on him' he got up made a fire boiled himself a great bowl of potatoes poured a bottle of oil and a bottle of vinegar over them, ate them and was well!! – You will like Capri, when the Ranch has gone out of your bones a little, it has charm and delicacy, I appreciate it all the more and to feel so many spots of the world are one's own and lovely if one only makes them so – What a pity your brother Oliver does'nt have a yacht and asks us all to go round with him and lives as we do! I thought perhaps you had bought *kilts* for L[awrence]! I am thrilled that you have some glad rags for me – I bought *nothing*, except 3 lovely aprons! but L has a new suit and 2 hats and an overcoat. My hair goes like that, it looks a little Jane Austenish

[sketch][4]

no I cant get it right – Murry's Christianity is to me like a hump, or a lame leg – The bit in him that's hard and wicked *I* like – I feel happy – for no reason – just feel like it and basta – L and I had a Xmas once in Capri – Go and see Faith McKenzie, you will like her, she has a little splendour, but I dont know her well – Give my love to the Brewsters – How nice your cover will look, any way

[1] Matthew viii.22.

[2] The MS for Johnson was 'A Little Moonshine with Lemon' (written on 25 November 1925); he included it in the DHL issue of *Laughing Horse*. The other is not certainly known; perhaps 'Europe Versus America'.

[3] DHL is recalling their stay there December 1919–February 1920 (see *Letters*, iii. 438ff).

[4] Frieda had drawn a rough outline of her head and hair over the account of Giovanni; here she adds a slightly less amateur sketch to illustrate her new hair style (cf. Letter 3539).

I hope so! We have a little white calf and 7 chickens, sent Rachel some butter moulds – L seems so *well*, so will you be when your cold is gone.

F

3553. To Earl and Achsah Brewster, 25 November 1925
Text: MS UT; Brewster 84–5.

Villa Bernarda. *Spotorno* (Genova)
25 Novem 1925

Dear Earl and Achsah

I had your letter forwarded from London, two days ago. Now I hear from Miss Brett that she is in Capri.

I'm sorry, really, we couldn't come down. I would rather have done so: the Riviera means nothing to me. But if Frieda is to have her children, and other visitors are to come, we have to be near enough. Capri is too far.

We've taken this house until end of March, but that doesn't mean we can't go away for a while. I should like to move south when the spring comes – to see Amalfi and Sicily in February, leaving the big luggage here. Are you really leaving Quattro Venti? And what are your plans afterwards? – Myself, I feel very vague. I don't even know if I want to go back to the ranch in the spring – though Frieda says she does. Vedremo!

Italy feels very familiar: almost too familiar, like the ghost of one's own self. But I am very glad to be by the Mediterranean again for a while. It seems so versatile and so young, after America, which is everywhere tense. I wish we were all richer, and could loiter around the coasts of the old world, Dalmatia, Isles of Greece, Constantinople, Egypt. But it's no good: we've got to go piano-piano.

It will soon be December, and the turn of the year. Let us make some little plan for the early New Year – end of January or in February.

Brett writes rather dismally – but I'm sure she will soon cheer up. Have you seen Faith Mackenzie? – and how is she? Rina Secker, here, is a bit out of sorts. Nobody seems very lively nowadays. Time we made a new start.

Frieda sends her love – it really *doesn't* seem so far away now.

a rivederci D. H. Lawrence

3554. To Hon. Dorothy Brett, [26 November 1925]
Text: MS UCin; Irvine, Brett 66.

Villa Bernarda, *Spotorno* (Genova)
Thursday

Dear Brett

I wish you would send me the 'melancholy' books – have nothing to read.

You can quite safely send anything by post, here. – And if you pack the flute carefully – get a shop to do it – you can send that by post too. The hotel would do it. There's no danger – and no duty. If there were duty, you could refund it to Cath Carswell.

Colds still hanging on, here. Froze in the night.

DHL

3555. To Martin Secker, 30 November 1925

Text: MS UInd; Postmark, Spotorno 30.11 25; Secker 67–8.

Villa Bernarda, *Spotorno* (Genova)
30 Novem 1925

Dear Secker

I return the letter about Douglas, signed. It bores me a bit, but if you think it should go to the *Times*, let it go.

We are settled in our cottage – quite comfortable. It has been cold, freezing at night, but we light the stove in the kitchen, and sit there at evening. Today is superbly sunny, and warm – so was yesterday. Rina usually comes with Adrian in the afternoon. She is much better now: was very *nervosa* at first, and a bit trying, no doubt, to her parents. But she gets better now every day. Adrian is not 'in the pink' but the scarlet. He is very bonny,[1] and growing fast, and perfectly happy and chirpy here. The change is trying for everybody, at first; from England, and especially silent Bridgefoot, to the Mediterranean. When Rina can leave the boy for a few hours with her mother, and get a good walk in the hills with us all, she'll be perfectly all right.

We shall be very pleased to see you – you'll have a second abode here – and we can go for walks when we like.

Did you mind about Knopf's not taking the *David* play?[2] And when will you have a set of proofs?

I'm not doing any serious work yet: just bits, that I have promised: and not much of those. Am a bit disgusted with work altogether.

Tomorrow is first of December – another year! But let time pass, what's it matter!

a rivederci D. H. Lawrence

3556. To Hon. Dorothy Brett, [5 December 1925]

Text: MS UCin; PC v. Spotorno – Pineta; Postmark, Spotorno 6 12 25; Huxley 643.

[Villa Bernarda, Spotorno, Genova]
Saturday

– Many thanks for the books: the 'ledgers' are most gaily imposing, I feel

[1] I.e. well in health, plump (northern dialect).

[2] Despite Knopf's initial disinclination to publish *David*, he subsequently agreed. His edition appeared on 23 April 1926 (Roberts A34).

nothing could go in them but scandalous stories. I've also the bit of MS. for Spud: but put enough stamps on your letters. I had 2.50 surcharge. Here it freezes, but is sunny. In France 14° below zero. What price the ranch! Went to Alassio yesterday to see F[rieda]'s daughter Barby. Alassio well begins Alas! for it's a chronic hole, awful! Barby is staying there pro tem. – Pa prefers she shouldn't house here.[1] – F. is panting for the glad rags. I had such a nice new hat a felt hat – left it in London – asked them to send it by Barby: and what has arrived? – a lady's black bowler riding hat!!!! Very chic!!! F. fancies herself in it. I'll get you one if you're envious.

DHL

Murry has taken a flat in the Vale of Health for the winter!! Insists he's coming here in January with Violet – ???

3557. To S. S. Koteliansky, 6 December 1925

Text: MS BL; Postmark, [Spot]orno 7 12 25; cited in Gransden 29–30.

Villa Bernarda, *Spotorno*, Prov di Genova
6 Decem 1925

My dear Kot

Curtis Browns sent me the letters – unless these are copies – they are, I see – and the £5. for the Bunin book.[2] Seltzer is hopeless, he ought to go bankrupt and have done with it. But his creditors won't *make* him bankrupt hoping to squeeze him bit by bit. – I wish he'd never existed, poor devil.

We've got this villa here till end of March – then what, I don't know: either back to America, to the ranch, or I think I'd like to go to Russia. Should I, do you think? and could I? I have a feeling inside me, I should like to go to Russia.

It's cold here, but sunny. Frieda's daughter Barbara is in Alassio, coming over tomorrow: the other daughter coming after Christmas. The Riviera doesn't interest me, and I'm a bit bored: but the sun shines on the Mediterranean, I like that. Brett is down in Capri. – I'm trying to clear off bits of work I've promised.

How is Sonia, and Ghita, and Grisha? Is 5 Acacia still cavernous? – with Fox for the prehistoric animal?[3] Bisogna sapere! –[4] And newspapers?

I wrote Barbara but haven't heard from her.[5] The world needs a move-on.

Sends us news, if there is any. – You are still Frieda's pet enemy, which is almost straining constancy.

stia bene DHL

[1] Barbara had continued to reside with the family of her father, Ernest Weekley (1865–1964), Professor of French, University College, Nottingham, who divorced Frieda in 1914 (see *Letters*, i. 374 n. 5).

[2] The reference is to Ivan Aleksyevich Bunin's *The Gentleman from San Francisco and Other Stories* (1922), trans. Leonard Woolf, Kot and DHL (see *Letters*, iv. 23 and n. 2).

[3] Ghita was the Farbmans' daughter and Fox their dog (cf. p. 81 n. 1).

[4] 'One needs to know! –'

[5] The letter to Barbara Low has not been found.

3558. To Donald Wells, 7 December 1925

Text: MS UT; Unpublished.

Villa Bernarda. *Spotorno* (Genova)
7 Decem 1925

Dear Mr Wells[1]

Thank you for your letter. Please do subtract the £19. odd from Secker's payment, to settle with Michael Borg for *Memoirs of the Foreign Legion*. I want him to have the money.

Yours truly D. H. Lawrence

3559. To Hon. Dorothy Brett, [8 December 1925]

Text: MS UCin; Moore 882–3.

Villa Bernarda. *Spotorno*, Prov. di Genova.
Tuesday.

Dear Brett.

Many thanks for the typescript. I used to buy those envelopes, in Capri. – I am sending two more stories. I promised Cynthia Asquith a ghost story, for a collection she is making. How will she swallow 'Gay Ghosts'?[2]

I am surprised at your adding one more to the list of Crucifixions. Whom are you popping on the Cross, to make him say 'too late.'?[3]

It's suddenly warmer: we had no rain at all, only high bitter wind, but sunshine. I am a bit chesty, but plasterless so far.

Why don't you grow a moustache, and have done with it? A turned-up one, like the Kaiser's, and the German advertisement *Es ist erreicht*! (Got it!) which used to advertise the moustache-tilter.[4]

Tell Achsah please not to send me books, I've got a bundle from England. And I *don't* want the back numbers of the *Adelphi*.

Mabel is sending me her MS. of the first fourteen – I think it's 14 – years of

[1] Donald Wells was on the staff of Curtis Brown's London office.

[2] See Letter 3633 and n.

[3] Brett (p. 288) described the picture she was painting as follows:

> The picture is of a crucifixion. The pale yellow Christ hangs on the Cross, against an orange sunset. With that final spurt of strength before death, he is staring at the vision of the figure in front of him. His eyes are visionary, his figure tense and aware. Before him, straddled across a rock, half curious, half smiling, is the figure of Pan, holding up a bunch of grapes to the dying Christ: a dark, reddish-gold figure with horns and hoofs. The heads of Pan and of Christ are both your [DHL's] head. Behind lies the sea. A deep curve of rocks brings the sea-line low in the middle of the picture; and below Pan's rock is just visible the tower of Quattro Venti.

[4] Cf. ['Return to Bestwood'], *Phoenix II*, p. 261: 'before the war, in Germany I used to see advertised in the newspapers a moustache-lifter, which you tied on at night and it would make your moustache stay turned up, like the immortal moustache of Kaiser Wilhelm II, whose moustache alone is immortal. This moustache-lifter was called: Es ist erreicht! In other words: It is reached! Consummatum est!'

her life: and will I write a foreword. – Will I put salt on its tail! – She's going back to Taos for a month, now – Tony is in California collecting money for Indian lawyers: and they are going to spend the spring, en famille so to speak, in Croton again, near New York.[1]

Haven't you seen the Brett-Youngs among all the rest? Nor Ferdinando di Chiara?[2] I feel you're not yet *au courant*.

I told you Jack and the Violet have taken a flat in the Vale of Health for the winter. They seem very friendly with Helen Thomas[3] – who wrote about the baby being born.

We'll see what the New Year will do for us – and the lugger. Remember me to everybody.

DHL

The three dollars is to buy new carbon paper!

[Frieda Lawrence begins]

Tuesday

Dear Brett,

Thrilled is'nt the word! The glad rags are triumphant rags! But are you sure you did'nt tear them from your own bosom? They are *all* large enough, how is that? The striped coat I love and Lawr had'nt a single woollen scarf, so he had the blue one – The black coat is very elegant only it will have to have such expensive other things, shoes and so on, it would be tight on my mother – And did you like the Quaker collar, that's fun – I will have a slip made to the little tigery coat – Thank you ever so much, did you hate making the parcel? We went to see Barby! Alassio an awful impression. Barby in a nice sunny warm pension but the two women told me how important it was that Barby started in the *best* set! and that General Wilson lived next door – I get so scared, as if they could pull me in and out of their 'sets'! Barby bewildered I think she is scared of L and me, God knows why – All I want of them is to learn to get something out of life, I dont care what they *feel* about me – But perhaps getting something out of life is a gift from the gods – Your Christ sounds splendid, I suppose the poor old or really rather young bird feels what he has *missed* and so he has – To be crucified only once, seems comparatively little, we have done that several times! So nothing to 'write home' about!! Lawr read some of the French

[1] See Letter 3176 and n. 3.

[2] Francis Brett Young (1884–1954), the novelist, and his wife Jessica, were friends of the Lawrences particularly during 1919–20 and 21. Ferdinando and his American wife Anna di Chiara had been known to DHL since early 1920 when they met in Capri.

[3] Helen Berenice Thomas (1877–1967), widow of the poet Edward Thomas (1878–1917). DHL met her in July 1919 (see *Letters*, iii. 372 and n. 1).

woman's translations yesterday, very interesting in French[1] – *Why* should Kot be cross with you? *Canaille* that's what they are to me, as to judging or condemning me, what do they matter? Carrion crows! Lawr is fairly well, but these last dying days of the year are always a trial, still he is glad to be in Europe, the ranch was a strain for him and the earth is good in many places – The Brewsters once offered us a picture from each of them, Lawr never answered, I wonder if they were hurt and tell them if you can delicately, we would like some, *small* ones – We have a nice little Bersaglieri officer to whom the villa belongs I am thrilled by his cockfeathers he is almost as nice as the feathers! I wish I knew of something to rejoice your heart as the rags did mine!

Yours ever F

Describe some of your own finery we cant imagine how you look!

3560. To Emily King, [12 December 1925]

Text: MS Lazarus; Unpublished.

Villa Bernarda: *Spotorno*, Prov. di Genova
Saturday

My dear Pamela

I was so sorry you had flu, and Joan whooping cough. No luck at all! Do hope the whoop is better.

So they hang on to Peg at that school! – they would, the brutes.

The weather's gone mild and cloudy again – which seems to have brought out colds in most people, ourselves included. But not much. – Martin Secker is here, staying with his wife's people down on the road. His wife is here with the baby – quite a sturdy lad of twenty months. But she's frightfully discontented: for no particular reason, that I can see.

Frieda's daughter Barby is in Alassio, about 25 miles away. She's not been over here yet: we went once there. She's enjoying herself all right with the five or six thousand English people out there, so she's all right.

I send you three pounds for Christmas: one pound for Peg. Don't send any parcels or anything out here, it's only a bother all round: unless you send a pound of decent tea – I like Ridgeways – Her Majesty's Blend – and a couple of tubes of Regesan Catarrh Jelly. But don't bother if it's a nuisance.

I do hope Joan's cough is better – lucky that Peg keeps all right.

Love to you all DHL

[1] See Letter 3700.

3561. To John Middleton Murry, 12 December 1925

Text: MS NYPL; Moore 869.

Villa Bernarda, *Spotorno*, Prov di Genova
12 Decem 1925

Dear Jack

I send back the Molly Skinner article – re-wrote the first four pages, and cleared the rest a bit.[1] But it needs re-typing. It's quite good, for a sort of 'note.' – But Molly Skinner is getting too vague and crazy. – I've just finished *Black Swans*. It irritates me, by its foolish facility. She herself knows life isn't like that – conceited slipshod nonsense – so why does she write it?

Hope you'll like Vale of Health – I hated it.[2]

Secker is here – with wife and child, down on the road, with her parents – for a month. He's gentle and nice, seems to me.

The Riviera isn't quite right, somehow – I prefer further south. But it does for a little while. The house is pleasant, and plenty of room, when you want to come.

Regards to you both from both DHL

If you print M. Skinner's article with my editing, *don't* mention me, to anybody – not to her. Just let her think your office did the editing.

3562. To Hon. Dorothy Brett, [12 December 1925]

Text: MS UCin; Huxley 646–7.

Villa Bernarda. *Spotorno* (GENOVA)
Mark the O It is just Genoa
Sat.

Dear Brett

Your p. c. – addressed to GEN*E*VA!! – I had the typing,[3] and very many thanks. –

The postal rate, *inside* Italy, is

letter – 60 centisimi
postcard – 40 "

But you can only send ½ ounce in a letter – very thin – so if it's a bit heavy, let them weigh it. The parcels were perfectly all right, so was the registered package. Sorry to bother you.

[1] Mollie Skinner had written a short story (about a goldfields hospital) entitled 'The Hand' and submitted it to Murry for the *Adelphi*. (See Skinner 161, and Letter 3671.)

[2] The Lawrences lived in a flat (1 Byron Villas) in the Vale-of-Health, Hampstead, 4 August–21 December 1915.

[3] Probably 'Smile' (see Letter 3571), subsequently published in *Nation and Athenæum*, xxxix (19 June 1926), 319–20 (Roberts C142). See also Letter 3711 and p. 452 n. 1.

I send you 'Sun'.[1] Perhaps better hold back the MS. when you send the typescript, so that if the package goes astray, we still have a copy.

I'm still struggling with my 'Gay Ghosts'. Alas and a thousand times alack, it's growing long – too long. Damn it! Even 'Sun' is a bit too long.

Am in bed for two days with that cold on the chest. But it's dissolving satisfactorily. Here it's cloudy, but not cold any more.

Martin Secker is here – with the Capellero family down by the road. He's a nice gentle soul, without a thrill: his wife a living block of discontent – why, I don't know, for she's not so perfect. But I think she's ill. – Myself, I feel like a chipmunk hibernating – I read Aldous Huxley's *Along the Road*.[2] I'd send it you, but it's Secker's copy. It's little essays about Italy – very nice in its way. He goes about in a 10. h.p. Citroen car, which seems to me a very good idea. If I could drive I might think of one.

F[rieda] is still charmed with her clothes. You will have had our letters. You should see her in the black step-downstairs coat and the bowler riding-hat! – I am swathed in the blue scarf, which if I were really a chippy I wouldn't be, only my own stripes.

Hope all goes well.

DHL

3563. To Ada Clarke, [15 December 1925]

Text: MS Clarke; Unpublished.

Villa Barnarda. *Spotorno* (Genova)
Tuesday. 15th

My dear Sister

I was forgetting to answer you about parcels: don't bother to send anything here. They're sure to hold the things up at the frontier, for God knows how long – and then charge duty. We must go in to Savona, and if we can find you some little thing, I'll put it in a letter. – Savona is only eight miles away, but the trains very inconvenient.

Barby was here for a day or two – has just gone back to Alassio. Quite nice. – Martin Secker also is here – they come up most days, so we aren't alone. – The passing of the cold bright weather left us all with colds – better now though. Brett writes from Capri that she isn't well. How damnable winter is. I do hope Pamela and Joan are better.

[1] 'Sun' was first printed by the London bookseller, Charles Lahr (see p. 572 n. 1) in his magazine, *New Coterie*, iv (Autumn 1926), 60–77. In September 1926 100 copies, or probably more, were separately published by Lahr (under his publisher's imprint, 'E. Archer'). Finally, in a longer, later form it was printed for Harry and Caresse Crosby by the Black Sun Press in Paris (October 1928). See Roberts A35.

[2] *Along the Road: Notes and Essays of a Tourist* (September 1925).

It would be awfully nice if you came in the New Year – but I suppose you mustn't bother poor Eddie too much yet. I believe the return fare, first, is only about £10. Murry wants to come with his wife, later in January.

It's a bit of a struggle in these houses, keeping warm. There are never any fireplaces. But we sit in the evening in the kitchen, where we have a good stove. The Seckers come up in the afternoon for tea, and chiefly to get warm by the stove. Sunny Italy can let you down. But it's never really bad.

Barby says that Elsa, her elder sister, is coming out in January too. They may take a little flat – their father prefers they don't stay with us. I'm glad. – But he's made provision for Frieda in his will!!!! See what it is to leave your husband.

I'll write when we've been to Savona.

Love to you all DHL

3564. To Baroness Anna von Richthofen, 16 December 1925

Text: MS UCB; Frieda Lawrence 196.

Villa Bernarda. *Spotorno*, Prov. di Genova
16 Dec 1925

Meine liebe Schwiegermutter

Gleich kommt Weihnacht wieder: hier haben die Kinder auf jeder Thüre: *Natale* geschrieben. Es ist aber keine grosse *Festa* in Italien. Ich war heute in Savona: man kann nicht viel dort kaufen: nicht viel interressantes. Ich habe Feigen und Datteln and Rosinen gekauft – die sind gut. Morgen machen wir ein Paket für dich, aus solchen Sachen. Hoffentlich bekommst du es, vor Weihnachten.

Wir haben wieder schönes Wetter. Gestern Abend, es wollte schneien: heut' morgen aber nichts davon, und schöne Sonne. Mein Verleger, Martin Secker, ist hier, und ging mit mir nach Savona. Er ist nett, aber kein funkelnder Mensch.

Jetzt ist's Abend: wir sitzen in der Küche, hoch unter dem Dach; der Abendsterne ist weiss, über den Berg gegenüber, unten liegen die Dorflichte wie Mandarin-orangen, kleine und glänzende. Die Frieda hat ihren Schlagrahm von Savona in einem Schluck gefressen, jetzt klagt dass sie es nicht behalten hat, um mit Kaffee und Kuchen nach Essen zu schmecken. Sie sitzt bei den Herd und liest. Die Suppe kocht. Gleich rufen wir nach unten, in die Tiefe: Venga Giovanni! è pronto il mangiare. Dann läuft der Alter wie einen glücklichen Hund, die Treppen hinauf, Nase in der Luft, riechend, schnüffelnd. Für ihn ist es schön, er weisst nimmer was für Gutes er bekommen soll.

Ich schicke dir ein wenig Geld, du müsst einkaufen, und dich immer noch als Stiftsherzogin vorbringen. Bleibe lustig.

DHL

[My dear Schwiegermutter

Christmas is almost back again: the children here have written: *Christmas* on every door. But it's not a big festival in Italy. I was in Savona today: one can't buy much there: not much that's interesting. I've bought figs and dates and raisins – those are good. Tomorrow we'll make up a parcel of such things for you. Hope you'll get it before Christmas.

We've got fine weather again. Last night, it wanted to snow; however, this morning nothing there, and lovely sun. My publisher, Martin Secker, is here, and went to Savona with me. He's nice, but not a sparkling person.

Now it's evening: we're sitting in the kitchen, high up under the roof; the evening star is white over the hills opposite, below lie the lights of the village like mandarin-oranges, small and bright. Frieda has gobbled up her whipped cream from Savona at one gulp, now she complains that she hasn't kept it to enjoy with coffee and cake after the meal. She is sitting by the stove reading. The soup is cooking. In a moment we'll call downstairs, into the depths: come on Giovanni! food's ready. Then the old man runs upstairs like a happy dog, nose in the air, smelling, sniffing. It's nice for him, he never knows what good things he's going to get.

I send you a little money, you have to shop and keep up the image of Duchess of the Stift, as ever. Stay jolly.

DHL]

3565. To S. S. Koteliansky, 18 December 1925

Text: MS BL; Postmark, Savona 18 12 25; cited in Gransden 30.

Villa Bernarda. *Spotorno*, Prov. di Genova.
18 Decem 1925

My dear Kot.

I had your letter. Oh, but don't let's bother any more about people and lies. I am so weary of human complications. I expect I know you well enough, of myself, no matter what anybody says – though they *don't* say anything. In the end one's very heart gets tired. But somewhere, inside myself, I don't change: and I don't think you do. We are both much simpler than a man like Murry, whom I don't really understand. – I remember very well the famous walk in the Lake district, how you suffered having to sleep in the same bed – and how we got water-lilies – and came down to Lewis' unattractive home, and it was war, and you departed in a cloud.[1] It's part of one's life and we don't live twice. Neither will Slatkovsky ever peep in again on our sour, sour herrings, in the Russian Law Bureau:[2] nor shall we ever see Maisie sit on Campbells knee.[3] Oh basta! We won't grow old yet. Son' tempi passati![4] – but there are other days. Next time we're in London we'll see if we really can't cheer up and rouse the neighbourhood: like Fox. – Does Ghita still call him *Foxie?* – The war, somehow, gave us a bad kick in the wind, all of us: and we felt the damage most, in the after years. Now we've *got* to begin to rouse up a bit, or we shall all be old before we know where we are.

As for Russia: I still think I should like to go, in spite of the 'rulers.' Don't I remember Litvinov in a stream of washing and boiled cabbage? And isn't he, too, in the Seats of the Mighty?[5] But there must be something there, besides and beyond.

So Sonya will never cook us another goose, only marmite pie and nut-cutlet. I tried that Shearns place,[6] and thought it horrid – a real blow-out. What is the cave coming to, with the cave-lady herbivorous!

But perhaps it is good for the headaches.

Make a bow for me, to your sacra famiglia – except Ghita isn't a bambino!

Tutte le buone cose![7] DHL

3566. To Hon. Dorothy Brett, [18 December 1925]

Text: MS UCin; PC v. Spotorno – Pineta; Postmark, Savona 18 12 25; Irvine, Brett 60.

[Villa Bernarda, Spotorno, Genova]

18 Decem.

– Sorry you're not feeling well: it's the big change, from the ranch, takes one some time to re-adjust oneself. I was laid up, but am better. F[rieda] too has a cold. – I heard tonight from William – just enough snow there to keep the roads deep in mud. He says it's awful. He's taken the horses down to his

[1] DHL, Kot and two companions (see *Letters*, ii. 268 n. 2) went on a walking-tour in Westmorland, 31 July–8 August 1914; when they returned to the home of A. P. Lewis in Barrow-in-Furness (ibid., 184 n. 3), they discovered that war had been declared. For a description of DHL's mood (and the water-lilies in his hat), see ibid., 268.

[2] R. S. Slatkowsky (d. 1918) was the proprietor of the Russian Law Bureau in High Holborn where Kot worked.

[3] DHL and Frieda stayed with Gordon Campbell (1885–1963), a barrister, and his wife Beatrice (see *Letters*, ii. 51 n. 1) when they returned from Germany in 1914 to be married. Maisie was the wife of William K. Horne, one of Kot's colleagues at the Law Bureau (see ibid., 205 n. 5).

[4] 'They are days gone by!'

[5] Maxim Litvinov was already a senior member of the Soviet Commissariat for Foreign Affairs and in 1930 would become Foreign Commissar. (See *Times* obituary, 3 January 1952.)

[6] Unidentified.

[7] 'All our best wishes!'

pasture at San Cristobal – says hay will be very dear – asks after you, complaining you've not written. We've been hunting for something for you for Christmas, but not a thing! – Barby came over for a few days last week-end: gone back now. Hope you're better. Suppose you have my 'Sun' story.

DHL

3567. To Earl and Achsah Brewster, 18 December 1925

Text: MS UT; Brewster 86–7.

Villa Bernarda. *Spotorno.* (Genova)
18 Dec. 1925

Dear Earl and Achsah

Very many thanks for your letters, and the *Adelphis*, and the poems. They are all safely here. And thanks awfully for being so kind to Miss Brett – we all call her 'the Brett.' Hope the shouting isn't a trial.

We go on very quietly here. I work a bit – not much – and walk in the hills, when the bitter cold winds havent laid me up with a chest. But it's better now. In the daytime we live in the sitting-room with a terrace over the village and the sea, but at night we dwell in the kitchen, with a good warm 'stufa economica'; which is anything but economical. Blessings on it, nevertheless. The Seckers come up in the afternoon, to get thawed out. Oh icy Italy, where is thy fireplace, thou heartless and bitter cold!

I was disappointed in *The White Stallion*. I am never very fond of abstract poetry, not even Blake. And the theme of this I prefer in the old hymns and Vedas, in the original, when it had a quivering which is gone here. I much prefer *Titans and Gods*![1] One *can't* put the mystery of Oriental philosophy, even that of the *Stallion*, in a rather brief, rhyming poem. But the other poems belong to us and our experience – I mean the ones like 'Foghorns', or 'Night Flying', many in *Titans and Gods*. But I wish Branford weren't so abstract – Spirits of the Heavens, and Earth: Breath, Beauty, all those capital letters on hollow bodies.

It is a pity we can't have Christmas together. I like Christmas in Capri, and very much wish we could have been there. But Frieda had her daughter over from Alassio for a few days: she is coming again: and the elder daughter in

[1] Frederick Victor Branford, a friend of the Brewsters, had published a collection of his poems (including 'On Hearing the Fog-Horns of a Warship' and 'Night-Flying') under the title *Titans and Gods*, in 1922. His second volume of poems, *The White Stallion*, appeared in June 1924. In his 'Foreword' to the latter Branford declared his philosophy to be rooted 'in the thought of the East, where Siva the Destroyer, Vishnu the Preserver, and Brahma the Creator, divide the empire of the Breath'. In March 1926 DHL, with Brett, visited Branford and 'his golden-haired wife', Martha, on Capri (Brett 269, 275). (DHL had come across his poems before: see *Letters*, iii. 342 and n. 5.)

January. It isn't the *house* that keeps one here. – But in the spring we'll really meet, and do something nice: when the almond blossom is out. I should love to walk with you – either in Calabria or Sicily. But it would have to be a bit warmer weather.

Many regards from us both, and a Happy Christmas DHL

Shall I send back your *Titans and Gods*?

3568. To William Hawk, 18 December 1925

Text: MS UT; Postmark, Savona 18 12 25; cited in Moore, *Intelligent Heart* 348.

Villa Bernarda. *Spotorno*, Prov. di Genova. Italy
18 Decem 1925

Dear William

We had your letter today: sounds dreary at the ranch, slush and mud. But probably by now it has frozen up, and is beautiful. You've taken the horses down to San Cristobal! Wonder what they'll think of that! Getting used to the level. – Thanks for shutting off the water, I hope we shall find those pipes uncollapsed, when the winter is over.

We've taken this house till end of March. It's on the sea, on the Riviera, about three hours from Monte Carlo. The village is just a quiet Italian village, but we have friends here. The house is nice, just under the Castle, in a big vineyard garden, with terrace over the roofs of the village, the sea beyond. We do the housework ourselves: Frieda obstinately refused a maid. But there's a gardener lives downstairs, he does all the fetching and carrying, goes shopping every morning at 7.30, pumps the water, and is there when we want him. We've got three floors: we live mostly on the top floor, high up, where there's a kitchen and bedroom and sitting-room, and a big terrace opening from the sitting-room: we sleep on the middle-floor: the bottom floor we store things in. It's real Italian country style – a pleasant sort of life, easier than America. The weather is on the whole sunny and dry, but we've had bitter cold winds. We go for walks in the hills – there are snow mountains behind – and do bits of things. Yesterday we got oranges from the trees and made marmalade, which I burnt a bit. But it's good. Frieda's youngest daughter Barbara is in Alassio, about 25 miles away. She comes over and stays a day or two with us. There are no horses to ride, no spring to fetch the water from. The pine-trees are those puffs of umbrella pines, all scattered separate on the stony slopes to the sea. It's very different. But then of course we're so used to it, the kind of life here: makes me wonder where I am, quite, and what we shall do next. At the present moment, I feel I don't know in the least when we shall get back to the ranch. It seems so far, and difficult, and another world. But when the year turns round, probably one's feelings will turn too. Yet I hardly like to ask you to keep a cow specially for me. You'd be sold if we didn't turn up.

Brett is down in Capri, about a day's journey from here. I believe she's having a good time, but she writes she doesn't feel well now. It's the big change from the ranch, difficult to adjust oneself again. She got a lot of clothes and things from her family, is quite smart, for her, and very social in Capri: and writes, with a wail, that only Prince loves her! But then, what is love! – We have promised to go south in the New Year, perhaps all go to Sicily for a while, with other old friends. But nothing is definite.

I hope you got the toys for the children, and didn't have to pay more duty than they were worth. I hate to think of Walton cooped up in the house. What a bore long winters are!

Do you think really of going to San Cristobal next year? I suppose you'll have to be on your own. But it seems a pity.

Well, the Lord knows what'll happen to us all. We shall have to wait and see.

Have you sold Susan, the black-eyed? Is Miss Wemyss reconciled to her old ma? How are Pueblo's pups, and Pueblo? – I hope Rachel has beheaded every unlaying hen she could lay hands on, the brutes! Did Aaron still have a sore over his eye, that Brett wrote me of? Is Scott Murray back in San Cristobal? I heard from Spud Johnson, and Mabel! – but no local news: save that Mabel thinks of moving to New York for the spring.

I enclose $25–, towards the horses.

Rachel, the letter of course is to you too.

Remember us warmly to your father and mother. I hope they're cheerful and well.

Anyhow you've got jolly wood fires – and probably bright crackly days, now. Keep well and cheerio!

D. H. Lawrence

3569. To Irita van Doren, 19 December 1925

Text: MS LC; Unpublished.

Villa Bernarda. *Spotorno*, Prov. di Genova, Italy
19 Decem 1925

Dear Mrs Van Doren

Thank you for your letter of Nov 24. The Jeffers poems haven't come yet, but I shall be interested to have a shot at them when they do.[1] Neither has the new book of Carl Van Doren's come from Knopfs, though they wrote they'd sent it.[2]

[1] Robinson Jeffers (1887–1962), *Roan Stallion, Tamar and Other Poems* (New York, 1925). (Mabel Luhan's *Lorenzo in Taos* is cast in the form of a letter to Jeffers. DHL never met him.)

[2] *Other Provinces* was published by Knopf in 1925.

I wrote you that I'd review *Doctor Transit*[1] and *Black Swans*, but neither is worth reviewing, in my poor opinion.

We've taken this villa till end of March, so if ever you feel like sending a book, send it direct, will you please?

The man who wrote it sent me *King John*.[2] Have you seen it? It's clever: and I suppose aims at the establishing of a new school of American literature. But the emotional body of the book is awful vieux jeu, and the form, the new prose form, is only an old jacket of *Ulysses* smartened up a bit. What a bore newness is!

All good wishes for New Year.

Sincerely D. H. Lawrence

3570. To John Clarke, 19 December 1925

Text: Lawrence–Gelder 133–4.

Villa Bernarda. Spotorno. Prov. di Genova.
19 Dec. 1925.

I'm sending you a pound, but it's only ten shillings to you. I want you to buy something for your Auntie Gertie with the other ten bob.

Tell your mother I couldn't find a thing for her in that beastly Savona: except rather lovely cups and plates and things – and she has enough of those. But if she'd like some, I could get her a parcel made up.

At last it's raining a bit here: rather nice, the country is so dry. Our old Giovanni is working away, planting his garden. One day you'll have to come with your mother to see everything and *parlare italiano*.

I do hope you get this in time. Write on your Auntie Gertie's present: *From Bert and Frieda*, and do it respectably, so as not to shame us, and don't be wessel-brained,[3] or there'll be death in the pot.

[1] This letter to Irita van Doren has not been found. *Doctor Transit* (New York, 1925, a novel satirising a man with the power to change the world) is by Isidore Schneider (1896–), American poet and novelist.

[2] *King John* (New York, 1925), a novel by Joseph Twadell Shipley (1893–), published in a limited edn of 500 copies and never reprinted. Shipley was a teacher and editor. DHL's comments on the novel are accurate: it is superficially Joycean, highly mannered in its contrived wittiness and sometimes unintelligible. What DHL does not remark on is his own presence in Shipley's pages, e.g.:

> Unconsciously trite he knew himself lord of creation. On the fifth day he made birds beasts and flowers D. H. Lawrence
>
> A snake came to my water trough
> On a hot, hot day and I in pyjamas for the heat
> (Wonder where he was when he wrote that)
> To drink there.
> In the deep, strange-scented shade of the great dark carob
> (Africa East Indies maybe must look it up carob) tree . . . (p. 2)

See also pp. 84–7.

[3] 'stupid' (dialect; literally, brain turned by drink).

Merry Christmas to you all: don't revel too much. And for heaven's sake, I hope the green family is better.

Love from your Auntie Frieda and your ever estimable Uncle Bert.

What have 'those pore collier's boys' been doing lately?

3571. To Nancy Pearn, 19 December 1925

Text: MS UT; Unpublished.

Villa Bernarda. *Spotorno.* Prov di Genova
19 Dec 1925

Dear Miss Pearn

Thanks for your letter, enclosing Edward O'Brien's. I'll write to him as soon as I've seen *The Golden Book.*[1] It's not come yet.

I enclose a little story: 'Smile!'[2] Will you please let the New York office have the duplicate. – There's another story being typed –[3] and I'm just finishing the ghost story: not very ghosty. – I had your letter about Cynthia Asquith: seems to me you don't like her butting in to literature. But I'll leave all the real arrangements to you, since it's your province.[4]

Best wishes: also from my wife. D. H. Lawrence

3572. To Joan King, [20 December 1925]

Text: MS Needham; PC v. 'Buon-Natale'; Postmark, Spotorno 20.12.25; Unpublished.

[Villa Bernarda, Spotorno, Genova]
[20 December 1925]

Merry Christmas, Joan!

DHL

3573. To Gertrude Cooper, [20 December 1925]

Text: MS Clarke; PC v. 'Buon-Natale'; Postmark, Spotorno 20.12.25; Unpublished.

[Villa Bernarda, Spotorno, Genova]
[20 December 1925]

Merry Christmas, Gertie!

DHL

[1] Nancy Pearn had forwarded a request from O'Brien that DHL should contribute to *The Golden Book*. DHL's essay, 'Morality and the Novel' was reprinted in *The Golden Book* (New York, 13 February 1926), pp. 248–50 (see p. 275 n. 4).

[2] See Letter 3562 and n. 3.

[3] 'Sun' (see Letter 3562).

[4] See p. 341 n. 2. Nancy Pearn responded to DHL's disclaimer on 30 December 1925 (TMSC UT):

> . . . As for the Ghost story, of course if you want Lady Cynthia Asquith to have this and the Publisher who is behind her pays reasonably well for it, then we shall feel that your interests are being protected and be quite happy about it. We are quite fond of Lady Cynthia as a matter of fact, but what we do not like is for a Publisher to get things cheap through a social medium so to speak.

3574. To Donald Wells, 20 December 1925

Text: MS UT; Unpublished.

Villa Bernarda, *Spotorno*, Prov di Genova, Italy
20 Dec 1925

Dear Mr Wells

I have a letter today from Mr Barmby, the New York Office, saying that he is paying Michael Borg for the share of royalties on *Memoirs of the Foreign Legion*. I don't know if he means they are paying direct from the New York office, to Borg in Malta. If so, you'll probably be making a double payment. Barmby says he is subtracting from my next American royalties.

Will you please see to this?

Yours Sincerely D. H. Lawrence

3575. To Curtis Brown, 23 December 1925

Text: MS UT; Unpublished.

Villa Bernarda. *Spotorno*, Prov. di Genova, Italy.
23 Dec 1925

Dear Curtis Brown

I wonder if you still think of coming out in January. If so, let me know. The weather was cold, but is now warm and just like spring.

Tell me what you would like to do, if you come: if you want to go to Florence and Rome, and perhaps down to Capri, or if you'd rather stay somewhere quietly. I suppose you'd rather travel. In that case I would come too. I have many friends in Capri urging me to go down, and we could do the other places on the way. But let me know, so that I could arrange. I'm afraid I've lost touch with my friends in Florence and Rome: but we might find them again. Would you come alone, or with your daughter?[1] I think we could manage quite inexpensively, if we tried. And it ought to be good fun.

Best wishes for New Year.

Sincerely D. H. Lawrence

3576. To Emily King, [24 December 1925]

Text: MS Needham; PC v. 'Buon-Natale'; Postmark, Spotorno 24.12 25; Unpublished.

[Villa Bernarda, Spotorno, Genova]
[24 December 1925]

I'm awfully sorry you're having such a time with Joan: had no idea she was in bed all this while. I *do* hope it's better! What a pity she can't be here – it's sunny and mild like spring now, and one can more or less live out of doors. –

[1] Beatrice Curtis Brown (1901–75?).

Don't you bother about sending that tea. I wouldn't have asked if I'd known. What about Peg's school?

love DHL

3577. To Hon. Dorothy Brett, [24 December 1925]

Text: MS UCin; Postmark, Spotorno 24.12 25; Moore 870.

Villa Bernarda, *Spotorno*, Prov di Genova
Thursday

Dear Brett

Thanks for the first part of 'Sun', which came today. I've done $\frac{3}{4}$ of 'Ghost of Silence',[1] and now gone stuck. But these colds one gets go away very irregularly, and leave one disinclined to literature. I feel at present I should love to throw my pen in the sea for ever, and call myself Abinadab Straw, no more D.H.L. walk under the heavens, nor books appear in his name.[2] Ah, if one were rich enough!

I bet you've not wangled your disoccupied millionaire. Those lantern slides will take a bit of bolting.[3]

Brett-Young is pompous Brummagen,[4] and Jessie is his proper help-meet.

I wanted to come down next week. But in London Curtis Brown asked me if I'd go with him for a fortnight in early January, around Italy. I said yes! Thought he'd forgotten it. Apparently he hasn't. I shall have to wait and see if he's really coming. If he does, I'll bring him along to Capri – but it won't be yet. Three weeks ahead perhaps. Tell Achsah, lest she make any preps. for me. – I do feel like roving off a bit. – No further sign of Barby Weekley. Those children of F[rieda]'s are duds. – You think Murry and Violet will turn up? My sister says she's coming in February. They'd better come together, in that case, and leave us January to ourselves. – Rachel's letter depressing! Suppose she'll have to go to that brother of hers. – Spud writes quite nicely: also Mrs Hughes. The thought of the ranch just now makes me shudder. F. has painted a watercolour of the campanile and roofs looking down. – No, there's absolutely nothing to buy here. But I send you two quid for a little wine. Try a bottle of *Strega*. It's a yellow liqueur made of citrons, on the Lago di Garda, near where we used to live. Try a glass first, then buy a bottle if you like it. Strega means witch, but absit omen! Tell Achsah I'll write the moment I hear from Curtis Brown.

DHL

[1] See Letter 3633 and n. 1.

[2] A possible reference to T. E. Lawrence (1888–1935) who, in order to achieve some anonymity, enlisted in the Royal Tank Corps as T. E. Shaw, in 1923.

[3] The allusion cannot be explained.

[4] Francis Brett Young was born at Halesowen and educated in Birmingham.

To keep your innards going, drink plenty of cold water, and at bed-time: or acqua di San Pelligrino – I'm disappointed in the French translations of *BirdsBeasts and Flowers*![1] The quickness has gone, and the music.

DHL

3578. To John Middleton Murry, [27 December 1925]

Text: MS NYPL; cited in Murry, *New Adelphi* 459.

Villa Bernarda. *Spotorno* (Genova)
Sunday 27 Decem

Dear Jack

Well Christmas is over, good thing. Most of Jesus' arrangements are tiresome: or in his name!

Let us roughly fix a date for your coming, will you? My sister wants to come in February: probably early in the month. That's a good time, the blossom is out. I wonder if you and Violet and she might come together. That would be nice for my sister, for the travelling. You would come by Turin, and go back, perhaps, by Nice.

In an unaware moment I promised Curtis Brown I'd make a little trip with him in Italy, in January, and apparently he's keeping me to my word. That would probably be about Jan 5th to 20th – I'm waiting for his definite letter.

Frieda has her daughter Barbara here at the moment. But if the other one turns up they'll have some little appartment of their own, perhaps in this village, or another.

Early Feb. should be very nice – and the hills behind are really wild and attractive. If you think well, you might definitely fix some date with my sister: Mrs L.A. Clarke. Gee St. *Ripley* (Derby).

Hope I shan't have got restive, and busted off to Moscow or Damascus. I wouldn't trust myself. Am not standing present conditions very well.

tanti buoni auguri. DHL

3579. To Adele Seltzer, 28 December 1925

Text: MS UTul; Lacy, *Seltzer* 151–2.

Villa Bernarda. *Spotorno*, Prov di Genova, Italy
28 Dec. 1925

Dear Adele

Thank you for your note, and the man (woman?) about translating.[2] The

[1] The translations were never published; they exist in typescript at UT and UCB. Cf. Letter 3700 and n. 4.

[2] The note is missing, and the translator unidentified.

Insel Verlag – Leipsig – have the translation rights of all my books, into German.

We've been here about six weeks: villa under the Castle, above the roofs of village, and the sea. It's quite nice, though the Riviera doesn't thrill me. Frieda has her daughter Barbara here, and probably the other one is coming: and I shall go off southwards, for a trip.

It's nice, now, to be in Europe again, away from the strain of America. One can relax, and laisser vaguer la galère.[1] I'm sick of being American-tightened-up.

At the present time I think the ranch is inaccessible – William Hawk wrote, deep deep *wet* snow. He and Rachel very down in the dumps, having to clear out from Del Monte, don't get on with the old man, everything gone wrong. – I don't know what we shall do about spring and our return. Frieda says she's happiest at the ranch. But as for me, I feel like staying outside that clenched grip of America for a bit. My imagination veers towards Russia, if only I can afford it. Bisogna aspettare un po![2]

Brett is down in Capri, seems to be enjoying it.

Hope things are going decently with you. Remember me to Thomas.

tanti buoni auguri D. H. Lawrence

3580. To Hon. Dorothy Brett, 29 December 1925

Text: MS UCin; Huxley 643–4.

Villa Bernarda, *Spotorno*, Prov. di Genova
29 Dec 1925

Dear Brett

The hankys came today, and are very nice indeed. But I wish you weren't so extravagant, presenting.

Barby Weekley is here since christmas day – nicer this time – she's busy painting, has faint hopes of one day selling something. But the Slade took all the life out of her work. That Slade is a criminal institution, and gets worse.[3]

We had a very mild Christmas Day – went down to the inn and had a turkey, (my dinner) with Seckers and Capelleros. But they *are* dull people. Now I'm waiting to hear any day from Curtis Brown, to know when *he* will appear. I shall meet him in Genoa or Florence, and come on. It's just possible still he won't come. But more probable he will. He's quite nice, but – absolutely a stranger, and fat and over fifty: Dio benedetto! We sort of let ourselves in for these things. If he comes, it will probably be next week – and then we'd drift on from Florence, Rome, Naples, to Capri – and he'll have to go back all alone. I dread the expense, rather! Why does everything cost, and nothing pay?

[1] 'drift'. [2] 'We must wait a little!' [3] Cf. p. 15 n. 3.

The weather has been sunny and lovely and warm. My cold is much better: Frieda says *she's* now feeling limp. The devil's in it.

Knopf is publishing *The Plumed Serpent* on Jan. 23rd., so by then we ought to have our copies. Strange that the *Porcupine* hasn't appeared.[1]

I have a sort of feeling, I should like to go to Russia, later in the spring. Nobody encourages me in the idea.

I send you another story, 'Glad Ghosts'. It's finished at last, and, usual woe, is much too long. Tell me, what impression it makes on you, I am curious to know. – I suppose you've about got through 'Sun'. Don't bother with the 'Ghosts', unless you wish. Perhaps you are painting fast.

There's no news: I haven't heard from anybody – drew an almost blank Christmas. Just as well, for I hate these strained rejoicings.

Where did you stay, in Rome? How dear was it, and was it nice? Ask Earl if he knows a moderate place. In Naples I suppose one goes to the Santa Lucia. – But I'm going to be tight, on that trip with Curtis Brown: I mean money, not wine.

Tanti buoni auguri per il nuovo anno. Come va il Cristo del Mundo crocifisso? Le piacerebbe, siccuro, lo mettere finalmente alla Croce; un' altra volta, ma l'ultima, questa! Povero uomaccio, perchè non aiutargli staccarsi! Cristo rifiutando alla Croce! Così lo farei io![2]

DHL

3581. To Ada Clarke, 3 January 1926
Text: MS Clarke; Unpublished.

Villa Bernarda, *Spotorno*, Prov di Genova
3 Jan 1926

My dear Sister

Well here's the New Year! – and a brilliant sunny day, with the sea bright. We had a sunny warm Christmas too: very quiet. Barby was here, and we painted pictures, rather nice. One day you must buy one, and help her on.

It will be great fun if you come in February. That can be a very nice month: but it *can* be cold. The almond blossom should be out, and ought to be quite a little forest of pink beneath us. – Murry said he too wanted to come, with his wife Violet – not the baby – about that time. I wrote him, perhaps you'd come with them. It would be very nice if you had them to travel with. – But if you'd rather come alone, only say so. – I expect they will stay a fortnight.

[1] See p. 240 n. 4.

[2] 'Many greetings for the new year. How goes Christ of the World crucified? You would certainly like finally to put him on the Cross; another time, but the last one, this! Poor fellow, why don't you help him to get himself down! Christ refusing the Cross! That's what I would do!'

Frieda also expects Elsa Weekley at the end of January. But perhaps she and Barby will take a little flat.

Brett is still in Capri, we have many friends there, who all want us to go down. Maybe later we shall do that. I don't feel particularly anxious to go back to the ranch this year. Rachel Hawk writes that it snows and thaws, snows and thaws, and is awful. – I feel that high altitude is a bit much for me. I am feeling much better, solider, here. The Mediterranean always does me good.

I was thankful to hear from Emily that Joan is a good deal better. I suppose they still make no move to get out of that hole of a business?[1] Hope Jack is better too. And poor Gertie, isn't it astonishing, to have only one single near relation in the world, and so much bother on the strength of it![2] Almost a record.

Martin Secker has been staying for a month with his in-laws, down in the Villa Maria. He's a nice mild soul. He leaves next week.

We haven't heard from BadenBaden since Christmas. I hope the Schwiegermutter is all right.

Love from us both DHL

What a blessing Bertie isn't a cougher!

Just heard from Murry, Violet is going to have another baby, and they cant come. It's a blow to him: and an added burden. – You might arrange to come with Elsa Weekley, she's nice.

3582. To S. S. Koteliansky, 4 January 1926

Text: MS BL; Postmark, Noli 4 I 26; Moore 876–7.

Villa Bernarda. *Spotorno*, Prov di Genova
4 Jan 1926

My dear Kot

I had Farbman's book, and actually read it all, with much interest.[3] It was really interesting. Many thanks for sending it.

I do hope the domestic tragedy in the cave was only a mishap. I simply feel I can't stand tragedies anywhere any more. Why can't things smooth out a bit? – But send a line, and say it was nothing serious.

It is very sunny and nice here today, feels like spring coming. We had a warm sunny Christmas. It is extraordinary, the change, when one crosses the Alps. I think on the whole I like the Mediterranean Countries best to live in. The ranch still doesn't attract me, though sometimes in my sleep I hear the

[1] 1919–27 Samuel King had a grocery business in Carlton, Nottingham; at this time it was not flourishing and he was indecisive about what action to take; in 1927 he took a shop in another suburb (Bulwell).

[2] Probably her niece Edna (see Letter 3895).

[3] Michael Farbman's *After Lenin: The New Phase in Russia* (1924). See also Letter 3587.

Indians drumming and singing. I still wish my old wish, that I had a little ship to sail this sea, and visit the Isles of Greece, and pass through the Bosphorus. That Rananim of ours, it has sunk out of sight.[1]

If you will send me a grammar book, I'll begin to learn Russian. Just an ordinary grammar book. Even if I never go to Russia, it'll do me no harm. And when I come to England you can give me a few lessons. I am forty years old now, but the world is still an unopened oyster, probably will always remain so. Nevertheless, one can go on trying to prise it open.

I wonder if Russia has had all her troubles and her revolutions, just to bring about a state of complete materialism and cheapness. That would be sad. But I suppose it's on the cards.

What are those people like, on the *Calendar*?[2] Do you know them?

I think Frieda has forsaken you, as a pet enemy. I won't tell you who the later one is, perhaps you've guessed. For my part, I wonder if we don't lose the faculty for making new connections, and if the old ones are all broken we're a bit lost. I feel suddenly rather grown up feel I'd better be a bit wary how I let fly.

Say nice things to Sonia from me, and to Ghita and Grisha.

DHL

I should be very pleased if you'd buy Ghita a small thing with the change, and give it her for a Valentine.

3583. To John Middleton Murry, 4 January 1926

Text: MS NYPL; Huxley 644–5.

Villa Bernarda. *Spotorno*, Prov di Genova
4 Jan 1926

Dear Jack

A la guerre comme à la guerre! Make up your mind to change your ways, and call the baby Benvenuto.

My dear Jack, *it's no good*! All you can do now, sanely, is to leave off. *A la vie comme à la vie.*[3] What a man has got to say, is never more than relatively important. To kill yourself, like Keats, for what you've got to say, is to mix the eggshell in with the omelette. That's Keats' poems to me. The very excess of beauty is the eggshell between one's teeth.

[1] For a description of 'Rananim', the new society DHL hoped to found, see *Letters*, ii. 259; for the origin of the name see ibid., 252 n. 3.

[2] The editors of the *Calendar of Modern Letters* (March 1925–July 1927) were Edgell Rickword (see Letter 3912 and n. 2), Douglas Garman and Bertram Higgins. (The title of the magazine, April 1926–July 1927, became *The Calendar*.)

[3] 'Take life as you find it.'

Carino, basta! Carito, deja, deja la canzon, cheto! Cheto, Cheto! Zitto, Zitto, Zitto! Basta la mossa![1]

In short, shut up. Throw the *Adelphi* to the devil, throw your own say after it, say goodbye to J.M.M. Filius Meus, Salvatore di Nessuno se non di se stesso,[2] and my dear fellow – *give it up*!

As for your humble, he says his say in bits, and pitches it as far from him as he can. And even then it's sometimes a boomerang.

Ach! du lieber Augustin, Augustin, Augustin – I don't care a straw who publishes me and who doesn't, nor where nor how, nor when nor why. I'll contrive, if I can, to get enough money to live on. But I don't take myself seriously, except between 8.0 and 10.0 a. m, and at the stroke of midnight. At other seasons, my say, like any butterfly, may settle where it likes: on the lily of the field or the horsetod in the road: or nowhere. It has departed from me.

My dear chap, people don't want the one-man show of you alone, nor the punch and Judy show of you and me. Why, oh why try to ram yourself down people's throats? Offer them a tasty tit-bit, and if they give you five quid, have a drink on it.

No no! I'm forty, and I want, in a good sense, to enjoy my life. Saying my say and seeing other people sup it up doesn't amount to a hill o' beans, as far as I go. I want to waste no time over it. That's why I have an agent. I want my own life to live. 'This is my body, keep your hands off!'[3]

Earn a bit of money journalistically, and kick your heels. You've perhaps got J.M.M. on the brain even more seriously than J[esus] C[hrist]. Don't you remember, we used to talk about having a little ship? The Mediterranean is glittering blue today. Bah, that one should be a mountain of mere words! Heavo-O! my boy! get out of it!

DHL

3584. To Baroness Anna von Richthofen, [4 January 1926]

Text: MS Schorer; PC v. Un Saluto da Noli – Il Castello e il Capo; Postmark, Spotorno 4. 1.26; Unpublished.

Spotorno.
Montag.

Vielen Dank für die Kritik – Wir haben deine Zeichnung – aber, obgleich es ähnlich ist, finde ich es sehr hässlich. Nein, du bist viel schöner, immernoch. – Noli ist unser nächstes Dorf, zwei Kilometer weg: das Schloss ganz nah, auf

1 'My dear chap, enough! Dear fellow, stop, stop your singing, silence! Silence, Silence! Quiet, Quiet, Quiet! The gesture is enough!'

2 'My Son, Saviour of no one except himself'.

3 Cf. Matthew xxvi. 26.

unsere Seite. – Sind die Bücher für die Else an dir gekommen? Ich will ihr etwas kaufen, wenn wir nach Florenz gehen: hier gibt's nichts. – Geht's der Frau Stötzer besser? – ich hoffe. – Die Barby ist noch in Alassio, hat noch nicht geschrieben, wann sie wiederkommt. Die Elsa bleibt in London bis erste Woche Februar: dann wahrscheinlich kommt meine Schwester Ada mit, zu uns. Es geht uns gut. Ich will an Else schreiben.

Saluti DHL

[Many thanks for the review – We have your drawing – but, even though it's like you, I find it very ugly. No, you are, still, much more beautiful. – Noli is our nearest village, two kilometers away: the castle very near, on our side. – Have the books for Else reached you? I want to buy her something when we go to Florence: here there's nothing. – Is Mrs Stötzer better now?[1] – I hope so. – Barby is still in Alassio, hasn't yet written when she comes back. Elsa stays in London till the first week of February: then my sister Ada probably comes with her, to us. We're fine. I want to write to Else.

Saluti DHL]

3585. To Curtis Brown, 4 January 1926

Text: MS UT; Unpublished.

Villa Bernarda, *Spotorno.* Prov di Genova
4 Jan 1926

Dear Curtis Brown

You didn't answer my letter of just before Christmas, to say whether you're coming down to Italy or not. Let me know, will you, because I must tell my friends when to expect me. The weather keeps pretty good, and I feel quite inclined for a jaunt, so long as we do it modestly.

The man who wrote from Vienna about plays seems to me cracked.[2]

Would you give to Donald Wells the address he asked me for:

Hon Dorothy Brett, Hotel Internationale, *Capri (Napoli), Italy.*

Martin Secker thinks to return to London on the 10th. He's had quite a good holiday here.

All the good wishes for the New Year, and send me a line.

Yrs D. H. Lawrence

One can't bother with this letter, can one! I feel bored stiff by all that Magnus stuff.

[1] Unidentified. [2] Unidentified.

3586. To Hon. Dorothy Brett, [6 January 1926]

Text: MS UCin; Postmark, Ventimiglia 7 GEN 26; Moore 877–8.

Villa Bernarda. *Spotorno* (Genova)
Wednesday 6 Jan Epiphany

Dear Brett

I have the rest of 'Sun', and have sent it off to Barmby and to Curtis Brown. Many thanks. From the latter I've not heard a word, since he wrote a day or two before Christmas and said he was hoping to come out and join me, for a trip. From their office they wrote for your address, wanting to send you the Knopf $50.00.[1]

It is most marvellous weather, and I wish I actually were making an excursion. But it is still a bit too early in the year for Calabria. It might turn very cold. The sea is most tempting, and I am really pining for the lugger. But I don't build on it, having wanted it for years, and being no nearer. – Barby was here for a few days: quite nice this time. We painted two pictures, which would amuse you: quite good[2] – I am correcting final proofs of *David*, and find it good. – No, Shaw is a pamphleteer rather than an artist. – Murry wrote, that because of Violet they won't be able to get out here. He seems very down: wants to transform the *Adelphi* into a one man, or two man (I'm the other) magazine. Says if I won't join him he'll write it *all* himself. Let him then. But I tell him to drop it, and get a bit clear from all that stuff. Why waste one's life entirely! – My sister says she's coming in February: and Frieda's daughter Elsa isn't coming till that month. This is the last winter I'll wait on people's comings and goings. – Martin Secker leaves for London next Monday. *The Plumed Serpent* is out on the 23rd. I'll order Earl and Achsah a London copy, but they won't like it. – If they want to read the stories I send you, let them, if you like. But I'll send the next to London to type, as you'll be fed up enough with 'Ghosts'. – I heard from Rachel, breaking her heart over the sale of Buster Brown and all the cows: and I dreamed that old Ambrose was lost. He's not likely to lose himself. Mabel is installing central heating! – at least Rachel said 'a heater.'

Hope you're feeling better – perhaps too much romance is not good for the inside. Remember me to everybody.

DHL

[1] Cf. Letter 3551 and n. 1.

[2] For Barbara Weekley's account of the joint activity, see Nehls, iii. 22.

3587. To Carl Seelig, 7 January 1926

Text: MS SIU; Unpublished.

Villa Bernarda. *Spotorno*, Prov di Genova
7. Jan 1926

Dear Carl Seelig

I was not surprised by your news: had seen the photographs of the Dutch-Java boy.[1] And I do really think, that you and your wife are not suited to one another: Therefore best make an end.

Here all goes quietly. My wife's daughter – by her first husband – is in Alassio, and comes to see us. But I am not the paternal sort. Am always glad I have no children.

Why don't you try translating one or two poems from *BirdsBeasts and Flowers*?[2] I should like to see what you'd make of them. A Frenchwoman has just turned them into the remorseless logic of French.

I still keep my idea of Russia in the later spring: have written to my Russian friends in London, and have even ordered a grammar-book, to start learning Russian. Look before you leap! – One friend, Michael Farbman, wrote quite a good book about Russia up to 1924. Have you read it? *After Lenin*, by Michael Farbman. I can send it you.

Did I thank you for the *Nachtgeschichten*.[3] They amused me. I sent them to my mother-in-law.

We have good weather here: mostly sunny and warm. Which is a great blessing. Perhaps soon we shall make a trip to Florence and Capri.

But for the next three months I shall merely wait and see what happens: like you and the Engelberg[4] and the Dutchman from Java. Leave it on the knees of the gods.

Greetings from us both, and remember us to your wife, and to the household in the châlet.

Sincerely D. H. Lawrence

[1] Seelig and his wife were divorced in 1928; in 1933 he married Martha, formerly the wife of a Dutchman, William Jacobus von Bosschart. It is not known if von Bosschart and the 'Dutch-Java boy' were one and the same.

[2] No translations of DHL by Seelig are known.

[3] Perhaps Otto Stoessel's *Nachtgeschichten* (Berlin, 1926). (In 1947 Seelig published a book under the same title.)

[4] A mountain resort near Lucerne.

3588. To John Middleton Murry, [9 January 1926]
Text: MS NYPL; Huxley 646.

Villa Bernarda. *Spotorno* (Genova)
9 Jan 1925

Dear Jack

Yes, I find the turn of the winter heavy too, and sometimes a struggle, and last year I nearly fell into the Styx. But I try as far as possible not to fight against the big currents. I don't care much about having my own way any more, even with myself. All I want is to live and be well alive, not constrainedly half dead.

That's why I should say to you, oh, don't bother any more about Jesus, or mankind, or yourself. Let it all go, and have the other sort of faith, as far as possible. I hate my enemies, but mostly I forget them. Let the *Adelphi* die, and say to it: Peace be to your ashes! I don't want any man for an adelphos, and adelphi are sure to drown one another, strangling round each others necks. Let loose! let loose!

I got my copy of *Reflections on the Death of a Porcupine* today. Did you get yours? A very handsome volume, my word! But if the doctrine inside isn't *amusing*, downright amusing, it's no good. Gaudeamus igitur!

It's very nice sunny weather here. The sun means a *lot*. It's almost the grace of God in itself. May a mackerel swallow the larvae of all Words!

Sta bene! DHL

3589. To Earl and Achsah Brewster, [9 January 1926]
Text: MS UT; Brewster 91–2.

Villa Bernarda. *Spotorno* (Genova)
9 Jan 1925.

Dear Earl and Achsah

This from Curtis Brown today, after holding me up since Christmas!

Now let's make some sort of a plan. Do you think we could manage a boat? Why couldn't we possibly hire a little lugger just for two months, and do the Isles of Greece that way? Surely it would be possible! – and it would be lovely. Start towards end of March, when it would be warm on the sea. I'd like that best.

Alternatives? – perhaps a little flight to Spain. It wouldn't cost more than a trip in Italy. – But I do hanker after a boat.

As you know, we've got this house till end of March. I was so frozen in Sardinia in January, I think it's best not to risk tours until March. In Feb. my sister is due to come here for a fortnight: but she might back out.

Now then, let's do something. The Ship for preference. Or Spain in March

– Balearic Isles, Majorca and Minorca – or central Sicily, that place, is it Castelvetrano, in the centre, where the flowers are really really a wonder, in March. It's where Persephone rose from hell, each spring. Or Calabria – though most people get typhoid there, with the filthy water. Or Tunis, and to Kairowan, to the edge of the desert. Or across Italy to Dalmatia, Spalato and Ragusa, very lovely; and Montenegro. But with the ship we could do all that to a marvel. I could put £100 sterling to the ship: at present exchange, that is Lire 12.000. Let us get down to brass tacks. The spring will be here before we know it. Meanwhile, in these few weeks we can economise. Call a council of war. And if we can go south, I shan't think of Russia this spring.

I have ordered you a copy of *The Plumed Serpent* from London, for you both. Hope you won't find it too heavy. Ask Brett if she's got her copy of *Reflections on the Death of a Porcupine*. My copy came this morning.

Let's run up a little flag, and declare for something.

Ever DHL

3590. To Hon. Dorothy Brett, [9 January 1926]

Text: MS UCin; PC v. Noli: Panorama; Postmark, Spo[to]rno 9.1.26; Irvine, Brett 61.

[Villa Bernarda, Spotorno, Genova]
Sat.

Heard from Curtis Brown he's going with *wife* to Taormina, and suggests my joining them. No! – I've written Earl and Achsah, to call a council and make real plans for end of Feb. or early March. Let us get something decided. – I got my copy of *Porcupine* today: very handsome. Have you got yours?

DHL

3591. To Curtis Brown, 9 January 1926

Text: MS Forster; Unpublished.

Villa Bernarda. *Spotorno*, Prov di Genova
9 Jan 1926

Dear Curtis Brown

I expect this will catch you before you leave London.

I hope you'll have a very jolly trip with Mrs Brown. Remember me to everybody in Taormina.

I am not sure now when exactly I shall go south: may take a walking tour with Brewster in Capri – which island, by the way, is only two hours by boat from Naples. – But you might send me a p. c.

c/o E. H. Brewster. Torre Quattro Venti, *Capri.* (Napoli)

when you are in that region, and if I am anywhere about, I'll run over to see you.

Again all good wishes for the trip.

Yrs D. H. Lawrence

3592. To S. S. Koteliansky, 11 January 1926

Text: MS BL; Postmark, Spotorno 11 1.26; cited in Gransden 30.

Villa Bernarda. *Spotorno*. (Genova)
11 Jan. 1926

My dear Kot

I have your letter – no doubt the Russian Grammar will soon come. Many thanks for sending it.

I have been thinking lately, the time has come to read Dostoevsky again: not as fiction, but as life. I am so weary of the English way of reading nothing but fiction in everything. I will order *Karamazov* at once.

Our little friend also wrote to me, asking would I write the *Adelphi* with him – just us two – as a sort of latter-day *Signature*. I told him, to drop it altogether, as the public wanted neither the one-man show of him alone, nor the Punch and Judy show of him and me. To which he replied with more spite and impudence than I have yet had from him, and which makes me imagine he must be nearing the end of his tether. 'The time was long, yet the time ran –'[1] Fra poco sarà finito, quella commedia sacra e buffa degli *Adelphi*. Per me, non sono adelphos di nessuno.[2]

Barbara has also written to Ivy Lowe, concerning my coming to Russia. Ha fatto bene?[3]

I am ordering you a copy of *Reflections on the Death of a Porcupine*, from Philadelphia, because it contains 'The Crown': in memory of *Signature* days. And I will order my new novel for Grisha, not expecting him to care for it. Many thanks to him for *Lenin*.

Yes, get a passport. It is time you moved out of England a bit. You could come and see us here, then: it is so sunny and nice. But wait a bit for me, and we'll go to Russia together: when the green leaves are coming, there.

Hope Ghita likes her purse: may it never be empty.

I had no idea our little friend had gone hawking the *Adelphi* around town. I believe he's in one of his money-panics, benedetto lui![4]

Greet Sonia, tutta la sacra famiglia.

DHL

If our little friend had stuck to me or my way a bit, he wouldn't be where he is.

Smerdyakov always suggested the French *merde* to me.[5] The beshitten!

Damn *all* magazines – except for the bit of money they pay.

[1] Dante Gabriel Rossetti, 'Sister Helen' l. 4 ['Time was . . .']. Cf. *Letters*, i. 159–60 and 160 n. 1.

[2] 'Before long that sacred and comic play of the *Adelphi* will be finished. As far as I'm concerned I am not adelphos to anyone.'

[3] 'Has she done well?'

[4] 'lucky him!'

[5] Smerdyakov is a character in Dostoievsky's *The Brothers Karamazov*. The verb 'smerdet' means to stink; it is probably related to French 'merde' through Latin 'merda', dung.

[Frieda Lawrence begins]

Halloh – Kot!

My greetings to you in the new year and *let*'s be friends.

Frieda

3593. To Harold Mason, 11 January 1926

Text: MS (Photocopy) UT; *Centaur* 25–6.

Villa Bernarda, *Spotorno* (Genova)
11 Jan 1926

Dear Mason

At last, yesterday, came the *Porcupines*, and I was afraid they had gone wrong. We are frightfully pleased with them. I love the Joseph's Coat with the canvas seams:[1] so does my wife. It's by far the jolliest-faced of all my books. Secker is here, and he had a bad five minutes when he saw it, he having no part in it. Murry wrote me spitefully about it, which I took as a left-handed compliment. Now, for your sakes, I hope it will go gaily in America.[2]

I shall send you immediately a copy of the English *Plumed Serpent*. Think you might like it.

Could you also send me, that is, send to two of my friends, a copy each of the *Porcupine*, and charge them to me? The addresses are

1. Dr David Eder. 2 Harley Place, Marylebone Rd. London.
1. S. Koteliansky. 5 Acacia Rd. St. Johns Wood. London N.W.8.

It is lovely sunny weather here. I do thank heaven for the sun, it's the love of God to me, any day.

I know John Macy, and like him very much, though I do think he lets the world use him badly:[3] *which one shouldn't do*. And one day I hope to meet Lawrence Stallings.[4] Tell him I wish he'd let me know, if ever he is within reach.

The sea is moving slowly into Noli bay, on a million little glitters. I am always so glad when it is morning, and the Mediterranean. They say Europe is

[1] The volume has attractively bright decorated back and front covers with a natural cloth covering on the spine.

[2] In a letter dated 9 January 1926 (TMSC Mason), which DHL would not yet have received, Mason expresses his pleasure that 375 copies of *Reflections* had been sold in the four weeks since publication, 'and the number increasing every day'. He also comments on the covers: 'People generally seem to like the appearance of the "scrambled eggs" boards we used . . . I hope you don't find them too frivolous.'

[3] John Macy (1877–1932) was literary editor of the *Nation*, 1922–3, and had reviewed *The Captain's Doll* and *Studies in Classic American Literature*; he wrote the introduction to the Modern Library edn of *Sons and Lovers* (1922). See *Letters*, iv. 477.

[4] Laurence Stallings (1894–1968), American novelist and dramatist. Journalist on the Washington *Times*, then drama critic for New York *World* where he reviewed DHL's *David*.

old: but it's not so old as the little roman hyacinths in the garden, and they've only just emerged, among the ivy. Ho quaranta anni, io! che me pare enorme![1]

Many greetings from us both to you both. D. H. Lawrence

3594. To Edward McDonald, 11 January 1926

Text: MS UT; Postmark, Spotorno 11. 1. 26; Moore 881.

Villa Bernarda. *Spotorno* (Genova), Italy
11 Jan 1926

Dear Dr McDonald

I never wrote you for the New Year, always looking to see the copies of the *Porcupine* – and they only arrived yesterday. I like the creature immensely: if ever the leopard handed over his spots, he did it this time. It's gayer than a geranium in a pot.

We are sitting quietly here, in this not very exciting village. But the house is on the hill above the roofs, just under the castle, and the sea goes in and out its bays, and glitters very bright. There is something forever cheerful and happy about the Mediterranean: I feel at home beside it. We've got a big garden of vines and almond trees, and an old peasant Giovanni, and so long as the sun shines, qui non se ne frega: we don't give a cent for the world. The 1924 wine from the garden is quite good. What a pity you and Mrs McDonald can't be here for a bit. It's only a glorified cottage, and we do the work ourselves. So, one's life is ones own.

If you want a year – or better, six months – in England, why don't you advertise in the *Times Lit. Sup.* that you want to exchange jobs for six months, or a year, with a professor of English at an English college. That's how they do it. I'm sure you'd find someone glad to go to The Drexel Institute for a summer.

I send you for a Valentine the first proofs of my *David* play, of which Secker is doing in March an edition of 500.[2] The proofs aren't corrected, but they may amuse you; I mean the play may. I like it.

ricordi, e tanti buoni saluti! – to you and Mrs McDonald, from us both.

D. H. Lawrence

3595. To S. S. Koteliansky, 15 January 1926

Text: MS BL; Postmark, Spotorno 16. 1.26; cited in Gransden 30.

Villa Bernarda. *Spotorno* (Genova)
15 Jan 1926

My dear Kot

I have the FOUR grammar books, and feel like the man who asked for a

[1] 'I am forty, I am! which seems a very big age to me!'

[2] The proofs (with minor corrections and additions in DHL's hand) are at UT.

piece of bread, and was given a field of corn. Why four, all at once? The extra three only frighten me.

But I bravely started, and am in the midst of those fearful и and ъ ы ь э and ж things. I hope the bolsheviks, with the end of the Romanovs, ended a few letters of the alphabet. Did they?

And where is Ghita's purse coming from, if all the money went on books? I enclose another ten bob, hope it'll reach. I thought you'd just buy *one* 5/- book.

It has actually *snowed* here, and been vilely cold. Today it is slackening off, hinting at mildness. The beastly Italian louts are out alla caccia, *hunting* – O Cacciatori![1] – the hedge sparrows, robins, larks and finches. The tiny birds are driven down by the snow, and I don't exaggerate when I say one hears five or six shots a minute, all day long. You hear a huge man say: sono cacciatore apassionato![2] – which means he's just shot a robin. Oh world of men![3]

My sister is coming out here for the second half of February, and is very thrilled. Martin Secker returns to London on Monday. He's quite nice, really, and perfectly unassuming – shy.

Nothing further from our little friend.

tanti saluti! DHL

3596. To Carl Seelig, [15 January 1926]

Text: MS SIU; PC v. Noli Ant[. . .]oggia; Postmark, Spotorno 15. 1.26; Unpublished.

[Villa Bernarda, Spotorno, Genova]
15. Jan.

You'll have to find some way of getting a passport. I have got a grammar book, and have started to learn Russian. – By the way, remember us to Herr Haas and the Frau Dr. – and tell them, if they come to Italy, to be sure to come this way. We might even go for a few days together, in March. Best wishes from both to both.

D. H. Lawrence

3597. To Ada Clarke, 15 January 1926

Text: MS Clarke; Unpublished.

Villa Bernarda. *Spotorno* (Genova)
15 Jan. 1926

My dear Sister

That will be great fun, if you come with Lizzie Booth.[4] We shall both be pleased to see her.

[1] 'at the hunt, *hunting* – O Hunters!' [2] 'I am a keen hunter!'

[3] DHL wrote an essay on the same subject, 'Man is a Hunter' (first published in *Phoenix* 32–4); this may be referred to in Letter 3903. See also Letters 3866, 3869.

[4] Lizzie and her husband, Harold Booth (headmaster of the village school at Hartshay, near Ripley, and later at Duffield), were close friends of Ada and Edwin Clarke.

I want you to decide whether you'd rather go to Genoa, Pisa, and Florence, than to Cannes or Monte Carlo. It will cost about the same. We'd make the trip with you at the end of the stay, and leave you on the Calais train in Genoa (Genova in Italian. Turin is Torino) – which would bring you straight to the boat.

I think I will meet you in Turin, and stay the night there, as you'll be tired of travelling by then. Will you sit up all night, or will you have a bed in the wagon-lit? If you do, you must book it in time: costs about £1. extra, I think – or maybe more.

We are only eight miles from Savona, and we shall probably motor here from there. So book your ticket either Turin – Savona – Genoa – Pisa – Florence and return Florence, Genoa, Turin, Paris. Or else book

Turin, Savona, Spotorno –

Spotorno, Ventimiglia (Ventimille), Paris

– whichever you please.

I suppose you'll leave London – *Victoria – Continental station* – at 11.0 in the morning, getting to Paris about 6.0 in the evening, and Turin about 5.30 following evening. Don't bring much luggage, just handbags that will go on the rack. It will save a lot of bother registering.

We've even had snow here: unheard of. But it's mild again today.

Martin Secker returns on Monday to London. He's a quiet little man, but very nice.

Did you get from America a copy of *Reflections on the Death of a Porcupine*? It's privately done, 1000 copies only.[1] I'm not quite sure if I ordered you one – will do so if not.

Did Jackie get my letter at Christmas, and cheque for £1? You never mentioned it, but I suppose he had it. I'm glad he's better.

love to all, and au revoir. DHL

3598. To Mabel Dodge Luhan, 16 January 1926

Text: MS Brill; Luhan 289–90.

Villa Bernarda. *Spotorno.* Prov di Genova
16 Jan. 1926

Dear Mabel

We had your Christmas Day letter, with the little story, yesterday. The story gives one the feeling of the pueblo and the country very much. I liked it.

I'm sorry I've mislaid Havelock Ellis' address. If you could tell him to send the MSS here, we could read them and tell you how they strike us. – Heaven knows what it is, to be honest in writing. One has to write from some point of

[1] The number of copies printed is disputed: see Roberts A32.

view, and leave all other aspects, from all the remaining points of view, to be conjectured. One can't write without feeling – and feeling is bias. The only thing to put down on paper is one's own honest-to-goodness feeling.

We actually had two days of snow here, and the cacciatori are banging away at the tiny birds, it's like a festa with all the crackers going off. The robins and finches fly about in perfect bewilderment – and occasionally in bits – La caccia!

It's a quiet winter, but pleasant. Thank heaven the sun shines warm again, the almond trees are budding. Europe is easy, when all's said and done. – Where, by the way, was your Florence villa?[1] If you'll send me the address we'll go and look at it, I expect we shall make a trip round about when my sister comes out in February.

I don't quite know what we shall do later in the spring. There is some talk of my going to Russia for a bit. But I don't know how that will turn out. How long are you staying in Croton? – I ordered you a copy of *The Plumed Serpent*. You may perhaps like it: not many people will: but I do, myself.

Brett is down in Capri. She seems to be enjoying it too, from what she writes. Frieda expects her daughter Barby this afternoon – la vita è tutta' altra. Quasi quasi non mi Conosco più.[2] I wonder very much what it's like at the ranch. William Hawk has taken the horses down to his pasture at San Cristobal.

Remember me to Spud and everybody – tanti buoni auguri!

DHL

My publisher Martin Secker is here – quiet little man. I think I'll give him this letter to post in England, he'll go back on Monday.

3599. To Martin Secker, [18 January 1926]

Text: MS UInd; PC v. Noli – La Marina; Postmark, Spotorno 19. 1.26.; Secker 68–9.

[Villa Bernarda, Spotorno, Genova]
Monday.

– Frieda, who is off the deep end in her translation of *David*,[3] says will you please send a German dictionary: English–German, German–English: it can come with *Karamazov* and *Hajji Baba*,[4] and please send me the bill. – At the moment you are in the train – povero lei![5] It's been a lovely day, Rina here to

[1] See Letter 3647 and n. 1.
[2] 'life is quite different. I very nearly don't know myself any more.'
[3] The trans. was not published; the MS is at UCB.
[4] See Letter 3610. DHL hoped to receive James Morier, *The Adventures of Hajji Baba of Ispahan* (1824); he was sent Morier's *Adventures of Hajji Baba of Ispahan in England* (1828).
[5] 'poor you!'

tea, after a small walk behind the castle. I'm glad I'm not being whirled Londonwards. I had a good whack at my gipsy story tonight, and nearly finished it:[1] over the climax, and on the short down slope to the end. – Rina thinks she would really like to start translating 'The Fox' or 'The Captain's Doll': you might send her that vol., and let her try.

Tanti Saluti! DHL

3600. To John Middleton Murry, 19 January 1926

Text: MS NYPL; cited in Murry, *New Adelphi* 460.

Villa Bernarda. *Spotorno* (Genova)
19 Jan 1926

Dear Jack

I would rather you didn't publish my things in the *Adelphi*. As man to man, if ever we were man to man, you and I, I would give them to you willingly. But as writer to writer, I feel it is a sort of self-betrayal. Surely you realise the complete incompatibility of my say with your say. Say your say, Caro! – and let *me* say mine. But for heavens sake, dont let us pretend to mix them.

Yrs DHL

3601. To Hon. Dorothy Brett, 19 January 1926

Text: MS UCin; Postmark, Spotorno 19 I 26; cited in Huxley 647.

Villa Bernarda. *Spotorno*, Prov di Genova
19 Jan 1926

Dear Brett

Just a line to thank you for the typescript of 'Glad Ghosts': the first bit of it.

Murry, I told you, wrote me impertinently about *The Porcupine*, that I am a professional heel-kicker. Lucky I'm not a professional behind-kicker. Now he adds insult to injury, asking if I will allow him to print the essay on power,[2] gratis, and various other things, gratis, in his *adelphi*; 'as the gift of one man to another.' To which I can only say; 'as one writer to another, I will give you nothing, paid for or unpaid for.' He's an incorrigible worm.

I had Earl's letter: a very old-maidish and mimping-pimping kind of letter too. Makes me want not to see him – smells too false.

So the time goes by. Martin Secker returned yesterday to London. He is nice, and unobtrusive. My sister is coming for a fortnight, the latter half of February. After that, I don't know what we'll do: wait a bit and see.

[1] *The Virgin and the Gipsy* (published by Giuseppe Orioli in Florence in May 1930).

[2] 'Blessed Are the Powerful' (originally entitled 'Power') was published in *Reflections*, pp. 145–60. (See *Reflections*, ed. Herbert, p. li n. 129.)

Your *porcupine* went to Callander.[1] Get it from them, it's such a gay-got-up book.

We had two days of snow, and cold, but it's sunny again. The hills behind here are nice, one can walk in them. Barby has not appeared again – no more painting! A cheery-o! letter from Mabel!

We'll have to wait and let time unravel itself a bit.

An impudent review of *Porcupine* in *N. York Times*, with large picture of me.[2] Quelle canaille!

Hasta otra vez! DHL

3602. To Edward McDonald, [19 January 1926]

Text: MS UT; PC v. Saluti da Noli; Postmark, Spotorno 19. 1.26; *Centaur* 26.

[Villa Bernarda, Spotorno, Genova]
19 Jan.

Had your letter today – and many thanks for the enclosure, and the hit back. What a piffling bit of writing that review! – I wrote you the other day and sent you proofs of the *David* play. – I doubt whether I shall return to America this year: think I shall stay in Europe, perhaps go to Russia. But we should like to see you in England. I can give you one or two letters etc – remind me as the time draws near. Would Mrs McDonald come with you? Noli is the next village – a mediaeval village republic. It's lovely and sunny again. Best wishes from both.

DHL

I'm ordering you a new little bi-monthly: *Word-Lore*.[3] Don't know if it's any good.

3603. To Martin Secker, 21 January 1926

Text: MS UInd; Secker 69.

Villa Bernarda. *Spotorno* (Genova)
21 Jan. 1926

Dear Secker

Here is the rest of the 'Gipsy' story. When it's typed, will you send me the

[1] Cf. Letter 3529.

[2] In *New York Times Book Review*, 27 December 1925, p. 5.

[3] MS reads: 'Word-Lore Word-Lore'.

Word-Lore: The 'folk' magazine (1926–8), ed. Douglas Macmillan. Readers were informed in the first number that '*Word-Lore* whilst aiming to be of a popular character, will nevertheless endeavour to be reliable and instructive . . . a unique repository of valuable and out-of-the-way records concerning a picturesque past that is rapidly fading out of remembrance.' Among the 'Founders' (who were prepared to subscribe a guinea) were listed DHL at Spotorno and 'Professor Ernest Weekley, 49 Harvard Road, Chiswick, W.4.'

MS so I can go over them! And the bill. And tell me please what you think of it – any crits. you have to make. I never mind altering these stories a bit. I'll let you see the 'Glad Ghosts' too, when I get the typescript.

Yesterday was the loveliest day, but today is cold and rainy. Barbara came last night. We wanted to go to Savona and buy colours, but the day's not good enough: leave it till tomorrow.

All well at the Villa Maria – the paraffin stove a great success. It will be useful today.

Saluti! DHL

3604. To John Hayward, 22 January 1926

Text: MS KCC; Unpublished.

Villa Bernarda, *Spotorno*, Prov. di Genova
22 Jan 1926

Dear Sir[1]

I'm sorry I can't promise to read a paper to the Heretics, as I don't know at all when I shall be in England.[2] But one day, I should like to.

Yours sincerely D. H. Lawrence

3605. To Hon. Dorothy Brett, 25 January 1926

Text: MS UCin; Huxley 648–9.

Villa Bernarda. *Spotorno* (Genova)
25 Jan. 1926

Dear Brett

I haven't thanked you yet for the second batch of 'Glad Ghosts', and your letter. – I suppose you'll be sending the last of it soon. – When I write another story, I'll send it on. At present I'm not doing anything. – January is always a hard month to climb through: it was at this time last year I got ill. This year I'm doing my best to avoid it: and I really feel much better. I think Italy really agrees with me better than America does: I feel sounder, solider. – My sister arrives on Feb 9th – for two weeks. Frieda's daughter Elsa on Feb. 12th. Barby is here since last Wed: and we're settling down better: do paintings. – I wish

[1] John Davy Hayward (1905–65) was, in 1926, an undergraduate at King's College, Cambridge. Despite his increasing incapacity from muscular dystrophy he became one of the most erudite editors and bibliophiles of his day. His edn of Rochester's *Collected Works* appeared in 1926, *The Poetry and Prose of John Donne* in 1929, etc.

[2] The 'Heretics' was a Cambridge society 'conspicuous in its heyday in the twenties for total freedom of thought, the sort of emancipated irreverence which one associates with the 18th century *philosophes*, and general moral free-wheeling' (T. E. B. Howarth, *Cambridge Between Two Wars*, 1978, pp. 50–1). Hayward was probably the secretary, Philip Sargant Florence, the economist, president.

we could really make some nice trip, when our visitors have left. – How is your primrose Jesus getting on?[1] I hear Murry's *Life of Jesus* was to appear in one of Lord Beaverbrook's papers – *Sunday Times* or something like that – it would have meant a nice bit of money. But apparently it's not coming off.[2] But he's got plenty of money, really, property and investments – richer than all of us put together – Murry, I mean. The photographs include Martin Secker and Rina's posterior. – I'll send you Lord Dufferin's *Letters from High Latitudes* to show you how nice a yacht can be.[3] I bought a few of these little books, for *our* yacht. Even the books must be small! Keep it in case we ever *do* get a yacht library. – I had a rather feeble review of *Plumed Serpent* from *Times Lit Sup.*[4] – My American copy hasn't come yet. Has your *porcupine*? – You must be getting smarter and smarter, in clothes. We, not! Hope you're well and cheerful.

DHL

Look out for your copy of *Plumed Serpent* – don't let it go to *Hotel Webster*.[5] (photographs enclosed!)

3606. To Martin Secker, [26 January 1926]

Text: MS UInd; PC v. Spotorno – Pineta; Postmark, [. . .] 26 GEN.26; Secker 68.

Villa Bernarda. *Spotorno*. (Genova), Italy.
27 Jan. 1926

Many thanks for *My Head*,[6] and typing, and dictionary, and *Karamazov*: do hope I haven't bothered you too much. I sent you the balance of the story[7] – You might keep the MS. for me, if it wouldn't be a nuisance to you – I have nowhere to store them. – Will you send me a bill for all the things, and I'll post you a cheque – it's simpler. – Barbara has been here a week: goes back tonight. My sister arrives this day fortnight: for two weeks. – Rina and Barby and I walked to the top of the ridge this afternoon, and made plans for outings when you come again. – *Did* you get the stupendous *Borzoi* calendar?[8] For vanity,

[1] See Letter 3559 and n. 3. For the phrase 'your primrose Jesus' see Brett 273.

[2] *The Life of Jesus* was published by Cape in October 1926, but beginning before that in Murry's *Adelphi*, in eleven parts, July 1926–June 1927.

[3] *Letters from High Latitudes: being some account of a voyage in the schooner yacht 'Foam' . . . to Iceland, Jan Mayen and Spitzbergen, in 1856* (1857), by Blackwood (F. T. H. Temple), Marquess of Dufferin and Ava.

[4] It was reviewed in *TLS*, 21 January 1926, p. 41, by Arthur Sydney MacDowall (1877–1933), author of *Nature and Men* (1923), *Thomas Hardy, A Critical Study* (1931), etc.

[5] Brett had intended staying in 'Hotel Webster'; she was actually staying with the Brewsters.

[6] In June 1925 Secker had published *My Head! My Head! Being the History of Elisha and the Shunamite Women* by Robert Graves (1895–1985).

[7] See Letter 3603.

[8] See Letter 3400 and n. 6 and also Letter 3617.

Knopf has it! I'll send you my copy if you didn't get one direct. Hope all will really go well. A feeble *Times* review!

DHL

3607. To Witter Bynner, 27 January 1926
Text: MS HU; Huxley 649.

Villa Bernarda. *Spotorno*. (Genova), Italy.
27 Jan. 1926

Dear Bynner

Caravan came today, and I have read it already, and like it very much. Surely you don't think me an enemy of life?[1] *My single constancy is love of life*![2] Caro, caro, is it *quite* true? But it's the only thing to be constant to, I'm with you entirely there: and against the old. But don't you go and get old just now. Do you see me merely as a cat? Sometimes a cat, anyhow. I like these the best of your poems, that I know. They are more really you. Even serving happiness is no joke! I hope you won't mind the little sketch of you in *The Plumed Serpent*.[3] I don't think it's unsympathetic – it only dislikes your spurious sort of love of happiness – the spurious side of it. Happiness is a subtle and aristocratic thing, and you mixed it up with the mob a bit. – Believe me, I'm not the enemy of your happiness: only of the false money with which you sometimes sought to buy happiness. You must know what I mean: these poems are very sincere and really deep in life, so you do know. – I hope, one day, when I've shed my fur and claws, and you've acknowledged your own fur and claws, we may be two men, and two friends: truly. – I don't know if I shall come back to America this year: it's a strain. I might go to Russia. Would you like to go with me? I've even learned my Russian A.B.C. – Frieda sends her greetings – hope everything goes well with you.

D. H. Lawrence

[1] Bynner had sent a copy of his volume of poems, *Caravan* (Knopf, 1925); it included one entitled 'D. H. Lawrence' (see Bynner 325–7). In it DHL is presented in feline imagery as one who consorts with 'men who are tired of being men / And . . . women who are tired of being women'. The poem ends with the writer wondering

Whether you are a man wishing to be an animal
Or an animal wishing to be a man.

[2] DHL here quotes the opening line of 'Epithalamium and Elegy' (*Caravan*, p. 65).

[3] Bynner appears as the American poet and socialist, Owen Rhys, who suffers from 'the despair of having lived in vain . . . Having missed something' (*The Plumed Serpent*, ed. L. D. Clark, Cambridge, 1987, p. 28).

3608. To John Middleton Murry, [29 January 1926]

Text: MS NYPL; Moore 886.

Villa Bernarda. *Spotorno* (Genova)
29 Jan.

Dear Jack

I don't mind if you use that criticism – nor about the Cuckoo poem.[1] I never pretend to be tolerant, though probably am so, as much as most folks. I can only repeat, I feel it's a betrayal of myself, as a writer of what I mean, to go into the *Adelphi*, so I'd rather stay out.[2]

There's nothing more to be said. You make it pretty clear, in your writings, what you stand for. I hope I do the same. If I don't, letters won't help. – And it's incompatible.

So don't look to me any more for help, after that crit., please. I can't go between the yellow covers of the *Adelphi* without taking on a tinge of yellow which is all right in itself, but not my colour for me.

Yrs D. H. Lawrence

3609. To Nancy Pearn, 29 January 1926

Text: MS UT; Huxley 650.

Villa Bernarda. *Spotorno* (Genova), Italy
29 Jan 1926

Dear Miss Pearn

I am sending you today two copies of the story 'Glad Ghosts'. I wrote it really for Lady Cynthia – but am not sure if it's suitable: 14,000 words anyhow. I shall send you next week a long story: 'The Virgin and the Gipsy' – about 25000 – or 30,000 words. Secker wants me to make another 3-story book like *The Ladybird*, and he rather fancies 'Glad Ghosts' and 'The Virgin' for two of them. But give me your advice, will you? – You got a copy of 'Sun': wonder if you liked it. I sent the duplicate straight to New York, so no need to bother about that.

[1] The 'criticism' was DHL's review of Pickthall's *Saïd the Fisherman*: see Letter 3481 and n. 4. The 'Cuckoo poem', entitled 'Creative Evolution', was printed in *Adelphi*, iii (February 1926), 608.

[2] Murry (*Reminiscences* 121–2) persuaded himself that DHL's rejection of him was on account of his failure to visit Spotorno. 'If our co-operation was to depend upon such intensely personal happenings, it was . . . merely an empty pretence, which it was better for both of us to have done with. I told him this' (p. 122). With the exception of two 'polite' communications (Letters 3724 and 3747), this was effectively the end of their correspondence until Murry wrote in February 1929.

Will you please send one copy of 'Glad Ghosts' on to Mrs McCord: though I doubt if theyll ever be able to use it.

Murry wanted me to give him things, gratis, for the *Adelphi*. I wouldn't mind a bit, if he didn't do such mean little things, and were not, *in what he says*, so very distasteful. After he's used that little crit. on *Säid the Fisherman* I don't want him to use anything else: he took a poem this month without any consent from me. I wouldn't mind a bit: but I *cant* get mixed up in the sickly yellow colour of his *Adelphi*sm. But this is private, please: though of course I've told him flatly. – It's rainy today – all the almond-blossom coming out. I like being in Italy again. Heard from Curtis Brown in Naples: sorry I can't join him.

D. H. Lawrence

3610. To Martin Secker, [30 January 1926]

Text: MS UInd; Postmark, Spotorno 30. 1.26; Secker 69.

Villa Bernarda, *Spotorno*, Genova
Sat.

Dear Secker

Many thanks for the complete typescript of the 'Virgin'. Let me know a bit in detail how the story strikes you. – It must be about 40,000 words.

We had a day of pouring rain yesterday, and it threatens again today.

I was so sad, the wrong *Hajji Baba* arrived. I've already got *Hajji Baba in England*. I wanted the *first* vol: *Hajji Baba in Ispahan*.[1] – So I sent it back to you. So sorry.

No further news here – all the plants are dead – but the almond blossom is already out, like the first flurry of snow, under the back door. I wish the sun would shine again. So, probably, do you.

Saluti D. H. Lawrence

3611. To Nancy Pearn, [30 January 1926]

Text: MS UT; Unpublished.

Villa Bernarda. *Spotorno* (Genova)
Sat.

Dear Miss Pearn

Of course, the moment I've posted you a letter, comes yours: many thanks. I'll remember the *Star*: 800 words should keep one sketchy.[2] I told you about 'Sun'.

I shouldn't write a *Sea and Sardinia* on the Riviera, though.

[1] See Letter 3599 and n. 4.

[2] Nancy Pearn had told DHL on 26 January 1926 (TMSC UT) that the literary editor of the *Star* would welcome travel sketches from him.

Will you please tell whoever it is that looks after poetry in the office, that Doran's have my permission to print 'Baby Asleep after Pain' in Miss Honde's anthology:[1] as for collecting a guinea, will you please use your discretion.

Pouring rain! but I dont suppose it will last.

My wife sends you greetings.

D. H. Lawrence

Don't you think old-fashioned people like Blackwoods might print me? – the reviews, as you say.

3612. To Harold Mason, 1 February 1926

Text: TMSC UT and MS Mason; Postmark, Spotorno 1 2. 26; *Centaur* 27.

Villa Bernarda, Spotorno, Prov. di Genova
1 Feb. 1926

Dear Mason,

Thanks for sending me that criticism. It's nice to be the best of the little writers.[2] Chi va piano va lontano – e va sano.[3] Who knows where we shall end.

How is my dear *Porcupine* disporting himself? I have an affection for that book. And did you get a copy of *The Plumed Serpent* I ordered for you. Povero di me,[4] I could weep over *that* book, I do so hate it's being published and going into the tuppenny hands of the tuppenny public. Small private editions are really *much* more to my taste. Odio profanum vulgum[5] – though it's not the vulgus, it's literatus literatibus.

Send a copy of *The Porcupine* to Martin Secker, 5 John St. Adelphi, W.C.2 will you please, at my expense. I nearly gave him one of my copies. Then, no! Why should I! I'll keep 'em both.

The almond blossom is all tipping out like flakes of snow on the hills: but now it rains, which is, here, almost a catastrophe.

Did I tell you, I half think of going to Russia, instead of coming to America this year. One has to be so tough in America Как хорошо здесь!

[1] It is not known whether 'Miss Honde's anthology' is identical with *Twelve Centuries of English Poetry and Prose*, ed. A. G. Newcomer *et al.* (New York, 1928) which includes 'A Baby Asleep After Pain'. (The poem had already appeared in *The Little Book of Modern British Verse*, ed. Jessie B. Rittenhouse, New York, 1924.)

[2] In the 'impudent review of *Porcupine* in *N. York Times*' (Letter 3601 and p. 381 n. 2) the anonymous reviewer referred to DHL as 'one of today's best little writers'. (In the auction sale, 24 June 1971, at which Charles Hamilton (New York) sold the MS of this letter, another item (no. 243) consisted of 'a group of five small original snapshots, ... several depicting Lawrence and all showing his surroundings in Italy ... One ... depicting Lawrence has been annotated in French ... in his handwriting, "The best of the little writers".')

[3] 'He who travels gently travels far – and healthily'.

[4] 'Poor me'.

[5] Horace, *Odes*, III. i. 1 ['Odi profanum vulgus': 'I despise the unitiated mob'].

That's just to show you what I *can* do, in the polyglottish line! I know already four words of Russian. Я радь.[1]

Perhaps you and Madame will come to Europe in the Summer or autumn, as McDonald is coming. Then we'll all have a meeting and drink white wine and red wine and black wine and brown wine, senza vergogna! At present I've got 30 bottles of the red, and 20 of the white, 1920 vintage, of this garden. It's nice, but on the over-dry side.

Secker took the snaps: so we write ourselves large. Tanti saluti buoni alla Signora ed a dio.[2] I hope I'll never write another serious novel!

D. H. Lawrence

3613. To Martin Secker, 1 February 1926

Text: MS UInd; Postmark, Spotorno 1 2.26; Secker 70.

Villa Bernarda. *Spotorno* (Genova)
1st Feb 1926

Dear Secker

Many thanks for the MS. of the 'Virgin': suppose you hadn't got my card asking you to keep it for me. – I enclose cheque, with 6/- towards the books. – *Jud Süss* is a vulgar affair.[3]

Frieda doesn't like the title of 'The Virgin and the Gipsy': she prefers something with Granny: like 'Granny Gone' or 'Granny on the Throne'.[4] What do you think? – I sent 'Glad Ghosts' to Miss Pearn at Curtis Browns. Ask her to let you see it. But really, I'd promised it for Lady Cynthia Asquith's collection of Ghost Stories – only I don't think it very suitable: and 14,000 words, too long. But Miss Pearn will send it you to read. – Only *don't count on a book for the autumn, really*. I feel at the moment I will never write another word. Why don't you defer the play a bit – perhaps even till autumn? That would do. Frieda is crazy, translating it. She loves it, and has become the authoress, I the cook and the captain bold,[5] and housemaid of the Villa B. – But on the 9th arrives my sister, with a friend, which will make an interlude,

[1] 'How nice it is here . . . I'm glad'.

[2] 'Many cordial greetings to your lady and to the almighty.'

[3] By Lion Feuchtwanger (1884–1958), the historical novel – based on the life of Josef Süss-Oppenheimer (1698–1738) – was translated by Willa and Edwin Muir, and published by Secker as *Jew Suss* in November 1926. See also Letter 3975.

[4] Frieda or DHL may have had in mind the immensely popular book by Frances Browne, *Granny's Wonderful Chair*; published in 1857, it reappeared in various forms for a century thereafter.

[5] The allusion is to Sir W. S. Gilbert, 'The Yarn of the Nancy Bell', in *The Bab Ballads* (1869). Cf. *Letters*, i. 293.

while Barby and Elsa Weekley are, apparently, going into the *Ligure*: with a friend, a Mrs Seaman.[1] Vive les femmes! e la stagione inglese![2]

A bit of friction down at the Villa Maria but probably its only the weather. Rain again today.

Saluti D. H. Lawrence

3614. To Hon. Dorothy Brett, 2 February 1926

Text: MS UCin; Postmark, Ventimiglia 2 FEB 26; Huxley 650–1.

Villa Bernarda. *Spotorno* (Genova)
2 Feb. 1926

Dear Brett

I got the whole of 'Glad Ghosts' – and have sent it off. But they'll never find a magazine to print it. They wrote that even 'Sun' was too 'pagan' for anything but a highbrow 'review'. Fools!

You are right, the London group are absolutely no good. Murry wrote asking me to define my position. Cheek! It's soon done with regard to him. Pour moi, vous n'existez pas, mon cher.[3]

It's beastly weather, cold and rainy, and all the almond blossom coming out in the chill. My sister arrives this day week – Tuesday – in Turin: I shall go up there to meet her.[4] She stays two weeks, and I hope we shall get a trip to Florence and Pisa: and I pray heaven the weather may be different.

What are your plans? Ours are very indefinite. I don't feel like going back to America. I love the ranch, but I feel a revulsion from America, from going west. I am even learning a bit of Russian, to go to Russia: though whether that will really come off, I don't know. We might keep this house on till April – But I simply don't know what I shall do. I wish I wanted to go to the ranch again: but I don't: not now. I just dont. The only thing is to wait a bit.

I've left off writing now: I am really awfully sick of writing. But now Frieda is at it, wildly translating the *David* play into German. She's even done it half. I wonder if it would be a great nuisance to you to post me my typewriter. F's daughter Elsa is a trained typist, and knows enough German to type out this MS. from F's rather muddled books. I tried to hire a type-writer in the village, but without success so far. But if you think it's not safe to post mine, or a lot of trouble, don't bother, and we'll try and get one, just for this job, from Savona. F's daughter Elsa is arriving next week also: but staying in the little hotel Ligure while my sister is here.

[1] Eileen Hilda Seaman (1873–1957), friend of the Weekley family and mother of Elsa's future husband (see Letter 3876 and n. 3). She was en route to visit her sister in Turin. For 'Ligure' see following letter.

[2] 'Long live the ladies! and the English season!'

[3] 'As far as I'm concerned, you don't exist, my dear chap.'

[4] MS reads 'here'.

If we go to Florence, you might have run up for a trip while we are there. But then, if you were going to England later on, it is a waste to come now. And we really might make a trip to Capri in March. – It all depends on your plans for returning to the ranch.

I send a couple of snapshots – Rina Secker takes them: they're good, for such a tiny camera, don't you think.

Sorry the Brewsters snubbed your Jesus.[1] Practise the tiger and the cheetah before you do your Buddha. The beasts come first.

Remember us to everybody – Brooks and all.[2]

DHL

3615. To Hon. Dorothy Brett, [11 February 1926]

Text: MS UCin; Postmark, Spotorno 12. 2.26; Huxley 651–2.

Spotorno.
Thursday

Dear Brett

I'm in bed these last six days with flu – don't see daylight yet. It gave me bronchial hemorrhage like at the ranch, only worse. The doctor says just keep still. My sister came yesterday with a friend – Mrs Booth – So they too are here in the fireless house. It pours with rain, is very cold, and has been like this, the weather, for nearly three weeks. My sister left Dover in bright sunshine, and a fine clear evening in Paris – no snow till Italy! F[rieda]'s daughter Elsa arrives in Ventimiglia tonight, Barby has gone to meet her. They come back tomorrow, stay in the little Hotel Ligure here till my sister has gone – she leaves on the 25th – then they two move up here. But I like Barby.

Chapter of dismalnesses!

I doubt if we shall ever see comfortable days together. Frieda declares an implacable intention of never seeing you again, and never speaking to you if she does see you – and I say nothing. Don't you say anything either, it only makes scenes: which is ridiculous. As for plans, I feel it's the Flood, the only thing is to build an Ark. I like that quot. from Keyserling:[3] but otherwise there's something snobbish and not quite real about his attitude. Though what you quote is right. He's often very right. Only, shall we say, nerveless, after-life. – I don't like Buddha, at the best: much prefer Hinduism.[4]

[1] Cf. Letter 3559 and n. 3.

[2] John Ellingham Brooks (1863–1929), a permanent (English) resident on Capri whom DHL had known since 1920. A friend of Douglas, Mackenzie and Maugham. See *Letters*, iii. 443 n. 2.

[3] Count Hermann Alexander Keyserling (1880–1946), a well-known popular philosopher; he founded the 'School of Wisdom' at Darmstadt in 1920. Brett's quotation may have come from his *Travel Diary of a Philosopher* (1925).

[4] MS reads 'Hunduism'.

I dreamed there had been a flood at San Cristobal, and Aaron lay drowned, and I could only find alive a bunch of weird, rather horrible pintos. – I enclose William's letter. – I don't give up the ranch, not at all! And I don't insist on Russia – not at all! I won't go unless I want to more than I do at this minute. Now, I say nothing, and let the rain pour down, and wait for the finger of the Lord.

So sorry to bother you about the typewriter. Pazienza! aspette! aspette pure![1]

DHL

3616. To Earl Brewster, [11 February 1926]

Text: MS UT; cited in Brewster 92–3.

Spotorno.
Thursday

Dear Earl

Being in bed with flu, I reply to your note on the only bit of paper I can reach. – The point to find out is whether Dutton is buying *sheets* from Routledge.[2] On a book which is not expected to have a big sale, an Amer. publisher usually arranges with his English representative to take from him 500 or 1000 or even 2000 copies of printed sheets, binds these up in the U.S.A., and this is called an American edition, though it doesn't really secure copyright, as a book produced in USA must be *printed* there. But it's quite all right, and every publisher on both sides makes such an arrangement. To buy sheets in England is much cheaper than to produce, for a small sale, in USA. And on a sale of sheets you only get the percentage from Routledge, and have no contract with Dutton: no connection with him at all.

If, however, Dutton *sets up* the book in U.S.A., you make a separate contract with him. – In the present[3] case it appears he is buying sheets. But write direct and ask him.

Brett says Achsah has a touch of flu. I've been in bed six days, and feel rather downcast. My sister is here with a friend, in this fireless house – and it pours with rain, is cold, and dismal as Hades: self in bed and Frieda cross. We've had awful weather for three weeks. My sister left Dover in bright sun.

Corraggio! Bisogna farse coraggio! e sempre pazienza!

tante cose![4] DHL

I didn't have a letter lately from Achsah. F. doesn't want to come to Capri, doesn't want to see Brett. È così!

[1] 'Patience! wait! do wait!'

[2] Brewster's *Life of Gotama the Buddha: from the Pali Canon* was published by Kegan Paul in October 1926, and by Dutton in New York.

[3] the present] this

[4] 'Courage! One must be brave! and still patience! Greetings!'

3617. To Martin Secker, [11 February 1926]

Text: MS UInd; Postmark, Spotorno, 12 2.26; Secker 70.

Spotorno.
Thursday

Dear Secker

Thanks for your letter. I've been in bed six days with flu – hope to be up tomorrow, however – not feeling very happy – and vile weather here, cold and wet. My sister came, with friend, last evening – entered Italy in snow and gloom then streaming rain: but still thrilled. Elsa Weekley arrives Ventimiglia tomorrow. But what with flu and weather, it's all disappointing and a bit of a burden.

The Knopfs' sent me the *wrong* inscribed Borzoi book! Want it back. I send it to you. Will you forward it to them when you've looked it through? – Send it please straight to Blanche A Knopf, 730 Fifth Avenue. New York. It had a case, but the case has disappeared!

Be well DHL

Patty went a-walking one fine day
Lost her breeches on the way – – !
Only it was Borzoi

3618. To Hon. Dorothy Brett, [16 February 1926]

Text: MS UCin; PC v. Spotorno – Hôtel Palace; Postmark, [. . .] 16 2 26; Moore 891–2.

Spotorno.
Shrove Tuesday.

Dear Brett.

The typewriter came yesterday – very many thanks. I'm sure you had a lot of bother. I haven't opened it yet, am not yet at the nail-pulling stage – but it looks all right. – I am up and creeping about, but hope to be more or less solid by the weekend. My sister's coming was occasion for another rumpus: F[rieda] abandoned the ship, and stays down in the little hotel with her two daughters, pro tem. On Saturday or at latest next Monday I hope to be able to go with my sister to Monte Carlo – or some little place near – for a week. She has booked her ticket home that way: returning on the 25th. After that I don't know what I shall do. I might stay alone in S. France for a while: I hardly feel up to F. and two daughters.[1] I'll let you know, however. – We've had two marvellous sunny days. – I like the jacket of the *Plumed Serpent* so much. Did

[1] For Frieda's account of strained relationships following the arrival of DHL's sister and her own daughters, see Frieda Lawrence 193–5.

you ever get your copy of the *Porcupine*? – Alas for the lugger, we seem to have no conjuring power, and we can't get it without.

tante cose. DHL

3619. To William Siebenhaar, 16 February 1926
Text: TMSC NWU; Unpublished.

Villa Bernarda, *Spotorno*, (Genova).
16 February 1926.

Dear Mr. Siebenhaar,

At last I heard from my New York agent, that Knopf will add *Max Havelaar* to his Blue Jade Library, if you are willing to accept the established honorarium of $250 – (two hundred and fifty dollars). It's not much, but I don't suppose you could do better, and the Blue Jade books are beautifully produced. Will you please write direct to

A.W.Barmby Esq., Curtis Brown Ltd., 116, West 39th. St.,
New York City.

I suppose the agents will take a 10% fee.

But I am glad Knopf has at last decided. I shall be glad to see the book in the Blue Jade Library.

I expect we shall be here till end of March, but am not sure. At the end of this week, though, I am going to Monte Carlo with my sister, who is returning to England. But I shall not stay long.

Best wishes to you and to Mrs. Siebenhaar. I hope you have had a good winter.

Yours Sincerely D. H. Lawrence

3620. To Mabel Dodge Luhan, [17 February 1926]
Text: MS Brill; PC; Postmark, Spotorno 17. 2.26; Luhan 291.

[Villa Bernarda, Spotorno, Genova]
Ash Wednesday

Nice of you to write so warmly about the *Plumed*. – I haven't got your MSS. yet, but expect they'll arrive. They'll be quite safe. I'm going to Monte Carlo for a bit, with my sister – it's lovely sunny weather, thank Heaven. Did Spud get the poems?[1]

DHL

[1] Most likely the two poems, both probably written in January 1926 (Tedlock, *Lawrence MSS* 101), which were published by Johnson in *Laughing Horse* (April 1926): 'Mediterranean in January' and 'Beyond the Rockies' (Roberts C139).

3621. To William Hopkin, [19 February 1926]

Text: MS NCL; PC v. Spotorno – Pineta; Postmark, Spotorno 19. 2 26; Unpublished.

[Ada Clarke begins]

Spotorno
Feb 19/26

This is a most beautiful place – our villa is perched high on the hill side behind the village and we have a most wonderful view of the bay. The hill slopes are covered with pink and white almond blossom with here and there yellow mimosa. Every day we get brilliant sunshine and my face is already burnt brick red. Next Monday we hope to go to Monte Carlo for a few days. Kind regards to Mrs Hopkin and yourself.[1]

Ada Clarke

[Lawrence begins]
Best wishes – hope I shall see you this summer.

D. H. Lawrence

3622. To William Hawk, 19 February 1926

Text: MS UT: Postmark, Spotorno 19 2 26; cited in Moore, *Intelligent Heart* 351.

Villa Bernarda. *Spotorno*. (Genova)
19 Feb. 1926

Dear William

Imagine Alaska! – are we really all going to bust away to the uttermost ends of the earth! What the devil's the matter with us all, and with everything! – I'm sorry Roany has shuffled off the mortal coil: he was a real friend of yours. Use one of our horses if you want a cart-horse. – I dreamed, by the way, they were all drowned in a flood.

I'm going away with my sister on Monday, to Monte Carlo for a few days: then probably on to Spain, alone. Frieda has her two daughters here, great tall girls, 21 and 23 years old. I feel absolutely swamped out, must go away by myself for a bit, or I shall give up the ghost. I expect Frieda will stay here till end of March: then I don't know where.

The almond blossom is out in clouds, here, and it's warm. That's one blessing. But somehow everything feels in a great muddle, with daughters that are by no means mine, and sister who doesn't see eye to eye with F. What a trial families are! Let's hope Walton and Shirley G[lenn] will sail a smooth course.[2]

I'm enclosing $50 towards the horses. Let us know if you really think of

[1] Hopkin, a widower for three years, had recently re-married (see p. 279 n. 4).
[2] William and Rachel Hawk's children.

going away. Brett still sits in Capri: she talks really of coming to the ranch for the summer. For myself, I don't know. If I can get away a bit by myself, I may get a clearer mind. At the moment I just feel muddled up.

I heard from Mabel, in Croton-on-Hudson: and from Adele Seltzer, rather pathetic, saying they've had a very bad winter. Poor Thomas, I'm afraid he's at his last gasp. But it's amazing how long the poor fish can keep gasping.

I'm glad those hens are owning up. I thought their heads had fallen long since. – Remember me to Scott Murray, hope he's all right in health. Wonder if it's snowed yet! We had two weeks of rain.

Tell Rachel to keep chirpy: we'll all get a new start on before long. Good luck to you! – let's look forward to a gay meeting in the nearish future: the present moment is a tight corner.

Ever. DHL

3623. To The Editor of *The New Statesman*, [ante 20 February 1926]

Text: 'The Late Mr. Maurice Magnus', *New Statesman*, xxvi (20 February 1926), 579.

[Villa Bernarda, Spotorno, Genova]
[ante 20 February 1926]

To the Editor of *The New Statesman*

Sir, – Referring to the review published in your last issue of Mr. Norman Douglas's *Experiments*, will you give me a little space in which to shake off Mr. Douglas's insinuations – to put it mildly – regarding my introduction to Maurice Magnus's *Memoirs of the Foreign Legion*?[1] When Mr. Douglas's 'pamphlet' first appeared I was in New Mexico, and it seemed too far off to trouble. But now that the essay is enshrined in Mr. Douglas's new book, *Experiments*, it is time that I said a word. One becomes weary of being slandered.

The whole circumstances of my acquaintance with Maurice Magnus, and the facts of his death, are told in my introduction as truthfully as a man can tell a thing. After the suicide of Magnus, I had continual letters from the two Maltese, whom I had met through Magnus, asking for redress. I knew them personally – which Douglas did not. Myself, I had not the money to repay Magnus's borrowings. All the literary remains were left to Douglas, in the terms of Magnus's will. But then, after his death, all Magnus's effects were confiscated, owing to his debts. There was really nothing to confiscate, since the very furniture of the house had been lent by the young Maltese, B[org].

[1] See Letter 3549 and n. 2. Norman Douglas's *Experiments* had been reviewed in the *New Statesman* on 13 February 1926. In the review DHL's introduction to Magnus's *Memoirs* was described as 'a brilliant but unfair portrait' (p. 554).

There were the MSS. – the bulk of them worthless. Only those *Memoirs of the Foreign Legion*, which I had gone over previously with Magnus, might be sold.

I wrote to B—— that Norman Douglas would no doubt get the *Memoirs* published. The reply came from Malta, B—— would never put anything into the hands of Douglas. I then wrote to Douglas – and, remembering the care with which he files all his letters, I kept his reply. Parts of this reply I quote here:

Florence,
26th December, 1921.

Dear Lawrence,

So many thanks for yours of the 20th.

Damn the Foreign Legion.... I have done my best, and if B—— had sent it to me the book would be published by this time, and B—— £30 or £50 the richer. Some folks are hard to please. By all means do what you like with the MS. As to M. himself, I may do some kind of memoir of him later on – independent of Foreign Legions. Put me into your introduction, if you like. . . .

Pocket all the cash yourself. B—— seems to be such a fool that he doesn't deserve any.

I'm out of it and, *for once in my life*, with a clean conscience. . . .

Yours always, Norman Douglas.

The italics in this letter are Douglas's own. As for his accusation of my 'unkindness' to Magnus, that too is funny. Certainly Magnus was generous with his money when he had any; who knew that better than Douglas? But did I make it appear otherwise? And when Magnus wanted *actual* help – not post-mortem sentiment – where did he look for it? To the young Maltese who would have no dealings whatsoever with Norman Douglas, after the suicide.

Then I am accused of making money out of Magnus's effects. I should never have dreamed of writing a word about Magnus, save for the continual painful letters from the Maltese. Then I did it solely and simply to discharge a certain obligation. For curiously enough, both B—— and S[alomonee] seemed to regard me as in some way responsible for their troubles with Magnus. I had been actually there with them and Magnus, and had driven in their motor-car. To discharge an obligation I do not admit, I wrote the Introduction. And when it was written, in the year 1922, it started the round of the publishers, as introducing the *Memoirs of the Foreign Legion*, and everywhere it was refused. More than one publisher said: 'We will publish the Introduction alone, without the Magnus *Memoirs*.' To which I said: 'That's no good. The Introduction only exists for the *Memoirs*.'

So, for two years, nothing happened. It is probable that I could have sold the Introduction to one of the large popular American magazines, as a 'personal' article. And that would have meant at least a thousand dollars for me. Whereas I shall never see a thousand dollars, by a long chalk, from this *Memoirs* book. Nevertheless, by this time B—— will have received in full the money he lent to Magnus. I shall have received as much – as much, perhaps, as I would get in America for a popular short story.

As for Mr. Douglas, he must gather himself haloes where he may.[1] —

Yours, etc., D. H. Lawrence

3624. To William Siebenhaar, [22 February 1926]

Text: TMSC NWU; PC; Unpublished.

Hotel Beau-Séjour, Monaco,
Monday.

I don't know what happened – but our train didn't stop at Diano M[arina]. We got in at Albenga as usual – but it must have been an earlier train much delayed. A quiet little hotel at 50 fs.

D. H. Lawrence

3625. To Emily King, [23 February 1926]

Text: MS Needham; PC v. Monaco: Vue sur Monte-Carlolet le Port; Postmark, Monaco 24 –2 26; Unpublished.

Monaco.
23 Feb

I had your letter – now Joan has chicken pox: what a shame! Let's hope it won't last! – I am still a bit shaky with my flu, but came along here with Ada. It's very nice. Frieda has her two girls in Spotorno. When Ada leaves – day after tomorrow – I think I shall go to Nice for a little while, quite near. Do hope you're all well by now.

DHL

3626. To S. S. Koteliansky, [24 February 1926]

Text: MS BL; PC v. Monaco. Monte Carlo et la Condamine; Postmark, Monaco 24 –2 26; Zytaruk 281.

Monte Carlo.
24 Feb.

I am here a few days with my sister – she leaves for England tomorrow: lovely hot weather, and romantic scenery, but the place rather come-down in style:

[1] Cf. Robert Herrick, 'To the Virgins, to Make Much of Time', *Hesperides* (1648), l. 1; see p. 563.

weary, weary people walking about. I'm going tomorrow to Nice, and perhaps alone to Spain. F[rieda] has her two daughters and another girl at the Villa Bernarda.

Am glad you liked those parts of the *Plumed Serpent*.[1]

DHL

3627. To Carl Seelig, [24 February 1926]

Text: MS SIU; PC v. [Monte Carlo]; Postmark, Monaco [. . .]; Unpublished.

[Monte Carlo]
24 Feb

Came here for a few days with my sister, but find it very stupid and boring. What are you doing?

DHL

3628. To Joan King, [24 February 1926]

Text: MS Needham; PC v. Monaco – Vue sur le Port, Rocher et le Palais; Postmark, M[onaco] 24 [. . .]; *Young Bert: An Exhibition of the Early Years of D. H. Lawrence* (Nottingham, 1972), pp. 92–3.

[Monte Carlo]
[24 February 1926]

Dear Joan

I do hope you've given your chicken pox to the chickens again, where it belongs. It's time you began to be a plump little bird. – I think your Auntie Ada likes Monte Carlo, but she hasn't gambled yet. Perhaps she is leaving it till the last day.

x x Love to you all. Uncle Bert
x
x x

3629. To Hon. Dorothy Brett, [24 February 1926]

Text: MS UCin; PC v. Monte-Carlo; Postmark, Monaco 24 –2 26; Irvine, Brett 62.

Monaco.
24 Feb.

Wonderful weather, romantic place to look at, but one gets awfully sick of it. It's rather common and come down – and there's no temptation to gamble. I go on to Nice tomorrow with my sister, who then leaves for England. I'll write from there.

DHL

[1] The 'parts' which particularly pleased Kot were 'the Quetzalcoatl hymns' (see Frieda's letter to Kot, mid-March 1926, E. W. Tedlock, ed., *Frieda Lawrence: The Memoirs and Correspondence*, 1961, p. 232).

3630. To George Conway, [24 February 1926]

Text: MS Sagar; PC v. Monte-Carlo, Vue Générale; Postmark, Monaco 25 -2 26; Moore, *Intelligent Heart* 351-2.

[Monte Carlo]
24 Feb

Staying here a few days with my sister – very sunny and bright, but as far as life goes, come-down, and boring – no temptation at all to gamble. Had your letter – so sorry you were ill – I wondered what had become of you and of Madame. We have a villa on the Italian Coast for the time being – but shall probably move in April, heaven knows where to. Many regards to you and to Mrs Conway.

D. H. Lawrence

3631. To Martin Secker, [24 February 1926]

Text: MS UInd; PC v. Monaco – Monte-Carlo, Vue Générale; Postmark, Monaco 25 -2 26; Secker 71.

[Monte Carlo]
24 Feb

You were right about the Riviera: it's deadly boring: but *very* sunny and rather romantic to look at. For the rest, it's third rate, and the temptation to gamble is nil. Even my sister won't try. We motor on the Grande Corniche to Nice tomorrow and in the afternoon she leaves for England. – I don't know where I shall go – but Italy is certainly much nicer than here. – I'll make up my mind tomorrow.

DHL

3632. To Ada Clarke, [25–6 February 1926]

Text: MS Clarke; Postmark, [. . .] 26 2 [. . .]; Unpublished.

Hotel Brice. rue Maréchal Joffre, Nice
25 Feb 1926

My dear Sister

I sat on the beach all the afternoon – still and sunny – then had a cup of tea. It *does* feel a bit lonely now, when I can't walk round and find you in your room. And I was awfully sorry we had all this upset: I was so looking forward to your coming and having a good time. But perhaps we managed for the best, after all.

I must owe you about 850 frs – which is about £6″7″0: then £3. English. – and Lizzie £2″10″0. So we'll call it twelve pounds, and you give Lizzie her £2″10″0 out of it. –

Lizzie is awfully nice, so peaceful to have with one.

I shan't make up my mind till morning, whether to go to that little place

Bormes, and sit by the sea a bit – it's very still and nice this evening – or whether to go straight to Florence. I think I'll do one or the other.

This hotel is just back of the sea-front: we needn't have walked those long streets.

I do hope you won't get too tired on the train. The best is not to let things worry you. I'll send an address the moment I decide.

Love. DHL

Friday morning

I thought of you two in the night! – I'm going to Capri for a bit.

3633. To Nancy Pearn, 25 February 1926
Text: MS UT; Unpublished.

Nice.
25 Feb 1926

Dear Miss Pearn

I send you 'The Rocking Horse Winner', for Lady Cynthia Asquith. Will you please have it typed, and hand it over to her. It will perhaps be more suitable, and spectral enough.[1]

Sincerely D. H. Lawrence

Going back to Italy tomorrow.

3634. To Hon. Dorothy Brett, 26 February 1926
Text: MS UT; Telegram; Unpublished.

Ventimiglia
26 February 1926

Vengo a Capri adesso.

Lawrence

[I'm coming to Capri now.]

3635. To Hon. Dorothy Brett, 27 February 1926
Text: MS UT; Telegram; Unpublished.

Roma
27 February 1926

Arrivo questa sera.

Lawrence

[I arrive this evening.]

[1] For Lady Cynthia Asquith's anthology, *The Ghost-Book* (Roberts B19), DHL had initially intended his contribution to be 'Glad Ghosts' (first called 'Gay Ghosts', then 'Ghost of Silence'). This was eventually considered unsuitable and, instead, he offered 'The Rocking-Horse Winner' which was accepted. (It first appeared in *Harper's Bazaar*, July 1926, Roberts C142.5.) *The Ghost-Book* was published by Hutchinson on 26 September 1926 but Secker wrote to Lady Cynthia on 5 February 1926 in an attempt to secure it for his own list (Secker Letter-Book, UIll).

3636. To Ada Clarke, 2 March 1926

Text: MS Clarke; Postmark, Capri 2. 3. 26; Unpublished.

presso Sig. E. H. Brewster, Torre Quattro Venti, *Capri* (Napoli)
2 March 1926

My dear Sister

I came straight down here on Friday,[1] got a 2nd Class wagon-lit in Genoa, to Rome, very comfortable, and was in Capri Sat. evening by 6.0. It's a long journey though: I only had half an hour to change in Rome. I'm staying for a few days with the Brewsters, who have a big and rather handsome villa. But they are sailing to India on March 16th – so I shan't stay long in the house. But the address holds good for a fortnight – or a bit less. Perhaps I shall move into an hotel here for a little while, or else go over with Brett to Ravello – we go by steamer – where we have more friends. Everybody here is very nice to me, so one can have a quiet time, at least. I haven't had any word from Spotorno – I didn't send my address till yesterday, and as it is very windy, the mail may not be able to arrive or leave, as the steamer can't land.

But let me know how you got on, and how you found everybody at home. – Here it's windy, and the wind is cold, there is much snow on the Apennines. But it's sunny, and there are many mauve anemones, and narcissus, and grape hyacinths out among the rocks, the wild crocuses just passing.

I'm so awfully sorry there was that bust-up to spoil your holiday – I had so wanted you to have a nice time. But there you are.

Love to all DHL

3637. To Martin Secker, [4 March 1926]

Text: MS UInd; Postmark, Capri 4. 3. 26; Secker 71.

Capri.
4 March

Dear Secker

I am in Capri with the Brewsters for a few days – they leave next week and sail for India. I saw Faith Mackenzie twice, and she seems cheerful; and am going to the Brett Youngs as soon as this very fierce and icy tramontana ceases blowing. It gets my chest. – Capri is about the same, only more built over, and rows of bathing houses on the Piccola Marina. Brooks is still quite brisk, but looks older.[2]

Will you please send a copy of *The Plumed Serpent* to

Catherine Carswell, Hawthorn Cottage, Great Kingshill, High Wycombe, Bucks.

[1] Friday] Tuesday

[2] For DHL's surprise visit to John Ellingham Brooks (see Letter 3614 and n. 2), see Brett 277–8.

I thought I'd ordered her one before.

When will you bring out *David*?

I'll let you know my next address.

Saluti. D. H. Lawrence

3638. To Catherine Carswell, [4 March 1926]

Text: MS YU; cited in Carswell 241.

Villa Bernarda, *Spotorno*, Prov. di Genova, Italy
4 March

Dear Catherine,

It has been a muddled unsatisfactory sort of winter. – I am actually in Capri for the time, Frieda is at Spotorno with her two daughters.

I am sure you are right to give up that cottage.[1] I am sure you are right to try putting John P[atrick] into a school. And I'm sure you are right to try to get free to work with your writing and make a way for yourself and family. I'm very glad you have decided. Let me know if I can help, with writing or anything. I am really glad you are cutting a bit loose again, from cottage housekeeping. It's a somewhat waste of time. Do the serial, and let's see it.

Italy is very much the same. I still like it, it is nice to live in. But I've had flu, and the cold tramontana wind gets my chest. I don't a bit know what we shall do this year – but I doubt if we shall go to the ranch. It's so far, and I feel I can't make any long efforts this year. I'm tired of straining with the world. Perhaps we shall come to England for the summer – I don't know. But I'll let you know. –

I ordered you a copy of *The Plumed Serpent*. I'm afraid you'll find it heavy.

Remember me to Don and the boy, and I do feel you're right in moving and *not* setting up a fixed ménage in London.

DHL

3639. To Ada Clarke, [11 March 1926]

Text: MS Clarke; Unpublished.

Hotel Palumbo. *Ravello*, Amalfi
11 March

My dear Sister

I came over here with Brett from Capri for a few days – It's a pretty place, high above the sea, looking south. We've got two other friends here – Miss

[1] DHL called at the cottage near High Wycombe on his way from London to the Midlands in October 1925 (Carswell 227).

Beveridge, who painted my portrait, is one.[1] I suppose I shall stay about a week, not time enough for you to answer. I've not heard yet if you got home all right. But surely you did! – Frieda writes much more mildly now, but still too much lay the law down. That sort of thing is no good.

I saw most of the old people in Capri, all very nice to me indeed, but the place not half so jolly as it used to be – going dead. Mrs Compton Mackenzie was there as usual, an unhappy soul, trying to pretend to be gay. She's another who loves her husband but can't live with him. Much good it does her!

The weather is still uncertain here, stormy, then too hot, then too cold – Rather chilly just now.

I do hope you're all all right – Send a line to Spotorno, it can be forwarded if I'm not there –

love DHL

3640. To S. S. Koteliansky, [12 March 1926]

Text: MS BL; PC v. Ravello – Campanile della Cattedrale e Fontana; Postmark, Rav[ello] [. . .]3 3 26; Zytaruk 282.

Ravello (Amalfi)
12 March

Came on here from Capri – Weather wildly cold, snowed yesterday – the sun hot again! How are you? – send me a line to Spotorno, expect to be back there soon.

tante cose! DHL

3641. To Margaret King, [12 March 1926]

Text: MS Needham; PC v. Ravello – Veduta della riviera di Amalfi; Postmark, [. . .]; Unpublished.

Ravello.
12 March.

I sent a book to your mother from Capri, for Dorothy Johnson[2] – hope it arrived. Though we are so far south here, on the Gulf of Salerno South of

[1] DHL met Anne Millicent Beveridge (1871–1955), Scottish painter, in Sicily in 1921; she painted his portrait c. 5–20 March 1921 (see *Letters*, iii. 683, 686, 701). She lived in Paris; the other friend to whom DHL refers – Mabel Harrison – was a fellow-artist who lived there too (Letter 3658) and to whom DHL later introduced Catherine Carswell (Carswell 241; see Letter 3691).

[2] Dorothy Johnson, daughter of a neighbour of the Kings and a near-contemporary of Margaret King, was a talented young painter in whose work DHL took an interest. The book, therefore, may have been related to pictorial art.

Naples, it snowed quite heavily yesterday. The sun is hot, and the wind cold: a funny mixture.

Hope you are all well.

DHL

3642. To Else Jaffe, [14 March 1926]
Text: PC; Frieda Lawrence, *Nur Der Wind*, p. 251.

Ravello – Amalfi
[14 March 1926]

Ich bin heute von Capri herüber gekommen, habe Freunde hier. Vor vorgestern hat es geschneit, heute ist es heiß. Ich weiß noch nicht, wann ich nach Spotorno zurück gehen werde. Wann gehst Du nach Irschenhausen? ich glaube, dort wäre ich gern, wenn der Enzian anfängt zu blühen. Brett läßt Friedel grüße. Tante Cose

DHL

[I've come over from Capri today, have friends here. Three days ago it snowed, today it's hot. I don't yet know when I shall go back to Spotorno. When are you going to Irschenhausen? I believe that's where I'd like to be most, when the gentians start to come out. Brett sends Friedel greetings. Many regards

DHL]

3643. To S. S. Koteliansky, [17 March 1926]
Text: MS BL; Postmark, Ravello 17. 3 26; Zytaruk 283.

Ravello.
17 March

My dear Kot

Will you tell me what you think of this letter.[1] Frieda sent it on. I don't know whether she *lost* the address mentioned in it. Is that a good address on the letter-head?

I shall probably go back to Spotorno next week: write me there, and send me the letter back, please.

It's rather horrid weather down here – feels earthquaky.

If you think I should write to these people, transcribe the address for me, will you? Since I had influenza I abandoned my Russian Grammar in despair.

[1] The letter is missing; consequently a number of DHL's allusions are obscure.

I think in April we shall go to Germany. From there to Moscow would not be so wildly far.

But send me a line.

tante cose DHL

3644. To Emily King, [17 March 1926]

Text: MS Needham; PCs v. Ravello – Panorama; Ravello – Villa Cimbrone – Belvedere e Panorama; Unpublished.

Ravello.
17 March

My dear Pamela

I am staying on here[1] a few days with friends. The weather is bad, and feels like earthquakes. Frieda wants to go to Germany on April 10th – I may go with them, or join them later. She is taking her daughters to see her mother. I suppose they will go back to England on Apr 30 – about. I find them a bit much, for me.

It is nearly your birthday. I am sending you £5. – but you must give Peg. £1. and Joan £1. – for their respective birthdays. I wonder how you all are? Write me a line to Spotorno. I've not had word from Ada even yet – but that's because of my moving round. I wonder how Peg is getting on – do hope she's all right. – Did you get the book for Dorothy Johnson?

Love DHL

3645. To Hon. Dorothy Brett, [17 March 1926]

Text: MS UCin; PC v. Ravello – Chiesa di S. Giovanni – Ambone Cosmatesco; Postmark, [. . .] 17. 3 26; Irvine, Brett 62.

[Ravello]
Wed

Awful day here, feels like earthquakes. Am sending your washing. Letter from Frieda – much milder. She wants to leave on Apr 10th and go to Germany. – I have moved up into the Dependances, and shall sit still for some days more, anyhow.

DHL

[1] DHL used two postcards showing Ravello, as notecards.

3646. To Hon. Dorothy Brett, [18 March 1926]

Text: MS UCin; Postmark, Ravell[o] 18 3.26; Huxley 653.

Hotel Palumbo. *Ravello*. Golfo di Salerno
Thursday

Dear Brett

Glad you got safely back. I'm sure it's better for you there, where you have a few friends, than mooning in an unknown place.

One has just to forget, and to accept what is good. We can't help being more or less damaged. What we have to do is to stick to the good part of ourselves, and of each other, and continue an understanding on that. I don't see why we shouldn't be *better* friends, instead of worse. But one must not try to force anything.

Frieda wrote much more quietly and humanly – she says, we must live more with other people: which I think is true. It's no use trying to be exclusive. There's a good *bit* in quite a lot of people. If we are to live, we must make the most of that, and not cut ourselves off.

I'll let you know my plans, as soon as I make any. Just be quiet, and leave things to the Lord.

DHL

Long and friendly letter from Mabel.[1] Did you keep her address:
Finney Farm, *Croton-on-Hudson*, N. Y.
You might send me Mrs Beckett's address.[2]

3647. To Mabel Dodge Luhan, 18 March 1926

Text: MS Brill; Luhan 291–2.

Ravello.
18 March 1926

Dear Mabel

I have been moving around a bit, while Frieda stays in Spotorno with her two daughters. Your article came along yesterday. I suppose it is true, one is struggling against all these mechanised emotions and motions, and one gets oneself a bit Laocoön-distorted in the process.[3] But à la guerre comme à la guerre. At the moment I'm feeling as if I'd had a kick dans le ventre.

[1] I.e. Mabel Luhan.

[2] Lucy ('Lucile') Katherine Beckett (1884–1979), daughter of the 2nd Baron Grimthorpe, was a friend of the Brewsters and an expatriate resident in Italy (see *Letters*, iii. 712 and n. 1). When in Ravello she lived in the family residence at the Palazzo Cimbrone (Letter 3970). Brett and DHL walked through the Cimbrone gardens (Brett 292).

[3] The famous marble sculpture in the Vatican shows Laocoon and his twin sons in their desperate, fatal struggle against two encircling sea-serpents.

There was a rather sniffy note from Edwin Dodge to say he is staying himself, con famiglia, in the villa.[1] You shouldn't have bothered him. I had no idea of staying there.

The plans for the summer are vague. Frieda talks of leaving Spotorno for good on Apr. 10th, and going to Germany. She has your MS. I shall read it as soon as I go up there again – perhaps next week – and let you know.

Brett may be coming to America quite soon. I gave her your address. I do think we are all changing pretty drastically, even she.

Best wishes DHL

3648. To Emily King, [20 March 1926]

Text: MS Needham; PC v. Ravello – Chiesa di S. Giovanni – Ambone cosmatesco; Postmark, Ravello [. . .] 26; Unpublished.

Ravello.
Saturday

I'm going to Rome on Monday, for a day or two, and shall go gradually on to Spotorno. Write to me there – I sent your birthday letter the other day. Frieda wants to go to Germany in Apr. with her daughters. Of myself, I'm not sure.

Love DHL

3649. To Hon. Dorothy Brett, [20 March 1926]

Text: MS UCin; PC v. Monte-Carlo. Le Port et le Casino; Postmark, Ravello 20. 3 26; Irvine, Brett 62.

[Ravello]
Sat.

Many thanks for the medicine, which came last night. I think it's good. – I am leaving for Rome on Monday – perhaps stay there a couple of days. Miss Harrison and Miss Beveridge are leaving too. – Do you remember the old Englishman with the plain daughter – we spoke to them as we played bezique. They are very nice – and coming to your hotel on Monday. I give them a note to you, perhaps you might show them the walks – Mr and Miss Williams.[2] They only stay till Apr. 1st. What about Faith Mc[kenzie] and the Russian?[3] I'm feeling better – weather dull.

DHL

[1] Mabel Luhan's second husband, the Bostonian architect; his Villa Curonia was at Arcetri, near Florence.

[2] Unidentified. (DHL's tone does not suggest that they were connected with the Leader-Williamses he had known in Sicily. Cf. *Letters*, iii. 637 and n. 2.)

[3] Presumably a reference to Nicolas Nadegin, a Russian baritone, the intimate friend and protégé of Faith Mackenzie from 1918 until his death in 1958 (see Compton Mackenzie, *My Life and Times: Octave Five 1915–1923*, 1966, pp. 137–8).

3650. To Hon. Dorothy Brett, [21 March 1926]

Text: MS UCin; Huxley 652–3.

Ravello.
Sunday.

Dear Brett

This is to introduce Miss Williams and her father. I hope you'll go a few walks together.

We leave for Rome early in the morning. I will write from there. Meanwhile, dont you mope and lie around, it's infra dig. The greatest virtue in life is real courage, that knows how to face facts and live beyond them. Don't be Murryish, pitying yourself and caving in. It's despicable. I should have thought, after a dose of that fellow, you'd have had too much desire to be different from him, to follow his sloppy self-indulgent melancholics, absolutely despicable. Rouse up and make a decent thing of your days, no matter what's happened. I do loathe cowardice, and sloppy emotion. My God, did you learn *nothing* from Murry, of how *not* to behave? Even you write the sort of letters he writes! Oh basta! Cut it out! Be something different from that, even to yourself.

DHL

3651. To Hon. Dorothy Brett, [22 March 1926]

Text: MS UCin; PC v. Roma, Via Appia; Postmark, Ro[ma] 22[. . .]; Irvine, Brett 62.

Rome.
Monday

Got here all right this afternoon – cloudy, but feels pleasant. Hope you're feeling all right.

DHL

3652. To Ada Clarke, [22 March 1926]

Text: MS Clarke; PC v. Roma – Acquedotto Claudio – Segione Lunga con buoi; Postmark, [. . .]; Unpublished.

Rome –
Monday

Got here this afternoon, staying a day or two.

DHL

3653. To Margaret King, [22 March 1926]

Text: MS Needham; PC v. Roma; Postmark, Ro[ma] 22[. . .]; Unpublished.

[Rome]
Monday

Came on here for a day or two – cloudy, but Rome is nice.

DHL

3654. To Hon. Dorothy Brett, [24 March 1926]

Text: MS UCin; PC v. [Pyramid of Caius Cestius (d. 43 B.C.) near St Paul's Gate]; Postmark, Roma 24 . III[. . .]; Irvine, Brett 63.

Rome.
Wed

I had your espresso forwarded from Ravello today – hope you're feeling all right – here it is pouring with rain all day – We go on tomorrow to Perugia, then to Florence.

DHL

3655. To Margaret King, [30 March 1926]

Text: MS Needham; PC v. Ritratto D'Incognita – Piero della Francesca (1415–1492); Postmark, Firenze 30.III 1926; Unpublished.

Florence.
30 March.

Am going on to Ravenna for a few days from here – but shall probably be in Spotorno for Sunday, and will write from there. Send me a line.

DHL

3656. To Hon. Dorothy Brett, [30 March 1926]

Text: MS UCin; PC v. La Vergine – Fra Filippo Lippi (1412–1469); Postmark, Firenze 30.III. 1926; Irvine, Brett 63.

Florence.
30 March

Am going on to Ravenna for a day or two – shall probably be in Spotorno for Easter Sunday – will write from there.

DHL

3657. To Ada Clarke, [30 March 1926]
Text: MS Clarke; PC v. Angelo Annunziante, Melozzo da Forli (1438–94); Postmark, Firenze 30.III 1926; Unpublished.

Florence.
30 March

Am going on to Ravenna for a few days – shall probably be in Spotorno for Easter Sunday, let you know how things are.

DHL

3658. To John and Helen Cournos, [30 March 1926]
Text: MS UT; Unpublished.

Hotel Washington
Tuesday

Dear Cournos e Signora[1]

We are going on to Ravenna this afternoon by the 4.30 – I tried every shop to get *The Plumed Serpent*, but sold out – so give you *St Mawr* – but am ordering the other to your London address.

Hope you'll have a good time – was very glad to have an evening with you and Mrs Cournos. – You can always get me

c/o Martin Secker, 5 John St, Adelphi

– or in Paris

c/o Miss Mabel Harrison, 49 Bvd Montparnasse.

Good luck for the future D. H. Lawrence

3659. To Hon. Dorothy Brett, [3 April 1926]
Text: MS UCin; Postmark, Spotorno 3. 4 26; Irvine, Brett 63.

Spotorno.
Saturday 3 April

Dear Brett

I've just got back here – we went to Ravenna for two days – had no idea you were in or near Florence.[2] – All very quiet and welcoming here – quite a change. I must hurry to the post with this, and will wire you – I'll write again tomorrow.

DHL

You might not get another letter in Florence if you leave Tuesday – but I'll address it there.

[1] John Cournos (1881–1966), Russian-born author, editor and autobiographer, living in London. Knew DHL from 1915. m. 1924, Helen Satterthwaite, née Kestner (1893–), novelist (pseudonym Sybil Norton). According to Cournos, he and his wife met DHL on the train between Assisi and Perugia and agreed to meet in Florence (Nehls, i. 327).

[2] Letter 3656 had been re-directed from Capri to Florence.

3660. To Hon. Dorothy Brett, 3 April 1926
Text: MS UT; Telegram; Unpublished.

Spotorno
3 April 1926

Sono arrivato cui oggi da Ravenna vi ho scritto –

Laprence

[I arrived here today from Ravenna I have written to you –]

3661. To Baroness Anna von Richthofen, [4 April 1926]
Text: MS UCB; Frieda Lawrence 197.

Villa Bernarda. *Spotorno*, Riviera Ponente
Oster Sonntag

Meine liebe Schwiegermutter

Ich bin wieder da! Die drei Frauenzimmer waren dort unten am Bahnhof, wenn ich angekommen bin, gestern, – feierlich geschmuckt – die Frauen, nicht ich. Ich bin für den Moment den Oster-Lamm. – Wann ich weg ging, war ich sehr ge-ärgert. Man muss aber doch viel vergessen und überleben. – Die Frieda ist erkältet, die Barby und Elsa aber sehr kräftig geworden, und die B. hat ein Paar ganz gute Bilder gemalt. Ich bin auch viel besser, gesund beinah wie früher, nur immer etwas bronchitis. Aber man sagt, ein Englander von 40 Jahren ist beinah immer bronchial.

Wir wissen nicht ganz was wir thun wollen. Wir lassen dieses Haus am 20n, ungefähr – und gehen, vielleicht, nach Perugia, zwischen Florenz und Rom, für sechs oder acht Wochen. Ich meine, ich hätte gern ein Buch über Umbria und die Etrusker schreiben: halb Reisebuch, wissenschaftlich auch. Vielleicht thue ich das. Dann kommen wir zu dir in Juni, wenn endlich, in Gottesnamen, es wird schönes wetter sein. Hier ist es immer grau, schwül, scirocco, ich glaube es kocht, langsam aber[1]

[My dear Schwiegermutter

I'm back! The three women were down at the station, when I arrived, yesterday, – dressed-up festively – the women, not me. For the moment I am the Easter Lamb. – When I went away, I was very cross. But really one has to forget a lot, and to live on. – Frieda has a cold, but Barby and Elsa have grown very strong, and B. has painted a couple of quite good pictures. I'm also much better, almost as in the past, only always a touch of bronchitis. But they say, an Englishman of 40 is almost always bronchial.

[1] MS incomplete: the word '*unfinished*', initialled 'CR', is written on the first page in an unknown hand. In the translation which follows, the final three words and the signature are taken from Frieda's translation in "*Not I, But the Wind . . .*".

We don't quite know what we want to do. We're leaving this house about the 20th – and go, perhaps, to Perugia, between Florence and Rome, for six or eight weeks. I think I'd like to write a book about Umbria and the Etruscans: half travel-book, scientific too.[1] Perhaps I'll do that. Then we come to you in June, when at last, for goodness sake, it'll be fine weather. Here it's always grey, close, scirocco, I think boiling, but slowly comes the spring.

DHL]

3662. To Hon. Dorothy Brett, [4 April 1926]

Text: MS UCin; Postmark, Spotorno 5. 4.26; Irvine, Brett 63–4.

Villa Bernarda. *Spotorno* (Genova)
Easter Sunday

Dear Brett

I had no idea you had come up to Florence – do hope you were not really ill. I went to Perugia and Ravenna with Mabel Harrison and Milly Beveridge – it was quite nice. I am really *much* better myself, in health.

Everybody here is as nice to me as possible – quite different. Frieda has a bad cold, the two girls are very well. We think to stay on till about the 20th – then either go to Germany, or perhaps to Perugia. I *might* stay a couple of months there, and do a book on Umbria and the Etruscan things: but am not sure.

I do think the best thing for you is to go to America. I hate to think of the ranch running waste. If only you could find someone congenial, you could live on our ranch, not down at the Hawks. Who knows how long it will take me to get tired of Europe, and hotels! – when I do, I shall come along to America. And now, I think we should find Frieda much more tolerant. But I don't want to go to America yet: and it's no use our trying anything in Europe.

Your money can't be lost, even if there is a delay. It must turn up. – Did you like Florence? I found it most horribly crowded.

Let me know what you decide.

DHL

3663. To Martin Secker, [4 April 1926]

Text: MS UInd; Postmark, Spotorno 5 4.26; Secker 71–2.

Villa Bernarda. Spotorno, Genova
4 April

Dear Secker

I was very sorry to miss you all. I had Rina's wire in Ravenna, so was prepared.

[1] The first mention of the work published posthumously as *Etruscan Places* (Secker, 1932).

Got back here yesterday afternoon, everybody very nice, and pleased to see me.

David looks very nice. Did you send out any copies for me? I wish you would send one each to my sisters,

Mrs L. A. Clarke. Gee St. *Ripley* (Derby)

Mrs S. King, 16 Brooklands Rd, Sneinton Hill, *Nottingham*.

Then please send a copy to

Mrs Ida Rauh (Mrs Andrew Dassburg), *Santa Fe*, New Mexico (registered)

and to

Hon. Dorothy Brett, Hotel Internazionale, *Capri* (Napoli)

and one to

Miss Barbara Low, 13 Guilford St. *W. C. 1*

That's the six!

We had two lovely days, but today again Scirocco.

We think to leave this house about 20th. Frieda is no longer so keen on Germany. We might go to Perugia, and I might do a book on Umbria and the Etruscan remains. What do you think? It would be half a travel book – of the region round Perugia, Assisi, Spoleto, Cortona, and the Maremma – and half a book about the Etruscan things, which interest me very much. – If you happen to know any good book, modern, on Etruscan things, I wish you'd order it for me. I've only read that old work, Dennis' – *Cities and Cemeteries of Etruria*.[1] There will be some lectures in Perugia.

Frieda thought she had your measles, but it's only the usual bad bronchial cold. I am much better, but still bronchial. I do wish the weather would *clear*. There will be an earthquake, ultimately.

I expect we shall see you in the summer. We might go to Scotland – and to Mackenzie's island without a roof[2] – who knows.

Let us know how the journey was, and all, and all!

D. H. Lawrence

3664. To Ada Clarke, [4 April 1926]

Text: MS Clarke; Postmark, Spotorno 5. 4.26; Unpublished.

Villa Bernarda, *Spotorno*, Riviera Ponente

Easter Sunday

My dear Sister

I got back here yesterday afternoon – the three females very glad to see me,

[1] George Dennis, *The Cities and Cemeteries of Etruria* (2 vols, 1848; rev. 1878).

[2] Mackenzie hoped that DHL's plan 'to visit Jethou in August would materialize' (*My Life and Times: Octave Six 1923–1930*, 1967, p. 84).

and very different in their tone. But there's bit of anger still working in my inside, I hope it'll work off.

I think I may go to Perugia, between Rome and Florence, for a couple of months, and perhaps write a book on Umbria and the Etruscans – or collect material for it. – We shall leave this house about the 20th, and Elsa and Barby will be back in England by the end of the month. It is long enough, Lord knows. I believe Frieda is sick of them. But I say nothing.

I had a very nice trip with friends who were always pleasant. I promised to come to England in July. – Have you got my play *David*? – I ordered it you. – Giovanni very pleased to see me, and asked if I'd been with you and Lizzie to *Philadelphia*. Why Philadelphia, heaven knows.

Let me know how you all are.

DHL

3665. To Elfie Rosebery, [4 April 1926]

Text: MS Secor; Unpublished.

Villa Bernarda, *Spotorno*, Prov di Genova
Easter Sunday

My dear Mrs Rosebery[1]

Many thanks for your letter which I found when I got back here, yesterday only. We made a little giro, to Assisi and Perugia, and Florence and Ravenna, so took a little time.

The boat seems to have sailed past us, for this season. I'll make enquiries now in Genova: but what I fear is that they'll expect us to pay hundreds of pounds sterling for any little sardine of a ship. The world is crazy.

I find my wife with a bad cold, but perfectly ready to sail off anywhere, if there were any deck to sail on. Failing that, we may go to Perugia for a time, and I may collect material for a book on Umbria. But I think we shall stay in this house till about the 20th, anyhow.

We had some horrid weather on our trip – then two sunny days – now again dark scirocco. Hope Ravello is nice! – Many thanks to Mr Rosebery for the

[1] Elfie Julia Rosebery, née Cahen (1883?–1948), American, m. Joseph Henry Rosebery (1863–1937). She graduated from Barnard College, Columbia University, in 1904; she was a talented (but not a professional) painter; and, with her husband, she lived in Italy for many years. From references to the Hotel Palumbo (Letters 3885 and 3969) it is virtually certain that DHL encountered the Roseberys in Ravello. They were close friends of the poet Robert Calverley Trevelyan (1872–1951) whom DHL first met in December 1913 (see *Letters*, ii. 116 and n. 1).

information. Remembrances to Mrs Lunn and to Mrs Ber – I've forgotten – with the baby:[1] and tanti saluti to the avvocato –

and a rivederci D. H. Lawrence

3666. To Curtis Brown, [5 April 1926]
Text: Huxley 654–5.

Villa Bernarda, Spotorno, Genova.
Easter Monday, 1926.

Dear Curtis Brown, –

I got back here day before yesterday – wandered round seeing friends for six weeks, and even then never got to Taormina. But I had a nice time: my wife stayed here with her two daughters, who are with us for another fortnight. We leave this house about the 20th – and then go either to Germany or to Perugia or Cortona. I fancied I might like to do a book, half travel and half study, on Umbria and the Etruscans. The Etruscan things interest me very much. We might stay at Perugia for a couple of months and get material. But heaven knows if I'll really do it – the book, I mean. I am 'off' writing – even letters – and most of my last fortnight's mail has gone lost.

Secker wrote he'd sold out his private edition of *David*. I suppose you'll arrange with Knopf to bring out a public, inexpensive edition over there, before the copyright goes wrong.[2] I agree with Knopf, these private editions are a bit of a swindle – fifteen bob for that bit of a book!

Don't mind if I have blank times when I don't write – I am like that. Hope you're feeling well.

D. H. Lawrence

3667. To Nancy Pearn, 6 April 1926
Text: MS UT; Unpublished.

Villa Bernarda, Spotorno (Genova)
6 April 1926

Dear Miss Pearn

I only got back two days ago from my little 'giro' round Capri and Ravello and Rome and Umbria and Ravenna – very nice! The mail, with your March 15th letter, which my wife sent after me, never reached me. – Of course it's all right, the £15. for the 'Rocking Horse' story, to Lady Cynthia: if she is suited.

Amusing to hear about the Capri photograph. I'd clean forgotten. It was a

[1] The two women cannot be identified.

[2] See p. 346 n. 2.

man for the *Tatler*, I think he said. But I've not seen the *Eve* – nor do I know if he did his Capri turn in the *Tatler*.[1]

We are leaving this house about the 20th of this month. I don't want to go back to America – don't feel like it. We may possibly go to Umbria – to Perugia or Cortona – and I may collect material for a book on Umbria and the Etruscan Remains. That would mean little Sketches for you to handle – if I did it.

Barmby writes that the *Dial* is printing the 'Glad Ghosts' story.[2]

It's funny scirocco sort of weather – I believe ultimately there'll be an earthquake.

Remembrances from us both D. H. Lawrence

3668. To Else Jaffe, [7 April 1926]

Text: MS UCB; Frieda Lawrence 198–9.

Villa Bernarda. *Spotorno* (Genova)
7 March 1926

Dear Else,

I got back here on Saturday, and found your letter. Frieda has a bad cold, but the two girls are very well. They are nice girls really, it is Frieda who, in a sense, has made a bad use of them, as far as I am concerned.

Frieda thinks to bring them to Baden Baden for a day or two, at the beginning of May. I shall stay in Florence presumably: and probably Frieda will come back there. I have an idea I might like to roam round in Umbria for a little while, and look at the Etruscan things, which interest me.

Thank you very much for offering us Irschenhausen. But I don't think, now, that I shall come to Germany till about July, so for heavens sake dont disappoint the young Ehepaar.[3] I'm leaving my plans quite indefinite.

I sent you Knopf's Almanach, I thought it would amuse you. He was

[1] Under the heading 'From Capri, The Land of Cypress and Myrtle', the *Tatler* (No. 1291, p. 513) of 24 March 1926 published a short piece on the 'beautiful island from which people can "see Naples and die," if they feel so disposed'. It was illustrated by four photographs, one of them of DHL. He was referred to as 'the well-known author–photographer'.

On 31 March 1926 *Eve* (xxiv, p. 655) published an illustrated article, 'More Pictures of Capri And some of its devotees'. Part of the text (relating to the photograph reproduced in this volume) ran as follows:

> On the right Mr. D. H. Lawrence is seen with the Hon. Dorothy Brett, Miss Harwood Brewster and Mr. and Mrs. Brewster, the American artists at Quartro Venti, the Brewsters' home at Capri. Mr. Lawrence always seems to attach some hidden significance to beards in his writings and should be an authority! Let us hope that he will dramatise Capri as excitingly as he interpreted Australia in his novel "Kangaroo" or as interestingly as he wrote about "Sea and Sardinia". . .'

[2] It was printed in two successive issues of the *Dial*, July and August 1926 (Roberts C143 and 144).

[3] The honeymoon couple have not been identified.

inspired to it by the Insel Verlag *Almanach*: but you see where his Hebraic-American vanity carried him! These copies must *cost* him three dollars each – and he just presents one to each of his authors. I also ordered you *again The Plumed Serpent*.

I'm glad you had a good time with Nusch – she is really very nice with me always. I'm sorry she couldn't come here.

Will you go the South of France with Alfred?[1] I was at Monte Carlo and at Nice, but I couldn't stand it. I didn't like it at all. But it isn't expensive – pension at the Beau Séjour in Monaco was frs 50–. They say that Borme, a little place off the railway, is very nice, with a very good hotel – not far from Toulon.

I shall be glad when this stupid and muddled winter is at last over. The weather is still very heavy and overcast, scirocco, not nice. It feels as if an earthquake were brewing somewhere.

We leave this house on the 20th., presumably for Florence.

I hope you'll have a good holiday. Remember me to Friedel, and Marianne.[2] Brett is sailing for America, for the ranch, at the end of the month.

tante cose DHL

3669. To Hon. Dorothy Brett, [8 April 1926]

Text: MS UCin; Postmark, S[pot]orno 8 4.26; Irvine, Brett 64–5.

Spotorno
Thursday.

Dear Brett

I had both your letters today. I think you are right to go back to the ranch, really: but I wish there were someone to be there too. Perhaps Ida knows somebody – or Spud. I gave you Mabel's address – Finney Farm. Croton-on-Hudson. N.Y.

I can't understand Gersons not getting your cheque through. I thought you had plenty of money in the N. York bank. I wish you'd be careful about those things. Let me know if your money has turned up.

Frieda wants to take her daughters to BadenBaden for a few days, and they are due to be in England by May 1st. So we think we shall leave this house on the 20th, en route for Germany. –

I don't think it would be any use our meeting again just now, we should only be upset. Better get a fresh start on all round: we need it badly.

I've not heard from William for a long time, though I sent him $50.

Let me know if you need any money.

[1] Dr Alfred Weber (1868–1958), Professor of Sociology and Political Science at the University of Heidelberg, and generally known to have been Else's lover for many years (cf. *Letters*, i. 413).

[2] Marianne was Else Jaffe's only daughter (b. 1905).

You know the German address:

c/o Frau von Richthofen, LudwigWilhelmstift, BadenBaden.

I used to know Reggie Turner – he is the last of the Oscar Wilde group.[1] Who introduced you to him?

We used to stay at the Lucchesi in the past. Is it nice now? Is it dear? – and very crowded? – I found the Washington very expensive.

Frieda will write you nice and amicably. – It's horrid scirocco weather.

DHL

3670. To S. S. Koteliansky, 10 April 1926

Text: TMS BL; Postmark, Spotorno 12 4 26; Moore 896–7.

Villa Bernarda, Spotorno, Italy,
10th April, 1926.

My dear Kot,

I came back here a couple of days ago, after wandering about and getting myself better after 'flu. Italy is still very nice, and I feel more at home here than in America.

I don't want to go to Russia now: I hear such dreary tales about it from people in Florence. As for those Nazcompros people, damn them![2] I could never stir Frieda to write to them, and as for myself, I am beyond it.

Swine that they wouldn't give you a naturalization paper.[3] Wasn't there anybody you could take by the nose? I suppose you will stay in the cave until you are a real grizzly. Sorry Farbman has 'flu. Everybody in Italy has it, and mine keeps flicking me in the eye with its tail.

Murry writes to me with sneaking impudence. I have not seen the letter, as Frieda destroyed it without sending it on. I shouldn't have answered it anyhow. Let the green mildew grow on him.

Brett says she is going back to America to look after the ranch. Myself, I don't quite know what I shall do, but I may go to Umbria, Perugia, and collect material for a book more or less about the Etruscans. We leave here on the 20th and are going to Florence.

[1] Reginald Turner (d. 1938), conversationalist, journalist and novelist and a prominent member of the expatriate colony in Florence. DHL had known him since 1920. See *Letters*, iii. 594 n. 4.

[2] Unidentified.

[3] His application for naturalisation was rejected but he became a 'British subject by Naturalization of Russian origin – Imperial Certificate London No. 17752 dated 27 November 1929' (Zytaruk 285 n. 2).

I have never met Gertrude Stein, but if you remember the deaf fellow in *Aaron's Rod*, that is her brother.[1] I really will write oftener once we are settled a little into quiet ways again.

Remember me to Sonia, Farbman and Ghita,

DHL

I actually dictated this letter to Frieda's daughter Elsa[2] – to see if I could do it. Hope you don't mind. F's daughters are really very funny: they sit on their mother with ferocity, simply won't stand her cheek, and fly at her very much in her own style. It leaves her a bit flabbergasted, and is very good for her, as you'll guess.

DHL

3671. To Mollie Skinner, 10 April 1926

Text: TMS WAPL; Skinner 165.

Villa Bernarda, Spotorno.
10th April, 1926.

Dear Molly Skinner,

I have been putting off writing to you because I was sad about *Black Swans*. It was too much of a cinema piece and stayed on the surface, and I wanted so much to like it and then really I didn't.

We have been here for some months, and now next week are moving on. I am awfully glad to be back in Italy. It seems so easy and it gives one a good deal.

What is *Men are We* about?[3] I do hope you will make it as real as you can, and not let it fly off into too much dramatics. Murry showed me your little sketch about the Hospital and I thought it was good;[4] but you ought to hold yourself in and discipline yourself as you write.

If I can help you with anything be sure to let me know. Write me c/o Curtis

[1] Leo Stein (1872–1947), brother of Gertrude Stein (1874–1946), was an American expatriate and art-collector. DHL met him in Settignano in 1919 (see *Letters*, iv. 111). The 'deaf fellow' in *Aaron's Rod* is Walter Rosen (ed. Mara Kalnins, Cambridge, 1988, p. 215 and n.).

[2] Her shorthand transcription is located at UCB as it is in the case of the two letters following. Three further letters exist only in Elsa Weekley's shorthand; regrettably they are indecipherable. All are conjecturally dated 10 April 1926; they were intended for: Bonner, an expatriate American whom DHL knew in Taormina in 1920 (see *Letters*, iii. 634; iv. 187); Alpha Barlow (1874–c. 1950), Achsah Brewster's sister; and Lilian Leader-Williams who, with her husband Basil Leader-Williams, was among DHL's acquaintances in Taormina (*Letters*, iv. 196).

[3] Mollie Skinner collected in *Men Are We* (Perth, 1927) her 'Aboriginal Stories' which first appeared in the *West Australian* newspaper. They reflected her attempt to penetrate 'the mystery of the aboriginal native of Australia' (Preface).

[4] See Letter 3561 and n. 1.

Brown. I should have written long ago except for feeling sad about *Black Swans*. One day we shall surely see you again, either in Australia or Europe. As soon as my play is out I shall send you a copy.

Yours ever, D. H. Lawrence

3672. To William Siebenhaar, 10 April 1926
Text: TMSC NWU; Unpublished.

Villa Bernarda, Spotorno,
10th. April 26.

Dear Mr. Siebenhaar,

I came back here a day or two ago and found your letters. I am glad you have fixed up the agreement with Knopf and do hope you will be able to push the *Havelaar* work on.

I wandered round and stayed with friends in Capri, Rome, Ravenna, etc., and liked it very much. Now we think of leaving next week for Florence and then perhaps for Germany.

It was awfully nice to see you in Monte Carlo and I hope you and Mrs. Siebenhaar will have a prosperous summer.

Yours sincerely D. H. Lawrence

3673. To Hon. Dorothy Brett, [11 April 1926]
Text: MS UCin; Postmark, Spotorno 12[. . .]26; Moore 897.

Spotorno
Sunday

Dear Brett

Your telegram last night, saying you were moving on to Perugia. I'm sure you'll like it. Go to the University museum and look at the Etruscan things. I might come down there later to see if I can do a book: but at present don't feel like making any effort of any sort.

We get on quite well here. Frieda's children are very fierce with her, and fall on her tooth and nail. They simply won't stand her egotism for a minute: she is furious, then becomes almost humble with us all. I think *they've* taught her a lesson. Being her own family, they can go for her exactly in her own way, and pretty well silence her. It makes me die with laughing. She's caught more than she bargained for, in her own offspring. Makes her really appreciative of me: and she quite sees that you too are not the most terrible person on earth.

I ordered your copy of *David* to the International.[1] Write and get it if you don't go back. And it just occurs to me, you may be in time for the American

[1] The hotel where Brett stayed in Capri (all DHL's letters to her in March were addressed there).

edition, if you do a cover design for the jacket. Get it off to Knopf as soon as you can. He's pretty sure to accept – and his edition isn't ready yet.

I wonder when you will sail? Frieda is secretly pining to go back to the ranch, and using her silent influence. It is I myself, who shrink away still. – I can't imagine why William hasn't written.

We shall leave this house on the 20th – I feel I don't care much where I go, so long as it's no effort.

Has your money come? Have you written to Earl and Achsah? Don't get yourself into financial straits, it is[1] such a handicap.

DHL

3674. To Earl and Achsah Brewster, [11 April 1926]

Text: MS UT; Brewster 94–5.

Spotorno.
Sunday 11 April

Dear Earl and Achsah

I have been home just a week. I stayed ten days or so in Ravello – very nice. Brett liked it too. Then with my friends I came slowly north, staying in Rome, Perugia, Assisi, Florence, Ravenna – and so here.

I find Frieda very much softened. Her daughters are very fierce with her. They simply will not stand her overbearing, and fly at her very much in her own way, which abashes and nonplusses her considerably. I am rather amused. Finding her own daughters so very much more brutal and uncompromising with her than I am, she seems to change her mind about a good many matters. – The young are courious. Their feelings don't seem to hurt them, or cost them so much, as ours have done. And they are very good and gallant fighting against anything they think false or unjust. Altogether it's a queer business, life!

We leave this house in a week's time, go to Florence for a bit. I may go down to Perugia for a couple of months, and collect material for a book on Umbria and *Etruscan* things – they interest me very much. Or we may go to Germany: I'm not sure. I don't mind immensely where I go, so long as there is no great effort. Only I don't want to go yet to America.

Brett came up to Florence too but not with me – but now I hear she is in Perugia, so probably she is moving south to Naples, to take her boat to America. She says she will sail, and I think it's best. She can't stand Capri any more: and I can't stand it when she clings too tight.

I had a note from Alpha asking how you were.

[1] MS reads 'it such'.

As soon as I get an address[1] I shall send you my play *David*. So write to me, and tell me all the news. I do hope you'll have a nice exhibition, and will sell things. Write me c/o Curtis Brown. 6 Henrietta St, London W. C. 2. Tell Harwood I shall expect her to be a gentle oriental angel next time I see her.

tante belle cose! D. H. Lawrence

3675. To Mabel Dodge Luhan, 12 April 1926

Text: MS Brill; Luhan 295–7.

Villa Bernarda, *Spotorno* (Genova)
12 April 1926

My dear Mabel

I have been back here a week, and in another week we leave the house, for where, I don't quite know. I don't want to come back to America just now – it's so hard and tense. I am weary of that tension, even the tension of the practice of relaxation. My I, my fourth centre, will look after me better than I should ever look after it. Which is all I feel about Gourdjieff.[2] You become perfect in the manipulation of your organism, and the I is in such perfect suspension[3]

[1] The Brewsters had left Capri for India (cf. Letter 3693).

[2] Georgei Ivanovitch Gurdjieff (1874?–1949), the self-proclaimed master of occult knowledge who had set up the 'Institute for the Harmonious Development of Man' at Fontainebleau in 1922 (where Katherine Mansfield died in January 1923). DHL's contempt for the Institute had been forcibly conveyed to Mabel Luhan on 9 January 1924: 'a rotten, false, self-conscious place of people playing a sickly stunt' (*Letters*, iv. 555). In this letter he is replying to hers of 3 April 1926 which reads in part (Luhan 293–4):

> Then Gurdjieff comes along with his Method or Solution, and it is this: if one will continue to go *on* instead of to drop down one's scale, a special effort is needed for self-creation. Nature, with heredity and sociology, has done all she's going to – has baited the hook all she can – has led us by the ego to *here*; now one has to do the rest oneself.
>
> Gurdjieff says quite calmly, here's a way. Sounds crazy, sounds awful. Try it. Observe this organism. Observe Mabel. Stand back a bit and see her. What she *does*, what she feels, what she thinks. It is enough to observe just her physical behaviour: her tone of voice, her movements, her changes of temperature, etc. Just behaviour, for that is a new language to learn . . . it is what her feelings and her thoughts are saying.
>
> This Mabel has three modes or centres: instinctive, mental, and emotional. They have eaten up the universe. She *must* create a fourth one herself – the I. Behind the brain there are potential muscles for the new mode. To develop them, observe yourself – all the time. Become conscious now of your self, it is a new universe, a cosmos, the world of self-consciousness. And it is terribly hard to know it. All the old life is against it. One can never make a habit of becoming conscious of this mechanism, one is so identified with it. One doesn't *feel like* becoming aware of it and at the same time non-identified with it.
>
> This is the only activity without wish – and it develops Will as opposed to Self-will. Gurdjieff says that little by little the by-products appear . . . in the old centres *new* emotions – active knowing and active creation. "Seek ye first the Kingdom of Heaven and all other things shall be added unto you."
>
> So that's his Method. Self-observation. First with *non-identification*, then *participation*, then *experiment*. *His* kind of alchemy.

[3] suspension] control

that if a dog barks the universe is shattered. Perhaps I should say, the I is also so perfectly self-controlled that nothing more ever can happen. Which perhaps is a goal and an end devoutly to be wished.

I do believe in self-discipline. And I don't believe in self-control.

In the end, if you Gourdjieff yourself to the very end, a dog that barks at you will be a dynamo sufficient to explode your universe. When you are final master of yourself, you are nothing, you can't even wag your tail or bark.

But the fact that your I is not your own makes necesssary a discipline more patient and flexible and long-lasting than any Gourdjieff's.

I wish you had not written to Edwin Dodge again about the Curonia. Myself, I don't want to go there to stay. An hour would be enough. Since your Duse story, basta![1] And Edwin Dodge's note to me was very sniffy, as if I were wanting something of him. Heaven forfend! But he was of course quite polite.

I have finished your Memoirs, sent the first part back to Havelock Ellis, will send him the rest tomorrow.

In the first place, why oh why didn't you change the names! My dear Mabel, call in all the copies, keep them under lock and key, and then carefully, scrupulously change the names: at least do that: before you let one page go out of your hands again. Remember, *other people* can be utterly remorseless, if they think you've given them away.

'Memoirs of a Born American' – they are frightfully depressing, leave me with my heart gone way down out of my shoes, so I haven't any heart at all, feel like a disembodied corpse, if you know what that means. At the same time, I should say it's the most serious 'confession' that ever came out of America, and perhaps the most heart-destroying revelation of the American life-process that ever has or ever will be produced. It's worse than *Œdipus* and *Medea*, and *Hamlet* and *Lear* and *Macbeth* are spinach and eggs in comparison. My dear Mabel, one could shed skyfuls of tears, except for the knowledge of the utter futility of shedding even one. The only thing to do is to close down for the time the fountains of emotion, and face life as far as possible emotionless. But you've said a sort of last word – *That's that*! – to Jesus' *Consummatum est*![2] – It's not the absolute truth – but then nothing ever is. It's not art, because art always gilds the pill, and this is hemlock in a cup. It seems to me so horribly near the truth, it makes me sick in my solar plexus, like death itself, which finally breaks the solar plexus. My dear Mabel, I do think it was pretty hard lines on all of you, to start with. Fate gave America gold and a ghoulish destiny. Heaven help us all! One thing, though, I do think we might learn: if we break,

[1] The famous Italian actress, Eleonora Duse (1858–1924) had stayed at the Villa Curonia with Mabel and Edwin Dodge; according to Mabel, Duse had made a violent sexual assault on her (Emily Hahn, *Mabel*, Boston, 1977, p. 46).

[2] 'It is finished!' (John xix. 30).

or conquer anyone – like Parmenter, it's like breaking the floor-joists, you're sure to go through into the cellar, and cripple yourself.[1] It's the broken snake that's the most dangerous. The unbroken slips away into the bushes of life.

Never win over any-body! – there's a motto. – I mean, never conquer, nor seek to conquer. And never be conquered, except by heaven. And if you don't set your will in opposition to heaven, there's no occasion for conquest there.

But one can't do more than live one's destiny, good or bad, destructive or constructive. One can do much *less*, like Bynner, and chew substitutes all one's life. Or like Edwin Dodge, not have much of a destiny anyhow.

Lord, what a life! It's pouring with rain, and I'm feeling weary to death of struggling with Frieda. I feel like turning to Buddha and crying basta! and sitting under a bho tree.[2]

DHL

Write

c/o Curtis Brown. 6 Henrietta St. *London W. C. 2.*

3676. To Lady Cynthia Asquith, 15 April 1926

Text: MS UT; Unpublished.

Spotorno.
15 April 1926

I got your little note of March 15th *today*, from Martin Secker. Heaven knows what he did with it in the interim. – Myself, I was moving round in the South seeing friends: – came back here to wind up the house. Frieda has been having her two daughters with her for the last two months: tall longlegged young women of 21 and 23: quite good friends, but as for mother and daughter, all bunk! – We leave here on Tuesday, stay in Florence a bit, then the two girls – you remember they are Ernest Weekley's daughters, who writes about words and gives radio lectures on words – they go back to England. I shall probably stay on in Italy for a while – perhaps in Umbria – and look up Etruscan things.

I'm glad you liked the 'Rocking Horse': I told Miss Pearn to agree with you for terms and all that. After all, I wrote the story for you, not the magazines. And I do hope the book will be a shining success. If it is, do a book of adventure stories: and a book of stories about the sun (not for adolescents this time): and a book of stories about the end of the world. It would be fun to have a sort of series.

[1] Dr John Parmenter (1862–1932), Buffalo physician, became Mabel's lover while she was married to her first husband, Karl Evans. The affair was ended when his wife Frances threatened to sue for divorce. Mabel Luhan omitted her account in the published memoirs (Lois Palken Rudnick, *Mabel Dodge Luhan*, Albuquerque, 1984, p. 26; letter to eds. from Ross Parmenter).

[2] I.e. a place for meditation (the Buddha sat under a bho tree when he achieved enlightenment).

I'm really glad to be back in Italy – I feel more at home here than in America. Today we were rowing to the little Bergeggi island.

You'd better ask somebody who is turfy if my racing and betting items are all right, in the 'Rocking Horse'. I'm by no means a dead cert!

I think Curtis Browns address finds me best – I shall be moving round.

tante belle cose! D. H. Lawrence

3677. To Hon. Dorothy Brett, [17 April 1926]

Text: MS UCin; Postmark, [V]entimiglia 17[. . .]6; Moore 900–1.

Spotorno.
Saturday 17 April

Dear Brett

Your wire this morning, saying you are back in Capri. How quickly you've moved! I suppose you didn't stay in Rome at all.

You will have had F[rieda]'s letter by now,[1] and the few books I sent. If you've room, you might take them to add to our little ranch library. If not, just abandon them.

We're packing up, to leave some time next week. Anyhow by the end of next week we shall be gone from this house. The girls are now beginning to regret they haven't seen more of Italy. But it's all very expensive.

I'm glad your money turned up. You cant possibly owe Gersons and those in Taos £50. You must have something to be going on with. Perhaps Mrs Hecksher will give you a bit.[2] But I do think you ought to keep track of your spending and incoming. It's very nasty to go back to Gersons and face unmet

[1] Frieda had written probably on 9 April 1926 (MS UCin):

Villa Bernarda, Spotorno
Friday

Dear Brett,

So you are going to the Ranch! Part of me goes with you! As you know! Do just as you like there and weep over the Azul for me! Lawrence is better – We had a good time with the children – I wish you had stayed with us here for a few days, it's a jolly place, the joy for me of having the children and making them rosy and fat – Now I am taking them to my mother – Her address – Frau Baronin von Richthofen, Ludwig Wilhelmstift, Baden-Baden, Germania – I have translated the play David quite well, I believe – I loved doing it – Do as you like at the ranch, perhaps the Spud would love to stay a bit. And dont think that we hate each other, only I am so impatient of any will that's put over me – You have given us much support also – But do get somebody to live with you at the ranch – You'll go queer alone – All good luck to you, we are sending you those 2 pictures of the Brewsters to take to the ranch if you would. Barby has done some quite nice things.

Travel well and greet the Ranch from me,

Ever yours Frieda

[2] The wife of Maurice Heckscher, brother to Brett's sister-in-law (cf. *Letters*, iv. 580–1 and n. 1).

cheques. I would loathe to draw a cheque if I thought it wouldn't be covered: it's sort of false.

You won't sail now until May 5. – you couldnt have caught the earlier boat. So you won't be at the ranch till about June. That will be late. I must write to Scott Murray to go up and see to the irrigating before then. I wish I heard from William. – Perhaps Mabel would be motoring back when you are there – she might take you.

I shan't bother you with Achsah's and Earls pictures: too much fag.

It's thunder and heavy rain here today. They write from Germany how beautiful it is there. But still I hanker after Umbria. I think I shall go and have a shot at that book, sooner or later. And Orvieto is one of the towns of the Etruscans. Anna di Chiara said Volterra was a good place, also. – I went to Assisi – the lower church of St. Francis *is* impressive: and the two Giotto pictures. But I like churches best outside. Isn't that a fascinating façade of the cathedral at Assisi?

I'll write again directly: do hope your cold is better: I am much better myself.

DHL

3678. To Richard Aldington, [18 April 1926]
Text: MS SIU; Moore 901–2.

Villa Bernarda. *Spotorno* (Genova)
Sunday

Dear Richard

Your letter this morning. Sounds nice, your little cottage (no, don't mention poor Margaret Radford, God's sake!).[1] Don't talk nonsense to me about primitive conditions, do you imagine I've suddenly turned my nose up at the brass tacks of life? I wash dishes and cook soup the same as ever – a little better, I hope.

I should like very much to come down and see you when I am in England – whenever that will be! So would Frieda (Arabella, we are expecting your letter full of *feminine* information)[2] – Perhaps in July or August. I thought Padworth was somewhere else – in Sussex or somewhere.

[1] Margaret was the younger daughter of Dollie (1864?–1920) and Ernest Radford (1857–1919) whom DHL knew from 1915 (see *Letters*, ii. 316 n. 2). From December 1917 to November 1919 the Lawrences lived for several periods in Dollie's cottage at Hermitage, Berks; during one visit Margaret Radford was there with them and DHL did not enjoy it (cf. *Letters*, iii. 349, 376). 1926–8 Aldington lived at Malthouse Cottage, Padworth near Reading.

[2] Aldington had separated from his wife Hilda Doolittle (divorced 1938) and from Autumn 1919 was living with Dorothy ('Arabella') Yorke (b. 1892), an American whom DHL used as a model for Josephine Ford in *Aaron's Rod*. (Cf. Letter 3700.)

But why dont you come and stroll around Tuscany and Umbria a bit with me. I thought I might do a sort of travel book about the Etruscans – heaven knows if I shall. But the Etruscan things appeal *very much* to my imagination. They are so curiously natural – somebody said bourgeois, but that's a lie, considering all the phallic monuments. I wish you'd come and read inscriptions, and do a bit of Etruscan deciphering – in Cortona and Viterbo and Volumni[1] and even Bologna. Seems to me you just need a bit of fresh ground. Come both of you, and we'll tramp round. Frieda is going to BadenBaden with her daughters – she may stay there, or come back and join me.

We leave on Tuesday for Florence –

Pensione Lucchesi, Lungarno Zecca, Firenze.

It's 45 Liras a day. But if you came, we'd go to little places and have a good time. I hate hotels.

Su, cari miei, su! avanti! vivete pericolosamente![2] as dear heroic Mussolini urges.

DHL

Send a line to Florence – I shall be there a week or fortnight anyhow.

3679. To Elfie Rosebery, [18 April 1926]

Text: MS Secor; PC v. Spotorno – Pineta; Postmark, Spotorno 19.4.26; Unpublished.

[Villa Bernarda, Spotorno, Genova]

Sunday.

– Your letter this morning: We are in the throes of packing, so excuse p.c. – There was nothing available in Genova, again, but expensive things beyond our pockets. We shall have to go down to a place like Palermo or Corfu, hire an ordinary lugger, and fit it up a bit. That's the only way. Next year! It *ought* to be done. – I'll keep your address. You can always get me c/o Curtis Brown. 6. Henrietta St. London W.C.2. We are going to Florence on Tuesday morning. If Mrs Lunn is still there, send her a line and tell her to let me know – at the Pensione Lucchesi, Lungarno Zecca, Florence – where she is, and I will call on her and pay my respects. I don't know how long I shall be there – but probably my wife will go to BadenBaden, and I shall linger on. – I remember Ravello very gratefully – it was nice there. ricordi al Signor Giuseppe – and to all the others that are left.[3]

D. H. Lawrence

[1] MS reads 'Volummni'.

[2] 'Come on, my dear ones, come on! forward! live dangerously!'

[3] I.e. left at the Hotel Palumbo, Ravello, where the card was addressed.

3680. To Baroness Anna von Richthofen, [19 April 1926]

Text: MS Clark; PC v. Ravello – Cattedrale – Parte superiore dell'Ambone – Sec. XIII; Postmark, Spotorno 19. 4.26; Unpublished.

Spotorno.
Montag

Wir reisen morgen nach Florenz: die Adresse dort ist

Pensione Lucchesi, Lungarno Zecca, Florenz.

Die drei Frauen bleiben eine Woche ungefähr, dann nach Baden. Ich werde dich später sehen.

Wie geht's dir?

DHL

[We go to Florence tomorrow: the address there is

Pension Lucchesi, Lungarno Zecca, Florence.

The three women stay for about a week, then go to Baden. I'll see you later.

How are you?

DHL]

3681. To Margaret King, [19 April 1926]

Text: MS Needham; PC v. Spotorno – Ospizio Marino Merello; Postmark, Spotorno 19. 4.26; Unpublished.

Spotorno
Monday

– Was very glad to have your letter with some consoling news: Joan better and you progressing. Never say die! – We leave tomorrow for Florence: address Pensione Lucchesi. Lungarno Zecca. Frieda will go with her daughters to Baden, but I think I shall stay on in Italy for a time, perhaps do a bit of work – and not come north till July. The snap of Joan is amusing.

DHL

3682. To William and Rachel Hawk, 19 April 1926

Text: MS UT; Unpublished.

Spotorno
Monday *19 April 1926*

Dear Rachel and William

I wonder very much why we have not heard from you in answer to my last. Did you get it, with the fifty dollars enclosed? – I hope to heaven you haven't already gone away from Del Monte.

We leave Spotorno tomorrow, and shall stay in Florence a while, then Frieda will go on with her daughters to Baden Baden, and I shall remain, I expect, in Italy until July. So write to me c/o Curtis Brown. 6 Henrietta St. London W.C. 2.

For about six weeks I was moving around, in Capri, Ravello, Rome etc – came back here a fortnight ago, to pack up. I saw Brett, of course, in Capri. She is sailing now on May 2nd for Boston: so she should be at Del Monte easily by June, if she has no difficulties. She is coming in on the quota,[1] so that she may remain in U.S.A. as long as she likes. I do hope they wont fuss and annoy her.

Myself, I simply don't want to take that long, weary journey. I don't even want to come to America very badly. But the ranch pulls, and I don't call the ranch America. Only, even the ranch is a sort of effort, a strain – and for the moment I don't want to make any efforts. I am so used to Italy, and so much at home here, I think I shall stay at least till July, then go to Germany and England, and perhaps to Scotland, where I have an invitation. Perhaps I shall do a bit of work here in Italy.

The thought of the ranch weighs on my mind. If you are not going away, William, I wish you'd look after it a bit for me, turn on the water and put the horses in the field, and just look at the fences. And make me a bill for all you do – and for the horses and everything. If you are going away, would you ask Scott Murray to do these things for me. I would write to him direct, but if you are there yourself, I would of course rather leave things to you, if you have time, and will do them.

Brett will probably want to live on our ranch. If she does, give her the keys. But she'll have to get someone to be there also. Alone is quite impossible, *don't let her* go up there alone. If she gets some workman of some sort, I will pay for any real work he does. But Brett is so scattered, someone would have to keep an eye on her. I was furious when she told me – only last week – that she had not left enough money in the New York bank to meet the cheque she drew to Gerson. So Gerson must have been on tenterhooks all winter. Rachel, if you are there, go for her tooth and nail about money. Don't let her go in for heavy expenses: tell her I say you're to prevent her, as I feel if she makes bills they'll only fall to me to pay, in the end. I haven't paid any yet – but I know she's about spent herself out again, and unless she collects money in New York, something will have to be done. Do, Rachel, be a real stepmother to her. Don't allow her to be nonsensical.

But perhaps you've gone away already to Alaska or some such hole. Dreadful thought! I wish you could have settled on our little ranch yourselves.

If a letter is on the way, it will be sent after me, wherever I am. I do wish I'd heard from you before we left here.

It is full spring here. The trees have finished blooming, the almonds are quite big, the young figs too, and the long flowers are on the vines. We are having peas from the garden, and the first few strawberries. – If one could only

[1] A yearly quota of immigrants was allowed from a particular country of origin.

stride over to the ranch! But the thought of that journey appals me, just now. – But I should like to see it all clean after snow – and those hairy lovely anemones under the pines, and the squawberry bushes coming green. It has a thrill of its own, so different from here.

I do hope things are going decently and pleasantly with you. We talk of you a good deal, as you may imagine. Remember us to Mr. and Mrs Hawk, and much affection to you both and to the children, from us both.

D. H. Lawrence

3683. To Nancy Pearn, [19 April 1926]

Text: MS UT; PC v. Ravello – Cattedrale – Capitello dell'Ambone Sec. XIII; Postmark, [Sp]otorno 19 4 26; Unpublished.

Spotorno.
Monday.

Nice to hear about the *Nation's* accepting 'Smile'.[1] We leave here tomorrow – address

Pensione Lucchesi, Lungarno Zecca, *Florence.*

Would you be so good as to tell the other departments, so that no more letters come here.

D. H. Lawrence

3684. To Mabel Dodge Luhan, 19 April 1926

Text: MS Brill; Luhan 297–9.

Spotorno.
19 April 1926

Dear Mabel

We leave here tomorrow, shall stay in Florence a few days. Then Frieda will go with her daughters to Baden Baden, and I shall probably stay in Umbria, and collect notes for that book on the Etruscans.

I heard from Brett that she is landing in Boston about May 16th: she sails from Naples on May 2nd. She wants to go back to Del Monte. She'll be able to keep an eye on the ranch. But heaven knows how she's going to be, out there alone. She must get some decent person. – And she's coming in on the quota: hope there won't be a fuss when she lands.

I discovered your little foreword to the Memoirs, when I was packing up: so it didn't get sent to H[avelock] Ellis with the rest of the MS. – It's a very clear

[1] See p. 351 n. 3.

statement of the very very very central malady of our civilisation, seems to me. To be born without any centre, any centrifugal I! – only this strange centripetal vortex of an ego. – I think everybody is born both: their souls go both ways, centrifugal and centripetal. But according to statement, yours was only centripetal, you only existed when something was pouring into you – some sensation, some conscious registering. Of course that's not quite true. There must be a last central you, or you couldnt *know*. Most people don't know. I believe the majority of people are like it. It's only that they have no definite I, and they exist in the group consciousness. They are so tribal, so entirely group conscious, that they don't need to have any individual consciousness. I think that's what the man meant when he said you never quite belonged to the human race. The group consciousness *of course* never knows the acute individual consciousness: and the acute individual consciousness is always half oblivious, half hostile, to the mass consciousness: the mass consciousness is hostile back again. You happen to have been born an individual, even if you were only, in your own terms, an individual vortex. Those other swine revolve slowly in the vast, obscene social or mass vortex, and so of course they never realise their own *null* negation. Yours anyhow was a fierce, direct negation: as there are gods of pure destruction pure in its way, and necessary as creation.

And that's what I think about Gourdjieff and all those things: they can only help you more competently *to make your own feelings*. They can never let you *have* any real feelings. – That only comes with an acute moment of self-knowledge: and you've had that: and a sort of anguish of repentance (it only means a turning back, or turning round, or the crucial pain of turning or revolving in the other direction). As for that, I dont know.

But the Foreword gives the book away, don't you see. All those terrible feelings, and none of them, ultimately, real. – But to *know it* immediately *makes* something real: in a sense, sets the whole thing in a rhythm of reality.

Heaven knows how it will all work out in actual living. Change is the coming of that which we don't expect. But the breaking of a lifelong habit is also *almost* impossible.

Collect your MSS and keep them all in a safe. Don't show them to anybody else, just now. Labour and wait. Dont be in a hurry. It's one of your habits you must break. Let some change come. Then, after a few years, take out your MSS again, and do what you wish with them. But not now. For the moment, let them lie still.

Write

c/o Curtis Brown, 6 Henrietta St, London W.C. 2.

tante cose! DHL

3685. To Ada Clarke, [19 April 1926]

Text: MS Clarke; PC v. Spotorno – Pineta; Postmark, Spotorno 19. 4.26; Lawrence–Gelder 135.

Spotorno.
Monday

Was glad to get your letter. I am very much better in health – getting on my own real feet again, and then one can stand firm. We leave for Florence tomorrow – address

Pensione Lucchesi, Lungarno Zecca.

Frieda will probably go to Baden after a week, with her daughters, but I think of staying on in Italy till July.

Will write from Florence.

DHL

Giovanni says, could you send him one of those photographs – to

Giovanni Rossi, Villa Bernarda.

I told you I never got your letter to Capri: it must have gone quite lost.[1]

3686. To Nancy Pearn, 19 April 1926

Text: MS UT; Unpublished.

Spotorno –
19 April 1926

Dear Miss Pearn

Murry told me he couldn't afford to pay anything for *Adelphi* contributions. – that he couldn't possibly pay the price for those 'Mornings in Mexico' articles. He has published one. If the *Criterion* has taken another, it leaves only two.[2] – Did Murry pay for the one he has already published? I'll bet not. – But don't bother him. Only, take the other two from him, because I cant stand the *Adelphi*, and because he writes to me with such a mixture of sweetness and impertinence, I won't stand that either.

[1] This second postscript was written on the verso of the PC.

[2] Murry had published 'Corasmin and the Parrots' – the 'one' referred to here – in December 1925 (iii, pp. 480–9, 502–6); cf. Letter 3711 and p. 451 n. 3. *New Criterion* published 'Market Day' as 'Mornings in Mexico, Saturday' in June 1926. (Murry later printed two more 'Mornings in Mexico' essays: 'The Mozo' in February 1927, iv, pp. 474–8, as 'Mornings in Mexico, The Mozo' and 'Walk to Huayapa' in March 1927. The last was reprinted in *Living Age*, 1 April 1927 as 'Sons of Montezuma'.) See Roberts C134, C140, C151 and C147.

We're all packed to leave. I sent you a p. c. with the address –
Pensione Lucchesi, Lungarno Zecca, Florence.
Yrs D. H. Lawrence

3687. To Hon. Dorothy Brett, [20 April 1926]

Text: MS UCin; PC v. Pisa – Lampada in bronzo detta di Galileo (Rossenti 1587); Postmark, Pisa 20 . IV [. . .]926; Irvine, Brett 66.

[Pisa]
[20 April 1926]

The women decided to make a small giro en route to Germany – got permission and some money from their father.[1] So by Thursday we shall be in Florence, at the Lucchesi. I am getting out of going to Germany just now, if possible – shall remain in Umbria. Hope you're feeling better.

DHL

3688. To John Cournos, 21 April 1926

Text: MS Cushman; Unpublished.

Pensione Lucchesi, Lungarno Zecca, Florence
21 April 1926

Dear Cournos

You may have seen me at Parma – but I changed at Piacenza to go round to Genova. – Yesterday we came to Florence, my wife and her daughters – they'll stay a week or so, I may stay on two months: then probably Paris.

Of course I recognised the people in *Miranda*: am afraid they won't be pleased. Will Hilda forgive you, or don't you want her to?[2]

It's the *Natale Romana* here: Fascist substitute for 1st May, and a great buzzing and playing of 'Giovanezza! Giovanezza!' in Piazza della Signoria.[3] But of course it is raining – always rains in Florence. – It is queer, this Fascist movement: one wonders what the end will be. – Interesting, in its way.

[1] I.e. Ernest Weekley.

[2] Cournos's novel, *Miranda Masters* (June 1926) is a very transparent, fictional presentation of the invariably tense and passionate interrelationships between himself ('Gombarov'), Hilda Aldington ('Miranda'), Richard Aldington ('Arnold') and Arabella Yorke ('Winifred'), c. 1916–18. The portrait of Miranda is unflattering: she is unfeeling about her stillborn child, attempts to seduce and then rejects Gombarov, thrusts Arnold into the (willing) arms of Winifred and has an affair with a young artist. (Cf. p. 426 n. 2.)

[3] The 'Birthday of Rome', one of the most important events in the Fascist calendar, was celebrated on 21 April (replacing 'Labour Day' on 1 May). (See *The Times*, 21 April 1926.) 'Giovanezza' is 'Youth'.

Remember me to Mrs Cournos – hope you're having a good time in Paris. Good luck! – and a bit more money in the family purse!

Yrs D. H. Lawrence[1]

3689. To Reginald Turner, [23 April 1926]
Text: TMSC NWU; Unpublished.

[Pensione Lucchesi, Lungarno Zecca, Florence]
[23 April 1926]

Reginald Turner Esq., Viale Milton, Citta

Dear Turner

I am here with my wife and her two daughters, the two Miss Weekleys, for a day or two. Miss Brett told me she had seen you.

Would you care to come to lunch with us, tomorrow or one day soon? It's an old-maidish place, but the food is about the ordinary – at 12.30!

remembrance from us both D. H. Lawrence

3690. To Hon. Dorothy Brett, [23 April 1926]
Text: MS UCin; Postmark, Fire[nz]e 25. IV 1926; Huxley 656–7.

Pensione Lucchesi. Lungarno Zecca, Firenze
Friday

Dear Brett

We are here in the most atrocious weather, pouring cold rain all the time. I loathe it. And we are still undecided about Germany. If this weather continues, I shall go. I feel the North Pole would be better than Florence, in any more of this weather.

I just got your letter. Why have you let yourself run so low in cash? To get to Santa Fe you need $150.00. The railway is about 93, the pullman about 40, and food to buy. But see if Mabel won't motor you over. Her Finney Farm is

[1] Associated with this MS, though not necessarily sent with it, is an unaddressed postcard (MS Cushman) dated 28 March 1926 and thus connected with DHL's earlier meeting with the Cournoses in Florence (see Letter 3658 and n. 1). The recto of the card is signed by DHL, Helen and John Cournos; it carries only a printed message, '*Italiani! Ricordiamo ed onoriamo i fattori della grande Italia*' ['Italians! Let us remember and honour the makers of Italy the great']; and it is stamped with the seal of the 'Associazione della "La Croce d'Oro" Firenze'. The verso shows a picture of (left) Mazzini, Vittorio Emanuele II, Garibaldi and Cavour, and (right) Vittorio Emanuele III, Thaon di Revel, Paolo Diaz and Mussolini; under the first group is the caption '1848–'49', under the second, '1922'; and applying to both, the words 'Per La Patria'.

The 'Croce d'Oro' was a mutual benefit or friendly society mainly consisting of business men with masonic leanings. DHL's interest in it, if any, cannot be explained.

between Boston and New York. – If you get really stuck for money, you'll have to borrow from me. I'll enclose a little note to Barmby.[1]

You'll have no-one to meet you in Boston, and I think you must be met by somebody. Usually the Y. W. C. A representative does it. – I hope you got that letter from your Father and from the Foreign Office – one can't stand being badgered about. What a curse the world is!

I asked Reggie Turner to lunch – don't know if he'll turn up.

Barbara and Elsa leave next Tuesday or Wednesday anyway. Frieda now won't go to BadenBaden unless I do. But that address is always good:
c/o Frau von Richthofen, Ludwig-Wilhelmstift, *BadenBaden*, Germany. *Otherwise c/o Curtis Brown. 6. Henrietta St. W. C. 2.* As for me, I feel absolutely numb to the soul, what with cold rain and the rest of things.

F. and I will be here another week, so write here. Did you get the woolly lamb, sent from Spotorno? – and a few little books. – Make your preparations carefully, before you go. *Ask about being met in Boston.*

DHL

3691. To Catherine Carswell, [23 April 1926]

Text: MS YU; PC v. Rome (Galerie Corsini). – Raphael. Étude pour la Madone du Prince Esterhazy; Unpublished.

Pensione Lucchesi. Lungarno Zecca, Florence.
Friday

My Dear Catherine

Your letter came on tonight – we are here for a week or ten days. – I do hope you are feeling more cheerful.[2] You are *bound* to find it hard at first – so is the boy. But let him stick it out for a time at least. I'm sure it's better for him to be separated from you just now – and better in the end for you.

I have written to Mabel Harrison, a very nice woman, in Paris, and asked her to write you and ask you to go and see her – She has a studio 49 Bvd Montparnasse just near the Gare de Montparnasse, where you come in from Versailles. So if she writes, go and see her, she'll help to cheer you up. – It's one of your crucial times, so you've just got to bear up and go through with it.

Here the weather is perfectly vile – for the first time, I hate Florence.

[1] The note is missing.

[2] Catherine and Donald Carswell were 'making a difficult experiment' (Carswell 241). She explained: 'I was living in a French village on half-a-crown a day, with John Patrick at school there and Donald with friends in London. Lawrence, who approved of the move, . . . sent me an introduction I was glad of to Mabel Harrison in Paris. At Jouy-en-Josas (our village) I was for days on end without a soul to speak to.' See also Letter 3733. (The letter from DHL to Mabel Harrison is missing.)

F[rieda]'s two daughters are here till next week, then they go back to England. I don't quite know what I shall do but I'll write.

Do hope you're feeling better now.

DHL

3692. To Jan Juta, [24 April 1926]
Text: Moore, *Intelligent Heart* 353–4.

Pensione Lucchesi, Florence,
24 April

Your letter arrived here this evening – we left Spotorno last Tuesday, for good. Frieda's two daughters are leaving next Tuesday for London, and we are either staying on in Tuscany or Umbria a couple of months, or else we shall go to Germany. I'm not sure yet. But we shall be here another ten days or so.

Your *Corsica* book looks nice: hope it'll be a success.[1]

What plan have you got? Another travel book? I wonder where! I myself was pining to get some sort of little ship, with about half a dozen of us, and do the Isles of Greece and Smyrna. I should have loved that. But the ship didn't turn up – too expensive, whatever offered. But we might keep that idea in mind.

The only other place that suggests itself is Spain – where I've never been.

I hope you've had a good time with your fresco. Italy doesn't seem to me so jolly as it used to be: Very little fun going. But Frieda rather wants to take a house – a villino – in the country here, till July: myself, I am doubtful. However, I don't care very much.

You wrote your address so dashingly, I'm dashed if I can read it. So hope this finds you.

[Frieda Lawrence begins]

It would have been fun if you had turned up at the Villa Bernarda!

I had such a jolly time with my long legged daughters! You might perhaps see us here sometime – But Elsa and Barby are going back on Tuesday –

3693. To Earl Brewster, 25 April 1926
Text: MS UT; Brewster 95–7.

Pensione Lucchesi. Lungarno Zecca, Florence
25 April 1926

Dear Earl

I had your letter from Port Said: so glad the journey was so pleasant, and you liked the books.

[1] *Concerning Corsica* by Réné Juta (Hansard) (Jan Juta's sister), with illustrations by Juta himself, was published by John Lane in March 1926.

We came here last Tuesday – it has poured with rain ever since, and is perfectly vile. Florence, too, is irritable and out of temper – over-crowded for one thing, and perhaps out of sorts with the present régime. I must say, I don't care for it. I had thought of staying perhaps a couple of months in and around Umbria, and doing a book on the Etruscans. But I notice, if ever I say I'll do a thing, I never bring it off. To tell the truth, I feel like going away – perhaps to Spain, or to Germany.

Frieda's two daughters leave on Tuesday, for London. Then F. and I will decide what we shall do. – They are nice girls, really. But the young are so disconcerting in that they have no centre of belief at all. No centre of real affirmation. They have epicurean and stoic qualities – courage and a certain endurance and honesty – very hostile to any form of tyranny or falsity – and then, nothing: a sort of blank. As if they could only put up resistances. They have, of course, a certain belief in pleasure, what is called 'enjoying yourself,' but even that doesn't go very deep. It's rather hard lines, really, they *inherited* unbelief: like children who expected to be left rich, when their parents died, and find themselves paupers.

The more I go around, the nearer I do come, in a certain way, to your position. I am convinced that every man needs a bho tree of some sort in his life. What ails us is, we have cut down all our bho trees. How long it takes a new one to grow, I don't know: probably many years. In a generation one can hack down forests of them. Still, here and there in the world a solitary bho tree must be standing: 'where two or three of ye have met together.'[1] And I'm going to sit right down under one, to be American about it, when I come across one.

Which is as good as saying, if you find a bit of bho-tree-shade in India, in that monastery of the hills or elsewhere, I'll probably come along. In the autumn, when the heats are over. Only let me know. You needn't advise *me* to come. Just tell me what you and Achsah and Harwood feel: all three of you, honest to God.

Because I really don't want to go to America: and I am getting weary, and wearier, of the outside world. I want the world from the inside, not from the outside. Which doesn't mean, for me, killing desire and anger. Greed, lust, yes! But desire and anger are from God. Give me anything which is from God, desire or anger or communion of saints, or even hurts. But nothing any more of the dreariness and the mechanism of man.

Brett sails for Boston on May 2nd. She wants to go, and I feel it is her direction. But in myself, every week seems to alienate my soul further from America. I don't want to go west.

I do hope you are having a nice time, and even selling some pictures. One reads of riots in Calcutta, but they won't really affect you.

[1] Matthew xviii. 20 ['. . . three are gathered together in my name'].

Yes, I do think there is a bit of real communion between us: so let's stick to it.

Hasta otra vez D. H. Lawrence
c/o Curtis Brown, 6 Henrietta St, London W.C. 2.

3694. To Rachel Hawk, 25 April 1926
Text: MS UT; Unpublished.

Florence. Italy
25 April 1926

Dear Rachel

I received your letter yesterday. What perfectly depressing news! you and William gone from the log cabin, some completely unknown Rasmussens[1] there, – and then all of you ill! Makes me feel I shall never never come back to the ranch. But things will have to straighten out. If you find it perfectly wretched looking for jobs out in the dreary world, why don't you go and live on our ranch? There's not much of a living to be made, that's true: but then the cost of living is also very small. When we come back, all we want, really, is a cabin to live in, and the horses to ride. And we could all do things together. It is perhaps nicer than San Cristobal.

Brett is sailing for Boston on May 2nd – I hope she has no troubles. But how she'll get on if you're not there, that I don't know. Everything is a muddle.

We came here to Florence last week – gave up the house. Frieda's daughters leave for London in three days' time, then F. and I must decide what we are going to do. Perhaps we shall stay on in Italy till July, then go to Germany, then to England. We might come to America in the autumn, and stay in Santa Fe or California till spring. Or we may winter again in the south of Europe, and sail for U. S. A. in the spring. I don't know. At the present moment, for some reason, I don't want to come back to America: just don't want to.

Be sure and write to me, wherever you go: don't disappear into the void. You and William will never be strangers to us, whatever happens: we shall always think of you, in a way, as part of the family. I wish I was rich enough to give Bill a wage, to live up on our little Kiowa. But perhaps he wouldn't want to.

Dreadful to think of weeks of slush and sleet! We've had four days of rain here, and are feeling furious. But the sun is coming out now, so perhaps there'll be a change.

I hear from Mabel – she says she'll make a short trip to Europe in May – and

[1] Joe and Maudie Rassmussen leased the Hawk ranch from Alfred Decker Hawk, 1926–7; they had three children and lived in Rachel and William Hawk's cabin (see p. 440 n. 1).

then go straight back to Taos.[1] In that case, I suppose we shall see her – though I doubt if I shall go to Paris in May.

You'll have to be careful what you do, Rachel. You might find some nice place, and good work, not too far off. You alone would be easy to provide for, you could soon earn your way. But there's the children, and there's William – and he's not just the average man, who can bang about among any traffic. You can but try. And then, if he gets really unhappy, away from the mountains, he'd best come back. Don't try and go against his nature, nor against your own. We're all made in our own peculiar way, and the only thing to do is to try and make two ways go together as naturally as possible, if you're two people, as far as they will go. William isn't quite the ordinary man, so you haven't got just the ordinary woman's job. I'm not the ordinary man myself, and don't want to be, and I hate anyone who tries to fit me into the ordinary man's shoes. – In this life, one can but try. But if the strain becomes too great, yield, and try something else. It is always better to give way, rather than break something which shouldn't be broken.

If ever I can help you, let me know. You know I shall be glad.

I enclose the twenty dollars I owe William.

affectionately D. H. Lawrence

Remember us kindly to Mr and Mrs Hawk.

DHL

c/o Curtis Brown, 6 Henrietta St. London W.C. 2.

3695. To Mabel Dodge Luhan, [25 April 1926]

Text: MS Brill; PC; Postmark, Firenze 26 . IV 1926; Luhan 299.

Florence.

25 Aprile.

– We are here for a while – if you come to Europe in May, let me know – but

c/o Curtis Brown. 6 Henrietta St. *London W.C.2.*

is the quickest.

Had your letter today. But I contend (although Gourdjieffs method is sound, for what it aims at) – that when the *I* finally emerges, that way, it will be half demon and half imbecile. That's the trajedy of that way. There's another way, but the change *has to take place* before you can start on it. However, every man to his own stride.

DHL

Don't you see Gourdjieffs ultimate I is the ultimate self important.

[1] Taos] Paris

3696. To Hon. Dorothy Brett, [25 April 1926]
Text: MS UCin; Postmark, Firenze 26 . IV 1926; Huxley 655–6.

Florence
Sunday –

Dear Brett –

Here is Rachel's letter – also very depressing![1] You'll probably find them gone when you arrive. – *Don't* go up alone to our Ranch: I expressly *dont want* you to go up there *alone*. If you have somebody decent with you, well and good. – I am a bit worried about the Ranch anyway. I feel very strongly it would be better to have some responsible person living there – like Scott Murray. I almost wish I'd asked Rachel and Wm. if they'd care to live there – I did just hint it, in my letter to them a week ago. I want you to be very careful, and cautiously feel around for what would be the best. Don't blindly dash into anything. – But for myself, I definitely feel it would be best to have some good man living permanently up there and making a bit of a living off the place. – It would *really* make it more livable for all of us – and make it more possible ultimately for us to plant a Buddha bho-tree – or a bho-tree of our own – up there, and foregather under its shade. It is what we ought to do, ultimately. Meanwhile we must build up to that. So do think carefully for the future, and

[1] DHL wrote to Brett on the letter to him from Rachel Hawk; it read:

Delmonte Ranch, Questa, N. Mex.
April 5, 1926.

Dear Mr. Lawrence,

I should have written long ago but we have been so busy and confused with packing and moving. We moved down here with the old folks last Tuesday. The Rasmossen family moved into our house on Saturday. Since coming down here we have all been sick in bed, first Bill, Walton, myself, the baby and now Mrs. Hawk. You wouldn't wonder tho if you could see the awful weather we are having. Nothing but sleet and wind. We have only had a wee peek of the sun four days in the last two weeks.

Betty, Louie and Barbara arrived yesterday. Betty will stay a short time. They had a terriable time getting out from Taos. It took them from 10 a.m. until 4 p.m. and then they had to leave the car at the top of the Lobo hill and pulled it up to-day with the team.

Your horses came up from San-Cristobal to-day. Mr. Rasmossen will feed them until there is enough grass up on your place for them to go up there.

I am sorry that we thought it wise to kill Moses. He got into a fight with the numerous other roosters and got by far the worst of the deal. And so considering his health and age, we killed him.

What is to become of Miss W[emyss]? Mother hates cats so, I can't ask her to care for her.

We do not know just where we will go. We have found out that the conditions of Alaska are not favorable to the raising of a family, so I guess we shall stay in the U. S. A. somewhere.

Your letters certainly sound as if you have no intention of returning this summer. I can't but wonder what will happen to all your things.

Hoping this finds you in the best of health and better spirits.

As ever Rachel Hawk

let us gradually shape the ranch the way it ought to go, for the final best: when we'll have a bho-tree as well as pine trees.

It is rather depressing here – vile weather – Florence very crowded and irritable. I don't like it much, and dont think I shall stay long. But another week, anyhow. – The two girls leave for London direct on Tuesday – then Frieda and I will have to decide what we do. – Mabel writes she will come to Paris in May, to see Gourdjieff in Fontainebleau. She thinks salvation lies that way. It may, for her.

If you get stuck for money, let me know. Any expenses incurred for the Ranch, I will pay. But be careful and thoughtful, don't do foolish things, and don't buy unnecessary ones. All our means, of all sorts, are definitely limited.

DHL

I can't stand Francis of Assisi – nor St Clare – nor St. Catherine. I didn't even like Assisi. They've killed so much of the precious interchange in life: most folks are half dead, maimed, because of those blighters. The indecency of sprinkling good food with ashes, and dirtying a sensitive mouth!

DHL

I still find I can't write to old Hawk. Say nice things to them from me, if you can.

3697. To Arthur Wilkinson, [27 April 1926]
Text: MS Schlaefle; Unpublished.

Pensione Lucchesi. Lungarno Zecca, Firenze
Tuesday 27 April

Dear Mr Wilkinson[1]

Many thanks for your letter and invitation.

My wife and I will be pleased to come to lunch with you and Mrs Wilkinson on Sunday, if the world is at all possible by then, and we'll catch the 10.30 tram. But I hope we shan't give you too much trouble.

It will be fun to see the flat – if only it's not too small.

Then a riverderci

Yours Sincerely D. H. Lawrence

[1] Arthur Gair Wilkinson (1882–1957), his wife Lilian ('Diddy') and children Frances ('Bim') and William ('Pino') lived at the Villa Poggi, San Paolo Mosciano, outside Florence, close to the Villa Mirenda where the Lawrences were to live. The adults had been introduced to one another on 26 April. They were neighbours May 1926–March 1928. Wilkinson was a landscape painter; he made puppets for his own puppet-theatre (cf. Letter 3705); and, with his family, pursued health and culture with great dedication. (See Sagar, Wilkinsons 62–75.)

3698. To Hon. Dorothy Brett, [28 April 1926]

Text: MS UCin; Postmark, Firenze 29 . IV 1926; Huxley 657.

Pensione Lucchesi. Lungarno Zecca, Firenze
Wednesday

Dear Brett

Your letter about the wave of the sea tonight. Don't you be saying bad things about the sea, you've got to sail on it just now.

The girls left at lunch time, for Milan, and tomorrow direct to Paris. Germany was put off at the last moment, by everybody. Frieda didn't want to go. The girls hated leaving Italy. We miss them – but they did make a *tightness* – that peculiar tightness that goes with more or less ordinary people – as if the landscape were shut in, and the air didn't move.

Perhaps now we shall take a little flat in the country here – outside Florence – for a couple of months, and I wander about to my Etruscans. I wouldn't care to live in Assisi – I was there – it is too museumish, not enough life of now in it. I really preferred Perugia. But I suppose I shall only go round and find my Etruscans for a bit.

I wrote to Rachel that if ever she and William felt sort of homeless, they could go and live on our ranch permanently, if they wanted. But of course it wouldn't be ambitious enough for Rachel. – I have not written to Scott Murray at all – feel a bit guilty about it, though.

Don't trouble at all about taking those $200.00 if you want them – and no hurry to pay them back. – I hope the Heckshers will be nice to you humanly. – I told you, Mabel says she is coming to Paris for a fortnight, in May, to see Gourdjieff, and be 'saved.' Benedetta lei![1]

This is the first sunny day. Even yesterday, when you said Capri was lovely, it poured! But today, when the girls left, it was at last warm and bright. Hard lines on them!

Did I tell you the 'Glad Ghosts' story is appearing in the *Dial*.[2]

I suppose this is the last letter that will catch you before you leave. Be wise and careful, and I feel you'll be really all right. And when you're on the other side, make wisdom and forethought your star. – I don't feel you'll have any troubles, serious ones.

Good luck, then, and *a rivederci*, and *tante cose*! – and let's hope for good days not far off, for us all.

DHL

The rose of St. Francis is a paper one – every decent rose has a thorn or two.

[1] 'Lucky her!' [2] Cf. Letter 3667 and n. 2.

3699. To Barbara Weekley, [post 28 April 1926]

Text: Nehls, iii. 54.

[Pensione Lucchesi, Lungarno Zecca, Florence]
[post 28 April 1926]

[Elsa] is wise, and will make the best of life. You are too inclined to throw everything away because of one irritating factor. There's been too much of that in all lives. You throw your soup at the waiter because it's too hot, or set fire to your bed, because there's a flea in it. Well, then you can lie on the ground.

3700. To Martin Secker, [29 April 1926]

Text: MS UInd; Postmark, Firenze 29 . IV 1926; Secker 72–3.

Pensione Lucchesi. Lungarno Zecca. Firenze
28 Aprile 1926[1]

Dear Secker

We came here ten days ago, and the girls only left yesterday, for London. It poured with rain all the time they were here – till the day they left, then it was gloriously sunny – as it is also today. Nevertheless they hated leaving. – Ask Rina to send them a line sometime: 49 Harvard Rd. Chiswick, W.

Florence is very full and noisy, but I still like Tuscany. Today we went out into the country – ½ hr. by tram, ½ hr. walk – to look at a villa. It's an old square sort of farm villa – the family only comes out from Florence very rarely – and we can have top floor and garden for Lit. 4,000 a year. There's one neighbouring villa with an English family, Wilkinsons – Arthur – artist – red beard, Rucksack, violin-case – you can see him – but seems nice. I think we shall take that apartment, and keep it as a pied à terre. The villa crowns a hill, as usual in old Tuscany, and looks far out over the Val d'Arno. It's just by the Church of San Paolo Mosciano, beyond Scandicci – but I forget, you don't know Florence. Tuscany is really much lovelier than the Genovese – but of course, doesn't get the winter sun as Spotorno does.

If ever you are riding that way, Rina, call on Richard Aldington and Dorothy Yorke (they have been living together for eight years, but Hilda Aldington won't divorce them) – at

Malthouse Cottage, *Padworth*. – near Reading.

It's not so very far from you, and I think you might like Arabella (Miss Yorke's nickname). But send them a line.

[1] The letter was written on the day following the departure of Frieda's daughters (cf. Letter 3698) and on the day of the Lawrences' first visit to Villa Mirenda (cf. following letter): i.e. on 29 April 1926.

The country here is very lovely now, with green wheat and flowers. I like it so much better than town. We lunched with Reggie Turner, who is getting on more or less – in bits – with his book. Doubt if he'll finish it.[1] Douglas is in Greece. Apparently he's deep deep in a book on 'The Flowers of the Greek Anthology':[2] actual flora. – I'm reading Italian books on the Etruscans – very interesting indeed. I'll join Vieusseux's library here – they will have more things.[3]

I heard from Jan Juta on the Riviera, wanting to come over 'in a friend's car' and see us. But we'd left. Oh, that 'friend's car.' – He said he'd a plan. But I should only want photographs reproduced in my Etruscan book, if I did it –

There are three poems from *Birds Beasts and Flowers* in *La Nouvelle Revue* this month – in French.[4] Not bad! Will you send a copy of *The Plumed Serpent* to the translator:

Mlle. Gabrielle Desgrand. Les Ronzières. *Vourles*. Rhône. France.

She's done the whole of the poems, and will try and get a book accepted.

What are you doing about the play?

How's Adrian? Hope you're all feeling well.

D. H. Lawrence

3701. To Arthur Wilkinson, [29 April 1926]

Text: MS Schlaefle; cited in Sagar, Wilkinsons 64.

Pensione Lucchesi. Lungarno Zecca. Firenze
Thursday evening

Dear Mr Wilkinson

We wanted to go into the country today, so found our way out to San Paolo Mosciano (they do say Polo!) – and we even went inside the Villa Miranda (the old woman calls *that* Merenda) – but not into the rooms, because the doors were locked. They said the padroni would be there on Sunday, and we said *we* would be lunching with you.

We both like the spot *immensely*: and the old house. I think surely we must take that apartment, and just keep it as a pied à terre. If we decide on it on Sunday – and I think we shall – I hope we can move in quickly. I do hate this sort of hotel-pension life.

[1] No publication of a book by Turner is recorded between 1926 and his death in 1938.

[2] Douglas's *Birds and Beasts of the Greek Anthology* was privately printed in Florence in 1927 (published London, 1928).

[3] Gabinetto G. P. Vieusseux is a well-known Florentine circulating library (housed in the Palazzo Strozzi), founded in 1819 and since 1921 run by the Commune of Florence. It was much used by British and other expatriates.

[4] *La Nouvelle Revue* does not contain the poems as DHL claims, nor can any trace be discovered of Mlle Desgrand.

Your house looked charming in the sun – and your little brown dog (is he yours?) went with us. I sent him sternly home! – We didn't like to call and intrude – But this is to say that we shall be very pleased to come on Sunday, and shall take the 10.30 tram; but as we now know the way to your house, please don't trouble to meet us.

tanti saluti D. H. Lawrence

3702. To Reginald Turner, [30 April 1926]
Text: MS UCLA; Postmark, Ferrovia 30. 4.26; Unpublished.

Pensione Lucchesi.
Friday.

Dear Reggie

What happened? You remember we agreed to meet last night – Thursday – at 7.30 at Gambrinus.[1] I was there from 7.30 till 8.0, but didn't find you. Did we miss one another, or did you forget? Anyhow I was there, waiting for you to go to dinner with me.

We shall probably take an apartment out beyond Vingone, in an old villa – lovely situation. I shall let you know, and you must come and see us.

Regards from us both, and regrets for the lost evening.

Sincerely D. H. Lawrence

3703. To Reginald Turner, [1 May 1926]
Text: MS UCLA; Moore 908.

Pensione Lucchesi.
Saturday[2]

Dear Reggie

Well what a shame! If I'd *only* sent you an espresso yesterday afternoon, as I so nearly did, you could have rung me up. I wish you'd telefoned anyhow, we were here.

I certainly *heard* Thursday, because I went straight down your stairs and told my wife and the girls, Thursday evening with Reggie. But I have to confess, it once happened to me in Mexico City, with the one man I really liked in that damnable town: only he said Thursday, and I heard Friday (I still believe he said Friday) – and I went and fixed Friday with some government people. But last night we were here, in this dulness! *Why* didn't you ring me up.

[1] The Gambrinus Halle 'Birreria and Caffeteria' is a large and popular bar, with a cinema attached, in the Via Brunelleschi.

[2] Saturday] Friday

But anyhow I'm awfully sorry, and a thousand apologies. Keep an evening early in the week, if you can, and let me know. Because we may move out to S. Paolo Mosciano – we're going tomorrow to decide.

I met Maugham in Mexico City too, and was annoyed with him. And for sure he didn't love me like a brother.[1] So don't expect us to be two roses on one stem. – But perhaps he's nice, I don't pretend I know him. And if he'd like to see me, I should like to see him. Honi soit etc.[2]

Many greetings from my wife and me. D. H. Lawrence

I feel depressed about the coal strike, innerly. But perhaps they'll smooth it out.[3]

3704. To William Siebenhaar, 1 May 1926

Text: TMSC NWU; Unpublished.

Pensione Lucchesi, Lungarno Zecca, Firenze,
1 May 1926.

Dear Siebenhaar,

I heard unexpectedly from Knopf today, asking if I'd do the introduction I promised, so long ago, to *Max Havelaar*. I hadn't thought more about it, because the Blue Jade Library doesn't have introductions. Now Knopf wants to keep me to my word.[4]

Have you got a copy of your Essay on Multatuli? – and an MS. copy of the book? I should like to read both once more, before I attempt an introd. And my copy of the Essay is in America, too.

This isn't a bad pensione L45 a day, if you fix terms beforehand. We shall possibly move out to a villa about 8 miles out, next week – tomorrow we are deciding. So send me a note here, please, and I'll reply by return, to let you know if we're moving, and the address, so you can send me the MSS., in case you have copies by you.

We've had some pretty rainy weather here – very unpleasant. It has been sunny these last three or four days, but feels like thunder again. The country, though, is lovely with flowers and green corn.

There are pensiones at L35 a day, not bad I believe, if one looks for them.

Regards to Mrs. Siebenhaar and to yourself.

Yours sincerely D. H. Lawrence

[1] Cf. Burns, 'Tam o'Shanter', l. 44.

[2] 'Honi soit qui mal y pense' ['Evil be to him who thinks evil'].

[3] Before midnight on 30 April the coal strike had officially begun, negotiations between unions and mine-owners having broken down. A General Strike was called by the Trades Union Congress from 4 May.

[4] Cf. Letters 3513 and n. 2, and 3619.

3705. To Margaret King, 3 May 1926

Text: MS Needham; cited in Vivian de Sola Pinto, ed., *D.H. Lawrence after Thirty Years, Catalogue of an Exhibition held in the Art Gallery of the University of Nottingham, 17 June–30 July, 1960* (Nottingham, 1960), p. 43.

Florence.
3 May 1926

My dear Peg

So there's the coal strike, and the rest all threatened. I do hope to heaven it *won't* develop into anything big, but I feel a bit sickish about it. Pray the Lord it may blow smooth again.

Barby and Elsa left last Wednesday, direct for London. Your Aunt Frieda didn't want to go to her family in BadenBaden just yet, so the girls didn't go either. – I more or less promised to do a sort of travel book about the old Etruscans and their remains here in Tuscany and Umbria. – So now we have taken a villa about 7 miles out of Florence here, in the country, and I can use that as a centre, when I have to go travelling round to Bologna and Cortona and Volterra and down to the Maremma to Tarquinia – quite a number of places in Tuscany and Umbria, where the best remains are. At present I am supposed to be reading up about my precious Etruschi!

As a matter of fact we are having to buy in things for that villa, which has got about five sticks of furniture in its big old brick-floored rooms. But there are two gardens, and lovely slopes of vines and olives, and three families of peasants to work the place – It is quite lovely in its way. – We have one family of English neighbours, who would send you into fits if you saw them: he's got the wildest red beard, sticking out all round – and wife and daughter and son, all with sandals and knapsacks. But they're jolly and very clever: paint, and play guitar and things. They used to have a very fine puppet show, puppets they made themselves, and play plays they wrote themselves, going with a caravan and giving shows in all the villages in England.[1] Rather fun! I want them to bring the caravan and puppets here, and I'll go with them and bang the drum, in the Italian villages.

We move up on Thursday. The address is:

Villa Mirenda, San Polo Mosciano, Scandicci – Florence.

We may keep this place as a pied à terre – we've got it for a year, anyhow. Then one day you can all come out and stay, and that will be fun.

[1] The family's skill in puppetry may be inferred from *The Peep Show* (1927) by Arthur Wilkinson's brother, Walter. The book, describing the author's experiences with his travelling puppet show in Somerset and Devon, is dedicated: 'To Lily and Arturo, Bim and Pino and all the other Gair Wilkinson Marionettes'.

I'm glad you like your shorthand. Hurry up and get a good job and save a bit of money, and then come out and see us for a time.

Hope Joan still likes school. – Oh heaven, if only there wouldn't be strikes, and all the worlds mischief!

Love to all. DHL

3706. To Ada Clarke, 3 May 1926

Text: MS Clarke; cited in Lawrence–Gelder 135–6.

Florence –
Monday 3 May 1926

My dear Sister

I had your letter today – and the coal-strike is on, and a general strike threatened, and altogether it feels like the end of the world. But let's hope something new and good will happen, so things can get clear again.

The weather here is pretty bad. It rained solidly for eight days, while the girls were here in Florence (they left, direct for London, last Wednesday) – Then it was hot and oppressive a few days, now it's steamy rain again. And it should be bright and dry in May.

Frieda didn't want to go to Germany with her children – was a bit afraid of her family, I think. So she stayed here, and yesterday we went and took a villa – the more habitable part of it – for a year. It's about ten miles out, about 1½ miles from the Vingone tram terminus, and two miles from any shops or post. But it's lovely country – and a big old heavy villa, square, perched on a hill and looking far out over the Valley of the Arno: it dates from Medici days. The family keep some downstairs rooms, and come out from Florence for a night, occasionally, and stay a month or so at wine harvest. They're quiet and nice – an old, now ineffectual family. There's very little furniture, and we have to buy linen and kitchen things. But the rent is only £25. a year, and we thought we might keep the place as a pied à terre. We can always come back to it. And sometimes, when F. is away, you can come and stay with me. Or if we were away, you could come with Eddie, one day, and stay a month or two.

If Stanley Clarke comes this way, tell him to come and see us.[1]

We are moving up on Thursday. The address is:

Villa Mirenda, San Polo Mosciano, Scandicci, *Florence.*

For myself, Secker has been urging me to write a travel book: and I don't want to do an ordinary travel book, just of places. So I thought I might stay here two months or so, and prepare[2] a book on the Etruscan cities – the dead

[1] Stanley (d. 1966?) was Edwin Clarke's brother, a teacher who emigrated to South Africa in the 1920s and taught at Rondebosch, near Cape Town.

[2] prepare] do

Etruscans. It would mean my travelling about a good deal, to Bologna, and Cortona and Perugia and Volterra and Chiusi, and down on the Maremma to Tarquinia. Frieda would stay in the villa – there is one family of neighbours, the Gair-Wilkinsons, a bit extraordinary, but nice – and I should go alone. I think I should enjoy it. That would be in June – at present I'm reading the Italian books on the Etruscans, getting the idea into shape. – That little story about the boy who betted on the horse-races, was sold in America for £50: and in England from Cynthia I only got £15. – I'll send it you when the book of Ghost Stories comes out.[1]

I do hope the strike will pass quickly, and the miners will feel all right about it. I feel rather bad, myself, about it.

Love. DHL

3707. To William Siebenhaar, 4 May 1926
Text: TMSC NWU; PC; Unpublished.

Florence,
4 May 1926.

Many thanks for your letter of this morning. We move out on Thursday to

Villa Mirenda, San Polo Mosciano, Scandicci – Firenze.

So better write me there. I'm glad I may see the MSS. Knopf is a very prompt payer.

Best wishes D. H. Lawrence

3708. To Miss Wells, 5 May 1926
Text: MS UT; Unpublished.

Florence.
5 May 1926

Dear Miss Wells[2]

Will you be so good as to make a record of my new address:

Villa Mirenda, San Polo Mosciano, *Scandicci – Florence.*

I've taken that villa – or the best part of it – for a year, so I can have a pied à terre. We're moving out – about eight miles out – tomorrow.

Will you please let Miss Pearn and the dramatic dept. have this address too. – And I wish you'd ask the girl who forwards the letters please to put the extra stamps on, for foreign mail, when necessary – expecially when forwarding

[1] See Letter 3633 and n. 1.
[2] DHL's correspondent was on the staff of Curtis Brown's London office; he may have confused this person and the recipient of Letters 3558 and 3574.

from America. The post people here make such a fuss. – Charge the stamps to me.

I'm sorry to give so much trouble.

Yours Sincerely. D. H. Lawrence

3709. To John Cournos, [8 May 1926]

Text: MS StaU; cited in Moore, *Poste Restante* 87.

Villa Mirenda. *Scandicci*, Florence. Italy
8 May

Dear Cournos

I didn't answer your letter, wondering when we should move. I told you, didn't I, we'd taken half this villa for a year. – Now we've decided to stay on here till 16th July, when go straight to BadenBaden for a fortnight, then to England for the month of August. So if you are in England, send me a line c/o Curtis Brown. 6 Henrietta St. W.C.2. and we can meet and have a talk. – Is Mrs Cournos with you in Paris, by the way, or has she gone off to America?

I heard from Mrs Knopf that they were sailing for Paris, so no doubt you will see them. Remember me to them.

Whom do you see in Paris? – Ford Hueffer? – and Joyce?[1] – all the crowd, or not many people? Here we are very quiet, thank god, though it's only an hour in to Florence.

If we meet in London, I should like to see Flint again, and Fletcher whom I've not met.[2]

Till then au revoir D. H. Lawrence

3710. To Reginald Turner, [12 May 1926]

Text: MS UCLA; Postmark, Scandicci 13. 5.26; Unpublished.

Villa Mirenda. San Polo Mosciano, Scandicci
Wednesday

Dear Reggie

Would you care to come to lunch on Sunday, with Orioli,[3] about 12.30. The country is very lovely now.

[1] Ford Madox Hueffer (Ford) (1873–1939), novelist and editor, whom DHL had known since 1909 and who introduced him to the London literary scene (see *Letters*, i. 138 n. 1). DHL had not met James Joyce (1882–1941) and confessed himself 'one of the people who can't read *Ulysses*' (ibid., iv. 340); but he knew Joyce's publisher Sylvia Beach (ibid., iv. 569) and therefore had some contact with the Parisian literary 'crowd'.

[2] It is not known when DHL met the poet, Frank Stewart Flint (1885–1960); their work had appeared together in *New Paths* (1918) (see *Letters*, iii. 261 n. 5). As for the poet John Gould Fletcher (1886–1950), DHL had indeed met him: they were introduced to one another by Cournos in 1917 (*Letters*, iii. 190 and n. 2).

[3] Giuseppe ('Pino') Orioli (1884–1942), Italian antiquarian bookseller and publisher; he and DHL met in Cornwall, 1916–17 (see *Letters*, iii. 591 n. 2). Orioli arranged for the printing and

You take the tram to the Vingone terminus, and walk *straight ahead* on the high-road, past the pagoda house, up the hill to the two cypresses. There turn to the left and come straight again. You see the house in front on the bluff, square and a bit stark, the old church behind. It's not far: about half an hour.

[map][1]

I haven't written to Orioli yet – so would you ask him, and let me know.

I do believe it's summer at last.

Don't expect us to be sumptuous it's very rough.

tante cose D. H. Lawrence

3711. To Nancy Pearn, 13 May 1926

Text: MS UT; Huxley 658.

Villa Mirenda. San Polo Mosciano, *Scandicci, Florence*, Italy
13 May 1926

Dear Miss Pearn

I send you a story, 'Two Blue Birds' – probably to be another tribulation to you.[2]

I also enclose Murry's letter to me, as he wants to vindicate himself in your sight.[3]

distribution of *Lady Chatterley's Lover* (1928) and published a number of DHL's other works. Orioli was a close friend of Turner who made him principal legatee to a considerable fortune. See Richard Aldington, *Pinorman* (1954).

1 DHL's sketch-map includes the tram terminus, the pagoda and the '2 cypresses' as well as 'V. Mirenda'.

2 'Two Blue Birds' was published in the *Dial*, lxxxii (April 1927), 287–301; it was collected in *Great Stories of All Nations*, ed. Max Lieber and Blanche Colton Williams (New York, September 1927) (Roberts C154); and included in *The Woman Who Rode Away*.

3 Murry wrote as follows (MS UT):

The Old Coastguard Station, Abbotsbury, Weymouth, Dorset
May 2 1926.

Dear Lorenzo,

You *are* an uncharitable bird. You might have answered my last effusion – at least have said to yourself that your friends like to know how you are.

I don't know whether you understand the position with regard to your 'Mornings in Mexico'. They were offered to me, purely as a business proposition over a year ago. I accepted three of them at a definite price, and my offer was accepted. Then I was asked to postpone publication until they had appeared in U.S.A. I agreed. Before I had published them came your note saying you didn't want to appear any more in *The Adelphi*. Unfortunately, one of them was already set up in type.

I don't want to hold you to this purely business arrangement if you don't want to be held. But you must tell Curtis Brown, who hold my written agreement to pay so much for the essays, that you want the essays back. Otherwise, my *bona fids* in regard to Curtis Brown is suspect. That's all. And certainly you misunderstood the situation when you said to C.B. that I wanted the essays for nothing. Their fate & price was decided by a definite arrangement with C.B. in which you had no part. I simply said to you that any future contributions would either be unpaid, or poorly paid. You replied you didn't want to contribute. Which was quite clear.

I had your note about the new *Masses* and 'Smile.'[1] Funny sort of home things find for themselves!

I feel bad about that strike. Italian papers say: 'The government will maintain an iron resistance.' Since the war, I've no belief in iron resistances. Flesh and blood and a bit of wisdom can do quite enough resisting, and a bit of adjusting into the bargain – and with iron one only hurts oneself and everybody. Damn iron!

Yrs D. H. Lawrence

not true.[2] He told me he wouldn't pay the price you'd asked for 'Mornings in Mexico', possibly. I don't care a bit, if he didn't always put my back up. – Will you, Miss Pearn, settle the matter just as you think well.

DHL

3712. To William Siebenhaar, 13 May 1926

Text: TMSC NWU; Huxley 658–9.

Villa Mirenda, San Polo Mosciano, Scandicci – Firenze.
13 May 1926.

Dear Siebenhaar,

I received the MS. of *Max Havelaar* a few days ago, and read it at once, and did a brief introduction, without waiting for your essay. The strike seems pretty bad, heaven knows when we shall get anything, beyond letters, out of England. So I shall send the MS. and introduction on to Knopf at once, as he seemed rather urgent.

I think your translation is excellent, so much in the spirit of the thing. And I came across no mistakes, except two slight slips which I altered. The only thing that pulled me up was the word 'disgruntled'. You use it two or three

Anyway, the whole thing isn't very important. And I'd rather not have any misunderstanding.

We came back to Dorsetshire on Saturday – two days ago. The second baby is due in a fortnight. With that one I shall have given sufficient hostages to future.

As you didn't answer my last, I don't know whether you think of coming to see us down here. It would be very nice if you would. But perhaps you'd rather not.

Finally, let me say I think it's silly for us to be out of temper with one another. Our ideas don't agree – well & good. But surely we are old enough & wise enough to ignore that. I've no designs upon you. I don't want to induce you to collaborate in *The Adelphi*. But I can't for the life of me see why we shouldn't be friendly disposed towards each other. I am only too ready to admit that I have much to gain from contact with you: but I also believe you might get something from contact with me.

My love to Frieda. Jack.

[1] The story (cf. p. 351 n. 3) had been accepted for publication in the very recently renamed *New Masses* (New York); it appeared there in June 1926. (*New Masses* was formerly called *Masses* and before that, *Liberator*.)

[2] DHL linked this commentary by a line to the remark in Murry's letter: 'any future contributions would either be unpaid . . .'

times. Is it *old* enough to have been used in 1850?[1] It feels modern to me, but it may actually not be so. It is merely a question of avoiding an obvious anachronism.

We are here in the country, very quiet, and the spring is very lovely. I only hope the sunny weather will continue.

Best wishes from both,

Yours Sincerely D. H. Lawrence

3713. To Hon. Dorothy Brett, 15 May 1926

Text: MS UCin; Postmark, Firenze 15 . V 1926; Huxley 659–60.

Villa Mirenda, S. Polo Mosciano, *Scandicci, Florence*, Italy
Sat 15 May 1926

Dear Brett

You will be drawing near to America now – I hope the sea has been decent and the landing will be all right: shall be waiting to hear.

We've taken the top half of this old villa out in the country about seven miles from Florence – crowning a little hilltop in the Tuscan style. Since the rent is only 3,000 Liras for a year – which is twenty-five pounds – I took the place for a year. Even if we go away, we can always keep it as a pied à terre and let friends live in it. It is nice – looking far out over the Arno valley – and very nice country, real country, pine woods, around. I am reading up my Etruscans, and if I get along with them, shall go round to Perugia and Volterra, Chiusi, Orvieto, Tarquinia. Meanwhile we can sit still and spend little. There's only one family of foreigners near – Wilkinsons – sort of village arty people who went round with a puppet show – quite nice, and not at all intrusive. Then the tram is only 1½ miles, at Vingone, and takes us in to Florence in ½ hour. This is a region of *no* foreigners.

The only thing to do is to sit still and let events work out. I count this as a sort of interval.

I shall wait to hear how you find the ranch, and how it treats you. I do hope there'll be somebody nice to go and live there too and help: you can*not* be there alone. I often dream of the Azul and Aaron, and Timsey. They seem to call one back, perhaps more strongly even than the place. – I don't know what it is in me, that I simply can't think of coming back to America just now: something in the whole continent that repulses me.

Murry wrote me, he expects his second baby in a fortnight – it may be here by now. But he is just the same – sort of underhand. I can't like him.

[1] The word was used in England in the seventeenth century. Nevertheless Siebenhaar appears to have taken DHL's advice and removed it from his translation.

Earl found your papers – I have them here – I won't send them to the ranch till I know you are there.

We've had horrid weather – then five days sun – now again grey and trying to rain – I never knew a spring so impotent, as if it couldn't emerge.

Knopf is printing *David* in America, so there should be time for your cover. If you'd like to see them, write to her, Mrs Blanche Knopf, 730 Fifth Avenue.

Things feel a bit dismal, with the strike in England and so on. There's nothing to do but to wait a bit, and see if one's spirits will really rouse up and give one a direction.

I still mistrust Earl – in his letter to me – about India.

Remember me to everybody – It seems so far – I don't know why.

DHL

3714. To Nelly Morrison, [16 May 1926]

Text: TMSC NWU; Unpublished.

Villa Mirenda, San Polo Mosciano, Scandicci, Firenze.
Sunday.

Dear Nelly Morrison,[1]

We've taken the top half of this little villa, and shall be glad to see you and Gino whenever you care to come out. Sometimes we go for long walks, so perhaps best send us a line. The country is very lovely.

You come to the *Vingone* tram terminus, walk straight ahead on the highroad, keeping the pagoda house on your right, on past the house written Podere Nuovo, to the two cypresses at the road joining: then turn to the left and come straight forward down the little hollow. Our house is the big square white one with a turret on the bluff above you: and behind it is the old church of San Polo Mosciano. A very easy road, about 25 minutes, and very pretty, so come soon.

I hope you enjoyed Venice.

Best wishes from us both and a rivederci D. H. Lawrence

3715. To S. S. Koteliansky, [17 May 1926]

Text: MS BL; Postmark, Firenze 17 . V 1926; cited in Gransden 30.

Villa Mirenda. San Polo Mosciano, Scandicci, Florence
17 May

My dear Kot

We've made another little move – taken the top half of this old villa about

[1] Nelly Morrison, born in India, the daughter of a Presbyterian doctor, lived in a flat (which the Lawrences had occupied late August–September 1921) at 32 Via dei Bardi in Florence. See *Letters*, iii. 720 and n. 1; iv. 81. (Gino's identity is not known.)

seven miles out of Florence, for a year. It's very cheap, only £25. the year, so we can leave it or lend it when we like. – Brett has gone back to America, to look after the ranch. I feel I don't want to go.

The weather is atrocious – a few fine days, then thunder and rain. Never was such a wet May. How is it in England?

We're right in the country, very pretty, and 1½ miles from the tram terminus. The tram takes us into Piazza in half an hour: very convenient.

I'm supposed to be preparing material for a book on the old Etruscans, but don't know if I shall do it. – The postcard is one of their things – called the Chimaera – Vth Century B. C.[1]

I hear from Murry – I suppose his second baby is born by now. He writes with the same impertinence, but I feel he is a defeated man.

The strike is over, apparently – I'm very glad. Myself, I'm scared of a class war in England. It would be the beginning of the end of all things. What do you think of it? – And why did the Lira fall so suddenly?

We may come to England in the later summer, then I shall see you. For the moment I am not deciding anything. – I only wish the weather would be dry, this wet is bad for one's bronchials.

Remember me to Sonia, and Grisha, and Ghita: also they will be glad the strike is over. What is Grisha doing? – My desire to go to Russia has disappeared again. I feel the Bolshevists are loutish and common. – I don't believe in them, except as disruptive and nihilistic agents. Boring!

What are you yourself doing?

tante cose! DHL

3716. To Earl Brewster, 17 May 1926

Text: MS UT; Brewster 97–9.

Villa Mirenda. San Polo Mosciano, Scandicci – Florence. Italy
17 May 1926

Dear Earl

Yesterday came your letter from Belur, or wherever it is,[2] enclosing the papers for Brett. She is due to land in New York tomorrow – povera lei! – and due to be at *Del Monte Ranch, Questa. New Mexico* in ten days time. I do hope she goes through without difficulty. I'm not sending her papers till I hear from her.

We have made a little move – taken the top half of this heavy old Tuscan villa for a year: it only costs 3,000 Liras per annum. It's very rough and no

[1] The postcard, presumably enclosed, is missing.

[2] Belur, in Mysore, is about 75 miles w. of Bangalore.

comforts, but nice: stands on a bluff looking over the Val d'Arno. It's about seven miles out of Florence – and we're 1½ miles from the Vingone tram-terminus: absolutely unspoiled country, one family of English neighbours, and then never another forestiere, ever. It's very pretty country – Tuscan – farms on little green hills, and pine woods fringing the ridges.

Only the weather is impossible: a few days sun, then more pouring rain, and more. I get very tired of it. Everywhere is much too green. If only the sun would drily shine!

I'm glad you find India interesting, more so than you thought. I gather from your tone, that it is more interesting than *sympatico* to you: but perhaps that's because you are too new to it. – It's nice to know the Swamis, and talk to them: but I don't see the point of bathing in the Ganges and reciting holy books merely. One needs a bho tree, but one doesn't want to be tied to it by the leg, like a chicken on a string. Somewhere *between* the east and the west, in that prophetically never-to-exist meeting point of the two, is really where one wants to be. – I think in the autumn, if you are still there and it's not too costly, I should like to come out, alone. I should like to try the contact, too. 'The way is not mine, or thine, but it lies between us.'[1]

I hope you'll have a good exhibition of your pictures, and sell some and get some money. If one doesn't want exactly to make friends unto oneself of the Mammon of Unrighteousness,[2] neither does one want to throw oneself on its mercy. There are gods of evil, even Mammon, to be placated. One can't have it all one's own way. – I'm going to try throwing a few sops to Cerberus myself – things like *The Plumed Serpent* have no profit in them, as far as Mammon goes.

I'm reading about the Etruscans, and looking at their remains. They interest me. I suppose they are the dead opposite of Buddha: but not of Brama or Siva.

I hope Achsah is really having a social good time, and Harwood is being a little angel to everybody.

a rivederci. D. H. Lawrence

3717. To Mabel Dodge Luhan, 17 May 1926

Text: MS Brill; Luhan 301–2.

Villa Mirenda. San Polo Mosciano, Scandicci – Florence.
17 May 1926

Dear Mabel

We've taken this old and bare sort of farm-villa: or at least, the top half of it,

[1] Unidentified (the sentiment appears Taoist).
[2] Luke xvi.9 ['Make to yourselves friends of the mammon . . .'].

for a year. But it costs very little, so we can just keep it as a pied à terre. It's very nice country, about seven miles out of Florence.

About your MSS. – I don't see much point in having them done into German – nobody would take half as much notice of them, if they came first in German. If you very carefully disguised all names, and your own identity, and got Orage and Little – Littell, whatever he is[1] – to swear secrecy – and were really careful – you might get them out in America. Or you might do as James Joyce did with *Ulysses*, get them published in a fat paper volume at the Shakspeare Library in Paris. You would have to see Miss Beach about it. But that strikes me as the best way. I think Frank Harris is doing something of the same with *My Life*.[2] Or you might come to Paris with Spud and *publish it yourself*, next winter. It's not at all impossible. I should think that *Miss Beach. Librairie Shakspeare. rue de l'Odeon. Paris* (I give the address from memory) – would tell you all about it.[3] She did the whole business of *Ulysses* herself, and you know what a great fat book that is. And she is very nice. – You could publish, if you like, the first vol. first, so that there would be nothing to startle the prudes: and when they were quite used to seeing *Intimate Memories* going through the mail, then send out the second and third volumes: ship them in bulk. You ought easily to get your money back. (But you must very carefully alter *all* names and disguise the locality.)

It may be, also, that you need a break in the continual writing. Nobody on earth can pour out three, four, five volumes without ever turning off the tap. Probably the Florence part would come better if you rested a bit – or if you were in Paris again. Europe is very unreal, in America. And in Europe,[4] America becomes like a sort of tormented dream to one.

Brett is due to land in New York tomorrow. I do hope she has no difficulties, and that she'll be able to look after the ranch this year. It is rather a burden on my mind.

As for Gourdjieff and Orage and the awakening of various centres and the ultimate *I* and all that – to tell you the truth, plainly, I don't know. History may repeat itself, but the repetition comes with such a difference, that you never can tell, till afterwards. There is no way mapped out, and never will be.

[1] Alfred Richard Orage (1873–1936) and perhaps Robert Littel (1896–1963). Orage, journalist and editor, co-edited the Fabian *New Age*, 1907–22; then promoted the teachings of Gurdjieff and lived in USA for this purpose, 1923–30. Author of *Frederick Nietzsche* (Edinburgh, 1906); *Readers and Writers, 1917–21* (1922); etc. Littel was assistant editor of the moderately radical *New Republic*, 1922–7, and may have had journalistic contact with Orage.

[2] James Thomas Frank Harris (1856–1931), journalist and miscellaneous writer, best known for his sensational autobiography, *My Life and Loves*. Vols 1–4 were privately printed in Paris, 1922–7.

[3] Sylvia Woodhouse Beach (1887–1962), American publisher and manager of Shakespeare and Company. See *Letters*, iv. 569 n.

[4] Europe,] America,

Only we know that the process is long, and painful, and dangerous, and you're more likely to die or to disintegrate than to come through, if you do *too* much about it.

I'm sorry Spuds *Horse* wants to be born with five legs and its tail at the end of its nose. Quel monstre!

I'll go and look at the outside of the Curonia, if I can find out where it is.[1] Somewhere up the Viale dei Colli, isnt it – behind Piazza Michelangelo?

I met a man called Loeser – is that how you write him?[2] – he spoke of you and 'Edwin' – why do Americans always talk about their friends by their christian names, to strangers and in piazza? I didn't care for him. – There's an unholy bunch of rich Americans here. – But I am weary of people who talk like that.

It rains a great deal, the country is much too green, and the proper spring and summer seem as if they'll never come. Which is very disappointing.

tante cose di noi due! DHL

3718. To William Siebenhaar, [17 May 1926]
Text: TMSC NWU; Unpublished.

S. Polo, Mosciano, Scandicci – Firenze.
Monday.

Dear Siebenhaar,

I wrote you that I had finished the introd. and sent it off with the MS. – as Knopf was urging to advertise the book.

I will try and get your essay from America. It went to Seltzer with the MS. of *Max* – and should be in the hands of my agent. But Seltzer isn't very reliable. I had quite a job to recover the MS. of *Max* from him, for Knopf. But I'll write to Barmby, Curtis Brown's New York manager, to ask him to send you the essay at once.

It is atrocious weather – continual cold rain. What is it like on the Riviera? Too disappointing here, really.

Tanti saluti, D. H. Lawrence

3719. To Catherine Carswell, 18 May 1926
Text: MS YU; cited in Carswell 241, 249.

Villa Mirenda. San Polo Mosciano. Scandicci. Florence.
18 May 1926

My dear Catherine

I nearly wrote you yesterday – now your letter just come. About the story, I

[1] See Letter 3647 and p. 407 n. 1. [2] Unidentified.

don't really know the magazines myself, because Curtis Browns do all my work. I did know a Hearst man in London, but he's out of it again. I know the *New Criterion*[1] in London, and could send your story there. And if we dare, I'm sure Curtis Brown, both in London and New York, would try to place your story, if I asked them. I find them really very good, they take a lot of trouble, and charge 10%. But are you bound to Pinker? If you are, you can't even legally place your things yourself without paying him his percentage. If you're not, then let me introduce you to Curtis Browns people: his magazine girl, Nancy Pearn, I find quite golden. Tell me your position with regard to Pinker. If you owe him nothing, you can dissolve any agreement with him at will. – And send me a copy of the story, anyhow, and I might suggest a paper. I know *Vanity Fair* in America, as it happens – and *The Dial.*

It's the same weather here as with you – always raining, cold, and like winter: perfectly awful, down here in Tuscany. We've taken the top half of this old villa, seven miles out of Florence, for a year: only £25. a year. I thought we could keep it as a pied à terre, and perhaps come and go, and lend it when we are away. The country is awfully nice round about, and no other forestiere except one family, the Gair-Wilkinsons, Gloster village-arty who used to have a puppet-show: they are quite nice. He's the King of all 'beavers,' with *his* red beard.

If only the weather cleared up, you might come and see us: and if F[rieda] feels like having a visitor. We'll see later. Florence isn't a bad place to live outside of. We are 1½ miles from the tram terminus – and ½ hour in to Florence, to the Duomo. It's the opposite direction from Fiesole, out of the Porta Romana the Vingone tram. – This is a sort of farm villa, really, and the padroni, quite nice people, only come out – a man of 35 and wife, he capitano di Cavalleria, but working in the *office*, most uncavalry-like man you ever saw[2] – just for the week-end, or one odd day, to see to the peasants. – But of course the house, though rather big, is bare and comfortless. It wouldn't matter at all if the weather were good.

I do hope the boys cold will be better. – Italy is dearer, a good deal, than France. – Jeka Kemp is quite nice, but not exciting.[3]

tante cose! DHL

[1] See Letter 3793 and p. 514 n. 1.

[2] The owner of the house was Raul Mirenda, 'an Army officer . . . passionately devoted to history and literature' (Nehls, iii. 59–63, 663 n. 16).

[3] Unidentified.

3720. To Curtis Brown, 18 May 1926

Text: MS Forster; Moore 913–14.

Villa Mirenda. San Polo Mosciano, Scandicci. Florence. Italy.
18 May 1926

Dear Curtis Brown

I wish Secker would let Jonathan Cape re-print *Sea and Sardinia*.[1] Secker is, I am afraid, one of those slow little birds who will *never* make headway for anybody. I feel while I am with him I shall never never get any forrarder, as they say. But I can't quite leave him. And he wrote me yesterday he was doing *Sea and Sardinia* himself this autumn at 7/6. Why always so expensive? And never the slightest bit of push. Never half alive!

Yes, I'm quite glad for Cape to do *Twilight in Italy* if he wants, and can arrange it with Duckworth.[2]

I am reading up the old Etruscans, and may this summer manage a book, half-travel and half description of Etruscan things, about those people. It would have quite a lot of photographs. But I know if Secker has to handle it, it will sell 3,000 and then stop. I doubt even if I trust him.

We've taken the top half of this old villa, seven miles out of Florence, for a year. But it only costs £25. a year, so we can just keep it as a pied à terre. When you come to Italy you must come here and see us.

The weather here is atrocious – thunder, rain, and rather cold. The country outside very nice indeed, no foreigners at all, very Tuscan – but green, green, over-green, to set your teeth on edge.

Nice that Knopf sets up the *David* play over there.

tanti saluti D. H. Lawrence

3721. To Arthur Wilkinson, [18? May 1926]

Text: MS Schlaefle; Sagar, Wilkinsons 64.

[Villa Mirenda, Scandicci, Florence]
Tuesday

Dear Wilkinson

Will you all come in this evening after supper, as there is a cake and the promised Kümmel, and, let us hope, a tune or two going.

Yrs D. H. Lawrence

[1] Secker had written to Curtis Brown on 8 May 1926 rejecting the enquiry from Cape; he wrote more abruptly to the same effect on 18 May (Secker Letter-Book, UIll). He told Brown of his intention to re-issue *Sea and Sardinia* without illustrations 'before very long'; the book was included in his 'New Adelphi Library' in April 1927.

[2] Cape issued *Twilight in Italy* in his 'Travellers' Library' in October 1926 at 3/6.

3722. To Carl Seelig, 21 May 1926
Text: MS SIU; Moore 915–16.

Villa Mirenda. San Polo Mosciano, *Scandicci*. Firenze. Italia
21 May 1926

Dear Carl Seelig

We neither of us went to Germany. Instead we have taken this villa about seven miles out of Florence – or at least, the top half of the villa – and are staying on probably until August. I suppose you still have no idea of coming to Italy.

My desire to go to Russia has died again. I hear such *dreary* accounts of it. Moscow so Americanised, the proletariat all becoming Yankee and mechanical. That bores me.

What is your wife doing about her divorce? Or is that all abandoned again, and you are happier together?

And what did Haas achieve in Paris? Did he get *his* divorce, and marry the Frau Doctor?

I am not very busy – I don't feel much like work. I have been reading up the ancient Etruscans. I thought perhaps in July, if the weather will clear up, I might go to Cortona and Chiusi and Volterra and Tarquinia and Orvieto, the old Etruscan places, and look at all the remains, and perhaps write a light Etruscan travel book, with many photograph reproductions. I think I might like it – if only the weather would be fine and hot.

Best wishes from both of us. Send us some news.

Yrs. D. H. Lawrence

[Frieda Lawrence begins]

Dass ich nicht schrieb: Ich komme mit meinen Töchtern, war reine Bescheidenheit – Aber kommen Sie – Es ist sehr schön! Eine alte Medici villa, aber sehr einfach, mehr wie einfach! Alles Gute Ihnen allen!

Frieda Lawrence

Ja, es ist gewiss schön an ihrem See!

[The fact that I didn't write: I'm coming with my daughters, was pure modesty – But do come – It is very beautiful! An old Medici villa, but very simple, more than simple! All the best to you all!

Frieda Lawrence

Yes, it is certainly beautiful by your lake!]

3723. To Mabel Dodge Luhan, 21 May 1926

Text: MS Brill; Luhan 302–4.

Villa Mirenda. San Polo Mosciano, *Scandicci* – Florence
21 May 1926

My dear Mabel

Your bit about the chauffeur, and the article on the Curonia came today. – I'll go and look at the outside of the villa very soon. – Probably your bit about the chauffeur boy[1] contains the germ of your resistance to these vols. You resist anything which is not resistance. The only other touch of real love in your book was for that clever girl in Paris – and that was deathly. With your men, you only want to resist them, fight them, and overthrow them: that was what you wanted with Parmenter: 'let's see who's stronger!' – With the chauffeur boy it was a touch of the real old physical love, not from the *will* like all the others. So you rejected it, as you must have rejected it all your life. And this makes one of the great losses of your life. Because in that kind of love you'd have had moments at least of escape from your ego. But you never finally wanted even the *momentary* escape from your ego. You wanted your ego *all the time*. – This makes you resist Italy, for Italy for the first time 'tempted' you. America never once tempted you, not even in the shadowy Uncle Carlos.[2] – And it is this which makes the peculiar rancid sort of bitterness one finds in Italy today: the permanent rejection, by the foreigner, of the natural physical flow, and the permanent insistence on the ego, the putting-it-over business. You'd better say to yourself: 'In rejecting the *best* of the Italian "thing", (as you always call it – and the chauffeur boy is an example, though personally he's not very important) – I made one of my life-mistakes.' – You know I always uphold, it is the sheer physical flow which is the healing and sustaining flow – At the height, it is sex, true sensual sex. But it has a thousand forms, and can even be only a mere flow in the air, to be enough. But one needs the physical flow. That's why I can't stay long in America.

Don't leave your MSS. to anybody. They'll all edit them to emasculation. Rouse up and publish them yourself. Do it in Paris, or even here. Norman Douglas publishes his works now himself, here in Florence. But Paris I believe is better.

And don't have introductions. Don't be introduced and discussed before you're there. Don't have anybody write an introduction. Don't ask for credentials and letters of recommendation. Publish your things blank straight as they are, without a word, and so put them down. If you sell a thousand it's quite enough to establish the book permanently. Print a thousand, or at most

[1] Gino (Hahn, *Mabel*, pp. 41–2).

[2] Carlos de Herédia, Sara Ganson's brother-in-law (ibid., p. 9).

two, and have done with it. Have it reviewed in about three good newpapers, and no more. As little publicity as possible, and the thing makes its own way and won't be quashed. And preserve your incognito as completely as you can, really. For once put your ego aside. After all, there's enough of your ego *in* the book, without having to write your name large on the title page. And never say die.

I do think one ought, if one can, to remove the fight (the fight *is* essential) from the field of one's personal relationships, and put it in the impersonal field of the combat[1] with this fixed and rotten society. – Put your fight into the publishing of your book, and let *people* alone. Even let your own salvation alone.

But there, you'll do what you need do.

It's been atrocious weather – rain, rain, rather cold, all the time. This afternoon I sit on the terrace in the sun, but there are mutters of thunder. I do wish it would clear up. – If you can, try and prevent Brett doing anything rash, like going up to live on the ranch all alone. I hope she'll find some substantial person to be up there with her.

If I were rich enough, I'd hire the Curonia for a bit just to show these English–American Florentines how completely one wants to ignore them. – But even from San Polo Mosciano one can do it enough.

DHL

3724. To John Middleton Murry, 25 May 1926

Text: MS NYPL; Unpublished.

Villa Mirenda, *Scandicci*, Florence
25 May 1926

Dear Jack

I don't know when we shall come to England – maybe in August. But I'll let you know. We took the top half of this villa, about seven miles out of Florence, for a year: one can keep it as a *pied à terre*. And while the weather's so bad, one may as well sit still. – It's bad here, as everywhere else: too much rain. The country is unnaturally green, and not a bit like Tuscany. But it's very pretty round about here.

I wonder if your second infant has arrived, and all is well![2]

Myself, I just go quietly on from day to day: paint the cupboard and window frames, go in to Florence, write a dozen lines of a short story: nothing more thrilling. But it's a long time since Frieda and I were alone: the Weekley girls were with F. for months: so I don't at all mind being slackened off.

[1] MS reads 'combat combat'.

[2] John Middleton Murry II arrived on 9 May 1926.

I'll let you know the next moves. I suppose you've got the *Adelphi* rigged afresh. – The Strike has left a hole somewhere in the social fabric, I feel: but I *don't* feel, like Hamlet, called upon to darn it up.[1]

Saluti DHL

3725. To Else Jaffe, 26 May 1926

Text: MS Jeffrey; cited in Frieda Lawrence 222–3.

Villa Mirenda. *Scandicci, Firenze*
26 May 1926

My dear Else

The Schwiegermutter wrote from Baden that you aren't well, and had a little operation. That's bad luck! I do hope you're better.

It isn't a good year, anyhow. Here it has rained and rained, till the country is turning yellow with wetness. But these last two days are sunny and warm: but not hot, as it should be.

We took the top half of this old villa, out on one of the little hills of Tuscany, about seven miles from Florence. We are two Kilometers from the tram, which takes us in to the Duomo in half an hour. The country around is pretty – all poderi and pine-woods, and no *walls* at all. I hope in the autumn, really, you'll come and stay a while: unless everything goes muddled again. For myself, I struggle to get back into a good humour, but don't succeed very well. – We've got the villa for a year, anyhow, so there should be time.

Myself, I am labouring at the moment to type out Frieda's MS. of the play *David*. It's a slow business, I'm no typist. But it is just as well for me to go through the MS myself, and it is good for me to learn some German, I suppose. Frieda's daughter Elsa typed the first 26 pages – and there are a fair number of alterations. But I shall send you the typescript as soon as it is finished: within a month, pray God! – I am interested, really, to see the play go into German, so much simpler and more direct than in English. English is really very complicated in its *meanings*. Perhaps the simpler a language becomes in its grammar and syntax, the more subtle and complex it becomes in its suggestions. Anyhow this play seems to me much more direct and dramatic in German, much less poetic and suggestive than in English. I shall be interested to know what you think of it.

I said to myself I would write perhaps a book about the Etruscans: nothing pretentious, but a sort of book for people who will actually be going to Florence and Cortona and Perugia and Volterra and those places, to look at the Etruscan things. They have a great attraction for me: there are lovely things in

[1] Cf. *Hamlet*, I. v. 189–90.

the Etruscan Museum here,[1] which no doubt you've seen. But I hope you'll come in the autumn and look at them again with me. Mommsen hated everything Etruscan, said the germ of all degeneracy was in the race.[2] But the bronzes and terra cottas are fascinating, so alive with physical life, with a powerful physicality which surely is as great, or sacred, ultimately, as the *ideal* of the Greeks and Germans. Anyhow, the real strength of Italy seems to me in this physicality, which is not at all Roman. I haven't yet seen any of the painted tombs at Tarquinii or Orvieto or down there on the Maremma. Have you seen F[ritz] Weege's *Etruskische Malerei*. 1921?[3] If there is a copy in one of your libraries, I wish you'd look at it and tell me if it has good reproductions. As for the text, I've read one or two books, and they're very dreary, repetition and surmise. It seems amazing that we should know so very very little about a race that lived alongside the Romans. But I can find very little *fact*. – I'll send you Ducati's book.[4] It's not worth reading: but glancing at. The Etruscans are on the *tapis* here in Tuscany. Italy is so wildly nationalistic, that I think Tuscany feels she may as well go one further back than Rome, and derive herself from Etruria. But they all feel scared, because Etruria was so luxurious and 'merely physical'. Let's hope the other parts of Italy will go and derive themselves from Samnites, Sabellians, Tapygians, and so forth.[5] The 'fascia' would then be a variegated one, and perhaps more fun.

We haven't made any definite plans. If I'm going to do anything about the Etruscans, I shall have to go to Bologna, and then down south. But perhaps I'll leave it till autumn. Anyhow I think we shall come to BadenBaden some time in July – and go to England in August – and perhaps return here in September. – But I shall see you somewhere or other.

How is Friedel? This time last year he came to us to[6] the ranch. Now Brett has gone out there alone. I haven't heard yet if she has landed in New York: I shall be relieved to hear, because she was going in on the immigrant quota, so she can stay as long as she likes. I hope the beastly immigration authorities won't make her trouble.

Remember me to Marianne. She's a young woman now, no longer a mere

1 Museo Archeologico.

2 Theodor Mommsen (1817–1903), *The History of Rome*, trans. W. P. Dickson (rev. edn, 1894). Mommsen makes many hostile remarks about the Etruscans, e.g. he refers to 'the internal decay of the nation, the seeds of which indeed were doubtless already deposited at a far earlier period'; or to 'the unbounded luxury of Etruscan life', 'Etruscan unchastity and Etruscan banquets' all of which 'leave no doubt as to the deep degeneracy of the nation' (II. iv. 435–6). See also I. xii. 232; I. xv. 309; II. ix. 124–5, 128.

3 Fritz Weege, (1880–), *Etruskische Malerei* (Halle, 1920; reprinted 1921).

4 Pericle Ducati (1880–), *Etruria Antica* (Turin, 1925).

5 Ancient peoples in the region of Rome (Sabines and Samnites, for whom DHL uses the ancient form of the name) and southern Italy (Iapygians).

6 to] with

girl. It is a strange thing to have a grown-up family: other people! Perhaps I could come for a little while to Irschenhausen to you, if you are there. Then I should see Hans, whom I shall hardly know.[1]

I hope Alfred is well. – The longer I live the more I realise it would shatter the nerves of an Aristotle or a Socrates, to have to think deeply about this world we've got ourselves into. It's no good taking long views: it's like looking down the crater of Vesuvius, you see nothing and you asphyxiate yourself. Best only tackle little problems and tidy up small corners. A man tears himself to bits grappling with the whole machine. That miserable strike in England looks like the beginning of another end!

But there, why think about it! Best go down to Scandicci and buy paint to paint these old doors and window-frames. Carpe diem, quam minimum etc.[2] No good thinking about what's coming after!

a rivederci DHL

3726. To Rachel Hawk, 29 May 1926

Text: MS UT; Postmark, Firenze 1 . VI 1926; Unpublished.

Villa Mirenda. *Scandicci*, Florence. Italy.
29 May 1926

Dear Rachel

Your letter of 9th May came today. I wrote you from Florence and sent William some money for the horses. – I haven't heard yet from Brett if she's landed safely: we are feeling a bit anxious. – I wish to heaven you *would* go up to our ranch and stay with her. Take the big house (big indeed!) for yourself, and use whatever you want. One can say that quite safely to *you*. Any stores, anything there is, make use of it. – I'm awfully sorry you didn't keep the Azul and ride him. I've told William many times to use the horses whenever he liked, for the buggy or to ride. And I want you, Rachel, to feel free to use any of the horses for any purpose. – If you go up with Brett, tell her I say you are to have the big house, and she pleases herself for the rest. – I hope William is well and *moderately* happy, at least. –

We took the upper half of this big old villa for a year: it's very cheap. It's about seven miles out of Florence, right in the country, and feels very easy and nice. I suppose in July we shall go to Germany, then to England, and probably return here in September. And perhaps by next spring we shall feel like coming west again.

I enclose the nine dollars for Mr Rasmussen, and a few odd ones for your trouble, looking after the water and things.

[1] Hans was Else Jaffe's younger son (b. 1909).

[2] Horace, *Odes*, IV. ix. 28 ['. . . minimum credula postero']: 'Enjoy today, trust as little as possible to the future'.

Your weather will be good by now. We too had a great spell of rain, till about a week ago. Now it is hot and summery, the cherries and strawberries are in full go, the roses are passing over. I am really very fond of Italy, the flow of life seems rich and easy.

I'm awfully sorry Mrs Hawk is lame in foot and arm: that's too bad, when she likes so much to be busy. I'll see if I can find any books to send her. And Frieda will find Shirley Glenn a little frock, Florence is the town for needlework. As for poor old Walton, he's cursed, like me, with bronchials, and a curse they are, though you don't easily die of them. The photograph is very pretty, of the children.

Remember me to Betty.[1] She seems to be a sort of grass widow, putting her little filly out to pasture a good deal. But I hope she gets a fairish good time, anyhow. Sometimes my heart sinks a bit, and I wish it was a hot afternoon, and you in your boots and Betty with a sash on her hips, very showy, were just coming round the corner to the porch, where we'd have tea. – And Brownie and the long-legged Selem tied under the trees! – But a year soon goes by. Un altro anno – !

How, by the way, is Eusebio?[2] Remember me to him.

You never told me who the Rasmussens are, and what arrangement you've made with them for your place.

Remember me to William and everybody. It will soon be time to cut alfalfa!

I'm glad Mr Hawk, at least, keeps well. And surely Mrs Hawk will be better, now the warm weather is here.

Don't call yourself our *ex*-neighbour. You've not gone right away yet, and I hope you won't. Anyhow don't start trailing after William round Forest Service camps. Go up to our ranch rather.

Frieda sends her love, and says she will write. But don't be *too* expectant of her letter.

Yours ever D. H. Lawrence

Do keep a financial watch on Brett! – Anything the ranch itself costs, I will pay – *let me know*.

3727. To Ada Clarke, 1 June 1926

Text: MS Clarke; cited in Lawrence–Gelder 136.

Villa Mirenda. *Scandicci*, Florence
1 June 1926

My dear Sister

I wonder how your business is going now, with the beastly strike. Really,

[1] Betty Cottam.

[2] One of the Mexican workers on Kiowa (Brett 248–50 and see Brett, *South Dakota Review* 68).

it's too bad they let it come to a strike: very dangerous too, because it may start a real class war, and England is the one country where that is most dangerous.

I am busy here typing the German translation of *David*, and painting the doors and windows: then two or three times a week I go in to Florence, where I have men friends. It makes all the difference in the world, having the town near like that, and yet being in the country so completely.

By the way, it's nearly your birthday.[1] I wonder what you'd like? Florence is a great town for leather – purses and sachels and cases of all sorts and colours, to match any dress, and not expensive. Then pottery, pictures, frames, and jewellery – all Florentine specialities. Tell me what you'd like.

We have promised to go to Baden Baden in mid July, then come on to England early in August. Probably we can have a friend's flat in Chelsea,[2] Frieda can stay there, and I shall come up and see you – either at Ripley or at the seaside. Have you made any plans for the holidays?

Here thank goodness it is nice and warm, one can go about in shirt and trousers and sandals. The fireflies are thick in the garden, and the peasants bring in baskets of cherries. I really like Tuscany much better than the Riviera. I like this far better than Spotorno. But perhaps you would prefer the sea.

We're going to lunch on Wednesday with Sir George Sitwell and Lady Ida. They have a castle about 14 miles out. But their home place is near Chesterfield: I guess you've heard of them, one way and another. It's their boys who write.[3]

We still haven't heard from Brett, whether she's landed in New York. I wonder what's happened to her. It's really time we heard.

Poor Jack, he loves long knives and pistols, but not stones through the bus window. I should have thought all those young Ripley Buffalo Bills would have shot a mob to pieces! How does Gertie get on? Does she collect any twopences?[4]

I'm feeling very much better now the real summer is here – almost my own self now. Certainly America isn't good for me: I'm thankful I made no move to go back. – Oh, Mabel Lujan thinks of coming to Europe next autumn, and bringing her Indian husband Tony! That'll be something of an event.

Arabella wanted to come out and see us, with Richard Aldington – you

[1] She was born 16 June 1887.

[2] See Letter 3732.

[3] Sir George Reresby Sitwell Bt (1860–1943), m. 1886, Lady Ida Emily Augusta Denison; they lived at the Castello di Montegufoni, Montagnana, Val Di Pesa, near Florence. Their 'boys' were (Sir) Osbert (1892–1969), poet, essayist, critic and autobiographer and (Sir) Sacheverell (1897–1988), art critic and essayist. Their daughter was (Dame) Edith Louisa (1887–1964), poet and critic. (The family seat in Derbyshire to which DHL was invited – Letter 3734 – was Renishaw Hall.)

[4] See Letter 3838 and n. 1.

know they've lived together since 1919. But apparently they're hard up. Yet he does leaders for the *Times Lit. Supplement*! It's too bad they pay so little.

I hope Stanley is having a good time. – Your garden must be nice now – here the roses are almost over. I do hope Eddie doesn't fret about the strike: I don't suppose it will have any lasting effect.

Remember me to everybody.

love DHL

3728. To Baroness Anna von Richthofen, [8 June 1926]

Text: MS Clark; PC v. Nemi – Panorama di Genzano; Postmark, Firenze [. . .] 6.[. . .]; Unpublished.

[Villa Mirenda, Scandicci, Florence]

Dienstag

Vielen Dank für den grünen Schlips, sehr schön, ich hab es sehr gern. So schmale sind sie wirklich besser. Ich habe dir nie für den andern, den pflaŭmen, gedankt: und ich trage ihn jetzt täglich. Ich hoffe es geht der Else besser. Sag ihr, sie soll mir schreiben. – Ist Friedel in Berlin? und was macht er dort? – Das Theaterstück braucht noch eine Woche, dann, wenn Gott hilft, ist es fertig. Ein schwieriges Arbeit, ich 'tippe' sehr ungern, und mache viele Fehler. – Mach einen schönen Ausflug mit der Else, du! wiedersehen

DHL

[Many thanks for the green tie, very beautiful, I like it very much. They're really better narrow like that. I've never thanked you for the other one, the plum-coloured one: and now I wear it every day. I hope Else is better. Tell her she should write to me. – Is Friedel in Berlin? and what's he doing there? – The play needs another week, then, God help me, it's done. Difficult work, I dislike 'typing' intensely, and make lots of mistakes. – Have a nice trip with Else, won't you! wiedersehen

DHL]

3729. To Hon. Dorothy Brett, [8 June 1926]

Text: MS UCin; Postmark, Scandicci 8. 6. 26; Moore 917–18.

Villa Mirenda, *Scandicci*, Firenze. Italia

8 May 1926[1]

Dear Brett

Had your note from The Shelton two days ago: so glad you had a pleasant

[1] The contents of the letter (e.g. DHL had not heard by 26 May that Brett had arrived in USA but has now received a cable from her; the visit to the Sitwells has taken place, etc.) as well as the postmark, prove the error in DHL's own dating and justify the conjectural 8 June 1926.

journey and enjoy New York. Now we shall hear from you at the Ranch, and have news of that too.

I heard from Rachel, maybe she will go up to our ranch with Walton and Shirley Glenn. I do hope she will. Then she can have the big house, and keep house, and you can have your dot again: or the milk house. That would be awfully nice all round. You would all feel at home.

Am enclosing Achsah's note to you. I heard from Earl – a bit lamentable – he's awfully interested in India, but doesn't really like it: says they can't leave before *October*: and do I think we might meet for the winter, perhaps winter on one of the Isles of Greece. – But perhaps, when he gets to the Monastery in the hills, he'll love it again.

We've been very quiet here – went out to the Sitwell father and mother – they have a castle some 14 miles out. – I'm busy typing out F[rieda]'s translation of *David* – be glad you don't have to do it – every noun in German a capital letter! – and having to re-translate F's translation – oh dear! But I've done three fourths. – I've not been able to go around for my Etruscans at all – shall have to do it when we come back in Sept.

We think to leave about July 16th – go to Baden for a fortnight – then to England for August. So write c/o Curtis Brown. 6 Henrietta St. W. C. 2. They are playing *David* in Sept. in London, just one performance, and I want to see what it's like, and how they get on with it.[1]

Sometimes I wish I was at the ranch – especially if the weather's good! here it's still unsettled. It was sunny for a spell, now again rain and high cloud.

How about your money? Are you managing? For heavens sake, *be careful.*

I heard from Murry, he has a son: such a tiny tiny baby, he says.

It's hard to believe that already you are way out at the ranch again. I expect we shall come in the spring – and it's already midsummer. The time flies by!

tante belle cose! DHL

[Frieda Lawrence begins]

Strange that this will find you at the ranch, it does'nt seem real! But I *love* it here, flowery mysterious Tuscany, we sit on a little hill and there are lots of other hills, it's an old Medici villa with some dignity! Ah, for the old times! Yes, I had my try with Elsa and Barby, they did quite a lot of things, and we had a really good time! Barby paints quite well, very sensitive! *Dont* live alone at the Ranch, not even for swank.! Now I am alone too and love my monastic peace. Will translate the *Plumed Serpent*! But dont you rely on making a life

[1] According to the programme (Lazarus collection), *David* was first produced by Ernest Milton (1890–1974) for the 300 Club and Stage Society at the Regent Theatre in London, 22–3 May 1927.

with L[awrence] and me – I may be a nun in 6 months or gone off with a bandit in the Abruzzi and goodness knows what L may do! May the Lord be with us all! The strike feels bad!

All good luck Frieda

3730. To Mabel Dodge Luhan, [8 June 1926]
Text: MS Brill; Luhan 299–301.

Villa Mirenda. *Scandicci.* Florence.
8 May 1926

Dear Mabel

I had your letter with 'Constance' – and also your following letter, where you say you – to put it short – don't feel anything any more. – I believe one has to go through that. It's the change of life. I feel all Italy is going through it: the strange change of life. It's the breaking down of the Gourdjieff 'habits.' But the habits that are hardest to break down are habits of feeling and consciousness, and above all, habits of relationship. Our habits of emotion go so deep, we almost die before they break: and our habits of relationship have so many cancer-like threads, any one of which will start the whole old thing again – it's a case of *poveri noi*! The process is organic and ultra-organic. I feel it's a painful, deadening process. But I don't feel that one can 'do' it, *make* it! There has to be something else pushing. And one has to be on the side of the new unknown. – Anyhow it's a weariness!

'Constance' is quite a good sketch, but has not much to do with you. It doesn't matter. You see in Europe you didn't *fight* – couldn't! And if you only live in and by the fight, you couldn't live. But perhaps that habit of the fight has to go, with all the rest. O poveri noi!

I think quite definitely you should publish those memoirs yourself, and do them in separate vols, with separate titles, so that the different vols *may* be quite different.

We think to stay here till about 16th July, then go to Baden for two weeks, then to England for August. So address me either c/o Curtis Brown. London – or else c/o Frau von Richthofen. Ludwig Wilhelmstift, *BadenBaden*.

Tell Spud I haven't had his *horses* yet, and shall write him the minute they come.

I heard from Brett, safe in New York, and thrilled by it. So probably you've seen her. I don't even want to be thrilled.

I suppose we shall be back here in Sept., and I shall go around to the Etruscan places. I'm afraid I shan't get anything much done before we leave.

One's got to leave off *wanting* to feel as one has felt – and enjoying what one has enjoyed – at least, in the old way.

The weather's always unsettled and unsatisfactory. They say there's an astronomical reason.

DHL

There just came from Taos about 1000 sheets of the drawing of me by Bynner for Spuds *Horse*.[1] Were they *all* really intended for me?

3731. To Martin Secker, 8 June 1926

Text: MS UInd; Postmark, Firenze 8 VI 1926; Secker 73–4.

Villa Mirenda. *Scandicci*. Florence
8 June 1926

Dear Secker

We are still here, in quiet – The weather is only so-so – keeps coming thunder and rain. I'm busy typing out and revising F[rieda]'s translation of *David* – such a job! I loathe the typewriter. But nobody else would do this particular job – would be able to do it!

We have decided to stay here till middle July, go to Baden for a fortnight, then to England for August. Do you know those people who are giving a performance of *David*? I've forgotten who they are. I wish you'd ask them if they keep the date fixed for the performance – if they fixed it – and tell them I shall be in London in August, and if they will be rehearsing then. I should like to have a finger in that particular pie.

We've been out very little – only to the Sitwell parents, Sir George and Lady Ida. They have a castle about fourteen miles out – queer old place – a bit disheartening. He collects, of all things, beds – room after room, bed after bed, as if he were providing for all the dead.

The weather's only so-so – a lot of rain and thunder. Don't like it.

Would you send a copy of *The Plumed Serpent* to

Prof. Aldo Sorani. 11. via E. Repetti, *Florence*.[2]

He is doing a critique on me – in Italian. Wonderful how well he knows my work.

I saw Douglas in a cafe and didn't speak to him: felt I couldn't stand him.

Would you send me another copy of *David* for myself – mine has gone!

[1] Bynner's is a pen and ink portrait included in the 'D. H. Lawrence Number' (p. 7) of the *Laughing Horse*, published in April 1926.

[2] Aldo Sorani (1883–1945) was well known in Florentine literary circles; he was particularly interested in English literature and politics; he was one of the founders of the British Institute of Florence in 1917 and received the MBE during World War I. Sorani was anti-Fascist; he signed Croce's *Manifesto* in 1925. His 'critique' – 'Incontri con D. H. Lawrence' ['Meetings with DHL'] – appeared after DHL's death in *Pegaso: Rassegna di lettere e arti* (Florence, 1932), iv. 702–10. It records DHL's love of Italy, memories of life at Villa Mirenda and a chance encounter when DHL showed Sorani proofs of *Lady Chatterley's Lover*. Sorani regarded the novel as a work of integrity and a challenge to the bourgeois world.

I hear the Knopfs are sailing – have sailed – for Europe. They'll probably be in Paris by now. But don't suppose I shall see them.

Hope all are well and cheerful.

tanti saluti D. H. Lawrence

3732. To Millicent Beveridge, 8 June 1926

Text: MS Hirst; Postmark, Scandicci 8 6. 26; Unpublished.

Villa Mirenda, *Scandicci*. Florence.
8 June 1926

Dear Milly

Many thanks for Fell, his book came a few days ago.[1] He's very thorough in washing out once more the few rags of information we have concerning the Etruscans: but not a thing has he to say. It's really disheartening: I shall just have to start in and go ahead, and be damned to all authorities! There really is next to nothing to be said, *scientifically*, about the Etruscans. Must take the imaginative line. – I was already enquiring in Germany about Wiege. I'll buy him when I come north.

So far I've not been out on my Etruscan travels. It's been poorish weather, and I've been painfully busy typing out Frieda's translation of *David*. I never use a typewriter – and then having to type German – and to alter F's translation all the way: a labour, I assure you. I wonder the typewriter hasn't gone off with a bang and a smell of sulphur.

We think to leave here about 16 July, go to Baden for a fortnight, then come to England. Are you really going to Scotland? If you are, could we rent your flat for the month of August? You know we are careful people. Myself, I expect to be away from London most of the time, seeing my people, etc. But it would be nice to have a pied à terre, and Frieda could stay there alone. I should think, in September we shall come back here, and I shall really spend the autumn over my Etruscans. I hope to heaven the autumn will be dry and decent, so I can go round all the places.

It's awfully nice here. You know, we've got the top half of this old square villa. I was hoping to get two nice, selfcontained rooms downstairs: but the lunatics are using them to store the corn in: beautiful big sitting-rooms. One day, though, you must try painting this country, it's so nice, and very paintable, so many nooks.

What a long time the Maggiore was returning to London. Was his case put off? And how did you find him?

We've only seen a few old acquaintances here: – except that we went out to

[1] Roland Arthur Lonsdale Fell, *Etruria and Rome* (Cambridge, 1924).

lunch with Sir George Sitwell, and Lady Ida: parents of the writing Sitwell trio. They have a castle about 14 miles out: strange old place: but it's very disheartening, because Sir G. collects *beds*: those four-poster golden venetian monsters that look like Mexican high-altars. Room after room, and nothing but bed after bed. I said 'but do you put your guests in them?' – Oh! he said. They're not to sleep in. They're museum pieces. Also gilt and wiggly-carved chairs. I sat on one. Oh! he said. Those chairs are not to sit in! – So I wriggled on the seat in the hopes it would come to pieces. Depressing! The trio will be out in September, so suppose we shall see them.

Brett safe in New York, and loving it: says it's so full of life. So is a gramophone!

I want to be in London a bit to see after those people who are going to give a performance of *David* in September. Seems to me I'd better have a finger in that pie. – Let us know about the flat, but don't bother in the least if you've made some other arrangement.

tante cose D. H. Lawrence

am enclosing the money for Fell.

3733. To Emily King, 14 June 1926
Text: MS Lazarus; Moore 918–19.

Villa Mirenda, *Scandicci*. Florence.
14 June 1926

My dear Pamela

The time slips by, and I've not written for so long. But nothing particular happens, and so there seems no particular reason to write. I've been busy typing out F[rieda]'s translation of *David* – such a sweat, typing German and making revisions. But it's done. Then we've been painting doors and windows, and making this old place look more alive. Then we go in to Florence about twice a week, and people come out here: so weeks are gone before one knows where one is.

We have promised to be in Baden for F's mother's birthday, on July 14th. Then I suppose we shall come to England first week in August. I haven't heard yet if we can have the flat in Chelsea – but it is probable. Ada writes she has taken a cottage at Mablethorpe for the month. That will be very nice. Then you and Joan and Peg can stay down there – and Sam can run down on the motorcycle – I'll send you some money for the holiday in my next letter. – I shall look forward to a week there with you all. – I have an invitation up to Scotland also – two invitations, Compton Mackenzie wants me to go to an Isle off Lewis, in the Outer Hebrides.[1] But

[1] The other invitation was to visit Millicent (and probably her sister Mary) Beveridge's house, 'Bailabhadan', in Newtonmore, Inverness.

I'm not sure. – I want to see what that stage society are doing with *David*. If they're rehearsing, I must keep an eye on them.

I'm a bit loath to leave here so soon, when we seem only just settled in. But also I want to be back for Vendemmia, – grape harvest – in September. Richard Aldington and Arabella said they would like to come back with us in September. – Arabella has been living with Richard ever since we knew them. They want to get married, but Hilda Aldington is a cat, and won't give them a divorce, though she herself went off with Gray.[1] – I wonder what Arabella will be like now. We shall see her in England. They live not far from Pangbourne. – By the way, Rosalind Baynes is married again, to a man, a widower, in the British Museum, and they live in London.[2] I'm glad she's settled down again.

Cath. Carswell is in France – she's put her boy in a French school near Versailles. She seems to hate it, the boy too.[3] They're very poor, and of course the husband Don is once more without a job. – What a life! – Murry has got another baby, and seems to be withdrawing from the 'world.' I haven't seen his Life of Christ yet.[4] – We heard from Brett – a cable – happily settled on the ranch with Rachel Hawk, our neighbour from below. Rachel is very responsible, and will look after everything. I'm very glad. They all write urging us to go out. But not this year, anyhow.

Is Peg nearly through with her course? And is she smart by now? How I hated typing my play! – I shall hear about everything when I come to England.

I'll write again very soon. Love to you all.

DHL

I'm sending a copy of the *laughing Horse* – a little magazine published by a young American friend away in Santa Fe. You'll be amused by it.

3734. To Ada Clarke, [14 June 1926]

Text: MS Clarke; Unpublished.

Villa Mirenda. *Scandicci.* Florence
Monday

My dear Sister

Your letter today – am very glad you are doing so well, all things considered. I was beginning to get worried. That coal strike is most awfully depressing, lasting so long, and no way out. The miners might just as well go back to the

[1] Cecil Gray (1895–1951), composer and music critic whom DHL knew well in Cornwall, 1917 (see *Letters*, iii. 128 n. 1). Hilda Aldington joined Gray, at Bosigran Castle, in Spring 1918; she was there in June (see ibid., iii. 254) but had left by September (ibid., iii. 280).

[2] Rosalind Popham (1891–1973) was divorced by her husband, Helton Godwin Baynes (1882–1943), in 1921; DHL had known both of them since 1912–13. In 1926 she married Arthur ('Hugh') Ewart Popham (1889–1970), art historian and bibliographer; his first wife was Brynhild Olivier (see *Letters*, ii. 230 n. 3, 321–2).

[3] See Letter 3691 and n. 2.

[4] See p. 383 n. 2.

eight hours day: better for them. But I suppose they feel a bit sore, too: which one can't wonder at.

I enclose £5. for the hammock: hope it'll be a nice one. I'm so glad your flowers are such a success: I often wondered about the bulbs Tom and I so carefully arranged.[1] Here the roses are gone, and the honeysuckle and the broom and the irises are finishing. But the bad weather is here again: yesterday it rained all day, and today it is fine, but blows like the devil. What ails it? Frieda's mother writes from Germany it is so cold and wet there – bitter! You say England is glorious: sounds good!

Frieda now isn't very anxious to go to Germany or to come to England. But we shall come. We are due to be in Baden on her mothers birthday, July 14th. – though it really is a bit of a bore, moving again when we are only just settled in here. One gets sick of moving, really.

We went out to the Sitwells – such an odd couple. They asked me to go to their place in August if I am in Derbyshire: so we might run over, when the three literary young ones are at home.

Brett cabled that she is happily settled on the ranch, with our neighbour, Rachel Hawk. Which puts one's mind at rest in that direction.

Richard Aldington and Arabella put off their coming here until autumn – which is just as well, all things considered. Perhaps you'll see Arabella again when we are in England.

The cottage at Mablethorpe sounds nice. I shall look forward to a week down there. Of course Pamela and Peg and Joan must be there part of the time. I'll send them some money for it. I don't suppose Sam is very 'flush.'

I'm sending you a *laughing Horse* – D.H.L. number. It's done by a young American friend in Santa Fe, and the advertisements will interest you, if nothing else does – show you how they do it in the South west![2]

The time goes quickly by. We shall be in England before we know where we are. Remember me to everybody.

Love. DHL

[1] Thomas Betts was a miner who worked for the Clarkes as gardener and handyman. DHL enjoyed any opportunity for a conversation with Betts whenever he visited his sister.

[2] Eight pages are devoted to advertisements. They extol the virtues of Zook's Pharmacy, Gerson Gusdorf's Navajo Blankets and S. Spitz's Mexican Filigree Jewelry, *et al.*; they offer real estate 'Direct from the King of Spain – And we furnish the papers to prove it'; and they cite DHL as one of the 'Celebrities [who] have had their Ice-Cream Sodas and Coca-Cola' at La Botica de Capital, La Plaza, Santa Fe.

3735. To Nancy Pearn, 22 June 1926
Text: MS UT; Huxley 660.

Villa Mirenda. *Scandicci*, Florence
22 June 1926

Dear Miss Pearn

I sent you a little western magazine – the *laughing Horse* – D.H.L number – thought it might amuse you: especially the advts. – I like my 'Mediterranean' poem – somebody might print it in a periodical. –

Seems to me there's something you asked me, which I've forgotten –

Would you ask the dramatic dept. if they've any news of the performance of *David* which was to be given by a private society – I forget which – in September. – I think we shall be in England for August – hope we shall see you – and I thought I might look at some of the rehearsals, if they're really going ahead. But maybe they're not.

We've planned to leave here for BadenBaden on July 12th.

Hope all goes jauntily.

Yrs D. H. Lawrence

3736. To Hon. Dorothy Brett, 23 June 1926
Text: MS UCin; Postmark, [. . .] 25[. . .]; Huxley 661–2.

Villa Mirenda. *Scandicci*, Florence.
23 June 1926

Dear Brett

Your first letters from the ranch. What a bore the rats had done so much chewing! But I thought all the mattresses had gone down to Del Monte! – And Frieda brought some – not all though – of the silver along with her. I'm sorry though that you had so much hard work. One just doesn't feel like drudgery, and I'm sure you hate being in an overall. But pray heaven, by now you are in your breeches and feeling like a real ranchero!

That scoundrel of an Azul, to run away! I can just see him. Were the others glad to have him back, or didn't they care? I can just imagine them, this afternoon, standing in a bunch under the scraggy trees near the wire gate, whisking their tails. It's an awful pity one can't just stride over, in one huge stride. Then we'd be there to tea in the porch.

Here it is real Italian summer at last. Everybody sleeps from one till three. Nay, it's quarter to four, and there's not a peasant in sight on all the poderi. But of course they get up at about 4.30 in the morning: we about six. I'm sitting on the little balcony upstairs – you can so easily imagine this old square whitish villa on a little hill all of its own, with the peasant houses and cypresses behind, and the vines and olives and corn on all the slopes. It's very picturesque, and many a paintable bit. Away in front lies the Arno valley, and mountains beyond. Behind are pine woods. The rooms inside are big and rather bare – with red-brick floors: spacious, rather nice, and very still. Life doesn't cost much here.

We go in to Florence once or twice a week. When we see Reggie Turner he always wants to be remembered to you. They all think you very bold, to go out there to the ranch.

But you are quite right when you say one shouldn't pretend to belong to one place exclusively. Italy is always lovely, and out there at the ranch it is always lovely. I am sure it is right for me to stay this year in the softness of the Mediterranean. But next year, in the spring, I want to come to the ranch, before the leaves come on the aspen trees, and the snow is gone. If one could but *stride* over!

Is the messiness of the old corral passing away? Are there very many flowers? Will there be many raspberries? Were there still humming birds round the squawberry bushes, or had they gone? Does the ditch run a nice stream?

Oh, by the way, tell me how much money you paid for clearing the ditch, and for Azul, and all those things. Because I will pay for them. You'll have no money. *Don't forget*!

Has the old tree down at the well – the old fallen aspen – still put out leaves? I often think of it. And has the big greasewood bush grown over the track to the well, so that it pushes your buckets aside?

What place have the Rasmussens got, and what is he ambitious about?

I am very much better in health now I can go about in shirt and trousers and sandals, and it's hot, and all relaxed. We live very quietly – picnic by the stream sometimes. I have finished typing out and revising *David* in German – he was a job! Did I tell you I had the little typewriter taken to pieces and cleaned: it goes very nicely. But I'm glad it's shut up again, it is an irritable thing, a typewriter.

Mabel said you were going to see her. May as well be friends with her. – I did think her book good.

I believe it's coming a thunder-storm: too bad: it's San Giovanni tomorrow, Florence's saint, and big festa-day.

Frieda doesn't want to go to Germany and England – says she wants to stay here. But probably we shall go.

tante belle cose! DHL

We're doing a fine embroidery – peacock, kid, and deer among the vines! – *How* is the big picture?

3737. To Margaret King, 24 June 1926

Text: MS Needham; cited in Pinto, *Renaissance and Modern Studies*, i. 6.

Villa Mirenda, *Scandicci*. Florence
24 June 1926

My dear Peg

I was very glad to have your letter and to hear that you've already got a job. That is smart work, and if the man you work for is nice, you'll be all right. I'm sure you'll like it better than teaching, which is a wearing, nerve-racking business[1] and you'll feel already independent, though 17/6 isn't a fortune. But for a year I taught school for 2/6 a week, so you're well ahead there.

That beastly coal strike, it sounds too dreary for words. Coal was the making of England, and it looks as if coal were to be the breaking of her too. But one can do nothing, so it's no good fuming. The weather, at any rate, has turned hot and really summery here, so probably it is the same in England, and you won't need fires any more.

I am always so glad when the real summer comes, and one can go about with light clothes on, and feet in sandals, and not bother about anything. Here everybody gets up about 4.30, and then, from 1.0 till about 3.30 in the afternoon the whole countryside goes to sleep, not a peasant anywhere in the corn or among the vines, all deep asleep. We take a siesta too. Then the evening comes cooler, and the nightingale starts singing again. There are many nightingales, in every little wood you can hear half a dozen singing away all day long, except in the hot hours, very lively. The wheat is very fine, and just turning yellow under the olive trees.

Today is San Giovanni, the Saint of Florence, and a great festa. So we shall go in to town this evening for dinner, and stay for the fireworks. They will illuminate the town, and everybody will be in full holiday rig. We usually go in to Florence twice a week – or I go alone. It's half an hours walk to the tram, and half an hour in the tram. But when we come home, the peasant boy comes to the tram with the pony trap, to meet us. We have usually so many parcels, and home is uphill.

We have promised to be in BadenBaden for Frieda's mothers birthday on July 14th: which would mean leaving here on Monday fortnight. Frieda now says she doesn't want to go: doesn't want to come to England either: wants to stay here. I must say, it's very lovely here, and seems a pity to go sweltering travelling those weary journeys in trains. I don't look forward, myself, to the effort of travelling again so soon. But we'll see.

[1] DHL advised his niece not to teach; she accepted his advice and, in January 1926, went to a commercial college in Nottingham. (c. June 1926 she became a secretary in the Nottingham office of the Confederation Life Association of Canada.)

I hear from Brett, she is settled on the ranch with Rachel Hawk and Rachel's two toddling children. She says it's very nice. Azul, Frieda's grey horse, jumped the fence and ran away. But Brett offered a reward, so a Mexican brought him back from away beyond Valdez.

I hope Joan is keeping well. Now the summer is here, I feel much better.

You get a quid to celebrate your entry into the ranks of the employed: and good luck for the future.

love to you all. DHL

3738. To Johanna Krug, [26 June 1926]
Text: MS UT; Unpublished.

Villa Mirenda, *Scandicci*, Firenze,
Samstag. 26 Juni

Meine liebe Nusch

Wo denn ist deiner Wörthersee? Wie weit von Wien? – und was kostet es? – und wann geht Ihr dahin? Ich glaube, wir werden auch kommen – fahren von hier am Ende Juli – ein paar Tage in Wien – und dann wenn Ihr reisset über Wien, können wir zusammen nach Wörthersee gehen. Müssen wir aber Zimmer bestellen? Ich glaube, es wäre schön. Jene Ecke von der Welt kenne ich nicht.

Dann können wir erst in September nach Baden gehen, wann es weniger voll ist, und frischer – gegen Ende September –

Es geht uns gut. – heiss hier – Korn schon geschnitten – Erde trocken – wie Herbst. Nur die jungen Weintrauben noch grün und hart und frisch.

Grüsse Emil, und sei gegrüsst – es wird schön sein, wenn wir uns in Kärten[1] alle zusammen finden.

DHL

[My dear Nusch

Where is your Wörthersee, then? How far from Vienna? – and what does it cost? – and when do you go there? I think we shall come too – leave from here at the end of July – a few days in Vienna – and then if you travel via Vienna, we can go to Wörthersee together. But do we have to book rooms? I think it would be nice. I don't know that corner of the world.

Then we're not able to go to Baden until September, when it's less crowded, and fresher – towards the end of September –

[1] It is presumed that DHL meant 'Kärnten' ('Carinthia' in s. Austria), but he clearly wrote 'Kärten'.

We're well. – hot here – corn already cut – earth dry – like autumn. Only the young grapes are still green and firm and fresh.

Greetings to Emil, and to yourself – it will be lovely when we all find ourselves together in Kärten.

DHL]

3739. To Curtis Brown, 26 June 1926
Text: MS UT; Unpublished.

Villa Mirenda, *Scandicci*, Florence
26 June 1926

Dear C[urtis] B[rown],

I enclose part of a letter from Secker. He wants to do a 7/6 edition of *Sea and Sardinia*, without pictures: which I think is all right.[1]

What do you think, though, of a 3/6 paper edition of the other books?[2] I don't, myself, quite know what to think of that. Am not sure it's wise: not at all sure. Will you tell me what you think?

And six shillings seems dear for a plain *David* play. But I suppose that's his affair.

I expect we shall be in England for August: we are due to leave here on July 14th for Baden Baden. I hope I shall see you in town. Or will you be gone away?

It's full, hot summer here at last: almost a pity to go away. But surely it will be nice everywhere?

Wonder if you've seen Knopf yet!

a rivederci D. H. Lawrence

We can shorten the address here a bit!

3740. To Nancy Pearn, 27 June 1926
Text: MS UT; Unpublished.

Villa Mirenda. *Scandicci*, Florence
27 June 1926

Dear Miss Pearn

Good news about *Nash's*![3] – If you think it's all right to let O'Brien put that story in 'This Years etc' – then let him do so.[4] Ça m'est égal!

[1] Cf. Letter 3720 and n. 1.

[2] This proposal about the ten fiction titles Secker published was mooted in his letter to Curtis Brown, 8 May 1926; it was subsequently raised by Secker with Duckworth with reference to the four titles he controlled, on 23 July (Secker Letter-Book, UIll).

[3] The 'good news' is not known.

[4] Edward O'Brien edited *The Best British Stories of 1926* (New York, November 1926); he included DHL's 'The Woman Who Rode Away' (Roberts B20).

But about the *Coterie*, do you mean to say I'm to sell a story and sign *100* booklets for £15?[1] Why Americans offer me $5.00 for a signature, and I never take it: never sign. I hate signing books for publishers – don't know why. – The rest of the business I don't mind: only the signing.

Vogue told Richard Aldington to ask me to do them little articles: paying £10. for 1,500[2] words: 1,500 words. I'm not doing anything else, so have written three little things – though they come about 2,000 – and I'll send them along in a day or two, soon as they're typed.[3] And will you offer them to *Vogue* – unless you think any of them quite unsuitable. Then I've another 'possible' story, nearly done.[4] – But little articles, if people like 'em, are much the easiest. In America, *Vanity Fair* asked me to do some. But the American *Vogue* might synchronise with the English one.

It's lovely summer here too, long hot days that I love. My wife says she doesn't want to leave Tuscany. But I expect we shall be in England for August, and then we must have a meal somewhere together.

hasta luego! D. H. Lawrence

You can shorten the address here a bit!

3741. To S. S. Koteliansky, 28 June 1926

Text: MS BL; Postmark, Firenze 30 . VI 192[. . .]; cited in Gransden 30.

Villa Mirenda, *Scandicci*. Florence
28 June 1926

My dear Kot

Your letter today – also a long screed from Barbara to Frieda.[5]

We are sitting very unobtrusively here: but think to leave this day fortnight, July 12th, for BadenBaden, and stay there a fortnight: then probably to England for August. Of course the thought of England, as it draws near, depresses me with infinite depression. But perhaps we may manage a month. Perhaps we may shirk it after all. But I'll tell you. – It is awfully nice here, now

[1] See p. 352 n. 1. The reference here is to the separately published *Sun*; none was signed: when Nancy Pearn replied on 10 July (TMSC UT); she described *Coterie*'s original suggestion as 'absurd'.

[2] 1,500] 15,000

[3] Two can be identified fairly confidently: 'The Nightingale' (cf. Letter 3804), published in *Forum*, lxxviii (September 1927), 382–7 (Roberts C158); 'Fireworks' which was probably written on 25 June 1926, the day after the Feast of the Nativity of St John the Baptist (cf. Letter 3737) and was published in *Nation and Athenæum*, xli (16 April 1927), 47–9 (Roberts C155). The third article is not known. None appeared in *Vogue*.

[4] 'The Man Who Loved Islands' (see Letter 3765) which was published in *Dial*, viii (July 1927), 1–25 and *London Mercury*, xvi (August 1927) (Roberts C157).

[5] I.e. Barbara Low.

the summer is hot and more or less steady, and the days pass by so quickly and without notice, it seems a pity to stir oneself up again.

I feel the same about Secker: absolute mistrust, which grows deeper instead of lighter. Why hadn't he sent you that £2.16. – long ago, if he owed it?[1] I think he is in low water. He keeps asking me to write another novel. But I don't want to. He can whistle. Why should I write books for any of 'em! I've had enough. – And if the New Agers smell no better than the Old Agers, they too can whistle, and keep their £1. per 1000.[2] – They hadn't written me. – Don't send me any of that miserable Shestov fragment. And if ever you want any money, tell me, and I'll send it along. Don't have a silly Jewish money complex. We've lived too long.

I haven't done any of the Etruscan book yet: and shan't do it, unless the mood changes. Why write books for the swine, unless one absolutely must!

I like it here. One can stay out and be quite remote. Or go into Florence in an hour, and see a few people who aren't exciting, but all the better. I don't ask excitement. I was very busy typing out F's translation of the *David* play – and working it up a bit. Thank heaven it's done, and just sent off. A real German play now! What next?

The parents of the Sitwells have a castle about 14 miles away. We went to see them: queer couple. Thursday I am lunching with the world's champion fencer.[3] How's that?

If we come to England, I expect we shall take a little flat Chelsea way for a month – then I shall go to my sisters for a week, probably to the seaside. – We shall see you – and we must make a little trip somewhere, like the memorable trip to the Lakes.[4] Aspettiamo! Shall we go down to Murry's Dorset together? – and see his second baby, son and heir, another John Middleton, ye Gods!

It seems I don't know anybody in London any more.

Remember me to Sonia and Ghita and Grisha.

tante cose! DHL

(note the address can be shortened).

[1] Secker had written to Kot, 14 June 1926, following up a statement of English sales of Shestov, *All Things Are Possible* – 105 copies on subscription ('settled April 27, 1920') and 80 copies since: presumably £2. 16 represented royalties on the latter. In USA the book had been remaindered; Secker wrote to the Robert MacBride Co., New York, 'asking them to account in detail for the disposal of their edition up to the date of remaindering' (Secker Letter-Book, UIll). See Letters 3942, 3947.

[2] Presumably an allusion to the *New Age*, edited by Orage until 1922 (see p. 457 n. 1) and from July 1923 by Arthur Benson (under whom it became the organ of the 'New Age Social Credit Society').

[3] Giorgio Chiavacci, the European champion at individual foil in 1926 (whether there was a world championship is a matter of dispute).

[4] See Letter 3565 and n. 1.

3742. To Willard Johnson, [July? 1926]
Text: MS YU; Unpublished.

[Villa Mirenda, Scandicci, Florence]
[July? 1926]

Dear Spud

Will you please send to

Curtis Brown Esq, 6 Henrietta St, Covent Garden, *London W.C. 2* half-a-dozen copies of my smiling gee-gee.[1] He is very much interested, and will use it for trade purposes.

Saluti! DHL

3743. To Earl Brewster, 2 July 1926
Text: MS UT; Brewster 100–2.

Villa Mirenda. *Scandicci*. Florence.
2 July 1926

Dear Earl

Your letter of 9th June today. I was wondering why you never answered my letters. I have written you three: and have received three – or four, counting the one today and the one from Port Said.

I am glad you are at Almora, among the mountains. – The feeling of India as bleak, rather ugly and dry-earth-treeless, has been gaining on me for some time. Yet it would, I think, interest me, because, as you say, of the life. I feel the spirituality of it has a curious physicality which must be a bit repellant, yet interesting too: a spirituality which is essentially physical.

We are still at this villa: I told you we'd taken the top half of it, six good big rooms, for a year – for Lire 3000. But we plan to leave for BadenBaden on July 12th – and to spend the month of August in England, then in September come back here. I like Tuscany, and especially here, it is charming.

Whether we shall stay all the winter is another matter. The isles of greece attract me very much: and one might go to Syra for a few months. I'm sure we should enjoy it. But do you imagine we should want to live there all our lives?[2] – Of course, one has to *try* first. One can't *fix* oneself on to an unknown spot. – And of course, one really hasn't enough money to keep on moving, and moving again. We would have to be wary. – How does one live, on Syra? – in hotel, or are there houses to be had? And one goes from Athens? – I should like to *see* Greece.

[1] The Lawrence issue of *Laughing Horse* (see p. 472 n. 1): hence the speculative dating of this letter. See also Letter 3745.

[2] The Brewsters explained this reference to Syra: 'On our way to India we heard the merits of Syra sung so enchantingly by one of the former residents of that Greek isle, that we decided to spend the rest of our days there if not in India . . . When we went there on our return from the East we found a rather treeless island devoted to market-gardening where our sojourn lasted only four days' (Brewster 99).

There is the question of the ranch – Brett is there now, and says she is very happy, with Rachel Hawk and the two babies. We shall have to settle something about that ranch. Perhaps we shall have to go out there next April or so. But it's terribly far, and expensive, and I am not drawn any more to America, even to New Mexico. It is difficult to say what one will do. – But probably for this winter we shall be here, or come to Syra, which after all is not so terribly far.

I am not seeing many people in Florence: just those I have known before. I don't want to go to the villas. Sometimes I think it would be good to take a *permanent* place, a little more remote than this, perhaps in the Appenines. You remember that villa you spoke of, north of Rome? But a place not too large or expensive, so that one felt free to travel a bit. For that reason, this place is good. While we sit still, we can save a few pounds. But we don't sit still long enough. – A place near Perugia might be good: somewhere unspoilt; and not too remote. We are getting to the age when we shall really have to think of establishing ourselves some little spot on the face of the earth. We can *try* Syra. But I am afraid of small islands.

Well, this is just to say *Saluti*! to you all. Write and tell me all the news. I have been wondering very much, lately, why nothing came from you.

a rivederci D. H. Lawrence

3744. To Mabel Dodge Luhan, 3 July 1926
Text: MS Brill; Luhan 304–7.

Villa Mirenda. Scandicci. Florence.
3 July 1926

Dear Mabel

I am sending back the MS. of the 'Villa' now. It seems to me all right as it is: a wee bit absurd, but expressive of the phase you want to describe. As for its lacking the human quality, it's aboundingly full of Mabel – which is all that is intended, for this time. It is a perfectly coherent part of the Memoirs.

I can see you don't want to publish the thing in English: and I think, all things considered, you are right. I wrote to Frieda's sister about getting it done in German. She did the *Boy in the Bush*, and did it splendidly. She replied that she would like to see the MS. very much, and would probably like to do the translation. – The difficulty is, with a book which has not yet appeared in English, the publisher would be willing to pay only very small translation rights – equivalent at most to \$200 – probably only \$100 – and it really is not worth while. You see you would, I presume, make a royalty contract with the publisher, as if the book were an original German work. You would have to make some arrangement with Else: either pay her a sum down for the translation, and keep all the rights and royalties for yourself: or else share the royalty rights with her; if she feels she can do it. You would have carefully to alter all the names before you sent the MS. to Germany, because of course many Americans read German: and you would have to take a nom de plume. Else knows the publishers and the publishing world pretty well, she no doubt would get the thing placed. Her husband used to edit a fat political-economy quarterly.[1] But think it over, then write to her yourself:

Frau Dr. Else Jaffe, Bismarkstrasse 17, *Heidelberg*, Germany.

We leave here in ten days time, for BadenBaden. I shall see Else and talk the matter over with her.

I don't think I want to go and see Gourdjieff. You don't imagine how little interest I have in those modes of salvation – or modes of anything. But later on, you go yourself to Fontainebleau for a while: it would do you good, even if you went away again deciding it was not for you. It would give you something to accept or reject.

I'm glad you met Brett and you got on well together. It's quite true, one should by now be old enough to take no notice of things said – specially things repeated – and we surely surely needn't get into 'states' any more.

The postman has this minute handed me the new batch of MS. I will read it at once. – Of course this vol. isn't so wildly interesting, but it's just as much an integral part of the memoirs, and just as necessary as the first two parts. – If you want to send it to Germany, don't send this Vol II yet awhile. Send only as far as where you leave Buffalo, after Parmenter. Better never offer too much at a time, to anybody. – You may take it as a fair test, that what didn't bore you to write, won't bore the reader to read. –

Best address me

c/o Curtis Brown. 6 Henrietta St. London. W.C. 2

– I expect we shall be in England for August.

Am glad you like Taos: it *is* very lovely there, with the fine pure air. I continue to like Tuscany: the cicalas are rattling away in the sun, the bells of all the little churches are ringing midday, the big white oxen are walking slowly home from under the olives. There is something eternal about it: apart, of course, from villas and furniture and antichità[2] and aesthetics. But we see few people, and live rough, which is what I prefer.

Frieda calls me for dinner. Remember me to everybody.

DHL[3]

[1] DHL was most likely thinking of *Archiv für Sozialwissenschaft und Sozialpolitik*, ed. Edgar Jaffe with Max Weber and Werner Sombart from 1904. (For two years, 1916–18, Jaffe was also co-editor with Heinrich von Frauendorfer of *Europäische Staats-und Wirtschafts-Zeitung*.)

[2] 'antiquity'.

[3] The remainder of the text is taken from Luhan 306–7; it is presumed that a portion of the MS became detached and was lost.

[I have read the new MS. and return it also.

The part about Edwin is excellent, and gives one a sense of true experience. The part about Bindo isn't so good.[1] You are never so good, apparently, when you are doing a relationship with one who is *not* an American. It was the same with Marcelle.[2] The hammer doesn't ring on the iron, quite. I don't know why that is. Even the Eyres the same.[3] – But it is just as well it is so, because that conveys the sense irrevocably that you *are* an American, and foreigners *don't* really come into immediate contact with you. It gives value to the Memoirs.

I wouldn't linger too much, I think, over occasional people in Florence. – But don't listen to me even there. – Do only that which *really interests you*, with a bit of burning interest. And anything that does burn in you, do it without reflection.

The part about Edwin is very good indeed. – But what about his feeling to *you*, as time goes on, in the Curonia? Do you give that?

DHL]

3745. To Nancy Pearn, [3 July 1926]

Text: MS UT; PC v. Firenze: Gruppo in terra cotta di Minerva e Dia da Orvieto. Sec. III av. C.; Postmark, Scand[icci] 4. 7. 26; Unpublished.

Villa Mirenda.
3 July.

I did send that *laughing Horse* for you – but I've ordered six more copies direct to Curtis Brown, and I'll write in one of those for you. – If any more are needed, then

Willard Johnson, *Taos*. New Mexico

will send all you want.

Yrs D. H. Lawrence

Have found two last copies.

3746. To Baroness Anna von Richthofen, [5 July 1926]

Text: MS UCB; Frieda Lawrence 264–5.

Villa Mirenda. *Scandicci*. Florence.
Montag.

Meine liebe Schwiegermutter

Ich freue mich, dass du einen so schönen Ausflug nach Herrenalp hattest.

[1] The Marchese Bindo Peruzzi de Medici, homosexual son of an American mother and a close friend of Mabel Luhan.

[2] Marcelle Senard, a friend of Mabel at the time of her marriage to Edwin Dodge.

[3] Charles and Eva Eyre, English friends in Florence. Eyre was Mabel's bank manager; Mabel and Edwin Dodge lived in the Eyres' house, the Villa Pazzi, while they searched for a house of their own.

Kommst du gern wieder nach Haus, oder möchst du lieber länger oben bleiben.

Wir kommen dann am 13n. Wir fahren nächsten Montag, 12 Juli, bis Mailand, und am Dienstag, 13n, von Mailand nach Baden-Baden; kommen erst am 6 uhr 48 abends an. Das ist aber nicht so spät! Kannst du uns ein Zimmer, oder vielleicht zwei Zimmer, in irgend einer Villa oder in einem Hotel finden? – dass wir essen können wo wir wollen. Und dann, nach einem Paar Tagen, können wir mit dir wieder nach Herrenalp gehen: oder wir können in Baden bleiben, oder in der Nähe, wie es dir gefällt. – Wir haben versprochen den ganzen Monat August in England zu sein. Aber das lasst uns zwanzig Tage in Deutschland, ungefähr. Es wird schön sein.

Ich habe immer sehr gern Baden und den Schwarzwald, und fühle mich immer wohl dort. Es wird herrlich Sommer sein, die Kirschen und Erdbeeren noch nicht fertig. Wir können im Waldkaffee essen, und Thee trinken, und die Frau Stötzer in ihrem Holzhäusle besuchen, und Ausflüge machen. Ja, es wird schön sein. Die Frieda kommt auch gern, wirklich. Betrübe dich nicht.

Hier ist es prachtvoll: so warm und still. Die Früchte sind schon hier: Feigen, Pfirrsich, Aprikosen, Pflaumen – alle grosse und schöne, da es so viel geregnet hat. Die Aprikosen sind wunderbar, beinah so gross wie Pfirrsiche. Und die erste kleine Birnen sind so süss, und hell-gelb. Ja, es ist voll Sommer.

Meinen Schwestern schreiben sehr betrübt, wegen den Streik: es hat kein Ende, und die beide verlieren viel Geld. – Man soll sein Leben aus Geld nicht machen. Verschwindet das Geld, ist das Leben kaput. Mit oder ohne Geld, habe ich mein Leben für mich, und sind nicht beschwindelt.

Der Friedel schrieb ganz nett, aus Berlin. Ich glaube er hat beinah genug vom Kapitalstadt, und wird gleich heimkehren. Die Else soll mir schreiben, wie es ihr das Theaterstück gefällt. – Man übersetzt schon *The Plumed Serpent* auf Schwedisch: ich bekomme aber nur 600 m.

Ich schicke dir ein wenig Geld, für deinen Geburtstag, dass du auch einkaufen kannst was du willst. Wir bringen nicht Geschenke, sie sind so langweilig.

Dann, Schwiegermutter, auf baldigen Wiedersehen.

DHL

[My dear Schwiegermutter

I'm glad that you had such a nice trip to Herrenalp.[1] Are you glad to come home again, or do you like staying up there longer.

We'll come then on the 13th. Next Monday, 12 July, we go as far as Milan,

[1] Herrenalb (pronounced with a final 'p') is a small health resort 10 miles e. of Baden-Baden.

and on Tuesday, 13th, from Milan to Baden-Baden; only get in at 6.48 in the evening. But that isn't so late! Can you find us a room, or perhaps two rooms, in some villa or in a hotel? – so we can eat where we want. And then, after a couple of days, we can go again to Herrenalp with you: or we can stay in Baden, or in the neighbourhood, as you like. – We've promised to be in England the whole of August. But that leaves us twenty days in Germany, roughly. It will be nice.

I'm always very fond of Baden and the Black Forest, and always feel well there. It will be glorious summer, the cherries and strawberries won't be over yet. We can eat at the Coffee house in the woods, and drink tea, and visit Mrs Stötzer in her little wooden house, and go on excursions. Yes, it will be beautiful. Frieda also loves coming, really. Don't be sad.

Here it's splendid: so warm and still. The fruit is here already: figs, peach, apricots, plums – all big and beautiful, since it's rained so much. The apricots are wonderful, almost as big as peaches. And the first little pears are so sweet, and pale-yellow. Yes, it's full summer.

My sisters write very sadly, because of the strike: there is no end to it, and both lose a lot of money. – One shouldn't make one's life out of money. If the money disappears, life is kaput. With or without money, I have my life for myself, and am not swindled.

Friedel wrote quite nicely, from Berlin. I think he's had about enough of the capital city, and will come straight back. Else ought to write to me how she likes the play. – They're already translating *The Plumed Serpent* into Swedish: but I only get 600 marks.[1]

I send you a little money, for your birthday, so you can buy what you like. We don't bring any presents, they're so boring.

So, Schwiegermutter, we'll see you soon.

DHL]

3747. To John Middleton Murry, [5 July 1926]

Text: MS NYPL; PC v. Firenze: Abesus etruscus ritratto funerario del Sec. III av. C.; Postmark, Scandicci 7. 7. 26; Unpublished.

[Villa Mirenda, Scandicci, Florence]

5 July

We leave here on the 12th for BadenBaden, stay there till the end of month, then spend August in England – all D. V. Am rather sorry to leave here – but hope it will be nice in the other places. Trust all goes well with you.

DHL

[1] The only recorded Swedish translation of a work by DHL in his lifetime was of *Sons and Lovers* by Gabriel Sanden (1925); *The Plumed Serpent*, trans. Artur Lundkvist, appeared in 1938.

3748. To Martin Secker, 5 July 1926

Text: MS UInd; Postmark, Scandicci 7. 7. 26; Huxley 662–3.

Villa Mirenda, *Scandicci*, Florence.
Monday 5 July 1926

Dear Secker

In the hot weather, the days slip by, and one does nothing, and loses count of time. I have never answered your letter about *Sea and Sardinia*. Every time I thought I'd said, it seems to me a good idea to do a 7/6 edition without pictures, and every time I forgot. But I hope you have gone ahead with it. – Do you think it's wise to start doing the other books as cheap as 3/6? – But we can talk about that when we come. –

In the real summer, I always lose interest in literature and publications. The cicalas rattle away all day in the trees, the girls sing, cutting the corn with the sickles, the sheaves of wheat lie all the afternoon like people dead asleep in the heat. E più non si frega.[1] – I don't work, except at an occasional scrap of an article. I don't feel much like doing a book, of any sort. Why do any more books? There are so many, and such a small demand for what there are. So why add to the burden, and waste one's vitality over it. Because it costs one a lot of blood. – Here we can live very modestly, and husband our resources. It is as good as earning money, to have very small expenses. Dunque –

and then we're silly enough to go away. We leave next Monday, the 12th. – for BadenBaden (c/o Frau von Richthofen, LudwigWilhelmstift) – and I expect we shall spend August in England. A friend is finding us a little flat in Chelsea. – So we shall see you and Rina – and I hope we'll have a pleasant time. – I want to be back here for September and vendemmia, because I like it best here. – The Tenente still writes occasionally from Porto Maurizio, where he is transferred: rather lachrymose and forlorn. And we had a postcard from your suocera.[2]

Reggie Turner came out the other day: he says he's doing that book. But I doubt if he'll ever finish it.

My sisters write extremely depressed about the strike. England seems crazy. Quos vult perdere Deus – ![3] Well, it's not my fault. – But building your life on money is worse than building your house on sand.[4]

Remember us both to Rina.

A rivederci D. H. Lawrence

[1] 'People don't care.' [2] 'mother-in-law'.

[3] James Duport, *Homeri Gnomologia* (1660): 'Those whom God would destroy [he first sends mad]'. Cf. *Letters*, iii. 48 and n. 1. [4] Cf. Matthew vii. 26.

3749. To Hon. Dorothy Brett, 7 July 1926
Text: MS UCin; Postmark, Firen[ze] 8[. . .]; Huxley 664–5.

Villa Mirenda. *Scandicci.* Firenze
7 July 1926

Dear Brett

Your letter today, saying the hay is cut. That will be wonderful, having a haystack, and being able to throw down the bunches of hay to the horses in winter, as I have often done at Del Monte. I feel Kiowa is gradually growing into a real self-respecting ranch again. – Friedel – he is in Berlin – sent us a photograph of the wagon with horses and Indians: very nice: gave one a wish to be back, too. – For some things, I wish I was really there. I would love to see the flowers, and ride up the raspberry canyon, and go along the ditch with a shovel. Then something else, I can't find out what it is, but it is something at the pit of my stomach, holds me away, at least for the moment. It is something connected with America itself, the whole America. – Yet of course I feel the tree in front of the house is my tree. And even the little aspens by the gate, I feel I have to keep my eye on them.

But I'm awfully sorry you have so much work to do. It would be really better to have Trinidad or somebody. – And be sure and tell me how much you spend for *labour*, for the ditch and the hay and those things. And I'll send the money along.

Here it is full summer: hot, quiet, the cicalas sing all day long like so many little sewing-machines in the leafy trees. The peasant girls and men are all cutting the wheat, with sickles, among the olive trees, and binding it into small, long sheaves. In some places they have already made the wheat stacks, and I hear the thresher away at a big farm. Fruit is in: big apricots, great big figs that they call fiori, peaches, plums, the first sweet little pears. But the grapes are green and hard yet. – It seems there is a great deal of fruit.

We have met various people: nobody thrilling, but some quite nice. Lord Berners came out to tea.[1] Do you know him? He was Tyrwitt, or something like that. He asked us to stay with him in Rome in October, and be motored round to the Etruscan places. We might try a day or two. He was very nice: and apparently rich, too rich: RollsRoycey.

We leave here next Monday – the 12th. I am sorry to go, except that the heat is a bit soaked in thunder, and heavy, and I think a little time rather high up in the Black Forest would be fresh and nice. How I should love to breathe the air at the ranch, and to taste the well water! What a pity there is such a strange

[1] Gerald Tyrwhitt-Wilson, 14th Baron Berners (1883–1950). He was a musical composer, novelist and talented landscape painter. An honorary attaché in the British Embassy in Rome, 1911–19, he owned a house overlooking the Forum (3 Foro Romano).

psychical gulf between America and Europe! One has to undergo a metamorphosis, and one can't always bear it. – We are due to spend August in England, then in early Sept come back here. I shall be glad to be back. – I haven't done any of my hill-towns yet. I must do them in the autumn. I was so busy with bits of things. – Secker and Knopf want me to write another novel, but I'm not going to lay myself waste again in such a hurry. Let the public read the old novels. – The Knopfs are in Europe, but don't suppose we shall see them. He says: 'it becomes harder and harder to sell good books.' Then let him sell bad ones. – The way for us to do is to live economically, so we don't need much money – that's how we live here: £300. a year would do me. Then one is independent of them.

How are your headaches? I hope the heat doesn't give you them. Occasionally I get one, an odd stunner.

Remember me to Rachel – also to Betty and Bobby. Is Bobby bad at all, or just a threat? I'm sorry she's not well.

My sisters in England are very depressed about the coal strike: no business doing, more ruin ahead. What a misery!

They've translated *Plumed Serpent* into Swedish. Hope it'll bite 'em. – How much butter do you get from the cow? – does she run and hide as Susan did. Eggs are abundant here: seven Liras a dozen: which is about 26 cents. – How are you for money? let me know. – I like the seal to your letter. Where did you find the bird? – Does Aaron still have a runny eye? – and Azul a jaw? – the poor creatures! – Is Prince a mild lamb with you?

DHL

3750. To Achsah Brewster, [8 July 1926]

Text: MS UT; PC v. Firenze – Panorama dal giardino di Boboli; Postmark, Ferrovia 8[. . .]26; Brewster 102.

Florence.
8 July

Down in Florence for a day – and it suddenly rains – hope it does so in India. We leave in four days for BadenBaden. Do hope you're all well.

DHL

3751. To Ada Clarke, [8 July 1926]

Text: MS Clarke; PC v. Firenze – Piazza Signoria; Postmark, [. . .]; Unpublished.

[Florence]
Thursday

We are leaving on Monday for BadenBaden – expect to be in London August 1st. – will write from Germany.

DHL

3752. To Margaret King, [8 July 1926]

Text: MS Needham; PC v. Firenze – Piazza Signoria; Postmark, Firenze [. . .] 7. 26; Unpublished.

[Florence]
Thursday

We leave on Monday for Baden – Did you get my letter? – have not heard from any of you for so long – shall see you in August.

DHL

3753. To William Siebenhaar, 9 July 1926

Text: TMSC NWU; PC; Unpublished.

[Villa Mirenda, Scandicci, Florence]
9 July 1926.

We leave here on the 12th. for Baden Baden and London. I had a letter from Curtis Brown's office – they can't find your essay – are now looking through Knopf's office – it probably went there with the MS. of *Max*. I'm sorry it doesn't turn up. You might send C.B. your address, in case it does. I suppose we shall be back here in Sept.

Best wishes D. H. Lawrence

3754. To Catherine Carswell, 10 July 1926

Text: MS YU; Unpublished.

Villa Mirenda, *Scandicci*, Florence
10 July 1926

My dear Catherine

I don't quite know where to address you – but will send this to the Villa Proust. – We are leaving here on Monday – in two day's time – for BadenBaden – per Adr. Frau von Richthofen. Ludwig-Wilhelmstift – where I expect we shall stay till 1st August – then to London, as I think we shall stay August in England – and back here in Sept. – Let me know if you are within reach, and if the boy is better. It's unhealthy sort of weather, anyhow. – I had your post-card, but no addresses. – Perhaps in London I could see your story and speak to somebody about your work. How is it going, anyhow? – We shall probably rent a little flat in London – Chelsea – as a base. I hope we shall see you.

DHL

3755. To Nancy Pearn, [10 July 1926]

Text: MS UT; PC v. Firenze – Via Cerretani; Postmark, Firenze 10 . VII 1926; Unpublished.

[Villa Mirenda, Scandicci, Florence]
Sat

We leave here Monday

c/o Frau von Richthofen, Ludwig Wilhelmstift, *BadenBaden.*

Would you mind telling the other depts. – They can keep the ordinary mail till I arrive, Aug 1st. – I send you MS of a story today.[1]

D. H. Lawrence

3756. To Emily King, [15 July 1926]

Text: MS Needham; PC v. Baden-Baden – Reiherbrunnen; Postmark, Baden-Baden 15 7. 26; Unpublished.

Baden.
Thursday

Hot sunny weather here – the country looking very nice. Yesterday was F[rieda]'s mother's 75th birthday – quite a feast. – I had your letter just before we left.

DHL

3757. To Hon. Dorothy Brett, [15 July 1926]

Text: MS UCin; PC v. [Chalet among trees]; Postmark, [. . .] 15 7. 26; Irvine, Brett 69.

BadenBaden.
15 July

Hot and sunny here – hotter than Italy – very leafy and nice, the Black Forest: had a busy day, yesterday: all the family here, celebrating F[rieda]'s mother's 75th birthday. Tell Rachel – thanks for her letter. – I expect we stay here till the 30th. – then England.

Grüsse. DHL

3758. To Harold Mason, [16 July 1926]

Text: MS Baker; PC v. Dorf und Ruine Ebersteinburg bei Baden-Baden; Postmark, Baden [-Baden] 16[. . .]; *Centaur* 28.

BadenBaden.
16 July

We are on the move again – stay here till Aug 1st, then to England. You, I suppose, are also summering somewhere. I was so sorry the *Porc*[*upine*] didn't

[1] Cf. Letter 3740 and p. 482 n. 4.

come home with his sack of dollars for you: perhaps if we'd cut him off without a 'Crown'! – It is funny thundery weather – how is U.S.A? Greetings to both.

D. H. Lawrence

c/o Curtis Brown, London is the best address.

3759. To Vere Collins, 16 July 1926

Text: MS UT; Unpublished.

c/o Frau von Richthofen, Ludwig-Wilhelmstift, Baden Baden
16 July 1926

Dear Collins

I got your letter today only. – I shall be very glad to leave to you the ungrateful task of revising the proofs of the Irish *Movements*, if you will be so good as to undertake it.[1]

We expect to be in London in August, when I hope to see you.

Yours D. H. Lawrence

3760. To Edward McDonald, 16 July 1926

Text: MS UT; Moore 926–7.

BadenBaden.
16 July 1926

Dear McDonald

I had your letter in Italy, a week or so ago: had often wondered why you hadn't written, but guessed you had your own reasons: or unreasons, as it seems.

So you have bought a house, and you roll the lawn, while your wife waters it with brine!! – it is what the ancients did, when they rased the strongholds of the enemy: strewed 'em with salt and watered them with bitter brine:[2] oh psychoanalysis, cast an eye on Mrs McDonald! what is she about? – So you have bought a house! It is the capitulation a man has to make sooner or later. The tortoise makes his hundred paces, then takes firmly to his shell. – Myself, I am still laboring over clod and furrow, but who knows how soon I shall 'buy a house' – that is, rent one and furnish it, not having £. s. d. to buy it. One does get dead sick of struggling ahead among the brick-bats and tin cans of our most modern world. The second half of one's life – I am forty – should surely be one's own, after one has more or less given away the first half, for a pound of imitation tea.

We came up from Italy three days ago, to celebrate my mother-in-law's

[1] See Letter 3543. [2] Cf. Judges ix. 45.

seventy fifth birthday. 'Wir alten, wir sind noch hier!' she says.[1] And here they mean to stay, having, through long and uninterrupted experience, become adepts at hanging on to their own lives, and letting anybody else who is fool enough cast bread upon the waters.[2] BadenBaden is a sort of Holbein *Totentanz*:[3] old, old people tottering their cautious dance of triumph: 'wir sind noch hier: hupf! hupf! hupf!'

In Italy, we moved away from the Riviera, which I never care for, to Tuscany, and have a top half of a villa about nine miles outside Florence, in the country – but one can go in to Florence by tram. I took the place for a year – for £25. – so it is rough. But I prefer it so. If ever you want to come to Italy, just descend on us, and we shall be delighted. We can give you a room, large enough, but without a single 'convenience' – à l'américaine – so that you will know you are abroad. – Florence, though overrun with tourists and irritable to a degree with fascism, is still one of the most intimate towns in the world. – We stay here about ten days longer, then go to England for the month of August. In Sept. we want to go back to Tuscany: – Villa Mirenda. *Scandicci*, Florence. But address me, if you write before Sept: c/o Curtis Brown. 6 Henrietta St. London W. C. 2.

Heaven knows how we shall find England. Italy, as I say, is *nervosa*, irritable, in a state of nerves and tension rather trying. Fascism is not natural to them. – Germany is fat and foody, a bit torpid at the moment, but seems to have force underneath: if it will ever rouse itself: – as for my own, my native land,[4] I always dread it a bit.

Of literary news, I have none. I wanted to write a book on the Etruscans and Etruscan cities – sort of half travel book. But I get such a distaste for committing myself any further into 'solid print,' I am holding off. Let the public read what there is to read.

When we were coming up the hill, home, in the half-dark last night, a young man, swinging downhill towards us, said as he came: 'Ihr kommt bald nach Egypte': – you'll soon come to Egypt. – Who he was and what he meant, we shall never know. But he swung past with a bright smile and a guten abend. – So if you hear we are in Egypt, you'll know we met a prophet. – Remember us kindly to Mrs MacDonald – and roll on, roll on, at the lawn!

D. H. Lawrence

[1] 'We old, we are still here!' [2] Cf. Ecclesiastes xi.1.

[3] Hans Holbein (1477–1543) produced the woodcuts for a very popular *Dance of Death* published in Lyon, 1538.

[4] Cf. Sir Walter Scott, *The Lay of the Last Minstrel* (1805), VI. i. 3.

3761. To Rolf Gardiner, 17 July 1926

Text: MS Lazarus; Huxley 666.

c/o Frau von Richthofen, Ludwig Wilhelmstift, *BadenBaden*
17 July 1926

Dear Gardiner

I was glad to get the circular letter and to realise that your *Youth* efforts had not gone entirely to the wall. I am very much inclined to agree that one must look for real guts and self-responsibility[1] to the Northern peoples. After a winter in Italy – and a while in France – I am a bit bored by the Latins, there is a sort of inner helplessness and lack of courage in them: so willing to go on deceiving themselves: with the only alternative of emigrating to America.

I expect to be in England for the month of August, perhaps we can arrange a meeting. And I can hear all about this new grouping. Let me know where you will be.

And don't be too ernest – earnest – how does one spell it? – nor overburdened by a mission: neither too self-willed. One must be simple and direct, and a bit free from oneself above all.

Hoping to see you then.

D. H. Lawrence

3762. To Willard Johnson, [19 July 1926]

Text: MS YU; PC v. 'Uhrmacher'; Postmark, B[ad]en[-]Baden 19 7 [. . .]; Unpublished.

BadenBaden
[19 July 1926]

Hot here – and mosquitoes in the forest. How is Taos? Did you have my letter and enclosure? – I heard from Mabel in Albuquerque – do hope Tony is better. Have you been up to the ranch yet? do go! – We leave for London on the 30th, F[rieda] will stay in town with her children, I shall probably go to Scotland. Write me a line.

DHL

3763. To Rina Secker, [19 July 1926]

Text: MS UInd; PC v. 'Elz- und Glottertal'; Postmark, Baden-Baden [. . .]9 7 26; Secker 41.

c/o Frau von Richthofen. LudwigWilhelmstift. BadenBaden
[19 July 1926]

Is it the same hot weather in England? – I suppose so: hotter here than

[1] MS reads 'self-responsibity'.

Tuscany. But I like it. How are you all? – We stay here till end of the month – then hope to see you.

DHL

3764. To Catherine Carswell, [19 July 1926]

Text: MS YU; cited in Moore, *Intelligent Heart* 356.

c/o Frau von Richthofen, Ludwig-Wilhelmstift, *Baden Baden*
Monday

My dear Catherine

Bad luck! By this same post comes the letter fixing up the little Chelsea flat, which a friend found, and I accepted. It costs £4. a week – yet I don't like, now everything is settled, to break off with no sufficient cause: and Frieda wants to be near her son in the S. Kensington Museum.[1] – I, at any rate, shall be most of the time away from London.

I don't know the dates of the play, nor anything about it, and feel a bit tepid.[2] God knows what these private societies are like! We have said we would be back in Italy first week in Sept. – but the Lord knows!

Here it is very hot, with constant threat of thunder which doesn't come. But I like it. I am rather fond of Baden and the woods.

I am relieved that the boy is better. Have you fixed for his autumn term? As for literature and publishing, I loathe the thought of it all, and wish I could afford never to appear in print again. Anyhow I am doing nothing at all now, and have no idea of beginning again. – I rather dread the thought of England. My sisters, of course, feel ruin in the near distance. So do I! – Germany seems very quiet.

We'll see you somewhere.

DHL

3765. To Nancy Pearn, [19 July 1926]

Text: MS UT; PC v. Sonntagnachmittag; Postmark, Baden-Baden 19 7 26; Unpublished.

c/o Frau v. Richthofen. Ludwig-Wilhelmstift, BadenBaden.
[19 July 1926]

As for that story and the £10. – I am cold about it.[3] It doesn't seem to me very worth while, but you decide. Are they nice people, anyhow? – It is very hot here, but the woods are cool. I always like the Black Forest. – We've taken a little flat in Chelsea for August – hope to see you there. Did you get the 'Islands' story?[4]

D. H. Lawrence

[1] Montague Weekley was an Assistant Keeper in the Victoria and Albert Museum from 1924.
[2] See p. 470 n. 1. [3] See Letter 3740. [4] See Letter 3740 and p. 482 n. 4.

3766. To Emily King, 21 July 1926

Text: MS Lazarus; Unpublished.

c/o Frau von Richthofen, Ludwig Wilhelmstift, BadenBaden
Wed. 21 July 1926

My dear Pamela

We have been here a week already – the time goes so quickly. Till yesterday, the weather was very hot – then we had a storm and torrents of rain, and today is grey. I suppose it is the same everywhere. The Rhine valley is a good deal flooded, and they are moaning for the corn. It's a crazy year.

Frieda's mother is very well – she seems to get younger rather than older – she was 75 a week ago. The old ladies here seem to live for ever. But it is a very soft and peaceful place. It always suits me very well, especially when I drink the water – I mean the hot water that rushes out of the earth. – On the whole, Germany is more agreeable than Italy just now, more friendly too. Italy is in such a state of nervous tension, with her fascism, it reacts on everything.

We have taken a flat in Chelsea for the month of August, so we expect to arrive in London on July 30th. I have an invitation to the north of Scotland, from friends who have a house there.[1] If I can afford it, I think I shall go. But this travelling is too expensive for me. Only I have no desire at all to be in London all August. Frieda stays in order to see her son, who is at the South Kensington Museum. But that is not my affair. – They want us to go to Bavaria on our way back to Italy, and stay there the month of September. We may do that.

I am afraid England will be rather depressed and depressing, owing to the coal strike. It really is very serious, and one wonders what the end will be. I am always thinking about you and Ada,[2] and your businesses, in the miserable affair. Really, nobody seems to have any imagination any more, nor any force.

They want me to go to Scotland in the first half of August. I might stop off at Nottingham on my way up, and at Derby on my way back – and so to Mablethorpe. But we must arrange it all when I am in London.

Anyhow I am glad Peg's got a job.

Love to you all DHL

I enclose £5. for the holiday, for the children.

[1] See Letter 3733 and p. 474 n. 1.

[2] The first eight words of this sentence are enclosed in brackets; it is not certain that the brackets were DHL's.

3767. To Arthur Wilkinson, [21 July 1926]

Text: MS Schlaefle; PCs v. Gutshof im Kammbachtal and Baden-Baden; cited in Sagar, Wilkinsons 65.

BadenBaden.[1]
Wed.

Dear Wilkinson

Thanks for your letter, and for forwarding the mail. I do hope it's not a nuisance: why does one get so much mail? – I had the two copies of the *Dial*[2] – hope they weren't sent parcel post, that's such a bore. But the Americans have no internal book post, so they send everything parcel – and a curse it is. Have a look at the book you have now, and tell me what it is. Probably I don't even want it. I enclose Liras for any possible extra stamps, and many apologies for troubling you. – We had a week of hot hot[3] weather, but yesterday heavy rain. For the time being, I like it better here than Italy, it seems more peaceful, not such a nervous tension. The forest here is very dense, this year the foliage is so thick and the little clearings are so bright green. It is country one can really walk in. On the whole, I think you'd find it no more expensive than Italy, if ever you wanted to come – and very friendly. – The relatives are pressing us to go to Bavaria for Sept, on the way back – instead of going straight to Italy. I am not sure, we might do so. – There are comparatively few visitors here, the hotels almost empty. Nobody seems to be spending any money – except ourselves. – We have taken a flat in Chelsea for the month of August – but I have promised to go to Scotland. I don't like London. – We often think of you at the Poggi – and 'our' Mirenda. – I hope you do your 'daily dozen' strictly, with Queenie and Tuppeny. (how awful!) regards to Mrs Wilkinson.

D. H. Lawrence

3768. To Giuseppe Orioli, [21 July 1926]

Text: MS NWU; PC v. 'Im Herbst'; Postmark, Baden-Baden 21 7. 26; Unpublished.

c/o Frau v. Richthofen. Ludwig-Wilhelmstift. *Baden-Baden*
[21 July 1926]

Germany is rather nice – not so nervoso as Italy, restful – and very green and leafy. The forest here is so still, it might be a thousand years ago. We stay till the 29th – then to London. I'll send you a line from there. – I have promised to go to Scotland – shall not be far from Elgin – shall I really go and see the C-C. Is it 'The College?'[4] Might be fun! We had very hot weather, but now it rains

[1] DHL used two postcards as notecards.

[2] See Letter 3667 and p. 416 n. 2.

[3] MS reads 'week hot hot'.

[4] Elgin Cathedral had an exceptionally large number of canonries; the canons' residences, disposed round the Cathedral precinct and surrounded by a wall, were collectively known as the 'College of Canons' or 'the College'.

again. I do nothing but have tea-parties with old baronesses and Excellencies and by-gone grandeurs – pity I'm not Reggie, under the circumstances.

DHL

3769. To S. S. Koteliansky, [22 July 1926]

Text: MS BL; PC v. Dorf und Ruine Ebersteinburg bei Baden-Baden; Postmark, Baden-Baden 22.7.26; Zytaruk 290.

BadenBaden
[22 July 1926]

Germany rather nice and peaceful – but a bit rainy again, after the heat. – We expect to arrive in London on the 30th., and go to a little flat:[1] 25 Rossetti Garden Mansions, Flood St. Chelsea, S.W.3 – So shall see you soon.

DHL

3770. To Rolf Gardiner, [22 July 1926]

Text: MS Lazarus; Huxley 666–7.

c/o Frau von Richthofen, Ludwig Wilhelmstift, *BadenBaden*
Thursday

Dear Rolf Gardiner

Your letter today: as usual, like a bluster in the weather. I am holding my hat on.

But do let us meet. We arrive in London on July 30th – and go to a little flat 25 Rossetti Garden Mansions. Flood St. Chelsea, S.W.3. We shall use it as a pied à terre. Myself, I have promised to spend some time with my sisters on the Lincs. coast – and to go to Scotland – various things.

I believe we are mutually a bit scared, I of weird movements, and you of me, I don't know why. But if you are in London even for a couple of days after the 30th, do come and see us, and we can talk a little, nervously. No, I shall ask you questions like a doctor of a patient he knows nothing about.

But I should like to come to Yorkshire, I should like even to try to dance a sword-dance with iron-stone miners above Whitby.[2] I should love to be connected with something, some few people, in something. As far as anything *matters*, I have always been very much alone, and regretted it. But I can't belong to clubs, or societies, or freemasons, or any other damn thing. So if

[1] In Letter 3732 DHL asked Millicent Beveridge if he could rent her flat; from Letters 3774 and 3775 it appears, however, that she could not oblige and arranged an alternative.

[2] This was a topic on which Gardiner and DHL exchanged views at their first meeting: 'we discussed magic dances, and I told Lawrence about the Morris and the sword dances of the Yorkshire miners, and he described the dances of the Mexican Indians' (Nehls, iii. 83).

there is, with you, an activity I *can* belong to, I shall thank my stars. But, of course, I shall be wary beyond words, of committing myself.

Everything needs a beginning, though – and I shall be very glad to abandon my rather meaningless isolation, and join in with some few other men, if I can. If only, in the dirty solution of this world, some new little crystal will begin to form.

Yrs D. H. Lawrence

3771. To Achsah Brewster, [22 July 1926]

Text: MS UT; PC v. Bei Hinterzarten; Postmark, Baden-Baden 22. 7.26; Brewster 102.

BadenBaden
[22 July 1926]

Very green and leafy and quiet here – I am wondering how you are – You'd like this Black Forest country. – We leave for London on the 29th – shall look for word from you there. F[rieda] sends many greetings, with mine.

DHL

3772. To Arthur Wilkinson, [28 July 1926]

Text: MS Schlaefle; Unpublished.

BadenBaden.
28 Juli

Lieber Wilkinson

I will send you the house address in London, in case any further mail arrives:

25 Rossetti Garden Mansions, *Chelsea, S. W. 3.*

We have taken that flat till August 28.

I hope you got my twenty Liras, in the last letter, to pay for the tips to the postman etc. I should have thought of it before.

We leave tomorrow evening, via Strassburg Brussels Ostende – and arrive London Friday. It takes only about 20 hrs. from here.

The weather is a mixture – a very lovely day – the next torrents and thunder – the next half fine, half wet – and so on. The woods steam. But still I like it. There are Concerts and Marionette Theatre in the Kurhaus – good orchestra three times a day. I drink the hot water, first: good for my miserable bronchi. – They want me to come back for three weeks in Sept. and take the inhalation cure: my sister-in-law wants us to go to Bavaria. Chi lo sa! I often think of S.

Polo, and wonder how you are: not too hot, I'll bet. I find Germany rather soothing, really, everybody very nice. – We shall find a line from you in London, I hope.

Viele Grüsse D. H. Lawrence

I do hope people will stop writing to S. Polo, to me, so you needn't be bothered any more.

DHL

3773. To Hon. Dorothy Brett, 29 July 1926
Text: MS UCin; Postmark, Baden-Baden [. . .]; Huxley 667–8.

BadenBaden.
29 July 1926

Dear Brett

Simply pouring with rain![1] The Rhine Valley all in floods. We leave tonight, via Strassburg, Brussels, Ostend, for London: through the night. It makes one shiver.

Your letters come rolling in – we are always quite thrilled by your descriptions of the ranch and life. How lovely the flowers must be! – there are strawberries, but you dont mention raspberries: here there are many in the woods. – Today came Rachel's letter to Frieda: she says rain and cold by you also. What one needs is an ark. I am going to begin making a collection of pairs of animals, seriously, it's awful! – and what will England be like? – I shan't see Murry – he is too much – or too little – for me. – Think I shall see the Sitwells, and Rolf Gardiner – do you remember how he wrote two years ago to the ranch? – As for the play, I know absolutely nothing of it so far – and have very few hopes.

We have a little flat

25 Rossetti Garden Mansions, Chelsea, S.W. 3

till August 28th. After that I don't know. The doctor wants me to come here for 20 days in Sept. and take the inhalation cure. You know the hot water comes gushing out of the earth – much hotter than Rio Grande springs – and one breathes the steam. I drink the waters, and they suit me: I may as well make an attack on those bronchials of mine before the winter comes – though they are much better. My sister-in-law wanted us to go to Bavaria – nr. Munich – for Sept. – I should have liked it so much. We must wait and see.

[1] 'Mercury' (*Phoenix* 35–9), which contains a vivid description of a thunder-storm, was written about this time (Roberts C152).

I shall not be very much in London, as I've promised to spend some time with my sisters on the Lincs. coast – also go to Scotland.

I am not doing any work at all: feel sufficiently disgusted with myself for having done so much and undermined my health, with so little return. Pity one has to write at all.

There is no news: nothing lately from India. Hope you're not living at ruinous expense there on the ranch: Indians aren't cheap. – I shall expect you to tell me in your next how much you have spent on ditching and haying etc – and I'll send a cheque. – Am so glad Azul's jaw is better – but Aaron's eye? – Did you see 'Glad Ghosts' in the *Dial*? – amusing. 'Smile!' – that little sketch of the dead wife – came in the English *Nation*. – In the *Adelphi*, the Life of Christ is relegated to the back pages,[1] and our little friend is discovering he is a pantheist: without a Pan, however: fryingpantheist!

A dwindling of money all round! and it rains, rains! – I left the typewriter in Italy. If I go to Scotland, shall I call on your father?

DHL

3774. To S. S. Koteliansky, [30 July 1926]

Text: MS BL; Postmark, Chelsea 30 JUL 1926; Zytaruk 290.

25 Rossetti Garden Mansions, Flood St. Chelsea, S.W. 3
Friday

Dear Kot

Got in this evening – very tired – found your note.

We shall expect you to tea tomorrow about 4.0: it's the very top floor, Mrs Stanley Fay's[2] flat. Hope you'll find it.

Wiedersehen DHL

3775. To Rolf Gardiner, [30 July 1926]

Text: MS Lazarus; Unpublished.

25 Rossetti Garden Mansions, Flood St. Chelsea, S. W. 3
Friday night

Dear Gardiner

Do come in here to lunch on Tuesday, if you can, about 12.30. It's the top floor, Mrs Stanley Fay's flat: quite easy. But poky!

So we shall expect you.

D. H. Lawrence

[1] See Letter 3605 and p. 383 n. 2.

[2] Unidentified.

3776. To Nancy Pearn, [31 July 1926]
Text: MS UT; Unpublished.

25 Rossetti Garden Mansions, Chelsea, S. W. 3.
Sat. 31 July

Dear Miss Pearn,

We got in here last night – have this little flat for a month, but I shall be going away next Thursday or Friday. Would you care to come in to tea before then – if you can? But perhaps you are away. Let me know – and we can fix something.

Would you give this address downstairs, so they can send me my letters here, please.

I'll come in to the office when there's a hope of finding anybody.

Yours D. H. Lawrence

3777. To Nancy Pearn, [4 August 1926]
Text: MS UT; Unpublished.

25 Rossetti Garden Mansions, Flood St. S.W.3
Wed.

Dear Miss Pearn

We shall be pleased to see you to tea tomorrow. Of course I got a cold – so shan't go north till the week-end. – You get off the bus on the Kings Rd at Chelsea Town hall, and walk back two blocks to Flood St. – and these 'Mansions' are at the bottom of the street.

Yes, I am quite content to let the *Coterie* people have 'Sun', now I needn't sign anything.[1]

Till tomorrow, then D. H. Lawrence

3778. To S. S. Koteliansky, [8 August 1926]
Text: MS BL; Postmark, Chelsea 8 AUG 1926; Zytaruk 291.

25 Rossetti Garden Mansions, Chelsea, S.W. 3.
Sunday.

My dear Kot

We have got back here today. The Aldingtons were very nice.[2] – I am leaving for Scotland tomorrow morning, Monday, at 9.50: so in the evening I should be in Edinburgh.

I forgot to tell you to take the *Early Greek Philosophies*.[3] If you would care for it, then tell Frieda, and come and fetch it.

[1] See p. 352 n. 1 and Letter 3740.
[2] The Lawrences visited them at Malthouse Cottage, Padworth (Nehls, iii. 84–7).
[3] John Burnet, *Early Greek Philosophy* (1892). Cf. *Letters*, ii. 364 n. 4.

My address is:
c/o Miss M. Beveridge, 'Bailabhadan', *Newtownmore* (Inverness), NB.
I hope Sonia came home safely, and is feeling well; and that I can see her when I come back.

I will write from Scotland.

au revoir DHL

3779. To Rachel Hawk, 8 August 1926

Text: MS UT; Unpublished.

25 Rossetti Garden Mansions. Chelsea. *London, S. W. 3*
8 August 1926

Dear Rachel

I had your letter and the tax notice – enclose the ten dollars. Tell me how much I owe you on the other things you mention, and I will send it.

We have been in London a week: it is quiet, not unpleasant, but I don't really care for it. Tomorrow I am going to Scotland – Inverness-shire – but Frieda is staying here till August 28th. I don't quite know how long we shall stay in England. The Stage Society are not beginning to rehearse *David* till the end of this month – and the productions will not be probably till November. I cant stay as long as that in England – but I must see the first rehearsals, when I get back from Scotland.

The weather isn't bad, for England, though not at all hot. The town is comparatively empty, nothing much doing. We went down to the country for the week-end, to stay with friends: the same small, green fields with big hedges, and slow canals with white water-lilies and yellow, and a kingfisher darting: the same old England, but as if it were asleep, or not alive. I am afraid I should never want to live in my native land again.

We are always glad to hear news of the ranch, and of everybody. How glad you will be to see William: I wonder so much if he likes the work, and being in the forest service. – I'm very glad that you and Brett get on together. I know it's not the easiest thing in life. But don't you take any notice of her calling the children brats, and so on. She only does it just to tease you. She likes them really – writes quite nicely about them, always. Perhaps it's a touch of the spinster in her, coming out sometimes. You have to take that into account.

I haven't yet been to see my sisters. They have taken a house by the sea for a month, and seem to enjoy it. I shall stop off as I return from Scotland, and stay a while with them at the seaside.

You must have had streams of visitors: the Gilletts and everybody: and the Crichtons. I think they're rather nice people, the Crichtons. Remember me to them when you see them.

The bells are ringing for Sunday evening service. I've got unused to the sound of peals of bells, makes me uneasy.

How is Ruffina? – a trial, I'll bet.

Hope Walton's cough is better – mine is fairly well. And remember me to Bobbie, I hope her chest is about all right.

Frieda says she'll write – perhaps one day she will.

So remember me to everybody.

DHL

3780. To Martin Secker, 8 August 1926

Text: MSC Lazarus; Secker 75.

25 Rossetti Garden Mansions. S.W.3[1]
8 Aug. 1926

Dear Secker

I am leaving in the morning on the 9.50 for Edinburgh. The address in Scotland is

c/o Miss M. Beveridge, Bailabhadan, Newtownmore. Inverness.

We went down to see Richard Aldington and his wife. They are very nice. I wish you would send her a copy of *Kangaroo*, and of *St. Mawr*, and of the *Serpent*.

All good wishes D. H. Lawrence

3781. To Baroness Anna von Richthofen, [11 August 1926]

Text: MS UCB; PC v. Inverness-shire; Postmark, [Invernes]s-shire 11[. . .]; Unpublished.

[Bailabhadan, Newtonmore, Inverness-shire]
11 Aug.

Ich bin seit gestern hier in Nord Schottland – schön, die Luft so frisch, und die Glockenblumen grad' wie im Schwarzwald: ich hab' es gern, viel lieber wie London. Ich glaube, die Frieda ist nicht glücklich, dort in London – es dauert aber nicht lang: und dann nimmermehr soll sie auf jenen Kindern warten – Deinen Brief an F. habe ich nicht lesen können. Wiedersehen

DHL

[I've been here in the North of Scotland since yesterday – beautiful, the air so fresh, and the harebells just like the Black Forest: I like it, much better than London. I believe Frieda isn't happy, there in London – but it won't be long:

[1] The text of this letter – as in the case of Letters 3894, 3899 and 3907 – is taken from a copy in the hand of Martin Secker.

and then she should never again wait around for those children – I've not been able to read your letter to F. Wiedersehen

DHL]

3782. To S. S. Koteliansky, [12 August 1926]

Text: MS BL; PC v. Newtonmore; Postmark, Newtonmo[re] 12 AU[. . .]6; Zytaruk 292.

[Bailabhadan, Newtonmore, Inverness-shire]

12 Aug.

Scotland is very nice, rather cold, and showers – but the shadows and lights on the low hills are queer and northern and alive. Of course there are motor-cars everywhere, which is a nuisance – and they are building new roads through the quiet valleys. – I hope Sonia is home, and feeling better.

au revoir. DHL

3783. To William Wilkinson, [12 August 1926]

Text: MS Schlaefle; PC v. On Loch-An-Ovie Near Newtonmore; Postmark, Newtonmore 12 AU[. . .]; Sagar, Wilkinsons 65.

Newtonmore. Inverness.

12 Aug.

Dear Pino –

Your card wandered on up here, where I'm staying another week or so. I was never in the Highlands before – find it rather attractive, though a bit cold and showery. Today grouse-shooting begins, but of course I'm not one to go banging at the birds. – The heather is just out – bell-heather dying – and the harebells are very lovely. The motor-cars spoil it all, though – they never cease passing, on these narrow little roads. We motor to the various lakes, and picnic, making fires with very damp wood. Which is my news. I am always glad to hear of you all. Ask your father to keep that *Harper's* for me![1]

tante cose! D. H. Lawrence

3784. To Rolf Gardiner, 14 August 1926

Text: MS Lazarus; Unpublished.

[Bailabhadan, Newtonmore, Inverness-shire.][2]

14 August 1926

Dear Gardiner

I came up here at the beginning of the week: find Scotland rather damp, and

[1] Probably a copy of *Harper's Bazaar* in which 'The Rocking-Horse Winner' first appeared (see p. 400 n. 1).

[2] DHL used headed paper for this and Letters 3785–6 and 3790.

somewhat obscured by tourists. I'm afraid it is *too* northern for me – one shrinks a little inside one's skin.

I've simply *got* to spend eight or nine days with my sisters in Mablethorpe, Lincs. – and I want to be back in London by the 26th – so it leaves me no time, I am afraid, to stop off in Yorkshire. I doubt if I could quite face a country house party, anyhow. We shall have to meet in some other place, some other time. – It's a case of *Schöpferische Pause* all round (by the way, thanks for the book, I'll send it back to you from here).[1] The only danger is lest the pause should be too long. It's a grey human twilight, for the time being.

I shall probably leave here next Wed. or Thursday: 18th or 19th. – and go straight down to Lincs. I suppose you wouldn't care to come down there? Probably anyhow it'll be horrid: and more family. Dio buono! Siamo tutti schiavi![2]

au revoir D. H. Lawrence

3785. To Hon. Dorothy Brett, 14 August 1926

Text: MS UCin; Postmark, [Newt]onmore [. . .] AU 26; cited in Huxley 668.

[Bailabhadan, Newtonmore, Inverness-shire.]
14 Aug. 1926

Dear Brett

So this is your Scotland. It is rather nice, but dampish and northern and one shrinks a trifle inside one's skin – For these countries, one should be amphibian. Grouse shooting began day before yesterday – an event for those that shoot, and a still bigger one for those that get shot. – The heather is out, the bell-heather dying. But the bluebells are best, they are very lovely, so big and tangled and blue. However, I have decided *not* to buy an estate in Scotland, etc etc.

Frieda sent on your letter, saying that you are again stumped for money. Your banking arrangements seem the most unsatisfactory. You know you can always get $200.00 by writing to Barmby – he'll give them you from my account. Meanwhile for goodness sake tell me about how much you've spent on my behalf. I'd send you the money now, but I left the cheque-book in London.

I suppose I shall be back in London about the 25th. Then I shall see if I can do anything about *David*. If I can, I shall have to stay a bit. If I can't, I shall depart to Baden for my cure. I want really to get my bronchials into form, before the winter comes.

[1] Fritz Klatt (1888–1945), *Die Schöpferische Pause* [*The Creative Pause*] (Jena, 1922), a work of educational theory. Cf. Letter 3825.

[2] 'Good God! We are all slaves!'

How I should dread a winter up here, so dark and dismal. And you, do you think you will stay on the ranch?

Remember me to Ida – I'm sorry she's so down. One has to bear up, and not give way to ones 'blood-pressures' any more than one can help.

Take care of the Ruffian[1] – she's a risky bit of goods. It's an awful pity you couldn't have had Joe and his wife – they are much more trustworthy – I mean the couple with two children, who were up last year.[2] But don't get into any sort of Indian tangle, over that Ruffian.

Tell Rachel I'll write to her. You seem altogether very social. I think it's better so: best not to be too isolated.

au revoir. DHL

3786. To Mabel Dodge Luhan, 14 August 1926

Text: MS Brill; Luhan 308–9.

[Bailabhadan, Newtonmore, Inverness-shire.]
14 August 1926

Dear Mabel

I am glad you are back in Taos. Poor Tony, I was thinking of him, sick there in Albuquerque. I think you mustn't take him so far from the Pueblo, really. I don't think he can stand it, it saps his vitality. Seems to me he ought not to do more than take little trips in the west.

As for publishing the *Memories*, I don't think it's wise, while your mother lives. Keep them safely locked away, and wait. And then one day publish them yourself.

I am up here in the north of Scotland for a couple of weeks. It is nice, but rather rainy. The heather is out on the moors: the so-called mountains are dumpy hills, rather sad and northern and forlorn: it is still daylight till about half-past nine in the evening. – But I wouldn't care to live up here. No!

We shall be in England for a week or two. The Stage Society is giving a couple of performances of the play *David* in Oct. or Novem. – I should like to see the first rehearsals, anyhow. But I don't want to stay long in England. I have said I will go back to BadenBaden and take an inhalation cure, in the Kurhaus, for my bronchials – for twenty days. Then towards the end of Sept., or in October, go back to Florence. That seems to be my programme for the moment.

The MSS. you sent are still in London – Frieda didn't forward them here. As soon as I get back, I shall read them and tell you my impression, and return

[1] I.e. Rufina Archuleta.

[2] Possibly Rufina's sister and her children (see Letter 3424).

them to you. I hear Spud has gone to New York. What will you do for a secretary?

I do hope Tony will be all right now. Remember me to Ida!

DHL

3787. To Arthur Wilkinson, [15 August 1926]

Text: MS Schlaefle; PC v. On the Calder, Newtonmore; Postmark, Newton[more] 1[. . .] AU 26; Pinto, *D. H. Lawrence after Thirty Years*, p. 43.

[Bailabhadan, Newtonmore, Inverness-shire]
15 Aug

I went to church this morning – the Church of Scotland. What do you think of that? We want to take a trip to the west, tomorrow – to the Isle of Skye: but of course, the weather is very Scottish and drizzly. Probably we shall go, in spite of all. – I would not like to live all my life in Scotland, but it's nice to see it. I sort of expect to meet Mrs Wilkinson coming striding off the moors, with a walking stick. It is rather obviously her country – only a bit too damp for human habitation. I expect to be in London about the 26th – afraid my wife will be getting bored. I hear Miss Morrison is in town. Best wishes to you all.

D. H. Lawrence

3788. To Hon. Dorothy Brett, [17 August 1926]

Text: MS UCin; PC v. The Storr Rock and Loch, near Portree, Skye; Postmark, [. . .]; Irvine, Brett 69.

Sligachan – Isle of Skye
[17 August 1926]

Came up here by steamer – a lovely day – and the west coast very lovely. Must say I like this island.

DHL

3789. To Ada Clarke, [17 August 1926]

Text: MS Clarke; PC v. In Glen Sligachan. Sgurr-nan-Gillean, Skye; Postmark, Sligachan 17 AU [. . .]6; Unpublished.

Slighachan. Isle of Skye
[17 August 1926]

very lovely here – we sailed up from Malaig, on the west coast – liked it very much. Hope to get to Newtonmore tomorrow evening.

DHL

3790. To Edward McDonald, 19 August 1926

Text: MS UT; Postmark, Newtonm[ore] 19 AU 26; *Centaur* 28.

[Bailabhadan, Newtonmore, Inverness-shire.]
19 August 1926

Dear McDonald

I have just got your letter – should like to see you very much – am going down to Mablethorpe, Lincolnshire, on Sunday, but expect to be in London, at least for two days, on the 26th. Send me a line to say where we might meet

at 'Ravenstone', George St. *Mablethorpe*, Lincolnshire.

au revoir D. H. Lawrence

3791. To Else Jaffe, 20 August 1926

Text: MS Jeffrey; Frieda Lawrence 226–7.

Bailabhadan, Newtonmore. Inverness.
20 August 1926

Dear Else

Frieda sent me on your letter from Irschenhausen. I am glad you like being there, but am surprised it is so cold. Here the weather is mild, mixed rainy and sunny. The heather is out on the moors: the day lasts till nine oclock: yet there is that dim, twilight feeling of the north. We made an excursion to the west, to Fort William and Mallaig, and sailed up from Mallaig to the Isle of Skye. I liked it very much. It rains and rains, and the white wet clouds blot over the mountains. But we had one perfect day, blue and iridescent, with the bare northern hills sloping green and sad and velvety to the silky blue sea. There is still something of an Odyssey up there, in among the islands and the silent lochs: like the twilight morning of the world, the herons fishing undisturbed by the water, and the sea running far in, for miles, between the wet, trickling hills, where the cottages are low and almost invisible, built into the earth. It is still out of the world, and like the very beginning of Europe: though of course, in August there are many tourists and motor-cars. But the country is almost uninhabited.

I am going south, tomorrow, to stay with my sisters in Lincolnshire for a little while, by the sea. Then really I should like to come to Bavaria, if only for a fortnight. I have a feeling, that I want to come again to Bavaria. I hope I shan't have to stay in England for that play. I would much rather come to Germany at the end of August. And Frieda, I know, has had enough, more than enough, of London. Perhaps after all we can come to Irschenhausen for the first part of September, and let that inhalation wait a while. – I am much better since I am here in Scotland: it suits me here: and probably the altitude of Irschenhausen would suit me too. Anyhow we could go back to Baden to do a bit of inhaling.

There is no hurry to get to Italy. – If only I need not stay in London for that play. – I find it most refreshing to get outside the made world, if only for a day – like to Skye. It restores the Old Adam in one. The made world is too deadening, and too dead.

So I am still hoping to see you all – Friedel will be there? – in Baiern, quite soon. Why should one be put off, from what one wants to do?

auf wiedersehen DHL

3792. To S. S. Koteliansky, [20 August 1926]

Text: MS BL; PC v. Sgurr-nan-Gillean and Lochan, from Carbost Road; Postmark, Newtonm[ore] 21 AU 26; Zytaruk 293.

Newtonmore.
Friday

I had your letter – so sorry Sonia has such a poor time. Frieda wrote she had seen you. – We had a trip to the West coast, and the Isle of Skye – very wet, but one lovely day: and I was very much impressed. It seemed so remote and uninhabited, so northern, and like the far-off old world, out there. One day I shall go again. – I hope to be in London at the end of next week, but will let you know. The address is 'Ravenstone', George St. Mablethorpe. Lincolnshire.

Remember me to all. DHL

3793. To Nancy Pearn, 20 August 1926

Text: MS UT; Unpublished.

Newtonmore. Inverness.
20 August 1926

Dear Miss Pearn

Here is the review of *The World of William Clissold*: probably too peppery for the unctuous *T.P.* – but really true.[1] Perhaps the *Nation* will have it, if *T.P.* doesnt: and in America too.

I am leaving here tomorrow: the address will be:

at 'Ravenstone', George St, *Mablethorpe*, Lincolnshire.

But I hope to be in London by the end of the month.

Hope you had a nice tea with my wife.[2]

Sincerely D. H. Lawrence

[1] DHL's review of H. G. Wells's *The World of William Clissold* (August 1926) appeared in *Calendar*, iii (October 1926), 254–7 (reprinted in *Phoenix* 346–50) (Roberts C146). It did not appear in *T. P.'s and Cassell's Weekly* or in *Nation* (New York).

[2] Frieda wanted to introduce Nancy Pearn to Rina Secker; they met on 19 August (Pearn to Frieda, 14 August 1926; TMSC UT).

I sent a pound to T. S. Eliot, just when the *Criterion* changed over to the *New Criterion*: and I asked them to send the two numbers with 'The Woman Who Rode Away',[1] and the subsequent two numbers, to my sister in law:

Frau Dr. Jaffe-Richthofen, Bismarkstr 17, *Heidelberg*, Germany.

I burned the cheque a fortnight ago, signed by Eliot and stamped with the *Criterion's* stamp. But if there is any muddle, it doesn't matter.

If *T.P.'s* should happen to like the review, then I will do others for them, if they wish. I rather like doing a serious review, for anybody, now and then. Seems to me there is need of a straightforward bit of criticism sometimes.

DHL

3794. To Hon. Dorothy Brett, 26 August 1926

Text: MS UCin; Postmark, [. . .]; Huxley 668–9.

Mablethorpe. Lincolnshire
26 Aug 1926

Dear Brett

I've been here a few days with my sisters, came on from Scotland. It's rather nice – quite common seaside place, not very big, with great sweeping sands that take the light, and little people that somehow seem lost in the light, and green sandhills. I'd paint it if I'd got paints, and could do it. I like it here, for a bit. Frieda is coming up for a fortnight or so; they don't begin rehearsing *David* till early September, I suppose I'll have to cast an eye on it, though I feel rather reluctant. Somehow I feel it will be a sham.

I wonder how you are getting on at the ranch, and if the money difficulties have settled themselves. I expect to hear in a day or two: and Frieda will bring me my little bag with cheque books etc. I don't know why, but everywhere seems so far off, from England. The ranch doesn't seem far from Italy. From here it seems like the Moon. Even Germany and Italy, here, seem as if they don't exist. But we shall go back to the Villa Mirenda some time in Sept., though probably towards the end.

England seems to suit my health – I feel very well here. But I don't write a line, and don't know when I shall begin again. I shall have to do something or other, soon.

Remember me to Rachel, and all the others. I do hope you're having a good time. It's rather cold here – but fine.

tante cose! DHL

1 See p. 71 n. 1. From January 1926 to January 1927 the magazine changed its title to *The New Criterion*; T. S. Eliot (1888–1965) was the editor. (The subsequent reference to the burning of the cheque alludes to the practice of a bank to return a cheque to the payer after it was signed by the payee and paid through the payer's account.)

3795. To Nancy Pearn, 26 August 1926
Text: MS UT; Unpublished.

'Duneville', Trusthorpe Road, *Sutton-on-Sea*, Lincolnshire
26 Aug 1926

Dear Miss Pearn

Thanks for your letter. This is just to send you our address for the next fortnight. My wife insists she wants to come to this coast again – It's rather nice, big sands and sky – so I have taken the little bungalow, and Mrs Lawrence comes tomorrow.

By now you'll have read my review: but read Wells' book, and see if it's not just.[1]

Yrs D. H. Lawrence

3796. To Else Jaffe, [26 August 1926]
Text: MS PM; Unpublished.

'Duneville', Trusthorpe Rd. *Sutton-on-Sea*, Lincolnshire.
26 August.

Dear Else

It is rather fine here at the seaside – big smooth sands that gleam when they are wet, and little people that seem gone in the gleam – and a hoarse sea. Frieda insists that we must see at least the beginnings of the play: and she insists also that she wants to come here for a time: so I have taken the bungalow 'Duneville' for two weeks – or perhaps a month. We shall have to see at the end of two weeks what we shall actually do. When will you leave Irschenhausen? – about the 28th September, or earlier?

Superficially everybody seems as careless and carefree and indifferent as only the English can be. But underneath, at least here in the Midlands, the coal strike is worrying them. I'm afraid it's a wound in the famous English unity, our dear Body Politic, this strike. It worries me too. I wish they'd come to a settlement. I am afraid of the class hatred which is the quiet volcano over which the English life is built. Above all things, it is dangerous, here in England: class hatred. Superficially one feels none at all – absolutely none. But there's something underneath. The English are not *really* apathetic: there's a power in them somewhere. But they seem absolutely indifferent. – I hope the translation goes well.[2] I'll write again.

DHL

[1] Cf. Letter 3793 and p. 513 n. 1.
[2] Presumably a reference to her translation of 'The Woman Who Rode Away' (cf. Letter 3793); see p. 288 n. 1.

3797. To Edward McDonald, [27 August 1926]

Text: MS UT; Postmark, [Ma]blethorp[e] [. . .] AU [. . .]; *Centaur* 28–9.

'Duneville', Trusthorpe Road, *Sutton-on-Sea*, Lincs.
27 Aug.

Dear McDonald

My wife has just arrived here – says she hasn't heard again from you.

We've taken this little bungalow by the sea, for a fortnight – we may stay a month. If you'd care to come up for a few days, just let me know: there is room. It's merely a flat sandy coast – but healthy, and I like it.

I shan't come to London now until they write to me that they are beginning the play. But when I *do* come, I shall let you know: if you are still here in England.

Yrs D. H. Lawrence

3798. To S. S. Koteliansky, [28 August 1926]

Text: MS BL; Postmark, [. . .]; Zytaruk 294.

Duneville, 'DUNEVILLE', Trusthorpe Rd. *Sutton-on-Sea*, Lincs.
28 Aug

My dear Kot

Frieda arrived last evening. I've taken this bungalow for two weeks – and for a month if we like it. The weather is lovely, and the sea very nice. I like this flat coast, it's where I first knew the sea.[1] – We're just moving now from Mablethorpe – Sutton is only two miles away – my sister departed yesterday. I'll write again.

DHL

P. S. – Do ask Gertler about a doctor to examine our friend Gertie, and about the sanatorium – how much it costs etc.[2]

I am so bored by the thought of all things literary – why not sell cigarettes!

DHL

3799. To Giuseppe Orioli, 29 August 1926

Text: MS UCLA; cited in Moore, *Intelligent Heart* 356.

'Duneville', Trusthorpe Rd, *Sutton-on-Sea*, Lincolnshire
29 Aug 1926

Dear Pino

Would you hate to do a little thing for me? Those leather boxes we bought (Frieda of course stuck to the coral brooch) were a great success, and I was so

[1] The Lawrence family spent a holiday at Mablethorpe in August 1906.

[2] Gertrude Cooper suffered from tuberculosis. In 1925 Gertler had himself been treated for it (see also Letter 3498 and n. 2).

rash as to promise two more to two envious ladies. You remember the long green box, that would hold about 100 cigarettes – I think it cost forty-five Liras: do you think you might get me two more, and send them for me? Do it some time when you're not busy. I wish you would send a blue one and a red one – or a brown – only not another green – to the two addresses:

Miss Mary Beveridge, 'Bailabhadan', *Newtonmore*, Inverness. Scotland

Miss Mabel Harrison, 49 Boulevard Montparnasse, Paris.

I enclose 150 Liras, and perhaps you will give your boy five Liras to do the posting for me. Don't be offended, will you, at my bothering you!

We are here by the seaside, in my native Midlands. It is rather nice, a big flat coast with a big sky above, and a low sea rumbling. I like it much better than London. We shall stay at least till September[1] 11th – two weeks, because I must go to London and see to the starting of my play *David*. They will give two performances, end of October. That will keep me in England. But I do hope to be back in Florence by the end of September.

I have no news of anybody: only Frieda saw Miss Morrison and Gino in London once or twice, while I was in Scotland. I think they are having a mildly pleasant time.

Remember me to Reggie – he'll be coming back to you soon, I suppose. Did you have a nice trip with your Doctor? – The weather here is sunny and fresh: I expect it's warm with you: on the cool side, here.

au revoir D. H. Lawrence

3800. To Earl Brewster, 29 August 1926

Text: MS UT; Brewster 103–4.

Sutton-on-Sea. Lincs.
29 Aug. 1926

Dear Earl

I have not heard from you for a long time, though I was glad to get Achsah's letter.

I came down to the seaside here to stay with my sisters, now Frieda has come, my sisters having returned to their homes. We shall stay at least two weeks longer, perhaps a month. I am waiting to hear from the people who are due to produce *David*: they will give two performances at the end of October, and are due to begin the study and rehearsing any time now. I want to make what suggestions I can, and see them start, before I leave England. – It is rather nice here on the Lincolnshire coast – flat country with big sweeps of sand, and a big sky, and a low sea. It was here I first knew the sea, on this coast.

[1] September] August

– I rather like being back in my own country, the Midlands. I don't care for London. But I feel my own regions give me something. And I liked Scotland.

I expect by the end of September we shall be going back to the Villa Mirenda, to Tuscany. The thought of the Isles of Greece appeals to me very much,[1] but I doubt if I could come till about Christmas time, or early January. Why don't you go first, and let us join you? I should like to come very much indeed, when the Tuscan winter begins to be dreary.

Write to me

c/o Curtis Brown. 6 Henrietta St, W.C. 2.

I hope you are enjoying these last months in India. Achsah says you want to do quite a lot of sightseeing before you leave: I expect it will really be quite thrilling.

a rivederci DHL

3801. To Arthur Wilkinson, 29 August 1926

Text: MS Schlaefle; cited in Sagar, Wilkinsons 66.

'Duneville', Trusthorpe Rd, *Sutton-on-Sea*, Lincs.
29 Aug 1926

Dear Wilkinson

We've taken this bungalow here by the sea, and may stay another month – but maybe not so long. I am detained by that play, which I must at least see started.

I like the Lincolnshire coast – knew it when I was a boy. It is so very bracing and tonicky – picks me up like a shot. There are not very many people – and the sands are so big, such a great sweep, and a big sky overhead, and a low sea growling in the wind. I think of you dipping in the pools of the stream behind San Polo. How much warmer it will be, than here. This is already on the cold side. But I can easily imagine you all sousing in this foam, too.

I gave a[2] letter of introduction for you to Richard Aldington and his wife. He is a poet, and critic on the *Times Lit. Sup.* – I told them, if ever they want to stay in our flat in the Mirenda, they are to apply to you and Mrs Wilkinson, and I know you'll do what you can for them.

I'm afraid we shan't be back for early September: but I do hope to be in San Polo again before that month is out. – I like England again though, especially up here in the Midlands. There's life in it – in spite of the coal strike: which last is looking pretty serious.

Greet Mrs Wilkinson from us – and Franceschina and Pino – and be greeted.

Yours D. H. Lawrence

[1] See Letter 3743 and n. 2.

[2] gave a] gave you a

3802. To Earl Brewster, 30 August 1926

Text: MS UT; Brewster 104–5.

Sutton-on-Sea. Lincs.
30 Aug. 1926

Dear Earl

Your letter of 3rd Aug reaches me today – after I'd posted mine to you this morning, to Almora.

I'm awfully sorry you and Achsah are so ill. It sounds to me as if you'd got malaria, though I hope you haven't. What altitude are you? – It may be mountain fever, owing to rarity.

I wish you were here – it is so blowy and blustery and sea-foamy and healthy, so very bracing. I like it. And I'm sad to think you won't see all those sights, Benares, Ajanta Caves etc. But perhaps you'll be feeling better, and try them. – Aldous Huxley came one evening: he too had simply hated India.[1] I wonder what it is. Is it a sort of *atavism* there, which one must resist.

I think you'll be all the better, though, for the experience. The best of Eastern thought is surely eternal: but one must maintain a more or less critical attitude. What irritated me in you in the past was a sort of way you had of looking on Buddhism as some sort of easy ether into which you could float away unresisted and unresisting. Believe me, no truth is like that. All truth – and real living is the only truth – has in it the elements of battle and repudiation. *Nothing is wholesale.* The problem of truth is: How can we most deeply *live*? – And the answer is different in every case. – And your Buddhism was, in a measure (I don't want to be wholesale either) – a form of side-tracking.

Believe me, you'll be happier, because you'll be truer to your own inner man, after this experience. You've got to get out of the vast lotus-pool of Buddhism on to the little firm island of your own single destiny. Your island can have its own little lotus pool, its own pink lotus. But *you yourself* must never try again to lose yourself in the universal lotus pool: the mud is too awful.

I shall be glad to hear you are safely on the way to Europe. I can promise, almost faithfully, to join you in Syra some time in the winter, if you go there. That is, I want to very much indeed. I am pining to see Athens and Greece.

Curiously, I like England again, now I am up in my own regions. It braces me up: and there seems a queer, odd sort of potentiality in the people,

[1] Aldous Huxley (1894–1963), novelist and essayist, first met DHL at Garsington in November 1915; within a month their correspondence had begun (see *Letters*, ii. 452 n. 2, 467–8). Huxley and his wife Maria, née Nys (1898–1955) became close friends of the Lawrences in the 1920s.
The Huxleys completed a ten-month round-the-world tour in July 1926 (see his travel diary, *Jesting Pilate*, published in October 1926); they spent four months in India.

especially the common people. One feels in them some odd, unaccustomed sort of plasm twinkling and nascent. They are not finished. And they have a funny sort of purity and gentleness, and at the same time, unbreakableness, that attracts one.

My best wishes to you and Achsah: and in hopes of a happy meeting soon.

DHL

write me c/o Curtis Brown, 6 Henrietta St. W. C. 2.

3803. To Edward McDonald, 31 August 1926

Text: MS UT; Postmark, Sutton-on-Sea 1 SP 26; Moore 934.

'Duneville', Trusthorpe Rd, *Sutton-on Sea.* Lincs
31 August[1] 1926

Dear McDonald

I'm sorry you can't come to Lincolnshire, for that means I shan't see you: which is a pity, for we might have had a few interesting hours. I sympathise, though, with your not wanting railway journeys: one does hate them.

It is very quiet here – and today, a wet day, with a dank sea and a dank wind: nobody bathing. Queer and forlorn this country is, this shore, as if still expecting the vikings and sea-roving Danes who came in such quantities.

I hope you won't have too bad an impression of England. I agree, that bad English cooking is the worst in the world: and that goes a long way to[2] depress anybody.

I haven't heard a word yet, about *David's* being *en train*. If I should have to run up to London at the week-end, I shall let you know. You say you don't sail till the 4th Sept.

I'm not going to give much of myself to that play, anyhow: am sceptical of it. Don't you give much of yourself, either, not to anything. It's mere waste.

Well, I suppose we shall meet somewhere, and somewhen: and let's hope we'll be feeling cheerful. Remember me very warmly to Mrs McDonald.

D. H. Lawrence

3804. To Nancy Pearn, 31 August 1926

Text: MS UT; Unpublished.

'Duneville', Trusthorpe Rd, *Sutton-on-Sea*, Lincs.
31 August 1926

Dear Miss Pearn

Show Harraps any little essays of mine that you have – if you wish. There is

[1] August] Sept. [2] MS reads 'long to'.

'The Nightingale' and those others I sent for *Vogue*.[1] – There is also this one, which I did in Baden and forgot.[2] I might manage another couple here, if the spirit will move.

Did you show 'Glad Ghosts' to Benn?[3] I should think the second half will have appeared by now in *The Dial*.

Suddenly a violent thunder here – and rain. It has been nice weather. I like this coast – so flat and fresh and open. And the bathing is very surfy and good. That's what my wife likes. – She wants to be remembered to you.

Yrs D. H. Lawrence

3805. To S. S. Koteliansky, [2 September 1926]

Text: MS BL; Postmark, Sutton-on-Sea 2 SP 26; cited in Gransden 30.

'Duneville', Trusthorpe Rd. Sutton on Sea. Lincs.
2 Sept.

My dear Kot

Many thanks for the booklet and letter. I am sending both on to my sister – I want to get Gertie away as soon as possible to some cure, she's delayed too long. I suppose I shall have to go over next week to see to the business – and probably take her to London – or direct to Mundesley.[4]

Frieda has asked her two daughters down here – whether they'll come or not, I don't know – I rather hope they wont.

I like being here. We've had now two dull days, with some rain, but I'm hoping it will brighten up today. I really rather like being back in my native Midlands. This is the first place – or Mablethorpe is – where we ever came for a holiday, to stay. It's all just flat sands – but very fresh and bracing – And the people are common, but alive. For the first time for years, I am rather glad to be at home in England. Though if the grey weather continues, I shall have to move off after the sun.

I haven't heard a word from the Whitworth people about the play.[5] When I

1 See Letter 3740 and p. 482 n. 3.

2 Probably 'Mercury' published in *Atlantic Monthly*, cxxxix (February 1927), 197–200, and in *Nation and Athenæum* (February 1927) (Roberts C152).

3 Almost exactly a year before (TMSC UT, 26 August 1925), Nancy Pearn had told DHL: 'Following the unexpectedly big success of their Augustan Books of English Poetry, published at sixpence, Messrs. Benn Ltd., propose to issue a similar series of short stories which have not previously appeared in any form in this country.' DHL was invited to contribute to the series. Further correspondence about it may have ensued; in what has survived this is DHL's first clear reference to it. See Letter 3807 and n. 3.

4 See Letters 3798 and 3498 and n. 2.

5 Geoffrey Whitworth (1883–1951), critic and dramatist. He founded the British Drama League, 1919; became drama critic of the *Christian Science Monitor*, 1923. m. 1910, Phyllis Bell (1884–1964). She founded the 'Three Hundred Club' in 1924 and agreed to its amalgamation with the Stage Society in 1926.

do I'll let you know: when I come to town. I must find some cheaper hotel to stay at, Garlands is too dear. But I'll let you know.

How is Gertler, by the way? I should like to see him when I come to London.

Frieda sends her Grüsse.

DHL

I wish you would address this letter to Mrs Whitworth –[1] hope I've spelled her right (I'm an ass – you don't know the address – she's the woman who is producing the play).

3806. To Martin Secker, 2 September 1926

Text: MS UInd; Postmark, Sutton-On[-Sea] 2 [. . .]; Secker 75–6.

'Duneville', Trusthorpe Rd. *Sutton on Sea.* Lincs
2 Sept. 1926

Dear Secker

Here we are in this little bungalow, one field away from the sea and sandhills. We've had two dull days now – otherwise it's been very nice. I like Lincolnshire myself very much – so flat, with a big sky, and sweeps of sands, and a low sea always making a noise. But of course it's where I first knew the sea, so I feel at home. It even makes me quite like being in England for a bit, being here. The Midlands are still much more alive than London. – But I expect you'd hate it.

I haven't heard yet from Mrs Whitworth about the play – thought I should have had some word by now. How long are they going to be, before they get a move on?

Tell Rina, Frieda says Mrs McElligotts maiden name was Selma Clifton, and she was then Mrs Bell.[2] Imagine that she has three little girls alive! Whatever will St. Peter say to her? I wouldn't be in her shoes, at heaven's gate.

We've got this place till Saturday week, but we can stay on till the end of Sept. if we like. I doubt if we shall, though.

I feel, if ever I were going to do an English novel, I'd have to come to England to do it. Perhaps this neighbourhood. But not now.

Have you got any books worth reading in the office. If you have, do send us a couple, for the lending library in the post-office seems to move between the narrow limits of Elinor Mordaunt and Stephen McKenna.[3] Very dull.

I'll let you know whenever I come to town.

Greetings to everybody. D. H. Lawrence

[1] For the reason given, DHL sent the letter to Secker (Letter 3806), instead of to Kot.

[2] Unidentified.

[3] Both were prolific novelists: Elinor Mordaunt (Evelyn May Mordaunt) (1877–1942) was fascinated by ships and the sea; Stephen McKenna (1888–1967) – best known for *Sonia* (1917) – took his material from London political and social life.

I wish you'd address this letter to Mrs Whitworth – hope I've spelled her right.[1]

3807. To Michael Joseph, 4 September 1926

Text: MS UT; Unpublished.

'Duneville', Trusthorpe Rd. Sutton-on-Sea, Lincs
4 Sept 1926

Dear Mr Joseph[2]

I have your letter about Ernest Benn Ltd and 'Glad Ghosts' – There would not be much money in the thing, from my point of view – but probably it would be good for publicity. And I don't think Secker would mind. The only thing I do object to, and there I object strongly, is signing five-hundred copies for a 6/- edition. I don't like these little books with authors autographs and prices beyond their real value. Five hundred of them I never would sign: I doubt if I'd sign five.[3] So with many thanks to you for the trouble you've taken, I think we'd better leave it at that. This autographing business puts me off completely.

Yours Sincerely D. H. Lawrence

I've never seen a specimen of this series. Why isn't it a straightforward shilling go, and no more!

3808. To Martin Secker, [5 September 1926]

Text: MS UInd; Postmark, Su[tton on Sea] [. . .]; Secker 76.

'Duneville.' Trusthorpe Rd, Sutton on Sea. Lincs.
Sunday

Dear Secker

Many thanks for *Polyglots* – don't you remember you lent it me last autumn, and I read it – when I met Gerhardi.[4] However, I'll send it back.

Curtis Browns ask me if I want to let Ernest Benn publish in his 1/- series that story 'Glad Ghosts' which has now appeared in the *Dial*. You didn't care for the story, so I suppose you don't mind. – But I doubt if I shall agree myself,

[1] This letter is missing.

[2] Michael Joseph (1897–1958), a director and later General Manager of Curtis Brown Ltd, 1926–35; in 1935 he founded his own publishing house, specialising in fiction and general books (Victor Gollancz was a co-director, Bertrand Russell and C. S. Forester were among his authors). Author of *The Commercial Side of Literature*, 1925. (See his obituary, *The Times*, 17 and 21 March 1958.)

[3] Ernest Benn published *Glad Ghosts*, November 1926; it was No. 2 in the 'Yellow Books' series (Roberts A36). 500 copies were printed in the limited first edn at 6/-; none was signed. An ordinary edn was published at 1/-.

[4] They met on 23 October 1925: see Letter 3516 and n. 2. DHL gave *The Polyglots* a 'jolly sort of approval' (Nehls, iii. 10).

as Benns want to include a 6/- edition of 500 autographed copies – and I'll see everybody in Hell before I autograph 500 – or 50 – copies.

And still I haven't heard a word from those Whitworth people about *David*.

A bit damp here today – and very quiet – wish it had kept like yesterday. I still like Lincs, this coast: but not too much damp. Frieda bathes – I'm still scared of my bronchials.

tanti saluti D. H. Lawrence

3809. To S. S. Koteliansky, [6 September 1926]

Text: MS BL; Postmark, Sutton-on-Sea 6 SP 26; Moore 934–5.

'Duneville', Trusthorpe Rd. Sutton on Sea. Lincs.
Monday

My dear Kot

Dull weather – rain and a low grey sky – not much fun here. I think we'll leave in a week's time. I wish you'd ask Gertler if he knows any place in Hampstead where we could have a couple of rooms, and eat in or eat out, doesn't matter which. I don't want to be down in town: and Frieda hated Chelsea. Or even your St. Johns Wood? – We'd then stay at least a week, and longer if it were necessary for the play – of which, so far, I've heard nothing. – It's being produced by the Stage Society and 300 combined – a Mrs Geoffrey Whitworth bossing the show, and Robert Aiken, who produced Shakspere at the Old Vic, producing it.[1] But how long do they think I'm going to wait in England for them? – I like it here all right, when it's fine – but in the rain and mist it's no good, and gives me another cold.

Apparently F's daughters aren't coming – that is, they've not written. Before I come to London I must go to Ripley. My sister thinks we might get Gertie examined *first* at Nottingham, and x-rayed there – and then proceed to other doctors if necessary. I think maybe she's right. I'll have to go at the week-end and talk it all over.

I'm writing also to Miss Morrison – who is at 1. Elm Row, Hampstead – to ask her if her people – in her house – know of rooms for a week or fortnight for us. I'll ask her to drop Gertler a line to Penn Studio, Rudal Cresc – is that right? – if she has wind of anything.

So I trust we shall see you next week. You will be no more a solitary.

au revoir. DHL

Frieda suddenly says that Miss Morrison will probably be away, and her house shut. If so, then let it be so!

[1] Robert Atkins (1886–1972), actor and stage director, was expected to produce *David* (May 1927), but see p. 470 n. 1. Atkins had produced Shakespeare with the Old Vic Company several times, most recently in June 1924.

3810. To Nelly Morrison, [6 September 1926]

Text: TMSC NWU; Moore 935.

'Duneville', Trusthorpe Rd., Sutton-on-Sea, Lincs.
August 1926.

Dear Nelly Morrison,

Here we are by the sea-sea-sea, and it's very nice, the big flat coast, when it doesn't rain. But when the sky hangs low and grey and damp and decomposing under it, it's the limit.

So we think we'll come to London. I shall have to be there a while for that play. I wish you would ask your host, (Jim Ede)[1] if he knows of rooms in Hampstead, or a decent little place where they would take in visitors, and where Frieda and I could go for a week or a fortnight. I don't want to be down in town any more. I wish we could get two rooms in Hampstead, it's healthier there, with meals or without, I don't care. We think of coming down to London this day week, the 13th., Monday. Or Frieda may come alone. I may have to stay a couple of days still with my sister.

I wrote and asked Mark Gertler also about rooms:[2] he is at Penn Studio, Rudall Crescent, Hampstead, a little way down the hill: he's a painter. I hope he's in town. But if you should be able to send me news of any definite place, would you hate to send him a line too?

I should like to see you and Gino in London, before we all go back to Italy again. I do hope you are rested. The grey skies make my thoughts turn to Florence, and[3] San Polo Mosciano. How do you feel about it?

Frieda suddenly says you may be away, and your host too. Well, heres the chance. Don't you *bother* about this, anyhow.

A riverderci, D. H. Lawrence

3811. To Ada Clarke, [6 September 1926]

Text: MS Clarke; Unpublished.

'Duneville', Trusthorpe Rd, Sutton on Sea. Lincs
Monday

My dear Sister

I have been thinking about Gertie. If she doesn't seem to you so very bad, then why drag her to London. Let us first have her thoroughly examined in Nottingham. I don't know the chest specialists there – I know Dr. Robinson is a good man.[4] But find out who would be best, and write him at once and ask for an appointment, in order to have Gertie thoroughly overhauled. Tell him her

[1] Unidentified. [2] The letter is missing. [3] TMSC reads 'and and'.

[4] Dr George E. J. Antoine Robinson (b. c. 1873); he was a surgeon rather than a 'chest specialist'.

case – ask for an examination as soon as possible, and tell him you would like an X-ray photograph. Be sure to tell him that. When we see how the thing is, if it has started, and how far it's gone, we shall know much better where we are. Ask him too if he would suggest an analysis of the sputum. But get an x ray photograph, and *don't tell Gertie* – let her imagine she is only being x-ray looked at. Then if the photograph is bad, you need never show it her. And if it isn't at all bad, which I don't believe it will be – then it will reassure her more than anything.

I think I will come over at the week-end – probably Saturday evening – and not return here: give this house up. If I have to be in London for that play – I've heard nothing yet, damn them – then this is too far and too expensive. We'd just take a place in Hampstead for a week or so – and if the play doesn't hurry up, then leave and go to Italy. It's bad weather here, and not much fun when one can't go out. – Frieda wants to stay here till Monday – today week – so I may do that too, if we can: then she can go to London and I come to Ripley.

Let me know about G. –

love. DHL

3812. To Else Jaffe, 7 September 1926

Text: MS Jeffrey; Frieda Lawrence 228.

Duneville. Trusthorpe Rd, Sutton on Sea. Lincs
7 Sept. 1926

My dear Else

I had your letter today. I'm very disappointed not to be able to come to Irschenhausen. Those fools are still delaying beginning the play. We go to London on Saturday – I'm not sure of the address – and I shall see what I can do. But I'm annoyed and bored beforehand.

But I doubt if we could get to Bavaria before the end of the month – Too late! I shall have to wait till spring, and go straight to Irschenhausen from Italy, if I may.

I expect we shall be in Baden, at least a day or two – travel over Paris. So we shall see you. I do hope you are feeling better. What makes you so knocked up?

It's dull weather here – a grey sky, a grey sea. My thoughts are turning south. The swifts are already going, and the swallows are gathering to go. Nothing to stay for.

auf wiedersehen DHL

3813. To Emily King, [7 September 1926]

Text: MS Needham; PC v. Studies at the Zoo. A Great Kangaroo with her Baby; Postmark, Sutton-on-Sea 7 SP 26; Unpublished.

['Duneville', Trusthorpe Rd, Sutton-on-Sea, Lincolnshire]
Tuesday

Had your letter this morning. I think we shall leave here for good on Saturday, or possibly Monday – and I shall come over to Ripley, via Nottingham, for a couple of days, Frieda will go straight to London. It's grey weather, heavy – not much fun any more. I'll let you know definitely.

love. DHL

3814. To William Siebenhaar, 7 September 1926

Text: TMSC NWU; Unpublished.

'Duneville', Trusthorpe Rd., Sutton-on-Sea, Lincs.
7 Sept. 1926.

Dear Siebenhaar,

I had your letter this morning – glad you had the proofs of *Max*. If you have gone through the proof of my 'introduction', don't bother to send it me, as I'm sure it will be all right.

I was in Scotland – then here awhile with my sisters. I think I shall leave Saturday – go for a few days to the Midlands – and be in London in about a week's time – about the 15th. that is. Do you know of a decent little hotel in London, not very dear? I always seem to land myself in for excessive expense.

No, I didn't see about Frank Harris. What have they done to him?[1]

How amazing to find Multatuli's widow. I hope to see you in London and hear about her.

Regards from me and my wife. I shall tell my sister, at the week-end, that I've heard from you.

Yours sincerely D. H. Lawrence

3815. To S. S. Koteliansky, [8 September 1926]

Text: MS BL; PC v. This is how I feel; Postmark, Sutton-on-Sea 8 SP 26; Zytaruk 298.

['Duneville', Trusthorpe Rd. Sutton-on-Sea, Lincolnshire]
Wed

Got your letter this evening in town – no time to go home. Frieda at least will

[1] The French government were believed to be preparing to prosecute Harris for corrupting public morals (cf. Letter 3824).

arrive Monday, and we shall be very glad of the rooms. You didn't give the address. But say we will take the rooms from Monday.

Send me the address. I shall go to Ripley for two days.

Many thanks for all your trouble.

DHL

3816. To Martin Secker, 8 September 1926

Text: MS UInd; Secker 77.

'Duneville.' Trusthorpe Rd, Sutton on Sea. Lincs
8 Sept 1926

Dear Secker

Many thanks for the books! Quite a noble parcel! May I keep the ones you publish yourself? The other two I'll return to you, anyhow.

It's been beastly weather here too: grey, overhung, with a grey slop of a sea and general unsightliness. That made us decide to leave on Saturday – or on Monday: Frieda will come straight to London, I'll stay a day or two with my sister. I'm not sure where we'll stay in London, probably in Hampstead, for a week or ten days: then set off back to Florence, via Paris and Baden.

So I shall see you in town, and Rina too, I hope.

Those Benns aren't worth bothering with.[1] – It's a fine day today, very.

Yrs D. H. Lawrence

3817. To Nancy Pearn, 8 September 1926

Text: MS UT; Unpublished.

'Duneville', Trusthorpe Rd, Sutton on Sea. Lincs
8 Sept 1926

Dear Miss Pearn

Herewith the proofs of 'Sun'.

We shall be leaving here next Monday – 13th. – so will you please not address me here after Saturday. Would you mind telling the other departments.

I expect we shall be in London some time next week. I'll let you know.

Yours Sincerely D. H. Lawrence

[1] Cf. Letter 3807 and n. 3.

3818. To Martin Secker, [8 September 1926]

Text: MS UT; Postmark, Sutton-on-Sea 8 SP 26; Unpublished.

[Frieda Lawrence begins]

Duneville, Trusthorpe Rd, Sutton-on-Sea
[8 September 1926]

Dear Martin,

Monty wrote a most enthusiastic letter about his visit to you, he loved Bridgfoot – It's jolly here on a fine day, but when it's damp and dull, then God help us! Lawrence seems fairly well – That man Geoffrey Whitworth has *not* written, Do impress him, that we are going away – *Why* does'nt he write? Anyhow we wont chase them – If they care so little, then they'd better be left – We shall be in London on Monday for a week I think – But Lawrence will let you know *where* – We dont know yet – My love to Rina – Tell Mrs Lamont how I liked the duck's egg! I had some good swimming here! What about Lawrence meeting Robert Aiken?

Best wishes Frieda

[Lawrence begins]

Dont bother with anybody – Aikens or Whitworths.

DHL

3819. To S. S. Koteliansky, [9 September 1926]

Text: MS BL; Postmark, Sutton[-on-Sea] 9 SP 26; Zytaruk 299.

Duneville. Trusthorpe Rd, Sutton on Sea, Lincs
Thursday.

My dear Kot

I hope you weren't shocked at the post card.[1] But I got your letter only at evening, on the beach, and had to scribble the nearest thing possible.

Very many thanks for finding us a place. It sounds very good, and I think we shall be all right there. But send me the address, wont you!

We leave here on Monday. I shall go to Ripley from here, but Frieda will come straight up to London, and take a taxi to the lodgings – arriving somewhere about tea-time. I'll let the landlady know, if I have her address.

So we shall see you soon. I do hope Sonia is feeling better. – I expect I shall be in town by Wednesday evening, or Thursday at latest.

auf wiedersehen. DHL

[1] See headnote to Letter 3815. The postcard was not characteristic of DHL, being of the slightly vulgar 'seaside' variety.

3820. To Emily King, [9 September 1926]

Text: MS Needham; PC v. Studies at the Zoo. The Leopard or Panther; Postmark, [Sutton] on Sea [. . .] SP 26; Unpublished.

['Duneville', Trusthorpe Road, Sutton-on-Sea, Lincolnshire]
Thursday

We've decided to leave here Monday – so I shall arrive in Nottingham on Monday afternoon, something after 4.0, I believe. If you have room, I should like to stay the night with you – but don't bother if Maud is still with you.[1] I'll go to Ripley on Tuesday, and fix up about Gertie. Weather's rather grey, but not bad.

Love. DHL

3821. To Hon. Dorothy Brett, 9 September 1926

Text: MS UCin; Moore 936–7.

Sutton-on-Sea. Lincs.
9 Sept 1926

Dear Brett

Your letter about the Chevrolet yesterday. How rash you are! You'll go bankrupt, you'll go over the edge of the Hondo Canyon, you'll run over Mexican babies, you'll – God knows what you won't do! And however will you hear when anything is tooting behind you? – I'm sure they weren't your friends who urged you to the Chevrolet. For the Lord's sake, go gingerly, in every respect.[2]

Your letter was full of news: what with Betty and Bobby's lungs, and the Ufer niece, the Ruffian, Agapeto and the rest. I do hope Rachel is calming down. What is she going to do for the winter? And William? Lord! how easy the world would be, save for people.

I had a very wailing letter from Earl. He hopes to leave that land of love, his dear India ('this trip to India is as bread to me' – it's turned out a stone)[3] in September – this month – and go to Greece: wants me to join him on the Isle of Syra, not far from Athens, some time during the winter. I might.

I've been here a fortnight with Frieda. I like this coast. But I haven't risked my bronchials in the ocean. We leave on Monday – I shall stay a few days with my sister – then to London for a bit. Those fools who are to do *David* haven't begun *yet* – here am I hanging on, feeling very bored with them. – But England isn't so bad, once you get into it again. It's not so scratchy as America – I dread even the sound of the Americans.

[1] Maud Beardsall was cousin to DHL and Emily King; she was the younger daughter of Herbert, Lydia Lawrence's youngest brother.

[2] Brett found driving 'was the beginning of a new independence' (*South Dakota Review* 29; see also p. 34).

[3] Cf. Matthew vii. 9.

What is it then that is so interesting between Mabel and Tony?

I shan't see Murry – but shall see Gertler, I suppose, in London – and Koteliansky. But there's no news in that direction: except that Waterlow is minister to *Siam*, having made himself objectionable to Chamberlain.[1]

Literary news none! I'm still feeling dead off writing altogether.

The photographs were very nice – especially the Azul. I'm glad Aaron too is better. Sometimes one dreams of them.

It's rather grey here – not much sun. But not bad. The air is fresh and strong.

I'm awfully bored going to London. But I'll wait a fortnight longer – then back to Italy. I feel like going south again.

Take care of the headaches. The thundery weather is bad for them. I've not had any lately.

I send a little money for the ex's. Am so afraid you'll go bust, what with Indian tribes and motor-cars etc.

Remember me to everybody.

DHL

3822. To William Siebenhaar, 10 September 1926

Text: TMSC NWU; Unpublished.

'Duneville', Trusthorpe Rd., Sutton-on-Sea, Lincs.
10 Sept. 1926.

Dear Siebenhaar,

That was very nice of you to wire me about the rooms – but I'm afraid expensive for you.

Friends in Hampstead have already got us a place there, for this time. But I shall certainly remember your place for another trip – Hampstead is so far.

I expect I shall arrive in London next Thursday: will let you know, and perhaps you will come and see us. The address will be 30 Willoughby Rd., Hampstead, N.W.3.

I am really very glad to have the Kensington Gardens Square address. The place sounds very reasonable, if it is decent. And the neighbourhood very nice. I shall call and look at it.

Very many thanks for your trouble. Trusting, then, that we shall see you in Hampstead,

Your Sincerely D. H. Lawrence

[1] (Sir) Sydney Philip Perigal Waterlow (1878–1944), CBE, diplomat. Educated at Eton and Trinity College, Cambridge; appointed British Minister at Bangkok in March 1926. According to DHL he fell foul of the Foreign Secretary, Sir Austen Chamberlain (1863–1937). Waterlow published translations of *Medea* and *Hippolytus* (1906); *Shelley* (1912), etc. He was second cousin to Katherine Mansfield and well known to Brett, Kot, Gertler, etc.

3823. To Giuseppe Orioli, 11 September 1926

Text: MS UCLA; cited in Moore, *Intelligent Heart* 356–7.

Sutton-on-Sea.
11 Sept. 1926

Dear Pino

Very nice of you to send the boxes! I haven't heard yet whether either of them has arrived, but I suppose they'll take a time.

We leave here on Monday – and Thursday I expect to be in London – at

30. Willoughby Rd, Hampstead. N. W. 3.

I'll see if I can summon up courage to go and look for Boris in Museum St.[1] – I'll have to see the people who are producing that play of mine – but don't suppose I shall stay longer than a week or ten days – then set off south, probably *via Paris*. If Reggie will still be there towards the end of the month, tell him to send me a line

c/o Miss M. Harrison, 49. Bvd. Montparnasse.

But I expect we shall be back at the Mirenda by the last of Sept, or early in October. It was nice here at the seaside, fresh and clean and tonicky. But I feel now like coming to Italy again.

Aldous Huxley came to see me in London – he has gone off to Cortina, in the Dolomites, to take a house there. He seemed no brisker than ever. I expect the Sitwells will have gone away from Renishaw now, so I shan't see them.[2]

Glad your trade is brisk. How is Florence feeling? cheerful, or nervosa? I rather dread that Italian nervosità.

Au revoir then. D. H. Lawrence

3824. To Millicent Beveridge, [11 September 1926]

Text: MS Lazarus; cited in Moore, *Poste Restante* 89.

Sutton on Sea.
Saturday

My dear Milly

We leave here on Monday – and I expect to be in London by Thursday.

Carlingford House, 30 Willoughby Rd, Hampstead, N. W. 3.

I am to see the people of the play as soon as I am in town. – But I don't expect we shall stay long in London – ten days or so. When do you expect to be back? – Frieda left a bundle of our things in your flat – c/o your charwoman – I hope you don't mind. I shall call and get them from the porter.

We had a lovely day yesterday – stayed all the time on the sands, in our little hut. There is a curious dolce far' niente charm about the seaside.

[1] Probably Boris de Croustchoff, Russian bibliographer whom DHL had met through Philip Heseltine in 1915 (*Letters*, ii. 448).

[2] Cf. p. 468 n. 3 and Letter 3734.

I'm enclosing the MS. of a story whose proofs I've just corrected for a paper I've never heard of – *The Coterie.*[1] – They'll publish the thing in their magazine, and also in a tiny booklet form – sounds daft. But I send it you to see if you recognise the garden at Fontana Vecchia, and where you used to sit and sketch, above the Lemon grove.[2] – Put the MS. in the fire when you've done with it – it's no good. – And I think some of the bits in Secker's catalogue are rather interesting.

Perhaps you will be in town before we go. Gertler found us these rooms. Do you know his paintings? – you wouldn't care for them. But you might like him. If you arrive in time, you must meet him.

There seems to be a lot of bitter feeling among the miners now – especially among the rougher class. This strike will have done more to preparing for industrial revolution, than fifty years of ordinary life would have done. It seems, for the first time as far as I know it, to have made the miners really class-conscious, and full of resentment.

What is this attack by the French government on Frank Harris? I've seen no details. – Have you seen his last recollections *My Life*? I only had a glance at it in Florence – but it seems to me the limit. Though it's probably all quite true, and if a man likes to turn himself inside out in a book, I don't see why the French, of all people, should prevent him. The way he tells some things is unpleasant and humiliating – but probably no more so than a dose of castor oil: and perhaps effective in the same way. It's only furtive things that should be suppressed.

I heard from Mabel. Probably we shall stay in Paris a few days, in the Littré, on our way out.

Remember me to everybody. I hope you're doing some nice painting.

DHL

3825. To Rolf Gardiner, 12 September 1926

Text: MS Lazarus; Huxley 669.

Sutton-on-Sea.
12 Sept. 1926

Dear Rolf Gardiner

I sent back *Schöpferische Pause* yesterday, to Lansdowne Rd. I read most of it, and was interested. Only the school-master part bored me. School-masters are terribly important to themselves: have to be, I suppose.

We leave here tomorrow – and by Thursday I expect to be in London:

at 30 Willoughby Rd, Hampstead N. W. 3.

[1] DHL included with his letter the typescript of 'Sun' (with autograph corrections and revisions). Cf. p. 352 n. 1.

[2] Cf. *Letters*, iii. 683.

Let me know if you will be in town, and we can meet. I expect to stay till towards the end of the month.

I feel the whole thing is a *Pause* just now. Let's hope it's Schöpferische.

Hope you had a decent time after all.

Sincerely D. H. Lawrence

3826. To Arthur Wilkinson, 12 September 1926

Text: MS Schlaefle; cited in Pinto, *D. H. Lawrence after Thirty Years*, p. 43.

Sutton on Sea.
12 Sept 1926

Dear Wilkinson

Your birthday budget was quite touching:[1] such nice letters from Mrs Wilkinson, and Pino – not to mention yourself: and as for Bim's Birthday Card, and your letter-head, why I was quite overwhelmed. Here I am, a forty-oner. And I don't care a straw, whether I'm one or one-and-ninety.

We leave here tomorrow – and I'm rather sorry. I've got quite into touch with my native land again, here – and feel at home. It's a lovely September morning, with bright sun and a wind, and nearly high tide, and long thin waves uncurling down the long, long sands. I think perhaps next year we may come here for five or six months. The sea side is such a good place for doing nothing in. One has a hut on the sands, and the sea does all the shuffling about that is necessary. And the people are amusing to watch. But there aren't many now.

So I'm sorry to go. I shall stay a day or two with my sister in Derbyshire, then we shall be in London, at

30. Willoughby Rd, Hampstead N. W. 3.

I have to see the Stage Society people who are producing my play *David* at end of October, so no doubt that will keep us till towards the end of the month. Then I've promised a day or two in Paris – and in Baden. But I do hope we shall get back to the Mirenda early in October. I shall get back penniless, for one wastes every sou in this moving around.

I heard from Orioli – he says everyone is coming back to Florence. Reggie Turner is in Paris. Miss Morrison and Gino have disappeared: gone into the country here somewhere, I suppose. Richard Aldington sent a line from San Gemignano – or however you spell it – but he and Arabella are moving on to Rome. They want us to come back, then they will come to the Mirenda. But they might turn up before we do.

The coal strike continues – and in the coal areas it's a serious business. For the first time, the iron seems to be entering the soul – or the consciousness – of

[1] To mark DHL's birthday on 11 September.

the workers. This will be the beginnings of a slow revolution, here in England – but a serious one. It's a funny country – so *safe*, and so kindly. And yet, way down, a certain ruthlessness.

I feel so furious to think that the Capitano, and Capitana don't come to the Mirenda when we're not there: and as soon as we appear, they'll turn up and shove us out of the house. It really takes away one's desire to be back. And otherwise it is so lovely.

I do hope, in the fresh autumn, we'll have some walks and picnics – and really discover the place a bit. I ought to do some work – I don't touch a pen, all this time – but the Lord sends the wet with the fine.

Tell Mrs Wilkinson to tie a string to her ankle, when she goes off into the 4th dimension, so that she can be pulled safely back when she's got beyond recall. Four is a dangerous number, as you realise when you're forty. Au revoir, then – and tanti saluti – tante cose!

D. H. Lawrence

3827. To Michael Joseph, [12 September 1926]

Text: MS UT; Unpublished.

Sutton on Sea.
12 Sept.

Dear Mr Joseph

Secker wrote that he doesn't want to see me on anybody else's list, except his own. But 'Glad Ghosts' after all is only a short story: and I do think it's good for publicity, to have it on Ernest Benn's list. Do you agree? Apart from that, of course, there's nothing in it, for I doubt if it will make me £10. But if it reaches a different set of readers, from Secker's, then it's all to the good, and I don't think Secker should mind.

We leave here tomorrow – and I shall be in London, I expect, by Thursday:
at 30. Willoughby Rd, Hampstead. N. W. 3.
Will you please write there.

Yours Sincerely D. H. Lawrence

3828. To S. S. Koteliansky, 15 September 1926

Text: MS BL; Postmark, Ripley 15 SP 26; Moore 937.

at Torestin, Gee St. Ripley, nr. Derby
15 Sept 1926

My dear Kot.

Of course it's grey and a bit rainy here: these Midlands![1]

[1] DHL paid his last visit to Eastwood on either 14 or 15 September (see W. E. Hopkin, 'D. H. Lawrence's Last Visit Home', *Nottingham Journal*, 11 September 1942).

Gertie doesn't seem so very bad. She was examined in Derby – the x ray shows a hole at the top of the left lung, but new. I have written to Dr Lucas, to ask when they can take her in to Mundesley.[1] The doctor said she couldn't do better than go there. So as soon as we hear there is room, my sister will take her over. She ought to be cured by Christmas.

I shall be coming to London tomorrow – dont know the time yet: probably in the evening.

This strike has done a lot of damage – and there is a lot of misery – families living on bread and margarine and potatoes – nothing more. The women have turned into fierce communists – you would hardly believe your eyes. It feels a different place: not pleasant at all.

I hope Sonia is better. You'll come up to Willoughby Rd.

wiedersehen DHL

3829. To Michael Joseph, 17 September 1926

Text: MS UT; Unpublished.

30 Willoughby Rd, Hampstead, N. W. 3.
Friday 17 Sept 1926

Dear Mr Joseph

I got here last night and found the Benn agreement. I talked to Secker about it: and he is against it. He showed me a copy of the Gerhardi shilling book: looks like a rather unimportant little yellow pamphlet.[2] Secker insists that, at least, I ought to retain the right to publish 'Glad Ghosts' later in a volume of short stories: that the agreement with Benn should only cover this present shilling edition. What do you think? I still think Benn might as well have a try with 'Glad Ghosts': but I don't want the story to be inhumed in this little yellow booklet – which I'm afraid will never sell much.

Sorry to trouble you again over such a small thing.

Yours Sincerely D. H. Lawrence

3830. To Enid Hilton, [20 September 1926]

Text: MS UCLA; Unpublished.

30 Willoughby Rd, Hampstead, N.W.3
Monday

Dear Enid[3]

Would you care to come to tea here on Wednesday about 4.0? We are out in the evenings.

[1] The letter to Dr Geoffrey Lucas (1872?–), a physician at Mundesley Sanatorium, has not been found.

[2] Gerhardie's *A Bad End* appeared as No. 1 in Benn's 'Yellow Books' series, in September 1926 (cf. Letter 3807 and n. 3). He signed a limited edn of 250 copies.

[3] Enid Hilton, née Hopkin (b. 1896), daughter of DHL's Eastwood friends, Willie and Sallie Hopkin. m. 1921?, Laurence Hilton.

If you come by bus, you walk up to the heath, up Willow Rd, and this is a turning off Willow Rd.

We shall expect you then.

D. H. Lawrence

3831. To Rachel Hawk, 20 September 1926

Text: MS UT; Unpublished.

London.
20 Sept. 1926

Dear Rachel

I was rather surprised – and at the same time not very surprised – by the contents of your letter. There is no doing anything with Brett, that's obvious. She'll have to run her course. I hope she won't suddenly abandon the ranch. I shall trust you to keep an eye on it.

I am wondering very much what we ought to do with it – the ranch. In my opinion, it would be better to sell it. I'm sure I shall never live there permanently, and it is too far, really too far, to go back and forth. If I had my way, I should sell it. – and I believe Frieda will come to agree. I know she will never come to stay there while Brett is on the place. – But don't say anything yet, to anybody, please, about our getting rid of the place. If Brett and Mabel heard, they'd fuss. – I wonder if it would be difficult to sell it? What do you think?

It is very hot, for September. I think we shall leave London next week, and go back to Florence: so write to

the Villa Mirenda, *Scandicci*, Florence. Italy.

It's a great nuisance for you, being badgered about from place to place: and if there is no Forest Service exam. this year, William will have no permanent job. You'll have to find yourself a little permanent place somewhere.

If there were a few dollars over, buy some little thing with them for the children.

Anyhow you'll be quite free down at the Danes cottage – nobody to bother you.

If you would like to have the Azul down at Del Monte, for your own personal use, for the time being, you fetch him down. I will tell the Brett.

I do hope Bobby and Betty are both well again. I'm afraid they fret against things.

Frieda sends her love. She says she will come, anyhow, to the ranch in the Spring, to see what is to be done: whether I come or not. But we'll see how we feel when the year turns.

I hope you'll be all right, and cheerful.

Remember me kindly to everybody.

D. H. Lawrence

3832. To Emily King, 21 September 1926

Text: MS Lazarus; Unpublished.

30 Willoughby Rd. Hampstead. N. W. 3.
21 Sept 1926

My dear Sister

I had your letter this morning: so glad the teeth are out. Now see if you're not a good deal better in every way. And if the constipation continues, try eating yeast: a little sandwich at about 11.0, and another before going to bed. You have to keep it up for some weeks – but usually it has a wonderful effect, freshening up the system.

Is there any further development about the wholesale business? When you are well enough, have a talk with that third partner, if you can get hold of him. Try to get a bit of grip on the affair.

If you find that Peg flags with too much evening work, just have her knock off again. The chief thing is that she shall be brisk and cheerful.

I haven't heard from Ada about Gertie – but Mark Gertler had a letter from the sanatorium saying they were offering Gertie a bed for this week-end. – Gertler seems very well, really: and he has had bad hemorrhages, far worse than Gertie.

The people are still slowly assembling the cast for *David*. I haven't seen them yet – and I don't feel inclined to stay longer in London. It is so expensive. So we shall leave next Tuesday – this day week – for Paris: stay a couple of days there – then go straight back to Florence. We shan't go to Baden again this time. Really, it costs too much, all the travelling. – I am thinking next year of taking a little house somewhere, for a permanency: perhaps here in England, in the country. We must have a bit of a permanent place somewhere – and the ranch is too far.

I hope Joan will keep well – she seems quite sparky now. And hope your mouth heals quickly.

Love. DHL

3833. To Catherine Carswell, [22 September 1926]

Text: MS YU; PC v. July. Falconry, hay harvest, chasing butterflies (British Museum MS); Postmark, Hampstead SEP 22 1926; Unpublished.

[30 Willoughby Rd. Hampstead, N. W. 3.]
Wed

I'd forgotten an elderly Australian – a Mr Siebenhaar – was coming to us to tea tomorrow. If he turns up I shall have to bring him along, and he's a bore, but inoffensive and you wont see him any more.

DHL

3834. To Michael Joseph, 22 September 1926
Text: MS UT; Unpublished.

30 Willoughby Rd, Hampstead, N. W. 3.
22 Sept 1926

Dear Mr Joseph

I was amused at the quick arrival of the proofs: quite right too. Secker can't have any more to complain of – so I enclose the signed agreement.

I shall be very much interested to know if Benn *can* sell these little yellow books.

Yrs D. H. Lawrence

3835. To William Siebenhaar, [22 September 1926]
Text: TMSC NWU; Unpublished.

30 Willoughby Rd., N.W.3.
Wednesday

Dear Siebenhaar,

I'm so sorry we were out – but our time is rather full up. We leave for Paris next Tuesday.

Would you care to come to tea tomorrow, about 4.0, if it is not too far? If only you'd sent a line yesterday, we could have got back. But we'll be in tomorrow, Thursday.

Hasta Luego D. H. Lawrence

3836. To S. S. Koteliansky, [23 September 1926]
Text: MS BL; Postmark, Hampstead SEP 23 1926; Zytaruk 301.

30 Willoughby Rd. Hampstead, N. W. 3.
Thursday

My dear Kot

Such a lot of people we see! – Tomorrow we are in after lunch – but that weary Enid Hopkin with husband threatens to come for tea – Margaret Radford threatens between 6.0 and 7.0 – and Frieda's son Monty is coming to dinner, and I expect we shall stay in the evening. If you feel like facing any of these people, come any time. – Saturday also we shall be here till evening – though Frieda's daughter comes to lunch, and maybe others to tea. But come when you like, notwithstanding.

We've fixed to leave on Tuesday.

Perhaps I'll be able to pop in at 5 Acacia on Monday.

DHL

3837. To Mabel Dodge Luhan, 23 September 1926
Text: MS Brill; Luhan 309–11.

30 Willoughby Rd. Hampstead, N W 3.
23 Sept. 1926

Dear Mabel

I am sending back all the MS. today. It is all very good – but towards the end gives a great feeling of weariness: the weariness you no doubt felt in Italy there. It depresses me, of course: the long, long indictment of our civilisation. The strange focussing of female power, upon object after object, in the process of decreation: or uncreation: as a sort of revenge for the compulsion of birth and procreation: becomes in the end like a sandhill slipping down on one. Ça ne finira jamais![1] It is as if the hourglass of time were reversed, and the sands of an eternity were streaming backwards, down on us. The struggle with the sands of time is worse than useless. Let the soft dry deluge continue, out of the reversed heavens. C'est la femme.

Tony's mother was your enemy – so she too is gone! – and I shall never see her look up at me again, sharply, as I sit in the car: with so much sharp understanding – and with so pathetically little, since our psyche is equipped with a whole extra box of tools.

Bobby Jones letter doesn't strike me as a pure bronze resonance of sincerity. To my feeling, it would be a bit cruel to bring Tony to Europe. But you will do what your doom makes you do, so why ragionare?[2] Jung is very interesting, in his own sort of fat muddled mystical way. Although he may be an initiate and a thrice-sealed adept, he's soft somewhere, and I've no doubt you'd find it fairly easy to bring his heavy posterior with a bump down off his apple-cart. I think Gourdjieff would be a tougher nut.

We leave here on Tuesday, and stay a few days in Paris, on our way to Florence. It is warm and sunny and autumnal, as I remember it in 1915 when we lived for a few months here in Hampstead. I have seen a few of the old people: and yesterday the Louis Untermeyers:[3] extraordinary, the ewige Jude,[4] by virtue of not having a real core to him, he is eternal. Plus ça change, plus c'est la même chose:[5] that is the whole history of the Jew, from Moses to Untermeyer: and all by virtue of having a little pebble at the middle of him, instead of an alive core.

The autumn sounds very lovely, in Taos and at the ranch. Part of me wishes

[1] 'That will never come to an end!' [2] 'argue about (it)?'

[3] Louis (1885–1977) and Jeanette Starr (1886–1970) Untermeyer, American poets. They had admired DHL for many years: in 1919 they sent him money (see *Letters*, iii. 445 and n.); in 1922, books (ibid., iv. 185). [4] 'the wandering Jew'.

[5] 'The more things change, the more they stay the same'.

I was there – part doesn't. I heard from Rachel Hawk she had left. Hope Brett will manage all right alone.

I suppose we shall be at the Villa Mirenda, *Scandicci* – Florence – by the first week in October. The grape harvest won't all be over.

Remember me to everybody. – You ought to number the pages of at least the sections of your MS.

DHL

3838. To Gertrude Cooper, 23 September 1926

Text: MS Clarke; Unpublished.

30 Willoughby Rd. Hampstead, N W 3.
23 Sept 1926

Dear Gertie

Now you must behave yourself, and eat and get fat. They'll simply make you eat at Mundesley, so make up your mind to it.

I wish I could have come to see you there – but we leave on Tuesday morning for Paris. The thing for you to do is simply to make up your mind to do everything to be well. Feroze's round matters so little – a few shillings here or there.[1] But your health through the years to come, that's the point. So don't fail in small matters like swallowing a drop of Pantanberge,[2] and a raw egg.

We shall be terribly anxious to hear how you are getting on – you must write to me, and we'll write to you. It would be the silliest thing in the world to fret about going away for a short time, to get quite well, when you know that staying neglectfully in Ripley leaves you faced with the danger of going away forever, from everybody.

Be sure and make up your mind to be wise in this matter, and put serious things first, not fritter away in rubbish like Feroze's round. You know we shall all be thinking about you, so you do your bit, and don't let us down.

DHL

3839. To Arthur Wilkinson, [23 September 1926]

Text: MS Schlaefle; PC v. A band of pilgrims on the way to Mecca (British Museum MS); Postmark, Hampstead SEP 23 1926; Unpublished.

30 Willoughby Rd. N. W. 3.
Thursday. 23 Sept

We leave here on Tuesday, for Paris – stay there only about a couple of days –

[1] Dr Dhunjabhai Furdunji Mullan-Feroze (1874–1959), the Clarkes' family doctor and a close friend (see *Letters*, iii. 313 n. 2). He employed Gertrude Cooper for a few years to collect from his patients their 'Lloyd George' insurance payments – the few pence per week which it cost to be a 'panel patient'. Her 'round' was mostly in the outlying villages near Ripley; she would travel by bus or on foot.

[2] See Letter 3394 and n. 4.

so on the 2nd Oct. or thereabouts we ought to be back at San Polo. I look forward to coming: will let you know definitely.

Be greeted, all of you.

D. H. Lawrence

3840. To William Siebenhaar, 24 September 1926
Text: TMSC NWU; Unpublished.

30 Willoughby Rd., Hampstead, N.W.3.
24 Sept. 1926.

Dear Siebenhaar,

What *does* happen to letters to you? I wrote Wednesday, as soon as I got home, and asked you to tea here Thursday – waited in for you – And I'm sure I put 18.

However – we leave for Paris on Tuesday – and are terribly full – I'll try to find time Monday – will send a line.

The publisher doesn't have any right to serial sales – you can offer any novel for serial purposes, no matter what contract you have with a publisher.[1] He has only the volume rights. And Cape would be delighted if Molly Skinner could get the *Atlantic Monthly* prize.

Many thanks for your essay. May I take it with me?

I'm so sorry we missed you. When do you leave England?

Yrs, D. H. Lawrence

If you are not engaged, we might meet on the steps of the National Gallery on Monday at 11.30. We have to lunch with people – but we might have a talk beforehand.

3841. To Richard Aldington, 24 September 1926
Text: MS Grover; Unpublished.

30 Willoughby Rd, Hampstead, N. W. 3.
24 Sept. 1926

Dear Richard

We are leaving here for Paris next Tuesday, 28th. – so I expect we shall be at the Villa Mirenda by October 2nd, as we have cut out Baden. The end of the month is near, so perhaps you will be in Rome when this letter gets there. Come and see us whenever you will, you and Arabella, at the Mirenda, and

[1] Presumably Siebenhaar was enquiring on Mollie Skinner's behalf regarding her novel *Black Swans* which Cape had published in 1925.

stay as long as you like. It is rather rough living, but you won't mind much, and we shall be pleased to see you.

Hope you've had a real good time, and are a bit fat. I prefer you a bit fatter than when I saw you last. And I hope Arabella feels warmed through, and nice and ruddy with red wine.

a rivederci D. H. Lawrence

3842. To Michael Joseph, 25 September 1926
Text: MS UT; Unpublished.

30 Willoughby Rd. N. W. 3
Saturday 25 Sept. 1926

Dear Mr Joseph

I hope you got the proofs and signed agreement of *Glad Ghosts*, which I sent off at once. I admire the quickness of Benns.

We leave here on Tuesday morning, early, for Paris – and then to Florence. The address will be

Villa Mirenda, *Scandicci*, *Florence*, Italy.

Would you mind giving it to the other departments.

I shall be so interested to know if Benns can sell *Glad Ghosts* at 1/-, in that little yellow jacket.

Yours Sincerely D. H. Lawrence

3843. To Emily King, [27 September 1926]
Text: MS Lazarus; Unpublished.

30 Willoughby Rd, N. W. 3.
Monday

My dear Pamela

We are off tomorrow for Paris – leave here at 8.0 and get there at 4.0 – not so long.

I lunched with Robert Atkins, who is producing *David*. He seemed keen on it. But they are putting off the actual performance till second week in December – to have time – and I have promised to come back for the later rehearsals and the play – so I *may* be home for Christmas.

At the present I'm rather glad to be off – we are out every night, and stay up too late.

How are you, with your teeth gone? Frieda's son Monty had to have eight perfectly good teeth removed, because of pyorrhea at the roots. They do poison the system.

How is Joan too? – Write me all the news to the
Villa Mirenda, *Scandicci*, Florence.
We should be there by Saturday.

Love DHL

3844. To Baroness Anna von Richthofen, [27 September 1926]

Text: MS UT; PC v. The sage Buzurjmihe discoursing to King Anūshirvan (British Museum MS); Postmark, Hampstead SEP 27 1926; Unpublished.

London.
Montag

Wir fahren morgen nach Paris – bleiben zwei oder drei Tage – und kommen Samstag an Florenz. Du hast die Adresse:
Villa Mirenda, *Scandicci*, Florenz.
Wir haben heute die *David* Leute gesehen. Ich glaube, sie werden es ganz gut thun. Sie spielen es in Mittel-Dezember – und wir haben versprochen, wieder hier zu sein. *Dann* können wir über Baden reisen, in der Weinachtszeit. Das wäre schöner. Wieder kalt hier. Schreib du nach Florenz.

DHL

[We go to Paris tomorrow – stay two or three days – and arrive Saturday in Florence. You have the address:
Villa Mirenda, *Scandicci*, Florence.
We saw the *David* people today. I believe they'll do it pretty well. They're producing it in mid-December – and we've promised to be back here. *Then* we can travel via Baden, at Christmas-time. That would be better. Cold again here. Write to Florence.

DHL]

3845. Olwen Bowen-Davies, 27 September 1926

Text: MS UT; Unpublished.

30 Willoughby Rd. Hampstead, N. W. 3
Monday 27 Sept 1926

Dear Miss Bowen-Davies[1]

The proof of the *William Clissold* review wandered in only this morning, from Lincolnshire.[2]

We are leaving tomorrow[3] morning for Paris, then on to Florence. Will you please make a note of the address:

[1] A member of Curtis Brown's office staff.

[2] See p. 513 n. 1.

[3] tomorrow] in the

Villa Mirenda, *Scandicci*, Florence. Italy.

I suppose Miss Pearn is not back yet: am sorry to miss her.

Sincerely D. H. Lawrence

3846. To Gertrude Cooper, 29 September 1926

Text: MS Clarke; Unpublished.

Paris.
29 Sept. 1926

My dear Gertie

Ada wrote me that Eddie took you to Mundesley, so there you are, staying the first few days in bed, I believe. I do hope you don't feel very strange and dismal. You're sure to get used to it, and like it in a little while. Be sure and write to me to the

Villa Mirenda, *Scandicci*, Florence, Italy.

We shall be there by Sunday, I think.

We had a very good journey here, came by Folkestone and Boulogne, and the journey so much easier, if a little longer, because there are fewer people. It was a lovely day on the sea, blue and fresh, and I wouldn't have minded sailing away somewhere not too far – only not to America.

Paris is warmer than London was when we left – and very much cheaper. I like it very much. The people are quite friendly, life is somehow simpler and more careless. We shall stay, I expect, till Friday, then travel another day to Switzerland, and stay the night there. Then one more day, to Milan, and from Milan to Florence, also a day. It takes a long time travelling only by day, but it's worth it.

I am very anxious to know what the doctors say of you after they've had you there for a few days, so be sure and write. And try and do as they tell you. But if they give you *too* much milk, then go to the doctor yourself and explain to him. You needn't die of suffocation from swallowing milk, either. – And when you're up, you'll see how they'll make you walk: just as if you were doing Feroze's round!

Make friends if you can, and don't be too shy. The great thing is to have the courage of life. Have the courage to live, and live well.

Frieda says she will write. We think of you every day, and shall be glad of a letter from you when we get home. – I may be home for Christmas, because of that play which is coming on then. So we shall all have a jolly Christmas together.

Love DHL

3847. To S. S. Koteliansky, [30 September 1926]

Text: MS BL; PC v. Notre-Dame de Paris – Chimere (le philosophe) Facade Ouest – Dans le fond, l'Eglise St. Sulpice; Postmark, Paris 30. IX 1926; Zytaruk 301.

Paris.
Thursday

very pleasant here, sunny and nice – We go on tomorrow as far as Lausanne – shall be at the Mirenda by Monday.

DHL

3848. To Ada Clarke, [30 September 1926]

Text: MS Lazarus; PC v. La Madeleine un matin d'hiver; Postmark, Paris 30. IX 1926; Unpublished.

Paris.
Thursday

Had very nice days here – shall go on tomorrow as far as Lausanne – write to the Mirenda.

DHL

3849. To Margaret King, [30 September 1926]

Text: MS Needham; PC v. Place de la Concorde et Groupe equestre par Coysevox; Postmark, Paris 30. IX 1926; Unpublished.

Paris
Thursday

Very nice weather here – have enjoyed these two days. We go on tomorrow – write to the Villa Mirenda.

DHL

3850. To Hon. Dorothy Brett, [30 September 1926]

Text: MS UCin; PC v. Notre-Dame de Paris; Postmark, Paris 1. X 1926; Irvine, Brett 70.

Paris
[30 September 1926]

Here for a few days on the way back to Italy – very pleasant autumn sunshine, the flowers very bright in the Luxembourg garden. Went up Montmartre this morning, and saw the world from there. – Hope you're all right, alone there. You'll have to be very careful, driving a car in that country. Hope everything is all right.

DHL

3851. To Gertrude Cooper, [30 September 1926]

Text: MS Clarke; PC v. Marché aux fleurs Quai de l'Horloge; Postmark, Paris 1. X 1926; Unpublished.

Paris
Thursday

Such nice sunny days here – hope it's the same with you.

DHL

3852. To Margaret King, [2 October 1926]

Text: MS Needham; PC v. Lausanne et les alpes; Postmark, Laus[anne] 2 X 26; Unpublished.

[Lausanne]
Sat

Got so far – cold here – we're off to Milan tomorrow, so should be at the Mirenda on Tuesday.

DHL

3853. To Gertrude Cooper, [2 October 1926]

Text: MS Clarke; PC v. Lausanne. La Cathédrale et les Alpes; Postmark, Laus[a]nne 2[. . .]; Unpublished.

[Lausanne]
Saturday

Got so far! It's cold here, we shall go on to Milan tomorrow. Hope all goes well!

DHL

3854. To Gertrude Cooper, 5 October 1926

Text: MS Clarke; cited in Lawrence–Gelder 137–8.

Villa Mirenda, *Scandicci*, Florence
5 Oct. 1926

My dear Gertie

I found your letter when we got back here last night. I knew you'd find the first week a bit stiff. But everybody is kept in bed for the beginning. And I'm sorry about the X ray: am anxious to hear that that has been done, and the result. Write and tell me. Although I know it's sickening for you to be stuck there in a sanatorium, I'm thankful you *are* there, just now, so that the best can be done.

It is almost hot, here – too hot to sit in the sun. And last night, the rooms being only just opened, it was so hot I could not sleep, and thought a good deal about you in Mundesley, and wished a bit of your cold wind would blow through my open window. These old villas are so massive, made of stone, that after a long spell of sunshine it takes weeks for the walls to cool off, on the south side.

It is very lovely, really – not like autumn, like summer. The peasants are bringing in the grapes, in a big wagon drawn by two big white oxen. Every hour or so, they roll up with a load, to go in the big vats in the ground-floor cellar. The grapes are very sweet this year – not very big – little and round and clear, and very sweet. It will be a good wine year, even if the bulk is not enormous.

But as for me, I ate so many bunches of grapes in the train yesterday, that today I am holding my innards! At the station at the top of the Appenines, Pracchia, where the train stops to gasp amid all its dust and puther,[1] they always sell fruit. When we came away in July, it was huge round balls of cherries. This time, it was grapes. – As a matter of fact, though, I think Frieda and I got the mild form of gastric flu which everybody has in Paris. I don't think it was the grapes at all. – I suppose, at Mundesley you'll be safe from gastric flu, anyhow.

Did I tell you Enid Hopkin came to tea with us at Hampstead? – she came twice, brought her husband the second time. He is very nice, but ordinary: too ordinary for Miss Enid. She is the most discontented thing I have seen for years: and heaven knows why. She's got everything she needs – a good husband too – but she is all of a work with discontent, like brewers' yeast. A trial, I can tell you. She says nobody wants her, and she has no friends. But can you wonder! And apparently all her bit of spare money has to go to help pay Willie's debts. She doesn't like that, either. Yet when her mother was alive, her Daddy was always the wonderful one, and she tried to look down a bit on Sallie, with some of that Hopkinish impudence. Now she knows her mistake. But she's impudent, a real Hopkin.

I think tomorrow Richard Aldington and Arabella are coming out to stay a little while here: hope they won't mind the hard beds. One doesn't realise how hard they are, till one comes back to them.

Tell Dr Lucas I want to come down and look at Mundesley, and meet him. Gertler told me about him. – You know I promised to be back in London for December, for that play of mine? We may all have a jolly Christmas together yet. Keep cheerful, now, and send a line.

DHL

[1] I.e. smoke or steam (Notts dialect).

3855. To Giuseppe Orioli, [6 October 1926]

Text: MS UCLA; Unpublished.

[Villa Mirenda, Scandicci, Florence]
[6 October 1926]

[My dear Orioli,

The most unfortunate thing has happened. Richard is not coming with me tomorrow, and wants to dine with me. I did my best to dissuade him but without success, and could not think of any excuse.

Do you think Douglas and the boys will think it very rude of me if I do not dine after all tonight.][1]

3856. To Emily King, 9 October 1926

Text: MS Lazarus; Unpublished.

Villa Mirenda, Scandicci, Florence
9 Oct. 1926

My dear Pamela

I found your letter here when we got back on Monday evening. So glad you are feeling better. Of course it will take a little time for your mouth to heal right up. But if once you can get yourself back into condition, you'll find everything will go much better.

Is there any further development with Sam and the business? This winter something will *have* to be decided about that. You can't hang on in Carlton.

We found it quite hot here still: and now it is close and sultry, I hope it will rain, it is too close.

They finished bringing in the grapes on Wed. evening: not a very big harvest, but the grapes very sweet and good. We've got them hanging in festoons in the rooms – eat them as we go – and if we don't eat them fast enough, they'll turn to raisins. But all the house smells of the queer sour smell of the great vats of grapes downstairs, that are waiting to soften off a bit, before the men tread on them.

Tell Peg I went and forgot her little book of songs in Paris; but I'll ask a friend if she can find me one.

Arabella and Richard Aldington are staying with us, till Monday – then they go back to England. They are very nice, it is nice having them. It is good, too, to be in one's own place and be quiet – We've rushed about so much lately, I'm really tired of it.

Peg won't overdo those evening classes – if they are too much, she can drop one. What about her correspondent in Havre, or Brest – or wherever it is.

Love. DHL

[1] The note is addressed in DHL's hand; the text is in another's. No explanation can be offered.

3857. To Mabel Dodge Luhan, 9 October 1926
Text: MS Brill; Luhan 311–12.

Villa Mirenda, *Scandicci*, Florence.
9 Oct. 1926

My dear Mabel

Your letter and the sketch came yesterday. I will offer the sketch to some magazine, but don't know if they'll take it. It's not really very good: not nearly so good as your Memoirs. As soon as you try writing from the imagination, not recording your own actual impressions, you become amateurish. Yet the most part of the Memoirs is not amateurish at all, very much to the point.

Richard Aldington says why not bequeath the Intimate Memoirs to the Académie Française. There they would be quite safe, and sure to be published some time. – But I myself know nothing about it.

By the way, did Frieda ask you to send an Indian bracelet to Arabella – Mrs Aldington? I only heard of it yesterday. Don't you be bothered about it: I don't see why Frieda troubles you, for such a thing. And if you did happen to send one, let me know what it cost. It's not *your* present to Arabella, mon Dieu! But if you haven't done anything about it, *don't*!

I do feel it's rather rash of Brett to have a motor car, in that country, on those roads, and with her deafness. But I suppose there is a special kind of providence for such cases.

We got back here four days ago. They were just finishing the vendemmia. It is hot, rather sultry – I shouldn't mind a little rain. I suppose Taos is all blue and gold. It is very lovely out there: much lovelier than here. If it weren't for a certain queer exalted or demonish *tension* in the atmosphere, I would so much rather be there than here. Italy, humanly, isn't very interesting nowadays. Fascism, whatever else it does, spreads the grand blight of boredom. But I suppose we shall stay here at least till spring.

Remember me to everbody!

DHL

Many thanks for *Lolly Willowes*.[1] I found it here. It was good, in a small way, and true. Only, like everybody else, she didn't know *how* to be a witch. Sabbaths and talks with satan are all beside the point. Being a witch is a much more serious, and strenuous matter.

Do you remember, by the way, the owl Manby sent over? – Is he just the same?[2]

[1] *Lolly Willowes: or, the Loving Huntsman* (1926), a novel by the English writer Sylvia Townsend Warner (1893–1978), was the first 'Book-of-the-Month' in USA.

[2] Probably Arthur Rockfort Manby (d. 1929), an eccentric expatriate English resident of Taos from whom Mabel and Maurice Sterne rented accommodation when they first moved there.

3858. To Nancy Pearn, 9 October 1926
Text: MS UT; Huxley 670.

Villa Mirenda, *Scandicci*, Florence
9 Oct. 1926

Dear Miss Pearn

Here we are back at home – nice to sit in the big empty rooms and be peaceful. They finished bringing in the grapes on Wednesday, so the whole place smells sourish, from the enormous vats of grapes downstairs, waiting to get a bit squashy, for the men to tread them out.

I am thinking about my own activities. I shall try just to do short stories and smaller things. Do you think any of the papers or magazines would care for me to do a review now and then? – they could choose the book. But they'd have to make it clear, whether I could say what I wanted or not.

And now, don't be very bored if I inflict a little burden on you. A friend to whom we are under a bit of an obligation in friendship, asks me if I can offer this sketch of hers to some periodical.[1] But I don't know any periodicals. Do you think it's any good trying it anywhere? If not, just tell me, and I can hand on your verdict.

Where did you go in Derbyshire? I was even there myself, but on the Matlock and Chesterfield side, for a bit. I hope you're feeling good and brisk. Here it is hot and sultry – shouldn't mind a breath of cold air.

Greetings from us both D. H. Lawrence

Just got your letter about the *Tribune* and critical articles. I should quite like to do any book that they think would be my line – only they would need to specify the book and the kind of article they want.[2]

DHL

3859. To Ada Clarke, [9 October 1926]
Text: MS Clarke; cited in Lawrence–Gelder 138–9.

Villa Mirenda. *Scandicci*, Florence.
Sat. 9 Oct.

My dear Sister

We got back here all right on Monday evening – everything very quiet – and

[1] See preceding letter. It seems that Mabel Luhan used a pseudonym on her 'sketch'. Nancy Pearn replied to DHL on 20 October 1926 (TMSC UT):

> Of course I was glad to read the story by *Miss Blanchard* since you sent it; but I am afraid my confidential question as a result must be: why did she do it? I think it would be kind to her to suggest other activities than literature.

(See the reference to 'M. Blanchard' in Letter 3876.)

[2] None of DHL's writings appeared in *Tribune*.

hot, rather sultry weather still: almost too hot. Arabella and Richard Aldington are here for a few days: leave on Monday for England. They are very nice, pleasant to have in the house. Apart from them, I haven't seen anyone in Florence, haven't let anybody know I am back. We saw so many people in London, it will be nice to be still for a bit.

They finished bringing in the grapes on Wednesday, and all the house smells sourish from the great vats where they're waiting to be squashed. We've got festoons of grapes hung up everywhere – if we don't eat them, they'll turn to raisins, they're very sweet.

I had one letter from Gertie, and am waiting to hear more. I shall be glad to know the result of a proper x-ray. I do hope it won't take a long time to get her started off on the right way to healing up. I'll write to her again now.

That coal strike is like an insanity. Are your men going back round Ripley? I feel I daren't read any more about it, it's so maddening stupid. – I suppose Bertie flourishes like the green bay tree![1]

love DHL

3860. To Rolf Gardiner, 11 October 1926
Text: MS Lazarus; Huxley 670–2.

Villa Mirenda. *Scandicci*, Florence. Italy
11 Oct. 1926

Dear Rolf Gardiner

We got tired of London and of feeling cooped up, and came back here. It is rather lovely, very warm, like summer, grape harvest just finished, and enough room in the house to spread oneself.

I wonder very much what your singing tour was like, and still more, what the Schleswig camp will be like. Let me know. I am sympathetic, fundamentally, but I feel how very hard it is to get anything *real* going. Until a few men have an active feeling that the world, the social world, can offer little or nothing any more; and until there can be some tangible desire for a new sort of relationship, between people; one is bound to beat about the bush. It is difficult not to fall into preciosity and a sort of faddism.

I think, one day, I shall take a place in the country, somewhere where perhaps one or two other men might like to settle in the neighbourhood, and we might possibly slowly evolve a new rhythm of life: learn to make the

[1] Cf. Psalm xxxvii. 36 (Book of Common Prayer).

creative pauses, and learn to dance and to sing together, without stunting, and perhaps also publish some little fighting periodical, keeping fully alert and alive to the world, living a different life in the midst of it, not merely apart. You see one cannot suddenly decapitate oneself. If barren idealism and intellectualism are a curse, it's not the head's fault. The head is really a quite sensible member, which knows what's what: or *must* know. One needs to establish a fuller relationship between oneself and the universe, and between oneself and ones fellow man and fellow woman. It doesn't mean cutting out the 'brothers in Christ' business simply: it means expanding it into a full relationship, where there can be also physical and passional meeting, as there used to be in the old dances and rituals. We have to know how to go out and meet one another, upon the third ground, the holy ground. You see you yourself go out intensely in the spirit, as it were, to meet some fellow men. But another part of yourself, the fighting and the passionate part, never issues – it seems to me – from its shell. – I may be all wrong, don't take any notice if I am. – We need to come forth and meet in the essential physical self, on some third holy ground. It used to be done in the old rituals, in the old dances, in the old fights between men. It could be done again. But the intelligent soul has to find the way in which to do it: it won't do itself. One has to be most intensely conscious: but not intellectual or ideal.

Let us think about it, and make some sort of start if it becomes possible. No use rushing into anything. If one can be sensible oneself, one will become the focus, or node, of a new sensibility.

Anyhow tell me about the Schleswig camp.[1]

D. H. Lawrence

3861. To Curtis Brown, 11 October 1926

Text: MS UT; Unpublished.

Villa Mirenda, *Scandicci*, Florence.
11 Oct. 1926

Dear Curtis Brown

Will you please answer this man for me – He has my permission, as far as

[1] Gardiner said in 1956 that the camp at Rendsburg in Schleswig-Holstein 'was an attempt to convene leaders of youth groups in Germany, Britain and Scandinavia. It was held at Rendsburg through the good offices of Theodor Steltzer who in 1944–45 was one of the Kreisauer Resistance group led by Helmut von Moltke against the Nazi tyranny' (Nehls, iii. 672 n. 135). For Gardiner's reply to DHL's letter, 28 November 1926, see Nehls, iii. 118–21.

that goes.[1] But I wish you'd decide whether he ought to make any return of any sort: and if Secker would have any objections.

Sincerely D. H. Lawrence

3862. To Else Jaffe, 12 October 1926

Text: MS Jeffrey; Frieda Lawrence 229–30.

Villa Mirenda, *Scandicci*, Florence
12 Oct. 1926

My dear Else

I have just had the enclosed letter from my agent.[2] My agreement with him is such, that the contracts for all the things I publish must be made through him, and all payments must be made to him. He deducts ten per cent for himself, and deposits the rest to my account.

Will you please tell me exactly what contract you made with the Insel-Verlag for *Der Fuchs*:[3] and what were the payments, apart from the translators fee? I know it was not much. But of course I owe Curtis Brown ten per-cent on it.

And in future will you see that everything goes through the agent's hands, or I shall be in trouble, as I am legally bound to him: and he is quite good to me. – It's my fault, I know, for not remembering sooner.

We have been back here just a week, and I am very glad to sit still in the peace of these quiet rooms. I am getting really tired of moving about, and cast round in my mind for a place which I shall keep as a permanency. Perhaps it will be in England.

It is warm here, almost hot still. The vendemmia finished last week, and we are all festooned with grapes. But the Schwiegermutter says that you too were

[1] The autograph letter from W. J. Glover (MS UT) reads as follows:

Oct. 4/26

Dear Sir

I am editing a Geography book for Messrs. Cassell, *entirely for use in schools*, and shall be very grateful if I may include two extracts from your fascinating book "Sea and Sardinia".

Due acknowledgment would of course be made, together with the name of book, author, & publisher.

May I suggest it would bring your work to the notice of many Head Teachers who otherwise, unfortunately for themselves, might miss it.

Trusting to secure your consent,

I am

Yours truly W. J. Glover.

No copy of the book – presumed to be *The Mediterranean Lands* (Cassell, 1928) – has been traced.

[2] The letter is missing but see Letter 3870.

[3] Else Jaffe's translation of 'The Fox' (*Der Fuchs*) was published by Insel Verlag in 1926.

in Venice. Venice is lovely in the autumn, if it's not too crowded. Do you feel content now, for the winter?

They are producing the *David* play in December, I saw the producer and the people concerned, and I promised to go to England to help them at the end of November. I'm not *very* sure if I shall do so, though. But if we do, we must come through Baden. I daren't say anything, because I know the Schwiegermutter was cross with us for putting off again this time. But we had moved so much, we were both feeling stupefied.

I wonder how the translation of the *Serpent* is going. You will find it a long job: I hope, not too tedious. Myself I am not working at anything particular: don't feel inclined.

I hope you're feeling well. Are the children all busy again, Friedel in Berlin? Here it seems so sleepy, the world is all vague.

Love. DHL

3863. To Curtis Brown, 12 October 1926
Text: MS UT; Unpublished.

Villa Mirenda, *Scandicci*, Florence.
12 Oct. 1926

Dear Curtis Brown

I've received today two copies of *Twilight in Italy*, in Cape's 'Traveller's Library.' I dont remember signing any contract for this, nor having any correspondence with you about it: though personally, I agree to it all right. But I know Secker will look down his nose: and I like to tell him plainly what I am doing. Have I really signed an agreement for *Twilight in Italy* with Cape? I think not. Will you tell me what arrangement you have made, so that I can tell Secker.

And would you mind telling me when the Oxford Press made their last payment for *Movements in European History*? – or when they are due to pay? It seems to me I have no track of them. – They wrote me that their Irish edition of the *History* is now ready – for use in the Free State Catholic High Schools. I believe the Oxford Press do so many numerous things, they are a bit vague.[1]

Sincerely D. H. Lawrence

[1] OUP imported sheets from the Educational Company of Ireland; they bound a 'Revised Edition for Irish Schools' and published it on 20 January 1927 for sale to 'Catholic Communities outside Ireland' (see Philip Crumpton, *DHL Review*, xiii, 105–18). The Irish edn itself was published in Dublin by the Educational Company in September 1926.

3864. To Martin Secker, 12 October 1926
Text: MS UInd; Postmark, Scandicci 13. 10 26; Secker 77–8.

Villa Mirenda, *Scandicci*, Florence.
12 Oct. 1926

Dear Secker

We got back here just a week ago – very warm, almost hot. Vendemmia finished last Wednesday, and we are hung all round with grapes. It is very nice, after so much moving, to be still, in these big, empty, silent rooms. I haven't yet let anybody in Florence know we are back – I don't feel keen on any more contacts, just yet.

A man wrote me from Bournemouth, that he wants to include two[1] extracts from 'my fascinating book, *Sea and Sardinia*' in a geography book he is publishing *entirely for use in schools*, for Cassell's. I sent the letter to Curtis Brown, for him to agree or not. Perhaps you have something to say. – How is the cheap edition of *S. and S.*?

I received two copies, from Cape, of *Twilight in Italy* this morning.[2] Have written to C. B. to ask who made any agreement, and when. I feel certain I have signed nothing.

Did I tell you, I saw the play people – and they're putting off the production of *David* till the second week in December, to have more time. Mrs Whitworth complained you never sent her the copy of the cheap edition. Did you forget? By the way, it would be better not to publish the cheap edition until after the play has actually been performed. So will you please hold it back until such time. –[3]

I promised to come to England at the end of November, to help them with the play. Whether I shall finally screw up my courage, I don't know. If I do, I suppose we shall stay over Christmas. It is so hot here still, it seems hard to imagine it should be so near.

Oh – and I promised in July to send a copy of *Kangaroo*, and *St. Mawr* and *The Plumed Serpent* to

Frau A. von Livonius, Bismarckstr. 10. *Baden Baden.*

This time I forgot. Will you please send the three books off for me.

How is Bridgefoot – and Rina and the boy. I guess it is lovely autumn there as here.

Sincerely D. H. Lawrence

[1] MS reads 'to'. [2] See Letter 3720 and n. 2.
[3] Secker's cheap edn of *David* was published in February 1927 at 6/-.

3865. To Robert Atkins, 16 October 1926

Text: MS DC; Postmark, Firenze 16 10 26; *New York Evening Post*, 30 November 1932.

Villa Mirenda, *Scandicci*, Florence.
16 Oct. 1926

Dear Atkins

I enclose the music I have written out for *David*.[1] It is very simple, needs only a pipe, tambourines, and a tom-tom drum. I hope it will do.

Let me know when you get the thing going a bit. I hope I can come to London and help, later, if you think it really worth while. If only one can get that feeling of primitive religious passion across to a London audience. If not, it's no good.

I'm wondering what sort of cast you are planning.[2]

Yours Sincerely D. H. Lawrence

3866. To S. S. Koteliansky, 17 October 1926

Text: MS BL; Postmark, Firenze 18 . X 1926; cited in Gransden 31.

Villa Mirenda. *Scandicci* (Florence)
Sunday 17 Oct 1926

My dear Kot

It's a fortnight tomorrow since we got back – we stayed a couple of days in Lausanne, Frieda having caught the gastric flu. which everybody had in Paris. But she's better. – And it is nice to be here in the big quiet rooms again, no traffic and no bothers. It is still very warm, at midday hot: but heavy mists in the morning. Lovely weather, though. The peasants finished the vendemmia two days after we got here – but the wine is still to be made. – I haven't told anybody in Florence that we are back, yet. It's so nice to be still.

I heard from Gertie, she has gained two pounds and a half in weight – but they are still keeping her in bed.

I sent off the music to *David* the other day. Wonder if you'll recognise the prophets singing Ranané Sadíkim.[3] But it won't sound the same. – Wonder if they'll make anything of the play, anyhow. I don't feel very sanguine.

[1] The music is reproduced in *A D. H. Lawrence Miscellany*, ed. Harry T. Moore (Carbondale, 1959), following p. 150.

[2] The cast of the production is given in Keith Sagar, ed. *A D. H. Lawrence Handbook* (Manchester, 1982), p. 295.

[3] For the Hebrew musical version of Psalm xxxi. 1 ('Ranani Zadikim . . .', 'Rejoice in the Lord, O ye righteous'), see *Letters*, ii. 252 n. 3.

Will you send me the Dobrée number in Well Walk, when you write, so I have their address.[1] I liked them – him too.

And don't forget, if you want to borrow some money, you can borrow from me as from the Lord, who doesn't mention payment till the Judgment Day, when all is over.

How is Sonia by now? quite well I hope. And Ghita, at Oxford, getting more superior every day, I'll bet.

There is an enormous fusillade going on in the boschi – shooting little birds as they go south – vivi pericolosamente! must have been intended for the uccellini![2] à la St. Francis.

Saluti! DHL

3867. To Else Jaffe, 18 October 1926

Text: MS Jeffrey; Frieda Lawrence 231.

Villa Mirenda, *Scandicci* (Firenze)
18 Oct. 1926

My dear Else

Kippenberg behaves as if he were the Great Cham of Tartary: whereas he's only a tiresome old buffer. I've told him once that, personally, I don't care for Franzius' pompous and heavy translations:[3] I'll tell him again, and to hell with him. Pity we cant change over to the people who did *Jack im Buschland*.[4] They are more up-to-date and go-ahead.

But anyhow Kip. has no right over magazine productions: so if you could get the 'Women Who Rode' into a Monatsheft,[5] you couldn't be interfered with, by him at least. – I get awfully bored, between publishers and agents and one set and another.

So now you'll be off to Vienna! Everybody seems to have been to Vienna, or to be going. Glad I needn't go, anyhow just now.

I'll tell Curtis Browns what you say about 'Fox'.

Sunny autumn here; still and nice: but an epidemic of typhoid in the neighbourhood: must look out.

[1] Bonamy Dobrée (1891–1974), lecturer in English, University of London, 1925–6; Professor of English, Egyptian University, Cairo, 1926–9; Professor of English, University of Leeds, 1936–55. m. 1913, Valentine Gladys Brooke-Pechell (d. 1974). Author of *Restoration Comedy* (1924); *The Lamp and the Lute* (which includes an essay on DHL) (1929); etc. (See obituary, *The Times*, 4 September 1974; see also Richard Hoggart, 'Bonamy Dobrée' in *Of Books and Humankind*, ed. J. Butt, 1964, pp. 195–208.)

[2] '. . . in the woods . . . south – live dangerously! . . . for the little birds!'

[3] Franzius's *Women in Love* and Else Jaffe's *The Plumed Serpent* were later rejected (GSArchiv).

[4] The title of the German translation of *The Boy in the Bush* (see p. 38 n. 2).

[5] 'a monthly magazine'.

I feel I'll never write another novel: that damned old Franzius turning the *Plumed Serpent* into a ponderous boa-constrictor! Oh Germania! It really *is* time you bobbed your philosophic hair!

Wiedersehen! DHL[1]

3868. To Hon. Dorothy Brett, 18 October 1926

Text: MS UCin; Postmark, Firenze 19 . X 1926; Moore 942–3.

Villa Mirenda, *Scandicci* (Florence)
18 Oct. 1926.

Dear Brett

So you are really driving your car, all alone, up to the ranch! I hope you say a proper prayer every time you start her, for it seems to me risky. And you are more or less alone on the ranch! If it gets monotonous, shut the place up. – Anyhow it's a mercy you can go down to Mabel's for a change. You seem to have quite a busy time of it, one way and another.

We have been here a fortnight now, stayed a day or two in Paris, and two days in Lausanne. In London we saw Kot and Gertler, I did not see Murry – Kot just the same, only very hard up – Gertler working away. He says he is well, but he doesn't seem to me to have much stamina. He and Mrs Dobree are friends.[2] But the Dobrees probably are going to Cairo, where Bonamy will be professor of English for three years. – I liked him, Dobree, and her too. – I don't think we saw any new people. – Mrs Farbman had had appendicitis, but is better after the operation: and Ghita is at Oxford, studying to go to Girton or Somerville or wherever it is. Frieda saw Ottoline – I didn't. She said she found her a little faded.

It is quite hot here, like summer, except that the mornings are misty. One can go about in thin things, and leave all the windows open, which is very nice. I haven't yet ordered the wood for the stoves. But I must do so. We live very quietly – I haven't yet told anybody in Florence that I am back. I feel how nice it is, in the soft, sunny days that are already none too long, to see nobody, but just leisurely to drift one's way. I do very little work of any sort. I wrote down the music to *David*. Did I tell you I more or less promised to go to London for December, for the play? But I shall see, when the time draws near, if it seems worth it.

This is a pretty, hilly part of Tuscany. The little pink cyclamens are out in

[1] Someone unknown wrote below DHL's signature: 'Den Brief musst Du auf heben' ('You must keep this letter').

[2] Valentine Dobrée sat for a portrait by Gertler in 1919 (see *Mark Gertler*, ed. Noel Carrington, pp. 172, 182); he though her 'the most genuine and satisfactory young woman [he had] as yet come across' (p. 186).

the woods, the pines smell sweet, the 'cacciatori' are banging away all day at the little birds, like the fools and true countrymen of St. Francis that they are.

You said you had some suggestion from Mabel, for my very private ear. I wonder what it is!

I haven't heard from the Brewsters lately. He gave me the address: Thomas Cook, Athens. – for the end of Oct.

I wonder if it's cold yet, at the ranch. The nights are, I suppose. Does the ditch run?

Aldous Huxley just telegraphed, asking us to lunch Friday – I thought he was in Cortina. – So this starts Florence again! – I do hope all is well!

DHL

3869. To Gertrude Cooper, 18 October 1926

Text: MS Clarke; Lawrence–Gelder 139–41.

Villa Mirenda, *Scandicci* (Florence)
18 Oct. 1926

My dear Gertie

We had your letter a day or two ago. I was very glad to hear of you putting on $2\frac{1}{2}$ pounds: but shall be glad to hear that you can get up and walk about a bit. It must be very monotonous, all the time in bed. You have been three full weeks at Mundesley now.

We are settling down here, in the big, quiet rooms. It is very nice to be quite still, to let the autumn days go by. It is still quite hot in the middle of the day, only misty in the mornings. But the windows stay open day and night, and we only wear cotton things: hot as summer. In the woods the little wild cyclamens, pink ones, are dotted under the leaves. I am very fond of them. And all the time, the famous Italian 'hunters' are banging away at the little birds, sparrows, larks, finches, any little bird that flutters. They are awful fools, in some respects, these people. To see a middle-aged man stalking a sparrow with as much intensity as if it were male rhinocerous, and letting bang at it with a great gun, is too much for my patience. They will offer you a string of little birds for a shilling, robins, finches, larks, even nightingales. Makes one tired!

The natives are scared because there is an epidemic of typhoid, from an infected well, two villages away. If it moves nearer, I think we shall leave for a while. No use running risks.

The days pass so quickly. I do very little work – go out for walks by myself in these hills – and talk a bit with our only neighbours, the Wilkinsons. I'll get them to take some snapshots for you, it might amuse you. – It still seems like summer – I do hope the winter will be a short one. We haven't ordered any wood yet, for firing. We cook on little charcoal fires. (at that very moment, the milk boils over!)

I do hope you are getting better. I haven't yet heard from Ada – the thought of that coal strike is terribly depressing. Write soon –

Love – also from Frieda DHL

3870. To Dr Anton Kippenberg, 18 October 1926
Text: MS GSArchiv; Unpublished.

Villa Mirenda, *Scandicci* (Florenz), Italien
18 Okt 1926

Dear Dr Kippenberg

I have a letter from Curtis Brown in London complaining that no contract has been made through him for *Der Fuchs*. He says you wrote to him, that the agreement had been made with Frau Dr Jaffe-Richthofen. She, however, writes that she made no agreement at all in the matter, that she merely received 300 Mark translator's fee.

I wish you would please settle with Curtis Brown, about this: and please make every agreement for each translation of my books, with him; as I am legally responsible to him for the placing of all my work.

I also hear from my sister-in-law, Frau Dr Jaffe-Richthofen, that you do not wish her to continue her translation of *The Plumed Serpent*, in spite of the fact that Frau Dr. Kippenberg had authorised her to begin the work. I am sorry; both for my sister-in-law's disappointment, and because I really prefer her translation, as far as I know it. It seems to me more flexible; not so heavy as Herr Franzius'. – However, I suppose you are the final judge here!

With all good wishes.

Yours Sincerely D. H. Lawrence

3871. To Earl and Achsah Brewster, 25 October 1926
Text: MS UT; Brewster 106–7.

Villa Mirenda, *Scandicci*, Florence. Italy.
25 Oct. 1926

Dear Earl and Achsah

I found a letter from you, when we got here just three weeks ago, saying you haven't heard from me. Yet I have written faithfully to Almora, and also to Bombay. Now I'll send this to Athens.

I hope you've had a good time now, in Benares and Delhi and Ajanta Caves. In spite of all, I should like to see those places: though not at any great cost to my liver. – Aldous Huxley was here on Friday. How he too loathed India! I think it frightened him with a sense of squalor.

We've been here three weeks, and it's been lovely warm weather, till it began storming three days ago. Now it's rather chilly, but sunny, and a lovely autumn, with the yellow leaves dropping off the vines, and the sumachs scarlet. I must go this afternoon and see about ordering wood. Soon we must light the stoves, I suppose. I'm always sorry when that begins.

I wonder if this will find you in Greece! I talked to John Mavrogordato about the Isles.[1] He says the lesser ones are more thrilling, but there's nowhere to stay. I shall be very anxious to hear about Syra. Perhaps, even, in the spring we might have a boat and sail from isle to isle. My old dream! It seems a little nearer! If only one had a bit more money. It's the eternal *if*.

Brett says she will stay on the ranch all winter. I wonder if she will. We shall be here for some time, at least I hope so. The Stage Society are giving two performances of *David* in mid-December, and want me to go over at the end of November to help. I wonder if I shall!

Your book came today, and looks very nice, and I am glad to have it.[2] I shall read it to Frieda, and we'll all learn the difference between a bho-tree and a crab-apple tree. I still haven't succeeded in raising a nice little bho-tree in a pot, which I can carry round with me. Ma spero sempre![3]

I shall be glad to hear you are in Europe. So write soon, and tell me how you are, you vicissitudinarians!

D. H. Lawrence

3872. To Martin Secker, 27 October 1926

Text: MS UInd; Postmark, [. . .]; Secker 78–9.

Villa Mirenda, *Scandicci*, Firenze
27 Oct. 1926

Dear Secker

Thanks for your letter and *Lo sa il Tonno*.[4] Of the latter I have struggled through 75 pages, in utter boredom. This kind of satire, the would-be Swiftian, has to be very good if it's going to amount to anything. I find the tunny feeble and amateurish. This kind of Italian humour, very verbose in the ironical manner, bores me stiff. It's bad enough in life, but page after page is just dreary. It would bore me far too much to translate the tunny. Besides, the very title would kill it, in English. Who, do you imagine, knows even what a tunny is! If it had been: 'The Sardine Knows', you'd have stood more chance.

[1] John Nicolas Mavrogordato (1882–1970), Hellenist. Educated at Eton and Oxford; subsequently Professor of Byzantine and Modern Greek in Oxford. m. 1914, Christine Humphreys. He and DHL probably met through their mutual friend, Gertler.

[2] *The Life of Gotama the Buddha* (October 1926).

[3] 'I keep on hoping!'

[4] Riccardo Bacchelli, *Lo Sa il Tonno* (Milan, 1923). This very mannered satire was never translated into English.

– However, I handed the thing on to Aldous Huxley, who was here with his wife to lunch, to see if he could raise a feeling about it. – It might be the sort of feebleness the public might like, but I doubt it extremely.

Huxley and wife came in a grand new Italian car – 61,000[1] Lire. They are living in Cortina, in the Dolomites, till next June. It rather bores them – steep stiff mountains. They are in Florence only for a bit, being dentisted. – Somebody said in his book *One or Two Graces*, or whatever it is, was an unflattering character of me.[2] But what's the odds? He never knew me, anyhow. – They were quite nice today, he and Maria, we like them. But triste: un uomo finito, to be sentimental and Italian. Weh mir, dass ich ein Enkel bin![3] is his sad motto.

We had a week of thunder and torrents (off and on) – but today was a perfectly beautiful day of pure sun, nippy air in the shade, snow on the distant Appenines.

I haven't heard anything more about the play – so am no nearer to making up my mind about coming to England in December. We're just busy getting ready the winter salotta, on the south side: had it whitewashed, now must see about buying stuoie[4] for the floor, and painting rosebuds on the furniture. Scatter ye roses while ye may![5] – I am working at a story – shortish – don't feel like a long effort.[6] – Haven't seen anybody but Huxleys and Orioli – not Reggie Turner. But take it from me, he'll never do that book. He's incapable of the sustained work necessary. – The publishers do seem to be in a state of flux. They publish too many books by half: so much cargo, nowhere to dump it, no wonder they founder.

It will be fun to see you and Rina here in January – the time flies by. – Do you want the *Tunny* back?

Sempre D. H. Lawrence

[1] 61,000] 51,000

[2] Huxley's *Two or Three Graces and Other Stories* was published in May 1926. The title-story contains a Lawrentian character, Kingham – red-bearded, talented, from a working-class background, a man who would never admit a mistake 'unless his passion for self-humiliation happened at the moment to be stronger than his passion for self-assertion'. Huxley denied that Kingham was modelled on DHL: the character 'was concocted before I knew him – at least I'd only seen him once' (*Letters of Aldous Huxley*, ed. Grover Smith, 1969, pp. 339–40).

On one of the visits from the Huxleys in October (cf. Letters 3874–5), Maria gave DHL four used canvases (see Letters 3887 and 3897). For a vivid description of the occasion and its consequences, see 'Making Pictures', *Phoenix II* 602–3.

[3] 'Woe is me, that I am a grandchild!' Cf. Mephistopheles in Goethe's *Faust*, Part I, l. 1977: 'Weh dir, dass du ein Enkel bist!' ('Woe to you, that you are a grandchild!').

[4] 'mats'.

[5] Herrick, 'To the Virgins, to Make Much of Time', l. 1 ['Gather . . . rosebuds . . .'].

[6] On 26 October 1926 DHL had written as far as p. 41 of the first version of *Lady Chatterley's Lover* (Tedlock, *Lawrence MSS* 20).

3873. To Margaret King, 28 October 1926
Text: MS Needham; Unpublished.

Villa Mirenda, *Scandicci*, Florence.
28 Oct. 1926

My dear Peg

Glad to get your letter – but what a bore about Joan's tonsils! But she did look as if she needed them out. What a creature the human being is, really! How is your mother since her teeth are out?

I write to Gertie regularly, and had a letter from her yesterday. She says she's gained five pounds – but is still mostly in bed. Which means that her temperature goes up every day: and they'll never let her get up until it stays rather on the *under-normal* side: which means the germ is no longer very active. But it's a fight, as I knew it would be.

I heard from Arabella that she was sending you a book of French songs I asked her to get for you as they passed through Paris. When it arrives, write and thank her:
Mrs Richard Aldington, Malthouse Cottage. Padworth, near Reading, Berks.

Write to me if you like in French, but don't expect me to answer in the same language – I get sick to death of languages. But I will correct your letter as best I can. Don't expect me to be very perfect, either. But it really is good practice for you to write in French. You'll have to find another girl-correspondent. Your last little hussy of the tavern was too flighty.

We've been having a week of storms, thunder, wind, rain in torrents, and hail. Today however, thank the Lord, it seems perfectly peaceful. The air is colder, there is snow on the Appenines across the Arno valley: but the day has been perfectly radiant, sunshine all day long, from dawn to sunset, I sat in the woods all morning, doing a bit of writing. But the sun was too hot – I had to get into the shade after a while. – And the distances marvellously clear. – I only hope it will last.

That coal-strike is too everlasting, too long even for the mercy of God! What is your father doing in the business? Is anything more said about the wholesale venture, or any other move? And I wonder how they are doing at Ripley? I haven't heard for a long time.

We've been busy getting the big sitting-room on the south side ready for winter. The peasants had quite a time, whitewashing it. They spray on the whitewash with the big spray they use for the vines – a garden spray – and it makes a beautiful surface. They of course just enjoy being in a big mess. – But it's done, thank goodness. Now we must buy thick matting for the floors, and when the stove is going, we should be cosy enough. But so far, we don't need any heating. – Well – tell me how Joan goes on, and how everything is, in French if you feel like it.

Love to you all. DHL

3874. To Ada Clarke, 28 October 1926

Text: MS Clarke; cited in Lawrence–Gelder 142.

Villa Mirenda, *Scandicci*, Florence.
28 Oct. 1926

My dear Sister

I haven't heard from you for a long time. Is it because you've got depressed, what with that everlasting and unspeakable strike, and one thing and another? Or is the business picking up, in spite of all? I'm sure it's a weariness beyond words, and what the miners themselves must be feeling, I don't like to think. Certainly it's one of the greatest disasters that has ever happened to England.

I heard from Gertie that she's still in bed, but has gained five pounds. It means, however, that her temperature goes up every evening. I know from Gertler that they won't let her go about until her temperature *never* rises above normal, but rather stays below. And that, in her case, will be difficult. I think I shall have to write to Dr. Lucas myself, and ask him what is his opinion of her. – But she's gained five pounds. And I knew it would be a bit of a fight with her.

I hear from Peggy, too, that Joan must have her tonsils cut. That child is a real misery! But she looked as if she needed her tonsils removing.

We've been having a week of stormy weather – thunder-storms all the time – and showers of pouring rain – and bursts of wind. Thank goodness, now it is quiet again – with snow on the tips of the Appenines opposite, a cold air, but a bright and blazing sunshine. Such days are very lovely. I go out in the morning and sit in the pine-woods alone and do a bit of writing – then take a walk. We see very few people – but I'm glad.

Today Aldous Huxley and his wife came out for lunch, in a grand new car. We used to know her at Ottolines. They were very nice, very pleasant, but sad, as if life had nothing for them. Really, people have no pep, they so easily go blank, and so young. – They offered me their old car – a good one – cheap: but I dont want it.

I haven't heard anything further about the play, so am not making any decision about coming to England. It's really nicer here. We've been getting ready the big sitting room on the south side of the house, for the winter. I must order wood for the stoves. We shall be able to keep warmer, I think, than in the Bernarda.

Let me know how you all are. I am always thinking about the strike. Has that Stanley sent the money back yet? And how is Jack in his school? – all right? – It's such lovely autumn here, the arbutus trees so pretty, with red and yellow balls dangling.

Love! DHL

3875. To Gertrude Cooper, 28 October 1926

Text: MS Clarke; cited in Lawrence–Gelder 141–2.

Villa Mirenda, *Scandicci*, Florence
28 Oct. 1926

My dear Gertie

Your letter yesterday! Bad luck that you are still in bed! So they can't get the temperature right down? You know, they keep you in bed until the temperature *never* rises above one degree *below* normal. I myself, at that rate, should be in bed for ever, for mine is always up and down. I haven't heard from Dr Lucas, but shall write to him and ask about you. – They won't try and ex-ray you till you're out of bed, now. – Oh, it's a bit of a fight, and I knew it would be! But you've gained five pounds, and that's the beginning of the victory, never you fear.

We here have had a series of violent thunder-storms, torrents of rain with sunshine between. Last night it suddenly turned cold, with snow on the mountains opposite. And today has been a perfectly beautiful day, clear sun from dawn to sunset, and the distances bright and lovely. Aldous Huxley – a writer – and his wife came for the day – in their fine new car. They want me to buy their old car, which is perfectly good. But I won't bother myself learning to drive, and struggling with a machine. I've no desire to scud about the face of the country, myself. It is much pleasanter to go quietly into the pine-woods and sit and do there what bit of work I do. Why rush from place to place!

I haven't heard from Ada for a long time. I don't know why she doesn't write. I suppose they're both depressed. I know they miss you a good deal: and then that everlasting strike is enough to ruin the nerves of a donkey-engine. I'm really thankful you're out of it, I know it was that which helped to pull you down. – Margaret King wrote that Joan must have her tonsils cut. What a child that is, always under the weather some way or other! Really, when will a bit of bright news come along?

We've been getting the sitting-room on the south side ready for winter. The sun pours in there. But the rooms are almost as high as a church, so the peasants spray the whitewash on with the garden-sprayer which they use for the vines. It makes a lovely surface: and a glorious mess, which they love.

Frieda wants to add a word, so I'll stop. – I shall be glad to hear you are getting up, it will mean the temperature is down, and that's a big stride. We've got to win all right.

Send us a line.

Love! DHL

[Frieda Lawrence begins]

How splendid gaining 5 lbs! I feel quite envious (not for myself, Lord preserve me) but for Lawr[ence]. It must be dreary, uphill work getting better and I wish I could send you some sunshine and grapes – More another day –

Yrs Frieda L –

3876. To Mabel Dodge Luhan, 30 October 1926

Text: MS Brill; Luhan 312–14.

Villa Mirenda, *Scandicci* (Florence)
30 Oct. 1926

My dear Mabel

My agents sent back the little M. Blanchard sketch, which I'd asked them to try round: said it wasn't good enough: and I agree with them. Why bother with those trifles! As I say, whenever you take a literary attitude, your stuff's no good. The novel, or[1] rather the *Memories*, is so good because you're not being literary: only occasionally a bit of a literary taint comes in. When you are only trying to put down your own truth, nothing else, the stuff becomes excellent. I do think the *Memories* extremely good. As for literature! – well, twenty years hence, Willa Cather's books will be where most other books are, under dust. Orage's books don't exist even now. There's nothing in it all, this literariiness.

I was talking to Aldous Huxley about *Intimate Memories*, and he was pining to read them. But don't send the MS. round any more than you need. – And when there does come a chance of printing it, print it, even if you only distribute a hundred copies at present.

I'm glad everything sounds so nice at Taos. That must have been a rare bean-feast, the Rodeo. It all sounds very jolly, really, and a lot of me wants to be back. We'll see how we feel when the winter turns.

I can hardly believe Tony's mother is dead. I caught her eye once or twice, and she did not look like a dier. – But a man can't have his mother for ever.

There are a few aspens on the hill here, and they drizzle slowly away in greeny-yellow. I think of the mountains at Taos and the ranch. No place can ever be more beautiful than that[2] is out there. If only oneself were a bit tougher!

[1] or] is [2] that] it

I've been painting pink roses on a dull yellow bureau: doesn't it sound Florentine?

It's a scirocco day, warm, moist, like a hot-house. – Remember me to Ida, to everybody.

D. H. Lawrence

If you send that bracelet, do let me know what it costs. The address is: Mrs Richard Aldington, Malthouse Cottage, *Padworth, near Reading*, Berks. *England*.

DHL

[Frieda Lawrence begins][1]

[Villa Mirenda

Dear Mabel

Yes, do send Arabella that bracelet. I will send you some of the lovely Florentine ribbons. Ever since in your novel I read about your Buffalo girl ribbon boxes, I wanted to send you some. Yes, your batches of novel are read with eagerness. You gave a good idea of the Duse, I am sure.[2] One has passed *that* milestone and with your novel you have had a marvellous spring cleaning of the human emotions, so now one ought to be able to get on. Lawrence seems well. We are getting a sunny winter room ready, painting the furniture – it needs it! I wonder if we shall come! Of course we love the ranch, but Lawrence is interested in Europe and there are the children, too. Elsa is engaged to a Teddy Seaman, he is learning to farm and the new young element is good in our lives.[3] Monty and Lawrence have also made friends, it's all come right – grazie a Dio! It's jolly here, too, our only neighbors 4 Wilkinsons, parents, a boy and a girl; had a well known puppet show. They have got them all: vegetarian, anti-vivisection, conscientious objector, socialism, etc. Of Florence we see little. I am bored with spite and that's all you get. . . . My love to Tony. You sound happy. The novel must have been a great thing for you.

My best wishes to you. F.

Why does A. think I am pining to get thin, or *ought* to be! My waistline is a great comfort to me and I wouldn't be cardboardy elegant, not I! Especially here in Italy. And why do you all think my life is a desperate struggle to hang on to Lawrence? It really does make me appear such a poor thing! I am jolly glad to be alone sometimes, so is he, but we are both glad to come together again, very glad! . . . Our lives, Lawrence's and mine, are so easy, if nobody

[1] MS of Frieda's letter is missing; the text is taken from Luhan 313–14.

[2] See Letter 3675 and p. 423 n. 1.

[3] Bernal Edward de Martelly Seaman (b. 1900) and Elsa Weekley m. 1929. (The allegation about farming was untrue.)

makes any mischief! . . . No, I am not such a fool as you all seem to think me; so there is a bit of temper for you; but then I ask for something else! Good luck to you.]

3877. To Barbara Weekley, [c. 31 October 1926]

Text: Nehls, iii. 189.

[Villa Mirenda, Scandicci, Florence]
[c. 31 October 1926]

Don't let [Elsa] marry a man unless she feels his physical presence warm to her . . . Passion has dignity; affection can be a very valuable thing, and one can make a life relationship with it.

3878. To Montague Weekley, [31 October 1926]

Text: MS NCL; Nehls, iii. 115–16.

[Frieda Lawrence begins]

Villa Mirenda, Scandicci
Sunday

Dear Monty,

It was *nice* to get your letter, and I'm so glad you are feeling better – From my window I can see a procession of lights going along, some Saint's day or other, Lawrence goes into the woods to write, he is writing a short long story, always breaking new ground, the curious class feeling this time or rather the soul against the body, no I dont explain it well, the *animal* part [Lawrence interjects: – Ooray!!! Eureka!] What are you doing? We are just getting such a jolly room ready, white, and lovely stuffs you get in Florence and the sun shines in all day [Lawrence interjects: (some days)], warm as toast! O dear and you are sitting over horrid gasfires and dark England, [Lawrence interjects: Poverino!!] But next spring we'll take a place in England and you must come for week ends and we'll have a connected life. Lawrence wants it too, wants to see something of the younger generation. I hope Elsa really has done the right thing and wont be bored with her Teddy – Dont be too spartan, but keep a steady core in yourself; but you'll get bored with my preaching – The Huxleys came, very nice he but such a weed 'Weh Dir, dass Du ein Enkel bist', Lawr said; and she was one of Lady Ottoline's protegées and never got over it.[1] Lawrence says, he'll say a word, *do* come at Xmas if you can?

Your mother

[1] See *Letters*, ii. 325 n. 1. For Lady Ottoline Morrell, see *Letters*, ii. 253 n. 3.

[Lawrence begins]
Dear Monty

Your Ma is wonderful at giving advice, and even more wonderful at taking it! In which latter, I think you're like her.

I haven't heard any more from those Stage Society people, so don't know if we shall come to London in December, for the play. I emphatically don't want to, but 'England expects' etc. – What about your coming here with Mistress Barby at Christmas time? If we're here, it might be fun. Your Ma is pining for somebody to think the house is grand: she gets no satisfaction out of me, that way. Anyhow it's Sunday evening, we sit in the kitchen with the lamp on the table, your Mother eats a persimmon with a spoon and offers me 'the other one' – while I write. So much for grandeur. – I have painted windowframes by the mile, doors by the acre, painted a chest of drawers till it turned into a bureau, and am not through, by a long chalk. This is living heroically, à la Frieda. Mussolini says vivi pericolosamente! and then makes millions of laws against anybody who takes a pot shot at him. Siamo così. Hope you're well!

DHL

3879. To Compton Mackenzie, [November 1926]

Text: The Gramophone, iv (December 1926), 264.

[Villa Mirenda, Scandicci, Florence]
[November 1926][1]

My favourite song is, I think, 'Kishmul's Galley', from the Hebridean Songs,[2] and my favourite composer, if one must be so selective, Mozart; and singer, a Red Indian singing to the drum, which sounds pretty stupid.

3880. To Nancy Pearn, 1 November 1926

Text: MS UT; Unpublished.

Villa Mirenda, *Scandicci* (Florence)
1 Nov 1926

Dear Miss Pearn

The Calendar, like most other little magazines, seems to have a swelled head

[1] Compton Mackenzie announced in the November 1926 issue of *The Gramophone* (of which he was editor) that he would publish in the December number a 'Symposium' of 'distinguished men and women' who had been willing to name their favourite song, composer, tune and singer. (It is clear from Mackenzie's *Life and Times: Octave Six*, p. 98, that Beerbohm's response had reached proof stage by 9 November.) Among others invited were Belloc, Chesterton, De la Mare, Galsworthy, Maugham and Shaw.

[2] DHL recalled this song (the title of which Mackenzie printed as 'Kishmul's Gallery') from Marjorie Kennedy-Fraser's *Songs of the Hebrides* (1909), p. 80. He had become acquainted with her book in 1917 (see *Letters*, iii. 164 and n. 6). DHL sang this song at a farewell party for the Brewsters, in late August 1928 (Brewster 292).

and a shrivelled pocket. I don't care a button whether I do a review for them or not: I call it charity work, at the price, and with all the pompous conditions. But if they send a book along, I'll review it, *if it interests me*.[1] That's my only condition.

Did you get a story I sent – 'More Modern Love' – ?[2] It was sent two weeks ago, but you didn't mention it in your letter.

All Saints today, and the natives trying to festivate in a phenominal rain. It's warm though – and has been rather good weather.

Saluti! D. H. Lawrence

3881. To Curtis Brown, [2 November 1926]

Text: Curtis Brown, *Contacts* (1935), p. 72.

[Villa Mirenda, Scandicci, Florence]
[2 November 1926]

Yesterday and to-day are All the Saints and All the Dead, so both days it's poured incessantly, and put all the candles out. It's been fine nearly all the time and warm – no fires yet. But this is one of Noah's opportunities.

3882. To Giuseppe Orioli, [7 November 1926]

Text: MS UCLA; Unpublished.

Villa Mirenda, *Scandicci*
Sunday

Dear Pino

We came to see you at midday yesterday, but found you shut up: do hope you aren't ill again. I don't suppose we shall be coming in again for a week or so. – Miss Morrison wrote that she is back.

Did you have my note about the stuoie? We're getting on with the salotta – bought a bed, so you can stay a night when you come out, if you wish. I'm painting doors and windows. The Italians say – loro si divertono! – If *they* were doing it, it would be: ma, un lavoro faticoso, sa![3]

Did you see my little story *Sun* printed by the *Coterie*. I'll show it you – you might sell one or two in your shop – But they only printed a hundred. It's got nice Sicilian background.

Remember us to Reggie, hope he's well.

DHL

[1] See Letter 3903 and n. 5.

[2] Published under the title 'In Love?' in *Dial*, lxxxiii (November 1927), 391–404, and collected in *The Woman Who Rode Away*.

[3] 'The Italians say – they are enjoying themselves! – . . . but, a tiring job, you know!'

3883. To Charles Lahr, 7 November 1926

Text: MS ULon; Postmark, Scandicci 9. 11.26; Unpublished.

Villa Mirenda, *Scandicci* (Florence), Italy
7 Novem. 1926

Dear Sir[1]

Thanks for the copies of *Sun* and the *Coterie*.[2] *Sun* looks very nice, and the *Coterie* is very amusing. I like its tone: and nobody airing their opinions is a relief. Will you please put me down for a years subscription.[3] I enclose cheque for ten shillings.

Yrs D. H. Lawrence

3884. To Nelly Morrison, [7 November 1926]

Text: TMSC NWU; Unpublished.

Villa Mirenda, Scandicci.
Sunday

Dear Nelly Morrison,

Glad to hear you're back. How are you – are you well? I was afraid you were ill when I saw, across the Arno, the flat shut up.

We've been here a month, quite a lovely month really. I don't care for big cities like London and Paris.

When will you come out and see us? We are getting ready the salotta on the south side for winter. I think it will be comfortable.

We were in town yesterday. Would have called and said Hallo! if we'd known you were there. Probably towards the end of the week we'll be in Florence again.

Remember us to Gino. How is Miss Hill? – the long one – and also the shorter one?[4] I hope they're in good form.

Au revoir from us both D. H. Lawrence

Country is quite lovely. Come out any sunny day.

[1] Charles Lahr (1885–1971), anarchist, bookseller, publisher and eccentric. b. Germany; 1905 fled to London to avoid conscription. Interned during World War I. Took over the Progressive Bookshop, 68 Red Lion Square, Holborn, in 1921; specialised in radical literature and modern first edns. Founded a quarterly, the *New Coterie*, 1925; contributors included DHL, Augustus John, Stanley Spencer, William Rothenstein; it ran for six issues. Published the unexpurgated edn of *Pansies*, 1929 (Roberts A47c and d). m. 1922, Esther Archer. See Kenneth Hopkins, *The Corruption of a Poet* (1954), pp. 97ff.; David Goodway, 'Charles Lahr', *London Magazine*, June/July 1977, 46–55; obituary, *The Times*, 18 August 1971.

[2] See p. 352 n. 1.

[3] The cheque, dated 9 November 1926 and drawn on the Aldwych Branch of the Westminster Bank (see *Letters*, ii. 189 n. 3), is attached to the MS.

[4] Unidentified.

3885. To Elfie Rosebery, 8 November 1926

Text: MS Secor; Postmark, Scandicci 8.11.26; Unpublished.

Villa Mirenda, *Scandicci* (Florence)
8 Novem 1926

Dear Mrs Rosebery

We are back here, after a time in BadenBaden and England and Scotland. Nice to be peaceful again. – I'm so sorry your husband has had such a miserable time doctoring. – I can imagine you'll welcome the peacefulness of the Palumbo – hope nothing will have gone any further wrong, there.

I wonder if you will go by Corfu, and hear anything of a ship. I should still love that Odyssey. I met John Mavrogordato in London – he owns one of the little isles – but says one can only do the archipelago if one has a ship to sleep in – no accommodation at all. – The Brewsters, from Capri (Americans, who went to India to be Buddhists, when we were there in March) – are leaving India, don't like it. He thinks they will winter in the Isle of Syra – or Sura – about eight hours from Athens – from the Piraeus. That was a summer resort island, so will have houses and hotel. He very much wants us to go there, when they are there. All might be done in a ship – if it weren't a fabulous cost, like the one in Naples.

I may have to go to England in December, but I hope not. Anyhow this address is always good.

Trusting you'll reach Ravello all right. Let me know any news.

Greetings from me and my wife.

Yrs Sincerely D. H. Lawrence

3886. To Nancy Pearn, 9 November 1926

Text: MS UT; Unpublished.

Villa Mirenda, *Scandicci* (Florence)
9 Novem. 1926

Dear Miss Pearn

I did the review quickly – feel I've been quite nice to Tomlinson.[1]

If the *T.P.'s* don't want it, they needn't pay for it. And if they want to cut it shorter, they can please themselves.

I never got the post card saying you had the story.[2]

Yrs D. H. Lawrence

[1] DHL's review of H. M. Tomlinson's *Gifts of Fortune* (October 1926) was published in *T. P.'s and Cassell's Weekly*, 1 January 1927 (Roberts C150).

[2] See Letter 3880 and n. 2.

3887. To Maria and Aldous Huxley, 11 November 1926
Text: Huxley 672.

Villa Mirenda, Scandicci, Firenze.
11 Novembre, 1926.

Dear Maria and Aldous, –

Many thanks for the photographs. I think *gli autori*[1] figure too often.

I've already painted a picture on one of the canvases. I've hung it up in the new *salotto*. I call it the 'Unholy Family',[2] because the *bambino* – with a *nimbus* – is just watching anxiously to see the young man give the semi-nude young woman *un gros baiser. Molto moderno!*

Hope it's nice at Cortina – it has emptied rain on us for days – but there's a clear moon this evening.

Haven't seen a soul. No news. *Tante cose.*

DHL

3888. To Thomas Seltzer, [13 November 1926]
Text: MS Forster; cited in Brown, *Contacts*, p. 73.

[Villa Mirenda, Scandicci, Florence]
[13 November 1926][3]

Dear Thomas Seltzer

Your letter, with Adele's, came a week ago. I don't know why it took so long. – I had, in all conscience, to ask Curtis Brown his opinion. I cant promise to come back to you, not now at least. – You say you will pay me the arrears if I come back, but not if I don't: which is a sort of threat. And you know why I left you: because you left *me* quite in the dark. – And Adele says I am to come back with a best seller under my arm. When I have written 'Sheik II' or 'Blondes Prefer Gentlemen', I'll come.[4] Why does anybody look to me for a best seller? I'm the wrong bird.

I'm awfully sorry things went to pieces. Blame me, if you like, for leaving you. But blame yourself, now as ever, for not knowing how to be simple and open with me.

And I do hope you will get rich one day – honestly I do.

Yrs DHL

[1] 'the authors'.

[2] Under the title *A Holy Family* the painting (30″ × 26″) is reproduced in *The Paintings of D. H. Lawrence* (Mandrake Press, 1929), plate [2]. DHL comments briefly on it in 'Making Pictures', *Phoenix II* 603. (On the 'canvases', see Letter 3897.)

[3] The text is printed from the copy of DHL's letter to Seltzer provided for Curtis Brown at the foot of the following letter; it is assumed that both were written on the same day.

[4] DHL alludes here to two famous best-sellers of the decade: *The Sheik* (1919), a *succès de scandale* by Edith Maude Hull which was filmed with Rudolph Valentino in the leading part and prompted the sequel, *Sons of the Sheik* (1925); and *Gentlemen Prefer Blondes* (1925) by Anita Loos (1893–1981), American novelist, which was dramatised in New York, 1926. DHL refers briefly to *The Sheik* in 'The Future of the Novel' (see *Study of Thomas Hardy*, ed. Steele, pp. 151, 153).

3889. To Curtis Brown, 13 November 1926

Text: MS Forster; Moore 945–6.

Villa Mirenda, *Scandicci* (Florence)
13 Nov. 1926

Dear C[urtis] B[rown]

I wrote to Seltzer – I'll send you a copy of the letter. Yes, he annoyed me too, with his tone!

The *Glad Ghosts* half-dozen came from Benns. Many thanks for your trouble.

What I feel about Secker is that he is so obscure, and his range is so definitely, and, I'm afraid, for ever limited and circumscribed. I like him personally. I don't want to leave him. But I feel that, even for *his* sake, if I am ever to get a wider public, some other publisher will have to help break down the fence. There's that to be thought of.

I'll copy out Seltzer's letter – mine to him, I mean. I dont want to do anything, with publishers, you don't know of from me.

Yrs D. H. Lawrence

3890. To Martin Secker, [15 November 1926]

Text: MS UInd; Postmark, Firenze 16 . XI 1926; Secker 79–80.

Villa Mirenda, Scandicci (Florence)
15 Nov.

Dear Secker

Your letter today. Do you really think those essays are good enough? It seems to me they are rather half baked, some of 'em. The four essays called 'Mornings in Mexico' – there must be four, they are a set – are good. But what about the others?[1] I doubt if I want them put in a book – they're not good enough. – The essays, other than 'The Crown', in *Reflections on the Death of a Porcupine*, are very much better. But I'm not keen on having those republished, either. – But be sure, if I don't want you to do this book, I wouldn't have Harrap or anybody else do it. I hate the thought of half baked essays in vol. form. Let me know exactly what you think – and send me the material you think genuinely suitable for a book, so I can look through it – if you have it. I feel very doubtful. – I will write and stop Curtis Browns going any further, when I hear from you. – Only about the four Mexico essays I feel quite sure – 'Corasmin and the Parrot' perhaps came in the *Adelphi*, also perhaps 'Market Day'. But I have 'Market Day' here, from an American periodical: *Travel*. – 'The Mozo' and 'The Walk to Huayapa' are the other two. Now what else?[2]

[1] See Letters 3740 and p. 482 n. 3 and 3804.

[2] See Letter 3321 and p. 186 n. 1. Four more essays were added to form *Mornings in Mexico* (Secker, 1927). See Letter 3894.

Yes, go ahead with the 3/6 novels in the spring, and we'll see the result. – I have begun a novel in the Derbyshire coal-mining districts – already rather improper. The gods alone know where it will end – if they'll help me out with it.

We've had too much rain, but today is lovely and warm and sunny. It's never been cold – no fires yet.

Saw Reggie Turner on Saturday. You'll never get a book out of him – nor will anyone else. – Our Tenente – now Capitano[1] – came for the day from Gradisca, in the Udine district – he is so miserable there, and descended on me with such a dense fog of that peculiar inert Italian misery, dreariness, that I am only just recovering. The Italians are certainly more dreary than the English, just now.

We've made the salotta on the south side – very nice – and I've painted a nice big picture that our vegetarian neighbours the Wilkinsons are afraid to look at, it's too 'suggestive'. Why do vegetarians always behave as if the world was vegetably propagated, even?

That Robert Atkins funked *David*. Mrs Whitworth is producing *The Widowing of Mrs Holroyd* in mid December, and *David* in March – with Nugent Monck for producer – whoever he is.[2] I am glad, because I needn't go to England now till end February, at least.

If you come to Florence I will find you a decent pensione for about 35 Liras, and you can often come out here for the day. You'll see it's not very convenient for guests to sleep here – not good enough. – The tram from Florence is only 1.50 – half an hour's ride.

Best wishes to you all – Frieda did write.

Yrs D. H. Lawrence[3]

[1] Ravagli.

[2] Phyllis Whitworth acted as impresario. *The Widowing of Mrs. Holroyd* was produced by Esmé Saville Percy (1887–1957), a distinguished actor who had considered producing the play in 1915 (see *Letters*, ii. 384); he staged it on 12, 13 and 19 December 1926 for the 300 Club and Stage Society at the Kingsway Theatre. Atkins did not produce *David* (see p. 470 n. 1). Nugent Monck (1877–1958) was well known as a producer associated with the Maddermarket Theatre in Norwich, from 1919.

[3] Secker's letter to Curtis Brown, 25 November 1926 (Secker Letter-Book, UIll) illuminates some points in DHL's and anticipates Letter 3894. It reads:

Dear Curtis Brown

Many thanks for yours. Lawrence ought not to be restive, for I am in constant communication with him at Scandicci, and he knows all my plans. "Sea and Sardinia" will be included in The New Adelphi Library early next year, (see enclosed), and composition is in hand. In his last letter to me, the author did not seem to think highly of the proposed collection of travel papers, the copy for which Pollinger submitted here, but I have told him that a short book, restricted to the Mexican sketches alone, would be good, and I have asked his permission to negotiate terms with you for this. I am awaiting his reply. Furthermore, we are starting next year a uniform thin-paper edition of his novels at 3/6, the first two titles being "The Lost Girl" and "The Plumed Serpent", so that Lawrence will be quite busy in our list during the early months of

3890a. To Bonamy Dobrée, 15 November 1926

Text: MS Dobrée; Unpublished.

Villa Mirenda, *Scandicci* (Florence)
15 Novem. 1926

Dear Dobrée

How are you and Mrs Dobrée – and where is Cairo, on your cards or off 'em? If you've not decided, do try and make it only for *one year* that you pledge yourself to those awful half-caste Egyptians, merest mongrels of all mongrels, and who will, I bet, try to ask you questions in bad French, during your good English lectures. A bas la canaille, – di qualunque colore.[1]

I heard from Mrs Whitworth today that that Robt Atkins man is not doing *David*. Tant mieux! he's not a miracle of finesse, by the looks of him. And guts! my boy, guts! will never sing a Psalm. – She, Mrs Whitworth, will do the *Widowing of Mrs Holroyd* in mid-December, and Nugent Monck, whoever he is, will produce *David* in March. Hope he'll be able to get it out of his sleeve, not like Atkins, whose white rabbit wouldn't materialise at his Hey! Presto! – And where will you be?

If you go to Egypt, remember we might come some day if you could tell me of a mild and non-social way of doing it. – We shan't come to England now, not until I am needed for casting an eye on *David* – in February or early March. Will you be wandering this way? If so, let me know in time.

I always laugh when I think of that fiaschetto[2] of a lunch in that pub. with you and Mrs Whitworth and the others. But that was a nice lunch we had at Well walk. How is Mrs Dobrée? is her cold better? – I've been reading Plato (in English) once more. Do you think all that myth stuff is Plato's own, and only the argumentative tiresomeness is Socrates'? Anyhow there's some sad gaps in Plato's philosophic mantle, and one sees odd bits of bare skin. I'll read the commentators one day.

Lovely warm autumn day – arbutus berries and mushrooms in the wood.

Best wishes D. H. Lawrence

3891. To Richard Aldington, 17 November 1926

Text: MS SIU; Moore 946.

Villa Mirenda, *Scandicci* (Florence)
17 Novem 1926

Dear Richard

Could you find out for Mabel Lujan *how* she might set about to leave her

next year. All this will help to carry-on while he is writing his new novel. I suggested some time ago that it would be as well if he gave us an English background for a change, and I was pleased to hear that his new book is to have a Derbyshire setting.

Yours sincerely

[1] 'Down with the rabble, – of whatever colour.'

[2] 'mini-disaster'.

MSS of her Memoirs in the hands of the Academie Française. It contains *such* things – and about so many living and known people – she is sure, if she happens to die, it will be destroyed. So she wants to leave it somewhere safe, and where it will have a chance ultimately of seeing the day – I wish you'd write direct to her and tell her how to proceed.

– Mrs Mabel Lujan, *Taos*, New Mexico, U S A.

and then she's pretty sure also to send Arabella that Indian bracelet: which would be nice. I'm sorry to bother you.

It's so hot here, hotter than when you were here – and sunny – the wild strawberries are coming out in a profusion of flowers. Uncanny!

How are you both?

DHL

3892. To Ada Clarke, 20 November 1926
Text: MS Clarke; Unpublished.

Villa Mirenda, Scandicci (Florence)
20 Novem 1926

My dear Sister

Our letters crossed last time. – I didn't write to Gertie's doctors – I know her left lung is much worse than we had thought – I suspected it all the time – and the fact that they can't get the temperature down means that they can't stop the germ's activity. But the fact that she's fatter also means the germ isn't making any headway. So they'll get the temperature down in time. It's a fight – and I was afraid it would be a long fight – but it's these first weeks that are the worst. Once the temperature *begins* to go down, it all goes much quicker. When the germ has got deep hold, it's much more difficult.

So the strike, at least, is over – though I haven't seen the English papers.[1]

I hear from the 300 Club that *David* is postponed till March, and that they're doing *The Widowing of Mrs Holroyd* in December. So we shan't come to London this year. I wonder if you'd like to go to London for *Mrs Holroyd* – about mid-December. I could get you a ticket, and you could go with Milly Beveridge, who will be a member of the 300. Let me know. Then I suppose I shall have to come to England about the end of February, for *David*, because that really needs me there. So we can stay here quietly for a time.

It's rained a great deal, thunder and lighting – but not cold – and sunshine between. So I go for good long walks by myself. And I have painted a biggish picture, about a yard long, ¾ wide in oils. It looks very nice – people – modern.

[1] In view of the accelerating, unofficial return to work, a Miners' Federation delegate conference voted on 19 November 1926 to end the strike.

I am rather pleased with it. It is easy to paint in these big rooms. We've made the sitting-room on the south side very nice, and quite cosy – so we have a warm room for the winter. – Now the Wilkinsons have gone into Florence for a couple of months – they are our only neighbours – she said she was tired of doing the cooking! They are vegetarians, and she boiled a few chestnuts now and then. Women can be the limit of selfishness: she certainly is.

I must write to Gertie. I keep wondering if there is anything I could send her, but have no inspiration. Can you suggest anything? And tell me what you'd like yourself for Christmas, and the children. I'm afraid G. will be in Mundesley for Christmas – but better there, than in the cemetery. It's a thing that's got to be fought out.

How is Joan? – I must write to her too. The time goes by so quickly. But the winter is only just beginning. Be sure to let me know about the play.

Love! DHL

3893. To Mabel Dodge Luhan, 23 November 1926

Text: MS Brill; Luhan 314–16.

Villa Mirenda, Scandicci (Florence)
23 Novem. 1926

My dear Mabel

Your letter and the two Florentine sketches of Craig and Savage Landor.[1] The last two are quite well enough, if you don't do any more like them. But you are losing the peculiar intimate flow that the *Memories* have had so far, and are getting a bit hard and journalistic. Perhaps people would like these two sketches very much: it's so smart and unhurt. But the genuine throb is going out of them. – Don't write if you're out of mood. Don't force yourself. And wait for grace.

I wrote at once to Richard Aldington, as you seemed keen on the Academie Française idea, to ask him to write to you direct, as soon as he had found out about the business of procedure. No doubt he will do so. – The other idea is to alter all the names, carefully, and print the thing yourself, not more than two hundred copies, and sell them by subscription to people you can really trust.

If you did it in Santa Fe – and did most of the work yourself – and didn't talk about it *at all* till it was finished, and then only very guardedly – you could secure the distribution of two hundred copies – then print no more, at least for

[1] Gordon Craig (1872–1966), artist and stage designer. The illegitimate son of the actress Ellen Terry, and father of Isadora Duncan's child, Craig was a vivid character who would interest Mabel Luhan. He opened an acting school in Florence and was known to Mabel and her first husband, Edwin Dodge. Walter Savage Landor (1775–1864), best known for his *Imaginary Conversations* (1824–8); another colourful English expatriate in Florence.

a time, but have the plates preserved. – This would be very little more than showing the MS. to people, as you have done: less dangerous, perhaps. – But a very good man to consult about this would be
Harold T. Mason. The Centaur Bookshop, 1224 Chancellor St. *Philadelphia.* Make it plain that it is not money you are after – and be careful. You can do most things, if you obviously *do not want* to attract attention.

I wish we could come over for a bit. I wish I could come today. It is rainy and heavily dull here – I'd welcome even the snow at Taos. But how can one take that long journey, so wearying and so expensive, all at once. We shall have to wait at least till March, and see then.

Many thanks for the Voltaire book: it interests me, but is sugared up horribly.[1] I detest the masturbating kind of style it is written in. I'm afraid I've nothing serious to send you in return – only a story!

I shrink rather from trespassing on Edwin Dodge's preserves, at the Curonia. Last time I heard of it, he'd got some impecunious American professor and family living there – How can I go and tread on their toes? It is known as *Mr* Dodge's villa now. Imagine my butting in! – It's not merely your abandoned relic, remember.

We live very quietly here, see far less company than you do at Taos. Sometimes I wish things were a little more convivial. But one has to take life as one finds it, and the kind of conviviality one *does* get doesn't help much.

I wouldn't worry about Bynner – he's a belated sort of mosquito.

Don't write your Memoirs unless you're really in the swing. And if you've had enough of Florence, finish that part off now.

Yrs D. H. Lawrence

3894. To Martin Secker, 23 November 1926
Text: MSC Lazarus; Secker 80–1.

Villa Mirenda, Scandicci. Florence.
23 Novem. 1926

Dear Secker

Your letter just come. The essay book sounds all right. I know that all of them are really good – except, it might be, 'Indians and Entertainment'. I think *Mornings in Mexico* is a good title. The four essays of that series are:

Mornings in Mexico {
'Corasmin and the Parrots'
'Walk to Huayapa'
'The Mozo'
'Market Day'

[1] Stephen G. Tallentyre's two-volume *Life of Voltaire* (1903). See Letter 3897.

then 'Indians and Entertainment'

'Dance of the Sprouting Corn'
'Hopi Snake Dance'.

The two Dance articles appeared in the New York *Theatre Arts Monthly*, in two issues, and had two drawings by me.[1] I think they printed both my drawings. But I *know* there is one, for the 'Sprouting Corn' dance. And I should like you to put that drawing in the book. I asked Miss Pearn if she could get you the two copies of the *Theatre Arts* from New York. If you wanted to put a tiny bit more in, you could use the poem and the little article from the *Laughing Horse*.[2] Tell me what you think of that. And for a title you could have 'Days and Dances in Mexico' or 'Mexican Days and Dances', because the dances are in New Mexico.

I enclose a copy of 'Market Day'. And you have a copy of *The Laughing Horse*. The first little article in the *Horse* could be the last in the book of essays. And the poem in the middle. So go ahead with this with C[urtis] B[rown] when you like. He can fix with Knopf.

Have you enquired when Knopf is to be ready with his *David*? All things considered, it seems to me much fairer to hold *David* until the end of February. Then the limited edition buyers won't feel swindled, and there will be an easy excuse for bringing it out cheaper. Don't bring it out now.

The novel goes pretty well – is already very improper – and will apparently be quite short.

Our neighbours, the Wilkinsons, have gone in to Florence for two months, until January 20th. Their house remains empty, and they would let it for a consideration of a pound a week. It's a very nice flat. If you and Rina would like it from Christmas till about the 20th. – say 18th. Jan – write *at once*. The W.'s would supply everything, and there is a woman to clean, though she doesn't cook. It's just two minutes from here. We'd have to know soon, as they may be letting it to others. Their address in Florence is

A. S. Wilkinson, Pensione Lucii, Borgo degli Albizzi 17. Florence.

Deluges here too. Arno floods. I've got a cold.

My picture is nice, I think. The bathing men are framed, and hang in

[1] For the 'Dance articles' see pp. 36 n. 2 and 103 n. 1; for the drawing see p. 27 n. 7. (No drawing appeared with 'Hopi Snake Dance'.) For 'Indians and Entertainment' see p. 36 n. 1.

[2] The article, 'A Little Moonshine with Lemon' was included in *Mornings in Mexico*; the poem, 'Beyond the Rockies', was not.

Frieda's room. I'm going to do a bigger picture, if I can – of Boccaccio's story of the nuns and the gardener.[1]

I enclose the 'Market Day' article.

Saluti DHL

P.S. Make a note, that I must say the Mexico articles have appeared in *The Theatre Arts Monthly*, *The Adelphi*, and *Travel*, will you – else they're always so offended.

3895. To Gertrude Cooper, 23 November 1926

Text: MS Clarke; cited in Lawrence–Gelder 143–5.

Villa Mirenda, *Scandicci* (Florence)
23 Novem 1926

My dear Gertie

We had been bothering about you, knowing how miserable you would be, still in bed, and the hope of going home deferred. But your letter sounded pretty cheerful, after all. And it must be rather cheering, to look in the mirror and see your face getting plump again, something as it used to be in Lynn Croft, when I was going to college.[2] – As for the lung, well, in a case like yours it's bound to be difficult to stop the germ working. And while the germ is active, you'll have a temperature. But the fact that you're getting fatter shows that the germ is making no headway at all. That's a great deal. And before long, you'll see the temperature will begin to go down. It's a fight, and as a fight we've got to look on it. I'm glad you're such a good patient. It's a weariness, being in bed. But then, anything for a cure!

I'm in bed these two days with a cold. We've had such deluges of rain, and I got wet coming up from Scandicci. Everything is steamy soggy wet, and there are great pale-brown floods out in the Arno Valley, we can see them from the window. And still it thunders and lightens at times – and it is warm. We only light the stove in the evening, for the damp.

This is the time of the year I dislike most, in any country. I wish it would come cold, and a bit crisp. The town is no better than the country, and the country isn't much better than the town. One can only grin and abide.

We shan't be coming to England yet. I hear they have postponed the *David* play until March, and in December are doing my first play, that I wrote when I was still in Croydon. *The Widowing of Mrs Holroyd*. It is a much simpler thing to produce on the stage, than *David*, so I needn't come home for it, though I should very much like to be there when it is done: about the middle of December. I hope Ada will go to London to see it. I have asked her if she will.

[1] The paintings referred to are *Men Bathing* and *Boccaccio Story* (28″ × 47″); the latter is reproduced in *The Paintings of D. H. Lawrence*, plate [8].

[2] I.e. in 1906–8.

She could probably stay with Milly Beveridge in Chelsea, who would look after her well.

We are rather cut off, in this wetness. Our neighbours, the only other English people within reach, have moved into Florence for a couple of months. They are vegetarians, and she says she is tired of *cooking*. But since she never seemed to do any cooking, it must be herself she is tired of. The more they have, the more selfish and empty some people become. – Only the other day three friends came to lunch, through the downpour. One was a young Russian woman, about twenty-five, I suppose.[1] But she had got herself up so exactly like a boy, with her Eton crop and black jacket and narrow skirt, that I gasped, and Giulia, our servant,[2] called her the signorino, the young gentleman. Why ever a pretty girl should want to appear just like a lad from a public school, passes my comprehension. To me it is just repulsive. Why can't women be women – and a bit charming!

Does your niece Edna write to you? I wonder how the young hussy is getting on! And Wilson – I wonder if he's hooked some fool of a woman yet! Fancy Brinsley turning out a specimen like him! But then fancy Dick Pogmore turning out such a flash guy![3] – I *must* ask Ada if there's any more news of him. – I forgot again to tell her about Enid Hopkin's discontented visit: and she asked me about it. It's a funny world, when one thinks of the people one has known.

If they play *David* in London in March, I suppose I shall have to come to England in February – towards the end. It is still a vile time: but at least the spring is coming. And then surely you'll be in Ripley again, and going about sprightly. – Don't bother about Feroze. Those little coloured people are little egoists, pure and simple: self and only self. They can't understand gratitude, and thoughtfulness.

I wonder so much if there is anything I could send you from Florence. Can you think of anything? – do tell me.

Love from us both. DHL

3896. To Nancy Pearn, 23 November 1926

Text: MS UT; Unpublished.

Villa Mirenda, *Scandicci*, Florence
23 Nov. 1926

Dear Miss Pearn

I'm rather sorry to have the 'Nightingale' clipped – but if it's only for a

[1] Unidentified.

[2] Giulia Pini, the daughter of one of the peasant families nearby. See also Letter 3921.

[3] 'Wilson' may have been William Joseph Wilson, the widowed husband of Florence (cf. p. 115 n. 1). Richard Pogmore was a companion of DHL's youth, and later a schoolteacher.

periodical, a mere weekly – and if they'll send me a proof – I suppose we may as well let 'em go ahead.[1] – I'll try some little sketches – I ought to be earning something.

Those essays for a little book, Secker wants to do it. And I want him to put in, with the two Indian Dance articles, my two drawings, that appeared in the two numbers of the New York *Theatre Arts Monthly*, a year or more ago. Do you think you could get him those two copies of the *Theatre Arts*?

Deluges of rain, and I've got a cold. How are you?

Would you hate to send this rather amusing letter (enclosed) down to the Foreign dept.[2] Do you even know what Urdu is?

Yrs D. H. Lawrence

3897. To Hon. Dorothy Brett, 24 November 1926

Text: MS UCin; Postmark, [Sc]andicci [. . .]11 26; Moore 948–50.

Villa Mirenda, *Scandicci* (Florence)
24 Novem 1926

My dear Brett,

In your last, it was already snow at the ranch: makes one shiver: yet the space and sunshine are lovely. Your letters are very good, telling one what happens. You seem so social, so many people – far more social out there in the desert, than we here, on the skirts of Florence. – Mabel says too you have fixed yourself up a little place down there, in which to type. That is a good idea. And very nice for you to be earning a bit. Twenty five cents is good: yes, you saved me a lot, doing my typing. Now, I do myself what bit is done. But it's very little.

If I don't write very often, there is no news. The weather is rainy, with thunder, and misty, and not cold. We are mostly alone. Our neighbours have gone into Florence, because she, Mrs Wilkinson, is so tired of cooking. She did extremely little – but no doubt you will sympathise with her. So we sit alone on the hill, now – save for the peasants. We've got the winter sitting-room ready – quite nice and comfortable, and a good warm stove, not a pig, and a good load of wood. So as far as material comforts go, we are all right. I have been very well – till this week, have got a cold, with all the wetness, I suppose. When it's fine enough, I go into the woods to write a bit. I'm doing a little novel – in the Midlands, in England – I hope to break it off quite soon, keep it quite short. – But lately it's been too wet to sit out. From the balcony we can see the wide

[1] See p. 482 n. 3. In addition to its appearance in *Forum*, 'The Nightingale' was published in the weekly *Spectator*, 10 September 1927.

[2] The enclosure is missing.

yellow floods in the Arno valley – I hate overmuch sloppy water, it is lugubrious.

I've not been in Florence for a fortnight. Then I saw Reggie Turner. Like most of the people there, he's going rather rapidly to pieces. Really, he's getting quite gaga! The town has a bad effect on one. I am glad to be in the country.

I would love to be able to stride over to the ranch, and Taos, for a bit: for the clear air, and a ride on Aaron, and a sight of the mountains, and to get away from Europe just for a bit. I feel my life is really over here, not in America. But at times one feels Europe very soggy and heavy – it would be marvellous if one could just fly over to New Mexico, now, for instance. Even to sit in Mabel's big room, in one of the chairs, near the big fire, and hear the snow drip outside – and put on a sheepskin and go over to José's corral: yes, I should like it very much indeed. Ma è troppo lontano, troppo lontano! Muy lejos![1] – I've forgotten my Spanish.

I'm glad you and Mabel are friends. It is very wise, to recognise those 'bouts' as sheer hysteric sickness, and treat them as such. It leaves at least tracts of safe ground. And friendship today is a difficult thing: we are inwardly more isolated, and the pegs that hold us firm are much more wobbly, than in Voltaire's day. Somehow, for friendship today, one has to be sadly disembodied. And though Voltaire liked being disembodied, I dislike it very much.

I am reading the *Life*.[2] It is interesting, but also false: far too jammy. Voltaire had made, acquired for himself, by the time he was my age, an *income* of £3,000 – equivalent at least to an income of twelve thousand pounds, today. How had he done it? – it means a capital of two hundred thousand pounds. Where had it come from? Ask yourself? – But that man Tallentyre is a cunning underhand biographer, who knows that women eat nothing but candy.

I have started painting, quite seriously, on my own. Maria Huxley – did I tell you, she came with Aldous? – brought me some canvases that her brother had daubed on: surely the worst beginnings that man ever made. I've done a nice biggish picture – that is, I like it – a man and woman in a pink room, and a child looking up – modern.[3] Now I am going to do a long one, about 1½ yards by ¾ yard – of Boccaccio's story of the gardener and the nunnery. It's rather fun, discovering one can paint one's own ideas and one's own feelings – and a change from writing.

The Huxleys' seem very bored. They are living pro. tem. up in Cortina,

[1] 'But it is too distant, too distant! Very distant!'

[2] See Letter 3893 and p. 580 n. 1.

[3] See Letter 3887 and n. 2.

north of Venice, in the higher mountains, because their child is supposed to have a lung. And they are very lonely, nobody there – And the voyage round the world seems to have taken the last gasp of breath out of Aldous' long body. Maria looks like a *very* small edition of Ottoline: like Ottoline's Cinderella daughter – same peculiar long cheeks, and rather nice eyes. I liked her, too. I wish they lived a bit nearer, so that I could walk over and see them. – But they think of coming to live in Florence next summer. – They arrived here in a very grand new motor-car, Maria driving.

I'm interested to know what will happen down at Del Monte. It all seems very unsettled and rather unreal. I don't believe Rachel and William would stay happily on the ranch, even if the old man were gone for ever. Does Rasmussen make it pay at all? He sounds jolly.

I haven't heard from the London friends for some time – save Kot, very dismal, feels he may have to do a job before long, to have money to live on. – But they don't seem to me very real.

Earl wrote, still from India – and a little more complacent this time. He'd got his liver right, and seems to have managed to rise superior to the Hindoos. He feared, for some time, they had no *breadth*. Now he doubts very severely whether they have even *depth*. In fact, whether they're not the most negligible of all people!

How American that is! – when they find the other party is not à l'Americaine! – they are sure to find it utterly negligible.

Earl says the Grecian isle, Syra, is now the Paradise of his imagination. How rash he is, *always* to take a ticket, first class, to his Paradise! But that is American too. That's why they travel so much. – I suppose they will be in Syra by January, at least. – I should like very much to go to Greece – it appeals to me just now. It needs money, though, like everything else. – And I may have to go to England end of February. They have postponed *David*. The producer funked it. So the 300 club are playing *The Widowing of Mrs Holroyd* in mid-december, and they have *David* down for mid-March. I shan't go to England for *Mrs Holroyd* – too wintry: but I feel I must go and give a helping hand to *David*. – So, if I must go to England in February, I shant go to Greece, and that's that! – However, it's still November.

I feel you've got quite a full and interesting life out there – and am very glad. It will be a great test if you can really pull off a winter successfully with Mabel – without the 'snarl of souls,' as the poem said.[1]

By the way, any news of Spud?

tante belle cose, e buoni auguri. DHL

[1] Unidentified.

3898. To Arthur, Lilian, William and Frances Wilkinson, [25 November 1926]

Text: MS Schlaefle; Sagar, Wilkinsons 67–8.

Villa Mirenda, Scandicci
Thursday

Dear W[ilkinson] and Mrs W[ilkinson] and P[ino] and B[im]

Ooray! you'll all come home as fat as porpoises with a fleshpot of Egypt[1] under each arm.

I've stopped in bed two days with a cold, but am rising now to blink an astonished welcome to that great stranger, the sun.

More borrowings! Did you take your easel to Florence? If you didn't, would you hate to lend it me, and I'll see if I can get that Scandicci carpenter to make me one like it. Cute idea!

My new picture – feel I should say 'pic chah!' – is going to be suggested by Boccaccio's scandalous story of the Nuns and the Gardener. Hope your virtuous easel won't swoon, and let my canvas fall from her arms.

We think to arrive at Lucii Albizzi – lots of eyes – about 2.30 Sunday afternoon, weather decent.

D. H. Lawrence

3899. To Martin Secker, [26 November 1926]

Text: MSC Lazarus; Secker 81–2.

Villa Mirenda, Scandicci, Florence
Friday

Dear Secker

I am sending you a copy of *Travel* with 'Walk to Huayapa' – and such excellent photographs of Mexico, it makes me feel it would be a good idea to put photograph illustrations in the book.[2] Let me know at once what you think of this, and we'll ask *Travel* for permission to use some of theirs: and I'll get some for the 'Snake Dance' from New Mexico, and the 'Corn Dance'. And I'll write just a little introduction to the book.

I wrote you to 5 John St. and said the Wilkinsons had left their house till 20th. January, and that if you're quick, you could have it till then – if you come out at Christmas or immediately after – and not pay them any rent – but give them the equivalent of about £1. a week. It's two minutes from here. There's a

[1] Cf. Exodus xvi. 3.

[2] The November issue of *Travel* (which included 'Walk to Huayapa', xlviii, pp. 30–5, 60 as 'Sunday Stroll in Sleepy Mexico') and the April issue (which included 'Market Day', xlvi, pp. 7–9, 44 as 'The Gentle Art of Marketing in Mexico') each contained six photographs of various aspects of Mexican life. None of them was reproduced in *Mornings in Mexico*.

cleaning woman for 20 liras a week and every thing provided. If it strikes Rina's fancy, write at once – write if you like to

Arthur S. Wilkinson, Pensione Lucii, Borgo degli Albizzi, Florence.

I had a bit of malaria, but am better. The sun shines, but raises a mist like the deuce. My design for my Boccaccio picture is so nice, if only I can get it on the canvas. The salotta is very nice. I've been painting the bookshelves and table-legs this morning. We practically never go into Florence – Plenty to do here: still more doors and windows to paint, as well as stair-rails – and my picture. But I must try and get the loan of Wilkinson's easel for that. Glad that Mackenzie seems all right and cheery. Adrian seems a real home-truther – that'll be an uncomprising generation by the looks of things.

Au revoir D. H. Lawrence

3900. To Vere Collins, 27 November 1926

Text: MS Lazarus; Unpublished.

Villa Mirenda, *Scandicci* (Florence)
27 Nov. 1926

Dear V[ere] H[enry]

I'm sending you a copy of *Glad Ghosts.*

And would you mind handing over the bill and the cheque, and asking them please to send me

1. Your catalogue – complete.
2. *The Oxford Book of Songs* (with music)[1]

Do I bore you with these little requests.

The world here is one vast steam, with sun overhead and illimitable puddle beneath.

I've taken to painting – also a little 'naughty' – and am now beginning a picture for Boccaccio's 'story of the Nuns and the Gardener'. It's amusing.

Where's your Byron's *Letters*?[2]

D. H. Lawrence

I want them to keep the balance of the cheque, at your office, so I can order books.

[1] *The Oxford Song Book*, ed. P. C. Buck (Oxford, 1916 and often reprinted). (OUP's catalogue described the book's contents as 'arranged . . . so that almost all the best songs of Britain may be sung in chorus by any company of men or boys which includes one pianist of mediocre ability'.)

[2] Collins' *Lord Byron in his Letters: Selections from his Letters and Journals* was published (by Murray) in March 1927.

3901. To Brigit Patmore, [December? 1926]

Text: Brigit Patmore, 'Conversations with D. H. Lawrence', *London Magazine*, iv (June 1957), 37.

[Villa Mirenda, Scandicci, Florence]
[December? 1926][1]

You have a curious sixth sense I like, an awareness which takes one to the fine edge of things into another world. The book is very like you.

3902. To Emily King, [1 December 1926]

Text: MS Lazarus; cited in Brian H. Finney, 'A Newly Discovered Text of D. H. Lawrence's "The Lovely Lady"', *Yale University Library Gazette*, xlix (January 1975), 246.

Villa Mirenda, *Scandicci* (Florence)
1 Decem

My dear Pamela

I'm awfully sorry Joan is starting again being bronchial. There's nothing to do but to take her to a place like Bournemouth, and leave her there for a time. You can find some nice people, I'm sure, who'll look after her. Ask Miss Jolyffe.[2] Or ask Gertie's cousins at Brighton. If you'll do this, I'll send you ten pounds towards expenses, so let me know. And don't tell me Joan wouldn't be happy away from you. She'd be perfectly all right, after the first day or so, if you found kindly people – and there are plenty. So that's what you'd better do.

It's raining here again, and cold, after two decent days. It certainly is a beastly autumn – everybody who writes, no matter where from, says the same. And all the Italians have throat colds. I had the same last week, but am all right again.

I heard from Gertie. I was afraid it would be a long fight, especially the first weeks. But the fact that she puts on flesh shows she can be pulled through, so let nobody croak. I have written now to Dr Lucas, to ask him for exact information.[3] I'll let you know when I hear.

[1] Brigit Patmore, née Ethel Elizabeth ('Brigit') Morrison-Scott (1882–1965), author. b. Ulster. Knew Violet Hunt, Alice Meynell, etc. through the 'South Lodge' circle, and met DHL there during the First World War. (She was the prototype for Clariss Browning in *Aaron's Rod*.) m. 1907, John Deighton Patmore (grandson of Coventry Patmore). A close friend of 'H. D.', she had a liaison with Richard Aldington, 1928–38; Aldington dedicated his poem 'A Dream in the Luxembourg' to her. Her book of short stories *This Impassioned Onlooker* was published in December 1926; she sent a copy to DHL and received this reply. (See *My Friends When Young* (1968); obituary, *The Times*, 22 September 1965.)

[2] When Gertrude Cooper went to Bournemouth for her health's sake, she stayed with Miss Jolyffe who presumably ran a boarding house.

[3] The letter is missing.

Tell Peg her letter in French was very good, hardly any mistakes, only a bit stiff. I'll answer it directly.

We have made ourselves pretty comfortable here, and got in a load of wood[1] for the stove – I think I shall try too to get briquettes, the stove is a roarer, and wood isn't cheap. Last year was much warmer, at this time. The devil's in the weather.

I have been painting pictures lately, to amuse myself this bad weather. But I doubt you wouldn't like them. They are big – in oil.

I have asked them to send you Cynthia Asquith's *Ghost Book*, which you mentioned[2] – You should have it in a day or two. – Now she wants me to do a murder story, for a murder book she has in mind.[3] My agents, Curtis Brown, get cross with her, using her name to get stuff out of authors and to plant these books. But like everybody else, she's on the make.

Let me know if there's anything I can send you from here, for Christmas – and ask Peg what she would like – embroidered things, leather work, bit of jewellery, or what. – There aren't many foreigners this season – they'll wait till spring, I expect.

I do hope Joan is better. Let me know.

Love DHL

3903. To Nancy Pearn, 1 December 1926

Text: MS UT; Unpublished.

Villa Mirenda, *Scandicci* (Florence)
1 Dec 1926

Dear Miss Pearn

Here's a little article[4] – Surely short enough – – let's see if that's the sort they want, and if it is, I'll do more. – I got Cunninghame Graham's book from the *Calender* – what a tiresome old fool he is, with a good subject![5] It will be rather fun to throw something at him – he's too complacent over other people's sufferings.

Sincerely D. H. Lawrence

[1] wood] briquettes

[2] See Letter 3633 and n. 1.

[3] For an account of the composition of 'The Lovely Lady' for Lady Cynthia Asquith's *The Black Cap: New Stories of Murder and Mystery* (Hutchinson, October 1927), see Finney, *Yale University Library Gazette*, xlix. 245–52.

[4] See p. 377 n. 3.

[5] The book was R. B. Cunninghame Graham's *Pedro de Valdivia, Conqueror of Chile*: DHL's review appeared in *Calendar*, iii (January 1927), 322–6 (Roberts C149).

3904. To Rolf Gardiner, 3 December 1926
Text: MS Lazarus; Huxley 672–5.

Villa Mirenda, *Scandicci* (Florence)
3 Decem. 1926

Dear Gardiner

I was glad to get your letter[1] – wondered often about the Baltic meeting – sounds a bit dreary. I think it's hardly worth while trying anything deliberately international – the start at home is so difficult – But the song-tour sounded splendid.

I'm sure you are doing the right thing, with hikes and dances and songs. But somehow it needs a central clue, or it will fizzle away again. There needs a centre of silence, and a heart of darkness – to borrow from Rider Haggard.[2] We'll have to establish some spot on earth, that will be the fissure into the under world, like the oracle at Delphos, where one can always come to. I will try to do it myself. I will try to come to England and make a place – some quiet house in the country – where one can begin – and from which the hikes, maybe, can branch out. Some place with a big barn and a bit of land – if one has enough money. Don't you think that is what it needs? And then one must set out and learn a deep discipline – and learn dances from all the world, and take whatsoever we can make into our own. And learn music the same; mass music, and canons, and wordless music like the Indians have. And try – keep on trying. It's a thing one has to feel one's way into. And perhaps work a small farm at the same time, to make the living cheap. It's what I want to do. Only I shrink from beginning. It is most difficult to begin. Yet I feel in my inside, one ought to do it. – You are doing the right things, in a skirmishing sort of way. But unless there is a headquarters, there will be no continuing. You yourself will tire. – What do you think? – If I did come to England to try such a thing, I should depend on you as the organiser of the activities, and the director of activities. About the dances and folk music, you know it all, I know practically nothing. – We need only be even two people, to start. I don't believe either in numbers, or haste. – But one has to drive one's peg down to the centre of the earth: or one's root: it's the same thing. And there must also be work connected – I mean earning a living – at least earning one's bread.

I'm not coming to England for the *Widowing of Mrs Holroyd*. – I begin to hate journeys – I've journeyed enough. Then my health is always risky. You remember the devil's cold I got coming to England in August. I've always had chest-bronchial troubles and pneumonia after-effects – so have to take care.

[1] See p. 553 n. 1.

[2] DHL seems to have borrowed a theme fairly common in the works of Rider Haggard (1856–1925) rather than an exact quotation.

How well I can see Hucknall Torkard and the miners! Didn't you go into the church to see the tablet, where Byron's heart is buried? – My father used to sing in Newstead Abbey choir, as a boy – But I've gone many times down Hucknall Long Lane to Watnall – and I like Watnall park – it's a great Sunday morning walk. Some of my happiest days I've spent haymaking in the fields just opposite the S. side of Greaseley Church – bottom of Watnall hill – adjoining the vicarage: Miriams father hired those fields.[1] If you're in those parts again, go to Eastwood, where I was born, and lived for my first 21 years. Go to Walker St – and stand in front of the third house – and look across at Crich on the left, Underwood in front – High Park Woods and Annesley on the right: I lived in that house from the age of 6 to 18, and I know that view better than any in the world. – Then walk down the fields to the Breach, and in the corner house facing the stile I lived from 1 to 6. – And walk up Engine Lane, over the level crossing at Moorgreen pit, along till you come to the highway (the Alfreton Rd) – turn to the left, towards Underwood, and go till you come to the lodge gate by the reservoir – go through the gate, and up the drive to the next gate, and continue on the *footpath* just below the drive on the left – on through the wood to Felley Mill. When you've crossed the brook, turn to the right (the *White Peacock* farm) through Felley Mill gate, and go up the footpath to Annesley. Or better still, turn to the right, uphill, *before* you descend to the brook, and go on uphill, up the rough deserted pasture – on past Annesley kennels – long empty – on to Annesley again. – That's the country of my heart. – From the hills, if you look across at Underwood wood, you'll see a tiny red farm on the edge of the wood – That was Miriam's farm – where I got my first incentive to write. – I'll go with you there some day.

I was at my sister's in September, and we drove round – I saw the miners – and pickets – and policeman – it was like a spear through one's heart. I tell you, we'd better buck up and do something for the England to come, for they've pushed the spear through the side of *my* England. – If you are in that district, anywhere near Ripley, do go and see my sister, she'd love it. Her husband has a tailor's shop and outlying tailor's trade among the colliers. They've 'got on,' so have a new house and a motor-car. – But they're nice.

Mrs W. E. Clarke, 'Torestin.' Gee St. *Ripley* (Derby)

Ripley is about 6 miles from Eastwood, by tram-car.

You should do a hike, from Nottingham – Nuttall[2] – Watnall – Moorgreen reservoir – Annesley – Blidworth or Papplewick – and across Sherwood forest, Ollerton – and round perhaps to Newark. – And another, do Langley Mill to Ripley – Ripley to Wingfield Manor (one of my favorite ruins) – Crich – and

[1] For 'Miriam' and the Chambers of Haggs Farm, see *Letters*, i. 22 nn. 1 and 2 and also p. 67 and n. 1.

[2] Local spelling of 'Nuthall'.

then down to Whatstandwell and up again to Alderswasley and so to Bole Hill and Wirksworth and over Via Gellia – or keep on the high ground from Crich and go round Tansley Moor round to Matlock Bridge – or where you like. But it's real England – the hard pith of England. I'll walk it with you one day.

Tell me what you think of *Mrs Holroyd*, if you see it.

If they give *David* in mid March, I shall come to England in mid-February. Then I hope to see you properly.

Keep the idea of a *centre* in mind – and look out for a house – not dear, because I don't make much money, but something we might gradually build up.

Yrs D. H. Lawrence

'Mrs Holyroyd' was an aunt of mine[1] – she lived in a tiny cottage just up the line from the railway-crossing at Brinsley, near Eastwood. My father was born in the cottage in the quarry hole just by Brinsley level crossing. But my uncle built the old cottage over again – all spoilt. There's a nice path goes down by the cottage, and up the fields to Coney Grey farm – then round to Eastwood or Moorgreen, as you like.[2]

3905. To Mabel Dodge Luhan, 6 December 1926

Text: MS Brill; Luhan 316–17.

Villa Mirenda, *Scandicci*, Firenze
6 Decem 1926

Dear Mabel

It's nearly Christmas, and Frieda hasn't sent you your ribbons yet. But we've not been in to Florence for quite a time. We'll go in and get them, though. I sent you a little book.

I went out the other evening and looked at the Curonia, from outside. I didn't go in: it was getting late: a grey evening, with the olives all washing up in silver, in a chill wind. You hadn't made me realise how splendidly the villa stands, looking out over everything. A beautiful place! I'll go again one day, now I know just where it is, and ask[3] for the gardener – Pietro, did you say.

It is tramontana here, and quite cold, but rather pleasant. We've got a good warm stove, and a nice room – and the olives and the pine-wood outside. And I've taken to painting for a change: now doing quite a biggish canvas of Boccaccio's story of the nuns who found the gardener asleep.

[1] The aunt was Mary Ellen ('Polly') (1854–95), wife of DHL's uncle, James Lawrence. See 'Odour of Chrysanthemums' in *The Prussian Officer and Other Stories*, ed. John Worthen (Cambridge, 1983), pp. 181–99 and note on 181:1.

[2] For Gardiner's reply on 13 December 1926, see Nehls, iii. 121–4.

[3] MS reads 'as'.

Secker wants to publish those Indian dance essays, that came in the *Theatre Arts* – also some Mexican essays – 'Mornings in Mexico' – in a smallish book in the spring. Knopf will do it in New York. And it is to have a few illustrations. You haven't one or two nice photographs of Indians dancing – or an Indian dancing – something a bit suave and beautiful – that we could reproduce, have you. If you have, I wish you'd send them to me. But be sure you have the right to reproduce them. – I'll dedicate the book to you, if you like: To Mabel Dodge Lujan, who called me to Taos.[1]

I'm glad you get on with the Brett, and that she has a comfortable corner to come to, in your house. The ranch weighs a bit on my mind. I think, when we come in the spring, we shall have to think if we should sell it. What do you think? Now there are oil kings about, it might be easier. And you would always let us a house of yours. I feel very uncertain about what the future will be.

The man Frayne sent me this letter:[2] very funny. He has never paid my taxes – and I never wanted him to. Why does he suddenly butt in? Would you hate to hand him the cheque, with thanks? Or let Brett do it. I suppose he *has* paid the money!

Hope you'll have a good Christmas.

D. H. Lawrence

Had a letter from Christine Hughes in Rome! – Suppose we shall see her soon.

I only did three Indian articles, didn't I? 'Corn Dance', 'Snake Dance', and 'Indians and Entertainment'.

3906. To Hon. Dorothy Brett, 6 December 1926

Text: MS UCin; Postmark, Scandicci 7 12 26; Irvine, Brett 70–2.

Villa Mirenda, *Scandicci* (Florence)
6 December 1926

Dear Brett

Cold weather here too, but not so icy as the ranch. Still, it's a tramontana wind, and the olives blow back bright silver in the gusts. But the umbrella pines, very green, stay still and velvety, like level rolls of green cloud.

The photographs came, and are very nice indeed, especially that of the wagon. They really came out marvellously. – I sent you a *Sun* and a *Glad Ghosts*: only 100 *Sun*'s were printed like that, so it will be a collector's trophy.[3] – And now they want to do 'Mornings in Mexico' in a book, with the Indian dance articles, and with a few photograph illustrations. I shall ask *Travel* – did you see the Nov. number? – if we could use one or two of the excellent

[1] The dedication simply reads: 'To Mabel Lujan'.

[2] The enclosure is missing.

[3] See p. 352 n. 1.

photographs they printed – and have asked Mabel if she has any dance photographs. – I've asked her too if she will pay that man Frayne the money he paid for the taxes – am sending her a cheque for it. If it bores her to do it, I wish *you* would hand over the cheque to him, so I know he has it. Rachel has always paid the taxes for me – why did Frayne suddenly butt in?

It is exciting to hear of bears and bucks, oil-kings and cow-boys and bear-hunters. Seems to grow more movie-like each day! – We were thinking, if we come in the spring – or when we come – whether it wouldn't be wiser to cast round for somebody to sell the ranch to. What do you think. I don't like you to feel tied to it, this bitter weather. What a mercy you have Mabel's comfortable house to go to.

We're very comfortable here, with a big, warm stove and a nice room – a hired piano – and paints. Suddenly I paint away. I'm doing a biggish canvas – about $1\frac{1}{2}$ yards by 1 yard – of Boccaccio's story of the nuns and the gardener: nice improper story, that tells itself. Painting suddenly interests me seriously – to get a certain feel into it. – You, meanwhile, how are you getting on with the book you are writing? or going to write?

The Huxleys are at

the Villa Ino Colli, Cortina d'Ampezzo, Italy.

Maria sends a dismal word to say it rains and freezes there.

I told you *David* is put off till March – so we dont go to England at least till mid-February. – Had a p. c. from Achsah, at the Taj Mahal. They're *on their way* to Greece.

You'll get this for Christmas. Do hope you'll have a good time.

DHL

I will of course pay for the horses' feed – so send me a bill as Rachel used to – don't forget.

3907. To Martin Secker, 6 December 1926
Text: MSC Lazarus; Secker 82.

Villa Mirenda, Scandicci, Florence
6 Decem. 1926

Dear Secker

Sorry you won't be coming out. It's cold here too – and how the stove eats up the wood!

I asked Curtis Brown – Miss Pearn – to get the *Theatre Arts* magazines with the Dance articles in – I think they are three, not two[1] – I think they published 'Indians and Entertainment' too.[2] When they come, decide if you want any of

[1] MSC reads 'too'. [2] See p. 36 n. 1.

their pictures, then ask them: or shall I? or shall Curtis Brown? I'm sending the copy of *Travel* now – with marked illustrations – and will you ask *them* too for permission – or do you want me to, or C.B? And hadn't Knopf better know about the pictures?

Novel goes nicely[1] – so does my Boccaccio picture!!

DHL

3908. To Curtis Brown, 6 December 1926

Text: MS UT; Unpublished.

Villa Mirenda, *Scandicci* (Florence)
6 December 1926

Dear C[urtis] B[rown]

Thanks for your letters. – I agree about Secker – as he's going ahead with a 3/6 edition, he's anyhow making what bid he can for a wider public.

I suggested, and he agrees, that he should put photograph illustrations in the book of essays: *Mornings in Mexico*. It will fatten the book out a bit. I will get Indian dance photographs – and the American periodical *Travel* printed some very good photographs of Mexico in their two numbers in which they did two of the Mexican sketches – Nov and Oct. Could one ask them for permission to use those photographs – or one or two of them? – Perhaps Knopf might have some idea for photographs. Would you mention it to him?

Would it trouble you to ask Benns to send me ten copies of *Glad Ghosts* – and the bill. It will do for a Christmas card.

Am working at another novel – scene Derbyshire coal area!! – Also I am painting quite a big (dimensionally) picture, and enjoying it very much. Hope you'll see it one day.

Yrs D. H. Lawrence

3908a. To Bonamy Dobrée, 6 December 1926

Text: MS Dobrée; Unpublished.

Villa Mirenda, *Scandicci* (Florence)
6 Decem. 1926

Dear Dobrée

Had your letter – so you're not gone to the land of mummies, anyhow! – What was the dialogue you wrote? Is it printed, and where?[2]

This is to say that our neighbours, the Wilkinsons, have left their villa – top

[1] *Lady Chatterley's Lover* (second version).

[2] Dobrée's *Histriophone* (Hogarth Essays No. 5, 1925). It is described in the 'stage-direction' as: 'A Dialogue on Dramatic Diction: persons, *Bentúas* and *Heltubáda*: scene, a library, in which every book wanted is immediately at elbow, and opens miraculously at the required place.'

half of it – till January 20th – and you can have it if you want – pay a nominal rent – 10/- or 15/- a week. It's two minutes from here – and we're about 7 miles out of Florence – come $5\frac{1}{2}$ miles by tram, then walk $1\frac{1}{2}$ miles – very nice country – flat is not wildly comfortable, but has everything in it. But probably you don't want to come away for the Christmas-New Year period.

Awfully nice to invite us to your flat – but it would be too much trouble for you.

Cold weather, but not bad, olive trees blowing up very silvery, air very bright. – I'm painting a picture of Boccaccio's Story of Nuns and the Gardener – penis and all – rather fun.

Tanti saluti di noi due a loro due![1]

D. H. Lawrence

3909. To Mabel Dodge Luhan, 10 December 1926

Text: MS Brill; Luhan 317–19.

Villa Mirenda, *Scandicci* (Florence)
10 Decem. 1926

Dear Mabel

We went in to Florence today – and here are your ribbons. I think there are sixteen bits – hope they're right colours. If you want any more, let us know and *say what colour* – send bit of stuff to match. We told the man in the shop it was a present – and he said *proprio un bel regalo, un bel regalo davvero!*[2] – but to me it seems not much of a show.

I hope the Piero della Francesca is the one you like.[3] Anyhow it's beautiful. If you had another in mind, tell me more in detail and I'll find it.

Tell Brett we are sending her a scarf – thin wool – gaudyish.

Hope you have a jolly Christmas.

DHL

I'll tell Huxley about the MS. if you really wish – but I'm scared of it going round with all names left. He is at

Villa Ino Colli, *Cortina d'Ampezzo*, Italia

it's in the Trento region – north Padua – in the mts.

When is Mary Foote due to appear?

tante belle cose! – tempo bellissimo qui, le montagne tutte nevicate, l'aria chiara e fresca – e un po'di allegria.[4]

[1] 'Many regards from the two of us to the two of you!'

[2] 'really a fine present, truly a fine present!'

[3] Presumably a reproduction of a picture by Piero della Francesca (c. 1410/20–92), perhaps the greatest of the quattrocento artists. Several of his paintings are in the Uffizi.

[4] 'all the best! very good weather here, the mountains all covered with snow, the air clear and fresh – and a bit of cheerfulness.'

[Frieda Lawrence begins][1]
[Dear Mabel

We got such a thrill out of your ribbons, just a shop full of boxes full of ribbons. I hope you like velvet ones, and the young man who sold them thrilled too! We are very cosy and quite 'elegant' for us, rushmatting all over the floor in a big, good room with bright, light things in it, and a piano and cyclamens, Lawrence painting on an easel – a Boccaccio picture *not at all* proper, and when it's fine, my word, it's fine – the weather, I mean. Of course it grieves me too much to think the ranch might go, but then we have so little money and Lawrence is so English. He is writing another short novel. We have a gay little dog for a friend and go down with a very small horse and a board of a waggon, driving like blazes and the peasants round us are very friendly. I think in Florence we're a myth. We hardly see anybody. One knows them! Of course we must come back to Taos. Lawrence seems awfully well this winter. Not many forestieri this year. We read 'Helen of Troy.'[2] They are doing Lawrence's play Mrs. Holroyd on Sunday. Good luck to you in the new year. If you came to Florence you would want to buy – such braids and silks and paper and embroidery, they have such clever hands! Thank you very much for Arabella's bracelet. Lawrence of course grumbled at me for taking it from you. You still have a lot to do for your novel, so many years!

Greetings to Tony. Frieda.

Christine Hughes wrote from Rome.

What about Spud?]

3910. To Ada Clarke, 10 December 1926

Text: MS Clarke; Unpublished.

Villa Mirenda, *Scandicci* (Florence)
10 Dec. 1926

My dear sister

I went to Florence today and bought a few Christmas things. The shop will pack them all in a box and send them all to you. I do hope you won't mind sending on the little parcel to Elsa Weekley, three things in one parcel – and a small tray to Milly Beveridge and one to Mary Beveridge. I put the names inside each thing. Give Joan one of the toys. If you want to change about a bit, do so – and let me know. Tell me if everything comes. – The toys, you work by

[1] The MS of Frieda's part is missing; the text is taken from Luhan.

[2] See Letter 3926 and n. 2.

sliding the little wooden bars at the bottom back and forth – they are just toys I bought in the street. – And let me know what Customs duty you have to pay, and I will send it.

Don't bother to send anything here – unless it is just a pair of woolen gloves for me – pale-coloured, pale cocoa or fawn. If you put them in a *letter*, you must write on the outside: contains pair woolen[1] gloves

may be opened

si può aprire

otherwise they make a fuss. But parcels, of course, go through customs automatically. Don't let the children see their things till Christmas. I had everything come in one parcel, because not only is it an awful fuss, awful, but it costs altogether about seven shillings a parcel.

It's lovely weather now, snow on the mountains, and the country a beautiful clear colour: more beautiful really than summer. We are very comfortable in the salotta – the new sitting room – the floor covered with thick rush matting – and a hired piano. The stove is a nice one built of stone, makes a good warmth. They used to have silk-worms up here in these big rooms, before the war, so of course they had to keep them warm.

You should get a copy of Cynthia Asquith's ghost book – and I'll send you two more small stories of mine for Christmas – they'll do for Christmas Cards.[2]

I wrote to Dr Lucas, but haven't heard from him. And I haven't heard from Gertie for a time. She must really spit on her hands now, and make an effort. It's time she made a fight now, from inside herself.

I'm sorry you won't see the play. Milly Beveridge would have looked after you.

I'm painting quite a big picture – yard and a half long. You'll see it one day, when you come to Italy again. It amuses me to paint.

If you find it an awful bother to make the parcels, get Emily to do it. She won't have too much to do. – I heard from her, Joan was better, and she'd taken her to a Father Santa Claus shop. She excites that child too much, instead of soothing her.

There's a bowl of pink roses and snapdragons on the table – so pretty.

Love DHL

When you send the other things, put a card in the parcels, will you?

If you want to change and give somebody else the box, you must do so.

[1] woolen] of

[2] One would be *Glad Ghosts* (cf. Letter 3908); the other, *Sun* (cf. Letter 3906).

3911. To Willard Johnson, 12 December 1926
Text: MS YU; Unpublished.

Villa Mirenda, *Scandicci* (Florence)
12 Decem. 1926

My dear Spud

Today came your letter – and I'll answer on the nail. I've asked a few times about you, of Mabel and Brett, but the void, or the vortex, I didn't know which, seemed to have swallowed you.

I'm very glad you've got that job, and aren't anybody's secretary or 'lady's help.' I hope it'll interest you enough to keep you going, or till you get something better. Liberty at any price, even at the price of a job! At least one can call one's soul one's own.

No, we're not in New Mexico: here in Italy. We think of going out, perhaps, in spring: and Frieda *may* sell the ranch. It's so far away – and somehow I shrink from America; I am more myself, less harassed in my feelings, here in Europe. People don't *get at one* so ferociously this side the water; I find I'm just blank scared of Americans, they never seem happy unless they're pulling one's guts out: the women[1] particularly.

We're very comfortable for the moment here in this old villa about eight miles out of Florence. The rooms are nice and big and bare, the stove is warm, the floor is covered with cosy rush matting, Frieda strums the piano and sings German songs, I pretend to write a novel – scene in England – but am much more of a *Maestro* painting a picture of Boccaccio's story of the nuns who find their gardener asleep in the garden on a hot afternoon, with his shirt blown back from what other people are pleased to call his *pudenda*, and which the nuns named his *glorietta*. Very nice picture! You must come one day and see it. When I've done enough – all with their shirt off – I'll have an exhibition of 'em in London.

Tonight they're playing *The Widowing of Mrs Holroyd* in London – the 300 club – and in March they're trying *David*. Let 'em try!

I heard from Christine: she and Mary C[hristine] may appear[2] – and we may go to Rome in the New Year. Mary C. has changed the limited flirtation company of Santa Fe for the much more unlimited one of Rome, the eternal city at the game. *Beata lei*![3] – Mabel and Brett are as thick as two peas, being the only ones left in the pod. But I'm glad if they're friends: – As for Bynner, the white mule seems to have kicked him across the last frontier – don't bother about him.

Yes, do do an edition of the horse called 'The Laughing Stallion', to be

[1] women] women women
[2] Mother and daughter; see p. 158 n. 1, and Letter 3931.
[3] 'Lucky her!'

followed by 'The Smiling Mare': he's been too long a gelding: and I'll send him something to keep his pecker up.

au revoir! all sorts of good wishes! DHL

3912. To Nancy Pearn, 13 December 1926

Text: MS UT; Unpublished.

Villa Mirenda, *Scandicci*, Florence
13 Dec 1926

Dear Miss Pearn

Would you mind sending the agreement downstairs.[1]

Would you mind asking the Rickword man, of the *Calendar*,[2] if he could please let me have a proof of the Cunninghame Grahame book-review, in case he prints it. I'd like to look through it.

Snap shot on the terrace here.[3]

D. H. Lawrence

3913. To S. S. Koteliansky, 14 December 1926

Text: MS BL; Postmark, Scandicci 16. 12 26; cited in Gransden 31.

Villa Mirenda, *Scandicci*, Florence
14 Dec 1926

My dear Kot

Here's Christmas near, and I've not written you for ages! But the life goes by so quietly and quickly. We are nice and comfortable here in the Mirenda, with a cosy room and a warm stove, and F[rieda] has hired a piano. I practically never go in to Florence, and really see nobody: which pleases me better. I've lost interest in people, and find I can amuse myself very well.

Lately I've been painting – quite a big picture, my last, about $1\frac{1}{2}$ yards by 1 yard – of Boccaccio's story of the nuns and the gardener. I'm sure it would amuse you – it does me. Think I'll turn into a painter, it costs one less, and probably would pay better than writing. Though for that matter I'm patiently doing a novel – scene in the Midlands.

How are you all? Have you found some way to make a living without emerging from the cave? Is Sonia better? – Is Gertler coming to Florence in the New Year? Tell him we shall be pleased to see him. – Wonder how *The*

[1] Perhaps the agreement for *Mornings in Mexico*.

[2] See p. 367 n. 2. Edgell Rickword (1898–1982), had published a book of poems (*Between the Eyes*, 1921) and a critical study of Rimbaud (1924), before he and Garman founded the *Calendar* (*of Modern Letters*). Its probing assessments of popular contemporaries became famous; Rickword's collection of them, *Scrutinies* (1928), contained DHL's essay, 'John Galsworthy' (cf. Letter 3968). Later Rickword edited *Left Review*, 1936–7 and *Our Time*, 1944–7.

[3] A note on the MS suggests that the photograph was of Huxley and DHL at the Villa Mirenda on 28 October 1926 (reproduced in Sagar, *The Life of D. H. Lawrence*, p. 212).

Widowing of Mrs Holroyd went off, on Sunday. Suppose I shall hear. But London seems remote.

I send you two quid for Christmas festivities. If I sent you more, you'd probably have a complex. If you want to feel you've earned them, sing *Good King Wenceslas* for me, for a carol. Anyhow have a good time, and buy a bottle of something cheerful.

Many greetings to all – Write me a word?

DHL

[Frieda Lawrence begins]

Dear Kot!

A merry Xmas, we often wish you and Gertler could come in for an evening! Glad we are no longer enemies!

Greetings to Sonia. F.

3914. To Giuseppe Orioli, [15 December 1926]

Text: MS UCLA; Unpublished.

Villa Mirenda, Scandicci, Firenze
Wednesday

Dear Pino

I wish you'd put Douglas' address on this letter – and I hope Giulia will put the stamp on.

I was amused at your little tea-party in the shop. Good idea! I always hated the tea places. Soon you can expect me too.

Do come and see us one of these lovely days – lunch or afternoon just as you like – and we can go into the woods a bit. But this year, there are no funghi!

Do come then!

DHL

3915. To Mabel Dodge Luhan, [16 December 1926]

Text: MS Brill; Luhan 319.

Villa Mirenda, Scandicci, Firenze
16 Dec.

Dear Mabel

I enclose R. Aldington's letter – you'll see he says more or less what I say.[1] – But you *must* alter names – no point in keeping them, absolutely.

[1] Aldington's letter (TMS Brill) read as follows:

Malthouse Cottage, Padworth, Near Reading, Berks.
11/12/26

Dear Lorenzo,

I have been slow in answering your last letter for several reasons. This is a busy season of the year with me because of the numbers of books which come for review. In addition I had to write

Awfully nice of you to keep Poppy for me – wonder when I'll ride her. Molta nebbia qui.[1]

DHL

We sent off the ribbons – have you got them?
No sign of Mary Foote.

3916. To Elfie Rosebery, [18? December 1926]

Text: MS Secor; Unpublished.

Villa Mirenda, *Scandicci*, Florence.
Sat.[2]

Dear Mrs Rosebery

I had your letter yesterday afternoon – So sorry about your colds – but we've got them the same, and hardly have the pep to struggle into Florence – takes more than an hour. – We're three chilometri from Scandicci too. – But I wish we had seen you – and that you both could have come out here. It's such pretty country, and we both should have been pleased. If you don't get away, let me know, and you must come out and see us.

Sincerely D. H. Lawrence

a lecture and then go to Newcastle to "deliver" it before the Literary and Philosophical Society. I got fifteen guineas thereby, and incidentally an invitation to lecture at Cambridge next year. I was a bit nervous for the first three minutes but afterwards rather enjoyed making them listen.

Now, to Mme Lujan and her affair. I consulted Professor Renwick about the project and he says that he thinks there is not the slightest chance than the Academie Francaise would undertake the job. They would only do so if it were both historical and French. I was therefore wrong in what I said.

The only alternative plan that occurs to me is this. There is a printer at Dijon who produced Ulysses. Might not Mme L. have her book privately printed by him, say 100 copies, and discreetly circulate them among her friends? This would ensure enough copies existing for the book not to perish. France has almost complete freedom in publication. I know the French representative at Geneva refused to give any but a formal ratification to Hugh Cecil's ridiculous resolution for the international suppression of "obscene" literature, on the grounds that such suppression was contrary to the law of France. Libel actions may be taken, but it would be practically impossible to bring a libel action against the author and printer of a book by an American privately printed in France. The one snag might be that she would not want this done in her life-time. Could she not have the book printed, wrap up and address the copies to various people, deposit them with the printer (who have to be well paid) with orders that they should be despatched directly she was dead?

All these posthumous arrangements sound rather ghoulish.

How are you getting on at Scandicci and what are you doing to conjure down that ennui which inevitably waits upon the Romantic Soul? All your "fixings" in the villa sound real dandy to me. Gee, you must be pining for a lil real home-life and a hundred per cent clean uplift.

Au revoir. We look forward to seeing you in March. Arabella sends love.

Richard

[1] 'A lot of mist here.'

[2] The letter is tentatively dated 18 December 1926 principally because DHL's references to his, Frieda's and the Roseberys' health seem to be echoed in Letter 3926.

3917. To Esmé Percy, 19 December 1926

Text: MS Lazarus; cited in Pinto, *D. H. Lawrence after Thirty Years*, p. 21.

Villa Mirenda, *Scandicci* (Florence)
19 Decem. 1926

Dear Mr Percy[1]

Mrs Whitworth sent me photographs and press-cuttings of your production of *The Widowing of Mrs Holroyd*.[2] I dearly wish I could have been there. You seem to have done the thing so well, and the actors, especially Miss Vanne, seem to have put such heart into it.[3] What a bore that the audience and the critics didn't like it! – Anyhow they all say plainly it was my fault – which no doubt it was: for an audience and a critic is always the same perfection unto itself. – Why do they never have the grace to say: But alas, perhaps I was an inefficient listener!

I have to confess it's years since I read the play myself. I wrote it fifteen years ago, when I was raw. Probably they're quite right when they say that the last act is too much taken up with washing the dead, instead of getting on a bit with life. I bet that would be my present opinion. If you've a moment to spare, tell me, will you, what you think – and what Miss Vanne thinks. – And then, if ever the play were to be done again, I'd re-model the end. I feel I should want to.

I should really be grateful for your criticism, and for that of any of the actors who wouldn't mind telling me how they feel.

Meanwhile many thanks to you and Miss Vanne and Colin Keith-Johnston and the others who did what they could, and evidently made the play live, even if there was no making it please the audience.

Yours Sincerely D. H. Lawrence

One of my friends thought the grandmother whined too much – and somebody else said Holroyd wasn't big enough, not the type[4] – but people all have their own fancies.

[1] See p. 576 n. 2.

[2] For reviews see Sagar, *A D. H. Lawrence Handbook*, pp. 288–94.

[3] Marda Vanne played Mrs Holroyd; Colin Keith-Johnston, Blackmore. (For Marda Vanne's reaction to the play see Nehls, iii. 673 n. 143.)

[4] The comment on Holroyd came from a letter (13 December 1926) from Rolf Gardiner (whose response to the play was generally favourable): 'the man who played *Holroyd* [Peter Earle] wasn't fine or big enough, I thought; not that touch of fire and physical splendour that I feel was the hidden ore in the body of him as you meant him perhaps' (Nehls, iii. 121).

3918. To Hon. Dorothy Brett, 19 December 1926
Text: MS UCin; Irvine, Brett 72–3.

[Frieda Lawrence begins]

[Villa Mirenda, Scandicci, Florence]
[19 December 1926]

Halloh, Brett, it's nearly Xmas, I suppose you'll spend it with Mabel! I'll do a Xmas tree for these 17! peasant children, they have never seen one! Lawrence is becoming a painter he has painted 3 big pictures and 2 little ones – *so* fine! So you are trying to learn to live alone – I suppose ultimately one is alone and thankful to be so – Outwardly you seem so independant, but you are'nt inwardly – I am sending one of your photos to Friedel, he will love it – Lawrence is well – we have had some beastly fog days – but some dreams of sunny ones – News from the play Mrs Holroyd: People very upset and disturbed, *well* acted – Bernard Shaw said, the dialect was superb, his own stuff was mere Fleet Street jargon compared to it![1] I wish I had seen it – Now I light the fire in our quite beautiful salotta – You write such good letters!

All good wishes F.

[Lawrence begins]

Villa Mirenda. *Scandicci* (Florence)
19 Dec 1926 –

Dear Brett

I am hoping to enclose this with your scarf tomorrow. We didn't find one to suit us the last time we were in Florence, and then five days of horrible fog kept us at home again. I shall never defend the Florence climate – though we are out on the hills, and better off than Florence. – Now it's a lovely sunny day, and I sat out in the wood this morning, working at my novel – which comes out of me slowly, and is good, I think, but a little too[2] deep in bits – sort of bottomless pools. –

I think the people didn't like *The Widowing of Mrs Holroyd* in London: too gloomy: perhaps it is, a bit. – Anyhow for *David* I shall have to go myself.

Don't you bother about me, I'm all right. My health is better than a year

[1] Frieda is quoting (inaccurately) from Rolf Gardiner's letter, 13 December. Gardiner wrote: 'Shaw . . . said the dialogue was the most magnificent he had ever heard, and his own stuff was "The Barber of Fleet Street" in comparison' (Nehls, iii. 121). Esmé Percy recalled another version of Shaw's remark: 'Compared with that, my prose is machine-made lace. You can hear the typewriter in it' (Sagar, *A D. H. Lawrence Handbook*, p. 288). A third version (again by Frieda) appears in Tedlock, *Frieda Lawrence*, p. 147.

[2] MS reads 'to'.

ago, a good deal, and one does learn to live alone. It is rather *simpatico* here – the country is quite lovely, and our own peasants, if numerous and not highly developed, have a decent feeling towards us. And it's not so hard as America.

I've finished my Boccaccio picture – quite nice, nuns in frocks like lavender crocuses – and I've done a quick one, *Fight with an Amazon*.[1] I like it best. Now I want to take some canvas down to Scandicci to have it stretched, and I'll do a landscape. The winter landscape, here, when the sun shines, is all a glitter of olives and layers of deep, soft green umbrella pines, and there are puffs of orange willow trees in the hollows. I wonder if I can do it! Anyhow I'll have a try. And the carpenter is making me a proper studio easel! What *will* Gertler say.

It sounds rather splendid at the ranch, though, so sunny and clear. Don't forget to send me a bill for the horses!

DHL

3919. To Giuseppe Orioli, [20 December 1926]

Text: MS UCLA; Unpublished.

Villa Mirenda
Monday

Dear Pino

All being well, weather included, we will come to Florence on Thursday morning. Tell Reggie, if he is in any way engaged, not to bother in the least – we will lunch in a restaurant. But we'll call at your shop when we arrive.

What a tea-party, my hat! We only needed a March hare.

Au revoir then DHL

3920. To Nancy Pearn, 20 December 1926

Text: MS UT; Unpublished.

Villa Mirenda, *Scandicci*, Florence
20 Dec 1926

Dear Miss Pearn

I don't really understand about the Basil Blackwell affair, though I have your letter and stand on my head. What I do make out is that six quid seems to be wandering homeless, and we may as well nab it before somebody else does, and then what? Anyhow, if you say nab then so do I, and we'll be a bit richer if no wiser.[2]

Yrs D. H. Lawrence

[1] Reproduced in *The Paintings of D. H. Lawrence*, plate [11].

[2] Cf. Letter 3427. Perhaps both payments represented DHL's share of royalties from *The New Decameron III* and *IV* published by Blackwell.

I sent you a copy of Benn's *Glad Ghosts* for a Christmas card – probably the Italian post will absorb it!

3921. To Emily King, [20 December 1926]

Text: MS Lazarus; cited in Keith Sagar, 'Six Paintings by D. H. Lawrence', *Words International*, i (November 1987), 24.

Villa Mirenda, Scandicci (Florence)
19 Dec 1926[1]

My dear Pamela,

I meant to have written before – but you'll get this by Christmas! I sent things from Florence for you all, to Ada: she will hand them on. I hope she has them by now. And I sent you two little paper-covered books, *Sun* and *Glad Ghosts*. There were only just 100 copies of *Sun* printed, so don't lose that one. – I hope you didn't bother to send anything here – it really isn't worth the fag, posting. Yes, you can send me a pound of good orange pekoe tea – that I always am glad of. But don't bother with anything else.

I was so glad to hear Joan was better, and enjoying herself at the Santa Claus show. Now if only you can keep her well!

I heard from Gertie – she seemed very cheerful. But truly it *is* a long job. The thing has got deep hold of that left lung, so it's a job to stop it. But they'll manage it. They've cured many a worse case.

We had four days of horrid foggy weather last week, very unusual here – sets everybody coughing. But thank goodness, it is bright and sunny again now. One minds nothing, so long as the sun shines, and one can go out. I sat in the sun in the wood, this morning, writing for a couple of hours. It is very nice when we can do that. – Yesterday, Sunday, we went to the popular Stenterello theatre in Florence, with some friends, and found it amusing.[2]

And Christmas is on Saturday! We are having friends out for the day. And on Friday we are having a bit of a Christmas tree for our own peasants. The trouble is, there are so many of them – three families, Orsini, Bandelli, and Pinis – over twenty: ten[3] children! But the grown-ups only get a cigar or a few sweets. They'll have to be allowed to come, all of them – they think it's so grand up here in the salotta, with the piano and the pictures and so on. – But they're very nice, always sending us in grapes or vegetables or nuts, whatever they've got.

I've been busy painting – done three biggish pictures. Aldous Huxley

[1] In the letter DHL refers to 'Yesterday, Sunday'; Sunday was 19 December; hence the letter should be dated 20 December 1926.

[2] Stenterello is the Florentine version of Harlequin, a satirical stock character.

[3] ten] and ten

brought me out some canvases, that his brother-in-law had left behind, so I started in, and had quite a good time. Now I'm going to take some canvas down to Scandicci to be stretched, and I think I shall do a landscape. The winter landscape here is very lovely, with the vivid green puffs of umbrella pines, pale olives, long cypresses, and bright orange willow-trees in the hollows. – Then tomorrow we must go to Florence with Giulia, the girl, to buy things for the Christmas tree. She of course is very thrilled, but it's a bit of a fag, so many of them! Yet one can't leave any out – and they're pining for the sight of a tree with candles.

Is anything special happening with you? We're very quiet, but I prefer it so. – I'm so glad to think the coal strike is over. – Peg says you bravely eat yeast. Does it agree with you? – And since the wholesale scheme is sinking into abeyance, does Sam have any other idea? Next year, really, he should make a move!

Love to you all! I do hope you'll have a nice Christmas.

DHL

3922. To Hon. Dorothy Brett, 21 December 1926

Text: MS UCin; Postmark, [Scandi]cci 21. 12 26; Irvine, Brett 73–4.

Villa Mirenda, *Scandicci* (Florence)
21 Dec. 1926

Dear Brett

F[rieda] got your scarf today – I didn't go in to Florence. She got you a thin one, because they are the most elegant. I'm afraid it'll be only for the look of the thing, not much for warmth. But it's pretty, don't you think?

Today is the shortest day – and a sunny nice day, freezing tonight. But I watch the sun going down behind the rim of pine-trees in the south-west, at soon after four, with real regret. I don't care for long winter evenings. It's much nicer to have the daylight. – Our sun is never so strong as yours, though. Yet I can sit out and write a bit.

I haven't heard from Brewster lately. They wrote from the Taj Mahal, that they were probably staying a month in Benares, and sailing for Greece in January. – It's queer, on the sunny winter days, one feels more like taking a trip, than in summer. But no doubt we shall sit still till we have to go to England – perhaps not before March – for the *David* play. I told you, I believe the audience hated *The Widowing of Mrs Holroyd*.

If you see Mabel, tell her I'll go one day to the *Curonia* about those books. But she knows I hate butting in to Edwin Dodge's house.

It'll be New Year already before you get this. I do hope it will be a decent year for us all round.

There's no news, because I wrote you yesterday. Hope you'll have a jolly Christmas at Mabel's – and that 1927 will be a real good turning-point year. It would do us all good to get round a corner.

DHL

3923. To Gertrude Cooper, 21 December 1926
Text: MS Clarke; Lawrence–Gelder 145–8.

Villa Mirenda, *Scandicci*, Florence.
21 Decem 1926

My dear Gertie

If I'm going to get you a letter for Christmas, I shall have to send it off today: only four days! How the time has flown! – and to you, probably it has seemed long. I'm awfully sorry you can't go home for Christmas. It is a real disappointment to us all. But when we're doing our best, we can do no more, and it's no use repining. I wish we had been in England, then I would have come to see you. But Ada says she is coming for a few days, with Lizzie Booth – and that will be good for you. – I sent you a purse of Florentine leather – hope it's not too gaudy. I sent it to Ada with her things, so she can forward it to you. I hope she has the parcel by now – on Saturday, it will be a fortnight since it was sent off. But the post is already slow.

I had your letter – is it still sunny with you? It is cold and sunny here now, thank goodness. Sometimes in the morning I sit out in the wood and do a bit of writing. The pine woods are lovely in winter, they still seem warm. You too have pine woods round Mundesley, don't you?

We are busy getting ready a Christmas tree for our peasants. There will be about twelve children, and I expect their parents will have to come to look. So many people work on this little estate. And the children are wild little things. They've never seen a Christmas tree, but they heard of some other English people who made one for the peasants, so they all had fits, hoping we'd do one. We've got all kinds of little wooden toys from Florence, and with a few glittering things, and some sweets and dates, and the candles, it'll do for them. They never get sweets or anything like that, from year's end to year's end. They're very much poorer than even the really poor, in England. You see there's no money. They just live on the wine and oil and corn and vegetables of the earth, and have no wages, no cash, unless they manage to sell a barrel of wine. But this year there wasn't much. – Here, the peasants are supposed to do all the work on the land, and then they take half the produce: the landlord taking the other half. But when it's a little hilly estate like this, no pasture, no cattle, all just the hard labour of wine and a bit of wheat, a few vegetables, and the olives, they don't come off very well. This bit of land round the villa has to support twenty-seven peasants, counting children. In England, it wouldn't support seven. – But we've no idea how poorly they live – like cattle. Still, they are nice, and when we give them things, they always send us back a few dried grapes, or figs, or olives.

We shall give them their Christmas tree on Friday evening at sundown. And if the twenty-seven all of them come, it'll be like Ripley fair in this salotta. The men will have to have a glass of sweet wine and a long cigar called a Toscana, and the women get a glass of wine and a few biscuits. There will be a buzz! I wish you could be here to help. But they talk such strong dialect, that even when you know Italian you have a job to follow them.

Ada said Bertie had been ill for a day or two – thank goodness he's better. It's very chesty weather. She was going down to London with Eddie to see my play – and then couldn't go. I'm sorry, I should like her to have seen it: though I believe most of the people found it too gloomy. I think, if it were being done again, I should alter the end, and make it more cheerful. Myself, I hate miserable endings, now. But it's so long since I wrote that play.

By the way, did you ever get a copy of a magazine called *Travel*, with one of my articles in it? It's of no importance, only I like to know when things arrive, and when they get lost in the post. The Italian post has a way of losing 'printed matter.' I suppose somebody just takes it, as it is not what they call first class matter.

Well really, I'm sorry to think of you still in Mundesley for the New Year. It's bitter. But I'm glad they are so kind to you. It might be much worse. And another year, we can look forward to real rejoicings. So we'll just have patience and courage!

Love from us both – and thank Dr Pearson for his letter, I was glad to have it.[1]

DHL

3924. To Nelly Morrison, [21 December 1926]
Text: TMSC NWU; Unpublished.

Villa Mirenda, Scandicci,
Tuesday.

Dear Nelly Morrison,

Nice of you to ask us to stay the night. We should like to.

[1] Dr Sidney Vere Pearson (1875–1950) was Senior Physician at Mundesley Sanatorium for forty-five years; he himself suffered from tuberculosis. Author of *The State Provision of Sanatoriums* (Cambridge, 1913), etc.

We are going to lunch the following Thursday with Orioli and Reggie – – so perhaps they'd be seeing too much of us.

Any friends of yours we would be pleased to see. The Miss Hills are away, aren't they?

May we just come in sometime in the afternoon, about 4 o'clock, and leave the little bag with the night things? We are going on to Miss Zimmern's to tea.[1]

If you don't answer, I shall take it all is O.K. Don't on any account stay in. We will leave the little bag with the maid.

Hope we'll have a fine warm cheerful evening on the Terrace.

Till then D. H. Lawrence

3925. To Dr Trigant Burrow, 25 December 1926

Text: MS (Photocopy) HU; Huxley 675–6.

Villa Mirenda, *Scandicci* (Florence), Italy
Christmas Day 1926

Dear Dr Burrow

Many thanks for the paper – 'Psychoanalysis in Theory and in Life'.[2] It's the first thing I've read for a long time that isn't out to bully somebody in some way or other. It is true, the essential self is so simple – and nobody lets it be. – But I wonder you ever get anybody to listen to you. My experience of people is, as soon as they think themselves clever enough to read a book or hear a lecture, they will only pay attention to some bullying suggestion in which they can take part – or against which they can raise an equally bullying protest. Really one gets sick of people – they cant let be. – And I who loathe sexuality so deeply am considered a lurid sexuality specialist – Mi fa male allo stomaco![3] – But I was really glad to hear a real peaceful word for once. You never thought you were writing a *Noël Noël* carol, did you? – But some times your sentences are like Laocoön snakes, one never knows where the head is, nor the tail.

Tell me some time – it seems rude – what old nation you belong to –

[1] Helen Zimmern (1846–1934), writer and journalist living in the Via Mattonaia. Author of *The Italy of the Italians* (1906), *New Italy* (1918), etc.

[2] The article appeared in the *Journal of Nervous and Mental Disease*, lxiv (1926), 209–24.

[3] 'It's bad for your stomach!'

England? Wales? surely not Jewish at all (that's not prejudice – only the psychology isnt Jewish).

Best wishes for the New Year D. H. Lawrence[1]

3926. To Elfie Rosebery, 25 December 1926

Text: MS Secor; PC v. Santo Domingo Indian; Postmark, Scandicci 27 12 26; Unpublished.

[Villa Mirenda, Scandicci, Florence]
christmas day 1926

Many thanks for your greeting. Did I ever thank you for *Helen*![2] – I meant to so hard, that I can't remember. It amused me very much. – So glad you're feeling better – we are still coughing – and it's trying to snow today here – I send you a little book[3] – Hope we shall come to Ravello this spring.

D. H. Lawrence[4]

[1] Burrow replied on 7 February 1927 (*A Search for Man's Sanity*, New York, 1958, pp. 163–4); he enclosed a copy of an article in the *British Journal of Medical Psychology*, vi (1926), 211–18. His acknowledgment of DHL's letter 'of January 12th' must refer to the date of its delivery. The letter read:

Dear D. H. Lawrence:

Many thanks for your good letter from Florence of January 12th. I am very glad you felt with me in my paper, 'Psychoanalysis in Theory and in Life.' What you say of my involved sentences is too terribly true. See if my language is not improving in this essay I am sending you today, 'The Reabsorbed Affect and Its Elimination.'

No, nobody listens to me. But I do not expect them to. I didn't listen myself. Circumstances, very unusual circumstances, *compelled* my mood to listen whether or no. And now and then I have the opportunity of compelling by extension this same mood acknowledgment in others. But it is only by compulsion that our willful mood is touched, not by persuasion. Intellectualism simply does not figure for a moment in the process.

No, I am not a Jew. I like them and they like me, but racially I am not one of them. My ancestry is chiefly French, though in recent generations depleted with English and Irish strains.

Your letters and their sympathetic encouragement have meant very much to me. You should have stopped to see me on your way from Mexico to England. This winter I am in New York in response to the group interest there on the part of several people. It has been an interesting experience, this fresh contact with a totally new environment and the opportunity to approach it from an entirely fresh mood basis. The response there has been more than I had had any expectation of. New York also has its soberness and its pain.

You are so fortunate to travel as much as you do. I think each year I shall set out but each year there are interests that stand momentarily in the way.

With my good wishes,

Sincerely yours,

[2] Perhaps the historical novel, *Helen: A Tale of Ancient Troy* (1925), by Edward Lucas White.

[3] The inscribed copy of *Glad Ghosts* is now in the Victoria University Library, Toronto.

[4] There follows (written upside down by DHL) the description of the postcard verso given in the headnote above.

3927. To Earl Brewster, 26 December 1926

Text: MS UT; Brewster 107–8.

Villa Mirenda, *Scandicci* (Florence), Italy
26 Decem. 1926

Dear Earl

I had your letter yesterday saying you were sailing for Port Said on Dec. 7th and would be in Athens for Christmas. Are you actually there? I am terribly anxious to know how you are, all three of you, and what it's like in Greece.

We are sitting here – comfortable indoors, thank heaven – but very cold out, and bits of snow. I haven't much to say for the Florentine climate: not enough sun: though the landscape out here among the hills is lovely.

Write as soon as you can to tell me about Syra. I am a bit held up, because I may have to go to London in mid-February to help with the production of *David*. They played *The Widowing of Mrs Holroyd* about a fortnight ago, and it made an impression, but was too tragic and gloomy in the last act, to please the audience. – But *David* is a much more difficult play to put on, I must go and help.

All the same, I'd love to come to Greece – even if not till after *David*, in March. So do write and tell me as soon as you can about Syra – how one manages, how dear it is, etc. – In the spring, Frieda may go to America to sell that ranch. If not, she'd come with me to Syra.

I do hope you're safely landed and feeling in good trim. One day I want to go to Benares. For me, it is the Hindu, Brahmin thing – that queer fluidity, and those lively, kicking legs, that attracts me: the pre-Buddha. I should very much like to see it, and try it. But Greece first: which is not so far, nor so costly.

Many good wishes from us both for the New Year, to you three. I do hope you've got the *sun* – we haven't!

au revoir. D. H. Lawrence

3928. To Nancy Pearn, [27 December 1926]

Text: MS UT; PC v. L'Umbria Illustrata Perugia – Ipogeo etrusco dei Volumni – Urna della Medusa; Unpublished.

Scandicci.
27 Decem

Dear Miss Pearn

Right-o about Hutchinsons![1] – do make the decision about price in future

[1] Negotiations perhaps related to Lady Cynthia's anthology, *Black Cap* (see p. 590 n. 3).

without bothering to refer to me, when you sell stories or things, – unless it's something very special. – Got your card today:

Cheer up!
Cheer up!!
Cheer up!!!

But am quite chirpy. It's sunny again. Auguri!

D. H. Lawrence

3929. To Maria Huxley, 28 December 1926
Text: Huxley 676–7.

Villa Mirenda, Scandicci, Firenze.
28th Dec., 1926.

Dear Maria, –

Glad you got the book. We had a Christmas tree and all the peasants – 27 of them! *They* liked it, and were nice. Then we had the Wilkinsons out one evening, but have seen nobody else. I find I'm best alone – unless I can choose rather squeamishly, but perhaps it's not really good for one.

We shall stay here if not howked out.[1] I shall probably have to go to London for the play *David* at end of February. But probably shall come back here. I like it here. I told you we'd fixed up the *salotto* nice and warm, with matting and stove going and Vallombrosa chairs. If you find a villa, find one between here and Galuzzo, if you can, so I can walk over.

I meant to thank you properly for those canvases; they were such a boon. My Boccaccio picture of the nuns and the gardener is finished – very nice and, as Wilkinson says: Well, not exactly *nice!* – on the long canvas – and the third picture, the *Fight with an Amazon*, is nearly done. So you see now you set me up! I'm really grateful.

I hope Aldous is flourishing – and the boy.[2] I see odd bits about him – *père*, not *fils* – in the papers – but journalists are all *canaille*.

Which reminds me, they played my *Widowing of Mrs. Holroyd* and I believe they hated it, and somebody says I ought to write about the class I come from, I've no right to venture into the Peerage – people educated above their class, etc.![3] *O tra-la-la! La gente invidiosa è la bestia più maleducata ancora. Come mai!*[4]

[1] I.e. dug out, cleared out (dialect).

[2] Matthew Huxley, b. 1920.

[3] Probably a reference to Ivor Brown's review of the play in the *Saturday Review*, cxlii (18 December 1926), 767–8. Brown remarks: 'Mr Lawrence . . . has also suggested how well he might have written . . . if he had stuck to the life he knows instead of plunging into the theory which is clamorously acclaimed by people who have been educated beyond their intelligence' (Sagar, *A D. H. Lawrence Handbook*, p. 291).

[4] 'Envious people are the rudest people indeed. How is that!'

3930. To Mabel Dodge Luhan, 29 December 1926

Text: MS Brill; Luhan 320–1.

Villa Mirenda, *Scandicci*, Florence.
29 Dec. 1926

Dear Mabel

– I have your letter with Romanelli's bill to you.[1] It seems enormous. When I go in to Florence I'll ask about it. But these people do now charge like the very devil. Florence is very expensive.

If I were you I'd *never* bother to have books sent all that way. Why $700. would print you the first two vols of your Memoirs – which surely is much more important to *you* than books to High Schools and such stuff. Why don't you have a small selection of the books, not more than 100 vols, made for your *own* library – and sell the rest in job lots in Florence. Give $100. worth of miscellaneous books to the library – and save the rest of the money. Seems to me madness to cart old books to Taos – madness. And let somebody bring the three pictures when they come – have a regular agent just ship them to the boat – or let someone like Gondrands ship them to New York, to somebody you can trust, then pick them up some time. Dont waste all that money on transport, when you can print your memoirs with it. – You got my letter with R. Aldingtons suggestion: that you print 100 copies of your memoirs, wrap them up addressed to the people you want to have them – to be forwarded after your death – or at your[2] order later on. – But I would always advise you to change *all* names, and names of places, before you send the thing to print. And ask the Centaur Bookshop about the business. – Bind just in paper wrappers, and keep it quiet.

If you really want me to look over those books in the Curonia, I shall have to wait for warmer weather. The villa will be icy as a church. But far better sell them here, and give the *proceeds* to the Taos library and the High School. Sheer waste of money sending the stuff 6000 miles.

Yrs D. H. Lawrence

3931. To Arthur Wilkinson, [30 December 1926]

Text: MS Schlaefle; Unpublished.

Villa Mirenda
Thursday

Dear Wilkinson

Yes, it was nice on Sunday – we enjoyed it.

Lovely day today. Am just undoing the Christmas tree.

[1] Unidentified.

[2] your] your your

Some friends want us to go to Rome – I don't want to bother. So I told Mrs Hughes – she's from Santa Fe, New Mexico – she could probably come with her daughter into your flat till January 12th if she liked. Is that right? If not, let me know – or just send her a line direct·

Mrs Christine Hughes, 19 Corso d'Italia, Rome.

She's a nice woman – daughter about 18, doing music in Rome. But how queer to see them in Italy!

Everything very still and very sleepy. When will you come out again?

Au revoir to all 4. D. H. Lawrence

3932. To Ada Clarke, 30 December 1926

Text: MS Clarke; Unpublished.

Villa Mirenda, *Scandicci* (Florence.)
Thursday 30 Decem. 1926

My dear Sister

I don't know if you've got my parcel yet – but there's no sign of yours. I tell you, it's not good bothering with foreign parcels. – My mother-in-law got the one sent off from the shop at the same time as yours: she had it well before Christmas. If yours doesn't come, I'll let you know and we'll make enquiries – same with mine to you.

We had a quiet Christmas, but that is as I prefer it. We had a jolly Christmas tree. Pietro[1] and Giulia went and cut one in the darkness before dawn, in the wood on the hill – a lovely young pine tree. With lots of candles and some Christmas glittery things, it looked lovely. The peasants all came up on Christmas Eve, with the children washed beyond recognition, the rascal Filiberto, who as a rule doesn't have much but dirt and his shirt to cover him, looking like a diminutive chauffeur, most amazing. We gave them wooden toys like those I sent, and sacks of sweets, and they were fascinated. The elder ones drank Marsala and sat still, and Tosca and Lilla and Teresina – damsels of 17 and 18 sang and danced. But we were worn out when they departed. Then friends came out for Sunday, for the rest we were alone, which I prefer. It was bitter cold for Christmas, even a sprinkle of snow, but today is sunny and hot as summer.

I think Miss Beveridge and her sister and Mabel Harrison will come in February and take the little Villa la Massa, just across the slope here – for three months. That will be very nice. But I wonder if I shall have to come to England in Feb. for *David*. – It was too bad you couldn't get to *Mrs Holroyd*. – I do

[1] Pietro Pini, Giulia's half-brother, was a young farmer; he modelled for DHL, possibly for his picture *Contadini* (Nehls, iii. 61–2).

hope the children are really well again – no more sickness, for heavens sake. It's enough having Gertie on one's mind. I haven't heard from her for Christmas. I do wish there was a turn for the better.

I've just dismantled the Christmas tree – I didn't want to keep it over the New Year. I wonder if we shall be here next year, to have the things again. The Brewsters have arrived in Greece, from India, and they want me to go there: to the isle of Syra. I should very much like to go to greece – but we'll see.

We have an invitation to Rome, too – but I don't think I want to bother to go to Rome.

Hope things are going well. Let me have a line –

love. DHL

3933. To Nancy Pearn, 31 December 1926

Text: MS UT; Unpublished.

Villa Mirenda, *Scandicci* (Firenze)
31 Decem. 1926

Dear Miss Pearn

The Rickworth young man of the *Calendar* asked me for poems. Here are 2 you can show him. – He said he was sending me a proof of that review, but it's not come yet.[1]

Last words I shall write this year!!!

Happy New Year to you D. H. Lawrence

3934. To Earl Brewster, 2 January 1927

Text: MS UT; PC v. Dintorni di Firenze – Ponte a Vingone – Via Roma; Brewster 111.

Villa Mirenda. *Scandicci*, Firenze.
2 Jan 1927

Dear Earl

Your Syra letter just come! – What a blow! – vegetable market-gardening, of all things![2]

Why don't you try this region? – it's very lovely, and *no foreigners*, and *beautiful* painting country – lovely old villas on each Tuscan hill – no doubt we could find you one for about 5,000 Liras a year[3] – our friends are just taking a villino across the hill for 3000 a year – *such* nice painting country. Let me know, and I'll ask about the villa Bianca. The best would be to say you'd go away for July and August – it full of villegiatura Italians then – we go to

[1] The poems were 'The Old Orchard' and 'Rainbow', published in *Calendar*, iv (April 1927), 67–73 (Roberts C153); for the review see Letter 3903 and n. 5.

[2] See p. 484 n. 2.

[3] year] month

England. – But I know Achsah doesn't like north of Rome. I find I like this unspoilt Tuscany very much. The tram comes to Vingone in ½ hour – and then we walk two kilometers – and there are pine woods, open and free, and beautiful.

I myself have taken to painting – quite biggish canvases – but figures mostly nude. Wonder what you'd say to 'em! – At Florence the Pensione Lucchesi is quite decent, 40 a day if you arrange. Hope you're all right.

Buoni auguri DHL

3935. To Margaret King, [3 January 1927]

Text: MS Needham; PC v. Dintorni di Firenze – Panorama di Ponte a Vingone; Postmark, Scandicci 4 I 27; Unpublished.

[Villa Mirenda, Scandicci, Florence]

3 Jan.

Many thanks for your letter. What a scandal that the hanks and socks were stolen: you have to *register* letters with things in them; and write outside 'may be opened'. – Ada's parcel has not come – they'll charge me 80% duty for silk – they might almost as well steal them. *Don't* send tea: keep it for when I come. – No more parcels.

love. DHL

3936. To Arthur Wilkinson, [3 January 1927]

Text: MS Schlaefle; PC v. Dintorni di Firenze – Ponte a Vingone – Via Roma; Postmark, Sca[ndicci] 4 I[. . .]; Unpublished.

[Villa Mirenda, Scandicci, Florence]

Jan 3rd

Sorry I bothered you about the villa – thought perhaps, if the people did come, they would have got it aired and warmed for you. But they wont come. Beastly weather, raining. Have got my new easel – twin to yours, exactly. – Tried briquettes in the stove: no good, so don't you try them.

Saluti Cordiali D. H. Lawrence

3937. To Mabel Dodge Luhan, [4 January 1927]

Text: MS Brill; Unpublished.

Villa Mirenda – Scandicci

4 Jan. 1926

Dear Mabel

Have been talking about your books. The transport agent *must* be a thief: if you must have the things sent, we could probably get G. Egidi. 28 Vigna

Nuo[va], Floren[ce] to send them for about $300.00. But *far* better sell them here – this man Orioli would more or less undertake it[1] – I know him – you wouldn't be much swindled. Let me know at once. And say if you'd like one box of books for yourself, and *which sort*. And I could arrange for the three pictures to be sent off, through Egidi. But you must authorise me properly. Decide and let me know quickly, as I may go to England.

Raining here, and dismal,

Yrs D. H. Lawrence

3938. To Martin Secker, 8 January 1927

Text: MS UInd; Postmark, Scandicci 10 1.27; Secker 82–3.

Villa Mirenda, *Scandicci* (Florence)
8 Jan 1927

Dear Secker

So long since I wrote you – or heard from either you or Rina. How are you, and all the family. We are pretty well – had a day or two of sunshine, but raining again now. Florence isn't much better than England, as far as climate goes.

We had a very quiet Christmas – only a Christmas tree for the peasants, which looked very jolly – it was a pine tree that Pietro stole from the hills. I think they liked it. The children anyhow were delighted – the handsome Tosca sang and capered – and all the twentyseven of the peasants came in relays – a real go. For the rest, nothing. I didn't see any of the English colony, didn't festivate that way at all. I find I've no desire left for seeing people who do nothing and who mean nothing and who make all life mean nothing, beyond a would-be-witty tea-party. I can't stand it.

I'm getting on with the novel. It's already what the world would call very improper – and not inclined towards popularity. But you won't be like Adele Seltzer and ask me to come back with a best seller under my arm.[2] It's very nice for those whose line it is, and very nasty for those whose line it isn't, to be called upon for best sellers. Anyhow it's the knees of the gods.

I finished my Boccaccio picture and also my *Fight with an Amazon*, and am doing a landscape with figures.[3] Painting is a much more amusing art than writing, and much less to it, costs one less, amuses one more. Think I shall try to sell pictures, and make a living that way.

I haven't thanked you even for the *Illus. London News* and *The Lit. Sup.*

[1] DHL's letter was written on Orioli's business notepaper (with part of the heading crossed out) and therefore probably in his shop.

[2] See Letter 3888 and n. 4.

[3] *Red Willow Trees*, reproduced in *The Paintings of D. H. Lawrence*, plate [3].

The first has sometimes a *very* interesting picture, like the nigger women with the ball.[1] And the second seems to me in a mild state of flux. – I want to pay for the *Lit Sup*.

I haven't heard yet about photographs for the *Mornings in Mexico* book, neither from Taos nor from *Travel*.[2] Time I did! Is there any hurry? You got the two copies of *Travel* did you. In one was an anti-Fascist article, so the Italians won't like it.[3]

Is there any news at all? I feel I wouldn't care about anything, if only the sun would shine. But send me a line to tell me how you are.

Yrs D. H. Lawrence

3939. To Nancy Pearn, 9 January 1927
Text: MS UT; Huxley 678–9.

Villa Mirenda, *Scandicci* (Florence)
9 Jan 1927

Dear Miss Pearn

The Insel Verlag asked me for a more or less personal article to put in their *Almanach*, in German. So I did them one. – I am sending you a duplicate, and I want you to read it, and decide whether we shall send it out into the world or not. If you think I should regret sending it out to editors, will you preserve it for me, as yours will be the only copy.[4] They're sure to cut the other one up, for translation, in Germany.

And how did you like the poems?[5] – I'm going to do some more. – But I'm slowly pegging at a novel, and painting my 4th. picture, very smart this last. Painting is more fun and less soul-work than writing. I may end as an R. A.

Yrs D. H. Lawrence

[1] The *Illustrated London News*, 25 December 1926, p. 1267, carried a photograph entitled: 'African Women take to European Sport: Exotic Push-Ball'. It shows a large group of women from the French colony of Oubangui-Chari keeping a gigantic ball in the air on their outstretched hands.

[2] Cf Letter 3899 and n. 2.

[3] The article, by George Raffalovich, is entitled 'What the Italians Think of America' (*Travel*, November 1926, 12–15, 52, 54, 58). Its tone is suggested by the topics covered, e.g. 'The Hatred of Italy', 'The Testimony of the Press', 'The Emigration Embroglio'.

[4] In her reply, 27 January 1927 (TMSC UT), Nancy Pearn wrote: 'I did find the article on "Becoming a Success" tremendously interesting . . . I cannot see any objection to having it published.' See also Letter 3966.

Perhaps the 'article' is the unpublished piece entitled 'Getting On' (MS UCin) – an early version of 'Autobiographical Sketch' in *Assorted Articles* (1930) – in which DHL gives his age as forty-one; he reiterates at length his views on Henry Saxton (cf. Letter 3950) and is critical about some of his mother's values. Other possibilities are 'Which Class I Belong To' (Roberts E428) and '[Return to Bestwood]' (Roberts E31).

[5] See Letter 3933 and n. 1.

3940. To Else Jaffe, 10 January 1927

Text: MS Jeffrey; Frieda Lawrence 235–6.

Villa Mirenda, *Scandicci* (Florence)
10[1] Jan 1927

My dear Else

That was a nice letter you wrote – and a very nice little purse you sent me for Christmas. I ought to have thanked you before – but something has happened to me about letters – in fact all writing. I seem to be losing my will-to-write altogether: in spite of the fact that I'm working at an English novel – but so differently from the way I've written before!

I spend much more time painting – have already done three, nearly four, fairly large pictures. I wonder what you'll say to them when you see them. Painting is more fun than writing, more of a game, and costs the soul far, far less.

I enclose a cross letter from Curtis Brown's foreign clerk. I have answered that I don't believe you have made any legal agreement whatsoever with the Insel Verlag.[2] Have you? Do let me know. – It is rather a bore, the high-handed way old Kippenberg behaves, as if he were the great Cham of publishers. I should like to get a bit of a slap at him.

It's very nice that Alfred is being feasted and rejoiced over. Congratulate him from me. It *is* nice to have a bit of grateful recognition, whatever one may say.

I am going to make another effort to get the two downstairs rooms with the big terrace, so you could have them as a little apartment when you come. They would be so nice.

They keep deferring the production of *David* – no doubt they are frightened of it. I believe they hated *The Widowing of Mrs Holroyd*. – Now they say *David* will probably be April, but I don't mind, because I'd much rather stay *here* till the sun warms up a bit in the north – one gets sick of winter – though it is a lovely day today.

Auf Wiedersehen, then. DHL

3941. To Baroness Anna von Richthofen, 12 January 1927

Text: MS UCB; Frieda Lawrence 259–60.

Villa Mirenda, *Scandicci* (Florenz)
12 Jan. 1927

Meine liebe Schwiegermutter

Für den schönen Schlips, der mir so viel gefällt, habe ich noch nicht dank!

[1] 10] 7

[2] The Curtis Brown letter is missing. Cf. Letter 3870.

gesagt. Jeh, ich bin roh! Aber jetzt ist mir ein Feder eine Schwierigkeit geworden. In meinem Leben habe ich so viel geschrieben, ich möchte schweigen. Aber du verstehst.

Wir sind wohl in Januar, und ich war noch nicht, diesen Winter, schlecht erkältet: ich danke der Herrgott, und bete, es mög so gut halten, bei mir. Auch bei dir geht es gut, nicht wahr?

Wir sitzen still, arbeiten viel, und das ist gesund. Leute machen man müde, und bringen Krankheit. Die Frieda näht viel, macht sich Kleider und Jäckele und Mantel, und sagt selber, sie ist besser wie Paquin: also gut! Ihre Hüte macht sie immer höher, wie der Turm von Babel, der so hoch gewachsen ist. Du sollst eine Tochter in der Frühling sehen, wie nie in deinem Leben.

Jetzt schreiben sie mir aus London, dass der *David* nur in April gespielt werden soll. Es gefällt mir aber besser: ich gehe viel lieber nach England, und nach Deutschland, wann Winter vorbei ist, und die Blumen geben auch Grüsse. Warte du nur, Schwiegermutter, und habe Geduld. Sommer ist die beste Zeit.

Wir haben schlechtes Wetter, nicht Regen, aber kalten Nebel, der ganz unnatürlich ist, hier in diesem Land. Inzwischen kommen schöne Tagen: wie Montag, wann ich an die Villa Curonia, Mabel's Villa auf dem Poggio Imperiale, zum erstenmal gegangen bin. Ach, eine grosse schöne schöne Villa, etwas nobel, aber traurig, traurig wie der Tod. Sie will Bücher heraus-reissen und nach Taos schicken lassen.

Lebewohl, du Schwiegermutter, bis wiedersehen

DHL

Was hat der D. Thomann gekostet? Ich zahl es dir.

[My dear Schwiegermutter

I haven't yet said thanks! for the beautiful tie, which I like so much. Dear me, I'm a brute! But now any pen has become a weariness to me. All my life I've written so much, I'd like to keep quiet. But you understand.

We're well into January, and I haven't had a bad cold yet this winter: I thank the Lord, and pray it'll keep on so well with me. Things are going well with you too, aren't they?

We sit quietly, working hard, and that's healthy. People make one tired, and bring illness. Frieda is sewing a lot, makes herself dresses and little jackets and a coat, and says herself she's better than Paquin:[1] all right! She's making her

[1] Mme Isidore Paquin (d. 1936) founder of the famous fashion house, Maison Paquin in Paris (1891–1956); 'Paquined' came to mean 'dressed in the most up-to-date fashion' (Sir James Murry and others, eds., *A New English Dictionary on Historical Principles: Supplement*, Oxford, 1911). Cf. *Reflections*, ed. Herbert, p. 152.

hats taller and taller, like the Tower of Babel, which grew so tall.[1] In the spring you should see a daughter such as never before in your life.

Now they write to me from London that *David* will be produced only in April. But that suits me better: I much prefer going to England, and to Germany, when winter is past, and the flowers greet one as well. Just wait, Schwiegermutter, and have patience. Summer is the best time.

We're having bad weather, not rain, but cold fog, which is totally unnatural for this country. In between come lovely lovely days: such as Monday, when I went for the first time to the Villa Curonia, Mabel's villa on the Poggio Imperiale. Oh dear, a big beautiful villa, rather superior, but sad, sad as death. She wants books torn out and sent to Taos.

Farewell, Schwiegermutter, till we meet

DHL

What did the D. Thomann cost?[2] I'll pay it you.]

3942. To Martin Secker, 12 January 1927

Text: MS UInd; Secker 83–4.

Villa Mirenda, *Scandicci* (Florence)
12 Jan. 1927

Dear Secker

I heard yesterday from Mrs Whitworth that *David* will probably not be produced till April. That suits me all right, as far as coming to England is concerned, but it seems late for the book. So if you like, then bring it out as soon as you wish – next month, perhaps. But ask Curtis Brown first about Knopf's date: I don't think the American edition can have come out, I've had no news of it whatsoever.[3] But if you get out *David* in February, the *Mornings in Mexico* will do very well in March: though I've not heard from *Travel* respecting illustrations. Have you? And have you the *Theatre Arts* Magazines yet, with the 'Dance' articles?

So long since I heard from you – hope you are all right. Is Rina in Italy? – she has given no sign. And what are you doing? The weather is dull and heavy here, not rain, but a sort of fog, very unpleasant – save for odd lovely days. But we don't go out much.

The new novel is getting on. The world will probably call it very improper. It isn't *really* – but there you are.

And I did a little picture of a negro wedding – fairly amusing. In the winter, one can but work.

Best wishes from both D. H. Lawrence

[1] Cf. Genesis xi. 4.
[2] The reference is obscure.
[3] Secker's first edn of *David* (March 1926) sold out in a month; he reprinted in February 1927. For Knopf's edn see p. 346 n. 2.

Your letter just come – Do pay Koteliansky, he hasn't a sou, suppose that makes him a weariness.[1] I believe he gives me half – Novel goes well, but is improper!

3943. To Earl Brewster, [14 January 1927]
Text: MS Picard; Telegram; Unpublished.

[Villa Mirenda, Scandicci, Florence]
[14 January 1927][2]

Aspettiamo Domenica ce letto per una persona tram a Vingone.

[We are expecting [you] on Sunday there is a bed for one person take the tram to Vingone.]

3944. To Mabel Dodge Luhan, 17 January 1927
Text: MS Brill; Luhan 321–2.

Villa Mirenda. *Scandicci* (Florence)
17 Jan 1927

Dear Mabel

We got the parcel of books and herbs yesterday: very nice of you to send them. The herbs smell *so* strong of Taos: when we went into the trattoria at Vingone, the padrona kept sniffing: cos' è? ma cos' è questo profumo?[3] – and we had to open the parcel and give her a bit.

[1] The reference is to Kot's claim that some royalty payment remained due to him on Shestov's *All Things Are Possible* (cf. Letter 3741 and n. 1). Secker asked Huebsch on 3 December 1926 (Secker Letter-Book, UIll) for

> the amount paid by the "Freeman" for the serial use of Shestov's "All Things are Possible" in June 1920. Our books record a single and final payment of £10, but the translator has somewhere or other unearthed evidence that he was to receive more than this amount on that account. It is all very ancient and probably unfounded, but to satisfy him we have promised to put the point to you in the extremely unlikely event of it still being within your recollection or investigation. Do not go to any trouble about it.

On 5 January 1927 Secker was able to assure Kot:

> we find that you were perfectly correct in reminding us that the sum of £10 paid in June 1920 was on account of serial used in "The Freeman" and not of the American edition of the book as we had assumed in good faith. The royalties on the McBride edition of the book to date therefore remain to be paid, and the proprietor's two-third share of these, on the basis of Messrs.McBride's statemnets already submitted to you, amounts to £7.9.2. We are communicating with Mr.D.H. Lawrence, whose authorisation we should like to have, and on receipt of his reply will forward you this cheque.

Finally, on 19 January 1927, Secker wrote again to Kot:

> we have now heard from Mr.Lawrence who authorises us to pay the proprietor's share of the royalties on Messrs.McBride's edition of "All Things Are Possible" to yourself. We accordingly enclose our cheque £7.9.2...
>
> P.S. Mr.Lawrence writes that his understanding is that one-half of the above cheque is due to himself.

[2] The text of the telegram is contained in a letter from Earl to Achsah Brewster. He told his wife, on 15 January 1927: 'This morning a telegram came from D.H.L. as follows: . . .' It is therefore assumed that the message was actually sent on Friday, 14 January.

[3] 'what is it? but what is this smell?'

I went to the Curonia a week ago with Orioli. We thought we'd be able to get in, without that Romanelli, who must be a marvellous thief, asking you $700 dollars, when $70 must be nearer the mark. – But we could find nobody – house shut up, cypress avenue empty and triste – the whole place of a tristezza da morire[1] – though a lovely day – on the big terrace a fat marble baby lying flat, but its tootsies broken off: and your old stone dogs! – After ages we found Pietro – he's very nice – remembers you affettuosamente – Acton had been up and told him you were *dead* – great blow to him.[2] But he had corrected that. – He and his wife are quite alone at the Curonia, and he says it is *molto triste*. I gave him money, as from you, and he sent you ringraziamenti e ricordi, no? – e tante cose, alla Signora Mebli![3] I like him. He told me how you made him do things, alla moda americana, subito, subito Pietro! E poi, quando era fatto – When he'd done it – it was some sort of a rockery – you came and said: Pietro, ho sbagliato. Porta tutto via.[4] – I can see it all. – We went in the downstairs, servants rooms – cold and sad – but all the fine copper pans! Pietro hadn't the keys of the living rooms – only that Romanelli. It is like Edwin Dodge to get into the hands of a swindler. – I hear Edwin D. wants $100,000 for the villa – which is Liras two-and-half million. He'll never get it. Lucky if he gets half. It's a lovely place, but sad, and oh, the cost of upkeep nowadays! You've no idea! – I shall go again as soon as there's a fine day, and get the Romanelli and really look at the books. According to Pietro, they are not so *very* many – a few quintali – and the heaviest are great bound vols. of magazines. Do you want those?

How did you like Buffalo? You'll be back now. – Tell Brett, Brewster is here for a day or two, looking round for a villa: but Achsah wants to *buy* one, near Rome – but not more than $6,000. Achsah and Harwood are in Capri.

Did you get the ribbons? How is Tony?

DHL

3945. To Nancy Pearn, 17 January 1927

Text: MS UT; Unpublished.

Villa Mirenda, *Scandicci* (Florence)
17 Jan 1927

Dear Miss Pearn

The *Forum* paid $75– for the nightingale, so I'm afraid they've put salt on

[1] 'sadness of death'.

[2] Arthur Mario Acton (1873–1953), art collector who bought and lived in the Villa La Pietra (overlooking Florence) where he established his fine collection of Italian primitives and created the splendid gardens.

[3] 'thanks and kind remembrances, would you believe it? – and greetings to Mrs Mebli!'

[4] 'in the American fashion, straight away, at once, Pietro! And then, when it was done . . . Pietro, I have made a mistake. Take everything away.'

the poor bird's tail, and will serve him out of season, to be luxurious. As for the *Spectator*, they wanted to cut him up, didn't they? So they can wait.[1] Damn them all.

I haven't *very* much feeling about 'Sixpenny Poets'.[2] Yet on principle I believe in cheap books. – Duckworth has two vols of my poems, and won't let Secker have 'em[3] – don't know if he'd let Benn. – As a matter of fact, I believe they, Benn's, asked me ages ago for a Sixpenny-worth of poems. – But let's try again, all round: Benn, Duckworth, Secker. I'm all for the nimble sixpence, and I loathe half-guineas and so on.

Yes, I sent the two poems for the *Calendar*, so give them to them for the £3.[4] No doubt it's munificente to them.

Are you managing illustrations for the *Mornings in Mexico* – from *Travel* and *The Theatre Arts*?

Yrs D. H. Lawrence

Rain!

3946. To Achsah Brewster, 19 January 1927

Text: MS UT; Brewster 113–14.

Villa Mirenda, Scandicci (Florence)
19 Jan 1927

Dear Achsah

We were so pleased to see Earl, and though he only stayed two days, it was very nice, and really friendly.[5] I think he's really got a lot out of India this time – the very disillusion is valuable, and then the glimpse of a new reality. I felt you'd had rather an anxious and nervous[6] time of it, and am glad to think of you sitting safely in the Villa Guilia. Don't wander far afield again, it's a big nervous expenditure: and you'll have all the motives for your work that you need for the rest of your days.

I wonder where you'll find a house. I think your idea of buying a place is a good one, so long as you *know* the locality and the spirit of place – and so long as you don't saddle yourself with a big house. This locality is lovely, but I know

[1] See pp. 482 n. 3 and 584 n. 1.

[2] Advertisements for Ernest Benn's series of pamphlets, *The Augustan Books of English Poetry*, included the sub-title 'The Sixpenny Poets'. Following the success of the first series (cf. p. 521 n. 3), edited by Edward Thompson, 1925–6, a second series was being prepared, ed. Humbert Wolfe. The first six titles (poems by Donne, George Herbert, Francis Thompson, Yeats, Monro and Rose Macaulay) appeared in April 1927. DHL's poems appeared in the series (No. 22) in February 1928 (Roberts A38).

[3] Duckworth published *Love Poems and Others* (1913) and *Amores* (1916).

[4] See Letter 3933.

[5] For Brewster's account of his stay, see Brewster 112–13.

[6] MS reads 'nevous'.

you don't want to come north of Rome, so won't press it. And there is nothing to prevent *our* coming south of Rome, later on. It would be nice if we could be neighbours.

We saw Magnelli and his work yesterday, and it was very interesting.[1] But today I feel as if some of the virtue had gone out of me.[2] These modern artists, who make art out of antipathy to life, always leave me feeling a little sick. It is as if they used all their skill and their effort to dress up a skeleton. Magnelli has lovely colour, and design – but underneath it is all empty, he pins all his beauty on to a dead nothingness. What's the good. I think I learned something from him – but rather, what not to be, than what to be. I'm afraid I am more modern even than these artistic anarchists.

Frieda sends many greetings to you, and is going to write – so she says. But she says it oftener than she does it. I am hoping we may all meet somewhere in the spring, in sunshine. We'll surely make a little trip south.

Remember me to Harwood, who, according to Earl, is becoming a real whopper. She'll be charading now with the Reynolds Girls, and having still another good time.[3] Happy soul, she has so many.

I do hope you're feeling rested and yourself again. I expect you have begun to work. – Do you mind giving Earl these Lembo letters? –[4]

a rivederci D. H. Lawrence

3947. To S. S. Koteliansky, 20 January 1927

Text: MS BL; Postmark, Scandicci 22 I 27; cited in Gransden 31.

Villa Mirenda, *Scandicci*, Florence
20 Jan 1927

Dear Kot

I had just heard from Secker, and told him to pay the money to you. – I'd sort of forgotten the Shestov. But annoying those things are! – I'll ask Secker why he didn't pay the money when he got it. It's an awful bore, that pettiness.

If I haven't written, it is because I'm finding it harder and harder to write letters. The will-to-write seems to be departing from me: though I do write

[1] Alberto Magnelli (1881–1971), Italian painter. He was acquainted with the Futurists (see *Letters*, ii. 180–1 nn.), though not one of them; he worked alongside the Cubists in Paris; but he returned to Florence (where he was born) in 1915 and became known for the bright, flat colours of his abstract paintings.

[2] Cf. Mark v. 30; Luke vi. 19 (AV).

[3] The Reynolds were an English family living in Anacapri. There were three daughters (Diana, Hermione and Pamela) roughly contemporary with Harwood Brewster who was very friendly with them.

[4] The reference is obscure. The Brewsters used 'Lembo's', a shop in Capri, for their art supplies, but the connection between that and DHL's remark cannot be explained.

my new novel in sudden intense whacks. And I paint away at my pictures, to amuse myself.

It's been bad weather – gave me a cold – but today the sun shines and one can sit still in the sun – which is all one asks, at the moment. It's not a winter to boast about, even here. Yet the time goes by quickly.

I had a letter from Dobrée, telling me we could stay in their house: very nice of him indeed. But now I think *David* is being put back until April, so that I should not need to come to England before end of March. The later the better, for me, in the hopes of spring.

There is no news at this end of the world. Frieda expects her children out in March.

Where is Gertler? Every day I mean to write to him, and thank him for the little book of pictures, and I never do it.[1] What's happened to me!

How is poor old Sonia? she does seem to be having hard luck lately. I'm awfully sorry.

Well, I'll really catch myself in a nice moment, and write a proper letter.

I'll tell Secker to deal with you for Shestov. In fact I'll send him your letter, as it contains nothing personal or libellous, and I'll add what I say to him.

Yrs D. H. Lawrence

When you get the money from Secker, keep it.

DHL[2]

3948. To Martin Secker, 20 January 1927
Text: MS UInd; Secker 84.

Villa Mirenda, *Scandicci* (Florence)
20 Jan. 1927

Dear Secker

I enclose Koteliansky's letter to me about the Shestov book. Will you in future deal with him entirely in the matter of the Shestov translation, as the work was really his. And it seems a pity you didn't pay in that small sum of American dues, at the time. – However, I suppose by now it is all settled.

Yrs D. H. Lawrence

[1] Perhaps DHL had received a copy of *Mark Gertler* (October 1925), introd. Hubert Wellington, the first in a series on 'British Artists of Today'.

[2] DHL then reproduced the text of Letter 3948 with the following variants: 'enclose letter from Koteliansky about the Shestov affair . . . seems to me a pity'.

3949. To Hon. Dorothy Brett, 20 January 1927
Text: MS UCin; Postmark, Scandicci 22 I 27; Moore 960–1.

Villa Mirenda, *Scandicci* (Florence)
20 Jan. 1927

Dear Brett.

This from Maria Huxley came today, so I send it on.[1] I gave Brewster the second of your photographs. He was here for three days, seemed very much the same, but improved, really, by India. He now has realised for good that a Bho-tree is probably phallic in shape; and that, of course, is a revolution. He was supposed to be looking for a house. Achsah and Harwood are in Anna di Chiara's frontispiece of a villa, the Villa Giulia. Anacapri, where they can stay till April 1st. – I think Achsah was scared stiff most of the time she was in India, and now would like to *buy* a house here in Italy. Myself, I think she's wise. Earl was nice, we both like him very much. He's gone off back to Capri.

Your last letter was a chapter from the book of Job, but you'll no doubt be in the Song of Songs or the 23rd Psalm by now. That's the best, and the worst, of letters. Of course Taos is lovely, very lovely in winter too. Id have *loved* to see the Christmas and New Year dances at the pueblo. I'd love to ride Poppy in a race with Prince. – But there you are, 6000 miles, a pot of money, and a great deal of travelling effort lie between, to say nothing of New York, which seems so paradisal to Maria Huxley. As for your coming to Europe, what's the good! We shall probably come to America soon.

As regards weather, it's a damp unpleasant winter, though today is sunny and nice. I've kept very well, on the whole: have got a cold now, but if the sun will only shine, it will go. I've been quite happy painting my pictures, and doing my novel. I did a little, small panel of a negro wedding in the jungle, which maybe I'll give you one day. If not that, then another. My men bathing and red willow trees is nearly done – How are your radishes? I shall be only too glad to have my eyes popping a bit. – I don't imagine Earl thought much of my pictures – but why should he? They're not modern enough – not mâte enough – not enough 'values' and colour-for-tone substitution. But I dont want those things, so nemmeno male! – He took me to see a Florentine painter Alberto Magnelli – very self-important and arch-priesty – worse than Gertler, revealing to one the body of the very divinity: very 'my work.' – Very clever work, quite lovely new colour and design, and inside it all, nothing – emptiness, ashes, an old bone. All that labour and immense self-conscious effort, and real technical achievement, over the cremated ashes of an inspiration! It put me in

[1] The enclosure is missing.

a vile temper, which I'm still in, and made me long for a bolshevist revolution, which won't come.

I told you *David* is put off probably till April, so I expect to stay here till end of March, anyhow: unless we do some little trip here in Italy. Christine Hughes very nicely invites us to Rome, but I don't feel Romish either.

Your little car seems to cost you a good deal of trouble, and I'm afraid, a lot of expense. I enclose fifty dollars on account of the horses' feed – but send me the whole bill. Did Mabel pay the taxes to Frayne? I like to know everything is straight.

I hear 12 Caprese sailed to America, all unknown to one another, from Naples on the *Mano Bianca*: including the Brett-Youngs. So you will[1] have Francis and Jessie with you in the States. He is to deliver 40 lectures. Better get him to give one in Taos, on Culture in Anacapri.

The narcissus flowers are out in the garden, but not yet by the brook. The Contadini call them tassette! – little cups. – Somehow I feel a certain inclination to go south for a bit. Perhaps it is Earl putting his will over me. – Dobrée has gone to Cairo to be English lecturer there,[2] and offers us their flat if we go to London. She stays in Hampstead till Sept. – I half believe Gertler is going to Spain. *The Merry go round*![3] – Murry, I hear, has a sort of pension from the government, for three years, to write two books on Shakspeare. So that lamb of Jesus[4] has again got the wind tempered for him, before he's shorn.

All the news – hasta otra vez! DHL

3950. To Ada Clarke, 23 January 1927

Text: MS Clarke; Postmark, Firenze 24 . I 1927; cited in Finney, *Yale University Library Gazette*, xlix. 248.

Villa Mirenda, *Scandicci* (Florence)
23 Jan. 1927

My dear Sister

Your letter from Mundesley, and the news about the operation for Gertie, does rather take the wind out of one's sails. I doubt if *I* should have the operation, if it was me. But I wouldn't say a word, one way or the other, to poor G. It is most awfully distressing. And one can do no more. One really has to refuse to think about it. But it leaves a little thorn stuck in one's mind, which makes one jump when it is touched.

We had such a lovely day, and a beautiful walk over the hills. The Appenines are white with snow, sweeping away to the north. But in the sun the

[1] will] will will [2] See p. 558 n. 1.
[3] Gertler's painting which, in October 1916, DHL considered 'the best *modern* picture' he had seen (*Letters*, ii. 660). [4] Cf. p. 383 n. 2.

lower land lies warm. It began to cloud over as we got home at tea-time. But it was a beautiful day.

Sunday evening is bad, though, for remembering the past as one doesn't want to remember it. One has to keep oneself on top of things, and not fret nor worry nor despond. Myself, I am pretty well just now, much better than last year. But I do hate to think of Gertie. It starts Lynn Croft all over again.

Did you hear if Willie Hopkin's father left him anything?[1] I hope he did, for Enid told me all *her* spare cash, and more than she could spare, had to go to help to keep him. Which seems pretty rough. So I hope he's got a bit of a windfall.

As for old Henry Saxton, I shall shed no tear in his memory, for I never liked him.[2] I hated him as Sunday School superintendent, so common and loud-mouthed. I often wonder why my mother respected him so much, and in a way looked up to him. Perhaps because he had such a fat successful belly, and bullied the poor parsons like Mr Reid.[3] Pax! He's left Camilla high and dry on the shelf forever, like the selfish mean brute he was. They need to run a chapel, such men do.

How is business now? And the Mansfield shop, is it rousing up?[4] I expect you are pretty busy. I hope so. – I heard from Pamela, a bit lachrymose. What in Hell's name ails the woman, if not injured self-importance? I suppose Sam is sticking on at Carlton?

We had Brewster here for a day or two: very nice. You remember they went to India from Capri, last year when I was there. They're just back. He went looking for sweet Buddha, but didn't find him. Now he's rather down in the mouth, with no Buddha to chase. But let him do without Buddha, and that old stuff. – They want us to move to South Italy. But I'm not moving yet.

I've got one or two novels to send you – old and new – when I get them packed up. – Cynthia Asquith asked me to write a murder story, to go in a murder book which is to follow the Ghost book.[5] I've not thought of it yet. I ask her, where[6] she'll end up, going from bad to worse. – If I don't feel murderous, I shall do no murder story – unless a bluff!

How are the children? I hope the winter is doing them no harm! The days

[1] Henry Hopkin, shoemaker and Wesleyan local preacher, died on 26 December 1926.

[2] Henry Saxton, an Eastwood grocer, was Superintendent of the Congregational Church Sunday School and prominent in local politics (chairman of Eastwood Council, 1906–8). m. Elizabeth Anne Askew; they had four children, one of whom was Camilla (who never married).

[3] Rev. Robert Reid (1868–1955), Congregational Minister at Eastwood, 1897–1911, whom DHL held in high regard (see *Letters*, i. 3, 4, 31 and n. 1).

[4] Edwin Clarke had opened a shop in Mansfield in 1926; it did not flourish (partly as a consequence of the 1926 strike) and was closed in 1930.

[5] See Letter 3902 and n. 3.

[6] where] where's

are already longer, and the narcissus are in flower in the garden. But not the little white wild ones yet. The contadini call them 'tassette' – which is 'little cups.' Rather nice. Remember me to Eddie!

Love DHL

Stamps for Jack!

Saargebiet – is the Saar occupied territory.

3951. To Gertrude Cooper, 23 January 1927

Text: MS Clarke; Lawrence–Gelder 148–52.

Villa Mirenda, *Scandicci* (Florence)
23 Jan. 1927

My dear Gertie

Ada wrote me from Mundesley, telling me the news, and about that operation they contemplate. It is very worrying: so worrying, one doesn't really know what to say, or how to write. If only we could be sure the bad lung wouldn't affect the good one, we needn't bother, because plenty of people live to eighty, with one lung. But with danger threatening to the other all the time, one doesn't know what to say. The right lung is perfectly sound! If only it could always remain so! – My God, what a fight for life! – It's no good trying to understand why these things should be. There's no explanation. One can only do one's best, and then live or die. One is between the hammer and the anvil. – For myself, I daren't say, either have the operation, or don't have it. It worries me too much. You must go way down into yourself, down till you really *feel* which would be right, to have it or not to have it. And then abide by what you feel, in your own still soul, would be the best.

Eh, one wishes things were different. But there's no help for it. One can only do one's best, and then stay brave. Don't weaken or fret. While we live, we must be game. And when we come to die, we'll die game too.

Listen to the doctors carefully, when they advise you. But when it comes to deciding finally, decide out of your own real self.

The days are already beginning to lengthen, and the narcissus flowers are out in the garden already: but the little white wild ones, down by the stream, aren't out yet, nor the wild crocuses. There are lots of Christmas roses wild, but they are greenish, they don't come really white, so they're not so pretty.

Brewster, an old friend, came for a day or two last week. They are just back from India, where he's been trailing round the Buddhist monasteries, hoping for Buddhism to cheer his soul. It hasn't done him much good. I said to him: Well, you've got your health and your freedom, do the rest for yourself! – But he's a nice man. They want us to go south, south of Rome, to live. I shan't move yet, though. We're quite well off here.

It's been a sunny day – Sunday. We went a walk over the other side of the hills, to San Vincenzo a Torri, and ate in a dark little village inn. These Italian small houses are dark holes inside. But they give you good food: always beef-tea and macaroni, and boiled beef, on Sundays. They have no meat at all during the week: just beans, or macaroni. So if it's week-day, they usually kill a couple of pigeons and fry them for you. We sat in the sun on the edge of the pine-wood, and listened to a shepherd playing a tin whistle – very badly. They make the weirdest noises, to call the sheep: grunts from the bottom of the stomach, then wild cat-hisses. I suppose it takes a peculiar sound to penetrate a sheep's stupid skull. The leading sheep, with the bell, was called Laura: 'Hoy! Laura! Hoy-a-hoy! Grunt-squish-squee!' – so the shepherd kept on at her. And she, like an old maid, munched a bit and tripped ahead, the rest trailing after her.

The mountains, the Appenines, are covered with deep snow, and they look very beautiful, sweeping away to the north, the farthest, up at Carrara, glimmering faint and pinkish in the far, far distance. And near at hand, the country lies in the sunshine, all open and rolling, with white buildings like dots here and there, and few people. It is very different from England. One day you must come and really get to know it. On a day like today, an odd butterfly comes flapping out, and there's a bee now and then. The sun is strong enough. I even saw the tail of a little lizard go whisking down a hole in the wall.

I heard from Pamela yesterday – not a very chirpy letter. She doesn't look on the rosy side of her life, I'm afraid. Yet she ought to be happy enough, she's nothing really to worry her. Do you remember in Lynn Croft, when we used to have autograph albums, and put verses and little paintings in them? I can remember Frances[1] chose for somebody's:

> But human bodies are such fools
> For all their colleges and schools
> That when no *real* ills perplex 'em
> They make enough themselves to vex 'em.[2]

And I think that is so true. When one gets a job like yours on hand, one thinks what fools people are, growsing[3] and grizzling and making their lives a misery, for nothing, instead of being thankful they've got off so lightly.

How is young Edna? Has she written? And the faithful Joseph, has he got hold of any other woman yet? – And do you hear from Jinny Bolton?[4] – I thought she was nice.

[1] Frances Amelia Cooper (1884–1918), Gertrude Cooper's sister; she died of tuberculosis.
[2] An anglicised version of Robert Burns' poem, 'Twa Dogs', ll. 195–8.
[3] Northern dialect spelling of 'grousing'.
[4] Sarah Jane Bolton (1877–1964).

So Willie Hopkin's old father is gone at last! I hope to goodness he left Willie a little inheritance, for he needed it badly enough. I was thinking today, how poor Sallie Hopkin would sit darning Willie's pants, till they were more darn than pants. All those years, always hard up! It seems rough! And then, at his age, he might have lived decently remembering her, not picking up with young rubbish like Rosy Swain, and then marrying a girl who *couldn't* really mean much to him.[1]

I suppose they're warbling away in Eastwood Congregational Chapel at this minute! Do you remember, how we all used to feel so sugary about the vesper verse: Lord keep us safe this night, secure from all our fears –?[2] Then off out into the dark, with Dicky Pogmore and the Chambers and all the rest. And how Alan used to love the lumps of mince-pie from the pantry?[3] And Frances did her hair up in brussel-sprouts, and made herself a cup of ovaltine or something of that sort! Sometimes it seems so far off. And sometimes it is like yesterday.

Well, keep as chirpy as you can, and don't worry us all out of our skins by getting downcast and depressed. It's a case of 'Onward Christian Soldiers'![4]

Love. DHL[5]

3952. To S. S. Koteliansky, 24 January 1927

Text: MS BL; Postmark, Firenze 24 . I 1927; Zytaruk 308.

Villa Mirenda, *Scandicci* (Florence)
24 Jan 1927

Dear Kot

Thanks for the cheque.[6] I am putting it in the fire, so you can say no more about it. – And I hope your letter will have some small effect on Secker. – But the world's a bad egg.

Yrs DHL

[1] Rosy Swain (1892–1974), a teacher at the British School, Eastwood (where DHL had been a pupil-teacher). DHL's remark about Hopkin's marrying Olive Lizzie Slack betrays a serious misjudgement.

[2] From a hymn (1792) by John Leland (1754–1841), an American Baptist minister. DHL used it as the closing hymn in 'Choir Correspondence' in *Mr Noon* (ed. Lindeth Vasey, Cambridge, 1984, p. 49).

[3] Alan Aubrey Chambers (1882–1946), Jessie Chambers's older brother and DHL's close friend in their youth. He was the prototype for George Saxton in *The White Peacock*.

[4] The famous hymn by Sabine Baring-Gould (1834–1924).

[5] A postscript of about six words ending with a question mark has been erased from the MS. Also, in a hand thought not to be Gertrude Cooper's though the instruction ends with her initials, someone added at the foot of the MS: 'Don't destroy this letter GC'.

[6] See Letter 3942 and p. 642 n. 1, the postscript to Secker's letter to Kot, 19 January 1927.

3953. To Emily King, [25 January 1927]

Text: MS Lazarus; Postmark, Scandicci 26. I . 27; Moore 958–9.

Villa Mirenda, *Scandicci* (Florence)
Tuesday

My dear Pamela

It is awfully upsetting about that operation of Gertie's. One doesn't even know whether to advise her to have it or not. My word, it's a hard fate some people have! We ought to count ourselves lucky, when no more ails us than does ail us. – By the way, how is Sarah Ann?[1] Is she avoiding the hospital?

I'm glad Joan is keeping better. Thank heaven, I've been pretty well so far. And perhaps now we shall have a spell of good weather, we've had bad long enough. Today is lovely, brilliant sun. I'm just going down to Scandicci, so shall go by the valley, by the stream, and see if the wild narcissus are out yet. Those in the garden are in flower.

Like you, I've got no news. Brewster, from Capri, was here for a day or two. They're just back from India. He went chasing Buddha, and didnt find him: in fact, found less of him in India than in Europe. So now he's a bit down in the mouth. But what do people want with Buddha or Jesus or those old heroes nowadays: any more than with Julius Caesar or Isis! It's all part of the past, and isn't really vital today. – So now the Brewsters are looking for another house in Italy. They gave up the Quattro Venti in Capri.

I wish you'd send some tea. If you've not got Orange Pekoe, send *two pounds* of *good* China – I don't mind if it's rather dear – by *parcel* post. It'll be best if the tea is in a made-up tin, or two pound tins. I bought[2] ¼ lb of Ridgeways yesterday, and it cost 16.50 – Liras: which is 3/6: which makes it 14/– a pound. Monstrous! So send two pounds at once, and we'll see how it comes, and how much it works out at. Let me know the cost, postage and all. And if possible, send it in the ready packed tins or packets, so they can't steal it without detection.

I'm just getting proofs of a little book of Red Indian and Mexican essays, which should be out this spring – with photograph illustrations. It'll be quite nice: small.

I told you I expect they'll do *David* in April, so I shouldn't come to London till end of March. And Frieda's sister wants us to go for the summer to Bavaria. That tempts me. I've not been since the war. And of course, the Taos people want us to go to the ranch. We'll see later on. Anyhow I shall be in England for the spring, I suppose.

I've just finished my landscape of red willow trees and men bathing. I like it best, now. It is fun to paint.

[1] Sarah Ann Wrath, née King (1882–1972) was Emily's sister-in-law.

[2] MS reads 'bough'.

Cynthia Asquith wants me to do a murder story – she wants to bring out a murder book. Bad to worse! I don't feel very murderous, either. So it remains to be seen if I do the story.

I do hope you're all keeping well! Remember me to Peg! and Joan!

Love DHL

3954. To Edith Isaacs, 27 January 1927
Text: MS WHist; Unpublished.

Villa Mirenda, *Scandicci* (Florence)
27 Jan. 1927

Dear Miss Isaacs

Your letter today! – As far as I am concerned, I am pleased for the two essays to go in the Little–Brown book. But haven't Curtis Browns told you that Martin Secker, and Knopf, are bringing out, either in late spring or early autumn, a little book of mine, *Mornings in Mexico*, which is to contain these two articles?[1] (also the 'Indians and Entertainment' article from *Theatre Arts*). And I wanted the book also to have the *illustrations*, mine and the others, which came in *Theatre Arts*. Haven't Curtis Brown's asked you for them?

Do you think the two books would clash at all? But probably not. *Mornings in Mexico* will have about eight essays in all.

I shall try to do an essay on the dance for you. It's a subject which *does* interest me – but not from a popular point of view. And if you don't care for my essay when it comes along, don't feel constrained to use it. No matter!

I nearly did you an article on the old subject, the Stenterello theatre here in Florence. But I didn't. – The Stage Society will probably produce *David* in London in April. I might do an article on that. What I *hoped* it would be like, on the stage, and what it *was* like.

All good wishes D. H. Lawrence

Will you anyhow please speak to Barmby about the essays for the Little Brown book.

DHL

3955. To Earl and Achsah Brewster, 6 February 1927
Text: MS UT; Brewster 115–16.

Villa Mirenda, *Scandicci*, Florence
6 Feb 1927

Dear Earl

Long since I had your letter – glad you find the Villa Giulia nice. Do you

[1] 'The Dance of the Sprouting Corn' and 'The Hopi Snake Dance', published in *Theatre Arts Monthly*. Edith Isaacs included the first essay in a collection she edited for Little, Brown & Co., *Theatre: Essays on the Arts of the Theatre* (Boston, 1927), pp. 246–56.

feel restored to Capri? and have you got a house there for yourselves? – Let me know: – From the Villa Bianca I have heard not a single syllable. Perhaps that little larvum of a man died outright, or went utterly speechless. – It's quite lovely weather here now, but much snow on the mountains. I find myself rather fond of this place. I've only been in to Florence once since you left – one afternoon: and saw nobody I knew. Magnelli has not been to see me, and never will. He didn't care for me: nor I for him. And when I think over his pictures, they seem to me pretentious rubbish, and about as formless as a paper-chase. Why does one take these little people seriously, even for half an hour. – I'm glad you like *Twilight in Italy*. They seem to be liking it in England: now, after twelve or thirteen years.[1] It takes them so long to creep up. I am expecting a packet of *David*s any day, and shall send you one the moment they come.

You remember they are supposed to be producing *David* in London in April – in which case I ought to go to England end of March – which knocks our walk. But perhaps they won't do it – and perhaps I shan't go. I feel an infinite disgust at the idea of having to be there while the fools mimble-pimble at the dialogue. They ruined *Mrs Holroyd* by trailing out the last scene all wrong. Why should I bother about them.

There's no news this end – we go on very quietly. I am in the thick of another picture: 'Eve Regaining Paradise'.[2] Don't take alarm at a title – that's another bit of modern nervousness. As for mâte surface, I find, for myself, I hate it. I like to paint rather wet, with oil, so the colour slips about and doesn't look like dried bone, as Magnelli's pictures do. And I'm not so conceited as to think that my marvellous ego and unparalleled technique will make a picture. I like a picture to be a picture to the whole sensual self, and as such it must have a meaning of its own, and concerted action. Thanks for telling about the hand and elbow: you're right. I love a bit of real advice.

Tell me when there's any news. – Oh, and if I owe Lembo anything, I *do* want to pay it. Did you speak to him. – And did you order the money from America in English or Italian. If in English, I'll put it to my English account, but if in Italian, I'll wait and not change much.

au revoir DHL

Dear Achsah –

You are right to let Harwood read *Glad Ghosts*. The sooner they read books that treat of sex *honestly* and with a bit of sincere reverence, the better for them, the young. Their great danger is that they are flippant, impertinent and

[1] Cf. Letter 3720 and n. 2.
[2] Reproduced as *Flight Back into Paradise* in *The Paintings of D. H. Lawrence*, plate [7].

contemptuous to sex – that secret, dirty thing – till they've made a mess of it, and lost their chance. – I hope you're working away gaily.

DHL

My new novel is three parts done, and is so *absolutely* improper, in words, and so really *good*, I hope, in spirit – that I don't know what's going to happen to it.

3956. To Martin Secker, 8 February 1927
Text: MS UInd; Postmark, Scandicci 9. 2 27; Secker 84–5.

Villa Mirenda, *Scandicci*, Florence
8 Feb 1927

Dear Secker

It won't take me very long, I think, to finish the novel; so it won't be too lengthy – 80 to 90 thousand, I suppose. But you'll probably hate it. I want to call it *Lady Chatterley's Lover*: nice and old-fashioned sounding. Do look up in *Debrett* or *Who's-Who* and see if there are any Chatterleys about, who might take offence. – It's what they'll call *very* improper – in fact, impossible to print. But they'll have to take it or leave it, I don't care. It's really, of course, very 'pure in heart.'[1] But the *words* are all used! Damn them anyhow.

We heard from Rina – she said she was going to Milan, so we asked her to come round this way and stay a day or two with us.[2] She hasn't answered yet. It's cold and grey these last two days: but has been warmer than last year. – I hear Knopf published *David* last September, and I never heard a word nor saw a sign. – Oh by the way, if you re-print *The Lost Girl* – do spell Ciccio with three c's.[3] – Could I have proofs, do you think? Or are you using the old plates? – No illustrations for *Mornings in Mexico*[4] have come from America – but I'm sure you can have those from the *Theatre Arts Monthly* – all of 'em. – And *Travel* said they'd give me what I liked – wrote very nicely. You do want to put a few pictures in, nowadays, for the wishy-washy public.

I hope you're having a decent time, and that Adrian flourishes. Remember me to Howe[5] – and both of us to Mrs Lamont.

D. H. Lawrence

[1] Matthew v. 8.
[2] DHL's letter to Rina Secker is missing.
[3] Secker re-issued the novel (in his Thin Paper Pocket Edition) in January 1927. He did not provide Ciccio with 'three c's'.
[4] *Mornings in Mexico*] *David*
[5] Percival Presland Howe (1887–1944) had been reader to Eveleigh Nash where he met Secker; he became Secker's partner in 1918. Author of *The Repertory Theatre* (1910), *Dramatic Portraits* (1913), *Life of William Hazlitt* (1922), etc. (See obituary, *The Times*, 22 March 1944.)

3957. To Hon. Dorothy Brett, 9 February 1927
Text: MS UCin; Postmark, [Firenz]e 10 . II 1927; Huxley 677–8.

Villa Mirenda, *Scandicci* (Florence)
9 Feb 1927

Dear Brett

Horrid the time you had with van Vechten and Dassburg[1] – there's a certain impotence about modern men, which runs to smuts. But no good bothering. The poor things have prurient itch. Anyhow I gather from Mabel's letter you are settled down and cosy again. For my part, people don't mean much to me, especially casuals: them I'd rather be without.

So you're in snow again, gleaming! I don't care for snow. It shines so cold on the bottom of one's heart. Here it's a fierce cold wind, olives splashing like water, but sunny. I don't mind when the sun shines. We are pretty comfortable indoors.

Thanks for the *Marriage* book – what a feeble lot of compromisers![2] It's no good talking about it: marriage, like homes, will last while our social system lasts, because it's the thing that holds our system together. But our system will collapse, and then marriage will be different – probably more tribal, men and women living a good deal apart, as in the old pueblo system, no little homes. It's the individual homes that are the real mischief. It all works back to individual property: even marriage is an arrangement for the holding of property together. A bore! But what a feeble lot of writers: no guts! – no balls, the colliers would say. That's how they are, though.

I've nearly done my novel – shall let it lie and settle down a bit, before I think of having it typed. And I challenge you to a pictorial contest. I'm just finishing a nice big canvas, Eve dodging back into Paradise, between Adam and the Angel at the Gate, who are having a fight about it – and leaving the world in flames in the far corner behind her. Great fun, and of course a capo lavoro!![3] I should like to do a middle picture – inside paradise, just as she bolts in, God Almighty astonished and indignant, and the new young god, who is just having a chat with the serpent, pleasantly amused. Then the third picture, Adam and Eve under the tree of knowledge, God Almighty disappearing in a dudgeon, and the animals skipping. Probably I shall never get them done – If I say I'll do a thing, I never do it. But I'll try. And you too have a shot, if the

[1] Carl van Vechten (1880–1964), music and dramatic critic, musicologist; Andrew Dasburg (see p. 159 n. 1); they were both close friends of Mabel Luhan.

[2] In view of Brett's earlier interest in Count Hermann Keyserling (see Letter 3615), it is probable that she had sent DHL a copy of his compilation, *The Book of Marriage: a new interpretation by 24 leaders of contemporary thought* (Cape, January 1927).

[3] 'a masterpiece!!'

subject tickles you. The tryptich! – Tell Mabel I'll see about the books and let her know.[1]

I found the first violet today – and the slope opposite is all bubb[led][2] over with little pale-gold bubbles of winter aconites. La primavera – wonder how the horses are! Did you get the money for their feed? Tell me how much more.

3958. To Arthur McLeod, 10 February 1927

Text: MS UT; Postmark, Scandicci 13 2 27; Moore, *Intelligent Heart* 362–3.

Villa Mirenda, *Scandicci* (Florence)
10 Feb. 1927

Dear Mac[3]

Is Philip Smith already at retiring age? Heaven help us, how quick! I'm 41 – and you're about 43, aren't you? – Why didn't you put in your news? Where are you now – are you a head-master somewhere, gravely ruling? Lord, how queer it all seems! No, one never forgets. What one was, one is. Only the years add so many other things, that my Addiscombe Rd self squirms when I look at it. I was thinking of Philip Smith a few days ago when I saw the winter aconites in flower on the poderes. He brought me the first I ever saw, from that place outside Croydon, where he lived. I can see him now, laying it before me on the table in Standard VI. Tempi passati! One of my troubled dreams, sleep-dreams, I mean, is that I'm teaching – and that I've clean forgotten to mark the register, and the class has gone home! Why should I feel so worried about not having marked the register? But I do.

How are you all? How are *you*? – and your mother? Do you still go to Devon in the summer? How is Miss Mason? – and Aylwin, do you know? And Humphreys, with his wife who jeered at him? – And is my landlord Jones still Attendance Officer? That baby I used to nurse must be nineteen now.[4] Santo cielo, potrei essere nonno![5] Tell me the news, but don't tell them all to write to me, or I shan't know what to say.

[1] Cf. Letters 3930 and 3944.

[2] MS torn.

[3] This is the last known letter to Arthur William McLeod (1885–1956), DHL's closest friend and colleague at Davidson Road School, Croydon (in 1927 McLeod was headmaster of Winterbourne School). They both taught at Davidson Road when Philip Frank Turner Smith (1866–1961) was headmaster. Smith was now retiring (from Norbury Manor School) and DHL sent £2 towards a retirement present. DHL's remark in the final sentence of the postscript was read out by McLeod at the farewell party for Smith in the Greyhound Hotel, Croydon, at the end of the Easter term. (See *Letters*, i. 84 n. 1; 136 n. 3.)

[4] Agnes Louise Eliza Mason (1871–c. 1950), Robert Henry Aylwin (1885–1931) and Ernest Arthur Humphreys (1882–) were all colleagues of DHL at Davidson Road School (see *Letters*, i. 194 and nn. 4, 6, 8). John William Jones (1868–1956), DHL's landlord at Colworth Road, Addiscombe, Croydon, was still the Superintendent School Attendance Officer (*Letters*, i. 82 and n. 2). DHL nursed his child, Hilda Mary Jones (b. 1908). (DHL wrote 'Alywin'.)

[5] 'Good heavens, I could be a grandfather!'

We are living here till the fit takes us to go and live somewhere else. My wife sends *saluti*!

I enclose two quid for P.S. – don't know if it's the sort of 'fitting amount.'

Do you ever see any of the boys of my period? I've never met a single one, in all my comings and goings.

Did I swindle you out of those proofs?[1] I'm so sorry. I've quite forgotten. I'll write out a poem when I think of one. Now I've only a *Glad Ghosts* to send you.

Souvenirs! D. H. Lawrence

I send you also Coppard's poems, which I find boring.[2] But you are more patient.

Remember me nicely to Philip Smith; he treated me always very decently.

DHL

3959. To Margaret King, [11 February 1927]

Text: MS Needham; PC v. Firenze – Piazza Signoria (Il David); Postmark, [. . .] 13. 2 27; Unpublished.

[Villa Mirenda, Scandicci, Florence]
Friday

I'm waiting for the tea – its not turned up yet – hope nobody's drinking it. It's lovely sunny weather. Are you all well? I'm waiting to hear about Gertie, how that goes off. So sorry you had flu – I'm pretty well. I'll write as soon as the tea comes.

Love DHL

3960. To Mabel Dodge Luhan, 14 February 1927

Text: MS Brill; Unpublished.

Villa Mirenda, Scandicci[3]
14 Feb. 1927

Dear Mabel

I've been to the Curonia with Orioli, and seen Romanelli there. We've

[1] In June 1914 when he was assembling material for *The Prussian Officer and Other Stories*, to be published by Duckworth in November, DHL asked McLeod: 'Have you any proofs or anything you could lend me . . . I really don't know what stories I've published' (*Letters*, ii. 187). Whatever was sent was obviously never returned.

[2] DHL had probably received a copy of *Yokohama, Garland, and Other Poems* by Alfred Edgar Coppard (1878–1957), published by Centaur Press, 1926 (see p. 284 n. 1), and was now sending it to McLeod.

[3] The letter was written on notepaper headed: J. I. Davis & G. M. Orioli, Libreria Antiquaria, Firenze (1), Lungarno Corsini 6. and London, 30 Museum Street.

decided to take away all the *sets* and things worth sending to America, bring them down here and get them sent off – ought to cost not more than fifty dollars. – Then take the most saleable of the novels, and Orioli will buy them – telling you first what they are – more or less – and the price he can give. But you won't be swindled. I'll buy just a few vols – perhaps Balzac. But there's a lot of rubbish – I expect the best have been picked out. And the rubbish we'll just leave at the Curonia.

I saw the picture of the child (nice), and the water-color by Bobby Jones (poor). About the third, there was a question. Romanelli said Edwin had told him a half-length woman with red hair and low dark-blue dress (rather nice) – I thought it was one of a woman in an orange sort of dress, full length, but a smallish picture. It *might* have been you – and rather nice. There's a huge horror upstairs of you by Miss Clarke in a pink dress.[1] I would have that burned.

There is Condamines *Apple Orchard* and some *Portraits of M*[*abel*] *D*[*odge*] *by Gertrude Stein*.[2] We'll send those by post. And the pictures, if we send the 3, aquerelle, child, and the orange dress – should cost only 25 or 30 dollars, if that, to send. Let me know if this sounds all right.

The villa is half empty, and desolate as the Marne battlefields. Terribly depressing. Dodge wants 10,000 Liras a month, to let. He'll not get ten cents.

The man Romanelli sent saluti – your poor Pietro looks forlorn. Romanelli I wouldn't trust as far as I could blow him, which isn't far, for he's fat. – But if I had to be custodian for places like the Curonia, I feel I might lose my honesty. There's something awful about it all.

I'll see if we cant pay the transport of all the 'sets' with the money from the oddments – but I don't promise it. There wasn't a single book of *value* that I could see – they must have been well picked over.

Till later, then! D. H. Lawrence

3961. To Ada Clarke, 16 February 1927

Text: MS Clarke; cited in Lawrence–Gelder 153.

Villa Mirenda, *Scandicci*, Florence.
16 Feb. 1927

My dear Sister

I had such a nice letter from Gertie from the hospital, quite chirpy and

[1] Rose ('Tante') Clark, Mabel Luhan's former art teacher at Buffalo who lived for a time in the Villa Curonia and acted as housekeeper and companion for Mabel's son, John Evans (Hahn, *Mabel*, pp. 14, 42, 54–5).

[2] *Apple Orchard* cannot be traced. (It is remotely possible that DHL had misread the title of Robert de La Condamine's book *The Upper Garden*, 1910.) Gertrude Stein wrote the *Portrait of Mabel Dodge* [1911]; Mabel had it printed and bound, and gave copies to her friends.

brave. I must say, the doctors are very nice. I wrote to Dr Pearson.[1] Poor G., she has never been so important and made so much of in her life. She says she does want to get well, 'to enjoy her food again.' I sympathise with her there, too. I hope the thing goes off decently – gives me the shudders, though.

I enclose a snap of the Villa Mirenda. The Wilkinsons, our only neighbours, took it from their window. It's the square building: we have the top floor: and that is Frieda, that speck in the window of the salotta, facing south. Below is the tiny church of San Paolo Mosciano, with the priest's house and peasant cottage. On this side are hills covered with umbrella pine. Beyond is the Arno valley, and Florence is out of sight on the right. It's very nice.

For a wonder, we've had a week of bright sunshine, rather lovely. The flowers are coming out: under the olives all the pale-gold bubbles of winter aconites, and many daisies: and I found the first wild violet and purple anemone. In the garden there are still lovely roses – and many narcissus. I suppose your snowdrops are out by now.

It is rather thrilling to hear of you launching out so in business. Let's hope nothing will happen again, to hinder it's being a real success. – A good thing Eddie has plenty to occupy him. – I feel like you about Sam. One can't bother any more. And after all, he's old enough to look after himself.

It seems to me rather awful if Willie Hopkin has a child. It's so unfitting. Why are people so messy. And if he's desperately hard up already, what a burden? But there, it's none of my business.

The tea Pamela sent me hasn't come yet. I wish it would, or I must start buying again. – Milly and Mary Beveridge and Mabel Harrison come next week to the little Villa La Massa just near. It will be nice having them in reach. – I've got some novels to send you, when I get them packed up. The post is such a bore.

I hope the children are all right. A lot of flu here. One does get nervous of sickness. But we're managing pretty well. Let me know about Gertie and everything.

love. DHL

3962. To Gertrude Cooper, 16 February 1927

Text: MS Clarke; cited in Lawrence–Gelder 153–4.

Villa Mirenda, *Scandicci*, Florence.
16 Feby. 1927

My dear Gertie

I was so glad to get quite a cheerful letter from you. One does feel worried at

[1] The letter is missing.

these times. The doctors must be awfully good. I had already written to thank Dr Pearson for looking after you. And when once you are well, I'll send him a book or something, to celebrate it, and as a mark of gratitude.

Our neighbours the Wilkinsons took this photograph of our villa, from their window. The big square building is the Villa Mirenda, and we have the top half. The speck in one of the windows is Frieda. The building below is the little church of San Paolo Mosciano, with the priest's house and the peasant's cottage. Away beyond is the flat valley of the Arno, and just round to the right is Florence, but you cant see it. One day you must come and get to know it all.

It is already beginning to be spring. Under the olive trees the winter aconites, such pretty pale yellow bubbles, are all out, and many daisies: and I found the first purple anemone. I wish I could send you some: but the post makes such a fuss, nowadays, about parcels, big or little. The wild tulips are peeping through, though they won't flower till Easter, and the grape hyacinths also are coming. We've had a week of lovely sunshine, and so far have both escaped the flu, thank heaven. There's a good deal about.

Miss Beveridge and Miss Harrison, the friends I stayed with in Scotland, are coming to a little villa near, next week. I do hope they'll be all right. One gets scared of people falling ill.

As for you, really you'll have seen quite a lot of the world, getting cured. I'm sure you'll feel you've been round the globe, and almost round the moon, by the time you get back to Ripley.

I do hope things will go easily. It's an anxious business all round. The doctors, though, really are wonderful, and we can do no more than trust to them. Frieda sends her love, with mine. I suppose we shall hear soon from somebody.

Love! DHL

3963. To Emily King, [20 February 1927]

Text: MS Lazarus; Unpublished.

Villa Mirenda, *Scandicci* (Firenze)
Sunday

My dear Pamela

The tea came yesterday – doesn't seem to have been stolen, though of course they open it and poke their fingers in it. I had to pay twenty-one Liras duty: about four shillings: but even then it's much cheaper than buying it here. It is awfully nice tea: I like that bouquet it has very much. You must send me some more, when you have a tin that holds just under 2 lbs, so you can get it packed for the 2 lb parcel rate. Send a tin if you can, one never has any here (tins). I enclose the money. And many thanks.

How do you like the photograph of the house: our neighbours the Wilkinsons took it from their window. It's the big square building at the back – and that speck in one of the windows is Frieda. We have the top floor – big rooms. In front is the little church of San Paolo Mosciano, with the priest's house and his peasants houses. Beyond lies the Arno valley, Florence out of sight to the right – and on this side there are pine woods.

We've had rather nice sunny weather lately – but today, though sunny, the wind is very cold, and the snow lies way down on the mountains. But the flowers are coming out: all the little yellow winter aconites, very gay, and I found the first purple anemone. In the garden are narcissus and little single hyacinths, and those pink Jerusalem cowslips: do you remember, we had them in the little front garden at Walker St,[1] near the mezereon tree that smelled so sweet. – I'm glad you've got your little greenhouse newly arranged. One can get a lot of fun out of flowers, as they come.

On Thursday the two Miss Beveridges and Mabel Harrison are coming to a little villa across the dip – there'll be great competitions painting! Frieda's girls have put off coming till April. I think Frieda is meeting them in Baden: but if I don't have to come to England early in April, I shall meet Brewster in Rome and go walking with him down the coast towards Naples: not go north. I don't much want to go north, this year.

How is Joan? – I hope she keeps well! And Peg, is she flourishing? I'll see if I haven't got a couple of books for her.

I had a very cheerful letter from Gertie in hospital, but the thought of that affair straight gives me the jim-jams. Am waiting for news.

I do hope it's fairly bright in England, and you're all feeling cheerful. Thanks again for the tea.

love! DHL

3964. To Angelo Ravagli, [20 February 1927]

Text: MS UT; PC v. [Villa Mirenda]; Postmark, Firenze 21 . II 1927; Unpublished.

[Villa Mirenda, Scandicci, Florence]

20 febbraio

Non le ho ancora ringraziato per la musica – ci ha fatto veramente un piacere. Mia moglie le suona con brio – ma parole non ci ne sono, per cantare. Come le pare la fotografia della Villa Mirenda, colla chiesa di San Paolo Mosciano. Fa bell' tempo, ma un vento fredissimo. Giovedì arrivano tre signorine inglesi (non sono più giovane) chi vanno stare nel villino La Massa, vicino. Sono

[1] The Eastwood address from which DHL's first surviving letter was written (*Letters*, i. 21); the family moved to Lynn Croft in 1903.

buone amice – le vedrà quando Lei vieni. voglio scrivere una lettera – ma Dio mio! scrivere!

DHL

[I have not yet thanked you for the music – it has given us much pleasure. My wife plays it with joy – but there are no words to sing it to. What do you think of the photograph of Villa Mirenda, with the church of San Paolo Mosciano. The weather is fine, but there's a very cold wind. On Thursday there will arrive three young English ladies (no longer young) who are going to stay in the little villa La Massa nearby. They are good friends – you will see them when you come. I want to write a letter – but my God! writing!

DHL]

3965. To Mabel Dodge Luhan, 21 February 1927
Text: MS Brill; Luhan 323–4.

[Lungarno Corsini 6. Firenze][1]
21 Feb 1927

Dear Mabel

Well, the books are here, and the three pictures – at Oriolis. We have been over to Egidi,[2] and it will probably cost about five or six hundred Liras to send the lot as far as Galveston, Texas. I will pay that, and you must pay the remainder. We are sending you *all* the sets: and everything worth having: *two*[3] *hundred and eighteen volumes*. The rest, hundreds of vols., we leave at the villa, just rubbish, as far as I can see: most disheartening. – Then I am taking ten, paper-cover Balzacs and about a dozen other trifles, mostly Tauchnitz for light reading.[4] I'll pay for them. Orioli is keeping about six Henry James, one or two Lafcadio Hearn, Burton's *Anatomy*[5] and one or two Stevensons to sell – in all about 42: of which one or two Henry James are first editions – the only things that are. He'll pay a proper price for them. We gave Pietro Liras 25.00 – and paid a cart. – The Condamine was *not* there – I never saw it – but Orioli thinks he has a copy of his own which he will send you along with the *Portraits of Mabel Dodge:* by post. – The Curonia, and especially the books, are most

[1] Cf. p. 641 n. 3. [2] Cf. Letter 3937.
[3] having: *two*] having: I think *two*
[4] The 'Collection of British and American Authors' and 'Collection of German Authors' (in English) produced by the Tauchnitz publishing house in Leipzig.
[5] Lafcadio Hearn (1850–1904), travel writer best known for his books about Japan (his adopted country). *The Anatomy of Melancholy* (1621), the learned and eccentric compendium by Robert Burton (1577–1640).

depressing. They must have been picked over very thoroughly, *all* the good things gone, and such a heap of rubbish – hundreds of vols. – The big yellow carpet is still on the hall floor – they say the moths rise[1] from it in clouds, in summer. There is a nice painted cupboard, and very nice copper pans in the kitchen. – As for the silver, that man Romanelli says it is nothing = *niente, niente*! But he's awful. If you send an order for Pietro to have it delivered here at Orioli's – Lungarno Corsini 6. – like the books – we can either send it you or sell it, as you wish. I've no idea what it is. – I think Romanelli hopes ultimately to lay hands on everything, and one feels like frustrating him.

I want to send you back all your MSS. You've wound up your Florence part. It's all right – just a wind-up. But you've lost the flow. The sketches aren't very good either. You've gone out of gear with your writing. But perhaps, innerly, you don't want to do any more. Let it rest, for a while.

I think it's going to snow here – and was so lovely. The wild tulips are all springing up.

I have Brett's 'adolescence.' Most people experience *something* the same. The worst is, the body, *the blood* forms its habits of hostility or sympathy, and these are practically unbreakable: they don't yield at all to the mind, but remain underneath like a rock substratum. The mind and spirit may play their own game, on top: but it never passes through the rock-bed.

But I'm glad you are friendly. Today is a day when I can imagine Taos.

D. H. Lawrence

3966. To Nancy Pearn, 25 February 1927
Text: MS UT; Unpublished.

Villa Mirenda. *Scandicci*, Florence
25 Feb. 1927

Dear Miss Pearn

Here is a review I did for *The Calendar*. Do you mind[2] having it typed and giving it them? They can cut it if it's too long: but it's four books.[3]

I've nearly done a story for Cynthia Asquith and her murder book – not very murderous. I'll send it you in a day or two.[4]

Have got a touch of flu – so has most everybody, including Huxley who has just come down from Cortina. But I think mine is light. – How are you?

I've done all I'm going to do of my novel for the time being, so shall have a shot at a few little things. They keep me going best. Seems quite a time since I

[1] moths rise] dust rises [2] mind] might

[3] In April 1927 the *Calendar* (iv, 17–21, 67–73) carried DHL's review of the following: Carl van Vechten, *Nigger Heaven*; Walter White, *Flight*; John Dos Passos, *Manhattan Transfer*; Ernest Hemingway, *In Our Time* (Roberts C153). [4] See Letter 3973.

heard from you. – By the way don't send out that autobiographical sketch of mine – 'On being a Success' – please. One day I'll have it back and write it up a bit.

tanti saluti D. H. Lawrence

3967. To Earl Brewster, 27 February 1927
Text: MS UT; Brewster 117–18.

Villa Mirenda, *Scandicci*, Florence.
27 Feb. 1927

Dear Earl

Imagine your having to move again! But I'm among the people who like Ravello – though Cimbrone is a bit too much of a good thing. Will you invite me? Frieda is probably going to Germany about the middle of March. If you and Achsah ask me, I'll come to Ravello for a week or ten days, then we'll go our walking trip. I don't think I shall go to England. Curse them, let them produce *David* as they like. Why should I mix myself up with them personally! I hate the very thought of them all.

Or should we meet in Rome and look at those Etruscan tombs? If I asked Lord Berners, he'd motor us to them all and have extra permits. But he's so rich – such a huge Rolls Royce. It goes dead against my stomach. I simply *can't* stand people at close quarters. Better tramp it our two selves. What do you think?

I do think it's awfully important to be honest: with oneself. I don't see how one can even begin to be honest with other people. And as I hate lying, I keep to myself as much as possible. You and I are at the *âge dangereuse* for men: when the whole rhythm of the psyche changes: when one no longer has an easy flow outwards: and when one rebels at a good many things. It is as well to know the thing is physiological: though that doesn't nullify the psychological reality. One resents bitterly a certain swindle about modern life, and especially a sex swindle. One is swindled out of one's proper sex life, a great deal. But it is nobody's individual fault: fault of the age: our own fault as well. The only thing is to wait; and to take the next wave as it rises. Pazienza! – I feel in you a terrible exasperation. One has to go through with it. I try and keep the *middle* of me harmonious to the *middle* of the universe. Outwardly, I know I'm in a bad temper, and let it go at that. I stick to what I told you, and put a phallus, a lingam you call it, in each one of my pictures somewhere. And I paint no picture that wont shock people's castrated social spirituality. I do this out of positive belief, that the phallus is a great sacred image: it represents a deep, deep life which has been denied in us, and still is denied. Women deny it horribly, with a grinning travesty of sex. But pazienza! pazienza! – One can still believe. And with the lingam, and belief in the mystery behind it, goes beauty. Oh, I'm with you there. But as for life, one can only be patient – which by nature I'm not. – I think men ought to be able to be honest, to a sufficient point, with one another. I've never succeeded yet. Vediamo! And meanwhile one has to preserve one's *central* innocence, and not get bittered. O pazienza! But one does need a bit of trust, mutual trust. You have so many defences, and fences. – Pazienza!

chi va piano va lontano![1]

a rivederci D. H. Lawrence

3968. To Nancy Pearn, 28 February 1927

Text: MS UT; Huxley 679.

Villa Mirenda – Scandicci. – Florence
28 Feb 1927

Dear Miss Pearn

I am sending a 'Scrutiny' on John Galsworthy, for a book of *Scrutinies* by the younger writers on the elder, which is being published by that *Calendar* young man Edgell Rickword.[2] – Will you please have it typed for me – I am ashamed of the scribbled MS: and will you please send me the typescript again, so I can go over it.

I'm afraid it is not very nice to Galsworthy – but really, reading one novel after another just nauseated me up to the nose. Probably you like him, though. – But I can't help it – either I must say what I say, or put the whole thing in the fire.

Yrs D. H. Lawrence

3969. To Earl Brewster, [6 March 1927]

Text: MS UT; Brewster 119–20.

Villa Mirenda, *Scandicci*, Florence
6 March

Dear Earl

Nice of you and Achsah to ask me to Ravello. Frieda says she'll go to Germany on the 17th. – a week next Thursday. I'd go that day to Rome, stay there a couple of days, and arrive at Amalfi on the 19th. I can find out when the boat leaves from Naples – but not, I think, till 10.0 oclock.

What *I* should most like to do, for the trip, would be to do the western half of the Etruscans – the Rome museums – then Veii and Cività Castellana and

[1] 'he who travels slowly goes a long way!'

[2] See p. 601 n. 2. ('John Galsworthy' was reprinted in *Phoenix* 539–50.)

Cervetri – which one does from Rome – then Corneto, just beyond Cività Vecchia in Maremma – then the Maremma coast-line – and Volterra. Do you know any of those places? I should like to do them very much. If there were time, we might get to Chiusi and Orvieto – we could see. I have a real feeling about the Etruscans.

Let me know how you feel about this. I can get hold of Berners in Rome – if he's there.

I think, alas, the fences and defences are born in one. One doesn't put them up. The devil is to put them down. Ones ancestors hand them on, dead barriers: just the wrong ones.

Raining today!

Glad you like Ravello. I liked the Hotel Palumbo very much last year – but *floods* of trippers come to lunch.

We'll talk when we meet. Say grüsse to Achsah for me – *and* to the imperturbable child, buddha-born.

DHL

What hotel did you mention in Rome? – tell me!

I'm afraid a couple of Americans I know are in the Palumbo – Mr and Mrs Rosebery – and *so* afraid they'd bore you.

3970. To Hon. Dorothy Brett, 8 March 1927

Text: MS UCin; Postmark, Scand[icci] 8. 3[. . .]; Huxley 679–81.

Villa Mirenda. *Scandicci.* Florence
8 March 1927

Dear Brett

Your letter from the De Vargas, and the one from Taos when you had got back, leaving Mabel and Tony in Santa Fe, have both come. Bad luck they got flu. I got my first slap of it ten days ago – bronchial the same – it went off in three days, but comes back – doesn't *quite* go yet. I have today dabbed on the last mustard plaster we bought in Amalfi – at this very moment I feel it nipping – so tomorrow I hope to be up – smiling. Too bad it got me, just at the end of Feb. February is the bad month. I hope Tony and Mabel are better.

It is already spring here – wild crocuses and anemones, big purple ones, and primroses and violets. We get some lovely sunny days, and some wet ones. But the country is looking lovely, with the almond blossoms out and the corn so green, and beans nearly in flower. Aldous and Maria and Mary Hutchinson came a week ago.[1] Aldous still absolutely gone in the grouches – is writing a

[1] Mary Hutchinson, née Barnes, m. 1910, St John ('Jack') Hutchinson (1884–1942), barrister. She was cousin to Lytton Strachey; the Hutchinsons were close friends of Gertler (see *Letters*, ii. 591 and n. 1; iii. 175 and n. 1).

political novel, heaven save him[1] – Maria seems to me ambitious – if you've got nothing else in your life, I suppose money and push make a life for you. Mary Hutchinson seems nice and gentle, very faded, poor dear – almost a little old woman. Clive Bell and Co. must be very wearing.[2] I feel myself in another world altogether. They seem to me like people from a dead planet, like the moon, where never again will the grass grow or the clouds turn red. It's no good, for me the human world becomes more and more unreal, more and more wearisome. I am really happiest when I don't see people and never go to town. Town just lays me out. I wont go to London for *David*. I simply wont go, to have my life spoilt by those people. They can maul and muck the play about as much as they like. They'd do it anyhow. Why should they suck my life into the bargain? I won't go.

Frieda wants to go to BadenBaden next week – stay a fortnight, and bring her two girls back here for a month. The Brewsters, did you know, have moved to Ravello, and are in Cimbrone, Lord Grimthorpes' place, you remember.[3] They invite me for a little while. I might go – but I don't know – It depends if I shake off this flu. What I've promised to do is to walk with Earl in the first weeks in April. I want to go the Etruscan places near Rome – Vei and Cervetri – then on the maremma coast, north of Cività Vecchia and south of Pisa – Corneto, Grosseto etc – and Volterra. The Etruscans interest me very much – and these are lonely places, with tombs – a dangerous malaria region in summer.

I doubt if we shall come to America this year. It's not a case of settling. But long journeys just don't appeal to me. I'd love the ranch if I could stride there. But America puts me off. Whatever else I am, I'm European. And at the moment, my desire to go far has left me. Probably it'll come back later. But for the moment, Italy will do for me. It seems awful to say it, but I feel I'd sell the ranch if it were mine. It's so far, and I'm not American. You say you'd buy it – but my dear Brett, what with?

I've done my novel – I like it – but it's so improper, according to the poor conventional fools, that it'll never be printed. And I will *not* cut it. Even my pictures, which seem to me absolutely innocent, I find people *can't even look* at them. They glance, and look quickly away. I wish I could print a picture that would just *kill* every cowardly and ill-minded person that looked at it. My word, what a slaughter! – How are your radishes? Since my 'Eve re-gaining

[1] *Point Counter Point* (1928).

[2] Arthur Clive Howard Bell (1881–1964), critic of art, literature and politics. m. 1907, Vanessa Stephen (sister of Virginia Woolf). DHL had known him since 1915 and then 'rather' liked him (*Letters*, ii. 435 and n. 5).

[3] Cf. p. 406 n. 2.

Paradise' I've not done anything. I began a *Resurrection*, but haven't worked at it.[1] In the spring, one slackens off. Then this cursed flu.

You've really got the automobile touch. Why not – round the world in the Flying Heart? – If there are any dollars over, use them for yourself. I did a review of Van Vechten's *Nigger Heaven* – poor stuff – and slapped him.[2]

We don't see a tenth part as many people as you do – so the Florence society is no menace. – I can see you bouncing on the little zegua!

DHL

3971. To Rachel Hawk, 8 March 1927

Text: MS UT; Postmark, Scandicci 9. 3 27; Unpublished.

Villa Mirenda, *Scandicci* (Florence), Italy.
8 March 1927

Dear Rachel

It is indeed a long time since we wrote to you – and only because one has had such a lot of bothering things to do, and we have felt so undecided as to plans: whether to come over to the ranch for the summer, or whether Frieda should come alone in the spring, to see if she could sell it. We feel still undecided. We both like it so much: and yet it is so far, and there are always complications. I am so tired of complications. And they seem inevitable.

My feeling is still to sell the place, and be free. We could always have a cabin for the summer, if we wanted to come, either on Del Monte or somewhere near. Have you any idea how much we could get for it, the ranch, as it stands, with the furniture and everything? You said you had somebody in mind. Could you get him to make an offer for the place? – including everything except just our personal things, clothes and books. I paid the taxes this winter, through Mabel, so everything is in order. Let me know about this if you can, will you? And one of us at least could come over and settle. But *please don't tell anybody*.

I'm awfully sorry Mr Hawk is so ill. I think New Mexico does perhaps tell on the nerves, in the long run. But it's jolly hard on Mrs Hawk, after so many years' struggle, when she could just do with a bit of peace. The only thing is, it would be very nice if you and William had the place again, without harassment. It was nicest that first winter, when the Danes were there, and everything was so quiet for us all.

We had the photograph of the children at Christmas time, and thought of

[1] *Resurrection*, an oil painting (38″ × 38″), was completed 27/8 May 1927. See *The Paintings of D. H. Lawrence*, plate [1].

[2] 'It is a false book by an author who lingers in nigger cabarets hoping to heaven to pick up something to write about and make a sensation – and, of course, money' (*Phoenix* 361).

you a great deal. How they grow! It does seem a shame that there are so many bothers in life that there needn't be. You and Bill ought to be able to live so nicely and happily there on Del Monte. You don't *want* a great deal of money, so why should you worry yourselves to death trying to make it. After all, what one wants is to *live*.

We've been very quiet here during the winter – but not a bad winter. I got a bit of flu last week, for the first time – bronchial, as usual. But it's not bad. How is Walton, that way? – Frieda is going to Germany for a month – then coming back here. I shall just go to Rome. Frieda is bringing her two daughters back with her, to stay awhile here. One is engaged to be married[1] – the other paints: great tall young women! – Brett writes constantly. All sorts of messages to William from us both. I *do* wish it were not so far. I should love to run over.

Ever Yours D. H. Lawrence

3972. To Emily King, 11 March 1927
Text: MS Lazarus; Unpublished.

Villa Mirenda, *Scandicci*, Florence
11 March 1927

My dear Pamela

The tea came yesterday – all safe in a nice tin – 21 Liras duty (the Lira 110 to a pound) – Today Ada writes that Joan has measles. Let's hope it's a mild attack, and no more. Everybody here has flu – I've been having it this last fortnight – twice thought it was gone, and went to Florence, and twice it came back. So now I go gingerly. But it's a sunny day, I'm going for a walk.

Frieda is going to Baden next Thursday – I expect she'll stay about three weeks. She expects to meet her children there, and bring them back here for a month. I don't want to go north – too much flu. The Brewsters asked me to go to them in Ravello – above the sea at Amalfi, south of Naples. I shall do that if I'm all right – leave on the 17th, stay a day or two in Rome, then on to Ravello. A change might be a good thing. Then in early April I'd like to walk with Brewster in Maremma, on the coast north of Rome, to look at Etruscan things and do some articles I was asked for – and earn a bit of money. I hope I can. I'd have to do it in April, later Maremma gets very bad with malaria. But I suppose I'll be back here by mid-April, or the end. – I'll send you a card if I leave next Thursday. If I stay, Giulia will look after me, and the Beveridge women.

It's lovely spring – lovely wild crocuses in the grassy places – purple and red

[1] See Letter 3876 and n. 3.

anemones in the green corn – and primroses and violets and grape hyacinths by the stream. Almond blossom is out, peach nearly out. Seems a shame the world is full of flu.

I send you £5. Buy something for Joan, and some of it is for you for your birthday. I do hope Joan is in for a light touch. Lucky that spring is here. Does Peg keep well? – I'm very much depressed about Gertie – feels bad, to me. But one just has to avoid thinking.

Love! DHL

3973. To Nancy Pearn, 11 March 1927
Text: MS UT; Huxley 681.

Villa Mirenda, *Scandicci*, Florence
11 March 1927

Dear Miss Pearn

I am sending today the MSS of 'The Lovely Lady', murder story (sic) for Cynthia Asquith. Hope you get it. Did you get that *very* untidy MS of the 'Scrutiny of John Galsworthy' which I sent without registering a week ago last monday?

I've had digs of flu – not bad, but beastly – this last fortnight. Hope it's about over.

I think if I'm well enough I'm going down to Ravello for a change next week – let you know.

When might you come here? Be sure to let us know in time, and we'll meet you.

Yrs D. H. Lawrence

3974. To Nancy Pearn, 12 March 1927
Text: MS UT; Unpublished.

Villa Mirenda, *Scandicci*, Florence.
12 March 1927

Dear Miss Pearn

Thanks for having the 'Scrutiny of John Galsworthy' typed for me. I'm returning it now. You remember it is for Edgell Rickwood, for a volume of *Scrutinies*. I don't suppose anybody will be very anxious to do it in magazine. But if you send a copy to America, you might mention to Barmby that a new magazine *Larus* – published in Boston or somewhere in Mass. – asked me for anything whatsoever that other papers weren't likely to want.[1]

Yrs D. H. Lawrence

3975. To Martin Secker, 15 March 1927

Text: MS UInd; Postmark, Firenze 16 . III 1927; Secker 85–6.

Villa Mirenda, *Scandicci*, Firenze
15 March 1927

Dear Secker

I thought to have had the *Mornings in Mexico* proofs before now, and waited for them before writing. But they don't turn up. Is there a delay?

Frieda is going on Thursday to Baden for about twenty days, and I'm going down to Ravello to stay with the Brewsters, who've got Lord Grimthorpe's house there for the time. But I've had flu nagging at me these last three weeks – seeming to get better, then coming back worse. If it's not gone a bit more surely than at the moment, I shall wait still a few days here. The address in Ravello is: Palazzo Cimbrone – Ravello. Prov. di Salerno. – I want to do a little Etruscan tour on my way back, and do a few articles on etruscan places that an American magazine[2] asked me for. It depends if I'm feeling fit. And one can't do it later than April, it is maremma coast, that gets so malarial.

I've finished my novel *Lady Chatterley's Lover* – not long – but about 80,000 I suppose – or ninety. It's verbally terribly improper – but I don't think I shall alter it. I'll send it you one of these days – am not keen, somehow, on letting it go out. What's the good of publishing things!

It's lovely spring here – the wheat full of big blue anemones, and primroses and many violets and grape hyacinths by the stream – and purple anemones and scarlet, and the wild tulips all in bud. Tuscany is very flowery. I'm sorry Rina didn't pop over. – Then she stayed much longer in Spotorno than she said! – We've still got the marionettes for Adrian – but they'll keep, and so will he! Wonder how he likes his new Gemma, or what is her name?[3] – How nice for you that *Jüd Süss* was so successful – yet it's not really good-false. But I'm absolutely no good at judging what the public might like.

I shan't come to England for *David* – don't want to – haven't heard when it

[1] *Larus, the Celestial Visitor*, edited from Lynn, Mass., ran from February 1927–June 1928. None of DHL's writings appeared in it.

[2] *Travel* printed four of the essays subsequently revised and collected in *Etruscan Places* (Roberts A60).

[3] Gemma was Adrian Secker's nanny in Spotorno.

will be. I hope you're feeling all right. I'm awfully tired of being nagged at by this flu. I'll send a p.c. if I leave Thursday.

Yrs D. H. Lawrence

Frieda says did Rina get the scarf? sent to Bridgefoot.

3976. To Enid Hopkin, 17 March 1927

Text: MS UCLA; cited in Moore, *Poste Restante* 90.

Villa Mirenda, *Scandicci*, Firenze
17 March 1927

Dear Enid

Your letter just caught me here. Frieda left today for Baden Baden, where she will stay a month or so – not definite – and come back with her daughters. That is her programme.

I am going to Rome tomorrow, and then south to Ravello, and shall likewise be back, I suppose, towards the end of April – or not much later. – I'm afraid we shall be full up with Frieda's daughters – and the country hasn't much to offer in the way of accommodations. It is quite peasant country out this side – the opposite from the Fiesole side in almost every respect. If you stay in Florence, you might try the Pensione Balestri, Piazza Mentana – and ask them what they charge for a room on the river. I think they're still pretty cheap, and some people said the other day, quite good. I suppose their terms *en pension* are about 30 Liras – and they'll always put you up a good lunch if you want to picnic.

We're about 8 miles out by tram – costs only 1.50 – and then nearly two miles to walk, from Vingone. Of course you'll come out and see us – but I'll write again as soon as I'm back.

It's lovely and sunny now – though it's rained heavily some days. But not a bad winter, on the whole. The flowers, red and blue anemones and all the rest, are very lovely – But May is a lovely month too.

I'm glad your father is a little easier. There was a rumour that there was a child! – thank heaven it's not true, it would mean more effort.

I have put off coming to England. I just feel I dont want to come north – feel a sort of migration instinct pushing me south rather than north.

There don't seem so many tourists this year: Swedes and Danes! – no Germans, not many English. Perhaps they'll roll in later. But its nicer when they are few.

I'll send you a line again shortly. Remember me to your husband.

Yrs D. H. Lawrence

3977. To Emily King, [18 March 1927]

Text: MS Needham; PC v. Firenze – Il Battistero; Postmark, Firenze 19 . III 1927; Unpublished.

[Villa Mirenda, Scandicci, Florence]
March 18.

Frieda has gone to Baden – I leave tomorrow for Rome. Write to me:
Palazzo Cimbrone, *Ravello*, Prov di Salerno.

Hope Joan is better.

love! DHL

3978. To Ada Clarke, [18 March 1927]

Text: MS Clarke; PC v. Firenze Piazza Signoria – Fontana (Particolare); Postmark, Firenze 19 . III 1927; Unpublished.

[Villa Mirenda, Scandicci, Florence]
18 March

Frieda left for Baden yesterday – I go to Rome tomorrow – then to
Palazzo Cimbrone, *Ravello*, Prov di Salerno.
Send a line at once.

DHL

3979. To Nancy Pearn, [18 March 1927]

Text: MS Lazarus; PC v. Firenze – Piazza Signoria; Postmark, Firenze 19 . III 1927; Unpublished.

[Villa Mirenda, Scandicci, Florence]
18 March

My wife has gone to BadenBaden – I leave tomorrow for Rome – my address for a fortnight or so
Palazzo Cimbrone, *Ravello*, Prov. di Salerno.

Had your letter – good about 'Mercury'[1] –

D. H. Lawrence

3980. To Joseph and Elfie Rosebery, [19 March 1927]

Text: MS Secor; PC v. Incontro di S. Gioacchino e S. Anna; Postmark, Firenze 19 . III 1927; Unpublished.

[Villa Mirenda, Scandicci, Florence]
March 19

I am expecting to come down to Ravello next week to stay a little while with the Brewsters in Cimbrone – so I hope to see you. My wife has gone to BadenBaden to her mother for a visit.

Yrs D. H. Lawrence

[1] See p. 521 n. 2.

INDEX

No distinction is made between a reference in the text or in a footnote.
All titles of writings by Lawrence are gathered under his name.
For localities, public buildings, etc. in London, see the comprehensive entry under the place-name; all biblical references are collected under 'Bible'.
A bold numeral indicates a biographical entry in a footnote.